VISIONS
OF
F·A·I·T·H

an anthology of reflections

Select, select: make an anthology
Of what's been given you by bold casual time.
Revise, omit; keep what's significant.
Fill, fill deserted time.
— Edwin Muir

VISIONS

OF

F·A·I·T·H

an anthology of reflections

Reverend William G.D. Sykes

Eden Press
Montréal

VISIONS OF FAITH
An Anthology of Reflections
by Reverend William G.D. Sykes

ISBN 0-920792-25-1

Copyright ©1986 Eden Press Inc.

Cover design: Luba Zagurak
Cover photograph: David Laforge
Page design: Evelyne Hertel and Luba Zagurak

Printed in Canada at Imprimerie Gagné.
Dépôt légal — premier trimestre 1986
Bibliothèque nationale du Québec

Eden Press
4626 St. Catherine Street W.
Montreal, Quebec   H3Z 1S3

Canadian Cataloguing in Publication Data

Sykes, William, G. D. (William George David)
   Visions of faith : an anthology of reflections.

ISBN 0-920792-25-1

1. Christian life—Quotations, maxims, etc.
2. Conduct of life—Quotations, maxims, etc.
3. Values—Quotations, maxims, etc.   4. Quotations, English.
I. Title

BV4501.2.S94 1986   248.4   C86-090032-0

TABLE OF CONTENTS

Introduction

This anthology came into being by accident. I was thirty, Chaplain to University College, London, and searching for a broader and deeper vision of faith than I had hitherto found. Then, in a bookstore in New York City, I bought a second-hand copy of *The Choice is Always Ours,* an anthology edited by Dorothy Berkley Phillips. What particularly excited me about the book was the emergence of a vision of faith of enormous dimensions, reaching out into many areas of life. As soon as I was back in London, I promptly ordered another twenty copies of *The Choice* — much to the amusement of the elderly shop assistant there who had originally recommended the book to me.

It took several months to digest the contents of the book. I gradually became aware of a still deeper and broader vision of faith. This in turn made me look again at the Bible and theology. What is more, it led me to explore literature, poetry, art, science, philosophy, psychology, music, and so on. I finally decided to compile my own anthology, based on this new vision of faith, not with any idea of publishing it, but solely for my own use and ministry. This task took sixteen years.

Three years ago I arranged the material under various topics and set them out in alphabetical order. There was no particular order within the topics. They were arranged with the biblical verses coming first, followed by the other material according to length, with the shortest quotations coming first.

I then started using this material. Close acquaintances began telling me it was worthy of publication. Eventually an old college friend dropped in on me during a visit from Canada. He'd heard about the compilation and wanted to have a look at it. After a few minutes of close scrutiny he said, "Well, if you want my candid opinion, you ought to get this published," and then added "What's more, I'll publish it. Let me have it in six months' time." Three years later, I handed the manuscript over to him.

What then is the underlying vision of faith behind this anthology? This is most easily described and best understood in biblical language and imagery. In the opening verses of the Bible, our attention is focussed on God the Creator. The Spirit of God is seen moving over the face of the waters, and the universe is brought into being. The psalmists, prophets, and people of faith saw in this process evidence of the Spirit of God at work. In the beauty of nature and in the order of creation is something of the Spirit of God at work.

In the story of the creation of man, God is depicted as making man in His own image and likeness, and of breathing life into man. Again people of faith have taken this to mean that God breathed something of His own nature into us, thus giving us a divine potential for life.

If we now turn to the Gospels, we can see this "something of God in man" being fully worked out in the person of our Lord. At the height of His ministry, following His baptism and sojourn in the wilderness, He tells His disciples, "He who has seen me has seen the Father. . . . Do you not believe that I am in the Father and the Father in me? The words that I say to you I do not speak on my own authority; but the Father who dwells in me does His works." In a similar vein on another occasion He is equally emphatic: "All things have been delivered to me by my Father."

If we look a little more closely at the record of the life of Christ we notice Him saying other things about Himself. He talks of Himself as light: "I am the light of the world; he who follows me will not walk in darkness, but will have the light of life." Elsewhere he spoke of Himself as joy, and stressed that "these things I have spoken to you, that my joy may be in you, and that your joy may be full." He also described Himself as truth and linked Himself with the gift of truth to the disciples: "If you love me, you will keep my commandments. And I will pray to the Father, and He will give you another Counsellor, to be with you for ever, even the Spirit of truth, whom the world cannot receive, because it neither sees Him nor knows Him; you know Him, for He dwells with you, and will be in you." Yet again He saw Himself as love, and revealed the richness of His inner relatedness to the Father with the words: "As the Father loved me, so have I loved you; abide in my love." On another occasion He described Himself as life. In the prologue of St. John's Gospel the writer recognizes that "in Him was life, and the life was the light of men," and the same writer pinpoints the purpose of Christ's life: "I came that they may have life, and have it abundantly."

It was the apostle Paul who made the exciting discovery that what Christ had experienced in His life, we can all in some measure experience. There is a large gap in our knowledge of Paul's life. It is thought that some years were spent in Arabia, where he thought through the implication's of Christ's life. When he reappeared he made some extraordinary statements: "I have been crucified with Christ; it is no longer I who live, but Christ who lives in me," and "For in Him (Christ) the whole fullness of deity dwells bodily and you have come to fullness of life in Him." In other words, we all have an enormous potential for life. This can be seen in a significant passage in his Letter to the Ephesians: "For this reason I bow my knees before the Father, from whom every family in heaven and earth is named, that according to the riches of His glory, He may grant you to be strengthened with might through his Spirit in the inner man, and that Christ may dwell in your hearts through faith; that you, being rooted and grounded in love, may have power to comprehend with all the saints what is the breadth and length and height and depth, and to know the love of Christ which surpasses knowledge, that you may be filled with all the fullness of God."

If we now go back to the Gospels, we can better understand the message that Jesus came to proclaim — namely the kingdom of God: "I must preach the good news of the kingdom of God . . . for I was sent for this purpose." In St. Luke's Gospel he says: "The kingdom of God is within you."

Commentators point out that the phrase "The kingdom of God is within you," can equally lend itself to another translation: "The kingdom of God is in the midst of you." A modern writer expands our vision of the kingdom of God by saying that "The outer world, with all its phenomena, is filled with divine splendour, but we must have experienced the divine within ourselves before we can hope to discover it in our environment."

What an exciting vision of faith. Could this be the original message of Jesus, the vision of faith of the early Church that we have sadly lost? At one level it means that we all have an enormous potential for life. At another level it means that once this becomes a living reality, it is as though scales are removed from our eyes, and we can see the kingdom of God both within and without ourselves. No wonder Evelyn Underhill could exclaim enthusiastically, "The best thing in life is the Kingdom of God. The best that can happen to anyone or the world, is to be filled with the fullness of God."

What then is the significance of the kingdom of God today? Albert Schweitzer summarized the importance and centrality of the kingdom of God in our era in the following words: "Modern faith finds the beginning of the Kingdom of God in Jesus and in the Spirit which came into the world with him. We no longer leave the fate of mankind to be decided at the end of the world. The time in which we live summons us to new faith in the Kingdom of God.

"We are no longer content . . . to believe in the kingdom that comes of itself at the end of time. Mankind today must either realise the Kingdom of God or perish. The question before us is whether we will use for beneficial purposes or for purposes of destruction the power that modern science has placed in our hands. . . . Our only hope is that the Spirit of God will strive with the spirit of the world and will prevail.

"The last petition of the Lord's Prayer has again its original meaning for us as a prayer for deliverance from the dominion of the evil powers of the world. These are no less real to us as working in men's minds, instead of being embodied in angelic beings opposed to God. The first believers set their hope solely upon the Kingdom of God in expectation of the end of the world; we do it in expectation of the end of the human race.

"The Spirit shows us the signs of the time and their meaning. Belief in the Kingdom of God makes the biggest demands of all the articles of the Christian faith. It means believing the seemingly impossible — the conquest of the spirit of the world by the Spirit of God. We look with confidence for the miracle to be wrought through the Spirit.

"The miracle must happen in us before it can happen in the world. We dare not set our hope on our own efforts to create the conditions of God's Kingdom in the world. . . . But there can be no Kingdom of God in the world with the Kingdom of God in our hearts. . . . Nothing can be achieved without inwardness. The Spirit of God will only strive against the spirit of the world when it has won its victory over that spirit in our hearts."

How then do we prepare to receive this gift of life as revealed in this vision of faith? If we go back to the Genesis story of the creation of man, we notice that that which is fashioned and shaped in the image and likeness of God is taken from the dust of the earth. The meaning behind this is that as well as having a divine potential, man is also born with an earthly, creaturely side to his nature. The trouble begins when this side of our nature occupies pride of place, and we become selfish, self-centred, egocentric and spoiled. If this kind of behaviour is persisted in during adolescence and into adulthood, life becomes restricted rather than enhanced and we end up frustrated, unhappy, and embittered. At some stage there has to be a shift of centre so that we stop being self-centred, and become instead God-centred.

The start of this process is baptism. In this sacrament (defined as an outward and visible sign of an inward and spiritual grace) our self-centredness is put to death by "drowning" in the waters of baptism. This is not just a cleansing, a purifying, a "putting off of the old man," but a ruthless "dying to self." This is where the Cross comes in, not just the historical Cross of Calvary, but the Cross *now* being experienced. One of the main actions in the baptismal service is the signing of the Cross on the forehead; then we leave the service, going back into everyday life to "take up our cross daily." It is a painful, costly business, which will continue to mean an involvement with physical, mental, and spiritual suffering. But let us not forget that our earthly, creaturely instinctive side remains, though with one major difference. It has been deposed from its top-most place. This part of human nature is being redeemed, being brought back and made to serve the growing personality. There is an awareness of a great availability of a creative source of energy and power.

Then there is the other side of baptism. The divine potential "breathed into" man is catalyzed and brought to life. There is a new birth, the birth of the Holy Spirit, or as some people prefer to call it — spiritual rebirth.

In one of His final appearances, Jesus breathes on His disciples (reminiscent of the Genesis story?), and says, "Receive the Holy Spirit." In Baptism, we are baptized "In the name of the Father, and of the Son, and of the Holy Spirit" — that is, into the whole fullness of God, as described earlier. In this there is resurrection, and by this we mean not just the historical resurrection, but resurrection in the present. A *re*-surrection — a rising again — of the divine from the depths of our being. And this has to continue on a day-to-day basis, so that like the apostle Paul, we come to know what it means to live in the power of the resurrection.

If we do all this, some other great Christian doctrines will come alive for us. The incarnation — God putting on human flesh in the person of Jesus Christ — will become part of our everyday experience. Once again God will be putting on human flesh — this time in *our* lives — and we shall come to know that divinity is the gracious art of how we become divine. Likewise the atonement — what Christ did for us on the Cross — assumes a present significance. We are actually able to enjoy our "at-one-ment" with God in the here and now. Surely all this is of the essence of what it means to be Christian.

Baptism then is exceedingly important; it opens up a spiritual dimension in which we are able to enjoy, here and now, eternal life, a quality of life that is so valuable that we can never conceive of it ending. In this we have a foretaste of heaven, in which the fear of death is transcended, and our departure from this life is seen as a gateway to something even greater.

After baptism, then, how do we grow in this vision of faith? The main way forward, as far as this book is concerned, is through reflection. This is a devotional form of thinking and feeling, of listening and seeing, with "the heart in the mind," as the Eastern Orthodox would say. It is a method of carrying out those two great commandments, a way of loving God with all our hearts and minds, and of loving our neighbour as ourselves. It leads on to thinking at a deep level, and of making a creative use of our feelings and emotions, which enriches our understanding and compassion. It is a way of becoming aware of the intuitive side of our nature, and of learning to trust and bide by it. It is a way of recalling the wisdom and knowledge of the past, and of feeding the mind on beauty, truth, and goodness. It is a way of going out of ourselves and of learning to love other people. It is a method whereby a constructive use is made of solitude, silence and stillness — in the presence of God. It leads on to meditation and contemplation, and as the mystics (i.e., the experts in the spiritual life) would claim, to a direct awareness and knowledge of God. Reflection is a stimulating and exciting undertaking in which maximum use is made of all our faculties. In it we experience moments of insight and illumination that result in a new consciousness, and a different way of seeing things.

The contents of the anthology are a skeleton of faith to encourage this practice of reflection. Lots of clues and hints are given, but it is up to the individual reader to put his or her own flesh and blood on it, through reflection. The contents are taken from two thousand years of Christian and religious experience, greatly expanded and enhanced by the words and writings of novelists, poets, artists, scientists, philosophers, musicians, statesmen, mystics, and playwrights, which are in line with the vision of faith. It is a vision, grounded in human experience (and perhaps more than human experience). To get the most out of this book it is important to understand this vision of faith.

We are now in a position to go one step further and ask a fundamental question: "What is the aim of this book?" To answer this we have to ask further questions. Not just the primary ones of "Who am I?" "Where did I come from?" and "Where am I going?" but the more searching ones of "What is life for?" and "What is the aim of life?"

I was helped in finding an answer to this question by a simple observation of nature. If a flower grows, blossoms, blooms, and then dies, nobody is particulary worried, because the flower has achieved what it set out to do. Now, in applying this observation to human beings, can we not say that our aim in life is to grow a soul (character, personality) that is us at our highest level of development and expression? Can we not also say that this is achieved not necessarily by stress and by striving, but by letting go and allowing God to work in us and through us? Can we not also say that this is largely achieved by being actively engaged in enabling other people to grow to their highest level of development and expression? And finally can we not say that we are only at our highest level of development and expression when we are properly related to nature, and to "the created order" — which takes us into the realm of politics, economics, and into the heart of the social order? This involves such things as the right use of money and power, and a right use and distribution of the world's resources. Ultimately what this book is about, and this might sound rather pretentious, is: fullness of life for everyone and world redemption.

How then do I personally use this book? Needless to say, I use it for reflection — an hour in the morning and an hour in the evening on a daily basis. I have reached the stage where I use the material as a catalyst for keeping a spiritual diary.

At the moment I am working through the book systematically from cover to cover and I try to spend an hour on a single phrase or sentence. For example, by way of illustration take the verse from Scripture: "For God did not give us a spirit of timidity but a spirit of power and love and self-control." If I was tackling this I would spend an hour reflecting on this verse, writing out in my journal everything that comes to mind as I carefully considered its contents. I would also consult my feelings, especially with such words as *timidity, power, love,* and *self control.* Sometimes I keep my mind focussed on the precise wording of the verse, repeating it quietly to myself from time to time, allowing the deep truths contained in the verse to penetrate to my inner being. At other times, I am very practical and down-to-earth and concentrate on working out its specific meaning. Quite frequently I allow my imagination to come into play and try to be aware of and sensitive to the intuitive side of my nature. All sorts of thoughts and feelings come to the surface and are committed to writing. Very rarely do I go back and read what I have written. The important part of the exercise lies in writing, and it leads, I believe, to a heightened apprehension.

In times of stress and confusion, when the mind is going round in circles, when decisions have to be made and I'm not sure what to do, I have resorted to the book and the journal. Once I start writing down possible solutions, and exploring various courses of action, new thoughts come from somewhere, and very often a breakthrough is made. Problems are frequently solved this way, and burdens lifted. The combination of the book and the journal has proved to be an invaluable source of guidance and a continual source of inspiration, understanding and insight. Progress through the book is slow, and this is as it should be. It might take as long as two years to get through, but it is well worth the effort that goes into it.

I also use the contents of the book for "reflection groups" in College. This can be with just one other person, or a small group of up to five people. We meet for an hour a week, equip ourselves with a cup of coffee, and then focus our attention on a topic for half an hour of silent reflection. The next half hour is spent in discussion, sharing insights, and learning from each other. Thirty hours a week of my time as a college chaplain are spent in such groups. I see them as a valuable part of education, drawing out something that is already there in the depths of the personality, leading on to wholeness and maturity.

How might other people use this book? Here are some suggestions. Those coming to the book for the first time might dip into in in spare moments, browsing through it at leisure. It's a good idea to follow up the topics and quotations you are particularly interested in.

Second, at a later stage, try to get an overall picture of the book, looking carefully at the vision of faith, and gradually assimilating the contents of the topics.

Third, go through it more systematically in a reflective way. This can mean repeating quotations to yourself slowly a couple of times, and concentrating on extracting all possible meaning from them. This involves thinking things through, using one's feelings and intuitions, imagination and memory. The words of the Collect for the Second Sunday in Advent (a prayer for the study of the Scriptures) has been helpful to some of those who have applied it to this anthology: ". . . Grant that we may in such wise hear them, read, mark, learn, and inwardly digest them . . ." Others have been helped in applying another way of looking at the Bible: "The Bible is like a telescope. If a man looks *through* his telescope, then he sees worlds beyond: but if he looks *at* his telescope, then he does not see anything but that. The Bible is a thing to be looked through to that which is beyond; but most people only look at it and so they see only the dead letter." Here we are close to the realm, not just of reflection, but of meditation and contemplation, and are approaching the book in a devotional way, "with the heart in the mind."

Fourth, I think we ought to be far more open to the message of the mystics and of what mysticism has to say than we have been in the past. A reader of this book in manuscript form wrote the following letter to me:

"When I got to page 225 . . . although I had read every word of every article up to that point I very nearly turned aside from the entire section headed "Mystics and Mysticism." But thank God I didn't for the article by Rufus Jones set the entire book on fire for me and brought me to the full realisation of the message you are trying to get across. The second article by Aldous Huxley plainly put a very distinguished mark on you. In view of my reaction set out above I feel that a paragraph should be included in the introduction to dispel any prejudice against mysticism, because many people may never reach page 225.

". . . The time has now come for the people of western countries to pay some attention to those of the east where Christ lived and taught and that the views of some of the mystics — Christ being the perfect one — puts an enlightening interpretation on the long-held doctrines of the Church which sadly have not been fully interpreted and understood. Phrases like 'the Kingdom of God is within you' have been bandied about sor so long that they have lost their meaning and are passed over as something one has heard so many times before. Instead of this why not say something like 'Everyone has a spark of God within them that needs to be developed, but this first step of approach has to be made by the individuals.' "

Finally, some people might also want to use the material, as I do, as a catalyst for keeping a journal, and working through the contents of the book over a long period of time.

A practical point: after each quotation, the author's name is given, along with the title of the book from which the quotation is taken, the name of the publishing firm, the edition, and the page number. This is to enable the reader to track down the quotation, to see it in context, and to facilitate follow-up reading.

This is very much an exploratory work. A second edition is planned. If any of the readers have favourite quotations not included in this book, I would be pleased to receive copies of them (with sources), and they will be duly considered for the next edition.

A

ACCEPTANCE

I have learned, in whatever state I am, to be content. I know how to be abased, and I know how to abound; in any and all circumstances I have learned the secret of facing plenty and hunger, abundance and want. I can do all things in him who strengthens me.

Philippians 4.11-13.

Accept the fact that you are accepted!
Paul Tillich, The Shaking of the Foundations, S.C.M. Press Ltd., 1949, p.162.

He who is in a state of rebellion cannot receive grace, to use the phrase of which the Church is so fond—so rightly fond, I dare say—for in life as in art the mood of rebellion closes up the channels of the soul, and shuts out the airs of heaven.

Oscar Wilde, The Works of Oscar Wilde, edited by G.F. Maine, William Collins Sons & Co. Ltd., 1948, "De Profundis," p.866.

There liveth no man on earth who may always have rest and peace without troubles and crosses, with whom things always go according to his will; there is always something to be suffered here, turn which way you will. And as soon as you are quit of one assault, perhaps two come in its place. Wherefore yield thyself willingly to them, and seek only that true peace of the heart, which none can take away from thee, that thou mayest overcome all assaults.

Thus then, Christ meant that inward peace which can break through all assaults and crosses of oppression, suffering, misery, humiliation and what more there may be of the like, so that a man may be joyful and patient therein, like the beloved disciples and followers of Christ. Now he who will in love give his whole diligence and might thereto, will verily come to know that true eternal peace which is God Himself, as far as it is possible to a creature; insomuch that what was bitter to him before, shall become sweet, and his heart shall remain unmoved among all changes....

Theologia Germanica, translated by Susanna Winkworth, Stuart & Watkins Ltd., 1966, p.53.

Nekhlyudov called to mind how at Kuzminskoye he had started to reflect over his life, trying to decide what he should do and how he should do it, and remembered how tangled up he had become, unable to arrive at any decision because there were so many considerations connected with each problem. He now put the same problems to himself and was surprised how easy they were. Everything was simple now because he was not thinking of what would be the result for himself—he was not even interested in that—but only of what he ought to do. And, strange to say, he had no idea what to do for his own needs, but knew beyond any doubt what he had to do for others....

The black cloud had spread until the whole sky was dark. Now it was not sheet - but fork-lightning that flashed vivid, lighting up the yard and outlining the crumbling house with its tumble-down porches, while thunder growled overhead. The birds were all silent but the leaves began to rustle and the wind reached the porch where Nekhlyudov sat....

Nekhlyudov went into the house.

"No, no," he thought, "the reason for what happens in our lives, all that we do, the meaning of it, is incomprehensible and must remain incomprehensible to me. Why did I have aunts? Why did Nikolenka Irtenyev die, while I am still alive? Why should there be a Katusha? What about my lunacy? Why that war? Why my reckless life afterwards? To understand all that, to understand the Master's purpose is beyond me. But to do His will, inscribed in my conscience—is in my power, and this I know unquestioningly. And when I am obeying His will, there is no doubt that my soul is at peace."

Leo Tolstoy, *Resurrection*, translated with an introduction by Rosemary Edmonds, Penguin Books Ltd., 1981, p.296.

ACTION

Christians are living in this sinful world and must bear its burden, they may not steal away from the battlefield.

Nicolas Berdyaev, *Christianity and Class War*, translated by Donald Attwater, Sheed & Ward Ltd., 1933, p.50.

The worst of partialities is to withhold oneself, the worst ignorance is not to act, the worst lie is to steal away.

Charles Péguy, *Basic Verities*, translated by Ann & Julian Green, Kegan Paul, Trench, Trubner & Co. Ltd., 1943, p.51.

Enlarging insight depends on expansion due to exercise; vision on action, on acting up to the limit of what has been glimpsed.

Anon.

Why stand we here trembling around
Calling on God for help, and not ourselves, in whom God dwells
Stretching a hand to save the falling Man?

William Blake, *The Complete Writings of William Blake*, edited by Geoffrey Keynes, Oxford University Press, 1974, "Jerusalem," p.672.

The end of man is an Action, and not a Thought, though it were the noblest?

Thomas Carlyle, *Sartor Resartus*, Ward, Lock & Co. Ltd., p.108.

"Tis God gives skill,
But not without men's hands: He could not make
Antonio Stradivari's violins Without Antonio.

George Eliot, *The Works of George Eliot*, Virtue & Co., 1913, Volume 18, *Jubal and Other Poems*, "Stradivarius," l.140, p.218.

In our era, the road to holiness necessarily passes through the world of action.

Dag Hammarskjold, *Markings,* translated by Leif Sjoberg & W.H. Auden, with a foreword by W.H. Auden, Faber and Faber Limited, 1964, p.108.

Perform every action as though it were your last.

Marcus Aurelius, *The Meditations of Marcus Aurelius,* translated by Jeremy Collier, with an introduction and notes by Alice Zimmern, Walter Scott, p.25.

What you theoretically know, vividly realize.

Francis Thompson, *The Works of Francis Thompson,* Burns & Oates Ltd., 1913, Volume III, "Shelley," p.2.

Action springs not from thought, but from a readiness for responsibility.

Dietrich Bonhoeffer, *Letters and Papers from Prison,* William Collins Sons & Co., Ltd., 1963, p.158.

Christians engaged actively in modern economic and social progress and in the struggle for justice and charity must be convinced that they have much to contribute to the prosperity of mankind and to world peace. Let them, as individuals and as group members, give a shining example to others. Endowed with the skill and experience so absolutely necessary for them, let them preserve a proper sense of values in their earthly activity in loyalty to Christ and his Gospel, in order that their lives, individual as well as social, may be inspired by the spirit of the Beatitudes, and in particular by the spirit of poverty.
Anyone who in obedience to Christ seeks first the kingdom of God will derive from it a stronger and purer love for helping all his brethren and for accomplishing the task of justice under the inspiration of charity.

Vatican Council II, *The Conciliar and Post Conciliar Documents,* 1981 Edition, general editor, Austin Flannery, O.P., Fowler Wright Books Ltd., p.979.

It is an indelible principle of Eternal truth, that practice and exercise is the Life of all. Should God give you worlds, and laws, and treasures, and worlds upon worlds, and Himself also in the Divinest manner, if you will be lazy and not meditate, you lose all. The soul is made for action, and cannot rest till it be employed. Idleness is its rust. Unless it will up and think and taste and see, all is in vain. Worlds of beauty and treasure and felicity may be round about it, and itself desolate. If therefore you would be happy, your life must be as full of operation as God of treasure. Your operation shall be treasure to Him, as His operation is delightful to you.

Thomas Traherne, *Centuries,* The Faith Press Ltd., 1969, p.217.

Two methods exist, of aiming at human improvement,—by adjusting circumstances without and by addressing the affections within; by creating facilities of position, or by developing force of character; by mechanism or by mind. The one is institutional and systematic, operating on a large scale; reaching individuals circuitously and at last; the other is personal and moral, the influence of soul on soul, life creating life, beginning in the regeneration of the individual and spreading thence over communities; the one, in short, reforming from the circumference to the centre, the other from the centre to the circumference. And in comparing these it is not difficult to show the superior triumphs of the latter, which was the method of Christ and Christianity.

James Martineau, *Endeavours after the Christian Life: Discourses,* Longmans, Green, Reader, & Dyer, 1876, p.90.

He would have urged all Christians to fulfil their duties as citizens in a world that still belongs to God despite its sin and shame. But equally firmly he would have declared that no scheme for social betterment, no international organization, no political or ecclesiastical reform can in themselves heal the wounds of humanity. In one way only men can be saved, by ridding their hearts of the selfishness that hides from them the knowledge of the love of God. Once that love can gain admittance, lighting up the whole universe as the sun breaks through the clouds at the end of a day of sodden rain, then the whole quality of life is changed and inevitably men will go out to help their fellow-men.

Florence Higham, said of F.D. Maurice in *Frederick Denison Maurice,* S.C.M. Press Ltd., 1947, p.126.

Seen with the eyes of the social historian, this three years' activity as a social revolutionary is the life of Jesus in its impact upon human history. What makes it unique is the scope of the vision which it embodies, and his profound insight into the conditions demanded for its accomplishment. The teaching of Jesus is not something separable from his life; it is the expression of the understanding which grew out of his life. Theory and practice are there completely unified. The one interprets and expounds the other. It is the fusion of insight and action that makes the life of Jesus the religious life *par excellence,* though it is far from being the kind of life that nowadays would be so described.

John Macmurray, *Creative Society,* S.C.M. Press Ltd., 1935, p.88.

God made man in His own image. Whatever that means, it means that man is important to God and is responsible to God. The Word became flesh and dwelt among us. God came to earth in the person of a humble carpenter, and thereby sanctified the individual. This means that what the individual believes, *is,* and does, counts.... We cannot foresee the results of our actions. It is our responsibility, not our helplessness, which appals me.... As each ... goes out to industry ... or university or family life, (his) influence, for good or bad, will radiate across the centuries. An act of kindness may help to mould a Gandhi, our failures may be creating a new Hitler. The progress of mankind has always depended upon those who, seemingly isolated and powerless in their own day, have seen their vision and remained true to it. In the darkening corridors of time they preserved integral their vision of the daylight at the end. This is a matter not of calculation but of faith. Our work may be small and its results invisible to us. But we may rest assured it will come to fruition in God's good time.

John Ferguson, *The Enthronement of Love, The Fellowship of Reconciliation,* 1950, p.102.

ADORATION

It is a beauteous evening, calm and free,
The holy time is quiet as a Nun
Breathless with adoration.

William Wordsworth, *The Poetical Works of William Wordsworth*, edited by E. de Selincourt and Helen Darbishire, Oxford at the Clarendon Press, 1954, Volume III, p.17, *Miscellaneous Sonnets*, "It is a Beauteous Evening," l.1.

Man is most truly himself, as the Eastern Church well knows, not when he toils but when he adores. And we are learning more and more that all innocent joy in life may be a form of adoration.

Vida D. Scudder, *The Privilege of Age*, J. M. Dent & Sons Ltd., 1939, p.230.

To worship is to quicken the conscience by the holiness of God, to feed the mind with the truth of God, to purge the imagination by the beauty of God, to open the heart to the love of God, to devote the will to the purpose of God. All this is gathered up in that emotion which most cleanses us from selfishness because it is the most selfless of all emotions—adoration.

William Temple, *The Hope of a New World*, S.C.M. Press Ltd., 1940, p.30.

To adore ... means to lose oneself in the unfathomable, to plunge into the inexhaustible, to find peace in the incorruptible, to be absorbed in defined immensity, to offer oneself to the fire and the transparency, to annihilate oneself in proportion as one becomes more deliberately conscious of oneself, and to give of one's deepest to that whose depth has no end.

Pierre Teilhard de Chardin, *Le Milieu Divin*, William Collins Sons & Co. Ltd., 1960, p.188.

Imagine an artist whose inspiration was ceaseless and continuously followed by realization— a Shakespeare or a Beethoven constantly at his best. All we can do to form an idea of God's personality should be in that direction, removing limitations all the time. That is prayer and that is adoration!

Ernest Dimnet, *What We Live By*, Jonathan Cape Ltd., 1932, p.67.

Worship is essentially an act of adoration, adoration of the one true God in whom we live and move and have our being. Forgetting our little selves, our petty ambitions, our puny triumphs, our foolish cares and fretful anxieties, we reach out towards the beauty and majesty of God. The religious life is not a dull, grim drive towards moral virtues, but a response to a vision of greatness.... The pattern prayer given by our Lord offers us the clue to right worship. It begins and ends with words of adoration.

Thomas F. Green, *Preparation For Worship*, (Swarthmore Lecture), George Allen & Unwin Ltd., 1952, p.17.

Adoration is the first and greatest of life's responses to its spiritual environment; the first and most fundamental of spirit's movements towards Spirit, the seed from which all other prayer must spring. It is among the most powerful of the educative forces which purify the understanding, form and develop the spiritual life. As we can never know the secret of great art or music until we have learned to look and listen with a

---

self-oblivious reverence, acknowledging a beauty that is beyond our grasp—so the claim and loveliness remain unrealized, till we have learned to look, to listen, to adore. Then only do we go beyond ourselves and our small vision, pour ourselves out to that which we know not, and so escape from our own pettiness and limitations into the universal life.

Evelyn Underhill, *The Golden Sequence,* Methuen & Co. Ltd., 1932, p. 162.

For Christian experience, the life and person of Christ stand apart as the greatness of these self-revelations; the perfect self-expression of the Holy in human terms, and the supreme school and focus of man's adoring prayer. For here the Invisible God, by the most wonderful of His condescensions, discloses His beauty and attraction—the brightness of His glory and the express image of His person—in a way that is mercifully adapted to our limitations, and meets us on our own ground. Therefore the events of Christ's life—alike the most strange and the most homely—are truly "mysteries." They contain far more than they reveal. They are charged with Spirit, and convey the supernatural to those who are content to watch and adore. Because of this, Christian devotion moves ever to and fro between adoring and intimate prayer; passing through the incarnational veil to the Absolute Beauty, and returning to find the Absolute Beauty shining through the incarnational veil. "Let thy thoughts be always upward to God and direct thy prayer to Christ continually," says Thomas à Kempis. Thus the great horizon gives its meaning to the welcoming figure; and the welcoming figure makes the great horizon safe and fair.

Evelyn Underhill, *The Golden Sequence,* Methuen & Co. Ltd., 1932, p. 165.

ADVERSITY

Gold is tried in the fire, and acceptable men in the furnace of adversity.

Ecclesiasticus 2.5 (A.V.).

Adversity introduces a man to himself.

Anon.

In prosperity, caution; in adversity, patience.

Dutch Proverb.

He knows not his own strength, that hath not met Adversity. Heaven prepares *good men* with *crosses*.

Ben Jonson, *Ben Jonson,* edited by C. H. Herford, Percy and Evelyn Simpson, Oxford at the Clarendon Press, 1947, Volume VIII, *The Poems, The Prose Works,* p. 563, "Explorata: or, Discoveries."

Sweet are the uses of adversity,
Which like the toad, ugly and venomous,
Wears yet a precious jewel in his head.

William Shakespeare, *As You Like It,* Act II, sc. i, l. 12.

Great and honest men take more courage in adversities and become stronger.
Irving Stone, *The Agony and the Ecstasy,* William Collins Sons & Co. Ltd., 1961, p.550.

He that wrestles with us strengthens our nerves, and sharpens our skill. Our antagonist is our helper.
Edmund Burke, *Reflections on the Revolution in France,* edited by Conor Cruise O'Brien, Penguin Books Ltd., 1969, p.278.

Prosperity doth best discover vice, but adversity doth best discover virtue.
Francis Bacon, *The Moral and Historical Works of Lord Bacon,* introductory dissertation, and notes, critical, explanatory, and historical, by Joseph Devey, Henry G. Bohn, 1852, p.14.

Adversity not only draws people together but brings forth that beautiful inward friendship, just as the cold winter forms ice-figures on the window-panes which the warmth of the sun effaces.
Søren Kierkegaard, *The Journals of Søren Kierkegaard,* a selection edited and translated by Alexander Dru, Oxford University Press, 1938, p.20.

In prosperous times I have sometimes felt my fancy and powers of language flag, but adversity is to me at least a tonic and bracer; the fountain is awakened from its inmost recesses, as if the spirit of affliction had troubled it in his passage.
Sir Walter Scott, *Sir Walter Scott's Journal, 1825-1832,* T. Nelson & Sons, Ltd., 1926, Volume I, p.99.

Now let us thank th'eternal pow'r: convinc'd,
That heav'n but tries our virtue by affliction:
That oft' the cloud which wraps the present hour,
Serves but to brighten all our future days!
John Brown, *Barbarossa, 1755,* Act V. sc.iii. p.56.

Let us be patient! These severe afflictions
Not from the ground arise,
But oftentimes celestial benedictions
Assume this dark disguise.
Henry Wadsworth Longfellow, *The Poetical Works of Longfellow,* Humphrey Milford, Oxford University Press, 1913, p.185, *By the Fireside,* "Resignation," st.iii, l.1.

Then, welcome each rebuff
That turns earth's smoothness rough,
Each sting that bids not sit nor stand, but go!
Be our joys three-parts pain!
Strive, and hold cheap the strain;
Learn, nor account the pang; dare, never grudge the throe!
Robert Browning, *The Poetical Works of Robert Browning,* Volume I, Smith, Elder & Co., 1899, p.581, *Dramatis Personae,* "Rabbi Ben Ezra," st.vi, l.1.

It is a good thing that we have to face difficulties and opposition from time to time, because this brings us back to ourselves; it makes us realize that we are exiles and cannot pin our hopes on anything in this world.

It is a good thing that we are maligned now and again, and are misjudged and disliked even when we mean and do well. This sort of thing is often a great help in achieving humility, and it keeps us from groundless self-satisfaction; for we are more ready to listen for God's assuring voice within, when those around believe the worst of us and treat us with contempt. That is why a man should build his life on God, for then he will not need to look for human consolation.

Thomas à Kempis, *The Imitation of Christ,* translated by Betty I. Knott, William Collins Sons & Co. Ltd., 1979, p.52.

AGE

He will not much remember the days of his life because God keeps him occupied with joy in his heart.

Ecclesiastes 5.20.

Stay with us, for it is toward evening and the day is now far spent.

Luke 24.29.

In seed time learn, in harvest teach, in winter enjoy.

William Blake, *The Complete Writings of William Blake,* edited by Geoffrey Keynes, Oxford University Press, 1974, p.150, *The Marriage of Heaven and Hell,* Plate 7, "Proverbs of Hell," l.1.

The evening of life brings with it its lamps.

Joseph Joubert, *Pensées and Letters,* George Routledge & Sons, Ltd., 1928, p.66.

I believe one has to be seventy before one is full of courage. The young are always half-hearted.

D.H. Lawrence, *The Selected Letters of D.H. Lawrence,* edited with an introduction by Diana Trilling, Farrar, Straus and Cudahy, Inc., 1958, p.212.

To know how to grow old is the master-work of wisdom, and one of the most difficult chapters in the great art of living.

Henri Frédéric Amiel, *Amiel's Journal,* translated by Mrs Humphry Ward, Macmillan & Co., Ltd., 1918, p.218.

Youth, large, lusty, loving—youth full of grace, force, fascination, Do you know that Old Age may come after you with equal grace, force, fascination?

Walt Whitman, *The Complete Poems,* edited by Francis Murphy, Penguin Books Ltd., 1982, p.254, "Youth, Day, Old Age and Night," l.1.

Old age has its pleasures, which, though different, are not less than the pleasures of youth.

W. Somerset Maugham, *The Summing Up,* Bernhard Tauchnitz, 1938, p.229.

Old places and old persons in their turn, when spirit dwells in them, have an intrinsic vitality of which youth is incapable; precisely the balance and wisdom that comes from long perspectives and broad foundations.

George Santayana, *My Host The World,* The Cresset Press Ltd., 1953, p.169.

Grow old along with me!
The best is yet to be,
The last of life, for which the first was made:
Our times are in His hand
Who saith, "A whole I planned,
Youth shows but half; trust God: see all nor be afraid!"

Robert Browning, *The Poetical Works of Robert Browning,* Volume I, Smith, Elder & Co., 1899, p.580, *Dramatis Personae,* "Rabbi Ben Ezra," st.i, l.1.

The soul's dark cottage, batter'd and decay'd,
Lets in new light, through chinks that time has made:
Stronger by weakness, wiser men become,
As they draw near to their eternal home:
Leaving the old, both worlds at once view,
That stand upon the threshold of the new.

Edmund Waller, *The Works of the English Poets, from Chaucer to Cowper,* Dr. Samuel Johnson, 1810, Volume VIII, p.81, "On The Foregoing Divine Poems."

For is it not possible that middle-age can be looked upon as a period of second flowering, second growth, even a kind of second adolescence?... Discontent, restlessness, doubt, despair, longing, are interpreted falsely as signs of decay. In youth one does not as often misinterpret the signs; one accepts them, quite rightly, as growing pains. One takes them seriously, listens to them, follows where they lead.

Anne Morrow Lindbergh, *Gift From The Sea,* Chatto & Windus Ltd., 1974, p.86.

Many people as they grow older fear the coming of old age. They regret the failing of physical and mental powers, the withdrawal from active life, posts of leadership and the satisfaction of being used creatively. These increasing diminishments can be seen as a hollowing-out of the material and the temporal, in order to be ready to be filled with the spiritual and the eternal.

George Appleton, *Journey for a Soul,* William Collins Sons & Co. Ltd., 1976, p.47.

The nearer we approach to the middle of life, and the better we have succeeded in entrenching ourselves in our personal standpoints and social positions, the more it appears as if we had discovered the right course and the right ideals and principles of behaviour.... We wholly overlook the essential fact that the achievements which society rewards are won at the cost of diminution of personality. Many—far too many—aspects of life which should also have been experienced lie in the lumber-room among dusty memories. Sometimes, even, they are glowing coals under grey ashes.

C.G. Jung, *Psychological Reflections,* selected and edited by Jolande Jacobi, Routledge & Kegan Paul Ltd., 1953, p.118.

When the signs of age begin to mark my body (and still more when they touch my mind); when the ill that is to diminish me or carry me off strikes from without or is born within me; when the painful moment comes in which I suddenly awaken to the fact that I am ill or growing old; and above all at that last moment when I feel I am losing hold of myself and am absolutely passive within the hands of the great unknown forces that have formed me; in all those dark moments, O God, grant that I may understand that it is You (provided only my faith is strong enough) who are painfully parting the fibres of my being in order to penetrate to the very marrow of my substance and bear me away within Yourself.

Pierre Teilhard de Chardin, *Le Milieu Divin*, William Collins Sons & Co. Ltd., 1960, p.69.

To a man of middle age, existence is no longer a dream, but a reality. He has not much more new to look forward to, for the character of his life is generally fixed by that time. His profession, his home, his occupations, will be for the most part what they are now. He will make few new acquaintances—no new friends. It is the solemn thought connected with middle age that life's last business is begun in earnest; and it is then, midway between the cradle and the grave, that a man begins to look back and marvel with a kind of remorseful feeling that he let the days of youth go by so half enjoyed. It is the pensive autumn feeling,—it is the sensation of half sadness that we experience when the longest day of the year is past, and every day that follows is shorter, and the lights fainter, and the feebler shadows, tell that nature is hastening with gigantic footsteps to her winter grave. So does man look back upon his youth. When the first grey hairs become visible—when the unwelcome truth fastens itself upon the mind, that a man is no longer going up the hill, but down, and that the sun is already westering, he looks back on things behind. Now this is a natural feeling, but is it the high Christian tone of feeling?... We may assuredly answer, No. We who have an inheritance incorruptible and undefiled, and that fadeth not away, what have we to do with things past? When we were children we thought as children. But now there lies before us manhood, with its earnest work: and then old age, and then the grave, and then home.
And so manhood in the Christian life is a better thing than boyhood, because it is a riper thing; and old age ought to be a brighter, and a calmer, and a more serene thing than manhod.

F.W. Robertson, *Sermons*, Kegan Paul, Trench, Trubner & Co. Ltd., 1893, First Series, p.63.

AMBITION

Put personal ambition away from you, and then you will find consolation in living or in dying, whatever may happen to you.

Henri Frédéric Amiel, *Amiel's Journal*, translated by Mrs. Humphry Ward, Macmillan & Co. Ltd., 1918, p.2.

All ambitions are lawful except those which climb upward on the miseries or credulities of mankind.

Joseph Conrad, *A Personal Record*, "A Familiar Preface," J.M. Dent & Sons Ltd., 1923, p.xx.

Where ambition ends, happiness begins.

Hungarian Proverb.

No bird soars too high, if he soars with his own wings.

William Blake, *The Complete Writings of William Blake,* edited by Geoffrey Keynes, Oxford University Press, 1974, p.151, *The Marriage of Heaven and Hell,* Plate 7, "Proverbs of Hell," l.15.

Such joy Ambition finds.

John Milton, *The Poetical Works of John Milton,* edited by the Rev. H.C. Beeching, Oxford at the Clarendon Press, 1900, p. 249, *Paradise Lost,* Bk. IV, l.92.

Ambition, like a torrent, ne're looks back;
And is a swelling, and the last affection
A high mind can put off.

Ben Johnson, *Ben Johnson,* edited by C. H. Herford and Percy Simpson, Oxford at the Clarendon Press, 1965, Volume V, p.477, "Catiline," Act III, l.247.

Ambition raises a secret tumult in the soul, it inflames the mind, and puts it into a violent hurry of thought: it is still reaching after an empty, imaginary good, that has not in it the power to abate or satisfy it. Most other things we long for can allay the cravings of their proper sense, and for a while set the appetite at rest: but fame is a good so wholly foreign to our natures, that we have no faculty in the soul adapted to it, nor any organ in the body to relish it; an object of desire placed out of the possibility of fruition. It may indeed fill the mind for a while with a giddy kind of pleasure, but it is such a pleasure as makes a man restless and uneasy under it; and which does not so much satisfy the present thirst, as it excites fresh desires, and sets the soul on new enterprises. For how few ambitious men are there, who have got as much fame as they desired, and whose thirst after it has not been as eager in the very height of their reputation, as it was before they became known and eminent among men!

Joseph Addison, *The Works of Joseph Addison,* notes by Richard Hurd, edited and published by Henry G. Bohn, 1856, Volume III, p.162.

ANXIETY

Envy and wrath shorten the life, and carefulness bringeth age before the time.

Ecclesiasticus 30.24 (A.V.).

Do not be anxious about your life, what you shall eat or what you shall drink, nor about your body, what you shall put on. Is not life more than food, and the body more than clothing? Look at the birds of the air: they neither sow nor reap nor gather into barns, and yet your heavenly Father feeds them. Are you not of more value than they? And which of you by being anxious can add one cubit to his span of life? And why are you anxious about clothing? Consider the lilies of the field, how they grow; they neither toil nor spin; yet I tell you, even Solomon in all his glory was not arrayed like one of these. But if God so clothes the grass of the field, which today is alive and tomorrow is thrown into the oven, will he not much more clothe you, O men of little faith? Therefore do not be anxious, saying, "What shall we eat?' or "What shall we drink?" or "What shall we wear?" For the Gentiles seek all these things; and your heavenly Father knows that you need them all. But seek first his kingdom and his righteousness, and all these things shall be yours as well. Therefore do not be anxious about tomorrow, for tomorrow will be anxious for itself. Let the day's own trouble be sufficient for the day.

Matthew 6.25-34.

Have no anxiety about anything, but in everything by prayer and supplication with thanksgiving let your requests be made known to God.

Philippians 4.6.

Humble yourselves therefore under the mighty hand of God, that in due time he may exalt you. Cast all your anxieties on him, for he cares about you.

1 Peter 5.6-7.

He has not learned the lesson of life who does not every day surmount a fear.

Ralph Waldo Emerson, *The Works of Ralph Waldo Emerson,* edited by George Sampson, George Bell & Sons, Ltd., 1906, Volume III, *Society and Solitude: Letters and Social Aims: Addresses,* p.147.

This bewilderment—this confusion as to who we are and what we should do—is the most painful thing about anxiety. But the positive and hopeful side is that just as anxiety destroys our self-awareness, so awareness of ourselves can destroy anxiety. That is to say, the stronger our consciousness of ourselves, the more we can take a stand against and overcome anxiety.

Rollo May, *Man's Search For Himself,* George Allen & Unwin Ltd., 1953, p.44.

Many people seem to think that worry is an expression of virtuous concern. On the contrary it is a subtle sin for it amounts to a distrust of God—his love, his will, his grace. Moreover, it makes one confused in mind and unable to think clearly. We should take any quiet forethought possible, and then trust God to guide and strengthen us to meet each duty, difficulty or emergency, as and when it comes.

George Appleton, *Journey for a Soul,* William Collins Sons & Co. Ltd., 1976, p.113.

Look at life carelessly. The only things worth being disappointed in or worrying about are in ourselves, not in externals. Take life as it comes and do what lies straight in front of you. It's only real carelessness about one's own will, and absolute hope and confidence in God's, that can teach one to believe that whatever is, is best. Don't you think this is the key to happiness in an apparently spoilt and disappointing life?

Edward Wilson, *Edward Wilson of the Antarctic,* George Seaver, John Murray Ltd., 1935, p.56.

"Anxiety and misgiving," wrote Fénelon, "proceed solely from love of self. The love of God accomplishes all things quietly and completely; it is not anxious or uncertain. The spirit of God rests continually in quietness. Perfect love casteth out fear. It is in forgetfulness of self that we find peace. Happy is he who yields himself completely, unconsciously, and finally to God. Listen to the inward whisper of His Spirit and follow it—that is enough; but to listen one must be silent, and to follow one must yield."

Lilian Whiting, *The Life Radiant,* Gay and Bird, 1904, p.320.

Most of our conflicts and difficulties come from trying to deal with the spiritual and practical aspects of our life separately instead of realising them as parts of one whole. If our practical life is centred on our own interests, cluttered up by possessions, distracted by ambitions, passions, wants and worries, beset by a sense of our own rights and importance, or anxieties for our own future, or longings for our own success, we need not expect that our spiritual life will be a contrast to all this. The soul's house is not built on such a convenient plan: there are few sound-proof partitions in it. Only when the conviction—not merely the idea—that the demand of the Spirit, however inconvenient, comes first and *is* first, rules the whole of it, will those objectionable noises die down which have a way of penetrating into the nicely furnished little oratory, and drowning all the quieter voices by their din. For a spiritual life is simply a life in which all that we do comes from the centre, where we are anchored in God: a life soaked through and through by a sense of His reality and claim, and self-given to the great movement of His will.

Evelyn Underhill, *The Spiritual Life*, Harper & Row, Publishers, Inc., 1936, p.37.

A great many worries can be diminished by realising the unimportance of the matter which is causing the anxiety. I have done in my time a considerable amount of public speaking; at first every audience terrified me, and nervousness made me speak very badly; I dreaded the ordeal so much that I always hoped I might break my leg before I had to make a speech, and when it was over I was exhausted from the nervous strain. Gradually I taught myself to feel that it did not matter whether I spoke well or ill, the universe would remain much the same in either case. I found that the less I cared whether I spoke well or badly, the less badly I spoke, and gradually the nervous strain diminished almost to vanishing point. A great deal of nervous fatigue can be dealt with in this way. Our doings are not so important as we naturally suppose; our successes and failures do not after all matter very much. Even great sorrows can be survived; troubles which seem as if they must put an end to happiness for life fade with the lapse of time until it becomes almost impossible to remember their poignancy. But over and above these self-centred considerations is the fact that one's ego is no very large part of the world. The man who can centre his thoughts and hopes upon something transcending self can find a certain peace in the ordinary troubles of life which is impossible to the pure egoist.

Bertrand Russell, *The Conquest of Happiness*, George Allen & Unwin Ltd., 1984, p.56.

ART

Fine art is that in which the hand, the head, and the *heart* of man go together.

John Ruskin, *The Two Paths*, George Allen, 1905, p.57.

Nature is a revelation of God; Art a revelation of man.

Henry Wadsworth Longfellow, *Hyperion*, George Routledge and Sons, 1887, p.196.

The art which is grand and yet simple is that which presupposes the greatest elevation both in artist and in public.

Henri Frédéric Amiel, *Amiel's Journal,* translated by Mrs. Humphry Ward, Macmillan & Co. Ltd., 1918, p.249.

Art, unless quickened from above and from within, has in it nothing beyond itself, which is visible beauty.

John Brown, *Horae Subsecivae,* T. Nelson & Sons, Ltd., 1928, p.176.

True art, is the desire of a man to express himself, to record the reactions of his personality to the world he lives in.

Amy Lowell, *Tendencies in Modern American Poetry,* The Macmillan Company, 1917, p.7.

Great art is an instant arrested in eternity.

James Huneker, *The Pathos of Distance,* T. Werner Laurie Ltd., 1913, p.120.

The Fine Arts once divorcing themselves from *truth,* are quite certain to fall mad, if they do not die.

Thomas Carlyle, *Latter-Day Pamphlets,* Chapman & Hall, 1899, p.271.

Art is the gift of God, and must be used
Unto His glory. That in Art is highest
Which aims at this.

Henry Wadsworth Longfellow, *The Poetical Works of Longfellow,* Humphrey Milford, Oxford University Press, 1913, p.793. *Michel Angelo,* Part I, section iii.

All great art is the work of the whole living creature, body and soul, and chiefly of the soul. But it is not only *the work* of the whole creature, it likewise *addresses* the whole creature.

John Ruskin, *The Stones of Venice,* edited and introduced by Jan Morris, Faber and Faber Limited, 1981, p.233.

Painting is an art, and art is not vague production, transitory and isolated, but a power which must be directed to the improvement and refinement of the human soul.

Wassily Kandinsky, *Concerning the Spiritual in Art,* translated with an introduction by M.T.H. Sadler, Dover Publications, Inc., 1977, p.54.

The man who has honesty, integrity, the love of inquiry, the desire to see beyond, is ready to appreciate good art. He needs no one to give him an art education; he is already qualified.

Robert Henri, *The Art Spirit,* compiled by Margery A. Ryerson, J.B. Lippincott Co., 1960, p.66.

But the artist appeals to that part of our being which is not dependant on wisdom; to that in us which is a gift and not an acquisition—and, therefore, more permanently enduring. He speaks to our capacity for delight and wonder, to the sense of mystery surrounding our lives; to our sense of pity, and beauty, and pain.

Joseph Conrad, *The Nigger Of The "Narcissus",* J.M. Dent & Sons Ltd., 1929, p.viii.

When the artist is alive in any person, whatever his kind of work may be, he becomes an inventive, searching, daring, self-expressing creature. He becomes interesting to other people. He disturbs, upsets, enlightens, and he opens ways for a better understanding. Where those who are not artists are trying to close the book, he opens it, shows there are still more pages possible.

Robert Henri, *The Art Spirit,* compiled by Margery A. Ryerson, J. B. Lippincott Co., 1960, p.15.

To draw a moral, to preach a doctrine, is like shouting at the north star. Life is a vast and awful business. The great artist sets down his vision of it and is silent.

Ludwig Lewisohn, *The Modern Drama,* B.W. Huebsch, 1915, p.109.

> So in Art's wide kingdoms ranges
> One sole meaning still the same:
> This is Truth, eternal Reason,
> Which from Beauty takes its dress,
> And serene through time and season
> Stands for aye in loveliness.

Johann Wolfgang von Goethe, *The Works of Thomas Carlyle,* Volume 24, "Wilhelm Meister's Apprenticeship and Travels," Chapman & Hall Limited, 1899, Volume II, p.329.

Art is a kind of innate drive that seizes a human being and makes him its instrument. The artist is not a person endowed with free will who seeks his own ends, but one who allows art to realize its purposes through him. As a human being he may have moods and a will and personal aims, but as an artist he is "man" in a higher sense— he is "collective man," a vehicle and moulder of the unconscious psychic life of mankind. That is his office, and it is sometimes so heavy a burden that he is fated to sacrifice happiness and everything that makes life worth living for the ordinary human being. As K.G. Carus says: "Strange are the ways by which genius is announced, for what distinguishes so supremely endowed a being is that, for all the freedom of his life and the clarity of his thought, he is everywhere hemmed round and prevailed upon by the Unconscious, the mysterious god within him; so that ideas flow to him—he knows not whence; he is driven to work and to create—he knows not to what end; and is mastered by an impulse for constant growth and development—he knows not whither."

C.G. Jung, *The Collected Works of C.G. Jung,* Volume 15, "The Spirit in Man, Art, and Literature," translated by R.F.C. Hull, Routledge & Kegan Paul Ltd., 1966, p.101.

ASPIRATION

> I have
> Immortal longings in me.

William Shakespeare, *Anthony and Cleopatra,* Act V. sc.ii. l.279.

> O Lord, I, a beggar, ask of Thee
> More than what a thousand kings may ask of Thee;
> Each one has something he needs to ask of Thee,
> I have come to ask Thee to give me Thyself.

Al-Ansari, *The Persian Mystics,* translated by Sardar Sir Jogendra Sing, John Murray Ltd., 1939, p.31. "The Invocations of Sheikh Abdullah Ansari of Herat."

An aspiration is a joy for ever, a possession as solid as a landed estate, a fortune which we can never exhaust and which gives year by year a revenue of pleasurable activity.

Robert Louis Stevenson, *Familiar Studies of Men and Books, Virginibus Puerisque, Selected Poems,* William Collins Sons & Co. Ltd., 1956, p.293.

The sensual man is at home in worldliness because he has no higher aspiration. The spiritual man, however much attracted to worldliness, cannot be at home in the world of sense because he is groping towards the world of spirit.

Hubert van Zeller, *Considerations,* Sheed & Ward Ltd., 1974, p.84.

By aspiring to a similitude of God in goodness or love, neither man nor angel ever transgressed, or shall transgress.

Francis Bacon, *The Advancement of Learning,* introduction by Henry Morley, Cassell and Company Ltd., 1905, p.156.

A good man, through obscurest aspiration,
Has still an instinct of the one true way.

Johann Wolfgang von Goethe, *Faust,* introduction by Dennis Wheatley, translated by Bayard Taylor, Sphere Books Ltd., 1974, p.26, Part I, "Prologue in Heaven," l.328.

Strong souls
Live like fire-hearted suns to spend their strength
In farthest striving action.

George Eliot, *The Spanish Gypsy. A Poem,* William Blackwood and Sons, 1868, p.303, Bk.iv.

Enflam'd with the study of learning, and the admiration of virtue; stirr'd up with high hopes of living to be brave men, and worthy patriots, dear to God, and famous to all ages.

John Milton, *Complete Prose Works of John Milton,* Oxford University Press, 1959, Volume II, 1643-1648, p.385, "Of Education."

And thou my mind aspire to higher things:
Grow rich in that which never taketh rust.

Sir Philip Sidney, *The Poems of Sir Philip Sidney,* edited by William A. Ringler, Jr., Oxford at the Clarendon Press, 1962, p.161: "Leave me, O Love."

For rigorous teachers seized my youth,
And purged its faith, and trimmed its fire,
Showed me the high, white star to Truth,
There bade me gaze, and there aspire.

Matthew Arnold, *The Poems of Matthew Arnold,* edited by Kenneth Allott, Longmans, Green & Co. Ltd., 1965, p.288, "Stanzas from the Grande Chartreuse," st.12, l.67.

My ... aspirations are my only friends.

Henry Wadsworth Longfellow, *The Poetical Works of Longfellow,* Humphrey Milford, Oxford University Press, 1913, p.688, "The Masque of Pandora," Part III, l.74.

Yet some there be that by due steps aspire
To lay their just hands on that golden key
That opes the palace of eternity.

John Milton, *The Poems of John Milton,* edited by John Carey & Alastair Fowler, Longmans, Green & Co. Ltd., 1968, p.176, "Comus," l.12.

It was my duty to have loved the highest:
It surely was my profit had I known:
It would have been my pleasure had I seen.
We needs must love the highest when we see it.

Alfred, Lord Tennyson, *The Poems of Tennyson,* edited by Christopher Ricks, Longmans, Green & Co. Ltd., 1969, p.1741, *Idylls of the King,* No.474, "Guinevere," l.652.

A man who loves Jesus and the truth, who is delivered from undisciplined desires and really lives the inward life, can turn to God with nothing to hold him back. In spirit he can rise beyond himself and rest in peace and joy.

Thomas à Kempis, *The Imitation of Christ,* translated by Betty I. Knott, William Collins Sons & Co. Ltd., 1979, p.85.

The religious spirit is in us. It preceded the religions, and their task as well as that of the prophets, of the initiated, consists in releasing, directing, and developing it. This mystical aspiration is an essentially human trait. It slumbers at the bottom of our souls awaiting the event, or the man capable, in the manner of an enzyme, of transforming it into true mysticism, into faith.

Lecomte du Noüy, *Human Destiny,* Longmans, Green & Co. Ltd., 1947, p.178.

I should like to make every man, woman, and child whom I meet discontented with themselves, even as I am discontented with myself. I should like to awaken in them, about their physical, their intellectual, their moral condition, that divine discontent which is the parent, first of upward aspiration and then of self-control, thought, effort to fulfil that aspiration even in part. For to be discontented with the divine discontent, and to be ashamed with the noble shame, is the very germ and first upgrowth of all virtue.

Charles Kingsley, *Health and Education,* W. Isbister & Co., 1874, p.20.

No aspiring soul ... has not at some time bowed in worship before the wonder, mystery and beauty of this world. The glorious forms and colours of sunset and dawn; the ripple of moonlight on the surface of some quiet lake; the majesty of mountain peaks; and the quaintly flowing music of mountain streams, remind every lover of Nature that God is not apart from His world, but can be found hidden there as the very Spirit of it all—"Beauty Itself among beautiful things." The beauty is there for all to see, but men dwell in the shadows of their own creation and their eyes are blind to it. We miss the joy of the beautiful so often, because we are wrapped up in ourselves.

Raynor C. Johnson, *A Pool of Reflections,* Hodder & Stoughton Ltd., 1975, p.143.

ATHEISM

The hope of the ungodly is like dust that is blown away with the wind.
Wisdom of Solomon 5.14.

The three great apostles and supporters of practical atheism are Wealth, Health, and Power.
C.C. Colton, *Lacon*, William Tegg, 1866, p.23.

The fearful Unbelief is unbelief in yourself.
Thomas Carlyle, *Sartor Resartus*, Ward, Lock & Co. Ltd., p.113.

Atheism is rather in the lip than in the heart of man.
Francis Bacon, *The Moral and Historical Works of Lord Bacon*, introductory dissertation, and notes, critical, explanatory, and historical, by Joseph Devey, Henry G. Bohn, 1852, p.46.

Some are Atheists by Neglect; others are so by Affectation: they, that think there is no God, at some times; do not think so, at all times.
Benjamin Whichcote, *Moral and Religious Aphorisms*, 1930, p.1, Century 1, No.1.

The atheist who is moved by love is moved by the spirit of God; an atheist who lives by love is saved by his faith in the God whose existence (under that name) he denies.
William Temple, *Nature, Man and God*, Macmillan & Co. Ltd., 1934, p.416.

Christianity founds hospitals, and atheists are cured in them, never knowing that they owe their cure to Christ.
William Temple, *Readings in St. John's Gospel* (First and Second Series), Macmillan & Co., Ltd., 1947, p.109.

My atheism, like that of Spinoza, is true piety towards the universe and denies only gods fashioned by men in their own image, to be servants of their human interests.
George Santayana, *Soliloquies in England and Later Soliloquies*, Constable and Company Ltd., 1922, p.246.

To every soul, even to one ignorant of the name of God, even one reared in atheism, grace offers ... that Reality of absolute goodness, which merits all our love and is able to save our life.
Jacques Maritain, *True Humanism*, translated by M.R. Adamson, Geoffrey Bles: The Centenary Press, 1938, p.56.

The growth of Christian experience over the centuries can be interpreted as some sort of conversation of faith, where people have learned to trust that the world has a meaning, and so have found one. Now you can say this is all fantasy; but the non-believer is then left with some rather difficult questions when he looks at the oddity of existence.
John Habgood, *Priestland's Progress*, Gerald Priestland, British Broadcasting Corporation, 1982, p.49.

They that deny a God destroy a man's nobility; for certainly man is of kin to the beasts by his body; and, if he be not of kin to God by his spirit, he is a base and ignoble creature. It destroys likewise magnanimity, and the raising of human nature.

Francis Bacon, *The Moral and Historical Works of Lord Bacon,* introductory dissertation and notes—critical, explanatory, and historical—by Joseph Devey, Henry G. Bohn, 1852, p.48.

One cannot escape the feeling that what modern atheism is revolting against is, in part at least, the objectified God, conceived by the atheists, as by many Christians, as an immensely magnified human person, with whom men can talk on equal terms and arraign His government of the world. But that ... is not God, but an idol and, in so far as modern atheism destroys that idol, it is doing a service to true religion.

J.H. Oldham, *Life is Commitment,* S.C.M. Press Ltd., 1953, p.47.

Forth from his dark and lonely hiding-place,
(Portentous sight!) the owlet Atheism,
Sailing on obscene wings athwart the noon,
Drops his blue-fringed lids, and holds them close,
And hooting at the glorious sun in Heaven,
Cries out, "Where is it?"

Samuel Taylor Coleridge, *Coleridge, Poetical Works,* edited by Ernest Hartley Coleridge, Oxford University Press, 1978, p.259, Fears in Solitude, l.81.

Not many years ago when I was an atheist, if anyone had asked me, "Why do you not believe in God?" my reply would have run something like this: "Look at the universe we live in. By far the greatest part of it consists of empty space, completely dark and unimaginably cold. The bodies which move in this space are so few and so small in comparison with the space itself that even if every one of them were known to be crowded as full as it could hold with perfectly happy creatures, it would still be difficult to believe that life and happiness were more than a bye-product to the power that made the universe.... History is largely a record of crime, war, disease, and terror, with just sufficient happiness interposed to give them, while it lasts, an agonised apprehension of losing it, and, when it is lost, the poignant misery of remembering. Every now and then they improve their condition a little and what we call a civilisation appears. But all civilisations pass away and, even while they remain, inflict peculiar sufferings of their own probably sufficient to outweigh what alleviations they may have brought to the normal pains of man.... If you ask me to believe that this is the work of a benevolent and omnipotent spirit, I reply that all the evidence points in the opposite direction. Either there is no spirit behind the universe, or else a spirit indifferent to good and evil, or else an evil spirit."
There was one question which I never dreamed of raising. I never noticed that the very strength and facility of the pessimists' case at once poses us a problem. If the universe is so bad, or even half so bad, how on earth did human beings ever come to attribute it to the activity of a wise and good Creator?

C.S. Lewis, *The Problem of Pain,* The Centenary Press, 1941, p.1.

Godlessness justifies itself on various grounds, scientific-positivistic, moral or social. In the second half of the nineteenth century a heavy stratum of both European and Russian intelligentsia convinced themselves that science had demonstrated that there was no God, that belief in God could not be combined with the existence of science. It must be said that this is the most naive and the feeblest of all the arguments of atheism. It was based on the belief that science is supreme not only over all knowledge, but over the whole of human life. Men thought that science had the answer to every question. In the twentieth-century positive science, specially physics and chemistry, have made colossal advances, but there is no longer the belief that science can solve all problems. Such a remarkable scholar as Eddington, astronomer and physicist, expresses his recognition of the results of science in these words: "something unknown does something unknown." The very existence of material, in which the earlier science believed so firmly, is now subject to doubt, consciously or unconsciously. Everything in the principal basis of science has become doubtful.... True science, always conscious of its limitations, can say nothing about God, positive or negative: it can neither prove nor disprove the existence of God. The problem of God's existence belongs in quite another sphere than that of science, which is concerned with the knowledge of the world of nature. The arguments of atheism based on the natural sciences are just as feeble as the arguments for God's existence, based on these same natural sciences. And Christian apologetics that refute the arguments of natural sciences against faith in God are very feeble and out-moded. We may ignore completely the arguments of natural science. But the Christian consciousness should be freed from all connection with the out-moded natural history with which it was linked in the past. Biblical natural history is the knowledge of humanity in its childhood; we cannot now consider it of serious importance. What is really important, is the possibility of a conflict between Christianity and the science of history. Historical knowledge may offer serious difficulties for the Christian faith in so far as this faith is to be based on the facts of history.... And only the worship of God in spirit and in truth rises above the difficulties connected with the science of history.

Nicolas Berdyaev, *Christian Existentialism*, edited and translated by Donald A. Lowrie, George Allen & Unwin Ltd., 1965, p.218.

AUTHORITY

Where there is no prophecy the people cast off restraint.

Proverbs 29.18.

And they were astonished at his teaching, for he taught them as one who had authority, and not as the scribes.

Mark 1.22.

The spiritual authority of the Gospel for those who accept it is secured by the fact that it is transmitted in a form which perpetually calls for private judgement.

William Temple, *Nature, Man and God*, Macmillan & Co. Ltd., 1934, p.351.

The spiritual authority of God Himself consists, not in His having the power to create and to destroy, but in His being the appropriate object of worship and love.

William Temple, *Nature, Man and God,* Macmillan & Co. Ltd., 1934, p.349.

The Gospel stories are not to be treated as something sacred, as a final authority, but as the means whereby we can come in touch with the living Christ who is the same yesterday, to-day, and for ever.

William Temple, *Basic Convictions,* Hamish Hamilton, 1937, p.46.

There is no authority short of God. Look up to him, expect his teachings. And though clouds of uncertainty may come, never let them make you turn your eyes away in discouragement, or think that on the earth you can find that guidance which is not a thing of earth, but which must come to us from heaven.

Phillips Brooks, *Series of Miscellaneous Illustrated Cards,* 1902, p.16.

There is only one authority in this field, and that is the authority which truth itself possesses when it is perceived to be true by the individual concerned; or, in other words, when it authenticates itself....
It is I who finally decide to submit to the authority.

Leslie D. Weatherhead, *The Christian Agnostic,* Hodder & Stoughton Ltd., 1965, p.21.

The spiritual authority of God is that which He exercises by displaying not His power, but His character. Holiness, not omnipotence, is the spring of His spiritual authority. In such a vision as that of Isaiah there is awe-inspiring majesty; but what leaps to the prophet's consciousness is not the sense of his powerlessness before the Almighty, but the sense of his uncleanness before the All-Holy.

William Temple, *Nature, Man and God,* Macmillan & Co. Ltd., 1934, p.348.

Therefore, lest the political community be ruined while everyone follows his own opinion, an authority is needed to guide the energies of all towards the common good— not mechanically or despotically, but by acting above all as a moral force based on freedom and a sense of responsibility.

Vatican Council II, *The Conciliar and Post Conciliar Documents,* 1981 Edition, general editor, Austin Flannery, O.P., Fowler Wright Books Ltd., p.981.

AWARENESS

Our most important task is to become aware of the fact that our new consciousness of space no longer admits the traditional religious imagery by which we represent to ourselves our encounter with God. At the same time, we must also recognize that this traditional imagery *was never essential to Christianity.* We must recover the New Testament awareness that our God does not need a temple (Acts 7.47-53) or even a cathedral. The New Testament teaches in fact that God has one indestructible temple:

which is man himself (1 Cor. 3.17). To understand that God is present in the world *in man* is in fact no new or radical idea. It is, on the contrary, one of the most elementary teachings of the New Testament.

Thomas Merton, *Conjectures of a Guilty Bystander*, Burns & Oates Ltd, 1968, p.274.

The Holy Spirit is that power which opens eyes that are closed, hearts that are unaware and minds that shrink from too much reality. If one is open towards God, one is open also to the beauty of the world, the truth of ideas, and the pain of disappointment and deformity. If one is closed up against being hurt, or blind towards one's fellow-men, one is inevitably shut off from God also. One cannot choose to be open in one direction and closed in another. Vision and vulnerability go together. Insensitivity also is an all-rounder. If for one reason or another we refuse really to *see* another person, we become incapable of sensing the presence of God.
The spirit of man is that facility which enables each of us to be truly present to another. The spirit of God is that power of communion which enables every other reality, and the God who is within and behind all realities, to be present to us.

John V. Taylor, *The Go-Between God*, S.C.M. Press Ltd., 1972, p.19.

Slowly on You, too, the meanings: the light-sparkles on water, tufts of weed in winter—the least thing—dandelion and groundsel.
Have you seen the wild bees' nest in the field, the cells, the grubs, the transparent white baby-bees, turning brown, hairy, the young bees beginning to fly, raking the moss down over the disturbed cells? the parasites?
Have you seen the face of your brother or sister? Have you seen the little robin hopping and peering under the bushes? Have you seen the sun rise, or set? I do not know—
I do not think that I have.
When your unquiet brain has ceased to spin its cobwebs over the calm and miraculous beauty of the world;
When the Air and Sunlight shall have penetrated your body through and through; and the Earth and Sea have become part of it;
When at last, like a sheath long concealing the swelling green shoot, the love of learning and the regard for elaborate art, wit, manners, dress, or anything rare or costly whatever, shall drop clean off from you;
When your Body—for to this it must inevitably return—is become shining and transparent before you in every part (however deformed);
Then (O blessed One!) these things also transparent possibly shall surrender themselves—the least thing shall speak to you words of deliverance.

Edward Carpenter, *Towards Democracy*, George Allen & Unwin Ltd., 1931, p.90.

Another lesson I learned was that the intensity of prayer is not measured by time, but by the reality and depth of one's awareness of unity with God. I learned to look on prayer not as a means of influencing the Creator in my favour, but as an awareness of the presence of God—everywhere.
I also learned a few helpful ideas about sin. Broadly speaking, I learned to recognize sin as the refusal to live up to the enlightenment we possess. To know the right order

of values and deliberately to choose the lower ones. To know that, however much these values may differ with different people at different stages of spiritual growth, for one's self there must be no compromise with that which one *knows* to be the lower value.

I learned, too, that to condemn others is a grave mistake, since hatred, and even the wrong kind of criticism, is an evil which recoils upon its author and poisons every human relationship.

That does not mean we should be blind to the weaknesses or wickednesses of others, any more than to our own, but that we should learn to look at them as the limitations of birth and circumstance, limitations which it is our duty to help them to rise above. In this I have found that example and service are more helpful than advice or preaching. It has enabled me to get some little glimpse of the meaning behind that great truth— that all the living are as one, in the Great Life of the Universe.

And it carries with it a deep sense of rest. It gives a meaning to life, and a happiness which nothing else can give and no one but ourselves can take away. It is a road to be travelled with a shout of joy—a most exciting road!

Margaret Bondfield, *What Life Has Taught Me,* introduced by Gilbert Murray, edited by Sir James Marchant, Odhams Press Limited, 1948, p.27.

B

BAPTISM

I baptize you with water for repentance, but he who is coming after me is mightier than I, whose sandals I am not worthy to carry; he will baptize you with the Holy Spirit and with fire.

Matthew 3.11.

Do you not know that all of us who have been baptized into Christ Jesus were baptized into his death? We were buried therefore with him by baptism into death, so that as Christ was raised from the dead by the glory of the Father, we too might walk in newness of life.

Romans 6.3-4.

He has put his seal upon us and given us his Spirit in our hearts as a guarantee.

2 Corinthians 1.22.

Hence I remind you to rekindle the gift of God that is within you through the laying on of my hands.

2 Timothy 1.6.

The true and availing baptism is a baptism into the life, death, and resurrection of Christ, and cleanses the soul of its sins and produces "a good conscience toward God"— the old sinful man is buried and a new and Christlike man is raised.

Rufus M. Jones, *Spiritual Reformers in the 16th and 17th Centuries,* Macmillan & Co. Ltd., 1914, p.110.

This birth must be wrought within you. The heart, or Son of God must arise in the birth of your life, and then you are in Christ and He is in you, and all that He and the Father have is yours; and as the Son is one with the Father, so also the new man is one with the Father and with the Son, one virtue, one power, one light, one life, one eternal paradise, one enduring substance, one Father, Son, and Holy Ghost, and thou His child!

Rufus M. Jones, *Spiritual Reformers in the 16th and 17th Centuries,* Macmillan & Co. Ltd., 1914, p.197.

The direct incoming of the Divine Spirit, producing a rebirth and a new creation in the man himself, is the only baptism which avails with God or which makes any difference in the actual condition of man. Baptism in its true significance is the reception of cleansing power, it is an inward process which purifies the heart, illuminates the conscience, and is not only necessary for salvation but in fact *is* salvation. Christian baptism is therefore not with water, but with Christ: it is the immersion of the soul in the life-giving streams of Christ's spiritual presence,... the reception of *Christ's real baptism,* an inner baptism, a baptism of spirit and power, by which the believing soul, the inner man, is clarified, strengthened, and made pure.

Rufus M. Jones, *Spiritual Reformers in the 16th and 17th Centuries,* Macmillan & Co. Ltd., 1914, p.80.

Imagine not infants but crowds of grown-up persons already changed in heart and feelings; their "life hidden with Christ and God," losing their personal consciousness in the laver of regeneration; rising again from the depths into the light of heaven, in communion with God and nature; met as they rose from the bath with the white raiment, which is "the righteousness of the saints," and ever after looking back on that moment as the instant of their new birth, of the putting off of the old man, and the putting on of Christ. Baptism was to them the figure of death, burial, and resurrection all in one, the most apt expression of the greatest change that can pass upon man, like the sudden change into another life when we leave the body.

Benjamin Jowett, *Select Passages from the Theological Writings of Benjamin Jowett,* edited by Lewis Campbell, John Murray, 1902, p.60.

For thousands of years, rites of initiation have been teaching spiritual rebirth; yet, strangely enough, man forgets again and again the meaning of divine procreation. This is surely no evidence of a strong life of the spirit; and yet the penalty of misunderstanding is heavy, for it is nothing less than neurotic decay, embitterment, atrophy and sterility. It is easy enough to drive the spirit out of the door, but when we have done so the salt of life grows flat—it loses its savour. Fortunately, we have proof that the spirit always renews its strength in the fact that the central teaching of the ancient initiations is handed on from generation to generation. Ever and again human beings arise who understand what is meant by the fact that God is our Father. The equal balance of the flesh and the spirit is not lost to the world.

C.G. Jung, *Modern Man in Search of a Soul,* translated by W. S. Dell & Cary F. Baynes, Kegan Paul, Trench, Trubner & Co. Ltd., 1933, p.142.

By the sacrament of Baptism, whenever it is properly conferred in the way the Lord determined and received with the proper dispositions of soul, man becomes truly incorporated into the crucified and glorified Christ and is reborn to a sharing of the divine life, as the Apostle says: "For you were buried together with him in baptism, and in him also rose again through faith in the working of God who raised him from the dead."

Baptism, therefore, constitutes the sacramental bond of unity existing among all who through it are reborn. But baptism, of itself, is only a beginning, a point of departure, for it is wholly directed toward the acquiring of fullness of life in Christ. Baptism is thus ordained toward a complete profession of faith, a complete incorporation into the system of salvation such as Christ himself willed it to be, and finally, toward a complete integration into eucharistic communion.

Vatican Council II, *The Conciliar and Post Conciliar Documents,* 1981 Edition, general editor, Austin Flannery, O.P., Fowler Wright Books Ltd., p.469.

BEAUTY

Know how much better the Lord of them is: for the first author of beauty hath created them ... for by the greatness and beauty of the creatures proportionably the maker of them is seen.

Wisdom of Solomon 13.3,5.

Though we travel the world over to find the beautiful, we must carry it with us, or we find it not.

Ralph Waldo Emerson, *The Works of Ralph Waldo Emerson*, edited by George Sampson, George Bell & Sons, Ltd., 1906, Volume I, *Essays and Representative Men*, p.191.

He has a daily beauty in his life.

William Shakespeare, *Othello*, Act V. sc.i. l.19.

Every bit of beauty in this world, the beauty of man, of nature, of a work of art, is a partial transfiguration of this world, a creative break-through to another.

Nicolas Berdyaev, *Christian Existentialism*, selected and translated by Donald A. Lowrie, George Allen & Unwin Ltd., 1965, p.323.

For beauty being the best of all we know
Sums up the unsearchable and secret aims
Of nature.

Robert Bridges, *Poetical Works of Robert Bridges*, Humphrey Milford, Oxford University Press, 1913, p.191, Sonnet: "The Growth of Love," st. viii, l.1.

Nothing in human life, least of all religion, is ever right until it is beautiful.

Harry Emerson Fosdick, *As I See Religion*, S.C.M. Press Ltd., 1932, p.128.

I want to help you to grow as beautiful as God meant you to be when he thought of you first.

George Macdonald, *The Marquis of Lossie*, Everett & Co. Ltd., 1912, p.68.

For, when with beauty we can virtue join,
We paint the semblance of a form divine,

Matthew Prior, *The Poetical Works of Matthew Prior*, edited by Charles Cowden Clarke, William P. Nimmo, 1868, p.401, "Verses spoken to Lady Henrietta Cavendish-Holles Harley, Countess of Oxford," l.17.

Physical beauty is the sign of an interior beauty, a spiritual and moral beauty which is the basis, the principle, and the unity of the beautiful.

Friedrich Schiller, *Essays, Aesthetical and Philosophical*, George Bell & Sons, Ltd., 1875, p.4.

The hours when the mind is absorbed by beauty are the only hours when we really live.

Richard Jefferies, *The Pageant of Summer*, Chatto & Windus, 1911, p.39.

(God) Himself has imparted of His own to all particular beings from that fountain of beauty—Himself. For the good and beautiful things in the world could never have

been what they are, save that they were made in the image of the archetype, which
is truly good and beautiful.

Philo, *Three Jewish Philosophers*, selections, edited by Hans Lewy, Harper & Row, Publishers, Inc., 1945, p.84.

But a celestial brightness—a more ethereal beauty—
Shone on her face and encircled her form, when, after confession,
Homeward serenely she walked with God's benediction upon her.
When she had passed, it seemed like the ceasing of exquisite music.

Henry Wadsworth Longfellow, *The Poetical Works of Longfellow*, Humphrey Milford, Oxford University Press, 1913, p.144, *Evangeline*, "Part the First," I. 1.59.

Spirit of Beauty, whose sweet impulses,
Flung like the rose of dawn across the sea,
Alone can flush the exalted consciousness
With shafts of sensible divinity—
Light of the World, essential loveliness.

Alan Seeger, *Poems*, introduction by William Archer, Constable and Company Ltd., 1917, "An Ode to Natural Beauty," p.4.

It's only now I am beginning to see again and to recognise again the beauty of the
world. Take the swallows to-day their flutter-flutter, their velvet-forked tails, their
transparent wings that are like the fins of fishes. The little dark head and breast golden
in the light. Then the beauty of the garden, and the beauty of raked paths.... Then,
the silence.

Katherine Mansfield, *Journal of Katherine Mansfield*, edited by J. Middleton Murry, Constable & Co. Ltd., 1927, p.242.

A thing of beauty is a joy for ever:
Its loveliness increases; it will never
Pass into nothingness; but still will keep
A bower quiet for us, and a sleep
Full of sweet dreams, and health, and quiet breathing.

John Keats, *The Poems of John Keats*, edited with an introduction and notes by E. de Selincourt, Methuen & Co. Ltd., 1907, p.53, "Endymion," Bk.I, l.1.

Man is so inclined to concern himself with the most ordinary things, while his mind
and senses are so easily blunted against impressions of beauty and perfection, that we
should use all means to preserve the capacity of feeling them.... Each day we should
at least hear one little song, read one good poem, see one first-rate picture and, if it
can be arranged, utter some sensible remarks.

Johann Wolfgang von Goethe, *William Meister's Years of Apprenticeship*, translated by H.M. Waidson, John Calder (Publishers) Ltd., 1978, Volume 2, p.74.

Beauty is something wonderful and strange that the artist fashions out of the chaos
of the world in the torment of his soul. And when he has made it, it is not given to
all to know it. To recognise it you must repeat the adventure of the artist. It is a

melody that he sings to you, and to hear it again in your own heart you want knowledge and sensitiveness and imagination.

W. Somerset Maugham, *The Moon and Sixpence*, William Heinemann Ltd., 1928, p.84.

The wonder of Creation suggests another gateway to worship: the door of Beauty. Whatever kind of beauty stirs us to delight or to painful longing, we can use as a ladder to rise above ourselves. For this love of beauty is divinely implanted. The touch of beauty, when we feel it, is not to be merely a passing delight: it is the call of God, inviting us gently and sweetly to turn to Him. St. Augustine says: "Thy whole creation praises Thee without ceasing ... to the end that, using Thy creatures as stepping stones, and passing on to Him who made them so wonderfully, our soul might shake off its despondence and soar up to Thee. There is refreshment and true courage." To the man or woman who "means only God" the beauty of Creation may become a transparent veil, half revealing and half concealing the presence of Love itself.

Olive Wyon, *The School of Prayer*, S.C.M. Press Ltd., 1943, p.89.

The Beautiful, says Hegel, is the spiritual making itself known sensuously. It represents, then, a direct message to us from the heart of Reality; ministers to us of more abundant life. Therefore the widening of our horizon which takes place when we turn in prayer to a greater world than that which the senses reveal to us, should bring with it a more poignant vision of loveliness, a more eager passion for Beauty as well as for Goodness and Truth. When St. Augustine strove to express the intensity of his regret for wasted years, it was to his neglect of the Beauty of God that he went to show the poignancy of his feelings, the immensity of his loss. "Oh Beauty so old and so new! too late have I loved thee!"
It needs a special training, I think—a special and deliberate use of our faculties—if we are to avoid this deprivation; and learn, as an integral part of our communion with Reality, to lay hold of the loveliness of the First and only Fair.

Evelyn Underhill, *The Essentials of Mysticism*, J.M. Dent & Sons Ltd., 1920, p.113.

The Beauty of the world, as many have felt, is the strongest evidence we have of the goodness and benevolence of the Creator. Not, of course, that the world was made beautiful for our sakes. It is beautiful because its Author is beautiful; and we should remember that when the old writers spoke of God as the Author of nature, they used the word in much the same sense as if we said that a man was the author of his own photograph. But we are allowed to see and enjoy beauty, although the gift cannot be proved to promote our own survival. It looks like a free gift of God. Beauty is a general quality of nature, and not only of organic nature; crystals are very beautiful. As in the case of the other ultimate values, the emotion of beauty is aroused by the meeting of mind and its object; and not only must the object be beautiful; the perceiving mind must also be beautiful and healthy. The vile or vulgar mind not only cannot discern beauty; it is a great destroyer of beauty everywhere.

The love of beauty is super-personal and disinterested, like all the spiritual values; it promotes common enjoyment and social sympathy. Unquestionably it is one of the three ultimate values, ranking with Goodness and Truth.

W.R. Inge, *Outspoken Essays*, Longmans, Green & Co. Ltd., 1922, Second Series, p.30.

Suppose a curious and fair woman. Some have seen the beauties of Heaven in such a person. It is a vain thing to say they loved too much. I dare say there are ten thousand beauties in that creature which they have not seen. They loved it not too much, but upon false causes. Not so much upon false ones, as only upon some little ones. They love a creature for sparkling eyes and curled hair, lily breasts and ruddy cheeks: which they should love moreover for being God's Image, Queen of the Universe, beloved by Angels, redeemed by Jesus Christ, an heiress of Heaven, and the temple of the Holy Ghost: a mine and fountain of all virtues, a treasury of graces, and a child of God. But these excellencies are unknown. They love her perhaps, but do not love God more: nor men as much: nor Heaven and Earth at all. And so, being defective to other things, perish by a seeming excess to that. We should be all Life and Mettle and Vigour and Love to everything; and that would poise us.... But God being beloved infinitely more, will be infinitely more our joy, and our heart will be more with Him, so that no man can be in danger by loving others too much, that loveth God as he ought.

Thomas Traherne, *Centuries*, The Faith Press Ltd., 1969, p.87.

BELIEF

I believe; help my unbelief!

Mark 9.24.

Have you believed because you have seen me? Blessed are those who have not seen and yet believe.

John 20.29.

There are three sources of belief: reason, custom, inspiration.

Blaise Pascal, *Pensées*, translated by W.F. Trotter, Random House Inc., 1941, p.87.

Belief consists in accepting the affirmations of the soul; unbelief, in denying them.

Ralph Waldo Emerson, *The Works of Ralph Waldo Emerson*, edited by George Sampson, George Bell & Sons, Ltd., 1906, Volume I, *Essays and Representative Men*, p.453.

It is your own assent to yourself, and the constant voice of your own reason, and not of others, that should make you believe.

Blaise Pascal, *Pensées*, translated by W.F. Trotter, Random House Inc., 1941, p.91.

So, once again, you chose for yourself—and opened the door to chaos. The chaos you become whenever God's hand does not rest upon your head.

Dag Hammarskjold, *Markings*, translated by Leif Sjoberg & W. H. Auden, with a foreword by W. H. Auden, Faber and Faber Limited, 1964, p.95.

Believe that life *is* worth living, and your belief will help create the fact.
William James, *The Will to Believe,* Longmans, Green & Co. Ltd., 1904, p.62.

That gracious Child, that thorn-crowned Man!
He lived while we believed.
Matthew Arnold, *The Poems of Matthew Arnold,* edited by Kenneth Allott, Longmans, Green & Co. Ltd., 1965, p.526, "Obermann Once More," l.167.

We all know people who tell us they cannot believe what cannot be proved. Of course it is not true. Of course they do in fact believe a great deal that they cannot prove— concerning the trustworthiness of their friends, for example.
William Temple, *The Hope of a New World,* S.C.M. Press Ltd., 1940, p.107.

Strong Son of God, immortal Love,
Whom we, that have not seen thy face,
By faith, and faith alone, embrace.
Believing where we cannot prove.
Alfred, Lord Tennyson, *The Poems of Tennyson,* edited by Christopher Ricks, Longmans, Green & Co. Ltd., 1969, p.861, No. 296, *In Memoriam A.H.H.,* "Prologue," l.1.

We have only to believe. And the more threatening and irreducible reality appears, the more firmly and desperately must we believe. Then, little by little, we shall see the universal horror unbend, and then smile upon us, and then take us in its more than human arms.
Pierre Teilhard de Chardin, *Le Milieu Divin,* William Collins Sons & Co. Ltd., 1960, p.129.

There is nothing that so sanctifies the heart of man, that keeps us in such habitual love, prayer, and delight in God: nothing that so kills all the roots of evil in our nature, that so renews and perfects all our virtues, that fills us with so much love, goodness, and good wishes to every creature as this faith that God is always present in us with His light and Holy Spirit.
William Law, *Selected Mystical Writings of William Law,* edited by Stephen Hobhouse, Rockliff, 1948, p.32.

The existence of God is fully credible only if evil is being transmuted into good; and that cannot—demonstrably cannot—finally be accomplished unless God the Supreme Good becomes the apparent good to every man.... The Supreme Good can only be my apparent good and so dominate my Self if it both is, and, in a form quickening my sympathy, manifestly displays itself as, utterly selfless love.
William Temple, *Nature, Man and God,* Macmillan & Co. Ltd., 1934, p.519.

I believe in one God, the creator of the universe. That he governs it by his Providence. That he ought to be worshipped. That the most acceptable service we can render to him is doing good to his other children. That the soul of man is immortal, and will be treated with justice in another life respecting its conduct in this. These I take to be the fundamental points in all sound religion, and I regard them as you do in whatever sect I meet with them. As to Jesus of Nazareth, my opinion of whom you particularly desire, I think the system of morals and his religion as he left them to us, the best the world saw or is like to see.

Benjamin Franklin, *The Private Correspondence of B. Franklin 1753-1790,* printed for Henry Colburn, 1817, p.131.

BIBLE

Thy word is a lamp to my feet and a light to my path.

Psalm 119.105.

All scripture is inspired by God and profitable for teaching, for reproof, for correction, and for training in righteousness.

2 Timothy 3.16.

If you knew the whole Bible off by heart and all the expositions of scholars, what good would it do you without the love and grace of God.

Thomas à Kempis, *The Imitation of Christ,* translated by Betty I. Knott, William Collins Sons & Co. Ltd., 1979, p.37.

That they might feel something *nearer* to them than the Scriptures, to wit, the *Word in the Heart,* from whence all Holy Scripture came, which is *Christ within them the Hope of their Glory.*

William Penn, *A Collection of the Works of William Penn,* in two volumes, 1726, Volume II, p.782.

I have sometimes seen more in a line of the Bible then I could well tell how to stand under, and yet at another time the whole Bible hath been to me as drie as a stick.

John Bunyan, *Grace Abounding and The Pilgrim's Progress,* edited with an introduction by Roger Sharrock, Oxford University Press, 1966, p.104.

When thou readest God's Word, then in everything that thou readest, constantly to say to thyself, "It is I that am addressed, to me this is spoken."

Søren Kierkegaard, *For Self-Examination and Judge For Yourselves,* translated by Walter Lowrie, Princeton University Press, 1968, p.61.

After the sacred volumes of God and the Scriptures, study, in the second place, that great volume of the works and creatures of God, strenuously, and before all books, which ought to be only regarded as commentaries.

Francis Bacon, *Letters and Remains of the Lord Chancellor Bacon,* collected by Robert Stephens, 1734, p.184, "To Trinity College, Cambridge."

You may learn the whole Bible by heart and speak to any point in divinity according to text and letter, and yet *know* nothing of God or of spiritual life.

Rufus M. Jones, *Spiritual Reformers in the 16th and 17th Centuries,* Macmillan & Co. Ltd., 1914, p.245.

But herein is the Bible itself greatly wronged. It nowhere lays claim to be regarded as *the* Word, *the* Way, *the* Truth. The Bible leads us to Jesus, the inexhaustible, the ever unfolding Revelation of God. It is Christ "in whom are hid all the treasures of wisdom and knowledge," not the Bible, save as leading to him.

George Macdonald, *Unspoken Sermons,* First Series, Alexander Strahan, Publisher, 1867, p.52.

In determining the intention of the sacred writers, attention must be paid, *inter alia,* to "literary forms for the fact is that truth is differently presented and expressed in the various types of historical writing, in prophetical and poetical texts," and in other forms of literary expression. Hence the exegete must look for that meaning which the sacred writer, in a determined situation and given the circumstances of his time and culture, intended to express, and did in fact express, through the medium of a contemporary literary form.

Vatican Council II, *The Conciliar and Post Conciliar Documents,* 1981 Edition, general editor, Austin Flannery, O.P., Fowler Wright Books Ltd., p.757.

If we come closer to the inner heart of Bible reading we are not just stuffing our minds with information; we are letting God feed us through his word, and this means letting the scriptures speak to imagination, conscience, feeling, and will, as well as to the mind.
As we read, and read slowly, we pause and let the truth of God come home to us. Our imagination is moved to *wonder,* our conscience is pricked to *penitence,* our feelings are moved to *love,* our will is stirred to *resolve,* and our mind to whatever *understanding* we can muster.
In that way we quietly let the passage of scripture come home to us, mould us, and be our food and drink.

Michael Ramsey, *Through the Year with Michael Ramsey,* edited by Margaret Duggan, Hodder & Stoughton Ltd., 1975, p.158.

Now concerning the Holy Scriptures, we do believe that they were given forth by the Holy Spirit of God through the holy men of God, who spoke, as the Scriptures of Truth saith, "As they were moved by the Holy Ghost" (2 Peter 1.21); and that they are to be read, and believed, and fulfilled, and he that fulfils them is Christ; and they are "profitable for doctrine, for reproof, for correction, for instruction in righteousness, that the man of God may be perfect, thoroughly furnished unto all good works" (2 Tim. 3. 16, 17) and are able to make us wise to salvation through faith in Christ Jesus.

George Fox, *The Journal of George Fox,* a revised edition by John L. Nickalls, Cambridge at the University Press, 1952, p.604.

I believe my early morning readings are the secret of my own happiness in life. Read chiefly the N.T., and in it chiefly the Gospels, and of them chiefly St. John's, and write out what you think each verse means in your own words as you read it, and in between each morning's reading put down shortly what has happened to you—I mean a sort of diary, only make it a mixture of self-examination and your prayers. Write out a short prayer or a short thanksgiving for anything that happens out of the way, no matter whether it has pleased you or not; for having once given your life and your will to God as a reasonable offering, *everything* that happens to you is sanctioned by Him because He allows only such things to happen to you, when once you have put your life in His hands, as can do you some good. Nine times out of ten you will be able to see. The tenth perhaps you won't—just make a note of it and ask God to show you. Only be quite sure that you have not given up your will to Him merely in so many words, but in reality, and then you will have every reason to take things exactly as they happen to come and find a blessing in the worst of them. God lives in and with those who get into this habit of thought, only it takes some perseverance to get out of the way of grumbling and impatience. I have been it at for some eight years now and I haven't succeeded yet, but it's worth sticking to.

Edward Wilson, *The Faith of Edward Wilson,* George Seaver, John Murray Ltd., 1949, p.14.

BLESSEDNESS

Bless the Lord, O my soul; and all that is within me, bless his holy name!
Psalm 103.1.

Blessed is the man who trusts in the Lord, whose trust is the Lord.
Jeremiah 17.7.

Blessed is he who has found his work; let him ask no other blessedness.
Thomas Carlyle, *Past and Present,* Ward, Lock & Co. Ltd., p.136.

There is in man a HIGHER than Love of Happiness: he can do without Happiness, and instead thereof find Blessedness.
Thomas Carlyle, *Sartor Resartus,* Ward, Lock & Co. Ltd., p.128.

He is blessed who is assured that the animal is dying out in him day by day, and the divine being established.
Henry David Thoreau, *Walden,* The New American Library of World Literature, Inc., 1960, p.149.

Amid my list of blessings infinite,
Stand this the foremost, "That my heart has bled."
Edward Young, *Night Thoughts,* Thomas Nelson, 1841, p.210.

Blesse mee in this life but with the peace of my conscience, command of my affections, the love of thy selfe and my dearest friend, and I shall be happy enough to pity *Caesar.*
Sir Thomas Browne, *The Works of Sir Thomas Browne,* edited by Geoffrey Keynes, Faber and Faber Limited, 1964, Volume One, *Religio Medici,* p.93.

Blessings, we enjoy daily. And for most of them, because they be so common, most men forget to pay their praises: but let not us; because it is a sacrifice so pleasing to Him that made that sun and us, and still protects us, and gives us flowers, and showers, and stomachs, and meat, and content, and leisure.
Izaak Walton, *The Complete Angler,* Macmillan & Co. Ltd., 1906, p.174.

Blessedness lieth not in much and many, but in One and oneness.... All the great works and wonders that God has ever wrought or shall ever work in or through the creatures, or even God Himself with all His goodness ... can never make me blessed, but only in so far as they exist and are done and loved, known, tasted and felt within me.

Theologia Germanica, translated by Susanna Winkworth, Stuart & Watkins Ltd., 1966, p.48.

You never enjoy the world aright, till the Sea itself floweth in your veins, till you are clothed with the heavens, and crowned with the stars; and perceive yourself to be the sole heir of the whole world, and more than so, because men are in it who are every one sole heirs as well as you. Till you can sing and rejoice and delight in God, as misers do in gold, and Kings in sceptres, you never enjoy the world....
All things were made to be yours, and you were made to prize them according to their value: which is your office and duty, the end for which you were created, and the means whereby you enjoy. The end for which you were created, is that by prizing all that God hath done, you may enjoy yourself and Him in Blessedness.

Thomas Traherne, *Centuries,* The Faith Press, Ltd., 1969, p.14, & p.6.

That blessed mood
In which the burthen of the mystery,
In which the heavy and the weary weight
Of all this unintelligible world,
Is lightened:—that serene and blessed mood,
In which the affections gently lead us on,—
Until, the breath of this corporeal frame
And even the motion of our human blood
Almost suspended, we are laid asleep
In body, and become a living soul:
While with an eye made quiet by the power
Of harmony, and the deep power of joy,
We see into the life of things.

William Wordsworth, *The Poetical Works of William Wordsworth,* edited by E. de Selincourt, Oxford at the Clarendon Press, 1944, Volume II, p.260, "Lines composed a few miles above Tintern Abbey," l.37.

Things worth remembering:
The value of time,
The success of perseverence,
The pleasure of working,
The dignity of simplicity,
The worth of character,
The improvement of talent,
The influence of example,
The obligation of duty,
The wisdom of economy,
The virtue of patience,
The joy of originating,
The power of kindness.

Anon.

Magnificent weather. The morning seems bathed in happy peace, and a heavenly fragrance rises from mountain and shore; it is as though a benediction were laid upon us.... One might believe oneself in a church—a vast temple in which every being and every natural beauty has its place. I dare not breathe for fear of putting the dream to flight,—a dream traversed by angels....

In these heavenly moments the cry of Pauline rises to one's lips. "I feel! I believe! I see!" All the miseries, the cares, the vexations of life, are forgotten; the universal joy absorbs us; we enter into the divine order, and into the blessedness of the Lord. Labour and tears, sin, pain, and death have passed away. To exist is to bless; life is happiness. In this sublime pause of things all dissonances have disappeared. It is as though creation were but one vast symphony, glorifying the God of goodness with an inexhaustible wealth of praise and harmony. We question no longer whether it is so or not. We have ourselves become notes in the great concert; and the soul breaks the silence of ecstasy only to vibrate in unison with the eternal joy.

Henri Frédéric Amiel, *Amiel's Journal,* translated by Mrs. Humphry Ward, Macmillan & Co. Ltd., 1918, p. 188.

You are as prone to love, as the sun is to shine; it being the most delightful and natural employment of the Soul of Man: without which you are dark and miserable. Consider therefore the extent of Love, its vigour and excellency. For certainly he that delights not in Love makes vain the universe, and is of necessity to himself the greatest burden. The whole world ministers to you as the theatre of your Love. It sustains you and all objects that you may continue to love them. Without which it were better for you to have no being. Life without objects is sensible emptiness, and that is a greater misery than Death nor Nothing. Objects without Love are the delusion of life. The Objects of Love are its greatest treasures: and without Love it is impossible they should be treasures.... To love all persons in all ages, all angels, all worlds, is divine and heavenly. To love all cities and all kingdoms, all kings and all peasants, and every person in all worlds with a natural intimate familiar love, as if him alone, is blessed. This makes a man effectually blessed in all worlds, a delightful lord of all things, a glorious friend to all persons, a concerned person in all transactions, and ever present with all affairs. So that he must ever be filled with company, ever in the midst of all nations, ever joyful, and ever blessed. The greatness of this man's love no man can measure; it is stable like the sun, it endureth for ever as the moon, it is a faithful witness in heaven. It is stronger and more great than all private affections. It representeth every person in the light of eternity, and loveth him with the love of all worlds, with a love conformable to God's, guided to the same ends, and founded upon the same causes. Which however lofty and divine it is, is ready to humble itself into the dust to serve the person beloved. And by how much the more sublime and glorious it is, is so much the more sweet and truly delightful, majesty and pleasure concurring together.

Now you may see what it is to be a son of God more clearly. Love in all its glory is the friend of the most High. It was begotten of Him, and is to sit in His Throne, and to reign in communion with Him. It is to please Him and to be pleased by Him, in all His works, ways, and operations. It is ordained to hold an eternal correspondence with Him in the highest heavens. It is here in its infancy, there in its manhood and perfect stature.

Thomas Traherne, *Centuries,* The Faith Press, Ltd., 1969, p.86.

BROTHERHOOD

Have we not all one father? Has not one God created us?

Malachi 2.10.

For you have one teacher, and you are all brethren.

Matthew 23.8.

Love one another with brotherly affection; outdo one another in showing honour. Never flag in zeal, be aglow with the Spirit, serve the Lord. Rejoice in your hope, be patient in tribulation, be constant in prayer. Contribute to the needs of the saints, practice hospitality.

Romans 12.10-13.

For he who sanctifies and those who are sanctified have all one origin. That is why he is not ashamed to call them brethren.

Hebrews 2.11.

Every experience proves that the real problem of our existence lies in the fact that we ought to love one another, but do not.

Reinhold Niebuhr, *Christian Realism and Political Problems,* Faber and Faber Limited, 1953, p.106.

It is easy enough to be friendly to one's friends. But to befriend the one who regards himself as your enemy, is the quintessence of true religion. The other is mere business.

Mohandas K. Gandhi, *Non-Violence in Peace & War,* Navajivan Publishing House, 1949, Volume 2, p.249.

Those who love not their fellow-beings, live unfruitful lives, and prepare for their old age a miserable grave.

Percy Bysshe Shelley, *The Poetical Works of Percy Bysshe Shelley,* edited with an introduction and memoir by H. Buxton Forman, George Bell & Sons, 1892, Volume I, p.141, "Alastor," Preface.

Of a truth, men are mystically united: a mystic bond of brotherhood makes all men one.

Thomas Carlyle, *The Works of Thomas Carlyle,* Chapman and Hall Limited, 1899, *Critical and Miscellaneous Essays,* Volume II, "Goethe's Works," p.388.

Whoever degrades another degrades me,
And whatever is done or said returns at last to me.

Walt Whitman, *The Complete Poems,* edited by Francis Murphy, Penguin Books Ltd., 1982, p.86, "Song of Myself," section 24, l.503.

No one can be perfectly free till all are free; no one can be perfectly moral till all are moral; no one can be perfectly happy till all are happy.

Herbert Spencer, *Social Statics,* Williams and Norgate, 1892, p.268.

We are beginning to discover that our problem is worldwide, and no one people of the earth can work out its salvation by detaching itself from others. Either we shall be saved together or drawn together into destruction.

Rabindranath Tagore, *Letters to a Friend,* George Allen & Unwin Ltd., 1928, p.133.

Only when man succeeds in developing his reason and love further than he has done so far, only when he can build a world based on human solidarity and justice, only when he can feel rooted in the experience of universal brotherliness, will he have found a new, human form of rootedness, will he have transformed his world into a truly human home.

Erich Fromm, *The Sane Society,* Routledge & Kegan Paul Ltd., 1956, p.60.

No man is an Iland, intire of it selfe; every man is a peece of the Continent, a part of the maine; if a Clod bee washed away by the Sea, Europe is the lesse, as well as if a Promontorie were, as well as if a Mannor of thy friends or of thine owne were; any mans death diminishes me, because I am involved in Mankinde; And therefore never send to know for whom the bell tolls; It tolls for thee.

John Donne, *Complete Poetry and Selected Prose,* edited by John Hayward, The Nonesuch Press, 1929, p.538, "Devotions," XVII.

C

CHARACTER

As he thinketh in his heart, so is he.
Proverbs 23.7 (A.V.).

A talent is formed in stillness, a character in the world's torrent.
Johann Wolfgang von Goethe, *Torquato Tasso*, 1709, Act I. sc.ii. l.66.

The foundation of every noble character is absolute sincerity.
Anon.

An honest man's the noblest work of God.
Alexander Pope, *An Essay on Man*, introduction by Henry Morley, Cassell and Company, Limited, 1905, "Epistle IV," p.52.

Character is higher than intellect.... A great soul will be strong to live, as well as strong to think.
Ralph Waldo Emerson, *The Works of Ralph Waldo Emerson*, edited by George Sampson, George Bell & Sons, Ltd., 1906, Volume III, *Society and Solitude: Letters and Social Aims: Addresses*, p.381.

Let us be true: this is the highest maxim of art and of life, the secret of eloquence and of virtue, and of all moral authority.
Henri Frédéric Amiel, *Amiel's Journal*, translated by Mrs. Humphry Ward, Macmillan & Co., Ltd., 1918, p.47.

(Jesus)—the most innocent, the most benevolent, the most eloquent and sublime character that ever has been exhibited to man.
Thomas Jefferson, *The Writings of Thomas Jefferson*, Taylor and Maury, 1854, Volume IV, p.476.

He was his Maker's Image undefac'd!
Samuel Taylor Coleridge, *The Poetical Works of Samuel Taylor Coleridge*, edited with a biographical introduction by James Dykes Campbell, Macmillan & Co., Ltd., 1893, p.372. *Remorse*, Act II, sc.i.

Happiness is not the end of life; character is.
Henry Ward Beecher, *Life Thoughts*, Alexander Strahan & Co., 1895, p.95.

This above all: to thine own self be true,
And it must follow as the night the day
Thou canst not then be false to any man.
William Shakespeare, *Hamlet*, Act I. sc.iii. l.78.

Friends, suffering, marriage, environment, study and recreation are influences which shape character. The strongest influence, if you are generous enough to yield to it, is the grace of God.

Hubert van Zeller, *Considerations,* Sheed & Ward Ltd., 1974, p.13.

Character cannot be developed in ease and quiet. Only through experiences of trial and suffering can the soul be strengthened, vision cleared, ambition inspired and success achieved.

Helen Keller, *Helen Keller's Journal,* Michael Joseph Ltd., 1938, p.66.

It is the character only of a good man to be able to deny and disown himself, and to make a full surrender of himself unto God; forgetting himself, and minding nothing but the will of his Creator; triumphing in nothing more than in his own nothingness, and in the allness of the Divinity. But indeed this, his being nothing, is the only way to be all things; this, his having nothing, the truest way of possessing all things.

John Smith the Platonist, *Select Discourses,* Cambridge at the University Press, 1859, p.401.

Our characters are shaped by our companions and by the objects to which we give most of our thoughts and with which we fill our imaginations. We cannot always be thinking even about Christ, but we can refuse to dwell on any thoughts which are out of tune with Him. We can, above all, quite deliberately turn our minds towards Him at any time when those thoughts come in.

William Temple, *Christian Faith and Life,* S.C.M Press Ltd., 1963, p.43.

What do we mean when we speak of a man of integrity? One who will be true to the highest he knows; who will never betray the truth or trifle with it; one who will never make a decision from self-regarding motives; one who will never yield to the persuasion of friends or the pressure of critics unless either conforms to his own standards of right and wrong; one who will face the consequences of his attitudes, decisions and actions, however costly they may be; one who will not be loud in self-justification, but quietly confident and humbly ready to explain.

George Appleton, *Journey for a Soul,* William Collins Sons & Co., Ltd., 1976, p.96.

Now these mental and moral possessions are their own reward. They cannot, like earthly possessions, be taken away from us. For those who know what they are worth, the world is a much brighter place than for those who think that a man's life consisteth in the abundance of the things which he possesseth. The man whose "mind to him a kingdom is" does not complain much of the injustices of life. Still less does the true Christian complain. He has found the joy that no man taketh from him. This world is not a bad place in his eyes, because he finds it full of love and beauty and wisdom. He knows that it is God's world, even though, in sad times like this, it seems to be "full of darkness and cruel habitations." Amid all the horrors of war and strife he sees the pure gold of love and heroism and devotion shining brightly.

W.R. Inge, *Personal Religion and the Life of Devotion,* Longmans, Green & Co. Ltd., 1924, p.59.

The crown and glory of life is character. It is the noblest possession of a man, constituting a rank in itself, and an estate in the general good-will; dignifying every station, and exalting every position in society. It exercises a greater power than wealth, and secures all the honour without the jealousies of fame. It carries with it an influence which always tells; for it is the result of proved honour, rectitude, and consistency—qualities which, perhaps more than any other, command the general confidence and respect of mankind.

Character is human nature in its best form. It is moral order embodied in the individual. Men of character are not only the conscience of society, but in every well-governed State they are its best motive power; for it is moral qualities in the main which rule the world.

Samuel Smiles, *Self-Help*, S.W. Partridge & Co., Ltd., 1912, p.285.

Where there is charity and wisdom
there is neither fear nor ignorance.
Where there is patience and humility,
there is neither anger nor disturbance.
Where there is poverty with joy,
there is neither covetousness nor avarice.
Where there is inner peace and meditation,
there is neither anxiousness nor dissipation.
Where there is fear of the Lord to guard the house (cf. Lk. 11.21),
there the enemy cannot gain entry.
Where there is mercy and discernment,
there is neither excess nor hardness of heart.

St. Francis of Assisi, *Francis and Clare, The Complete Works*, translated with an introduction by Regis J. Armstrong, O.F.M. Cap., & Ignatius C. Brady, O.F.M., preface by John Vaughn, O.F.M., S.P.C.K., 1982, p.35, *The Writings*, XXVII, "How virtue drives out vice."

The unity is one of character and its ideal. That character of the completed man, raised above what is poor and low, and governed by noble tempers and pure principles, has in Spenser two conspicuous elements. In the first place, it is based on manliness.... It is not merely courage, it is not merely energy, it is not merely strength. It is the quality of soul which frankly accepts the conditions in human life, of labour, of obedience, of effort, of unequal success, which does not quarrel with them or evade them, but takes for granted with unquestioning alacrity that man is called—by his call to high aims and destiny—to a continual struggle with difficulty, with pain, with evil, and makes it the point of honour not to be dismayed or wearied out by them. It is a cheerful and serious willingness for hard work and endurance, as being inevitable and very bearable necessities, together with even a pleasure in encountering trials which put a man on his mettle, an enjoyment of the contest and the risk, even in play. It is the quality which seizes on the paramount idea of duty, as something which leaves a man no choice; which despises and breaks through the inferior considerations and motives—trouble, uncertainty, doubt, curiosity—which hang about and impede duty; which is impatient with the idleness and childishness of a life of mere amusement, or mere looking on, of continued and self-satisfied levity, of vacillation, of clever and ingenious trifling.

R. W. Church, *Spenser, English Men of Letters*, edited by John Morley, Macmillan & Co., Ltd., 1883, p.151.

CHARITY

Did universal charity prevail, earth would be a heaven, and hell a fable.

C.C. Colton, *Lacon*, William Tegg, 1866, p.39.

Charity and personal force are the only investments worth any thing.

Walt Whitman, *The Complete Poems*, edited by Francis Murphy, Penguin Books Ltd., 1982, p.396, "Song of Prudence," l.15.

Charity is a virtue of the heart, and not of the hands.

Joseph Addison, *The Works of Joseph Addison*, notes by Richard Hurd, edited and published by Henry G. Bohn, 1856, Volume IV, p.321.

For this I think (is) charity, to love God for himselfe, and our neighbour for God.

Sir Thomas Browne, *The Works of Sir Thomas Browne*, edited by Geoffrey Keynes, Faber and Faber Limited, 1964, Volume One, *Religio Medici*, p.92.

No sound ought to be heard in the church but the healing voice of Christian charity.

Edmund Burke, *Reflections on the Revolution in France*, edited by Conor Cruise O'Brien, Penguin Books Ltd., 1969, p.94.

To do him any wrong was to beget
A kindness from him, for his heart was rich,
Of such fine mould, that if you sow'd therein
The seed of Hate, it blossom'd Charity.

Alfred, Lord Tennyson, *Queen Mary, A Drama*, Henry S. King & Co., 1875, p. 188, Act IV. sc.i.

God is love, and he that has learnt to live in the Spirit of love has learnt to live and dwell in God. Love was the beginner of all the works of God, and from eternity to eternity nothing can come from God but a variety of wonders and works of love over all nature and creature.

William Law, *Selected Mystical Writings of William Law*, edited by Stephen Hobhouse, Rockliff, 1948, p.182.

Now Scripture enjoins nothing except charity and condemns nothing except lust, and in that way informs the practices of men.... I mean by charity that affection of the mind which aims at the enjoyment of God for His own sake and of one's self and one's neighbour for God's sake. By lust I mean that affection of the mind which aims at the enjoyment of one's self and one's neighbour without reference to God.... Now in proportion as the dominion of lust is pulled down, in the same proportion that of charity is built up.

St. Augustine, *An Augustine Synthesis*, arranged by Erich Przywara, S.J., Sheed & Ward Ltd., 1945, p.347.

We call it charity when men gave away what they did not want themselves in order to patch up evils and ameliorate bad conditions which their greed, slackness, or stupidity have helped to create. This is not charity, and it is blasphemy to call it by that splendid name. We call it charity when we give a poor devil half a crown to get shut of him and rid ourselves of the sight of his misery, that is blasphemy too. Real charity is not easy, it is always hard, it means that we must be ready to take time, trouble, and infinite pains to create life. The business man who seeks to give good value for money, who prides himself on his fellow workers in the business, and whose aim is to see that by efficiency, and energy his business produces and sustains fine life, he is the charitable man. Our faith is that God is Charity—that His charity is so great that he spares Himself no suffering and no agony in order to create in the world fine life. We are meant to be like Him.

G.A. Studdert Kennedy, *The New Man in Christ,* edited by the Dean of Worcester, Hodder and Stoughton Ltd., 1932, p.230.

God is love, or rather Charity; generous, out-flowing, self-giving love, *Agape*. When all the qualities which human thought attributes to Reality are set aside, this remains. Charity is the colour of the Divine personality, the spectrum of Holiness. We believe that the tendency to give, to share, to cherish, is the mainspring of the universe, ultimate cause of all that is, and reveals the Nature of God: and therefore that when we are most generous we are most living and most real.... To enter the Divine order then, achieve the full life for which we are made, means entering an existence which only has meaning as the channel and expression of an infinite, self-spending love.... When we look out towards this Love that moves the stars and stirs in the child's heart, and claims our total allegiance and remember that this alone is Reality and we are only real so far as we conform to its demands, we see our human situation from a fresh angle; and perceive that it is both more humble and dependent, and more splendid, than we had dreamed. We are surrounded and penetrated by great spiritual forces, of which we hardly know anything. Yet the outward events of our life cannot be understood, except in their relation to that unseen and intensely living world, the Infinite Charity which penetrates and supports us, the God whom we resist and yet for whom we thirst; who is ever at work, transforming the self-centred desire of the natural creature into the wide-spreading, outpouring love of the citizen of Heaven.

Evelyn Underhill, *The School of Charity,* Longmans, Green & Co. Ltd., 1956, p.10.

CHEERFULNESS

A cheerful heart is a good medicine, but a downcast spirit dries up the bones.
Proverbs 17.22.

Be of good cheer.
Matthew 14.27 (A.V.).

That which befits us ... is cheerfulness and courage.
Ralph Waldo Emerson, *The Works of Ralph Waldo Emerson*, edited by George Sampson, George Bell & Sons, Ltd., 1906, Volume I, *Essays and Representative Men*, p.353.

Health and cheerfulness mutually beget each other.
Joseph Addison, *The Works of Joseph Addison*, notes by Richard Hurd, edited and published by Henry G. Bohn, 1856, Volume III, p.363.

A cheerful temper, joined with innocence, will make beauty attractive, knowledge delightful, and wit good-natured.
Joseph Addison, *The Works of Joseph Addison*, notes by Richard Hurd, edited and published by Henry G. Bohn, 1856, Volume II, p.153.

And so of cheerfulness, or a good temper—the more it is spent, the more of it remains.
Ralph Waldo Emerson, *The Conduct of Life, Nature, and Other Essays*, J.M. Dent & Sons Ltd., 1911, p.279.

Good nature is worth more than knowledge, more than money, more than honour, to the persons who possess it, and certainly to everybody who dwells with them, in so far as mere happiness is concerned.
Henry Ward Beecher, *Proverbs From Plymouth Pulpit*, Charles Burnet & Co., 1887, p.20.

I have always preferred cheerfulness to mirth. The latter I consider as an act, the former as an habit of the mind. Mirth is short and transient, cheerfulness fixed and permanent.
Joseph Addison, *The Works of Joseph Addison*, notes by Richard Hurd, edited and published by Henry G. Bohn, 1856, Volume III, p.356.

Mirth is like a flash of lightning, that breaks through a gloom of clouds and glitters for a moment; cheerfulness keeps up a kind of day-light in the mind, and fills it with a steady and perpetual serenity.
Joseph Addison, *The Works of Joseph Addison*, notes by Richard Hurd, edited and published by Henry G. Bohn, 1856, Volume III, p.356.

CHRISTIAN

O noble testimony of the soul by nature Christian!
Tertullian, *The Writings of Tertullian*, Hamilton & Co., 1869, Volume I, p.87, "Apology No. 17."

A Christian is the highest style of man
Edward Young, *Night Thoughts*, Thomas Nelson, 1841, p.64.

If a man cannot be a Christian in the place where he is, he cannot be a Christian anywhere.
Henry Ward Beecher, *Life Thoughts*, Alexander Strahan & Co., 1859, p.135.

The greatest of all blessings, as it is the most ennobling of all privileges, is to be indeed a Christian.
Samuel Taylor Coleridge, *Letters of Samuel Taylor Coleridge*, edited by Ernest Hartley Coleridge, William Heinemann Ltd., 1895, Volume II, p.775, Letter No. ccix.

Those who reject Christian beliefs, cannot count on keeping Christian morals.

Sir Richard Livingstone, *On Education,* Cambridge at the University Press, 1954, p.133.

The only absolute for the Christian is love, and on *that* you have got to be prepared to take *unconditional* stands and say, "Here I stand, I can no other."

John A. T. Robinson, *The Roots of a Radical,* S.C.M. Press Ltd., 1980, p.55.

The Christian is the man who has ceased to do what he likes, and who has dedicated his life to do as Christ likes.

William Barclay, *The Gospel of Matthew,* The Saint Andrew Press, 1974, Volume One, p.21.

He only is a Christian in fact in whom Christ dwelleth, liveth and hath His being, in whom Christ hath arisen as the eternal ground of the soul. He only is a Christian who has this high title in himself, and has entered with mind and soul into that Eternal Word which has manifested itself as the life of our humanity.

Rufus M. Jones, *Spiritual Reformers in the 16th and 17th Centuries,* Macmillan & Co. Ltd., 1914, p.170.

To be a Christian does not mean to be religious in a particular way, to make something of oneself (a sinner, a penitent, or a saint) on the basis of some method or other, but to be a man—not a type of man, but the man that Christ creates in us. It is not the religious act that makes the Christian, but participation in the sufferings of God in the secular life.

Dietrich Bonhoeffer, *Letters and Papers from Prison,* edited by Eberhard Bethge, S.C.M. Press Ltd., 1967, Second Revised Edition, p.198.

It is not *Opinion,* or *Speculation,* or *Notions* of what is true; or Assent to, or the Subscription of Articles, or Propositions, tho' never so soundly worded, that ... makes a Man a *True* Believer, or a *True* Christian. But it is a *Conformity* of Mind and Practice to the *Will of God,* in all Holiness of Conversation, according to the Dictates of this Divine Principle of Light and Life in the Soul, which denotes a Person *truly* a Child of God.

William Penn, *A Collection of the Works of William Penn,* in two volumes, 1726, Volume II. p.781.

He (Sebastian Franck) is especially interesting and important as an exponent and interpreter of a religion based on inward authority because he unites, in an unusual manner, the intellectual ideals of the Humanist with the experience and attitude of the Mystic. In him we have a Christian thinker who is able to detach himself from the theological formulations of his own and of earlier times, and who could draw, with a breadth of mind and depth of insight, from the wells of the great original thinkers of all ages, and who, besides, in his own deep and serious soul could feel the inner flow of central realities.

Rufus M. Jones, *Spiritual Reformers in the 16th and 17th Centuries,* Macmillan & Co. Ltd., 1914, p.46.

He is a Christian that wholly giveth himself up into Christ's incarnation, suffering, and death, and dieth to his hypocrisy in the death of Christ, and riseth from the death of Christ in a new will and obedience, and who, according to his inward ground, is and liveth in Christ, who himself becometh the temple of Christ, wherein Christ workerh wirh his power and virtue, and thereby killeth sin in the flesh. Such a one is a Christian in Christ, and may rightly enter into the resemblance of Christ, and exercise his Christianity therein. Such a one will hear God's word, and keep and ponder it in his heart.

Jacob Boehme, *Mysterium Magnum*, translated by John Sparrow, John M. Watkins, 1924, Volume II, p.714.

It is quite easy to be a genial libertine—friendly with everyone you meet, if you have for yourself and them no moral standard. And it is fairly easy for you to set up a moral standard for yourself and others—no doubt underlining the words *for others*—if you allow yourself in the process to become hypercritical, unsympathetic and censorious, which is to be a Pharisee. But to set up a standard for others and yourself— with the words *for yourself* underlined—and still show sympathy and love to those who fail to reach it, without letting the standard down, that is very hard. But that is to be a Christian.

William Temple, *The Church Looks Forward*, Macmillan & Co. Ltd., 1944, p.166.

The indwelling Spirit of Christ radiates its benign influence as Life, as Light, and as Love. Christ is the eternal principle of life in all that lives. "That which came into being, in Him was Life, and the Life was the Light of men." He came "that we might have Life, and have it more abundantly." The call of Christ is the call to a more vivid, earnest, strenuous life. It has been said of a great man that he passed through the dream of life as one awake; and that is what all Christians ought to do. "Now it is high time to awake out of sleep." Spiritual wakefulness means concentration of purpose. The world may be divided into those who have a purpose in life, and those who have none, or who fluctuate between several. Few things are more striking than the change which comes over even the outward appearance of a man or woman between youth and old age, according to whether he or she has or not a fixed purpose which is being carried out day by day. The face of the man who has found his work shows, in each decade of his life until the failure of his powers, increasing strength and dignity, and even beauty; while the man who lets himself drift shows in every line of his face that his will has been overpowered by disorderly impulses, or has simply abdicated. The portraits of good and great men at various ages, and the faces of those who are neither good nor great, are instructive in this way.

W.R. Inge, *Personal Religion and the Life of Devotion*, Longmans, Green & Co. Ltd., 1924, p.73.

CHRISTIANITY

Christianity is the highest perfection of humanity.

Samuel Johnson, *Boswell's Life of Johnson*, edited by G.B. Hill, revised by L.F. Powell, Oxford at the Clarendon Press, 1934, Volume II, p.27.

I still & shall to Eternity Embrace Christianity and Adore Him who is the Express image of God.

William Blake, *The Complete Writings of William Blake*, edited by Geoffrey Keynes, Oxford University Press, 1974, p.815, *The Letters*, No.23.

The true religion of Christ is written in the soul and Spirit of man, by the Spirit of God; and the believer is the only book, in which God himself writes his New Testament.

William Dell, *Select Works of William Dell,* printed for John Kendall, 1773, p.438.

For what is now called the Christian religion existed even among the ancients and was not lacking from the beginning of the human race until "Christ came in the flesh." From that time, true religion, which already existed, began to be called Christian.

St. Augustine, *The Retractions,* Series: "The Fathers of the Church," Volume 60, translated by Sister Mary Inez Bogan, The Catholic University of America Press, Inc., 1968, p.52.

Christianity is not primarily a system of ideas divinely communicated, nor a way of life divinely enjoined or guided, nor a method of worship divinely taught. It is primarily a self-revelation of God in a historical Person, and in that Person's life, death and resurrection.

William Temple, *Nature, Man and God,* Macmillan & Co. Ltd., 1934, p.436.

We may be suspicious of the clergy and refuse to have anything to do with catechisms, and yet love the Holy and the Just, who came to save and not to curse. Jesus will always supply us with the best criticism of Christianity, and when Christianity has passed away the religion of Jesus will in all probability survive. After Jesus as God we shall come back to faith in the God of Jesus.

Henri Frédéric Amiel, *Amiel's Journal,* translated by Mrs. Humphry Ward, Macmillan & Co. Ltd., 1918, p.140.

Christianity can never be merely a pleasant or consoling religion. It is a stern business. It is concerned with the salvation through sacrifice and love of a world in which, as we can all see now, evil and cruelty are rampant. Its supreme symbol is the Crucifix— the total and loving self-giving of man to the redeeming purposes of God.

Evelyn Underhill, *The Fruits of the Spirit,* Longmans, Green & Co. Ltd., 1949, p.71.

Christ's teaching is better than all the teaching of the saints, and any man who has the Spirit will find *the hidden manna* there. It so happens that many people hear the Gospel frequently and yet feel little desire, and this is because they do not have the Spirit of Christ. Anyone who wishes to understand and to savour the words of Christ to the full must try to make his whole life conform to the pattern of Christ.

Thomas à Kempis, *The Imitation of Christ,* translated by Betty I. Knott, William Collins Sons & Co. Ltd., 1979, p.37.

It is not easy to take the principles of Christianity and to deduce how a Christian should behave in a concrete case in order to be, without any doubt, a Christian. For Christianity is not a philosophical problem composed of lifeless abstract principles. It is, on the contrary, of its very principles that every individual can always be under the living providence of the living God in every particular case—and then there is nothing to deduce, for God is freedom.

Theodor Haecker, *Journal in the Night,* translated by Alexander Dru, The Harvill Press Ltd., 1950, p.80.

The claim of Christianity is simply the claim of Christ Himself: "I am come that you may have life and have it more abundantly." He set Himself to teach us what full living means, to show us how to become really alive. "I am the way," He said, "the truth and the life." Those who heard Him and watched Him got tremendously excited about Him. Christ was a revolutionary. He had a secret which altered people's lives, that put spring and energy and youth and joy into them, the joy of living.

R.L. Smith, *Man's Dilemma and God's Answer, Broadcast Talks*, S.C.M. Press Ltd., 1944, p.70.

In one fundamental sense ... it seems to me that Christianity alone attacks the seat of evil in the kind of world we have been considering, and has a solvent for the intellectual predicaments which arise in such a world. It addresses itself precisely to that crust of self-righteousness which, by the nature of its teaching, it has to dissolve before it can do anything else with a man. The more human beings are lacking in imagination, the more we shall find that their self-righteousness hardens, so that it is just the thick-skinned who are more sure of being right than anybody else.

Herbert Butterfield, *Christianity and History*, G. Bell & Sons Ltd., 1949, p.41.

Christianity in its origin was essentially a rich and vivid consciousness of God, rising to a perfect experience of union with God in mind, and heart, and soul. It was a personal exhibition of the Divine in the human, the Eternal in the midst of time. The direct impact and power of Christ's life on His followers is the most extraordinary thing in the Gospels—it, and not any portents, caused the realization that He was Divine. Christ always taught His disciples to expect a personal experience of God like His own, though less in degree. Thus Christianity is, in its very heart, a mystical religion. The first Church was a mystical fellowship, in which each member had received the Holy Ghost. In St. Paul the mystical element is very strong. Christ's "method of inwardness," His directions as to prayer, His idealism and attitude towards wealth, towards death; His emphasis on love—all His teaching implied, we may say, a mystical view of life.

W.R. Inge, *The Awakening of the Soul*, edited by Prebendary A.F. Judd, A.R. Mowbray & Co. Ltd., 1959, p.29.

Christianity ... does not consist in the mere knowing of history and applying the history-knowledge to ourselves, saying: "Christ died for us; He hath paid the ransom for us, so that we need do nothing but comfort ourselves therewith and steadfastly believe that it is so." The "doctors" and "the wise world" and "the makers of opinion" will have it that Christ suffered on the Cross for all our sins, and that we can be justified and acquitted of all our transgressions by what He did for us, but it is no true, safe way for the soul. To stake faith upon a history that once was, to look for "satisfaction" through the sufferings which Christ endured before we were born is to be "the child of an assumed grace," is to possess a mere external and historical faith that leaves the dim, weak soul where it was before.

Rufus M. Jones, *Spiritual Reformers in the 16th and 17th Centuries*, Macmillan & Co. Ltd., 1914, p.192.

Let us never forget what it means that the revelation of which the Church is "repository and trustee" is not a book but a person. It is this which makes Christianity compatible with progress, and indeed a constant source of progress; it is this which fits it for universality. For here we have no code of rules that can only be obeyed in the circumstances of their origin, no scheme of thought which can only be understood in the terms in which it was first conceived, but a Person to whom we can be loyal in all circumstances whatever, with that infinite flexibility and delicacy of adjustment which are compatible with a loyalty that remains absolute and unalterable.

Here we see God self-revealed, and we must admit to our minds no thought or image of God that is not a reflection in us of His personality.

William Temple, *Thoughts On Some Problems Of The Day*, Macmillan & Co. Ltd., 1931, p.28.

The fundamental principle of Christianity is simple to state. Christ said, The time is fulfilled, and the Kingdom of God is at hand. Christianity is no more and no less than the advent of the Kingdom of God. Some people extract "God" from the Kingdom of God to construct a philosophy upon, while others seize on "Kingdom" to carry out a social movement. The latter choice has resulted in social theories and political parties. Thomas Aquinas, on the other hand, emphasized the idea of God. As that system gradually declined, it became an individualistic religion, in which God was separated from the daily life of mankind.

True Christianity, however, is not an individualistic religion, but a superindividualistic one. While it is a social movement, it involves the co-operation between God and men. This point should be made clear.

The idea of the Kingdom of God was not clear even to the disciples. That was why Jesus was finally crucified. Judas Iscariot exchanged the Kingdom of God for a "Kingdom" movement, leaving out "God." Seeing that Jesus would not become a king, Judas betrayed him.

Peter, on the contrary, excluded all but God, and forgot the element of love to which he should have bent his energies. Even in the Bible we find places where the idea of the Kingdom of God is sundered and dim. We must consider the meaning of the Kingdom of God in its totality and clarity.

Toyohiko Kagawa, *Meditations*, translated by Jiro Takenaka, Harper & Brothers, 1950, No.15.

CHURCH

Unless the Lord builds the house, those who build it labour in vain.

Psalm 127.1.

They devoted themselves to the apostles' teaching and fellowship, to the breaking of bread and the prayers.

Acts 2.42.

Religion that is not embedded in the common life too soon degenerates into religiosity, and an inward-looking Church is a dying Church.

F.R. Barry, *Christian Ethics and Secular Society*, Hodder & Stoughton Ltd., 1966, p.117.

It is the Church of the saints and martyrs and prophets, who have been the lights of the world in their several generations, that has the demand upon your allegiance—

not the Church which has been corrupted by wealth and worldly power. But the true
Church is embedded in the existing Churches—you will not find it elsewhere.

Alec R. Vidler, *God's Demand And Man's Response,* John Hermitage, The Unicorn Press, 1938, p.102.

To be of no church is dangerous. Religion, of which the rewards are distant, and
which is animated only by Faith and Hope, will glide by degrees out of the mind
unless it be invigorated and reimpressed by external ordinances, by stated calls to
worship, and the salutary influence of example.

Samuel Johnson, *Lives of the English Poets,* edited by G.B. Hill, Oxford at the Clarendon Press, 1905, Volume
I, *Milton,* p.155.

The Church is the community of the Spirit, not as having a monopoly of the Spirit,
but as having been called into existence by God and entrusted with the word and the
sacraments. In the Church there should be going on in a concentrated way the work
of the Spirit, which in a diffuse way is going on throughout creation. When the
Church is truly the Church it is introducing a new dimension into the social situation,
thus giving hope for an eventual transformation.

George Appleton, *Journey for a Soul,* William Collins Sons & Co. Ltd., 1976, p.166.

If it seems to you that the Church as organised has somehow lost sense of proportion,
remember that only through the Church has the Gospel ever reached you, and that
only through the Church can it reach the ages far ahead. And you will do more to
the cause of Christ by bringing what reality you can into its life than you can ever
render by staying outside and doing what seems possible to you, or you and your few
friends, in isolation.

William Temple, *Christian Faith and Life,* S.C.M. Press Ltd., 1963, p.131.

Meanwhile, the special work assigned to the Church of England would seem to be
the development of a *Johannine* Christianity, which shall be both Catholic and Evangelical without being either Roman or Protestant. It has been abundantly proved that
neither Romanism nor Protestantism, regarded as alternatives, possesses enough of
the truth to satisfy the religious needs of the present day. But is it not probable that,
as the theology of the Fourth Gospel acted as a reconciling principle between the
opposing sections in the early Church, so it may be found to contain the teaching
which is most needed by both parties in our own communion? In St. John and St.
Paul we find all the principles of a sound and sober Christian Mysticism; and it is to
these "fresh springs" of the spiritual life that we must turn, if the Church is to renew
her youth.

W.R. Inge, *Christian Mysticism,* Methuen & Co., 1899, p.324.

What do I mean by saying that Christianity is unthinkable apart from the Church?
In the first place, if Christianity is the revelation of the depths of the personal and of
love as the ultimate meaning of the universe, it can find expression only in a community. Love can exist only between persons. It demands community. Christ is not Christ
without the community of love which He founded. In contrast with all other forms
of association which exist for particular, limited purposes, the Church is the association

which unites persons with persons, inclusive of all ages— the tiniest infants are admitted by baptism—all occupations, all classes, all races.

The Church is indispensable, secondly, as the society which has to do with men's ultimate concern. Our ultimate concern is about our fundamental being and the meaning of our life and destiny. Other associations have to do with men's immediate concerns in their temporal existence. If one admits that men have an ultimate concern, distinct from the endless variety of their immediate interests, and if one believes or hopes that the universe is not indifferent to that ultimate concern, then there must be an association in which that ultimate concern finds expression in religious worship. Take away the Church with its centres of worship, and life becomes wholly this-worldly and loses immeasurably in depth.

Thirdly, the Church is necessary because Christianity is essentially the proclamation, not of a demand, but of fulfilment. It is not the insistence on love as an ideal to be striven after, but the joyful news that God is love and that we know this because His love has been manifested in history. Grace and truth came by Jesus Christ. The Church is the witness to that revelation and the continuing embodiment of that new life. Take away the Church and Christianity itself disappears. It is a delusion to suppose that we can cut out twenty centuries of lived experience and establish a direct relation between ourselves and the historic Jesus. As historical criticism has proved, we can never reach back to Him behind the witness which His disciples bear to Him. He continues to live in the memory, experience and lives of His disciples. Jesus confronts us today not merely as an individual who lived and acted in Palestine in the first thirty years of our era, but as the source of all the influences that have emanated from Him through the centuries. If we relate ourselves to Him, it is as those who stand in the living stream of tradition and are caught up and borne forward by it.

Fourthly, the coming of this new being and life, when it is apprehended by the mind, is found to imply certain conceptions about God, the world and man, that is to say a theology. The Church is the guardian of the new message and proclamation, and has to see that they are preserved in their purity and power and protected against error, misrepresentation and emasculation.

These considerations seem to me conclusive and unanswerable.

J.H. Oldham, *Life Is Commitment*, S.C.M. Press Ltd., 1953, p.79.

COMMITMENT

Of the many half-truths floating about in sermons and articles today I know few so misleading as this: "Religion is life." It is misleading just because it is not obviously false. It contains important truths. For one thing, it says this: Religion, wherever it exists, spreads over the whole of life. One cannot take it up as one takes up golf— by giving it a couple of afternoons a week. That kind of amateur religion is not religion. Religion is either the whole of one's life, or else it is not religion, no matter how much fuss is made over it. This is true, and dangerously true. "Religion is life," so understood, cuts with condemnation. To all those who want religion, but want it "in its place," that is, apart from their business, their politics, their luxuries or their conveniences, or anything else, this says, "My good friend, what you call your "religion" is something or other, but you had better find its name and call it by its name; don't call it religion."

Religion can never be lived except with one's whole life, and what cannot be humanly lived is not religion or any concern of religion. So far "religion is life" makes sense. But how much farther? Does it hint at the all-important fact that religion is not any kind of life, but a difficult and exacting way to which many are called but few chosen? Does it suggest just what it is that marks off religion from all the other kinds of lives that have been lived and can be lived—the life of the dilettante or of the egotist or the cynic or the romantic, or of the healthy cabbage? Jesus told Nicodemus, "You must be born again." He told the rich young ruler, "Sell all you have," and the disciples, "He who would save his life must lose it." Could you have guessed any of these things from "religion is life"? Where is the way of the cross, the demand for decision, the necessity for absolute loyalty? Something slips between the fingers of this plausible generality and this something is commitment.

Commitment is all-important in our understanding of religion because it expresses clearly, as "life" does not, this fact: Religion is a relationship. This may sound like a truism. Yet even a truism is significant when it is denied. Every kind of subjectivism is such a denial. Nothing is so attractive to the tired sophisticate as the call to leave awhile the world that is too much with him and retreat to a place of stillness within his own soul. That there is such a place is an exciting discovery, and so is the art of finding it, steering safely to it, and avoiding the dangerous turmoils of the world of outer fact or the world of the inner self, both full of confusion and strife. To explore this middle ground of introspection and reverie, and flavour its precarious peace, is an engrossing adventure, especially when it is dignified with the name of religion.

To such religious romanticism the word "commitment" brings a rude corrective. It reminds one inescapably of the essential thing in religion—God. It is easy to forget God when one is most concerned about one's inner experiences. It is not so easy to forget Him when one is concerned about commitment. One can give oneself only to something which is there, which can be observed, understood and obeyed; to something which makes demands and holds out promises and obligations. It warns against subjectivity. One's own subjectivity can hide God from one just as much as the pressure of work or the hypocrisies of polite society.

If one is not clear about God, one will always tend to shy away toward something more accessible, like one's own conscious states. To talk about commitment brings one face to face with the question of God, so that one cannot dodge it.... God is that within and beyond the universe which expresses the greatest good which now is and ever can be: the direction of life against death, the direction of unity against discord, the direction of creation and increasing growth against destruction and decay. God is the power of good in all its various forms: in the order and structure of inorganic matter, in the process of growth and sensitivity in the realm of life, in the conditions of intelligence, cooperation, appreciation and creative love on the human level.

This cosmic reach in our description of God must not distract our attention from the specific human focus within which our experiences of the good are most intense and most decisive. It is here most of all that we know God as a daily fact. We have tried the ways of ambition, of self-aggrandizement, of aggressive opportunism, and we have seen the kind of flimsy success to which they lead, we have tasted the bitter poisons they generate, we have known the conflict, the disgust, the inner division, the outer isolation that follow in their wake. We have also tried in some small measure the other way, and known that every man and woman must have love; that there is no life or peace without love; only strife, waste, madness, destruction, death. There is that in life which makes it necessary that men should find the way of truth, of under-standing, of justice, or else destroy themselves and each other. You have not seen it? You cannot move a step but you stumble into it; it is in the structure of your world; you cannot live a day or an hour without saying either yes or no to it, without finding life through it or death without it.

Even a faint glimpse of this reality brings you back to yourself. Whither do you move? With it or without it? The alternatives are simple—terrifyingly simple and clear. To compromise in this matter is to decide; to waver is to decide; to postpone and evade decision is to decide; to hide the matter is to decide. There is no escape. You must say yes, or no. There are a thousand ways of saying no; one way of saying yes; and no way of saying anything else.

Gregory Vlastos, *The Religious Way and The Religious Person in the World Today*, National Board of the Young Women's Christian Association of the U.S.A., 1934.

COMMUNITY

I am a part of all that I have met.

Alfred, Lord Tennyson, *The Poems of Tennyson*, edited by Christopher Ricks, Longmans, Green & Co. Ltd., 1969, p.563, No.217, *Ulysses*, l.18.

The community stagnates without the impulse of the individual. The impulse dies away without the sympathy of the community.

William James, *The Will To Believe*, Longmans, Green & Co. Ltd., 1904, p.232.

All are but parts of one stupendous whole,
Whose body Nature is, and God the soul.

Alexander Pope, *An Essay on Man*, introduction by Henry Morley, Cassell & Company, Limited, 1905, Epistle I, p.23.

We don't live alone. We are members of one body. We are responsible for each other. And I tell you that the time will soon come when, if men will not learn that lesson, then they will be taught it in fire and blood and anguish.

J.B. Priestley, *An Inspector Calls*, William Heinemann Ltd., 1947, p.57, Act III.

Life is the one universal soul, which by virtue of the enlivening BREATH, and the informing WORD, all organized bodies have in common, each *after its kind*.

Samuel Taylor Coleridge, *Coleridge, Select Poetry & Prose*, edited by Stephen Potter, The Nonesuch Press, p.449, "Aids to Reflection," Aphorism ix, l.1.

We cannot imagine a human being living from birth without any contact with fellow-men. Without other people we could not achieve worthwhile self-consciousness. Human personality cannot develop in isolation. Human society cannot function without understanding, communication and co-operation between people. I *am* only through relationship with others.

George Appleton, *Journey for a Soul,* William Collins Sons & Co. Ltd., 1976, p.26.

The individual, if left alone from birth, would remain primitive and beastlike in his thoughts and feelings to a degree that we can hardly conceive. The individual is what he is and has the significance that he has not so much in virtue of his individuality, but rather as a member of a great human community, which directs his material and spiritual existence from the cradle to the grave.

Albert Einstein, *Ideas and Opinions,* Souvenir Press (Educational & Academic) Ltd., 1973, p.13.

No amount of philosophical theories are worth much compared with a simple picture of home life. It is these common relations of life which are most awful and sacred. The highest life we know is, I think I may say with reverence, family life—life of Father and Son; family life on earth is a faint picture of something better in heaven. We shall be surprised some day to find that, while we have been searching for the noble and divine, we have it all the while at home.

Forbes Robinson, *Letters to his Friends,* S.C.M. Press Ltd., 1938, p.60.

I want you to form the nucleus of a new community which shall start a new life amongst us—a life in which the only riches is integrity of character. So that each one may fulfil his own nature and deep desires to the utmost, but wherein the ultimate satisfaction and joy is in the completeness of us all as one. Let us be good all together, instead of just in the privacy of our chambers, let us know that the intrinsic part of all of us is the best part, the believing part, the passionate, generous part. We can all come croppers, but what does it matter. We can laugh at each other, and dislike each other, but the good remains, and we know it. And the new community shall be established upon the known, eternal good part in us.... I hold this the most sacred duty—the gathering together of a number of people who shall so agree to live by the best they know, that they shall be *free* to live by the *best* they know. The ideal, the religion, must now be *lived, practised.*

D.H. Lawrence, *The Letters of D.H. Lawrence,* edited by George J. Zytaruk & James T. Boulton, Cambridge University Press, 1981, Volume II, p.271.

COMPASSION

Have unity of spirit, sympathy, love of the brethren, a tender heart and a humble mind.

1 Peter 3.8.

Compassion was the chief and, perhaps, the only law of all human existence.

Fyodor Dostoyevsky, *The Idiot,* translated with an introduction by David Magarshack, Penguin Books Ltd., 1983, p.248.

Jesus *found him.* The man did not find Jesus; Jesus found him. That is the deepest truth of Christian faith; Jesus found me. Our fellowship with Him is rooted in His compassion.

William Temple, *Readings in St. John's Gospel* (First and Second Series), Macmillan & Co. Ltd., 1947, p.160.

Pity may represent little more than the impersonal concern which prompts the mailing of a cheque, but true sympathy is the personal concern which demands the giving of one's soul.

Martin Luther King, *Strength to Love,* William Collins Sons & Co., Ltd, 1980, p.32.

If you think of your fellow-creatures, then you only want to cry, you could really cry the whole day long. The only thing to do is to pray that God will perform a miracle and save some of them. And I hope that I am doing that enough!

Anne Frank, *The Diary of Anne Frank,* Pan Books Ltd., 1954, p.111.

Jesus' "lack of moral principles." He sat at meal with publicans and sinners, he consorted with harlots. Did he do this to obtain their votes? Or did he think that, perhaps he could convert them by such "appeasement"? Or was his humanity rich and deep enough to make contact, even in them, with that in human nature which is common to all men, indestructible, and upon which the future has to be built?

Dag Hammarskjold, *Markings,* translated by Leif Sjoberg and W.H. Auden, with a foreword by W.H. Auden, Faber and Faber Limited, 1964, p.134.

But to share with Christ his passion, his crucifixion, his death, means to accept unreservedly all these events, in the same spirit as he did, that is, to accept them in an act of free will, to suffer together with the man of sorrows, to be there in silence, the very silence of Christ, interrupted only by a few decisive words, the silence of real communion; not just the silence of pity, but of compassion, which allows us to grow into complete oneness with the other so that there is no longer one and the other, but only one life and one death.

Anthony Bloom, *Living Prayer,* Darton, Longman & Todd Ltd., 1966, p.16.

In his feeling I see him (Christ) supremely as a man of compassion. That is, he entered into every aspect and event of human life, knowing it in its truth and reality, sharing all that human beings experienced, not only perceiving what women and men felt, but feeling with them. With those who needed tenderness he was tender, but his love was not always gentle. He would not spare people the truth, even when it had to hurt. He could love the rich young man and yet say to him that he could not inherit eternal life if he did not give up his riches. He flayed the oppressors of the poor with the most biting invective that has ever been used. His love could be gentle, but it could also be stern and austere, intensely demanding.
I see him deeply involved in the conflict of his time, not standing aside offering advice or principles from on high, but deeply involved, right in the conflict, followed round by contentious groups, supported or attacked, applauded or derided, loved or feared. He was a man of passion, not only in his suffering, but throughout his life and ministry.

Kenneth C. Barnes, *The Creative Imagination* (Swarthmore Lecture Pamphlet), Friends Home Service Committee, 1967, p.33.

The fact that human love or sympathy is the guide who conducts us to the heart of life, revealing to us God and Nature and ourselves, is proof that part of our life is bound up with the life of the world, and that if we live in these our true relations we shall not entirely die so long as human beings remain alive upon this earth. The progress of the race, the diminution of sin and misery, the advancing kingdom of Christ on earth,—these are matters in which we have a *personal* interest. The strong desire that we feel—and the best of us feel it most strongly—that the human race may be better, wiser, and happier in the future than they are now or have been in the past, is neither due to a false association of ideas, nor to pure unselfishness. There is a sense in which death would not be the end of everything for us, even though in this life only we had hope in Christ.

W.R. Inge, *Christian Mysticism,* Methuen & Co., 1899, p.327.

Out of kindliness springs compassion, which is a fellow-feeling with all men; for none can share the griefs of all, save him who is kind. Compassion is an inward movement of the heart, stirred by pity for the bodily and ghostly griefs of all men. This compassion makes a man suffer with Christ in His passion; for he who is compassionate marks the wherefore of His pains and the way of His resignation; of His love, His wounds, His tenderness; of His grief and His nobleness; of the disgrace, the misery, and the shame He endured; of the way in which He was despised; of His crown; of the nails; of His mercifulness; of His destruction and dying in patience. These manifold and unheard-of sorrows of Christ our Saviour and our Bridegroom, move all kindly men to pity and compassion with Christ.

Compassion makes a man look into himself and recognize his faults, his feebleness in virtues and in the worship of God, his lukewarmness, his laziness, his many failings, the time he has wasted and his present imperfection in moral and other virtues; all this makes a man feel true pity and compassion for himself. Further, compassion marks the errors and disorders of our fellow-creatures, how little they care for their God and their eternal blessedness, their ingratitude for all the good things which God has done for them, and the pains He suffered for their sake; how they are strangers to virtue, unskilled and unpractised in it, but skilful and cunning in every wickedness; how attentive they are to the loss and gain of earthly goods, how careless and reckless they are of God, of eternal things, and their eternal bliss. When he marks this, a good man is moved to compassion for the salvation of all men.

Such a man will also regard with pity the bodily needs of his neighbours, and the manifold suffering of human nature; seeing men hungry, thirsty, cold, naked, sick, poor, and abject; the manifold oppressions of the poor, the grief caused by loss of kinsmen, friends, goods, honour, peace; all the countless sorrows which befall the nature of man. These things move the just to compassion, so that they share the sorrows of all.

John of Ruysbroeck, *The Adornment of the Spiritual Marriage,* translated by C.A. Wynschenk Dom, edited with an introduction and notes by Evelyn Underhill, John M. Watkins, 1951, p.30.

CONSCIENCE

So I always take pains to have a clear conscience toward God and toward men.
Acts 24.16.

The still small voice.
William Cowper, *The Poetical Works of Cowper*, edited by H.S. Milford, Oxford University Press, 1950, p.214, *The Task*, Bk.V. 1.685.

Conscience is the voice of the soul, the passions are the voice of the body.
Jean Jacques Rousseau, *Emile* or *Education*, translated by Barbara Foxley, J.M. Dent & Sons Ltd., 1911, p.249.

Labour to keep alive in your breast that little spark of celestial fire, called conscience.
George Washington, *The Life of George Washington*, Jared Sparks, Henry Colburn, Publisher, 1839, p.401.

In early days the conscience has in most
A quickness, which in later life is lost.
William Cowper, *The Poetical Works of Cowper*, edited by H.S. Milford, Oxford University Press, 1950, p.244, "Tirocinium," 1.109.

The church must be reminded that it is not the master or the servant of the state, but rather the conscience of the state.
Martin Luther King, *Strength to Love*, William Collins Sons & Co. Ltd., 1980, p.62.

Our secret thoughts are rarely heard except in secret. No man knows what conscience is until he understands what solitude can teach him concerning it.
Joseph Cook, *Conscience*, R.D. Dickinson, 1879, p.90.

Yet still there whispers the small voice within,
Heard through Gain's silence, and o'er Glory's din:
Whatever creed be taught, or land be trod,
Man's conscience is the Oracle of God.
Lord Byron, *The Poetical Works of Lord Byron*, edited, with a memoir by Ernest Hartley Coleridge, John Murray, 1948, p.759, *The Island*, "Canto the First," st.vi. 1.120.

By "conscience" I mean the individual's conviction concerning right and wrong. Sometimes it is a reflective judgement, sometimes an emotional reaction, sometimes an intuitive perception. At its best it combines all three.
William Temple, *Citizen and Churchman*, Eyre & Spottiswoode, Ltd., 1941, p.29.

Some good must come by clinging to the right. Conscience is a man's compass, and though the needle sometimes deviates, though one often perceives irregularities in directing one's course by it, still one must try to follow its direction.
Vincent van Gogh, *Dear Theo: An Autobiography of Vincent van Gogh*, edited by Irving Stone, Constable & Company Ltd., 1937, p.208.

The more productively one lives, the stronger is one's conscience, and, in turn, the more it furthers one's productiveness. The less productively one lives, the weaker becomes one's conscience; the paradoxical—and tragic—situation of man is that his conscience is weakest when he needs it most.

Erich Fromm, *Man For Himself*, Routledge & Kegan Paul Ltd., 1975, p.160.

The glory of a good man is the witness of a good conscience. Have a good conscience, and you will always have gladness; for a good conscience is able to endure a great deal, and be glad even in adversity, whereas a bad conscience is always fearful and restless. You will enjoy quiet rest if conscience does not condemn you.

Thomas à Kempis, *The Imitation of Christ*, translated by Betty I. Knott, William Collins Sons & Co. Ltd., 1979, p.91.

Deep within his conscience man discovers a law which he has not laid upon himself but which he must obey. Its voice, ever calling him to love and to do what is good and to avoid evil, tells him inwardly at the right moment: do this, shun that. For man has in his heart a law inscribed by God. His dignity lies in observing this law, and by it he will be judged. His conscience is man's most secret core, and his sanctuary. There he is alone with God whose voice echoes in his depths. By conscience, in a wonderful way, that law is made known which is fulfilled in the love of God and of one's neighbour.

Vatican Council II, *The Conciliar and Post Conciliar Documents*, 1981 Edition, general editor, Austin Flannery, O.P., Fowler Wright Books Ltd., p.916.

Conscience is that depth of human nature at which it comes in touch with God, where it receives God's message and hears His voice.... Conscience is the remembrance, in our sinful life, of God and of life Divine. When, in the most sinful and criminal man, conscience awakes, this means that he remembers about God, and how it is to live a godly life, although he may not express it in these words. Conscience is the organ of reception of religious revelation of truth, of good, of integral truth. It is not a separate side of human nature or a special function; it is the wholeness of man's spiritual nature, its very heart.... Conscience is also the source of original primary judgements about the world, and about life. More than this, conscience judges God, or about God, because it is an organ of the perception of God. Conscience may judge about God only because it is an organ of the perception of God. God acts on man's conscience, awakens his conscience, awakens his memories of a higher world. Conscience is the remembrance of what man is, to what world he belongs by the idea of his creation, by whom he was created, how and why he was created. Conscience is a spiritual, supernatural element in man, and it is not at all of social origin. What is of social origin is rather an obstruction or deformation of conscience. Conscience is that depth of human nature where it has not fallen completely away from God, where it has maintained contact with the Divine world.

Nicolas Berdyaev, *Christian Existentialism*, selected & translated by Donald A. Lowrie, George Allen & Unwin Ltd., 1965, p.88.

CONTEMPLATION

What we plant in the soil of contemplation we shall reap in the harvest of action.

Meister Eckhart, *Meister Eckhart,* translated by Raymond B. Blakney, Harper & Row, Publishers, Inc., 1941, p.111.

Contemplatives are not useful, they are only indispensable.

Ernest Dimnet, *What We Live By,* Jonathan Cape Ltd., 1932, p.195.

All civil mankind have agreed in leaving one day for contemplation against six for practice.

Ralph Waldo Emerson, *The Works of Ralph Waldo Emerson,* edited by George Sampson, George Bell & Sons Ltd., 1906, Volume IV, *Miscellaneous Pieces,* p.431.

I think there is a place both inside and outside of religion for a sort of contemplation of the Good, not just by dedicated experts but by ordinary people: an attention which is not just the planning of particular good actions but an attempt to look right away from self towards a distant transcendent perfection, a source of uncontaminated energy, a source of *new* and quite undreamt-of virtue.

Iris Murdoch, *The Sovereignty Of Good Over Other Concepts,* Cambridge University Press, 1967, p.34.

For not, surely, by deliberate effort of thought does a man grow wise. The truths of life are not discovered by us. At moments unforeseen, some gracious influence descends upon the soul, touching it to an emotion which, we know not how, the mind transmutes into thought. This can happen only in a calm of the senses, a surrender of the whole being to passionless contemplation. I understand, now, the intellectual mood of the quietist.

George Gissing, *The Private Papers of Henry Rycroft,* J.M. Dent & Sons Ltd., 1964, p.134.

Contemplation is the state of union with the divine Ground of all being. The highest prayer is the most passive. Inevitably; for the less there is of self, the more there is of God. That is why the path to passive or infused contemplation is so hard and, for many, so painful—a passage through successive or simultaneous Dark Nights, in which the pilgrim must die to the life of sense as an end in itself, to the life of private and even of traditionally hallowed thinking and believing, and finally to the deep source of all ignorance and evil, the life of the separate, individualized will.

Aldous Huxley, *The Perennial Philosophy,* Chatto & Windus Ltd., 1974, p.259.

Prayer is one of the means towards the end, as the mystic strives to attain the goal. There must be continued and unbroken perseverence in prayer, in order to secure unmoved tranquillity of mind and perpetual purity. Pure and sincere prayer is only obtained by laying aside all anxiety about material things, and all distractions. When purification and cleansing have done their part, there must be no self-satisfaction, but only a deep humility: then the soul must concentrate its thoughts and little by little it will begin to rise to the contemplation of God and to spiritual insight.

John Cassian, in *Studies in Early Mysticism in the Near and Middle East,* Margaret Smith, Sheldon Press, 1931, p.67.

The contemplation of God—and contemplative prayer is, I believe, not necessarily an advanced state but something accessible to us very backward Christians—the waiting upon God in quietness can be our greatest service to the world if in our apartness the love for people is on our heart. As Aaron went into the holy of holies wearing a breastplate with jewels representing the twelve tribes upon it, so the Christian puts himself deliberately into the presence of God with the needs and sorrows of humanity upon his heart. And he does this best not by the vocal skill with which he informs the Deity about the world's needs but by the simplicity of his own exposure to God's greatness and the world's need. "As the soul is in the body" wrote the unknown author of the Letter to Diognetus, "so are the Christians in the world."

Michael Ramsey, *Spirituality For Today,* edited by Eric James, S.C.M. Press Ltd., 1968, p.139.

We like to look on the spiritual life as something very noble, very holy; but also very peaceful and consoling. The word "contemplation" easily tempts those who have not tried it to think that the mystical life consists in looking at the Everlasting Hills, and having nice feelings about God. But the world of contemplation is really continuous with the world of prayer, in the same way as the high Alps are continuous with the lower pastures. To enter it means exchanging the lovely view for the austere reality; penetrating the strange hill-country, slogging up stony tracks in heavy boots, bearing fatigue and risking fog and storm, helping fellow-climbers at one's own cost. It means renouncing the hotel-life level of religion with its comforts and conveniences, and setting our face towards the snows; not for any personal ambition or enjoyment, but driven by the strange mountain love. "Thou hast made us for Thyself and our hearts shall have no rest save in Thee." Narrow rough paths, slippery shale, the glimpse of awful crevasses, terrible storms, cold, bewildering fog and darkness—all these wait for the genuine mountaineer. The great mystics experience all of them, and are well content so to do.

One of the best of all guides to these summits, St. John of the Cross, drew for his disciples a picturesque map of the route. It starts straight up a very narrow path. There are two much wider and better paths going left and right; one of them is marked "the advantages of this world" and the other "the advantages of the next world." Both must be avoided; for both end in the foothills, with no road further on. The real path goes very steeply up the mountain, to a place where St. John has written, "After this there is no path at all"; and the climber says with St. Paul, "Having nothing I possess all things."

Here we are already a long way from the valley; and have reached the stage which is familiar to all climbers, where we feel exhilarated because we think we see the top, but are really about to begin the true climb. This is the Illuminative Life; and here, says St. John, on these levels, the majority of souls come to a halt. For the next thing he shows us is an immense precipice; towering above us, and separating the lovely Alpine pastures of the spiritual life from the awful silence of the Godhead, the mysterious region of the everlasting snows. No one can tell the climber how to tackle the precipice. Here he must be led by the Spirit of God; and his success must depend on his self-abandonment and his courage—his willingness to risk, to trust, and to endure to the very end. Every one suffers on the precipice. Here all landmarks and all guides seem to fail, and the naked soul must cling as best it can to the naked rock of reality. This is the experience which St. John calls in another place the Dark Night of the Spirit. It is a rare experience, but the only way to the real summit; the supernatural life of perfect union with the self-giving and outpouring love of God. There His reality, His honour and His glory alone remain; the very substance of the soul's perpetual joy. And that, and only that, is the mystic goal.

Evelyn Underhill, *Collected Papers of Evelyn Underhill,* Longmans, Green & Co. Ltd., 1946, p.118.

CONTENTMENT

The lines have fallen for me in pleasant places;
yea, I have a goodly heritage.
Psalm 16.6.

The noblest mind the best contentment has.

Edmund Spenser, *Spenser's Faerie Queene,* edited by J.C. Smith, Oxford at the Clarendon Press, 1964, p.13, Bk.I. Canto I. st.xxxv. l.4.

A contented mind is a continual feast.
English Proverb.

A mind content, both Crown and Kingdom is.

Robert Greene, *Farewell to Folly,* 1587, st.ii. l.12.

Content is Wealth, the Riches of the Mind;
And happy He who can that Treasure find.

John Dryden, *The Poems of John Dryden,* edited by James Kinsley, Oxford at the Clarendon Press, 1958, Volume IV, p.1715, "The Wife of Bath Her Tale," l.466.

Those who face that which is actually before them, unburdened by the past, undistracted by the future, these are they who live, who make the best use of their lives; these are those who have found the secret of contentment.

Alban Goodier, S.J., *The School of Love,* Burns Oates & Washbourne Ltd., 1920, p.68.

My crown is in my heart, not on my head;
Not deck'd with diamonds and Indian stones,
Nor to be seen: my crown is call'd content;
A crown it is that seldom kings enjoy.

William Shakespeare, *King Henry VI,* Part III, Act III. sc.i. l.62.

For not that, which men covet most, is best,
Nor that thing worst, which men do most refuse;
But fittest is, that all contented rest
With that they hold: each hath his fortune in his brest.

Edmund Spenser, *Spenser's Faerie Queene,* edited by J.C. Smith, Oxford at the Clarendon Press, 1964, p.414, Bk.VI. Canto IX. st.xxix. l.6.

How calm and quiet a delight
It is alone,
To read, and meditate, and write,
By none offended, nor offending none;
To walk, ride, sit, or sleep at one's own ease,
And pleasing a man's self, none other to displease!

Charles Cotton, *Poems,* chosen and edited by J.R. Tutin, published by the Editor, 1903, "The Retirement," p.16.

To live content with small means; to seek elegance rather than luxury, and refinement rather than fashion; to be worthy, not respectable, and wealthy, not rich; to study hard, to think quietly, talk gently, act frankly; to listen to stars and birds, to babes and sages, with open heart; to bear all cheerfully, do all bravely, await occasions, hurry never. In a word, to let the spiritual, unbidden and unconscious, grow up through the common. This is to be my symphony.

William E. Channing, *A Series of Miscellaneous Illustrated Cards,* 1902, "My Symphony," p.37.

Contentedness, in all accidents brings great peace of spirit.... If I fall into the hands of thieves or of publicans and sequestrators: what now? They have left me the sun and moon, fire and water, a lovely wife, and friends to pity me, and some to relieve me, and I can still discourse; and unless I list, they have not taken away my merry countenance, and my cheerful spirit, and a good conscience: they still have left me the providence of God, and all the promises of the gospel, and my religion, and my hopes of heaven, and my charity to them too; and still I sleep and digest, I eat and drink, I read and meditate; I can walk in my neighbour's pleasant fields, and see the varieties of natural beauties, and delight in all that in which God delights—that is, in virtue and wisdom, in the whole creation, and in God himself.

Jeremy Taylor, *Holy Living,* abridged by Anne Lamb, The Langford Press, 1970, pp.62, 65.

CONVERSION

Suddenly I heard the words of Christ and I understood them, and life and death ceased to seem to me evil, and instead of despair I experienced happiness and the joy of life undisturbed by death.

Leo Tolstoy, *A Confession* and *What I Believe,* translated with an introduction by Aylmer Maude, Humphrey Milford, Oxford University Press, 1921, p.105.

There may have been a neurotic element in the make-up of Saul of Tarsus, John Bunyan and George Fox, and this may account for some features in the story of the conversion of each. But in all three examples, the man is re-made psychologically, morally and intellectually by his vision. This does not happen to the drug addict.

H.G. Wood, *Belief And Unbelief Since 1850,* Cambridge at the University Press, 1955, p.84.

The life of communion which the conversion sets going, the humble and arduous year by year acceptance and using every experience in supernatural regard: this it is which gradually converts the penitent into the saint, as a real garden is made, not by sticking in plants, but by long and unremitting cultivation of the soil.

Evelyn Underhill, *Man and The Supernatural,* Methuen & Co. Ltd., 1927, p.220.

Five years ago I came to believe in Christ's teaching, and my life suddenly changed; I ceased to desire what I had previously desired, and began to desire what I formerly did not want. What had previously seemed to me good seemed evil, and what had seemed evil seemed good. It happened to me as it happens to a man who goes out on some business and on the way suddenly decides that the business is unnecessary and returns home. All that was on his right is now on his left, and all that was on his left is now on his right.

Leo Tolstoy, *A Confession* and *What I Believe,* translated with an introduction by Aylmer Maude, Humphrey Milford, Oxford University Press, 1921, p.103.

Give Me the greedy heart and the little creeping treasons,
Give Me the proud heart and the blind, obstinate eyes (to Caiaphas);
Give me the shallow heart, and the vain lust, and the folly (to Herod);
Give me the coward heart and the spiritless refusals (to Pilate);
Give me the confused self that you can do nothing with;
I can do something.

Dorothy L. Sayers, *The Just Vengeance,* Victor Gollancz Ltd., 1946, p.68.

What is quite certain is that the self cannot by any effort of its own lift itself off its own self as centre and resystematise itself about God as its centre. Such radical conversion must be the act of God, and that too by some process other than the gradual self-purification of a self-centred soul assisted by the ever-present influence of God diffused through nature, including human nature. It cannot be a process only of enlightenment. Nothing can suffice but a redemptive act. Something impinging upon the self from without must deliver it from the freedom which is perfect bondage to the bondage which is its only perfect freedom.

William Temple, *Nature, Man and God,* Macmillan & Co., Ltd., 1934, p.397.

Everyone who lives in this deplorable exile of ours knows that he cannot be filled with a love of eternity, or anointed with the sweet oil of heaven, unless he be truly converted to God. Before he can experience even a little of God's love he must really be turned to him, and, in mind at least, be wholly turned from every earthly thing. The turning indeed is a matter of daily ordered love, so that, first, he loves what he ought to love and not what he ought not, and, second, his love kindles more towards the former than to the latter.

Richard Rolle, *The Fire of Love,* translated with an introduction by Clifton Wolters, Penguin Books Ltd., 1981, p.48.

While I silently ponder on that change wrought in me, I find no language equal to convey to another a clear idea of it. I looked upon the works of God in this visible creation, and an awfulness covered me. My heart was tender and often contrite, and universal love to my fellow-creatures increased in me. This will be understood by such as have trodden the same path. Some glances of real beauty may be seen in their faces, who dwell in true meekness. There is a harmony in the sound of that voice to which divine love gives utterance, and some appearance of right order in their temper and conduct, whose passions are regulated; yet these do not fully show forth that inward life to those who have not felt it; this ... new name is only known rightly by such as receive it.

John Woolman, *The Journal of John Woolman,* Edward Marsh, 1857, p.8.

During the two years just before and after I was twenty I had two experiences which led to religious conversion. The first occurred when I was waiting at a bus stop on a wet afternoon. It was opposite the Odeon cinema, outside the station, and I was surrounded by people, shops, cars. A friend was with me. All of a sudden, for no apparent reason, everything looked different. Everything I could see shone, vibrated, throbbed with joy and with meaning. I knew that it had done this all along, and would go on doing it, but that usually I couldn't see it. It was all over in a minute or two. I climbed on to the bus, saying nothing to my friend—it seemed impossible to explain—and sat stunned with astonishment and happiness.

The second experience occurred some months later. I left my office at lunch-time, stopped at a small Greek café in Fleet Street to buy some rolls and fruit, and walked up Chancery Lane. It was an August day, quite warm but cloudy, with the sun glaringly, painfully bright, behind the clouds. I had a strong sense that something was about to happen. I sat on a seat in the garden of Lincoln's Inn waiting for whatever it was to occur. The sun behind the clouds grew brighter and brighter, the clouds assumed a shape which fascinated me, and between one moment and the next, although no word had been uttered, I felt myself spoken to. I was aware of being regarded by love, of being wholly accepted, accused, forgiven, all at once. The joy of it was the greatest I had ever known in my life. I felt I had been born for this moment and had marked time till it occurred.

Monica Furlong, *Travelling In,* Hodder and Stoughton Ltd., 1971, p.26.

COURAGE

Be strong and of good courage; be not frightened, neither be dismayed; for the Lord your God is with you wherever you go.

Joshua 1.9.

Great things are done more through courage than through wisdom.

German Proverb.

Where true Fortitude dwells, Loyalty, Bounty, Friendship and Fidelity may be found.

Sir Thomas Browne, *The Works of Sir Thomas Browne,* edited by Geoffrey Keynes, Faber and Faber Limited, 1964, Volume I, Christian Morals, p.258.

Courage is not simply *one* of the virtues but the form of every virtue at the testing point, which means at the point of highest reality.

C.S. Lewis, in *The Unquiet Grave,* Cyril Connolly, Hamish Hamilton, 1945, p.75.

The stout heart is also a warm and kind one: Affection dwells with Danger, all the holier and the lovelier for such stern environment.

Thomas Carlyle, *The Works of Thomas Carlyle*, Chapman & Hall Limited, 1899, Critical and Miscellaneous Essays, Volume III, *Corn-Law Rhymes*, p.147.

Courage is what it takes to stand up and speak; courage is also what it takes to sit down, and listen.

Anon.

The Courage we desire and prize is not the Courage to die decently, but to live manfully.

Thomas Carlyle, *The Works of Thomas Carlyle*, Chapman & Hall Limited, 1899, *Critical and Miscellaneous Essays*, Volume III, "Boswell's Life of Johnson," p.123.

Oh courage ... oh yes! If only one had that.... Then life might be liveable, in spite of everything.

Henrik Ibsen, *Hedda Gabler*, edited by James Walter McFarlane, translated by Jens Arup & James Walter McFarlane, Oxford University Press, 1966, Volume VII, p.225, Act II.

Courage is the basic virtue for everyone so long as he continues to grow, to move ahead.

Rollo May, *Man's Search For Himself*, George Allen & Unwin Ltd., 1953, p.224.

Courage is sustained, not only by prayer, but by calling up anew the vision of the goal.

A.D. Sertillanges, O.P., *The Intellectual Life*, translated by Mary Ryan, The Mercier Press, 1948, p.157.

The greatest virtue in life is real courage, that knows how to face facts and live beyond them.

D.H. Lawrence, *The Selected Letters of D.H. Lawrence*, edited with an introduction by Diana Trilling, Farrar, Strauss and Cudahy, Inc., 1958, p.243.

It requires moral courage to grieve; it requires religious courage to rejoice.

Søren Kierkegaard, *The Journals of Søren Kierkegaard*, a selection edited and translated by Alexander Dru, Oxford University Press, 1938, p.87.

Heroism is the brilliant triumph of the soul over the flesh—that is to say, over fear; fear of poverty, of suffering, of calumny, of sickness, of isolation, and of death. There is no serious piety without heroism. Heroism is the dazzling and glorious concentration of courage.

Henri Frédéric Amiel, *Amiel's Journal*, translated by Mrs. Humphry Ward, Macmillan & Co. Ltd., 1918, p.4.

Unbounded courage and compassion joined,
Tempering each other in the victor's mind,
Alternately proclaim him good and great,
And make the hero and the man complete.

Joseph Addison, *The Works of Joseph Addison*, notes by Richard Hurd, edited and published by Henry G. Bohn, 1856, Volume I, The Campaign, p.48.

Yet I argue not
Against heavens hand or will, nor bate a jot
Of heart or hope; but still bear up, and steer
Right onward.

John Milton, *The Poetical Works of Milton,* edited by the Rev. H.C. Beeching, Oxford at the University Press, 1900, p.89, "To Mr. Cyriack Skinner upon his Blindness," 1.6.

Courage is required not only in a person's occasional crucial decision for his own freedom, but in the little hour-to-hour decisions which place the bricks in the structure of his building of himself into a person who acts with freedom and responsibility.

Rollo May, *Man's Search For Himself,* George Allen & Unwin Ltd., 1953, p.229.

We must accept our existence as far as ever it is possible; everything, even the unheard of, must be possible there. That is fundamentally the only courage which is demanded of us: to be brave in the face of the strangest, most singular and most inexplicable things that can befall us.

Rainer Maria Rilke, *Letters to a Young Poet,* translation, introduction and commentary by Reginald Snell, Sidgwick and Jackson, 1945, p.38.

Courage cannot be explained with reference solely to itself. A courageous man is one who has courage to do something, to be something. That is, he believes that there is more to be done with life than prolong it. It is said that a man must have the courage of his convictions, but he can have no courage unless he has convictions.
The New Testament in general, and the Sermon on the Mount in particular, makes it clear that the courageous man's first victory is a conquest over anxiety. Anxiety can be described under these headings: 1) *Material*—Fear of increased prices, inflation, unemployment, changes in trade, nationally and internationally, illness, infirmity. These might be summarized as a general, though vague, feeling of political and economic insecurity. 2) *Spiritual*—Fear of loss of freedom and power to keep one's identity. Fear of being a hypocrite or incapable of significant action. Fear of being inadequate in personal relationships especially in the family. 3) *Religious*—Fear of the failure and disappearance of the church on account of the small number of practising members. Fear through a reluctance to think and live in the light of the fact that Christians walk by faith and not by sight and therefore cannot answer all the questions men may ask. Christians do not claim that only Christians can be courageous but that a man, or woman, requires courage to be a Christian in any century—whether in facing violence, torture and death or enduring the constant battle to be fought out against anxiety.
It is brave to accept dangers oneself but it is even braver to allow and even exhort others to be courageous in their particular spheres of living—for example, a bishop ordaining clergy, parents encouraging their sons and daughters to leave home and take full responsibility for themselves, friend helping friend to make a decision where one should be made no matter at what cost.
Christians learn that courage is a necessity rather than a virtue through their frequent meditation on the passion and triumph of our Lord. In every generation orthodox

doctrine and individual piety are most clearly expressed in the compassion and courage of church members. Where there is no courage, compassion dwindles and where compassion is absent courage tends to become arrogant self-display.

R.E.C. Browne, in *A Dictionary of Christian Ethics*, edited by John Macquarrie, S.C.M. Press Ltd., 1967, "Courage," p.76.

CREATION

Any child knows that the earth was not made in six days. But not everyone knows that God made the world through his Spirit and man in his own image.

Dietrich Bonhoeffer, *The Collected Works of Dietrich Bonhoeffer*, Volume I, *No Rusty Swords*, "Letters, Lectures and Notes 1928-1936," edited with an introduction by Edwin H. Robertson, translated by Edwin H. Robertson and John Bowden, William Collins Sons & Co. Ltd., 1965, p.143.

Two things fill the mind with ever new and increasing admiration and awe, the oftener and the more steadily they are reflected on: the starry heavens above me and the moral law within me.

Immanuel Kant, *Critique of Practical Reason*, translated and edited with an introduction by Lewis White Beck, The University of Chicago Press, 1949, p.258.

All creatures are living in the hand of God; the senses perceive only the action of the creature, but faith sees the action of God in everything.

Jean Pierre de Caussade, S.J., *Self-Abandonment To Divine Providence*, edited by Father John Joyce, S. J., introduction by David Knowles, Burns & Oates Ltd., 1962, p.18.

The essence of the doctrine of Creation is not that God inaugurated the existence of the world at a particular moment of time, but that it owes its existence—not only its beginning—to His volitional activity.

William Temple, *Nature, Man And God*, Macmillan & Co. Ltd., 1934, p.301.

> Flower in the crannied wall,
> I pluck you out of the crannies,
> I hold you here, root and all, in my hand,
> Little flower—but *if* I could understand
> What you are, root and all, and all in all,
> I should know what God and man is.

Alfred, Lord Tennyson, *The Poems of Tennyson*, edited by Christopher Ricks, Longmans, Green & Co. Ltd., 1969, p.1193, No.349, "Flower in the crannied wall," l.1.

Every man, in the course of his life, must not only show himself obedient and docile. By his fidelity he must *build*—starting with the most natural territory of his own self—a work ... into which something enters from all the elements of the earth. He *makes his own soul* throughout all his earthly days; and at the same time he collaborates in another work, which infinitely transcends ... the perspectives of his individual achievement: the completing of the world.

Pierre Teilhard de Chardin, *Le Milieu Divin*, William Collins Sons & Co. Ltd., 1960, p.32.

God is *in* the world, or nowhere, creating continually in us and around us. This creative principle is everywhere, in animate and so-called inanimate matter, in the ether, water, earth, human hearts. But this creation is a continuing process, and 'the process is itself the actuality,' since no sooner do you arrive than you start on a fresh journey. In so far as man partakes of this creative process does he partake of the divine, of God, and that participation is his immortality, reducing the question of whether his individuality survives death of the body to the estate of an irrelevancy. His true destiny as co-creator in the universe is his dignity and his grandeur.

Alfred North Whitehead, *Dialogues of Alfred North Whitehead*, as recorded by Lucien Price, Max Reinhardt, 1954, p.366.

> For I have learned
> To look on nature, not as in the hour
> Of thoughtless youth; but hearing oftentimes
> The still, sad music of humanity,
> Nor harsh nor grating, though of ample power
> To chasten and subdue. And I have felt
> A presence that disturbs me with the joy
> Of elevated thoughts; a sense sublime
> Of something far more deeply interfused,
> Whose dwelling is the light of setting suns,
> And the round ocean and the living air,
> And the blue sky, and in the mind of man:
> A motion and a spirit, that impels
> All thinking things, all objects of all thought,
> And rolls through all things.

William Wordsworth, *The Poetical Works of William Wordsworth*, edited by E. de Selincourt, Oxford at the Clarendon Press, 1944, Volume II, p.261, "Lines composed a few miles above Tintern Abbey," l.88.

> The spacious firmament on high,
> With all the blue ethereal sky,
> And spangled heavens, a shining frame,
> Their great Original proclaim:
> The unwearied sun from day to day
> Does his Creator's power display,
> And publishes to every land
> The work of an Almighty hand.
>
> Soon as the evening shades prevail,
> The moon takes up the wondrous tale,
> And nightly to the listening earth
> Repeats the story of her birth:
> Whilst all the stars that round her burn,
> And all the planets, in their turn,
> Confirm the tidings as they roll,
> And spread the truth from pole to pole.

What though, in solemn silence, all
Move round the dark terrestrial ball?
What though nor real voice nor sound
Amid their radiant orbs be found?
In reason's ear they all rejoice,
And utter forth a glorious voice,
For ever singing, as they shine,
"The hand that made us is Divine."

Joseph Addison, *The Works of Joseph Addison,* notes by Richard Hurd, edited and published by Henry G. Bohn, 1856, Volume III, p.485.

Sometimes I look about me with a feeling of complete dismay. In the confusion that afflicts the world today, I see a disrespect for the very values of life. Beauty is all about us, but how many are blind to it! They look at the wonder of this earth—and seem to see nothing. People move hectically but give little thought to where they are going. They seek excitement for its mere sake, as if they were lost and desperate. They take little pleasure in the natural and quiet and simple things of life.

Each second we live is a new and unique moment of the universe, a moment that never was before and will never be again. And what do we teach our children in School? We teach them that two and two make four, and that Paris is the capital of France. When will we also teach them what they are? We should say to each one of them: Do you know what you are? You are a marvel. You are unique. In all of the world there is no other child exactly like you. In the millions of years that have passed there never has been another child like you. And look at your body—what a wonder it is! Your legs, your arms, your cunning fingers, the way you move! You may become a Shakespeare, a Michelangelo, a Beethoven. You have the capacity for anything. Yes, you are a marvel. And when you grow up, can you then harm another who is, like you, a marvel? You must cherish one another. You must work—we all must work— to make the world worthy of its children....

The love of one's country is a natural thing. But why should love stop at the border? Our family is one—each of us has a duty to his brothers. We are all leaves of a tree, and the tree is humanity.

Pablo Casals, *Joys and Sorrows: Reflections by Pablo Casals,* as told to Albert E. Kahn, Macdonald and Co. (Publishers) Ltd., 1970, p.295.

What we have to find is a metaphysical landscape, a way of seeing the world, which shall justify the saint, the artist and the scientist, and give each his full rights. Not a doctrine of watertight compartments, an opposition of "appearance" to "reality." Rather, a doctrine of the indwelling of this visible world by an invisible, yet truly existent, world of spirit; which, while infinitely transcending, yet everywhere supports and permeates the natural scene. Even to say this, is to blur the true issue by resort to the deceptive spatial language which colours and controls our thoughts, and translate the dynamic and spiritual into static and intellectual terms.

The first demand we must make of such a diagram is, that it shall at least safeguard, though it can never represent, all the best that man has learned to apprehend of the distinct and rich reality of God.... For that which above all a genuine theism requires of our human ways of thinking, is the acknowledgement of two sorts or stages of reality, which can never be washed down into one: of a two-foldness that goes right through man's experience, and cannot without impoverishment be resolved. We may call these two sorts of reality, this two-foldness, by various names—Supernature and Nature, Eternity and Time, God and the World, Infinite and Finite, Creator and Creature. These terms do but emphasize one or another aspect of a total fact too great for us to grasp, without infringing the central truth of its mysterious duality: for "God," as Plotinus says, "never was the All. That would make Him dependent on His universe."

Evelyn Underhill, *Man and The Supernatural,* Methuen & Co. Ltd., 1927, p.54.

CROSS

This was why the Jews sought all the more to kill him, because he not only broke the sabbath but also called God his own Father, making himself equal with God.

John 5.18.

I have been crucified with Christ; it is no longer I who live, but Christ who lives in me; and the life I now live in the flesh I live by faith in the Son of God, who loved me and gave himself for me.

Galatians 2.20.

The cross is "I" crossed out.

Anon.

No Cross, No Crown

William Penn, title of pamphlet, 1669.

The way to God is the way of the Cross. Christ Himself is the pattern and His way of Life is the typical way for all who would find God.

Rufus M. Jones, *Spiritual Reformers in the 16th and 17th Centuries,* Macmillan & Co. Ltd., 1914, p.250.

The Way of the Cross winds through our towns and cities, our hospitals and factories, and through our battlefields; it takes the road of poverty and suffering in every form. It is in front of these new Stations of the Cross that we must stop and meditate and pray to the suffering Christ for strength to love him enough to act.

Michel Quoist, *Prayers of Life,* translated by Anne Marie de Commaile & Agnes Mitchell Forsyth, Gill & Macmillan Ltd., 1963, p.5.

After all, the fundamental idea both of St. John and of St. Paul is simply that the death of Christ, the culminating act in a life of self-sacrifice, is the supreme manifestation of Christ's love, and therefore of the love of the Father whom He reveals; and that the contemplation of that life and death gives other men the power, as nothing else has done, to overcome temptation and to lead lives of love like His.

Hastings Rashdall, *The Idea of Atonement in Christian Theology,* Macmillan & Co. Ltd., 1920, p.184.

We Christians often use the words "Christ died to save us from our sins." He shows us the limitless measure of God's love and that draws our hearts to him. He makes known to us God's forgiveness, not only in his teaching, but by the fact of his own forgiveness of those who brought him to the cross. There is something more which it is difficult to describe— he works within us, assuring us of God's forgiveness, changing our hearts towards sin and selfishness, and sharing his risen life so that sin, though it may attack us, need find no entry.

George Appleton, *Journey for a Soul,* William Collins Sons & Co. Ltd., 1976, p.178.

(How could Christ die for our sins?) This is the hardest thing for people to realise intellectually. You can tell them about it, but I believe the experience of Christ's death, the freedom from sin, can only be experienced personally. You can hear about it and know about it, but I think this is the gap across which a person has to leap by experience or by faith.

George Reindorp, in *Priestland's Progress,* Gerald Priestland, British Broadcasting Corporation, 1982, p.79.

THE CROSS IS NOT a) the angry Father appeasing his wrath by taking it out of his loving Son; b) the Son standing in my place to take the punishment I ought to have. *THE CROSS IS* God accepting in his own person the worst evil of the world he has created and, by accepting the worst that men can do, assuring us that all men, however bad, are accepted by his love.

Hugh Montefiore, *My Confirmation Notebook,* S.P.C.K., 1983, p.28.

The Cross is the glory of God because self-sacrifice is the expression of love. That glory would be complete in itself even if it had no consequences. But in fact what is revealed in the Cross is not only the perfection of the divine love, but its triumph. For by its sacrifice the divine love wins those who can appreciate it out of their selfishness which is spiritual death into loving fellowship with itself which is true life.

William Temple, *Readings in St. John's Gospel* (First and Second Series), Macmillan & Co. Ltd., 1947, p.308.

The Cross was not a transaction. It was the culmination of this mighty Love, for "here on the cross hung God and man"—God's Love springing forth in a soul strong enough to show it in its full scope.
But let no person think that he can "cover himself with the purple mantle of Christ's sufferings and death," and so win his salvation: "Thou thyself," he says, "must go through Christ's whole journey, and enter wholly into His process."

Rufus M. Jones, *Spiritual Reformers in the 16th and 17th Centuries,* Macmillan & Co. Ltd., 1914, p.194.

I simply argue that the Cross be raised again at the centre of the market place as well as on the steeple of the church. I am recovering the claim that Jesus was not crucified in a Cathedral between two candles, but on a Cross between two thieves; on the town garbage heap; at a crossroad so cosmopolitan that they had to write his title in Hebrew and in Latin and in Greek (or shall we say in English, in Bantu and in Afrikaans?); at the kind of place where cynics talk smut, and thieves curse, and soldiers gamble.

Because that is where He died. And that is what He died about. And that is where churchmen should be and what churchmen should be about.

George F. Macleod, *Only One Way Left,* The Iona Community, 1956, p.38.

"There cannot be a God' of love," men say, "because if there were, and He looked upon this world, His heart would break."
The Church points to the Cross and says, "His heart does break."
"It is God who has made the world," men say, "it is He who is responsible and it is He who should bear the load."
The Church points to the Cross and says, "He does bear it."
"God is beyond men's comprehension, and it is blasphemy to say you know Him";
and the Church answers, "We do not know Him perfectly; but we worship the majesty we see."

William Temple, *The Preacher's Theme To-day,* S.P.C.K., 1936, p.62.

You can say that Christ died for our sins. You may say that the Father has forgiven us because Christ has done for us what we ought to have done. You may say that we are washed in the blood of the Lamb. You may say that Christ has defeated death. They are all true. If any of them do not appeal to you, leave it alone and get on with the formula that does. And, whatever you do, do not start quarrelling with other people because they use a different formula from yours.

C.S. Lewis, *Mere Christianity,* William Collins Sons & Co. Ltd., 1961, p.153.

The great message of the *Cross* stands or falls with the divinity of Christ. Is it not the truth that all the rivals of Christianity fail just here? All the religious philosophies of antiquity, it seems to me, shrink, in the last resort, from grasping the nettle of suffering quite firmly. They all want to make us invulnerable, somehow. There must always be a back-door of escape if the ills of life become too overpowering. Either defiant resistence, or suicide, or complete detachment, is recommended. By some means or other, the man himself must be rescued from circumstance, he must provide himself with a magic impenetrable armour. And *therefore,* the sting of pain is never drawn. The good news of Christianity is that suffering is itself divine. It is not foreign to the experience of God Himself. "In all their afflictions He was afflicted." "Surely He hath borne our griefs and carried our sorrows." "If thou be the Son of God," said His enemies, "come down from the Cross." No; not while any man remains unredeemed. The divine suffering is not an episode, but a revelation. It is the necessary form which divine love takes, when it is brought into contact with evil. To overcome evil with good means to suffer unjustly and willingly.

W.R. Inge, *Speculum Animae,* Longmans, Green and Co. Ltd., 1911, p.22.

I think the traditional accounts of Atonement and Redemption have tended to start with an assumption about the Creation and Fall. They see Creation as something that was perfect at the beginning, which men then spoiled with their sins, and which at some point in history had to be restored to proper relationship by something dramatic. Now seeing the Creation and Fall as a story (I'll avoid the word myth), I believe in Creation as something continuous that is going on all the time. So I see Redemption as something that is going on all the time, as the fundamental character of God's creative activity. And I see the Cross as focussing this truth of God's reconciling love working for the harmony of His Creation....

Crucifixion seems to me to show that the way this reconciliation may be achieved is by breaking the continual process of revenge. And Resurrection expresses the confidence that this is the way the world is ultimately built. It is a long-term process, and it does not do away with the fact that very often this is the way of disaster for those who practise it. But it does express the conviction that in the long run this is the only way in which human violence and self-destruction can be overcome.

Maurice Wiles, in *Priestland's Progress*, Gerald Priestland, British Broadcasting Corporation, 1982, p.87.

D

DARKNESS

Into each life some rain must fall,
Some days must be dark and dreary.

Henry Wadsworth Longfellow, *The Poetical Works of Longfellow*, Humphrey Milford, Oxford University Press, 1913, p.63, "The Rainy Day," st.iii. 1.4.

Resolve to be thyself; and know that he,
Who finds himself, loses his misery!

Matthew Arnold, *The Poems of Matthew Arnold*, edited by Kenneth Allott, Longmans, Green & Co. Ltd., 1965, p.144, "Self-Dependence," 1.31.

Darkness is more productive of sublime ideas than light.

Edmund Burke, *Burke's Works*, printed for J. Dodsley, Volume I, p.145, Part II, sec.xiv, "Light: On the Sublime and Beautiful," 1.17.

And out of darkness came the hands
That reach through nature, moulding men.

Alfred, Lord Tennyson, *The Poems of Tennyson*, edited by Christopher Ricks, Longmans, Green & Co. Ltd., 1969, p.974, No.296, "In Memoriam A.H.H.," st.cxxiv. 1.23.

The mass of men lead lives of quiet desperation.

Henry David Thoreau, *Walden*, The New American Library of World Literature, Inc., 1960, p.10.

That Jesus fought despair and triumphed we know from his prayers on the cross which began with "My God, why have you forsaken me?" and ended with "Into your hand, Lord, I commend my spirit." However near we come to despair, we have this precedent to refer to.

Hubert van Zeller, *Considerations*, Sheed & Ward Ltd., 1974, p.76.

And when he can no longer *feel* the truth, he shall not therefore die. He lives because God is true; and he is able to know that he lives because he knows, having once understood the word, that God is truth. He believes in the God of former vision, lives by that word therefore, when all is dark and there is no vision.

George Macdonald, *Unspoken Sermons*, First Series, Alexander Strahan, Publisher, 1867, p.144.

He wandered aimlessly. The sun was setting. A special form of misery had begun to oppress him of late. There was nothing poignant, nothing acute about it; but there was a feeling of permanence, of eternity about it; it brought a foretaste of hopeless years of this cold leaden misery, a foretaste of an eternity "on a square yard of space."

Fyodor Dostoyevsky, *Crime and Punishment*, translated by Constance Garnett, Folio Society, 1957, p.353.

If I stoop
Into a dark tremendous sea of cloud,
It is but for a time; I press God's lamp
Close to my breast; its splendour, soon or late,
Will pierce the gloom: I shall emerge one day.

Robert Browning, *The Poetical Works of Robert Browning*, Smith, Elder & Co., 1899, Volume I, *Paracelsus V*, p.72.

When the heart is hard and parched up, come upon me with a shower of mercy.
When grace is lost from life, come with a burst of song.
When tumultuous work raises its din on all sides shutting me out from beyond, come
to me, my lord of silence, with thy peace and rest.
When my beggarly heart sits crouched, shut up in a corner, break open the door, my
king, and come with the ceremony of a king.
When desire blinds the mind with delusion and dust, O thou holy one, thou wakeful,
come with thy light and thy thunder.

Rabindranath Tagore, *Gitanjali*, Macmillan & Co. Ltd., 1971, p.30.

For the rest, I was utterly derelict. I felt myself banished from life and from God.
And I was quite hopeless: not approximately, not in the sense people often intend
when they play with this terrible word, but in the sense that to have had the very
tiniest of hopes, for the very briefest of instants, would have been wholly inconceivable.
The doom that I lived with in eternity was the doom that I must live in eternity with
a self I detested, and must live with it alone.

Victor Gollancz, *More For Timothy*, Victor Gollancz Ltd., 1953, p.92.

The man of to-day pursues his dark journey in a time of darkness, as one who has no
freedom, no mental collectedness, no all-round development, as one who loses himself
in an atmosphere of inhumanity, who surrenders his spiritual independence and his
moral judgment to the organised society in which he lives, and who finds himself in
every direction up against hindrances to the temper of true civilisation. Of the dangerous position in which he is placed philosophy has no understanding, and therefore
makes no attempt to help him. She does not even urge him to reflection on what is
happening to himself.

Albert Schweitzer, in *Albert Schweitzer: Christian Revolutionary*, by George Seaver, James Clarke & Co. Ltd.,
1944, p.94.

Oh, how dare I mention the dark feeling of mysterious dread which comes over the
mind, and which the lamp of reason, though burning bright the while, is unable to
dispel! Art thou, as leeches say, the concomitant of disease—the result of shattered
nerves? Nay, rather the principle of woe itself, the fountain head of all sorrow co-
existent with man, whose influence he feels when yet unborn;... for ... woe doth he
bring with him into the world, even thyself, dark one, terrible one, causeless, unbe-
gotten, without a father.... Then is it not lawful for man to exclaim, "Better that I
had never been born!" Fool, for thyself wast not born, but to fulfil the inscrutable
decrees of thy Creator; and how dost thou know that this dark principle is not, after

all, thy best friend; that it is not that which tempers the whole mass of thy corruption? It may be, for what thou knowest, the mother of wisdom, and of great works: it is the dread of the horror of the night that makes the pilgrim hasten on his way. When thou feelest it nigh, let thy safety word be "Onward"; if thou tarry, thou art over-whelmed. Courage! build great works—'tis urging thee—it is ever nearest the favour-ites of God—the fool knows little of it. Thou wouldst be joyous, wouldst thou? then be a fool. What great work was ever the result of joy, the puny one? Who have been the wise ones, the mighty ones, the conquering ones of this earth? the joyous? I believe
not.

George Borrow, *Lavengro*, Thomas Nelson and Sons, Ltd., 1933, p.119.

For an hour past I have been the prey of a vague anxiety; I recognise my old enemy.... It is a sense of void and anguish; a sense of something lacking: what? Love, peace,—God perhaps. The feeling is one of pure want unmixed with hope, and there is anguish in it because I can clearly distinguish neither the evil nor its remedy.... Of all the hours of the day, in fine weather, the afternoon, about 3 o'clock, is the time which to me is most difficult to bear. I never feel more strongly than I do then, *"le vide effrayant de la vie,"* the stress of mental anxiety, or the painful thirst for happiness. This torture born of the sunlight is a strange phenomenon. Is it that the sun, just as it brings out the stain upon a garment, the wrinkles in a face, or the discoloration of the hair, so also it illumines with inexorable distinctness the scars and rents of the heart? Does it rouse in us a sort of shame of existence? In any case the bright hours of the day are capable of flooding the whole soul with melancholy, of kindling in us the passion for death, or suicide, or annihilation, or of driving us to that which is next akin to death, the deadening of the senses by the pursuit of pleasure. They rouse in the lonely man a horror of himself; they make him long to escape from his own
misery and solitude ...
People talk of the temptations to crime connected with darkness, but the dumb sense of desolation which is often the product of the most brilliant moment of daylight must not be forgotten either. From the one, as from the other, God is absent; but in the first case a man follows his senses and the cry of his passion; in the second, he
feels himself lost and bewildered, a creature forsaken by all the world.

Henri Frédéric Amiel, *Amiel's Journal*, translated by Mrs. Humphry Ward, Macmillan & Co. Ltd., 1918, p.200.

DEATH

A good life has a peaceful death.
French Proverb.

I came from God, and I'm going back to God, and I won't have any gaps of death
in the middle of my life.

George Macdonald, *Mary Marston, Sampson Low*, Marston, Searle, & Rivington, 1881, Volume III, p.317.

To die is poignantly bitter, but the idea of having to die without having lived is unbearable.

Erich Fromm, *Man For Himself*, Routledge & Kegan Paul Ltd., 1975, p.162.

As a well-spent day brings happy sleep, so life well used brings happy death.

Leonardo da Vinci, *The Notebooks of Leonardo da Vinci*, arranged, rendered into English, with an introduction by Edward MacCurdy, Jonathan Cape Ltd., 1977, Volume I, p.65.

The only religious way to think of death is as part and parcel of life; to regard it, with the understanding and with the emotions, as the inviolable condition of life.

Thomas Mann, *The Magic Mountain*, translated by H.T. Lowe-Porter, Penguin Books Ltd., 1983, p.200.

Do not seek death. Death will find you. But seek the road which makes death a fulfilment.

Dag Hammarskjold, *Markings*, translated by Leif Sjoberg & W.H. Auden, with a foreword by W.H. Auden, Faber and Faber Limited, 1964, p.136.

It takes so many years
To learn that one is dead!

T.S. Eliot, *The Complete Poems and Plays of T.S. Eliot*, Faber and Faber Limited, 1975, *The Family Reunion*, p.343, Act II. sc.iii.

What do I dread most? The answer nearly always is having to face this or that ordeal alone. It is being cut off. It is not the ordeal itself; it is the being with it on my own. Death is one such ordeal. Not the moment or the pain, but the being out of reach.

Hubert van Zeller, *Considerations*, Sheed & Ward Ltd., 1974, p.19.

On the day when death will knock at thy door what wilt thou offer to him? Oh, I will set before my guest the full vessel of my life—I will never let him go with empty hands.
All the sweet vintage of all my autumn days and summer nights, all the earnings and gleanings of my busy life will I place before him at the close of my days when death will knock at my door.

Rabindranath Tagore, *Gitanjali*, Macmillan & Co. Ltd., 1971, p.83.

Our attitude to all men would be Christian if we regarded them as though they were dying, and determined our relation to them in the light of death, both of their death and our own. A person who is dying calls forth a special kind of feeling. Our attitude to him is at once softened and lifted on to a higher plane. We then can feel compassion for people whom we did not love. But every man is dying, I too am dying and must never forget about death.

Nicolas Berdyaev, *The Destiny of Man*, translated by Natalie Duddington, Geoffrey Bles, The Centenary Press, 1937, p.156.

The Lord does not promise that anyone who keeps His word shall avoid the physical incident called death; but that if his mind is turned towards that word it will not pay any attention to death: death will be to it irrelevant. It may truly be said that such a man will not "experience" death, because, though it will happen to him, it will matter to him no more than the fall of a leaf from a tree under which he might be reading a book.

William Temple, *Readings in St. John's Gospel* (First and Second Series), Macmillan & Co. Ltd., 1947, p. 147.

The birth of a human being is pregnant with meaning; then why is this not true of death also? Twenty years or more of a young man's life are spent in preparation for the full unfolding of his individual existence; why then should he not spend twenty years or more preparing for his end?...

I am convinced that it is hygienic—if I may use the word—to discover in death a goal towards which one can strive, and that shrinking away from it is something unhealthy and abnormal which robs the second half of life of its purpose.

C.G. Jung, *Psychological Reflections,* selected and edited by Jolande Jacobi, Routledge & Kegan Paul Ltd., 1953, p. 287.

God must, in some way or other, make room for Himself, hollowing us out and emptying us, if He is finally to penetrate into us. And in order to assimilate us in Him, He must break the molecules of our being so as to re-cast and re-model us. The function of death is to provide the necessary entrance into our inmost selves. It will make us undergo the required dissociation. It will put us into the state organically needed if the divine fire is to descend upon us. And in that way its fatal power to decompose and dissolve will be harnessed to the most sublime operations of life. What was by nature empty and void, a return to bits and pieces, can, in any human existence, become fullness and unity in God.

Pierre Teilhard de Chardin, *Le Milieu Divin,* William Collins Sons & Co. Ltd., 1960, p. 68.

For dying is an art, which has to be learned in the practice of life by allowing it to dissolve our assertive will and refine our perceptions, until we come to feel habitually the mystery of death in each new-born moment and to see with wonder in all around us that mutual embrace of light and shadow, of idea and substance in which life and death unite. This is the art to which those who are growing old should in particular devote themselves, thus helping to form the new body or bodies within them in which they are soon to live. Yet an assent to death is as much a grace of ardent youth, though unconscious then, as it is of an old age fulfilled in wisdom and understanding. In fact the whole of our life, with its physical and mental changes and its continual demands upon us to adapt to new circumstances and pressures from within and without, is a testing of our capacity to maintain and consciously deepen the union between living and dying by which we are created and can ourselves create.

Hugh L'Anson Fausset, *Fruits of Silence,* Abelard-Schuman Ltd., 1963, p. 215.

DISCIPLESHIP

There are two words used a great deal by Jesus in the Gospels. One is "Come" and the other is "Go." It's no use coming unless you go, and it's no use going unless you come.

Anon.

When we fail in our discipleship it is always for one of two reasons; either we are not trying to be loyal, or else we are trying in our own strength and find that it is not enough.

William Temple, *Readings in St. John's Gospel* (First and Second Series), Macmillan & Co. Ltd., 1947, p.225.

To him who obeys, and thus opens the doors of his heart to receive the eternal gift, God gives the spirit of his Son, the spirit of himself, to be in him, and lead him to the understanding of all truth; that the true disciple shall thus always know what he ought to do, though not necessarily what another ought to do.

George Macdonald, *Unspoken Sermons,* Third Series, Longmans, Green & Co., 1889, p.155.

There is a kind of Church-worker for whom our age even more urgently calls, and on whom the life and example of Christ set more immediately the seal of discipleship— the man who, to the glory of God and for the good of his fellows, does honest work of the everyday sort.

Archibald C. Craig, *University Sermons,* James Clarke & Co. Ltd., 1937, p.147.

He prepared His disciples for a change after the critical moment was passed; with the Cross and Resurrection His Kingdom would have come with power, and they were no longer to be apart from the world, bringing to it *ab extra* the divine act of redemption which is itself the revelation of God, but were to carry its power into the world as leaven that should leaven the whole lump.

William Temple, *Citizen And Churchman,* Eyre and Spottiswoode, Ltd., 1941, p.65.

Every disciple knows that the aim of his life is to grow like his Lord. To achieve this he will study the earliest records of the divine life lived among men. He will want to get back behind the words to their meaning, behind the actions to the mind and character which inspired those actions. He will be eager to enter into intimate touch with him who promised to be with men and to live within the inmost being of each man. So with the outer study and the inner communion he will come to understand and acquire something of the mind of Christ.

George Appleton, *Journey for a Soul,* William Collins Sons & Co. Ltd., 1976, p.157.

On one occasion three would-be disciples came to Jesus and offered their discipleship with reservations or delays. He warned them that discipleship involved hardship, with total, immediate and life-long commitment (Luke 9.57-62). When we begin to follow we shall soon realize that more is needed, and if we are honest enough or rash enough to ask "What do I still lack?" he will unerringly put his finger on the one thing we are least ready to surrender.

George Appleton, *Journey for a Soul,* William Collins Sons & Co. Ltd., 1976, p.188.

The Christian who reads, in these verses (Luke 14.25-35), of the price of discipleship will see that, if he is to take the divine words seriously, he must learn not to be too much "entangled in the affairs of this life," whether human affairs or relationships, or personal and material things. He must learn to think of these as things that he can do without, including life itself. No one knows what he may be called upon one day to face or to do in loyalty to his profession as a Christian disciple—especially in a world as dangerous and uncertain as that in which our lives are cast. The man who is bogged down by worldly ties and considerations will find obedience much harder if God should call him one day to some sacrificial act.

The price of discipleship, therefore, is to be willing to give up everything if occasion should demand it, and, in the meanwhile, to live as men "looking for their Lord," with loins girt and lamps burning, ready for action when the word is given. Discipleship is, or may be, a very costly thing. It may cost us all we have. In this passage, therefore, Jesus introduces a fourth condition, and that is that we should not go into it except with our eyes wide open. He does this in the form of three little parables, those of the tower builder who carefully surveys his material; the warrior-king who closely considers his chances of success; and the salt, which, if it cannot last out, goes bad.

Jesus bids us count the cost of discipleship. Can we face it? Is it going to be too much for us? Dare we risk failure and be cast out?

"He that hath ears to hear let him hear." Let him hear: let him ponder: let him decide.

J.R.H. Moorman, *The Path To Glory*, S.P.C.K. and Seabury Press, 1960, p.182.

DIVINITY

He who is of God hears the words of God; the reason why you do not hear them is that you are not of God.

John 8.47.

Little children, you are of God, and have overcome them; for he who is in you is greater than he who is in the world.

1 John 4.4.

We know that we are of God.

1 John 5.19.

There's a divinity that shapes our ends,
Rough-hew them how we will.

William Shakespeare, *Hamlet*, Act V. sc.ii. l.10.

There is surely a peece of Divinity in us, something that was before the Elements, and owes no homage unto the Sun.

Sir Thomas Browne, *The Works of Sir Thomas Browne*, edited by Geoffrey Keynes, Faber and Faber Limited, 1964, Volume I, *Religio Medici*, p.87.

The mystery of a Person, indeed, is ever divine, to him that has a sense for the Godlike.

Thomas Carlyle, *Sartor Resartus*, Ward, Lock & Co. Ltd., p.92.

Were I indeed to define divinity, I should rather call it a *divine life,* than a *divine science;* it being something rather to be understood by a spiritual sensation, than by any verbal description ...

John Smith the Platonist, *Select Discourses,* Cambridge at the University Press, 1859, p.1.

Reason is our Soules left hand, Faith her right,
By these we reach divinity.

John Donne, *The Satires, Epigrams and Verse Letters,* Oxford at the Clarendon Press, 1967, p.90, Verse Letters: "To the Countess of Bedford," l.1.

There is a power in the soul untouched by time and flesh, flowing from the Spirit, remaining in the Spirit, altogether spiritual. In this power is God, ever verdant, flowering in all the joy and glory of his actual self.

Meister Eckhart, *Meister Eckhart,* Franz Pfeiffer, translated by C. de B. Evans, John M. Watkins, 1956, Volume I, p.36.

Strong is the soul, and wise, and beautiful;
The seeds of godlike power are in us still;
Gods are we, bards, saints, heroes, if we will!

Matthew Arnold, *The Poems of Matthew Arnold,* edited by Kenneth Allott, Longmans, Green & Co. Ltd., 1965, p.53, "Written in Emerson's Essays," l.11.

That only which we have within, can we see without. If we meet no gods, it is because we harbour none. If there is grandeur in you, you will find grandeur in porters and sweeps. He only is rightly immortal, to whom all things are immortal.

Ralph Waldo Emerson, *The Conduct of Life, Nature, and Other Essays,* J.M. Dent & Sons Ltd., 1911, p.262.

Divinity is essentially the first of the professions, because it is necessary for all at all times; law and physic are only necessary for some at some times. I speak of them, of course, not in their abstract existence, but in their applicability to man.

Samuel Taylor Coleridge, *Table Talk of Samuel Taylor Coleridge,* introduction by Henry Morley, George Routledge and Sons, 1884, p.186.

Since it is through the possession of happiness that people become happy, and since happiness is in fact divinity, it is clear that it is through the possession of divinity that they become happy. But by the same logic as men become just through the possession of justice, or wise through the possession of wisdom, so those who possess divinity necessarily become divine. Each individual is therefore divine. While only God is so by nature, as many as you like may become so by participation.

Boethius, *The Consolation of Philosophy,* translated with an introduction by V.E. Watts, Penguin Books Ltd., 1969, p.102.

In the life which wells up in me and in the matter which sustains me, I find much more than Your gifts. It is You Yourself whom I find, You who makes me participate in Your being, You who moulds me. Truly in the ruling and in the first disciplining of my living strength, in the continually beneficent play of secondary causes, I touch, as near as possible, the two faces of Your creative action, and I encounter, and kiss,

Your two marvellous hands—the one which holds us so firmly that it is merged, in us, with the sources of life, and the other whose embrace is so wide that, at its slightest pressure, all the springs of the universe respond harmoniously together.

Pierre Teilhard de Chardin, *Le Milieu Divin*, William Collins Sons & Co. Ltd., 1960, p.56.

The Scriptures say of human beings that there is an outward man and, along with him, an inner man.

To the outward man belong those things that depend on the soul but are connected with the flesh and blended with it, and the co-operative functions of the several members such as the eye, the ear, the tongue, the hand, and so on. The Scripture speaks of all this as the old man, the earthy man, the outward person, the enemy, the servant.

Within us all is the other person, the inner man, whom the Scripture calls the new man, the heavenly man, the young person, a friend, the aristocrat ...

The seed of God is in us. Given an intelligent farmer and a diligent fieldhand, it will thrive and grow up to God whose seed it is and, accordingly, its fruit will be God-nature. Pear seeds grow into pear trees; nut seeds into nut trees, and God-seed into God!

Meister Eckhart, *Meister Eckhart*, translated by Raymond B. Blakney, Harper & Row, Publishers, Inc., 1941, p.74.

The centre of life is neither in thought nor in feeling, nor in will, nor even in consciousness, so far as it thinks, feels, or wishes. For moral truth may have been penetrated and possessed in all these ways, and escape us still. Deeper even than consciousness there is our being itself, our very substance, our nature. Only those truths which have entered into this last region, which have become ourselves, become spontaneous and involuntary, instinctive and unconscious, are really our life—that is to say, something more than our property. So long as we are able to distinguish any space whatever between the truth and us we remain outside it. The thought, the feeling, the desire, the consciousness of life, are not yet quite life. But peace and repose can nowhere be found except in life and in eternal life, and the eternal life is the divine life, is God. To become divine is then the aim of life: then only can truth be said to be ours beyond the possibility of loss, because it is no longer outside of us, nor even in us, but we are it, and it is we; we ourselves are a truth, a will, a work of God. Liberty has become nature; the creature is one with its creator—one through love. It is what it ought to be; its education is finished, and its final happiness begins. The sun of time declines and the light of eternal blessedness arises.

Our fleshly hearts may call this mysticism. It is the mysticism of Jesus: "I am one with my Father; ye shall be one with me. We will be one with you."

Henri Frédéric Amiel, *Amiel's Journal*, translated by Mrs. Humphry Ward, Macmillan & Co. Ltd., 1918, p.44.

DOUBT

Feed your faith, and your doubts will starve to death.

Anon.

If Christ has grappled our hearts to Himself at all, then it were surely wise to trust
His certainties and not our own doubts, however persistent.

Herbert H. Farmer, *The Healing Cross*, Nisbet & Co. Ltd., 1938, p.208.

If a man will begin with certainties, he shall end in doubts; but if he will be content
to begin with doubts, he shall end in certainties.

Francis Bacon, *The Advancement of Learning*, introduction by Henry Morley, Cassell and Company Ltd., 1905,
p.38.

Modest doubt is call'd
The beacon of the wise.

William Shakespeare, *Troilus and Cressida*, Act II. sc.ii. l.15.

There lives more faith in honest doubt,
Believe me, than in half the creeds.

Alfred, Lord Tennyson. *The Poems of Tennyson*, edited by Christopher Ricks, Longmans, Green & Co. Ltd., 1969,
p.948, No.296, "In Memoriam A.H.H.," st.xcvi. l.11.

You call for faith:
I show you doubt, to prove that faith exists.
The more of doubt, the stronger faith, I say,
If faith o'ercomes doubt.

Robert Browning, *The Poetical Works of Robert Browning*, Volume I, Smith, Elder & Co., 1899, p.536, *Men and
Women*, "Bishop Blougram's Apology."

For nothing worthy proving can be proven,
Nor yet disproven: wherefore thou be wise,
Cleave ever to the sunnier side of doubt,
And cling to Faith beyond the forms of Faith!

Alfred, Lord Tennyson, *The Poems of Tennyson*, edited by Christopher Ricks, Longmans, Green & Co. Ltd., 1969,
p.1351, No. 415, "The Ancient Sage," l.66.

There is an increasing number of people to whom everything they are doing seems
futile. They are still under the spell of the slogans which preach faith in the secular
paradise of success and glamour. But doubt, the fertile condition of all progress, has
begun to beset them and has made them ready to ask what their real self-interest as
human beings is.

Erich Fromm, *Man For Himself*, Routledge & Kegan Paul Ltd., 1975, p.140.

And your doubt can become a good quality if you train it. It must become *aware,* it
must become criticism. Ask it, whenever it wants to spoil something for you, *why*
something is ugly, demand proofs from it, test it, and you will perhaps find it helpless
and nonplussed, perhaps also aggressive. But do not give way, demand arguments
and conduct yourself thus carefully and consistently every single time, and the day
will dawn when it will become, instead of a subverter, one of your best workmen,—
perhaps the cleverest of all who are building at your life.

Rainer Maria Rilke, *Letters to a Young Poet*, translation, introduction and commentary by Reginald Snell, Sidgwick
and Jackson, 1945, p.42.

Doubt and perplexity will often be the lot of travellers on this life's journey. Beyond the questions arising in our daily thought and conduct are those greater difficulties which seem to stop our progress and to render existence an insoluble riddle. Doubt has many sources. It may be true that some could find the origin of their doubts in an unwillingness to face their moral condition and obey the demands of duty. But at the present day, doubt frequently arises from a sense that received dogmas do not correspond with the facts of life or with the moral values which our truest insight reveals. In other cases there may be not so much perplexity and doubt as an exhilarating spirit of inquiry and exploration driving a man forward on the quest for truth for himself and all men. We strongly deprecate the attitude of mind, still too often current, which brands as unbelief that criticism of accepted ideas without which progress is impossible. We may often attain to a fuller understanding of the truth that God intends for us through doubts of the orthodoxy of the past. For true faith is not a passive acceptance of authority, but is an inner assurance of truth, asking, seeking, knocking until the door is opened. The enjoyment of idle questionings may indeed become an excuse for living a poor and careless life, but the genuine seeker is obeying the very call of God within him.

Christian faith and practice in the experience of the Society of Friends, London Yearly Meeting of the Religious Society of Friends, 1972, No.119, 1911, 1925.

DYING TO SELF

And every one who has left houses or brothers or sisters or father or mother or children or lands, for my name's sake, will receive a hundredfold, and inherit eternal life.

Matthew 19.29.

If any man would come after me, let him deny himself and take up his cross daily and follow me. For whoever would save his life will lose it; and whoever loses his life for my sake, he will save it. For what does it profit a man if he gains the whole world and loses or forfeits himself?

Luke 9.23-25.

Sell your possessions, and give alms; provide yourselves with purses that do not grow old, with a treasure in the heavens that does not fail.... For where your treasure is, there will your heart be also.

Luke 12.33-34.

The kingdom of heaven is like treasure hidden in a field, which a man found and covered up; then in his joy he goes and sells all that he has and buys that field. Again, the kingdom of heaven is like a merchant in search of fine pearls, who, on finding one pearl of great value, went and sold all that he had and bought it.

Matthew 13.44-46.

If any one purifies himself from what is ignoble, then he will be a vessel for noble use, consecrated and useful to the master of the house, ready for any good work.

2 Timothy 2.21.

It is the crushed grape that yields the wine.

Anon.

A man there was, though some did count him mad,
The more he cast away the more he had.

John Bunyan, *The Pilgrim's Progress,* introduction and notes by G.B. Harrison, J.M. Dent & Sons Ltd., 1964,
p.263.

All the activity of man in the works of self-denial has no good in itself, but is only
to open an entrance for the one only Good, the light of God, to operate upon us.

William Law, *Selected Mystical Writings of William Law,* edited by Stephen Hobhouse, Rockliff, 1948, p.99.

Know, that when thou learnest to lose thy self,
Thou wilt reach the Beloved.
There is no other secret to be revealed,
And more than this is not known to me.

Al-Ansari, *The Persian Mystics,* translated by Sardar Sir Jogendra Sing, John Murray Ltd., 1939, p.40.

In all your doing and thinking you should act on the assumption that you are going
to die today ... Try to live in such a way now that when the hour of death comes you
may feel joy, not fear. Learn to die to the world now, so that you may begin to live
with Christ then.

Thomas à Kempis, *The Imitation of Christ,* translated by Betty I. Knott, William Collins Sons & Co. Ltd., 1979,
pp.72,74.

Except the seed die.... It has to die in order to liberate the energy it bears within it
so that with this energy new forms may be developed.
So we have to die in order to liberate a *tied up* energy, in order to possess an energy
which is free and capable of understanding the true relationship of things.

Simone Weil, *Gravity and Grace,* Routledge & Kegan Paul Ltd., 1972, p.30.

"Our kingdom go" is the necessary and unavoidable corollary of "Thy Kingdom come."
For the more there is of self, the less there is of God. The divine eternal fullness of
life can be gained only by those who have deliberately lost the partial, separative life
of craving and self-interest, of egocentric thinking, feeling, wishing and acting.

Aldous Huxley, *The Perennial Philosophy,* Chatto & Windus Ltd., 1974, p.113.

Batter my heart, three person'd God; for, you
As yet but knocke, breathe, shine, and seeke to mend;
That I may rise, and stand, o'erthrow mee, 'and bend
Your force, to breake, blowe, burn and make me new.

John Donne, *Poetical Works,* edited by Sir Herbert Grierson, Oxford University Press, p.299, "Divine Poems,
Holy Sonnets" XIV, l.1.

We must learn to detach ourselves from all that is capable of being lost, to bind
ourselves absolutely only to what is absolute and eternal.

Henri Frédéric Amiel, *Amiel's Journal,* translated by Mrs. Humphry Ward, Macmillan & Co. Ltd., 1918, p.1.

Therefore we should make ourselves poor, that we may fundamentally die, and in this dying be made alive again. Therefore Christ said, "Unless the grain of corn fall into the ground and die it cannot bring forth fruit. But if it die it bringeth forth much fruit." So also is it in truth. Whoso wisheth to have all the fruit of life must suffer all manner of death.... And whoso doth not entirely die cannot either fully live.

John Tauler, *The Following of Christ,* translated by J.R. Morell, Burns & Oates, 1886, p.175.

The proper good of a creature is to surrender itself to its Creator—to enact intellectually, volitionally, and emotionally, that relationship which is given in the mere fact of its being a creature.... In the world as we now know it, the problem is how to recover this self-surrender. We are not merely imperfect creatures who must be improved: we are, as Newman said, rebels who must lay down our arms ... to surrender a self-will inflamed and swollen with years of usurpation is a kind of death.... Hence the necessity to die daily: however often we think we have broken the rebellious self we shall still find it alive.

C.S. Lewis, *The Problem of Pain,* The Centenary Press, 1941, p.78.

There is, of course, a negative element or aspect in all genuine religion. No person can grow rich in spiritual experience or can gain an intimate acquaintance with a God of purity and truth without negating the easy ways of instinct, the low pursuits of life which end in self, the habits of thought and action which limit and hamper the realization of the diviner posssibilities of the whole nature. Sometimes the eye that hinders must be plucked out or the right hand cut off and thrust away for the sake of a freer pursuit of the soul's kingdom. There is, too, a still deeper principle of negativity involved in the very fibre of personal life itself. No one can advance without surrender, no one can have gains without losses, no one can reach great goals without giving up many things in themselves desirable. There is "a rivalry of mes" which no person can ever escape, for in order to choose and achieve one typical self another possible self must be sternly sacrificed. In a very real sense it remains forever true that we must die to live, we must die to the narrow self in order to be raised to the wider and richer self.

Rufus M. Jones, *Spiritual Reformers in the 16th and 17th Centuries,* Macmillan & Co. Ltd., 1914, p.xxv.

E

EDUCATION

The direction in which education starts a man will determine his future life.

Plato, *The Republic of Plato,* translation, analyses and introduction by B. Jowett, Oxford at the Clarendon Press, 1881, p.110, Bk.IV, 425B.

Finally, education, alone, can conduct us to that enjoyment which is, at once, best in quality and infinite in quantity.

Horace Mann, *Lectures and Reports on Education,* Cambridge: Published for the Editor, 1867, p.84.

Deep verst in books and shallow in himself.

John Milton, *The Poetical Works of Milton,* edited by the Rev. H.C. Beeching, Oxford at the Clarendon Press, 1900, p.495, *Paradise Regain'd,* Bk.IV. l.327.

Education has for a chief object the formation of character.

Herbert Spencer, *Social Statics,* Williams and Norgate, 1892, p.81.

Education is not learning; it is the exercise and development of the powers of the mind; and the two great methods by which this end may be accomplished are in the halls of learning or in the conflicts of life.

Anon.

To be what we are, and to become what we are capable of becoming, is the only end of life.

Robert Louis Stevenson, *Familiar Studies of Men and Books, Virginibus Puerisque, Selected Poems,* William Collins Sons & Co. Ltd., 1956, p.112.

But warm, eager, living life—to be rooted in life—to learn, to desire, to know, to feel, to think, to act. That is what I want. And nothing less. That is what I must try for.

Katherine Mansfield, *Journal of Katherine Mansfield,* edited by J. Middleton Murry, Constable & Co. Ltd., 1927, p.251.

Education ... is the leading human souls to what is best, and making what is best out of them; and these two objects are always attainable together, and by the same means; the training which makes men happiest in themselves, also makes them most serviceable to others.

John Ruskin, *The Stones of Venice,* edited by Ernest Rhys, J.M. Dent & Co., 1907, Volume III, p.197.

One impulse from a vernal wood
May teach you more of man,

Of moral evil and of good,
Than all the sages can.

William Wordsworth, *The Poetical Works of William Wordsworth,* edited by E. de Selincourt and Helen Darbishire, Oxford at the Clarendon Press, 1958, Volume IV, p.57, "The Tables Turned," st.vi. l.21.

An education which is not religious is atheistic; there is no middle way. If you give to children an account of the world from which God is left out, you are teaching them to understand the world without reference to God. If He is then introduced, He is an excrescence. He becomes an appendix to His own creation.

William Temple, *The Hope of a New World,* S.C.M. Press Ltd., 1940, p.12.

One person who has mastered life is better than a thousand persons who have mastered only the contents of books, but no one can get anything out of life without God. If I were looking for a master of learning, I should go to Paris to the colleges where the higher studies are pursued, but if I wanted to know about the perfection of life, they could not tell me there.

Meister Eckhart, *Meister Eckhart,* translated by Raymond B. Blakney, Harper & Row, Publishers, Inc., 1941, p.230.

Most people live, whether physically, intellectually or morally, in a very restricted circle of their potential being. They *make use* of a very small portion of their possible consciousness, and of their soul's resources in general, much like a man who, out of his whole bodily organism, should get into a habit of using and moving only his little finger. Great emergencies and crises show us how much greater our vital resources are than we had supposed.

William James, *The Letters of William James,* edited by Henry James, Longmans, Green & Co. Ltd., 1926, p.253.

Life should be a giving birth to the soul, the development of a higher mode of reality. The animal must be humanised: flesh must be made spirit; physiological activity must be transmuted into intellect and conscience, into reason, justice, and generosity, as the torch is transmuted into life and warmth. The blind, greedy, selfish nature of man must put on beauty and nobleness. This heavenly alchemy is what justifies our presence on the earth: it is our mission and our glory.

Henri Frédéric Amiel, *Amiel's Journal,* translated by Mrs. Humphry Ward, Macmillan & Co. Ltd., 1918, p.285.

What is a complete human being? Again I shall take the Greek answer to this question. Human beings have bodies, minds and characters. Each of these is capable of what the Greeks called "virtue" *(aretn)* or what we might call "excellence." The virtue or excellence of the body is health and fitness and strength, the firm and sensitive hand, the clear eye; the excellence of the mind is to know and to understand and to think, to have some idea of what the world is and of what man has done and has been and can be; the excellence of the character lies in the great virtues. This trinity of body, mind and character is man: man's aim, besides earning his living, is to make the most of all three, to have as good a mind, body and character as possible; and a liberal education, a free man's education, is to help him to this; not because a sound body, mind and character help to success, or even because they help to happiness, but because they are good things in themselves, and because what is good is worth while, simply because it is good.

Sir Richard Livingstone, *On Education,* Cambridge at the University Press, 1954, p.61.

ETERNAL LIFE

This is eternal life, that they know thee the only true God, and Jesus Christ whom thou hast sent.

John 17.3.

We feel and know that we are eternal.

Spinoza, *Spinoza's Ethics and De Intellectus Emendatione,* introduction by T.S. Gregory, J.M. Dent & Sons Ltd., 1955, p.214.

To have the sense of the eternal in life is a short flight for the soul. To have had it, is the soul's vitality.

George Meredith, *Diana of the Crossways,* Archibald Constable and Company Ltd., 1909, p.11.

But felt through all this fleshly dresse
Bright *shootes* of everlastingnesse.

Henry Vaughan, *The Works of Henry Vaughan,* edited by L.C. Martin, Oxford at the Clarendon Press, 1957, "Silex Scintillans," p.419.

Every creative act of ours in relation to other people—an act of love, of pity, of help, of peacemaking—not merely has a future but is eternal.

Nicolas Berdyaev, *The Destiny of Man,* translated by Natalie Duddington, Geoffrey Bles, The Centenary Press, 1937, p.189.

Eternal life is the life of God, and to have eternal life is to share the life of God. Here we are at the very heart of the matter. Eternal life is nothing less than God's life.

William Barclay, *The Plain Man Looks at the Apostles' Creed,* William Collins Sons & Co. Ltd., 1967, p.374.

It is eternity now. I am in the midst of it. It is about me in the sunshine; I am in it, as the butterfly floats in the light-laden air. Nothing has to come: it is now. Now is eternity; now is the immortal life.

Richard Jefferies, *The Story of My Heart,* Duckworth & Co., 1923, p.30.

If a man once knows the Spirit within him, the source of all his aspiration after holiness, as indeed the Spirit of Jesus Christ, and if he knows this Spirit of Jesus Christ within himself as none other than the Spirit of the Eternal and Almighty God, what more can he want? *This is the eternal life.*

William Temple, *Readings in St. John's Gospel* (First and Second Series), Macmillan & Co. Ltd., 1947, p.310.

The eternal life is not the future life; it is life in harmony with the true order of things,—life in God. We must learn to look upon time as a movement of eternity, as an undulation in the ocean of being. To live, so as to keep this consciousness of

ours in perpetual relation with the eternal, is to be wise; to live, so as to personify
and embody the eternal, is to be religious.

Henri Frédéric Amiel, *Amiel's Journal,* translated by Mrs. Humphry Ward, Macmillan & Co. Ltd., 1918, p.96.

Religion, in its fullest development, essentially requires, not only this our little span
of earthly years, but a life beyond. Neither an Eternal Life that is already fully achieved
here below, nor an Eternal Life already to be begun and known solely in the beyond,
satisfies these requirements. Only an Eternal Life already begun and truly known in
part here, though fully to be achieved and completely to be understood hereafter,
corresponds to the deepest longings of man's spirit as touched by the prevenient Spirit,
God.

Friedrich von Hugel, *Eternal Life,* T & T. Clarke, 1913, p.396.

Jesus did not promise to men simply life after death, but a quality of life now. He
promised us eternal life, the sharing of God's life, participation in his own risen life.
He said that he had come to give men abundant life—sufficient to keep the body in
health and strength, to illuminate and guide the mind, to bring peace to the heart.
If we have that life within us now, we shall not worry about our last migration into
the spiritual world, for we shall know a good deal about it already.

George Appleton, *Journey for a Soul,* William Collins Sons & Co. Ltd., 1976, p.212.

Eternal life is not just everlasting life, a continuation of what goes on at present, for
that might not be too joyful for many people. It is a quality of life, the kind of life
which Jesus had, human life permeated by the grace and love of God, and so invulnerable to physical death. Jesus taught his disciples that they could have eternal life
now, just as in the teaching of the Buddha the sphere of bliss and blessing which he
called Nirvana can be enjoyed now. The perfection of both will come in the dimension
beyond death.

George Appleton, *Journey for a Soul,* William Collins Sons & Co. Ltd., 1976, p.213.

Our hearts tell us of a higher form of existence, in which the doom of death is not
merely deferred but abolished. This eternal world we here see through a glass darkly:
at best we can apprehend but the outskirts of God's ways, and hear a small whisper
of His voice; but our conviction is that, though our earthly house be dissolved (as
dissolved it must be), we have a home not made with hands, eternal in the heavens.
In this hope we may include all creation; and trust that in some way neither more
nor less incomprehensible than the deliverance which we expect for ourselves, all God's
creatures, according to their several capacities, may be set free from the bondage of
corruption and participate in the final triumph over death and sin. Most firmly do I
believe that this faith in immortality, though formless and inpalpable as the air we
breathe, and incapable of definite presentation except under inadequate and self-contra-
dictory symbols, is nevertheless enthroned in the centre of our being, and that those
who have steadily set their affections on things above, and lived the risen life even on
earth, receive in themselves an assurance which robs death of its sting, and is an earnest
of a final victory over the grave.

W.R. Inge, *Christian Mysticism,* Methuen & Co., 1899, p.328.

EUCHARIST

For my flesh is food indeed, and my blood is drink indeed. He who eats my flesh and drinks my blood abides in me, and I in him.

John 6.55-56.

That we should "take" and "eat" is an indispensable aid which the sincere Christian cannot omit; but the one thing that matters is that we should "feed upon him in our hearts."

William Temple, *Readings in St. John's Gospel* (First and Second Series), Macmillan & Co. Ltd., 1947, p.95.

The Eucharist to the Christian is the culminating point of all sacramental rites.... For this Sacrament is the constantly repeated act from which the soul draws its spiritual food. Its virtue resides in its repetition; it is repeated again and again, just because it is constantly needed to effect that contact with divine life and power which, in its aspect of communion, is all its meaning. Here the Christian believes that he takes into himself the very life which makes him one with God.

Oliver Quick, *The Christian Sacraments,* Nisbet & Co. Ltd., 1952, p.185, 186.

The Prayer of the Chalice

Father, to Thee I raise my whole being, a vessel emptied of self. Accept, Lord, this my emptiness, and so fill me with Thyself—Thy Light, Thy Love, Thy Life—that these Thy precious gifts may radiate through me and overflow the chalice of my heart into the hearts of all with whom I come into contact this day revealing unto them the beauty of Thy Joy and Wholeness and the serenity of Thy Peace which nothing can destroy.

Anon.

The idea is that you appropriate to yourself and assimilate the essence of his sacrifice, symbolically represented by the bread and wine of the Eucharist. A man who was completely innocent offered himself as a sacrifice for the good of others, including his enemies and became the ransom of the world. It was a perfect act.

Mohandas K. Gandhi, *Non-Violence in Peace & War,* Navajivan Publishing House, 1949, Volume II, p.166.

I believe that when I take that piece of bread and it becomes part of my frame, it is woven into my nerves and muscles, so that as I do that in faith I receive Jesus Christ, the Bread of Life, who strengthens me and passes into my being; so that I can say, "I live, yet no longer I, but Christ liveth in me." And I believe that the sacrament is a vehicle of divine grace and—receiving it in faith and humility and penitence—that new life comes into me.

Francis Glasson, in *Priestland's Progress,* Gerald Priestland, British Broadcasting Corporation, 1982, p.174.

Two men stand before some great picture. Both see the same colours and the same lines—one sees beauty, the other sees nothing significant. But the one who sees the beauty does not make it—the artist made it.—And so when you listen to beautiful music, where is the beauty? You do not create it: you do not invent it—you find it.

And yet you will not find it unless you have the understanding of music which qualifies you to be sensitive to it. It is the same with beauty everywhere.... And so in the Holy Communion Christ offers Himself in all His fullness of holiness and love to be ours, but whether you receive Him depends on the insight of your faith, on how far you are conscious of your need of Him, on how far you are sincere in seeking to be united with Him in His offering of Himself to the Father.

William Temple, Christian Faith and Life, S.C.M. Press Ltd., 1963, p.122.

I do believe that when we address to the Lord our prayer to send down His Holy Spirit upon this bread and wine, it does happen. I have no theory about how it happens. But it happens with the same simple certainty which I would attach to the incarnation. If God could unite Himself to a human flesh and soul, he can unite Himself as completely to this bread and wine. And when we receive communion, I believe that God reaches out to us on the most primitive and simple level. A babe can receive a small particle of bread and a drop of wine, and with it be reached by God.

Anthony Bloom, in Priestland's Progress, Gerald Priestland, British Broadcasting Corporation, 1982, p.185.

The Holy Communion is the Sacrament in and by which we are to remember Him, and in remembering to be united to Him. The culmination of the life of prayer is the reception of the life of God within us, and this is the mystery of the Eucharist. Whether or not it be true, as the mystics of all ages have taught,... that there is a "soul centre" which is as it were the natural point of contact with the Divine, an unquenchable spark from the altar in heaven, a principle which does not and cannot consent to sin, and which, as William Law says, "is so infinite that nothing can satisfy it, or give it any rest, but the infinity of God," at any rate in this sacrament the "medicine of immortality" is offered us, and offered in the name and through the mediation of Jesus Christ. "Whoso eateth my flesh and drinketh my blood hath eternal life."

W.R. Inge, Speculum Animae, Longmans, Green & Co. Ltd., 1911, p.15.

When we receive the Holy Communion, we express our belief that the mysterious Divine presence, of which we are conscious in prayer (using, once more, the word prayer of all communings of the soul with the unseen spiritual world)—that this mysterious Divine presence is not only God, or the Spirit of God, but "the Spirit of *Jesus*," to use a phrase which the Revised Version has restored to our New Testament. We are identifying the living well-spring of our faith, the source of our hope and our happiness, the guide and inspirer of our lives, with a historical character who lived nearly two thousand years ago.

W.R. Inge, Speculum Animae, Longmans, Green & Co. Ltd., 1911, p.17.

EVIL

Fret not yourself because of the wicked, be not envious of wrongdoers! For they will soon fade like the grass, and wither like the green herb.

Psalm 37.1-2.

Do not be overcome by evil, but overcome evil with good.

Romans 12.21.

A belief in a supernatural source of evil is not necessary; men alone are quite capable of every wickedness.

Joseph Conrad, *Under Western Eyes*, J.M. Dent & Sons Ltd., 1923, p.151.

The only thing necessary for the triumph of evil is for good men to do nothing.

Attributed to Edmund Burke.

He who passively accepts evil is as much involved in it as he who helps to perpetrate it. He who accepts evil without protesting against it is really operating with it.

Martin Luther King, *Stride Toward Freedom*, Harper & Row, Publishers, Inc., 1958, p.51.

There is no explanation for evil. It must be looked upon as a necessary part of the order of the universe. To ignore it is childish; to bewail it senseless.

W. Somerset Maugham, *The Summing Up*, Bernhard Tauchnitz, 1938, p.225.

Every minute you are thinking of evil, you might have been thinking of good instead. Refuse to pander to a morbid interest in your own misdeeds. Pick yourself up, be sorry, shake yourself, and go on again.

Evelyn Underhill, *The Letters of Evelyn Underhill,* edited with an introduction by Charles Williams, Longmans, Green & Co. Ltd., 1947, p.72.

It is the evil that lies in ourselves that is ever least tolerant of the evil that dwells within others.

Maurice Maeterlinck, *Wisdom and Destiny,* translated by Alfred Sutro, George Allen, 1898, p.342.

There is some soul of goodness in things evil,
Would men observingly distil it out.

William Shakespeare, *Henry V,* Act IV. sc.i. l.4.

Wickedness is always easier than virtue; for it takes the short cut to every thing.

Samuel Johnson, *Boswell's Life of Johnson,* edited by G.B. Hill, revised by L.F. Powell, Oxford at the Clarendon Press, 1950, Volume V, p.218.

Must I do all the evil I can, before I learn to shun it? Is it not enough to know the evil to shun it? If not, we should be sincere enough to admit that we love evil too well to give it up.

Mohandas K. Gandhi, *Non-Violence in Peace & War,* Navajivan Publishing House, 1949, Volume II, p.74.

The germs of all things are in every heart, and the greatest criminals as well as the greatest heroes are but different modes of ourselves. Only evil grows of itself, while for goodness we want effort and courage.

Henri Frédéric Amiel, *Amiel's Journal,* translated by Mrs. Humphry Ward, Macmillan & Co. Ltd., 1918, p.101.

The mystery of evil is the deepest one of all. It is the mystery of the primal creative act, when God called into existence the human soul, made in His own image, and presented it with the terrifying choice, to centre itself upon itself, or to centre itself upon Him without whom it could not subsist at all.... The mystery renews itself daily in me, as it does in every man born of woman.

Morris West, *The Shoes of the Fisherman*, William Heinemann Ltd., 1963, p.302.

I much prefer absolute silence about things which with the best will in the world I do not understand, to the semi, forced explanations that leave a bitter taste in my mind.
It is so easy to say God permits evil—and what evil!—in order to bring good out of it. I confess that while I understand that, it has never *entirely* satisfied me. And so I prefer to be silent in the abyss of my ignorance, and to pray.

Theodor Haecker, *Journal in the Night*, translated by Alexander Dru, The Harvill Press Ltd., 1950, p.195.

At all times, all too many Christians have behaved as though the devil were a First Principle, on the same footing as God. They have paid more attention to evil and the problem of its eradications than to good and the methods by which individual goodness may be deepened, and the sum of goodness increased. The effects which follow too constant and intense a concentration upon evil are always disastrous. Those who crusade, not *for* God in themselves, but *against* the devil in others, never succeed in making the world better, but leave it either as it was, or sometimes even perceptibly worse than it was, before the crusade began. By thinking primarily of evil we tend, however excellent our intentions, to create occasions for evil to manifest itself.

Aldous Huxley, *The Devils of Loudun*, Penguin Books Ltd., 1973, p.175.

Hatred of evil destroys the spiritual world of man just as much as hatred of the good, which does not mean to say that our attitude towards evil must not be ruthless nor that there can be any question of a truce with it. Hence our attitude to evil must be twofold: we must be tolerant of it as the Creator is tolerant, and we must mercilessly struggle against it. True spirituality consists in believing in the power of good rather than that of ill, in God rather than Satan.

Nicolas Berdyaev, *Freedom and the Spirit*, translated by Oliver Fielding Clarke, Geoffrey Bles, The Centenary Press, 1935, pp.183, 182; and *The Destiny of Man*, translated by Natalie Duddington, Geoffrey Bles, The Centenary Press, 1937, p.190.

EVOLUTION

Progress is
The law of life, man is not Man as yet.

Robert Browning, *The Poetical Works of Robert Browning*, Smith, Elder, & Co., 1899, Volume I, "Paracelsus V," p.70.

It is always worth while to inquire how far the doctrine of evolution has anything to do with any reasonable notion of progress.... If you take an unarmed saint and confront him with a hungry tiger, there will be a struggle for existence culminating in the survival of the fittest, which means, of course, the fittest to survive in those conditions;

but it will not be a survival of the ethically best. There is no reason to suppose that the struggle for existence always favours what is ethically admirable any more than there is any reason to suppose that a social order, if it may have the name, characterized by cut-throat competition, will always bring its best citizens to the top.

William Temple, *The Preacher's Theme To-day*, S.P.C.K., 1936, p.32.

If we do not develop within ourselves this deeply rooted feeling that there is something higher than ourselves, we shall never find the strength to evolve to something higher.... The heights of the spirit can only be climbed by passing through the portals of humility. You can only acquire right knowledge when you have learnt to esteem it.... Whoever seeks for higher knowledge, must create it for himself. He must instil it into his soul. It cannot be done by study; it can only be done through life.

Rudolf Steiner, *Knowledge of the Higher Worlds and its Attainment*, Rudolf Steiner Press, 1936, p.18.

The last end of man, the ultimate reason for human existence, is unitive knowledge of the divine Ground—the knowledge that can come only to those who are prepared to "die to self" and so make room, as it were, for God. Out of any given generation of men and women very few will achieve the final end of human existence; but the opportunity for coming to unitive knowledge will, in one way or another, continually be offered until all sentient beings realize Who in fact they are.

Aldous Huxley, *The Perennial Philosophy*, Chatto & Windus Ltd., 1974, p.29.

Let every man remember that the destiny of mankind is incomparable and that it depends greatly on his will to collaborate in the transcendent task. Let him remember that the Law is, and always has been, to struggle and that the fight has lost nothing of its violence by being transposed from the material onto the spiritual plane; let him remember that his own dignity, his nobility as a human being, must emerge from his efforts to liberate himself from his bondage and to obey his deepest aspirations. And let him above all never forget that the divine spark is in him, in him alone, and that he is free to disregard it, to kill it, or to come closer to God by showing his eagerness to work with Him, and for Him.

Lecomte du Noüy, *Human Destiny*, Longmans, Green & Co. Ltd., 1947, p.273.

To read the gospel with an open mind is to see beyond all possibility of doubt that Jesus came to bring us new truths concerning our destiny: not only a new life superior to that we are conscious of, but also in a very real sense a new physical power of acting upon our *temporal* world.
Through a failure to grasp the exact nature of this power newly bestowed on all who put their confidence in God—a failure due either to a hesitation in face of what seems to us so unlikely or to a fear of falling into illuminism—many christians neglect this earthly aspect of the promises of the Master, or at least do not give themselves to it with that complete hardihood which he nevertheless never tires of asking of us, if only we have ears to hear him.

We must not allow timidity or modesty to turn us into poor craftsmen. If it is true that the development of the world can be influenced by our faith in Christ, then to let this power lie dormant within us would indeed be unpardonable.

Pierre Teilhard de Chardin, *Hymn of the Universe*, William Collins Sons & Co. Ltd., 1961, p.143.

EXPERIENCE

Yet he is not far from each one of us, for "In him we live and move and have our being."

Acts 17.27.

The essential meaning of religion is not to know God as one knows a friend; it is to become God, for to know Him is to take Him into our inmost self as the fulfilment of that self; and it is only in becoming Him that we know Him.

Anon.

I have learnt to love you late, Beauty at once so ancient and so new! I have learnt to love you late! You were within me, and I was in the world outside myself. I searched for you outside myself and, disfigured as I was, I fell upon the lovely things of your creation. You were with me. But I was not with you.

St. Augustine, *Confessions*, translated with an introduction by R.S. Pine-Coffin, Penguin Books Ltd., 1964, p.231.

People today are not prepared to take their faith from the tradition in which they were born, nor from other people. They want to deduce it from their own experience of life. They do not need theories, but the experience which will be the source of their own interpretation. They are suspicious of anything which seems to escape from life into theory, from experience into doctrine, or from the thing itself into talk about it.
The method they want to follow is the inductive one rather than the deductive.

George Appleton, *Journey for a Soul*, William Collins Sons & Co. Ltd., 1976, p.37.

By religious experience we ought to mean an experience which is religious through and through—an experiencing of all things in the light of the knowledge of God. It is this, and not any moment of illumination, of which we may say that it is self-authenticating; for in such an experience all things increasingly fit together in a single intelligible whole.

William Temple, *Thoughts On Some Problems Of The Day*, Macmillan & Co. Ltd., 1931, p.25.

The significant features of the experience are the consciousness of fresh springs of life, the release of new energies, the inner integration and unification of personality, the inauguration of a sense of mission, the flooding of the life with hope and gladness, and the conviction, amounting in the mind of the recipient to certainty, that God is found as an environing and vitalizing presence.

Rufus M. Jones, *Spiritual Reformers in the 16th and 17th Centuries*, Macmillan & Co. Ltd., 1914, p.xxi.

He comes to us as One unknown, without a name, as of old, by the lake-side, He came to those men who knew Him not. He speaks to us the same word: "Follow thou me!" and sets us to the tasks which He has to fulfil for our time. He commands. And to those who obey Him, whether they be wise or simple, He will reveal Himself in the toils, the conflicts, the sufferings which they shall pass through in His fellowship, and, as an ineffable mystery, they shall learn in their own experience Who He is.

Albert Schweitzer, *The Quest of the Historical Jesus,* A. & C. Black Limited, 1954, p.401.

What must we do to gain this knowledge of "That which is ..."?
Study, experiment, and live it as far as possible in your ordinary lives until the time comes when you can absorb it into your own rhythm. The grace of Supreme Love will reveal it to you in time. The flow is continuous between the seed and the fruit. What is written in books does not touch the heart of a reader unless he experiences what he learns. What is taught cannot reach the soul of a listener until he lives what he hears.

One can no more pass on the Truth than one can acquire it from others....
Nevertheless, there is Life of the heart. Speak to your hearts, speak slowly, clearly, *using no words.* Give birth to that Life that lies concealed therein. Feel it! Know it!

Lizelle Reymond, *My Life With A Brahmin Family,* translated by Lucy Norton, Rider & Company, 1958, p.177.

The spiritual life is a grand experiment which ends in an experience; but it is not merely a leap in the dark; throughout its whole course there is a progressive verification of its fundamental hypothesis, which makes us quite sure that we are on the right road. It is much like climbing a mountain. We are too much occupied with finding our way and securing footholds to think much about the elevation which we have reached; but from time to time we observe that we are nearer the summit, by the larger prospect which has opened around us. For the fuller revelation we look forward. Our world is still in the making, and we are in the making too. We look to the *"Christus futurus"* to interpret the Christ of past history, and to the *homo futurus* to show us what is the meaning of human personality.

W.R. Inge, *Speculum Animae,* Longmans, Green & Co. Ltd., 1911, p.42.

These lectures (attended as a trade union organizer) opened up a new world of adventure, a spiritual world—an introduction to the mystery and dynamic force of prayer. Unlike other turns in the road of life, this experience was of slow growth—full of retreat, of backsliding, to use an old evangelical word. I do not think it possible to exaggerate the importance of the discoveries I made about life, and the relation of the self to the unseen world of the Spirit, and yet I find it hard to speak about; these are matters that cannot be taken on trust, they must be individually experienced and have no validity otherwise. In my case, a course of reading brought to me a sense of the *quality* of service given to the world by people like the Lady Julian of Norwich, Catherine of Sienna, the Quaker Saints, Josephine Butler, and that great host of dedicated lives. My everyday trade union work took on a deeper significance. The doing of ordinary everyday things became lit up with that inner light of the Spirit which gave one strength and effectiveness; strength to meet defeat with a smile; to face success with a sense of responsibility; to be willing to do one's best without thought of reward; to bear misrepresentation without giving way to futile bitterness. Saint Theresa declared that: "There are only two duties required of us—the love of God and the love of our neighbour, and the surest sign of discovering whether we observe these duties is the love of our neighbour"; and a great scholar has asserted that this love of God is not an emotion, although that may be experienced, it is a *principle of action*—it reinforces effort, it demands that we *do* something, not merely talk or feel sympathetic, we've got to use the new strength or it will break us.

That is the vital difference between those who drift with the stream, as I did at first, and those who, like the great souls down the ages, inspire, revive, and strengthen the corporate life of their generation.

Margaret Bondfield, in *What Life Has Taught Me*, introduced by Gilbert Murray, and edited by Sir James Marchant, Odhams Press Ltd., 1948, p.26.

F

FAITH

Now faith is the assurance of things hoped for, the conviction of things not seen.
Hebrews 11.1.

Faith is kept alive in us, and gathers strength, from practice more than from speculation.
Joseph Addison, *The Works of Joseph Addison,* notes by Richard Hurd, edited and published by Henry G. Bohn, 1856, Volume III, p.484.

The only faith that wears well and holds its colour in all weathers is that which is woven of conviction and set with the sharp mordant of experience.
J.R. Lowell, *My Study Windows,* George Routledge & Sons, Ltd., 1905, p.142.

Faith is a kind of winged intellect. The great workmen of history have been men who believed like giants.
Charles H. Parkhurst, *The Pattern in the Mount and Other Sermons,* R.D. Dickinson, 1890, p.57.

Reason saw not till *Faith* sprung the Light.
John Dryden, *The Poems of John Dryden,* edited by James Kinsley, Oxford at the Clarendon Press, 1958, Volume I, p.313, "Religio Laici," 1.69.

Faith is a certitude without proofs ... Faith is a sentiment, for it is a hope; it is an instinct, for it precedes all outward instruction.
Henri Frédéric Amiel, *Amiel's Journal,* translated by Mrs. Humphry Ward, Macmillan & Co. Ltd., 1918, p.192.

Religious faith does not consist in supposing that there is a God; it consists in personal trust in God rising to personal fellowship with God.
William Temple, *Basic Convictions,* Hamish Hamilton, 1937, p.16.

It is faith that is expected of you and honest living, not profound understanding and deep knowledge of the mysteries of God.
Thomas à Kempis, *The Imitation of Christ,* translated by Betty I. Knott, William Collins Sons & Co. Ltd., 1979, p.249.

One in whom persuasion and belief
Had ripened into faith, and faith become
A passionate intuition.
William Wordsworth, *The Poetical Works of William Wordsworth,* edited by E. de Selincourt and Helen Darbishire, Oxford at the Clarendon Press, 1959, Volume V, p.150, *The Excursion,* Bk. IV, 1.1294.

It is neither *necessary*, nor indeed *possible*, to understand any matter of Faith; farther than it is Revealed.

Benjamin Whichcote, *Moral and Religious Aphorisms*, 1930, p.136, Century XIII, No.1168.

Relying on God has to begin all over again every day as if nothing had yet been done.

C.S. Lewis, *Letters of C.S. Lewis*, edited, with a Memoir by W.H. Lewis, Geoffrey Bles Ltd., 1966, p.220.

That man is perfect in faith who can come to God in the utter dearth of his feelings and his desires, without a glow or an inspiration, with the weight of low thoughts, failures, neglects, and wandering forgetfulness, and say to him, "Thou art my refuge, because thou art my home."

George Macdonald, *Unspoken Sermons*, First Series, Alexander Strahan, Publisher, 1867, p.25.

Faith is not knowledge or certainty. It is often contrasted with reason, but the true contrast is with the evidence of the senses. Faith is a kind of spiritual sight, an in-seeing into realities. It always wants to get beyond the superficial surface of things, into the spiritual behind the material. It wants to go beyond the outside symptoms into the causes of them. It consists of following knowledge and reason as far as they will take us, and then going beyond, in the same direction. There is a risk about faith, which can only be tested by taking the leap when the sure path comes to an end.

George Appleton, *Journey for a Soul*, William Collins Sons & Co. Ltd., 1976, p.118.

Faith enables us to get free from:
The domination of place and time, for it gives the additional dimension of the spiritual and the eternal.
The domination of happenings, for we are not at the mercy of circumstances, but can draw upon the inexhaustible wisdom and grace of God.
The domination of the written word, for we do not identify it with the inerrant word of God, but test it by the incarnate word.
The domination of theology, for men's thoughts about God change, and our theories, however good, are seen to be imperfect.
The domination of puritanism, for we see that truth and love must be decisive about action.
The domination of conscience, for conscience constantly needs educating from our growing knowledge of God.

George Appleton, *Journey for a Soul*, William Collins Sons & Co. Ltd., 1976, p.182.

The creeds are not objects of faith; they are expressions of a faith of which Christ is the object, and in regard to all such personal relationship there is scope for at least a great width of intellectual movement as we seek more and more perfectly to understand and to interpret the character with which we are confronted.

William Temple, *The Preacher's Theme To-day*, S.P.C.K., 1936, p.31.

Faith is an act of self-consecration, in which the will, the intellect, and the affections all have their place. It is the resolve to live as if certain things were true, in the confident assurance that they are true, and that we shall one day find out for ourselves that they are true. The process of verification begins as soon as we have honestly set out to climb. We ourselves change, and the world changes to our sight. The landscape opens out more and more as we get further up the hill.

W.R. Inge, *Personal Religion and the Life of Devotion*, Longmans, Green & Co. Ltd., 1924, p.45.

Faith is a state of the mind and the soul.... The language of religion is a set of formulas which register a basic spiritual experience. It must not be regarded as describing in terms to be defined by philosophy, the reality which is accessible to our senses and which we can analyse with the tools of logic. I was late in understanding what this meant. When I finally reached that point, the beliefs in which I was once brought up and which, in fact, had given my life direction even while my intellect still challenged their validity, were recognised by me as mine in their own right and by my free choice.... The explanation of how man should live a life of active social service in full harmony with himself as a member of the community of the spirit, I found in the writings of those great medieval mystics for whom "self-surrender" had been the way to self-realisation, and who in "singleness of mind" and "inwardness" had found strength to say Yes to every demand which the needs of their neighbours made them face, and to say Yes also to every fate life had in store for them.... Love—that much misused and misinterpreted word—for them meant simply an overflowing of the strength with which they felt themselves filled when living in true self-oblivion. And this love found natural expression in an unhesitant fulfilment of duty and an unreserved acceptance of life, whatever it brought them personally of toil, suffering—or happiness.

Dag Hammarskjold, *Markings*, translated by Leif Sjoberg & W.H. Auden, with a foreword by W.H. Auden, Faber and Faber Limited, 1964, p.10.

This approach of Faith, this appreciation of the nature of God as He has been unveiled in the ethical processes of history, especially in the Person of Christ, and in His expanding conquest of the world, must always be one of the great factors of spiritual religion....

Once at least there shone through the thin veil of matter a personal Life which brought another kind of world than this world of natural law and utilitarian aims full into light. There broke through here in the face of Jesus Christ a revelation of Purpose in the universe so far beyond the vague trend of purpose dimly felt in slowly evolving life that it is possible here to catch an illuminating vision of what the goal of the long drama may be—the unveiling of sons of God. Here the discovery can be made that the deepest Reality towards which Reason points, and which the mystical experience *feels,* is no vague Something Beyond, but a living, loving Some One, dealing with us as Person with person. In Him there comes to focus in a Life that we can love and appreciate a personal character which impresses us as being absolutely good, and as being in its inexhaustible depth of Love and Grace worthy to be taken as the revelation of the true nature of the God whom all human hearts long for. And finally through this personal revelation of God in Christ there has come to us a clear insight that pain and suffering and tragedy can be taken up into a self-chosen Life and absorbed without spoiling its immense joy, and that precisely through suffering-love, joyously accepted, a Person expressing in the world the heart of God may become the moral and spiritual Saviour of others....

Nowhere else in the universe—above us or within us—has the moral significance of life come so full into sight, or the reality of actual divine fellowship, whether in our aspirations or in our failures, been raised to such a pitch of practical certainty as in the personal life and death and resurrection and steady historical triumph of Jesus Christ.... He shows the moral supremacy, even in this imperfect empirical world, of the perfectly good will, and He impresses those who *see* Him—see Him, I mean, with eyes that can penetrate through the temporal to the eternal and find His real nature— as being the supreme personal unveiling of God,... strong enough in His infinite Grace and divine self-giving to convince us of the eternal co-operation of God with our struggling humanity, and to settle our Faith in the essential Saviourhood of God. He who sees *that* in Christ has found a real way to God and discovered a genuine way of salvation. It is the way of Faith, but Faith in no airy and unsubstantial road, no capricious leap. There is no kind of aimful living conceivable that does not involve faith in something trans-subjective—faith in something not given in present empirical experience. Even in our most elementary life-adjustments there is something operative in us which far underlies our conscious perceiving and the logic of our conclusions. We are moved, not alone by what we clearly picture and coldly analyse, but by deeply-lying instincts which defy analysis, by background and foreground fringes of consciousness, by immanent and penetrative intelligence which cannot be brought to definite focus, by the vast reservoirs of accumulated wisdom through which we *feel* the way to go, though we can pictorially envisage no "spotted trees" that mark the trail. This religious and saving Faith, through which the soul discovers God and makes the supreme life-adjustment to Him, is profoundly moral and, in the best sense of the word, rational. It does not begin with an assumption, blind or otherwise, as to Christ's metaphysical nature, it does not depend upon the adoption of systematically formulated doctrines; it becomes operative through the discovery of a personal Life, historically lived— and continued through the centuries as a transforming Spirit—rich enough in its experience to exhibit the infinite significance of life, inwardly deep enough in its spiritual resources to reveal the character of God, and strong enough in sympathy, in tenderness, in patience, and in self-giving love to beget forever trust and confidence and love on the part of all who thus find Him.

The God whom we learn to know in Christ—the God historically revealed—is no vague first Cause, no abstract Reality, no all-negating Absolute. He is a concrete Person, whose traits of character are intensely moral and spiritual. His will is no fateful swing of mechanical law; it is a morally good will which works patiently and forever toward a harmonized world, a Kingdom of God. The central trait of His character is Love. He does not *become* Father. He is not reconciled to us by persuasive offerings and sacrifices. He is inherently and by essential disposition Father and the God of all Grace. He is not remote and absentee—making a world "in the beginning," and leaving it to run by law, or only occasionally interrupting its normal processes—He is immanent Spirit, working always,—the God of beauty and organizing purpose. He is Life and Light and Truth, an Immanuel God who can and does show Himself in a personal Incarnation, and so exhibits the course and goal of the race.

Rufus M. Jones, *Spiritual Reformers in the 16th and 17th Centuries*, Macmillan & Co. Ltd., 1914, p.xi.

FELLOWSHIP

No one enters into fellowship with God but one who has given much time to the recollection of Him, for perfect fellowship means that the mind and the understanding have become absorbed in the joy of inward converse with their Lord, as one who talks with his beloved.

Al-Ghazali, in *Al-Ghazali the Mystic*, Margaret Smith, Luzac & Co., 1944, p.182.

Fellowship with Christ is participation in the divine life which finds its fullest expression in triumph over death. Life is a larger word than Resurrection; but Resurrection is, so to speak, the crucial quality of Life.

William Temple, *Readings in St. John's Gospel* (First and Second Series), Macmillan & Co. Ltd., 1947, p.181.

Is our fellowship in Christ a reality more profound and effective than our membership of our earthly fellowships—family, school, party, class, nation, race—and able in consequence to unite us in love across all natural divisions and hostilities? Of course not. And the reason is that we do not truly abide in Him.

William Temple, *Readings in St. John's Gospel* (First and Second Series), Macmillan & Co. Ltd., 1947, p.267.

The fundamental fact about human life is that God in His love, has entered into fellowship with us; the loftiest hope for human life is that we may, in answering love, enter into fellowship with Him. This is not to be found in the devotional life alone, nor in the practical life alone, but only in the perfect blend of both.

William Temple, *Lent with William Temple*, edited by G.P. Millick Belshaw, A.R. Mowbray & Co. Ltd., 1966, p.7.

In the Apostles' Creed Christians confess their faith in a communion of saints, a fellowship of holy, loving people of all generations who have tried to live according to the light they have received. There is a fellowship of saintliness, a kinship of character and dedication, which is not confined to the Christian religion only, but comprises all who live by the highest they know and are glad to recognize a similar dedication in other people.

George Appleton, *Journey for a Soul*, William Collins Sons & Co. Ltd., 1976, p.191.

And moreover, in these first words (Our Father), the praying soul accepts once for all its true status as a member of the whole family of man. Our Father. It can never again enter into prayer as a ring-fenced individual, intent on a private relation with God; for this is a violation of the law of Charity. Its prayer must overflow the boundaries of selfhood to include the life, the needs of the race; accepting as a corollary of its filial relation with God a brotherly relation with all other souls however diverse, and at every point replacing "mine" by "ours." This widespreading love, this refusal of private advantage is the very condition of Christian prayer; for that prayer is an instrument of redemptive action, not merely of personal achievement.

Evelyn Underhill, *Abba,* Longmans, Green & Co. Ltd., 1940. p.14.

The Church of these spiritual Reformers (sixteenth and seventeenth centuries) was a Fellowship, a Society, a Family, rather than a mysterious and supernatural entity. They felt once again, as powerfully perhaps as it was possible in their centuries to feel it, the immense significance of the Pauline conception of the Church as the continued embodiment and revelation of Christ, the communion of saints past and present who live or have lived by the Spirit. Through this spiritual group, part of whom are visible and part invisible, they held that the divine revelation is continued and the eternal Word of God is being uttered to the race. "The true religion of Christ," as one of these spiritual teachers well puts it, "is written in the soul and spirit of man by the Spirit of God; and the believer is the only book in which God now writes His New Testament." This Church of the Spirit is always being built. Its power is proportional to the spiritual vitality of the membership, to the measure of apprehension of divine resources, to the depth of insight and grasp of truth, to the prevalence of love and brotherhood, to the character of service, which the members exhibit. It possesses no other kind of power or authority than the power and authority of personal lives formed into a community by living correspondence with God, and acting as human channels and organs of His Life and Spirit. Such a Church can meet new formulations of science and history and social ideals with no authoritative and conclusive word of God which automatically settles the issue. Its only weapons are truth and light, and these have to be continually re-discovered and re-fashioned to fit the facts which the age has found and verified. Its mission is *prophetic.* It does not dogmatically decide what facts must be believed, but it sees and announces the spiritual significance of the facts that are discovered and verified. It was, thus, in their thought a growing, changing, ever-adjusting body—the living body of Christ in the World.

Rufus M. Jones, *Spiritual Reformers in the 16th and 17th Centuries,* Macmillan & Co. Ltd., 1914, p.1.

FINDING GOD

People are generally better persuaded by the reasons which they have themselves discovered than by those which have come into the mind of others.

Blaise Pascal, *Pensées,* translated by W.F. Trotter, Random House, Inc., 1941, p.7.

Console thyself, thou wouldst not seek Me, if thou hadst not found me.

Blaise Pascal, *Pensées,* translated by W.R. Trotter, Random House Inc., 1941, p.177.

Humble recognition of what your nature is will lead more surely to God than profound searching for knowledge.

Thomas à Kempis, *The Imitation of Christ,* translated by Betty I. Knott, William Collins Sons & Co. Ltd., 1979, p.41.

Thy hand be on the latch to open the door at his first knock. Shouldst thou open the door and not see him, do not say he did not knock, but understand that he is there, and wants thee to go out to him. It may be he has something for thee to do for him. Go and do it, and perhaps thou wilt return with a new prayer, to find a new window in thy soul.

George Macdonald, *Unspoken Sermons,* Third Series, Longmans, Green & Co., 1889, p.227.

Especially four ways among the many in which the human creature experiences the fact of God, and God is self-disclosed to men, stand out before us.

First, in History we find the Supernatural penetrating Process and revealed through it.

Next, in Incarnation—and, depending from this, in the fact of sanctity—we find the Supernatural penetrating Personality and revealed through it.

Thirdly, in Sacraments and Symbols we find the Supernatural penetrating created Things, and revealed to the soul through the channels of sense.

Last, in Prayer we find the Supernatural in immediate contact with created spirit; self-revealed and self-active within the Individual Soul.

Evelyn Underhill, *Man And The Supernatural,* Methuen & Co. Ltd., 1927, p.90.

For this turning to the Light and Spirit of God within Thee, is thy *only true* turning unto God, there is no other way of finding Him but in that Place where he dwelleth in Thee. For though God be everywhere present, yet He is only present to Thee in the deepest, and most central Part of thy Soul. Thy natural *Senses* cannot possess God, or unite Thee to Him, nay thy inward Faculties of *Understanding, Will*, and *Memory,* can only reach after God, but cannot be the *Place* of his Habitation in Thee. But there is a *Root*, or *Depth* in Thee, from whence all these Faculties come forth, as Lines from a *Centre,* or as Branches from the Body of the Tree. This Depth is called the *Centre*, the *Fund* or *Bottom* of the Soul. This Depth is the *Unity*, the *Eternity*, I had almost said, the *Infinity* of thy Soul; for it is so infinite, that nothing can satisfy it, or give it any Rest, but the infinity of God.

William Law, *The Spirit of Prayer,* full text, edited with an introduction and notes by Sidney Spencer, James Clarke & Co. Ltd., 1969, p.44.

How many of us feel a secret longing to find God; and this usually accompanied by the perception that we are confronted by an impenetrable barrier—we cannot find Him. We waste too much time looking for Him in impossible directions and by impossible means. He is not to be found by merely studying lengthy arguments, brilliant explanations of theological statements, or controversies upon the meaning of obscure dogmas. He is not even to be found through organising charity concerts and social reforms, however useful. We shall find Him through a self stripped bare of all other interests and pretentions—stripped bare of everything but a humble and passionately seeking heart. He says to the soul, "Long for Me, and I will show Myself. Desire Me with a great desire and I will be found" ... the hound of God must have in his heart no plan of his own. It is hard for the heart to say, "I have no wishes of my own; I have no interests, no plans, no ambitions, no schemes, no desires, no love, no will. Thy desire is my desire. Thy love is my all. I am empty of all things, that I may be a channel for the stream of Thy will."

Anon.

In ancient times the love of the beauty of the world had a very important place in men's thoughts and surrounded the whole of life with marvellous poetry. This was the case in every nation; in China, in India, and in Greece....

The example of Saint Francis shows how great a place the beauty of the world can have in Christian thought. Not only in his actual poem perfect poetry, but all his life was perfect poetry in action. His very choice of places for solitary retreats or for the foundations of his convents was in itself the most beautiful poetry in action. Vagabondage and poverty were poetry with him; he stripped himself naked in order to have immediate contact with the beauty of the world....

Today one might think that the white races had almost lost all feeling for the beauty of the world, and that they had taken upon them the task of making it disappear from all the continents where they have penetrated with their armies, their trade and their religion. As Christ said to the Pharisees: "Woe to you for ye have taken away the key of knowledge; ye entered not in yourselves and they that were entering in ye hindered." (Luke 11.52)

And yet at the present time, in the countries of the white races, the beauty of the world is almost the only way by which we can allow God to penetrate us, for we are still further removed from the other two. Real love and respect for religious practices are rare even among those who are most assiduous in observing them, and are practically never to be found in others. Most people do not even conceive them to be possible. As regards the supernatural purpose of affliction, compassion and gratitude are not only rare but have become almost unintelligible for almost everyone today. The very idea of them has almost disappeared; the very meaning of the words has been debased. On the other hand a sense of beauty, although mutilated, distorted and soiled, remains rooted in the heart of man as a powerful incentive. It is present in all the preoccupations of secular life. If it were made true and pure it would sweep all secular life in a body to the feet of God, it would make the total incarnation of the faith possible.

Moreover, speaking generally, the beauty of the world is the commonest, easiest and most natural way of approach.

Simone Weil, *Waiting on God,* translated by Emma Craufurd, William Collins Sons & Co. Ltd., 1974, p.115.

FORGIVENESS

Father, forgive them; for they know not what they do.
Luke 23.34.

And be kind to one another, tenderhearted, forgiving one another, as God in Christ forgave you.
Ephesians 4.32.

Forgive us our sins as we forgive those who sin against us.
Lord's Prayer—ASB.

The one final and utter failure of the church would be its ceasing to be able to bring sinners assurance of forgiveness.

Leonard Hodgson, *The Doctrine of the Atonement*, Nisbet & Co. Ltd., 1951, p.150.

The brave know only how to forgive;... but a coward never forgave. It is not in his nature.

Laurence Sterne, *Sermons of Laurence Sterne*, 1779, p.153.

"I can forgive, but I cannot forget," is only another way of saying, *"I will not forgive."*

Henry Ward Beecher, *Life Thoughts*, Alexander Strahan & Co., 1859, p.67.

There is not one Moral Virtue that Jesus Inculcated but Plato & Cicero did Inculcate before him; what then did Christ Inculcate? Forgiveness of Sins. This alone is the Gospel, & this is the Life & Immortality brought to light by Jesus.

William Blake, *The Complete Writings of William Blake*, edited by Geoffrey Keynes, Oxford University Press, 1974, p.757, "The Everlasting Gospel," supplementary passages, written not before 1818, 1.1.

A wise man will make haste to forgive, because he knows the true value of time, and will not suffer it to pass away in unnecessary pain.

Samuel Johnson, *The Yale Edition of the Works of Samuel Johnson*, edited by W.J. Bate and Albrecht B. Strauss, Yale University Press, 1969, Volume V, p.208, "The Rambler," No.15.

If we are to love others as we love ourselves, then we must learn to love the little self which so often needs to be forgiven for doing the things we do not want to do and saying the things we do not want to say.

Rebecca Beard, *Everyman's Search*, Arthur James, 1951, p.122.

To ask that one's own higher self should forgive one s own trespasses is the hardest prayer to answer that we can ever offer up. If we can breathe this prayer, and find it truly answered in a harmony of exalted comprehension and acceptance, then we shall have learnt what forgiveness is. There is no other way to learn forgiveness.

Havelock Ellis, *Selected Essays*, J.M. Dent & Sons Ltd., 1936, p.324.

If forgiveness meant letting off the criminal it would be a violation of the love-commandment. We have no right to be turning other people's cheeks, leaving other people's children to be raped or lonely old ladies to be beaten up, allowing thieves and murderers to run loose. But in Christian theology, forgiveness does not mean being let off the consequences. Forgiveness means reconciliation.

F.R. Barry, *Christian Ethics and Secular Society*, Hodder and Stoughton Ltd., 1966, p.240.

Forgiveness is the answer to the child's dream of a miracle by which what is broken is made whole again, what is soiled is again made clean. The dream explains why we need to be forgiven, and why we must forgive. In the presence of God, nothing stands between Him and us—we *are* forgiven. But we *cannot* feel his presence if anything is allowed to stand between ourselves and others.

Dag Hammarskjold, *Markings*, translated by Leif Sjoberg & W.H. Auden, with a foreword by W.H. Auden, Faber and Faber Limited, 1964, p.110.

Forgiveness breaks the chain of causality because he who "forgives" you—out of love—takes upon himself the consequences of what *you* have done. Forgiveness, therefore, always entails a sacrifice.
The price you must pay for your own liberation through another's sacrifice, is that you in turn must be willing to liberate in the same way, irrespective of the consequences to yourself.

Dag Hammarskjold, *Markings*, translated by Leif Sjoberg & W.H. Auden, with a foreword by W.H. Auden, Faber and Faber Limited, 1964, p.163.

The Christian who has heard his word of pardon from the lips of Christ upon the Cross is never in danger of supposing that God does not mind. He minds, like that. And so, as St. Paul says, Christ as set forth upon the Cross shows the righteousness of God in the very act of forgiveness. This is part—I know not whether it be the whole, but this is part—at least of that which Christian tradition has stood for in its insistence that the mere appeal of love to our souls is not sufficient as an account of the Atonement—that there must also be in a true sense a propitiation toward God.

William Temple, *The Preacher's Theme To-day*, S.P.C.K., 1936, p.58.

What is the Christian method of correction? Not retributive, nor deterrent, nor even reformative punishment, but the conversion of the offender's heart and will by the readiness of his victim to suffer at his hands. That is the Christian method of meeting wrong-doing; it is revealed in the Passion of Christ to be the nature of God, and it is the point in God's purification which is singled out for us to imitate: "Love your enemies and pray for them that persecute you; that ye may be the sons of your Father which is in Heaven; for He maketh His sun to rise on the evil and the good, and sendeth rain on the just and unjust ... ye therefore shall be perfect as your heavenly Father is perfect." There is the Christian principle beyond all doubt. The good man will not be given to taking care that the bad man is punished, but he will convert the bad man by consenting to suffer, at his hands.

William Temple, *The Kingdom of God*, Macmillan & Co. Ltd., 1912, p.80.

Why do I forgive anyone? Ordinary ethics say, because I feel sympathy with him. They allow men to seem to themselves, when they pardon others, frightfully good, and allow them to practise a style of pardoning which is not free from humiliation of the other. They thus make forgiveness a sweetened triumph of self-devotion.
The ethic of Reverence for Life does away with this unpurified view. All acts of forbearance and of pardon are for it acts forced from one by veracity toward oneself. I must practise unlimited forgiveness because, if I did not, I should be wanting in veracity to myself, for it would be acting as if I myself were not guilty in the same way as the other has been guilty towards me. Because my life is so liberally spotted with falsehood, I must forgive falsehood which has been practised upon me; because I myself have been in so many cases wanting in love, and guilty of hatred, slander, deceit, or arrogance, I must pardon any want of love, and all hatred, slander, deceit, or arrogance which have been directed against myself. I must forgive quietly and without drawing attention to it; in fact, I do not really pardon at all, for I do not let

things develop to any such act of judgement. Nor is this any eccentric proceeding; it is only a necessary widening and refinement of ordinary ethics.

The struggle against the evil that is in mankind we have to carry on not by judging others, but by judging ourselves. Struggle with oneself and veracity towards oneself are the means by which we work upon others. We quietly draw them into our efforts after the deep spiritual self-assertion which springs out of reverence for one's own life. Power makes no noise. It is there, and works. True ethics begin where the use of language ceases.

The innermost element then, in activist ethics, even if it appears as self-devotion, comes from the compulsion to veracity towards oneself, and obtains therein its true value; the whole ethic of being other than the world flows pure only when it comes from this source. It is not from kindness to others that I am tender-hearted, peaceable, forbearing, and friendly, but because by such behaviour I prove my own deepest self-assertion to be true. Reverence for Life which I apply to my own existence, and Reverence for Life which keeps me in a temper of devotion to other existence than mine, interpenetrate each other.

Albert Schweitzer, in *Albert Schweitzer: Christian Revolutionary*, George Seaver, James Clarke & Co. Ltd., 1944, p.91.

FREEDOM

So if the Son makes you free, you will be free indeed.
John 8.36.

So free we seem, so fettered fast we are!
Robert Browning, *The Poetical Works of Robert Browning*, Volume I, Smith, Elder & Co., 1899, p.524, *Men and Women*, "Andrea Del Sarto," l.51.

The freedom of the heart from all that is other than God is needful if it is to be pre-occupied with the love of Him and the direct experience of Him.
Al-Ghazali, in *Al-Ghazali, The Mystic*, Margaret Smith, Luzac & Co., 1944, p.106.

Anything is free when it spontaneously expresses its own nature to the full in activity.
John Macmurray, *Freedom in the Modern World*, Faber and Faber Limited, 1935, p.101.

But what is Freedom? Rightly understood,
A universal licence to be good.
Hartley Coleridge, *The Complete Poetical Works of Hartley Coleridge*, edited with an introduction by Ramsay Colles, George Routledge & Sons, Ltd., 1908, "Liberty," p.106.

Yes! to this thought I hold with firm persistence;
The final word of all that's wise and true:
He only earns his freedom and existence,
Who daily conquers them anew.
Johann Wolfgang von Goethe, *Faust*, introduction by Dennis Wheatley, translated by Bayard Taylor, Sphere Books Ltd., 1974, p.424, Part 2, Act V. sc.vi. l.11573.

Every man has freedom to do all that he wills, provided he infringes not the equal freedom of any other man.

Herbert Spencer, *Social Statics*, Williams and Norgate, 1892, p.54.

When freedom is not an inner idea which imparts strength to our activities and breadth to our creations, when it is merely a thing of external circumstance, it is like an open space to one who is blindfolded.

Rabindranath Tagore, *Creative Unity*, Macmillan & Co. Ltd., 1922, p.133.

The coming of the Son of God and the Messiah in His power and glory as the King of the world and as a conqueror would have been the end of the freedom of the human spirit and the realization of the Kingdom of God by means of necessity and compulsion.

Nicolas Berdyaev, *Freedom and the Spirit*, Geoffrey Bles, The Centenary Press, 1935, p.140.

God compels nobody, for He will have no one saved by compulsion. God has given freewill to men that they may choose for themselves, either the good or the bad. Christ said to His disciples, "Will ye go away?" as though He would say, "You are under no compulsion." God forces no one, for love cannot compel, and God's service is, therefore, a thing of complete freedom.

Rufus M. Jones, *Spiritual Reformers in the 16th and 17th Centuries*, Macmillan & Co. Ltd., 1914, p.22.

All creation is for him (God) a communication of his very being, that is, he can only create free beings. He can only call into existence beings that he calls upon to make themselves.

Louis Lavelle, in *Existentialism*, Paul Foulquié, translated by Kathleen Raine, Dennis Dobson Ltd., 1947, p.113.

Freedom in Christ is not freedom to do what I like, but freedom to be what I am meant to be. It is freedom from all the chains which hold me back from being my true self. It is freedom from all imposed limitations and external pressures. It is to share in Christ's freedom to do God's will, and then to help others find a similar freedom.

George Appleton, *Journey for a Soul*, William Collins Sons & Co. Ltd., 1976, p.181.

God has laid upon man the duty of being free, of safeguarding freedom of spirit, no matter how difficult that may be, or how much sacrifice and suffering it may require.

Nicolas Berdyaev, *The Fate of Man in the Modern World*, translated by Donald A. Lowrie, S.C.M. Press Ltd., 1935, p.44.

If we would have a living thing, we must give that thing some degree of liberty—even though liberty bring with it risk. If we would debar all liberty and all risk, then we can have only the mummy and the dead husk of the thing.

Edward Carpenter, *Love's Coming-Of-Age*, George Allen & Unwin Ltd., 1923, p.108.

Our emancipation lies through the path of suffering. We must unlock the gate of joy by the key of pain. Our heart is like a fountain. So long as it is driven through the narrow channel of self it is full of fear and doubt and sorrow; for then it is dark and does not know its end. But when it comes out into the open, on the bosom of the All, then it glistens in the light and sings in the joy of freedom.

Rabindranath Tagore, *Letters to a Friend*, George Allen & Unwin Ltd., 1928, p.80.

It may now be very easily conceived what is human freedom, which I define to be this: it is, namely, a firm reality which our understanding acquires through direct union with God, so that it can bring forth ideas in itself, and effects outside itself, in complete harmony with its nature; without, however, its effects being subjected to any external causes, so as to be capable of being changed or transformed by them.

Spinoza, *Short Treatise on God, Man, and His Well-Being*, translated and edited, with an introduction and commentary and a life of Spinoza by A. Wolf, Adam and Charles Black, 1910, p.148.

My experience in the West, where I have realised the immense power of money and of organised propaganda,—working everywhere behind screens of camouflage, creating an atmosphere of distrust, timidity, and antipathy,—has impressed me deeply with the truth that real freedom is of the mind and spirit; it can never come to us from outside. He only has freedom who ideally loves freedom himself and is glad to extend it to others. He who cares to have slaves must chain himself to them; he who builds walls to create exclusion for others builds walls across his own freedom; he who distrusts freedom in others loses his moral right to it. Sooner or later he is lured into the meshes of physical and moral servility.

Rabindranath Tagore, *Creative Unity*, Macmillan & Co. Ltd., 1922, p.136.

FREE WILL AND DETERMINISM

We moderns are faced with the necessity of rediscovering the life of the spirit; we must experience it anew for ourselves. It is the only way in which we can break the spell that binds us to the cycle of biological events.

C.G. Jung, *Modern Man in Search of a Soul*, translated by W.S. Dell & Cary F. Baynes, Kegan Paul, Trench, Trubner & Co. Ltd., 1933, p.140.

The important thing to grasp is that while we are born in a determined condition, we do have the freedom to acquire insight, maturity, responsibility to make something of the materials entrusted to us. That's where redemption as new freedom leads us into the communion of saints, where we realise our full stature.

John Bowker, in *Priestland's Progress*, Gerald Priestland, British Broadcasting Corporation, 1982, p.65.

Man is a passion which brings a will into play, which works an intelligence,—and thus the organs which seem to be in the service of intelligence, are in reality only the agents of passion. For all the commoner sorts of being, determinism is true: inward liberty exists only as an exception and as the result of self-conquest. And even he who has tasted liberty is only free intermittently and by moments. True liberty, then, is not a continuous state: it is not an indefeasible and invariable quality. We are free only so far as we are not dupes of ourselves, our pretexts, our instincts, our temperament. We are freed by energy and the critical spirit—that is to say, by detachment of soul, by self-government. So that we are enslaved, but susceptible of freedom; we are bound, but capable of shaking off our bonds. The soul is caged, but it has power to flutter within its cage.

Henri Frédéric Amiel, *Amiel's Journal,* translated by Mrs. Humphry Ward, Macmillan & Co. Ltd., 1918, p.285.

We are faced with the determined everyday world where processes are going on in time, and the future seems inexorable. Man is burdened and bound. He both strives toward freedom and fears it. The paradox of liberation lies in the fact that to maintain freedom and struggle from freedom, it is somehow necessary to be free, to have freedom in oneself. He who is a slave to the depths of his being does not know the word freedom and hence cannot struggle for it. The ancient taboos surround man on every side, cramp his moral life. And to liberate himself from their power, man must first feel himself inwardly free, and only then can he struggle externally for freedom. The inward conquest of enslavement is the basic task of moral living. And this means conquest of enslavement to the past as well as to the future, conquest of enslavement to the external world and enslavement to oneself, to one's lower self. To arouse man's creative energy means inward liberation, and this is accompanied by a sense of freedom. Creativity is the way of liberation.

Nicolas Berdyaev, *Christian Existentialism,* selected and translated by Donald A. Lowrie, George Allen & Unwin Ltd., 1965, p.142.

It must be freely admitted that, in this experimental world, to which God has given the risky privilege of free-will, there are inevitable "ills and accidents." Moreover, the cumulative effect over the centuries of millions of individuals' choosing to please themselves rather than the Designer of "the whole show" has infected the whole planet. That is what the theologians mean when they call this a "sinful" world. This naturally means that, so far as this world is concerned, the tough, insensitive, and selfish, will frequently appear to get away with it, while the weak and sensitive will often suffer. Once we admit the possibilities of free will we can see that injustices and grievances are inevitable. (As Christ once said: "It must needs be that offences come.") We may not agree with the risk that God took in giving Man the power to choose—we might even have preferred God to have made a race of robots who were unfailingly good and cheerful and kind....

The people who feel that God is a Disappointment have not understood the terms on which we inhabit this planet. They are wanting a world in which good is rewarded and evil is punished—as in a well-run kindergarten. They want to see the good man prosper invariably, and the evil man suffer invariably, here and now. There is, of course, nothing wrong with their sense of justice. But they misunderstand the conditions of this present temporary life in which God witholds His Hand, in order, so to speak, to allow room for His plan of freewill to work itself out.

J.B. Phillips, *Your God Is Too Small,* The Epworth Press, 1952, p.44.

FRIENDSHIP

A faithful friend is a strong defence: and he that hath found such an one hath found
a treasure.

Ecclesiasticus 6.14 (A.V.).

No longer do I call you servants, for the servant does not know what his master is
doing; but I have called you friends, for all that I have heard from my Father I have
made known to you.

John 15.15.

I am wealthy in my friends.

William Shakespeare, *Timon of Athens*, Act II. sc.ii. l.189.

A friend may well be reckoned the masterpiece of nature.

Ralph Waldo Emerson, *Essays,* Bernhard Tauchnitz Edition, 1915, p.147, "Friendship."

The essence of friendship is entireness, a total magnanimity and trust.

Ralph Waldo Emerson, *Essays,* Bernhard Tauchnitz Edition, 1915, p.156, "Friendship."

Nor do I question for a moment that Affection is responsible for nine-tenths of whatever
solid and durable happiness there is in our natural lives.

C.S. Lewis, *The Four Loves,* William Collins Sons & Co. Ltd., 1981, p.52.

The only way to have a friend is to be one.

Ralph Waldo Emerson, *Essays,* Bernhard Tauchnitz Edition, 1915, p.153, "Friendship."

To be a strong hand in the dark to another in the time of need.

Hugh Black, *Friendship,* Hodder & Stoughton, 1897, p.43.

Friendship ... is an union of spirits, a marriage of hearts, and the bond thereof virtue.

William Penn, *Fruits of Solitude,* in "Reflections and Maxims, relating to The Conduct of Human Life," A.W.
Bennett, 1863, p.23.

A true friend unbosoms freely, advises justly, assists readily, adventures boldly, takes
all patiently, defends courageously, and continues a friend unchangeably.

William Penn, *Fruits of Solitude,* in "Reflections and Maxims, relating to, The Conduct of Human Life," A.W.
Bennett, 1863, p.24.

Friendship requires great communication between friends. Otherwise, it can neither
be born nor exist.

St. Francis de Sales, *Introduction to the Devout Life,* translated and edited by John K. Ryan, Longmans, Green
and Co. Ltd., 1962, p.186.

If a man does not make new acquaintance as he advances through life, he will soon
find himself alone. A man, Sir, should keep his friendship *in constant repair.*

Samuel Johnson, *Boswell's Life of Johnson,* edited by G.B. Hill, revised by L.F. Powell, Oxford at the Clarendon
Press, 1934, Volume I, p.300.

That friendship may be at once fond and lasting, there must not only be equal virtue on each part, but virtue of the same kind; not only the same end must be proposed, but the same means must be approved by both.

Samuel Johnson, *The Yale Edition of the Works of Samuel Johnson,* edited by W.J. Bate and Albrecht B. Strauss, Yale University Press, 1969, Volume III, p.341, "The Rambler," No.64.

I dream'd in a dream I saw a city invincible to the attacks of the whole of the rest of the earth,
I dream'd that was the new city of Friends,
Nothing was greater there than the quality of robust love, it led the rest,
It was seen every hour in the actions of the men of that city,
And in all their looks and words.

Walt Whitman, *The Complete Poems,* edited by Francis Murphy, Penguin Books Ltd., 1982, "I Dream'd in a Dream," l. 1.

To be honest, to be kind—to earn a little and to spend a little less, to make upon the whole a family happier for his presence, to renounce when that shall be necessary and not be embittered, to keep a few friends, but these without capitulation—above all, on the same grim condition, to keep friends with himself—here is a task for all that a man has of fortitude and delicacy.

Robert Louis Stevenson, *Across the Plains,* T. Nelson & Sons, Ltd., 1892, p.274.

Like everyone else I feel the need of relations and friendship, of affection, of friendly intercourse, and I am not made of stone or iron, so I cannot miss these things without feeling, as does any other intelligent and honest man, a void and deep need. I tell you this to let you know how much good your visit has done me.

Vincent van Gogh, *Dear Theo: An Autobiography of Vincent van Gogh,* edited by Irving Stone, Constable & Company Ltd., 1937, p.39.

Speak to us of Friendship.
And he answered, saying:
Your friend is your needs answered.
He is your field which you sow with love and reap with thanksgiving.
And he is your board and your fireside.
For you come to him with your hunger, and you seek him for peace.
When your friend speaks his mind you fear not the "nay" in your own mind, nor do you with-hold the "ay."
And when he is silent your heart ceases not to listen to his heart;
For without words, in friendship, all thoughts, all desires, all expectations are born and shared, with joy that is unacclaimed.
When you part from your friend, you grieve not;
For that which you love most in him may be clearer in his absence, as the mountain to the climber is clearer from the plain.
And let there be no purpose in friendship save the deepening of the spirit.
For love that seeks aught but the disclosure of its own mystery is not love but a net cast forth: and only the unprofitable is caught.

And let your best be for your friend.
If he must know the ebb of your tide, let him know its flood also.
For what is your friend that you should seek him with hours to kill?
Seek him always with hours to live.
For it is his to fill your need, but not your emptiness.
And in the sweetness of friendship let there be laughter, and sharing of pleasures.
For in the dew of little things the heart finds its morning and is refreshed.

Kahlil Gibran, The Prophet, William Heinemann Ltd., 1970, p.69.

FULFILMENT

For he satisfies him who is thirsty, and the hungry he fills with good things.

Psalm 107.9.

For this reason I bow my knees before the Father, from whom every family in heaven and on earth is named, that according to the riches of his glory he may grant you to be strengthened with might through his Spirit in the inner man, and that Christ may dwell in your hearts through faith; that you, being rooted and grounded in love, may have power to comprehend with all the saints what is the breadth and length and height and depth, and to know the love of Christ which surpasses knowledge, that you may be filled with all the fulness of God.

Ephesians 3.14-19.

None save God can fill the perfect whole.

P.J. Bailey, Festus, William Pickering, 1839, p.51.

Happiness lies in the fulfilment of the spirit through the body.

Cyril Connolly, The Unquiet Grave, Hamish Hamilton, 1945, p.26.

The moment one is on the side of life "peace and security" drop out of consciousness. The only peace, the only security, is in fulfilment.

Henry Miller, The Wisdom of the Heart, New Directions Books, 1941, p.87.

It is the sign of a feeble character to seek for a short-cut to fulfilment through the favour of those whose interest lies in keeping it barred—the one path to fulfilment is the difficult path of suffering and self-sacrifice.

Rabindranath Tagore, Letters to a Friend, George Allen & Unwin Ltd., 1928, p.88.

There is certainly no greater happiness, than to be able to look back on a life usefully and virtuously employed, to trace our own progress in existence, by such tokens as excite neither shame nor sorrow.

Samuel Johnson, The Yale Edition of the Works of Samuel Johnson, edited by W.J. Bate and Albrecht B. Strauss, Yale University Press, 1969, Volume III, p.225, "The Rambler," No.41.

As long as anyone believes that his ideal and purpose is outside him, that it is above the clouds, in the past or in the future, he will go outside himself and seek fulfillment where it can not be found. He will look for solutions and answers at every point except the one where they can be found—in himself.

Erich Fromm, *Man For Himself*, Routledge & Kegan Paul Ltd., 1975, p.249.

Give me fulness of life like to the sea and the sun, to the earth and the air; give me fulness of physical life, mind equal and beyond their fulness; give me a greatness and perfection of soul higher than all things; give me my inexpressible desire which swells in me like a tide—give it to me with all the force of the sea....
My heart has been lifted the higher towards perfection of soul.... Fulness of physical life ever brings to me a more eager desire of soul-life.

Richard Jefferies, *The Story of My Heart*, Duckworth & Co., 1923, pp.79,86.

Our own insufficiency is that we live in a fraction of ourselves, in a narrow *I*, in a narrow vision, *in time*, in a belief that the material universe of the moment is *all*. The perfecting of oneself, the attainment of unity, is connected with grasping the idea of pleroma, with a full-filling which must mean, to begin with, an overcoming of our narrow temporal vision—so that now we can understand better why the Hermetist advises the exercise of thinking of the life *as living at all points,* as a movement towards "eternal life." But time—life—is only one track through the fullness of things.

Maurice Nicoll, *Living Time*, Vincent Stuart Publishers Ltd., 1952, p.136.

Love alone is capable of uniting living beings in such a way as to complete and fulfil them, for it alone takes them and joins them by what is deepest in themselves.... Does not love every instant achieve all around us, in the couple or the team, the magic feat,... of "personalising" by totalising? And if that is what it can achieve daily on a small scale, why should it not repeat this one day on world-wide dimensions?

Pierre Teilhard de Chardin, *The Phenomenon of Man*, William Collins Sons & Co. Ltd., 1982, p.291.

It would seem that the amount of destructiveness to be found in individuals is proportionate to the amount to which expansiveness of life is curtailed. By this we do not refer to individual frustrations of this or that instinctive desire but to the thwarting of the whole of life, the blockage of spontaneity of the growth and expression of man's sensuous, emotional, and intellectual capacities. Life has an inner dynamism of its own; it tends to grow, to be expressed, to be lived. It seems that if this tendency is thwarted the energy directed towards life undergoes a process of decomposition and changes into energies directed towards destruction. In other words: the drive for life and the drive for destruction are not mutually independent factors but are in a reversed interdependence. The more the drive towards life is thwarted, the stronger is the drive towards destruction; the more life is realized, the less is the strength of destructiveness.
Destructiveness is the outcome of unlived life.

Erich Fromm, *The Fear of Freedom*, Routledge & Kegan Paul Ltd., 1961, p.158.

To be happy here on earth we must live a full life. But there is no truly full life for us unless we live at a level above our natural powers as reasoning beings. So, if God is not to make nonsense of His own plan, He must add to our natural powers an extra capacity which will lift us to His own level. And unless we use that extra capacity, we shall not know the fullest life possible to us, nor shall we satisfy certain powers within us if we don't even know they exist. And all this shows that to bother about super-nature, to talk about another level of life than our natural life, is not to trail off into vague abstractions and dreams, but to appreciate our own possibilities. That other level of life is so definite as to belong to one actual Being just as my life belongs to me. What could be more concrete than that? And it is surely the most practical thing in the world to learn about all our powers, all our capabilities. Physiology tells us about our bodies, education exercises our minds, philosophy tells us about our powers of reasoning, art opens up possibilities of enjoying beauty. And now religion comes along and shows us that we have further powers still—the crown of all our natural powers. We shall be losers if we refuse to listen, merely on the ground that they are supernatural powers, for they will still be there whether we choose to recognize them or not. We are definitely refusing to rise to those heights because we are refusing to learn about them. That may take some doing. It takes courage and stamina to climb a mountain, but we cannot see the view from its summit if we stay in the plain. And the view is worth all the effort.

R.L. Smith, in *Man's Dilemma and God's Answer*, Broadcast Talks, S.C.M. Press Ltd., 1944, p.76.

G

GENIUS

In every man of genius a new strange force is brought into the world.
Havelock Ellis, *Selected Essays*, J.M. Dent & Sons Ltd., 1936, p.111.

Geniuses are the luckiest of mortals because what they must do is the same as what they most want to do.
W.H. Auden, "Foreword," *Markings*, Dag Hammarskjold, Faber and Faber Limited, 1964, p.17.

The true Genius is a mind of large general powers, accidentally determined to some particular direction.
Samuel Johnson, *Lives of the English Poets*, edited by G.B. Hill, Oxford at the Clarendon Press, 1905, Volume I, p.2, "Cowley."

Genius is mainly an affair of energy.
Matthew Arnold, *The Complete Prose Works of Matthew Arnold*, Volume III, edited by R.H. Super, *Lectures and Essays in Criticism*, Ann Arbor, The University of Michigan Press, 1962, "The Literary Influence of Academics," p.238.

Men of genius do not excel in any profession because they labour in it, but they labour in it because they excel.
William Hazlitt, *Hazlitt's Characteristics*, Elkin Mathews & Marrot Ltd., 1827, p.123.

To believe your own thought, to believe that what is true for you in your private heart is true for all men,—that is genius.
Ralph Waldo Emerson, *Essays*, Bernhard Tauchnitz Edition, 1915, p.34, "Self-Reliance."

Time, Place, and Action, may with pains be wrought,
But Genius must be born, and never can be taught.
John Dryden, *The Poems of John Dryden*, edited by James Kinsley, Oxford at the Clarendon Press, 1958, Volume II, p.853, "To my Dear Friend Mr. Congreve," 1.59.

Hast thou any notion what a Man of Genius is? Genius is "the inspired gift of God." It is the clearer presence of God Most High in a man. Dim, potential in all men; in this man it has become clear, actual.
Thomas Carlyle, *Past and Present*, Ward, Lock & Co. Ltd., p.199.

Genius is the unreserved devotion of the whole soul to the divine, poetic arts, and through them to God; deeming all else, even to our daily bread, only valuable as it helps us to unveil the heavenly face of Beauty.
Samuel Palmer, in *Visionary and Dreamer*, Lord David Cecil, Constable & Company Ltd., 1969, p.63.

117

There are two kinds of genius. The first and highest may be said to speak out of the eternal to the present, and must compel its age to understand *it;* the second understands its age, and tells it what it wishes to be told.

J.R. Lowell, *My Study Windows,* George Routledge & Sons, Ltd., 1905, p.383.

I know now that revelation is from the self, but from that age-long memorised self, that shapes the elaborate shell of the mollusc and the child in the womb, that teaches the birds to make their nest; and that genius is a crisis that joins that buried self for certain moments to our trivial daily mind.

W.B. Yeats, *Autobiographies,* Macmillan & Co. Ltd., 1966, p.272.

Genius is not a single power, but a combination of great powers. It reasons, but it is not reasoning; it judges, but it is not judgement; it imagines, but it is not imagination; it feels deeply and fiercely, but it is not passion. It is neither, because it is all. It is another name for the perfection of human nature, for Genius is not a fact but an ideal. It is nothing less than the possession of all the powers and impulses of humanity, in their greatest possible strength and most harmonious combination; and the genius of any particular man is great in proportion as he approaches this ideal of universal genius.

Edwin P. Whipple, *Literature And Life.* Lectures, John Chapman, 1851, p.81.

GLORY

The heavens are telling the glory of God; and the firmament proclaims his handiwork.

Psalm 19.1.

And the Word became flesh and dwelt among us, full of grace and truth; we have beheld his glory, glory as of the only Son from the Father.

John 1.14.

The glory which thou hast given me I have given to them, that they may be one even as we are one, I in them and thou in me, that they may become perfectly one.

John 17.22-23.

Through him we have obtained access to this grace in which we stand, and we rejoice in our hope of sharing the glory of God.

Romans 5.2.

Do you not know that your body is a temple of the Holy Spirit within you, which you have from God? You are not your own; you were bought with a price. So glorify God in your body.

1 Corinthians 6.19-20.

To them God chose to make known how great among the Gentiles are the riches of the glory of this mystery, which is Christ in you, the hope of glory.

Colossians 1.27.

That the God of our Lord Jesus Christ, the Father of glory, may give you a spirit of wisdom and of revelation in the knowledge of him, having the eyes of your hearts enlightened, that you may know what is the hope to which he has called you, what are the riches of his glorious inheritance in the saints, and what is the immeasurable greatness of his power in us who believe, according to the working of his great might.

Ephesians 1.17-19.

The glory of God is a living Man. (i.e., a man fully alive).

S. Irenaeus, *Five Books of S. Irenaeus Against Heresies,* translated by the Rev. John Keble, James Parker & Co., 1872, p.369, Bk. IV.

When one candle is lighted ... we light many by it, and when God hath kindled the Life of His glory in one man's Heart he often enkindles many by the flame of that.

Rufus M. Jones, *Spiritual Reformers in the 16th and 17th Centuries,* Macmillan & Co. Ltd., 1914, p.287.

That is what gives Him the greatest glory—the achieving of great things through the weakest and most improbable means.

Thomas Merton, *The Sign of Jonas,* Sheldon Press, 1976, p.76.

What is the freedom of the godly man? Being absolutely nothing to and wanting absolutely nothing for himself but only the glory of God in all his works.

Meister Eckhart, *Meister Eckhart,* Franz Pfeiffer, translated by C. de B. Evans, John M. Watkins, 1956, Volume I, p.287.

The noble hart, that harbours vertuous thought,
And is with child of glorious great intent,
Can never rest, untill it forth have brought
Th'eternall brood of glorie excellent.

Edmund Spenser, *Spenser's Faerie Queene,* edited by J.C. Smith, Oxford at the Clarendon Press, 1964, p.55, Bk.I, canto v, st.i, l.1.

The principle that governs the universe "became flesh and dwelt among us and we beheld His glory," and the impression was as of something that shone through Him from beyond—"glory as of an Only Begotten Son from a Father"; of One who perfectly represented something and who is perfectly united with it.

William Temple, *Christian Faith and Life,* S.C.M. Press Ltd., 1963, p.34.

As we become forgetful of ourselves and entirely filled with His glory, the glory of His righteousness and love, we become transformed into His image ... from glory to glory; and because we are more like Him, we shall live more like Him; because we live more like Him, we shall do something that is far more truly His will than what we might have planned out for ourselves in an eager and perhaps impatient generosity.

William Temple, *Basic Convictions,* Hamish Hamilton, 1937, p.29.

A man does not direct all his actions to the glory of God by forming a conception in his mind, or stirring up a strong imagination upon any action, that that must be for the glory of God: it is not thinking of God's glory that is glorifying of Him....

We rather glorify God by entertaining the impressions of His glory upon us, than by communicating any kind of glory to Him. Then does a good man become the tabernacle of God, wherein the divine Shechinah does rest, and which the Divine glory fills, when the frame of his mind and life is wholly according to that idea and pattern which he receives from the mount. We best glorify Him when we grow most like to Him: and we then act most for His glory, when a true spirit of sanctity, justice, meekness, &c., runs through all our actions; when we so live in the world as becomes those that converse with the great Mind and Wisdom of the whole world; with that Almighty Spirit that made, supports, and governs all things; with that Being from whence all good flows, and in which there is no spot, stain, or shadow of evil; and so, being captivated and overcome by the sense of the Divine loveliness and goodness, we endeavour to be like Him, and conform ourselves, as much as may be, to Him.

John Smith the Platonist, *Select Discourses,* Cambridge at the University Press, 1859, p.417.

GOD

Be still, and know that I am God.

Psalm 46.10.

God is not an optional extra, He's an absolute must.

A girl of fourteen.

God isn't a think; He's a feel.

Joyce Grenfell, *In Pleasant Places,* MacDonald Futura Publishers Ltd., 1983, p.161.

I will tell you, Scholar, I have heard a grave Divine say, that God has two dwellings; one in heaven, and the other in a meek and thankful heart.

Izaak Walton, *The Complete Angler,* Macmillan & Co. Ltd., 1906, p.175.

From thee, great God, we spring, to thee we tend,
Path, motive, guide, original and end.

Samuel Johnson, *The Yale Edition of the Works of Samuel Johnson,* edited by W.J. Bate and Albrecht B. Strauss, Yale University Press, 1969, Volume III, p.36, "Motto for The Rambler," No.7.

God! Thou art love! I build my faith on that.

Robert Browning, *The Poetical Works of Robert Browning,* Smith, Elder, & Co., 1899, Volume I, "Paracelsus V," p.61.

None but God can satisfy the longings of an immortal soul; that, as the heart was made for Him, so He only can fill it.

Richard Chenevix Trench, *Notes on the Parables of our Lord,* Pickering & Inglis Ltd., 1953, p.400.

The Father is our ground and origin, in which we begin our being and our life.

John of Ruysbroeck, *The Adornment of the Spiritual Marriage,* translated by C.A. Wynschenk Dom, edited with an introduction and notes by Evelyn Underhill, John M. Watkins, 1951, p.173.

God shall be my hope,
My stay, my guide, and lantern to my feet.
William Shakespeare, *King Henry VI, Part II,* Act II. sc.iii. l.24.

The Divine Essence itself is Love and Wisdom.
Emanuel Swedenborg, *The Divine Love and Wisdom,* J.M. Dent & Sons Ltd., 1914, p.12.

A voice is in the wind I do not know;
A meaning on the face of the high hills,
Whose utterance I cannot comprehend.
A something is behind them: that is God.
George Macdonald, *Within And Without,* Longman, Brown, Green, and Longmans, 1855, p.9.

What is that light whose gentle beams now and again strike through to my heart, causing me to shudder in awe yet firing me with their warmth? I shudder to feel how different I am from it: yet in so far as I am like it, I am aglow with its fire.
St. Augustine, *Confessions,* translated with an introduction by R.S. Pine-Coffin, Penguin Books Ltd., 1964, p.260.

Thou must not think that God is a Being who is off in an upper heaven, or that when the soul departs it goes many hundred thousands of miles aloft. It does not need to do that, for as soon as it has entered the innermost Birth it is in heaven already with God—*near and far in God is one thing....* There is only one "place" to look for God and that is in one's own soul, there is only one "region" in which to find heaven or hell, and that is in the nature and character of the person's own desire and will.
Rufus M. Jones, *Spiritual Reformers in the 16th and 17th Centuries,* Macmillan & Co. Ltd., 1914, p.186.

I regularly and repeatedly find the whole notion of God quite incomprehensible. Faith, I always believe, takes us to where the language bends and I'm jumping for analogy and metaphor. But in worship, in private meditation and in service, yes I do get a sense of the transcendent and the holy, a presence that is more than the universe and yet personal and benevolent towards me—I'm not sure if I know the meaning of the word love, but there's a very strong benevolence there. And I think at that level I know God.
Stuart Miller, in *Priestland's Progress,* Gerald Priestland, British Broadcasting Corporation, 1982, p.58.

Why should I wish to see God better than this day?
I see something of God each hour of the twenty-four, and each moment then,
In the faces of men and women I see God, and in my own face in the glass,
I find letters from God dropt in the street, and every one is sign'd by God's name,
And I leave them where they are, for I know that wheresoe'er I go,
Others will punctually come for ever and ever.
Walt Whitman, *The Complete Poems,* edited by Francis Murphy, Penguin Books Ltd., 1982, p.121, "Song of Myself," section 48, l.1283.

Every man, though he realizes that he was conceived by a bodily father in his mother's womb, is conscious also that he has within him a spirit that is free, intelligent, and independent of the body.

That eternal spirit proceeding from the infinite, is the origin of all and is what we call God.

Leo Tolstoy, *A Confession, The Gospel in Brief*, and *What I Believe*, translated with an introduction by Aylmer Maude, Oxford University Press, 1940, p.267.

The word "God" is used in most cases as by no means a term of science or exact knowledge, but a term of poetry and eloquence, a term *thrown out*, so to speak, at a not fully grasped object of the speaker's consciousness, a *literary* term, in short; and mankind mean different things by it as their consciousness differs.

Matthew Arnold, *The Complete Prose Works of Matthew Arnold*, Volume VI, *Dissent and Dogma*, edited by R.H. Super, Ann Arbor, The University of Michigan Press, 1968, "Literature and Dogma," Ch.I, p.171.

When Bishop Robinson was asked how he prayed "to the ground of your being" he replied:

"I do not pray to the ground of my being. I pray to God as Father. Prayer, for the Christian, is the opening of oneself to that utterly gracious personal reality which Jesus could only address as 'Abba, Father!' I have no interest in a God conceived in some vaguely impersonal pantheistic terms. The only God who meets my need as a Christian is 'the God of Abraham, Isaac and Jacob,' the God and Father of our Lord Jesus Christ."

John B. Coburn, in *Spirituality For Today*, edited by Eric James, S.C.M. Press Ltd., 1968, p.26.

The word for "Father," which the earliest Christians learnt from Jesus ... was the intimate mode of address from child to father.... We must suppose that Jesus used it, by choice, because it is the appropriate way of speaking about the personal life with God which was his concern.... He was aware that there were sophisticated types who could not take his teaching.... "I thank thee, Father," he is recorded to have said, "for hiding these things from the learned and wise, and revealing them to the simple...." And again, "Unless you turn round and become like children, you will never enter the kingdom of God...." This "turning round" is a large part of what is meant by "repentance" in the gospels. It is learning to think of God as your Father and of yourself as his child, quite simply.

C.H. Dodd, *The Founder of Christianity*, William Collins Sons & Co. Ltd., 1979, p.72.

Over the infinity of space and time, the infinitely more infinite love of God comes to possess us. He comes at his own time. We have the power to consent to receive him or refuse. If we remain deaf, he comes back again and again like a beggar, but also, like a beggar, one day he stops coming. If we consent, God puts a little seed in us and he goes away again. The seed grows. A day comes when the soul belongs to God, when it not only consents to love but when truly and effectively it loves. Then in its turn it must cross the universe to go to God. The soul does not love like a creature with created love. The love within it is divine, uncreated; for it is the love of God for God which is passing through it. God alone is capable of loving God. We can only consent to give up our own feelings so as to allow free passage in one soul for this love. We are created for this consent, and for this alone.

Victor Gollancz, *More For Timothy*, Victor Gollancz Ltd., 1953, p.95.

It is clearly necessary, from the beginning to the end of time, that God's way of revealing Himself to His creatures should be a *simple* way, which *all* those creatures may understand. Whether taught or untaught, whether of mean capacity or enlarged, it is necessary that communion with their Creator should be possible to all; and the admission to such communion must be rested, not on their having a knowledge of astronomy, but on their having a human soul. In order to render this communion possible, the Deity has stooped from His throne, and has not only, in the person of His Son, taken upon Him the veil of our human *flesh,* but, in the person of the Father, taken upon Him the veil of our human *thoughts,* and permitted *us,* by His own spoken authority, to conceive Him simply and clearly as a loving Father and Friend;—a being to be walked with and reasoned with; to be moved by our entreaties, angered by our rebellion, alienated by our coldness, pleased by our love, and glorified by our labour; and finally, to be beheld in immediate and active presence in all the powers and changes of creation. This conception of God, which is the child's, is evidently the only one which can be universal, and therefore the only one which *for us* can be true.

John Ruskin, *Modern Painters*, George Allen & Sons, 1910, Volume IV, Part V, Ch.VI, p.90.

GOD WITHIN

I myself believe that the evidence for God lies primarily in inner personal experiences.

William James, *Pragmatism*, Longmans, Green & Co. Ltd., 1943, p.109.

The name of this infinite and inexhaustible depth and ground of all being is *God.*

Paul Tillich, *The Shaking of the Foundations*, S.C.M. Press Ltd., 1949, p.57.

Where the creature ends, there God begins to be. God only asks that you get out of his way, in so far as you are creature, and let him be God in you.

Meister Eckhart, *Meister Eckhart*, translated by Raymond B. Blakney, Harper & Row, Publishers, Inc., 1941, p.127.

To get at the core of God at his greatest, one must first get into the core of himself at his least, for no one can know God who has not first known himself. Go to the depths of the soul, the secret place of the Most High, to the roots, to the heights; for all that God can do is focussed there.

Meister Eckhart, *Meister Eckhart*, translated by Raymond B. Blakney, Harper & Row, Publishers, Inc., 1941, p.246.

Christian education has done all that is humanly possible; but it has not been enough. Too few people have experienced the divine image as the innermost possession of their own souls.

C.G. Jung, *Psychological Reflections*, selected and edited by Jolande Jacobi, Routledge & Kegan Paul Ltd., 1953, p.308.

Remember how Saint Augustine tells us about his seeking God in many places and eventually finding Him within himself. Do you suppose it is of little importance that a soul which is often distracted should come to understand this truth and to find that, in order to speak to its Eternal Father and to take its delight in Him, it has no need to go to Heaven or to speak in a loud voice? However quietly we speak, He is so near that He will hear us: we need no wings to go in search of Him but have only to find a place where we can be alone and look upon Him present within us.

St. Teresa of Avila, *The Complete Works of St. Teresa of Jesus,* translated by E. Allison Peers, Sheed & Ward Ltd., 1978, Volume II, "Way of Perfection," p. 114.

"Oh, if only it were possible to find understanding," Joseph exclaimed. "If only there were a dogma to believe in. Everything is contradictory, everything tangential; there are no certainties anywhere. Everything can be interpreted one way and then again interpreted in the opposite sense. The whole of world history can be explained as development and progress and can also be seen as nothing but decadence and meaninglessness. Isn't there any truth? Is there no real and valid doctrine?"
The Master had never heard him speak so fervently. He walked on in silence for a little, then said: "There is truth, my boy. But the doctrine you desire, absolute, perfect dogma that alone provides wisdom, does not exist. Nor should you long for a perfect doctrine, my friend. Rather, you should long for the perfection of yourself. The deity is within *you,* not in ideas and books. Truth is lived, not taught. Be prepared for conflicts, Joseph Knecht—I can see they have already begun."

Herman Hesse, *The Glass Bead Game,* translated by Richard and Clara Winston, Penguin Books Ltd., 1979, p. 79.

There is a young man,
who lives in a world of progress.
He used to worship a God
who was kind to him.
This God had a long white beard,
He lived in the clouds,
but all the same
He was close to the solemn child
who had secretly
shut Him up, in a picture book.
But now,
the man is enlightened.
Now he has been to school,
and has learned to kick a ball,
and to be abject
in the face of public opinion.
He knows too,
that men are hardly removed from monkeys.
You see, he lives in the light
of the twentieth century.

He works, twelve hours a day,
and is able to rent a room,
in a lodging house,
that is not a home.
At night he hangs
a wretched coat
up on a peg on the door
and stares
at the awful jug and basin,
and goes to bed.
And the poor coat,
worn to the man's shape,
round-shouldered and abject,
watches him, asleep,
dreaming of all
the essential
holy things,
that he cannot hope to obtain
for two pounds ten a week.

Very soon
he will put off his body,
like the dejected coat
that he hates.
And his body will be
worn to the shape
of twelve hours' work a day
for two pounds ten a week.
If he had only known
that the God in the picture book,
is not an old man in the clouds
but the seed of life in his soul,
the man would have lived.
And his life would have flowered
with the flower of limitless joy.

But he does not know,
and in him
the Holy Ghost
is a poor little bird
in a cage,
who never sings,
and never opens his wings,
yet never, never
desires to be gone away.

Caryll Houselander, "The Young Man," in *Let There Be God,* compiled by T.H. Parker and F. J. Teskey, The
Religious Education Press Ltd., 1968, p.123.

GOOD

And God saw everything that he had made, and behold, it was very good.
Genesis 1.31.

I am the good shepherd. The good shepherd lays down his life for the sheep.
John 10.11.

And Jesus said to him, "Why do you call me good? No one is good but God alone."
Luke 18.19.

He went about doing good.
Acts 10.38.

He was a good man, full of the Holy Spirit and of faith.
Acts 11.24.

Let us never tire of doing good.
Galatians 6.9 (N.E.B.).

We know that in everything God works for good with those who love him, who are
called according to his purpose.
Romans 8.28.

For we are his workmanship, created in Christ Jesus for good works, which God
prepared beforehand, that we should walk in them.
Ephesians 2.10.

I am larger, better than I thought,
I did not know I held so much goodness.
Walt Whitman, *The Complete Poems*, edited by Francis Murphy, Penguin Books Ltd., 1982, p.181, "Song of
the Open Road," section 5, 1.60.

Be good yourself and the world will be good.
Hindu Proverb.

Goodness is a special kind of truth and beauty. It is truth and beauty in human
behaviour.
H.A. Overstreet, *The Enduring Quest*, foreword by J.W.N. Sullivan, Jonathan Cape Ltd., 1931, p.174.

Loving-kindness is the better part of goodness. It lends grace to the sterner qualities
of which this consists.
W. Somerset Maugham, *The Summing Up*, Bernhard Tauchnitz, 1938, p.242.

Anyone who proposes to do good must not expect people to roll stones out of his way,
but must accept his lot calmly if they even roll a few more upon it.
Albert Schweitzer, *Out of My Life and Thought*, Henry Holt and Company Inc., 1949, p.92.

Look around the Habitable World, how few
Know their own Good; or knowing it, pursue.

John Dryden, *The Poems of John Dryden*, Oxford at the Clarendon Press, 1958, Volume II, p.720, *The Satires of Juvenal*, "The Tenth Satyr," 1.1.

Good, the more
Communicated, more abundant grows.

John Milton, *The Poetical Works of John Milton*, edited by the Rev. H.C. Beeching, Oxford at the Clarendon Press, 1900, p.274, *Paradise Lost*, Bk.V, 1.71.

(Goodness) needeth not to enter into the soul, for it is there already, only it is unperceived.

Theologia Germanica, translated by Susanna Winkworth, Stuart & Watkins Ltd., 1966, p.48.

There is but one unconditional commandment, which is that we should seek incessantly, with fear and trembling, so to vote and to act as to bring about the very largest total universe of good which we can see.

William James, *The Will To Believe*, Longmans, Green & Co. Ltd., 1904, p.209.

He said to Judas, when he betrayed Him: "Friend, wherefore art thou come?" Just as if He had said: "Thou hatest Me and art Mine enemy: yet I love thee and am thy friend...." As though God in human nature were saying: "I am pure, simple Goodness, and therefore I cannot will, or desire, or rejoice in, or do or give anything but goodness. If I am to reward thee for any evil and wickedness, I must do it with goodness, for I am and have nothing else."

Theologia Germanica, translated by Susanna Winkworth, Stuart & Watkins Ltd., 1966, p.87.

He lived in a continuous enjoyment of God and perpetually drew nearer to the Centre of his soul's rest and always stayed God's time of advancement. His spirit was absorbed in the business and employment of becoming perfect in his art and profession—which was the art *of being a good man.*

Rufus M. Jones, said of John Smith in *Spiritual Reformers in the 16th and 17th Centuries*, Macmillan & Co. Ltd., 1914, p.308.

And when we come to think of it, goodness *is* uneventful. It does not flash, it glows. It is deep, quiet, and very simple. It passes not with oratory, it is commonly foreign to riches, nor does it often sit in the places of the mighty: but may be felt in the touch of a friendly hand or the look of a kindly eye.

David Grayson, *Adventures in Contentment*, Andrew Melrose, Ltd., 1946, p.192.

The Father was all in all to the Son, and the Son no more thought of his own goodness than an honest man thinks of his honesty. When the good man sees goodness, he thinks of his own evil: Jesus had no evil to think of, but neither does he think of his goodness; he delights in his Father's. "Why callest thou me good?"

George Macdonald, *Unspoken Sermons*, Second Series, Longmans, Green & Co. Ltd., 1885, p.6.

Those people work more wisely who seek to achieve good in their own small corner of the world and then leave the leaven to leaven the whole lump, than those who are for ever thinking that life is vain unless one can act through the central government, carry legislation, achieve political power and do big things.

Herbert Butterfield, *Christianity and History*, G. Bell & Sons Ltd., 1949, p.104.

And what rule do you think I walked by? Truly a strange one, but the best in the whole world. I was guided by an implicit faith in God's goodness: and therefore led to the study of the most obvious and common things. For thus I thought within myself: God being, as we generally believe, infinite in goodness, it is most consonant and agreeable with His nature, that the best things should be the most common. For nothing is more natural to infinite goodness, than to make the best things most frequent; and only things worthless scarce.

Thomas Traherne, *Centuries*, The Faith Press Ltd., 1969, p.138.

GRACE

And from his fulness have we all received, grace upon grace.

John 1.16.

But by the grace of God I am what I am, and his grace toward me was not in vain. On the contrary, I worked harder than any of them, though it was not I, but the grace of God which is with me.

1 Corinthians 15.10.

My grace is sufficient for you, for my power is made perfect in weakness.

2 Corinthians 12.9.

Since you are joint heirs of the grace of life.

1 Peter 3.7.

And after you have suffered a little while, the God of all grace, who has called you to his eternal glory in Christ, will himself restore, establish, and strengthen you.

1 Peter 5.10.

The power of grace always remains God's power but it becomes operative in man and thus fulfils, sustains, and renews human nature.

Daniel D. Williams, in *A Dictionary of Christian Ethics*, edited by John Macquarrie, S.C.M. Press Ltd., 1967, p.139, "Grace."

Grace is not something other than God, imparted by Him; it is the very Love of God (which is Himself) approaching and seeking entry to the soul of man.

William Temple, *Nature, Man and God*, Macmillan & Co., Ltd., 1934, p.485.

If you knew how to annihilate self-interest and cast out all affection for the created world, then I would come, and my grace would well up abundantly within you.

Thomas à Kempis, *The Imitation of Christ*, translated by Betty I. Knott, William Collins Sons & Co. Ltd., 1979, p.175.

This gift is from God and not of man's deserving. But certainly no one ever receives such a great grace without tremendous labour and burning desire.

Richard of Saint-Victor, *Selected Writings on Contemplation,* translated by Clare Kirchberger, Faber and Faber Limited, 1957, p.111.

But O! th'exceeding grace
Of highest God, that loves his creatures so,
And all his works with mercy doth embrace.

Edmund Spenser, *Spenser's Faerie Queene,* edited by J.C. Smith, Oxford at the Clarendon Press, 1964, p.258, Bk.II, Canto VIII, st.i, l.5.

Let nobody presume upon his own powers for such exaltation or uplifting of the heart or ascribe it to his own merits. For it is certain that this comes not from human deserving but is a divine gift.

Richard of Saint-Victor, *Selected Writings on Contemplation,* translated by Clare Kirchberger, Faber and Faber Limited, 1957, p.205.

O Lord, I need your grace so much if I am to start anything good, or go on with it, or bring it to completion. Without grace, I have no power to do anything—but nothing is beyond my powers, if your grace gives strength to me.

Thomas à Kempis, *The Imitation of Christ,* translated by Betty I. Knott, William Collins Sons & Co. Ltd., 1979, p.202.

No one is suddenly endowed with all graces, but when God, the source of all grace, helps and teaches a soul, it can attain this state by sustained spiritual exercises and wisely ordered activity. For without His especial help and inner guidance no soul can reach a state of perfection.

Walter Hilton, *The Ladder of Perfection,* translated with an introduction by Leo Sherley-Price, Penguin Books Ltd., 1957, p.146.

I am aware
Of my own unworthiness,
But I am certain
Of Thy boundless grace.

Al-Ansari, *The Persian Mystics,* translated by Sardar Sir Jogendra Sing, John Murray Ltd., 1939, p.51.

Whoso walks in solitude,
And inhabiteth the wood,
Choosing light, wave, rock, and bird,
Before the money-loving herd,
Into that forester shall pass,
From these companions, power and grace.

Ralph Waldo Emerson, *The Works of Ralph Waldo Emerson,* edited by George Sampson, George Bell & Sons, Ltd., 1906, Volume V, *Poems,* "Woodnotes," p.37.

For the Goodness of God is the highest prayer, and it cometh down to the lowest part of our need. It quickeneth our soul and bringeth it on life, and maketh it for to waxen in grace and virtue. It is nearest in nature; and readiest in grace: for *it* is the same

grace that the soul seeketh, and ever shall seek till we know verily that He hath us
all in Himself enclosed.

Lady Julian of Norwich, *Revelations of Divine Love,* edited by Grace Warrack, Methuen & Co. Ltd., 1949, p.13.

GREATNESS

Great souls care only for what is great.

Henri Frédéric Amiel, *Amiel's Journal,* translated by Mrs. Humphry Ward, Macmillan & Co. Ltd., 1918, p.137.

Great Hopes make great Men.

Thomas Fuller, M.D., *Gnomologia,* 1732, Dublin, p.67, No.1759.

Great men are the guide-posts and landmarks in the state.

Edmund Burke, *Speeches and Letters on American Affairs,* J.M. Dent & Sons Ltd., 1961, p.51.

Nothing great or new can be done without enthusiasm.

Dr. Harvey Cushing, in *Dialogues of Alfred North Whitehead,* as recorded by Lucien Price, Max Reinhardt, 1954, p.47.

It is a rough road that leads to the heights of greatness.

Seneca, *Epistulae Morales,* Richard M. Gummere, William Heinemann, Volume II, p.285.

No great man lives in vain. The History of the world is but the Biography of great
men.

Thomas Carlyle, *Sartor Resartus,* "Lectures on Heroes," Chapman and Hall, 1840, p.206.

And I smiled to think God's greatness flowed around our incompleteness,—
Round our restlessness, His rest.

E.B. Browning, *Elizabeth Barrett Browning's Poetical Works,* Smith, Elder, & Co., 1873, Volume II, p.82.,
"Rhyme of the Duchess May," st. xi.

Great Truths are portions of the soul of man;
Great souls are portions of Eternity.

J.R. Lowell, *The Poetical Works of James Russell Lowell,* introduction by William Michael Rossetti, Ward, Lock
& Co. Ltd., 1911, p.110, Sonnet No.vi.

Man's Unhappiness, as I construe, comes of his Greatness; it is because there is an
Infinite in him, which with all his cunning he cannot quite bury under the Finite.

Thomas Carlyle, *Sartor Resartus,* Ward, Locke & Co. Ltd., p.127.

Great men are the true men, the men in whom Nature has succeeded. They are not
extraordinary—they are in the true order. It is the other species of men who are not
what they ought to be.

Henri Frédéric Amiel, *Amiel's Journal,* translated by Mrs. Humphry Ward, Macmillan & Co. Ltd., 1918, p.112.

Greatness after all, in spite of its name, appears to be not so much a certain size as
a certain quality in human lives. It may be present in lives whose range is very small.

Phillips Brooks, *Sermons,* Richard D. Dickinson, 1879, p.14.

Greatness is a spiritual condition worthy to excite love, interest, and admiration; and the outward proof of possessing greatness is that we excite love, interest, and admiration.
Matthew Arnold, *The Complete Prose Works of Matthew Arnold*, Volume V, *Culture and Anarchy*, edited by R.H. Super, Ann Arbor, The University of Michigan Press, 1965, "Sweetness and Light," p.96.

It is difficult to achieve greatness of mind and character where our responsibility is diminutive and fragmentary, where our whole life occupies and affects an extremely limited area.
Rabindranath Tagore, *Letters to a Friend*, George Allen & Unwin Ltd., 1928, p.90.

Altogether it will be found that a quiet life is characteristic of great men, and that their pleasures have not been of the sort that would look exciting to the outward eye.
Bertrand Russell, *The Conquest of Happiness*, George Allen & Unwin Ltd., 1984, p.49.

All things that we see standing accomplished in the world are properly the outer material result, the practical realisation and embodiment, of Thoughts that dwelt in the Great Men sent into the world.
Thomas Carlyle, *Sartor Resartus*, "Lectures on Heroes," Chapman and Hall, 1840, p.185.

The heights by great men reached and kept
Were not attained by sudden flight,
But they, while their companions slept,
Were toiling upward in the night.
Henry Wadsworth Longfellow, *The Poetical Works of Longfellow*, Humphrey Milford, Oxford University Press, 1913, p.299, "The Ladder of St. Augustine," st.x. l.1.

The greatest man is he who chooses the Right with invincible resolution, who resists the sorest temptations from within and without, who bears the heaviest burdens cheerfully, who is calmest in storms and most fearless under menace and frowns, whose reliance on truth, on virtue, on God is most unfaltering; and is this a greatness, which is apt to make a show, or which is most likely to abound in conspicuous station?
William E. Channing, *Self-Culture*, Dutton and Wentworth, Printers, 1838, p.9.

He alone deserves the appellation of great, who either achieves great things himself, or teaches how they may be achieved; or who describes with suitable dignity the great achievements of others. But those things only are great, which either make this life of ours happy, or at least comfortable and agreeable as far as is consistent with honesty, or which lead to another and a happier life.
John Milton, *The Works of John Milton*, Columbia University Press, 1933, Volume VIII, p.95, "Second Defence of the People of England."

GRIEF

Grief is itself a med'cine.
William Cowper, *The Poetical Works of Cowper*, edited by H.S. Milford, Oxford University Press, 1950, p.79, "Charity," l.159.

Time and thinking tame the strongest grief.

English Proverb.

In mourning let grief suffice as its highest expression.

Confucius, *The Analects of Confucius,* translated by William Edward Soothill, edited by Lady Hosie, Oxford University Press, 1937, p.213.

Those who have known real grief seldom seem sad.

Benjamin Disraeli, *Endymion,* Longmans, Green, & Co. Ltd., 1880, Volume I, p.42.

See how Time makes all griefs decay.

Adelaide Anne Procter, *The Complete Works of Adelaide Anne Procter,* introduction by Charles Dickens, George Bell and Sons Ltd., 1905, p.169, "Life in Death and Death in Life."

For grief once told brings somewhat back of peace.

William Morris, *The Earthly Paradise,* Reeves and Turner, 1896, Volume I, "Prologue, The Wanderers," p.5.

To weep is to make less the depth of grief.

William Shakespeare, *King Henry VI, Part III,* Act II. sc.i. l.85.

You cannot prevent the birds of sorrow from flying over your head, but you can prevent them from building nests in your hair.

Chinese Proverb.

Grief melts away
Like snow in May,
As if there were no such cold thing.

George Herbert, *The Works of George Herbert,* edited by F.E. Hutchinson, Oxford at the Clarendon Press, 1972, p.165, "The Church, The Flower," st.i, l.5.

It is dangerous to abandon oneself to the luxury of grief; it deprives one of courage, and even the wish for recovery.

Henri Frédéric Amiel, *Amiel's Journal,* translated by Mrs. Humphry Ward, Macmillan & Co. Ltd., 1918, p.192.

No bond
In closer union knits two human hearts
Than fellowship in grief.

Robert Southey, *Joan of Arc and Minor Poems,* George Routledge and Co., 1854, p.9.

To spare oneself from grief at all cost can be achieved only at the price of total detachment, which excludes the ability to experience happiness.

Erich Fromm, *Man For Himself,* Routledge & Kegan Paul Ltd., 1975, p.190.

That Man, who is from God sent forth,
Doth yet again to God return?—
Such ebb and flow must ever be,
Then wherefore should we mourn?

William Wordsworth, *The Poetical Works of William Wordsworth,* edited by E. de Selincourt and Helen Darbishire, Oxford at the Clarendon Press, 1958, Volume IV, p.267, "Lines on the Expected Dissolution of Mr. Fox," st.vi, l.21.

Can I see another's woe,
And not be in sorrow too?
Can I see another's grief,
And not seek for kind relief?

William Blake, *The Complete Writings of William Blake*, edited by Geoffrey Keynes, Oxford University Press, 1974, p.122, *Songs of Innocence*, "On Another's Sorrow," l.1.

Oh! then indulge thy grief, nor fear to tell
The gentle source from whence thy sorrows flow!
Nor think it weakness when we love to feel,
Nor think it weakness what we feel to show.

William Cowper, *The Poetical Works of Cowper*, edited by H.S. Milford, Oxford University Press, 1950, p.278, "To Delia: On her endeavouring to conceal her grief at parting," l.17.

I can only tell you what I have felt to be the only thing which makes life endurable at a time of real sorrow—God Himself. He comes unutterably near in trouble. In fact, one scarcely knows He exists until one loves or sorrows. There is no "getting over" sorrow. I hate the idea. But there is a "getting into" sorrow, and finding right in the heart of it the dearest thing of all human beings—the Man of Sorrows, a God.

Forbes Robinson, *Letters to his Friends*, S.C.M. Press Ltd., 1938, p.68.

I would maintain the sanctity of human joy and human grief. I bow in reverence before the emotions of every melted heart. We have a human right to our sorrow. To blame the deep grief which bereavement awakens, is to censure all strong human attachments. The more intense the delight in their presence, the more poignant the impression of their absence; and you cannot destroy the anguish unless you forbid the joy. A morality which rebukes sorrow rebukes love. When the tears of bereavement
have had their natural flow, they lead us again to life and love's generous joy.

James Martineau, *Endeavours after the Christian Life: Discourses*, Longmans, Green, Reader, and Dyer, 1876, p.45.

If we will but be still and *listen*, I think we shall hear these sad trials talking to us; saying as it were, "You have known life and enjoyed it, you have tried and suffered from it; your tent has been pitched in pleasant places among those dear relations and tried friends, and now they are disappearing from around you. The stakes are loosened one by one, and the canvas is torn away, with no vestige left behind, and you want something which will *not* be taken away. You want something large enough to fill your heart, and imperishable enough to make it immortal like itself. That something
is God.

Samuel Palmer, letter from Samuel Palmer to a bereaved person, in *Visionary and Dreamer*, Lord David Cecil, Constable & Company, 1969, p.103.

Almighty God, who hast shown us in the life and teaching of Thy Son the true way of blessedness, Thou hast also shown us in His suffering and death that the path of love may lead to the Cross, and the reward of faithfulness may be a crown of thorns. Give us grace to learn these hard lessons. May we take up our cross and follow Christ, in the strength of patience and the constancy of faith; and see even in our darkest
hour of trial and anguish the shining of the eternal light.

A Prayer.

GROWING

Big oaks from little acorns grow.

Anon.

Why stay we on the earth unless to grow?

Robert Browning, *The Poetical Works of Robert Browning*, Volume I, Smith, Elder & Co., 1899, p.543, *Men and Women*, "Cleon," l.114.

All growth that is not towards God
Is growing to decay.

George Macdonald, *Within and Without*, Longman, Brown, Green, and Longmans, 1855, p.16.

A child-like man is not a man whose development has been arrested; on the contrary, he is a man who has given himself a chance of continuing to develop long after most adults have muffled themselves in the cocoon of middle-aged habit and convention.

Aldous Huxley, *Music At Night*, Chatto & Windus Ltd., 1970, p.332.

To regret one's own experience is to arrest one's own development. To deny one's own experience is to put a lie into the lips of one's own life. It is no less than a denial of the soul.

Oscar Wilde, *The Works of Oscar Wilde*, edited by G.F. Maine, William Collins Sons & Co. Ltd., 1948, *De Profundis*, p.860.

Let us not always say
"Spite of this flesh to-day
I strove, made head, gained ground upon the whole!"
As the bird wings and sings,
Let us cry "All good things
Are ours, nor soul helps flesh more, now, than flesh helps soul."

Robert Browning, *The Poetical Works of Robert Browning*, Volume I, Smith, Elder, & Co., 1899, p.581, *Dramatis Personae*, "Rabbi Ben Ezra," st.xii. l.1.

I would finally just like to advise you to grow through your development quietly and seriously; you can interrupt it in no more violent manner than by looking outwards, and expecting answer from outside to questions which perhaps only your innermost feeling in your most silent hour can answer.

Rainer Maria Rilke, *Letters to a Young Poet*, translation, introduction and commentary by Reginald Snell, Sidgwick and Jackson, 1945, p.13.

All the growth of the Christian is the more and more life he is receiving. At first his religion may hardly be distinguishable from the mere prudent desire to save his soul; but at last he loses that very soul in the glory of love, and so saves it; self becomes but the cloud on which the white light of God divides into harmonies unspeakable.

George Macdonald, *Unspoken Sermons*, Second Series, Longmans, Green, & Co. Ltd., 1885, p.173.

In this strange life we grow through adversity rather than through success. The greatest lessons we have to learn are those concerned with loss, not gain. Although worldly wisdom emphasises the importance of winning the race to success and affluence, the spiritual path teaches us how to become good and gracious losers. The man who seeks his life will lose it when he dies, but the man who is prepared to lose everything he possesses for the sake of righteousness, enters a new field of experience that is completely at variance with anything he had previously glimpsed.

Martin Israel, The Pain That Heals, Hodder and Stoughton Limited, 1981, p.9.

God does not offer Himself to our finite beings as a thing all complete and ready to be embraced. For us He is eternal discovery and eternal growth. The more we think we understand Him, the more He reveals Himself as otherwise. The more we think we hold Him, the further He withdraws, drawing us into the depths of Himself. The nearer we approach Him through all the efforts of nature and grace, the more He increases, in one and the same movement, His attraction over our powers, and the receptivity of our powers to that divine attraction.

Pierre Teilhard de Chardin, Le Milieu Divin, William Collins Sons & Co. Ltd., 1960, p.131.

Victorious living does not mean freedom from temptation. *Nor does it mean freedom from mistakes.* We are personalities in the making, limited and grappling with things too high for us. Obviously we, at our very best, will make many mistakes. But these mistakes need not be sins. Our actions are the result of our intentions and our intelligence. Our intentions may be very good, but because the intelligence is limited the action may turn out to be a mistake—a mistake, but not necessarily a sin. For sin comes out of a wrong intention.
Therefore the action carries a sense of incompleteness and frustration, but not of guilt. Victorious living does not mean perfect living in the sense of living without a flaw, but it does mean adequate living and that can be consistent with many mistakes.
Nor does it mean maturity. It does mean a cleansing away of things that keep from growth, but it is not full growth. In addition to many mistakes in our lives, there will be many immaturities. Purity is not maturity. This Gospel of ours is called the Way. Our feet are on that Way, but only on that Way, we have not arrived at the goal.
Nor does it mean that we may not occasionally lapse into a wrong act, which may be called a sin. At that point we may have lost a skirmish, but it doesn't mean we may not still win the battle. We may even lose a battle and still win the war. One of the differences between a sheep and a swine is that when a sheep falls into a mud hole it bleats to get out, while the swine loves it and wallows in it. In saying that an occasional lapse is consistent with victorious living I am possibly opening the door to provide for such lapses. This is dangerous and weakening. There must be no such provision in the mind. There must be an absoluteness about the whole thing. But nevertheless, victorious living can be consistent with occasional failure.

E. Stanley Jones, Victorious Living, Hodder & Stoughton Limited, 1941, p.78.

GUIDANCE

I will put my law within them, and I will write it upon their hearts; and I will be their God, and they shall be my people.

Jeremiah 31.33.

Your ears shall hear a word behind you, saying, "This is the way, walk in it," when you turn to the right or when you turn to the left.

Isaiah 30.21.

If you love me, you will keep my commandments. And I will pray the Father, and he will give you another Counsellor, to be with you for ever, even the Spirit of truth, whom the world cannot receive, because it neither sees him nor knows him; you know him, for he dwells with you, and will be in you.

John 14.15-17.

But the Counsellor, the Holy Spirit, whom the Father will send in my name, he will teach you all things, and bring to your remembrance all that I have said to you.

John 14.26.

When they deliver you up, do not be anxious how you are to speak or what you are to say; for what you are to say will be given to you in that hour; for it is not you who speak, but the Spirit of your Father speaking through you.

Matthew 10.19-20.

For a time will come when your innermost voice will speak to you, saying: "This is *my* path; here I shall find peace. I will pursue this path, come what may."

Grace Cooke, *Spiritual Unfoldment*, The White Eagle Publishing Trust, 1961, p.13.

I give you the end of a golden string:
Only wind it into a ball,
It will lead you in at Heaven's Gate
Built in Jerusalem's wall.

William Blake, *The Complete Writings of William Blake*, edited by Geoffrey Keynes, Oxford University Press, 1974, p.551, Epigrams, Verses, and Fragments from the Note-Book, Written about 1808-1811, No.66.

Jesus promised that his Spirit would guide his disciples into all truth, both truth of mind and direction of life. There can be no hesitation in the choice between what is good and what is evil, what is loving and what is selfish, what is true and what is false. Sometimes, however, the choice is between two goods or between two paths neither of which is completely good. How do we seek the Spirit's guidance?

George Appleton, *Journey for a Soul*, William Collins Sons & Co. Ltd., 1976, p.207.

Conditions for being shown God's will:
Readiness to accept and do God's will without any conditions or reservations.
Reference to God of all the problems, attitudes, opportunities and decisions of our lives.

Readiness to receive insights from others but not let them decide for us.
Examination of any intuitions to discover any ulterior motives or reluctance.
Patient waiting upon God until a persistent feeling of oughtness comes.
Quiet putting into practice of the guidance received without dithering or looking back.

George Appleton, *Journey for a Soul*, William Collins Sons & Co. Ltd., 1976, p.207.

Let us, then, labour for an inward stillness,—
An inward stillness and an inward healing;
That perfect silence where the lips and heart
Are still, and we no longer entertain
Our own imperfect thoughts and vain opinions,
But God alone speaks in us, and we wait
In singleness of heart, that we may know
His will, and in the silence of our spirits,
That we may do His will, and do that only!

Henry Wadsworth Longfellow, *The Poetical Works of Longfellow*, Humphrey Milford, Oxford University Press, 1913, p.571, *John Endicott*, Act I. sc.iii.

H

HAPPINESS

Happiness is neither without us nor within us. It is in God, both without us and within us.

Blaise Pascal, *Pensées,* translated by W.F. Trotter, Random House Inc., 1941, p.154.

Look inwards, for you have a lasting fountain of happiness at home that will always bubble up if you will but dig for it.

Marcus Aurelius, *The Meditations of Marcus Aurelius,* translated by Jeremy Collier, with an introduction and notes by Alice Zimmern, Walter Scott, p.116.

The happy people are those who are producing something; the bored people are those who are consuming much and producing nothing.

W.R. Inge, in *The Wit and Wisdom of Dean Inge,* compiled by Sir James Marchant, Longmans, Green & Co. Ltd., 1927, p.55.

In every part and corner of our life, to lose oneself is to be gainer; to forget oneself is to be happy.

Robert Louis Stevenson, *Memories & Portraits,* Chatto & Windus Ltd., 1887, p.48.

A happy life must be to a great extent a quiet life, for it is only in an atmosphere of quiet that true joy can live.

Bertrand Russell, *The Conquest of Happiness,* George Allen & Unwin Ltd., 1984, p.52.

Happiness is more than anything that serene, secure, happy freedom from guilt.

Henrik Ibsen, *Rosmersholm,* translated and edited by James Walter McFarlane, Oxford University Press, 1960, Volume VI, p.349, Act III.

Wherein lies happiness? In that which becks
Our ready minds to fellowship divine,
A fellowship with essence.

John Keats, *The Poems of John Keats,* edited with an introduction and notes by E. de Selincourt, Methuen & Co. Ltd., 1907, p.70, "Endymion," Bk.I. l.777.

I have come to know happy individuals, by the way, who are happy only because they are whole. Even the lowliest, provided he is whole, can be happy and in his own way perfect.

Johann Wolfgang von Goethe, *Wisdom and Experience,* selections by Ludwig Curtius, translated and edited, with an introduction by Hermann J. Weigand, Routledge & Kegan Paul Ltd., 1949, p.213.

A happiness that is sought for ourselves alone can never be found: for a happiness that is diminished by being shared is not big enough to make us happy.

Thomas Merton, *No Man is an Island,* Burns & Oates Ltd., 1974, p.1.

Happy the Man, and happy he alone,
He, who can call to day his own:
He, who secure within, can say
Tomorrow do thy worst, for I have liv'd to day.

John Dryden, *The Poems of John Dryden,* edited by James Kinsley, Oxford at the Clarendon Press, 1958, Volume
I, p.436, *Horace,* Ode 29, Bk.3. st.viii. 1.65.

If we were to ask the question: "What is human life's chief concern?" one of the
answers we should receive would be: "It is happiness." How to gain, how to keep,
how to recover happiness, is in fact for most men at all times the secret motive of all
they do, and of all they are willing to endure.

William James, *The Varieties of Religious Experience,* William Collins Sons & Co. Ltd., 1974, p.92.

Is not making others happy the best happiness? To illuminate for an instant the depths
of a deep soul ... is to me a blessing and a precious privilege. There is a sort of religious
joy in helping to renew the strength and courage of noble minds. We are surprised
to find ourselves the possessors of a power of which we are not worthy, and we long
to exercise it purely and seriously.

Henri Frédéric Amiel, *Amiel's Journal,* translated by Mrs. Humphry Ward, Macmillan & Co. Ltd., 1918, p.239.

True happiness is of a retired nature, and an enemy to pomp and noise: it arises, in
the first place, from the enjoyment of one's self; and in the next, from the friendship
and conversation of a few select companions.

Joseph Addison, *The Works of Joseph Addison,* notes by Richard Hurd, edited and published by Henry G. Bohn,
1856, Volume II, p.264.

Happiness is nothing else, as we usually describe it to ourselves, but the enjoyment
of some chief good: and therefore the Deity is so boundlessly happy, because it is
every way one with its own immense perfection; and every thing so much the more
feelingly lives upon happiness, by how much the more it comes to partake of God,
and to be made like Him.... And, as it is impossible to enjoy happiness without a
fruition of God; so it is impossible to enjoy Him without an assimilation and conformity
of our natures to Him in a way of true goodness and godlike perfection.

John Smith the Platonist, *Select Discourses,* Cambridge at the University Press, 1859, p.150.

A sentence that I harped on years ago, and one that used to comfort me—so well—
was this, "What I do thou knowest not now, but thou shalt know hereafter." That
saying has always been a perfect treasure to me; I have never been able to get along
without it.
A happy life is not built up of tours abroad and pleasant holidays, but of little clumps
of violets noticed by the roadside, hidden away almost so that only those can see them
who have God's peace and love in their hearts; in one long continuous chain of little
joys; little whispers from the spiritual world; little gleams of sunshine on our daily
work.... So long as I have stuck to Nature and the New Testament I have only got
happier and happier every day.

Edward Wilson, in *Edward Wilson of the Antarctic,* George Seaver, John Murray Ltd., 1935, p.71.

At its highest level ... happiness is the ecstasy which mystics have inadequately described. At more humdrum levels it is human love; the delights and beauties of our dear earth, its colours and shapes and sounds; the enchantment of understanding and laughing, and all other exercise of such faculties as we possess; the marvel of the meaning of everything, fitfully glimpsed, inadequately expounded, but ever-present.

Such is happiness: not compressible into a pill; not translatable into a sensation; lost to whoever would grasp it to himself alone; not to be gorged out of a trough, or torn out of another's body, or paid into a bank, or driven along on an autoroute, or fired in gun-salutes, or discovered in the stratosphere. Existing, intangible, in every true response to life, and absent in every false one; propounded through the centuries in every noteworthy word and thought and deed; expressed in art and literature and music; in vast cathedrals and tiny melodies; in everything that is harmonious, and in the unending heroism of imperfect men reaching after perfection.

Malcolm Muggeridge, *Muggeridge Through The Microphone*, edited by Christopher Ralling, British Broadcasting Corporation, 1967, p.64.

There are various ways of being happy, and every man has the capacity to make his life what it needs to be for him to have a reasonable amount of peace in it. Why then do we persecute ourselves with illusory demands, never content until we feel we have conformed to some standard of happiness that is not good for us only, but for *everyone?* Why can we not be content with the secret gift of happiness that God offers us, without consulting the rest of the world? Why do we insist, rather, on a happiness that is approved by the magazines and TV? Perhaps because we do not believe in a happiness that is given to us for nothing. We do not think we can be happy with a happiness that has no price tag on it.

If we are fools enough to remain at the mercy of the people who want to sell us happiness, it will be impossible for us ever to be content with anything. How would they profit if we became content? We would no longer need their new product.

The last thing the salesman wants is for the buyer to become content. You are of no use in our affluent society unless you are always just about to grasp what you never have.

Thomas Merton, *Conjectures of a Guilty Bystander*, Burns & Oates Ltd., 1968, p.84.

Fundamental happiness depends more than anything else upon what may be called a friendly interest in persons and things.

A friendly interest in persons is a form of affectionateness, but not the form which is grasping and possessive and seeking always an emphatic response. This latter form is very frequently a source of unhappiness. The kind that makes for happiness is the kind that likes to observe people and finds pleasure in their individual traits, that wishes to afford scope for the interests and pleasures of those with whom it is brought into contact without desiring to acquire power over them or to secure their enthusiastic admiration. The person whose attitude towards others is genuinely of this kind will be a source of happiness and a recipient of reciprocal kindness. His relations with others, whether slight or serious, will satisfy both his interests and his affections; he will not be soured by ingratitude, since he will seldom suffer it and will not notice it when he does. The same idiosyncrasies which would get on another man's nerves to the point of exasperation will be to him a source of gentle amusement. He will achieve without effort results which another man, after long struggles, will find to be unattainable. Being happy in himself, he will be a pleasant companion, and this in turn will increase his happiness. But all this must be genuine; it must not spring from an idea of self-sacrifice inspired by a sense of duty. A sense of duty is useful in work, but offensive in personal relations. People wish to be liked, not to be endured with patient resignation. To like many people spontaneously and without effort is perhaps the greatest of all sources of personal happiness.

I spoke also of what I call a friendly interest in things. This phrase may perhaps seem forced; it may be said that it is impossible to feel friendly to things. Nevertheless, there is something analagous to friendliness in the kind of interest that a geologist takes in rocks, or an archeologist in ruins, and this interest ought to be an element in our attitude to individuals or societies. It is possible to have an interest in things which is hostile rather than friendly. A man might collect facts concerning the habitats of spiders because he hated spiders and wished to live where they were few. This kind of interest would not afford the same satisfaction as the geologist derives from his rocks. An interest in impersonal things, though perhaps less valuable as an ingredient in everyday happiness than a friendly attitude towards our fellow creatures, is nevertheless very important. The world is vast and our powers are limited. If all our happiness is bound up entirely in our personal circumstances it is difficult not to demand of life more than it has to give. And to demand too much is the surest way of getting even less than is possible. The man who can forget his worries by means of a genuine interest in, say, the Council of Trent, or the life history of stars, will find that, when he returns from his excursion into the impersonal world, he has acquired a poise and calm which enable him to deal with his worries in the best way, and he will in the meantime have experienced a genuine even if temporary happiness.

The secret of happiness is this: let your interests be as wide as possible, and let your reactions to the things and persons that interest you be as far as possible friendly rather than hostile.

Bertrand Russell, *The Conquest of Happiness*, George Allen & Unwin, Unwin Paperbacks, 1978, p.120.

HEART

Walk in the ways of your heart.
Ecclesiastes 11.9.

Keep your heart with all vigilance; for from it flow the springs of life.
Proverbs 4.23.

Create in me a clean heart, O God, and put a new and right spirit within me.
Psalm 51.10.

Out of the abundance of the heart the mouth speaks.
Matthew 12.34.

But in your hearts reverence Christ as Lord.
1 Peter 3.15.

The "heart" in the biblical sense is not the inner life, but the whole man in relation to God.
Dietrich Bonhoeffer, *Letters and Papers from Prison,* edited by Eberhard Bethge, S.C.M. Press Ltd., 1967, Second Revised Edition, p.192.

Man *becomes* man only by the intelligence, but he *is* man by the heart.
Henri Frédéric Amiel, *Amiel's Journal,* translated by Mrs. Humphry Ward, Macmillan & Co. Ltd., 1918, p.12.

It is the heart which experiences God, and not the reason.
Blaise Pascal, *Pensées,* translated by W.F. Trotter, Random House Inc., 1941, p.95.

Go to your bosom,
Knock there, and ask your heart what it doth know.
William Shakespeare, *Measure For Measure,* Act II. sc.ii. l.136.

Better to have the poet's heart than brain,
To feel than write.
George Macdonald, *Within and Without,* Longman, Brown, Green, and Longmans, 1855, p.93.

His heart was as great as the world, but there was no room in it to hold the memory of a wrong.
Ralph Waldo Emerson, *The Works of Ralph Waldo Emerson,* edited by George Sampson, George Bell & Sons Ltd., 1906, Volume III, *Society and Solitude: Letters and Social Aims: Addresses,* p.350.

Ye whose hearts are fresh and simple,
Who have faith in God and Nature.
Henry Wadsworth Longfellow, *The Poetical Works of Longfellow,* Humphrey Milford, Oxford University Press, 1913, p.203, *Hiawatha,* "Introduction," l.88.

The logic of the heart is usually better than the logic of the head, and the consistency of sympathy is superior as a rule for life to the consistency of the intellect.
Randolph Bourne, *Youth and Life,* Constable & Co. Ltd., 1913, p.244.

And about feelings: all feelings are pure which gather you and lift you up; a feeling is impure which takes hold of only one side of your being and so distorts you.
Rainer Maria Rilke, *Letters to a Young Poet,* translation, introduction and commentary by Reginald Snell, Sidgwick and Jackson, 1945, p.41.

True conviction springs from the heart. As the real seat of conscience, it is a far more reliable judge than the understanding of what is permissible and what is not. The latter, for all its subtlety and discernment, is likely to miss the central point.
Johann Wolfgang von Goethe, *Wisdom and Experience,* selections by Ludwig Curtius, translated and edited, with an introduction by Hermann J. Weigand, Routledge & Kegan Paul Ltd., 1949, p.133.

Do not cry out to God.
Your own heart is the source

---

from which He flows unceasingly
unless you stop its course.

Angelus Silesius, *The Book of Angelus Silesius*, translated, drawn, and handwritten by Frederick Franck, Wildwood House Ltd., 1976, p.120.

The heart has its reasons, which reason does not know. We feel it in a thousand things. I say that the heart naturally loves the Universal Being, and also itself naturally, according as it gives itself to them; and it hardens itself against one or the other at its will. You have rejected the one, and kept the other. Is it by reason that you love yourself?

Blaise Pascal, *Pensées*, translated by W.F. Trotter, Random House Inc., 1941, p.95.

Yet if, putting aside for the moment all conventions and custom, one will look quietly within himself, he will perceive that there are most distinct and inviolable inner forces, binding him by different ties to different people, and with different and inevitable results according to the quality and the nature of the affection bestowed—that there is in fact in that world of the heart a kind of cosmical harmony and variety, and an order almost astronomical.

Edward Carpenter, *Love's Coming-of-Age*, George Allen & Unwin Ltd., 1923, p.176.

It is a fine thing to establish one's own religion in one's heart, not to be dependent on tradition and second hand ideals. Life will seem to you, later, not a lesser, but a greater thing. This which is a great torment now, will be a noble thing to you later on.

D.H. Lawrence, *The Letters of D.H. Lawrence*, edited by James T. Boulton, Cambridge University Press, 1979, Volume I, p.256.

The heart is to be understood here, not in its ordinary meaning, but in the sense of the "inner man." We have within us an inner man, according to the Apostle Paul, or a hidden man of the heart, according to the Apostle Peter. It is the God-like spirit that was breathed into the first man, and it remains with us continuously, even after the Fall. It shows itself in the fear of God, which is founded on the certainty of God's existence, and in the awareness of our complete dependence on Him, in the stirrings of conscience and in our lack of contentment with all that is material.

Theophan the Recluse, in *The Art of Prayer, An Orthodox Anthology*, compiled by Igumen Chariton of Valamo, translated by E. Kadloubovsky and E.M. Palmer, edited with an introduction by Timothy Ware, Faber and Faber Limited, 1973, p.191.

We are what we see; we create what we see; our rank in the scale of being is determined by the objects of our interest and love. There is absolutely no other way of rising in the scale of being, of realizing our true destiny, of filling our allotted place in the chain of spiritual life, than by ascending in heart and mind to the spiritual world, having our conversation there, setting our affections on things above....
We can transcend the limitations of our finite existence; we can live the life of the hidden man of the heart. Such a life is not foreign to the nature of the soul. The way

to it is by love and yearning, which are natural to the soul when she sees glimpses of her father's house, and the home from which she has been exiled.

W. R. Inge, *The Awakening of the Soul*, edited by Prebendary A.F. Judd, A.R. Mowbray & Co. Ltd., 1959, pp.30,26.

HEAVEN

Heaven means to be one with God.

Frederick W. Farrar, *Eternal Hope*, Macmillan & Co. Ltd., 1892, p.25.

Heaven is nothing but Grace perfected, 'tis of the same nature of that you enjoy here when you are united by faith to Christ.

Rufus M. Jones, *Spiritual Reformers in the 16th and 17th Centuries*, Macmillan & Co. Ltd., 1914, p.252.

How good is the presence of God! Right in the depths, in the heaven of my soul, I find him, for he never abandons me. God in me and I in him—that is my whole life.

Elizabeth of Dijon, in *Elizabeth of Dijon*, Hans Urs von Balthasar, translated and adapted by A.V. Littledale, The Harvill Press Ltd., 1956, p.76.

The Second Person of the Blessed Trinity was no less *in heaven* during the period of the earthly ministry than either before or after it. What we see as we watch the life of Jesus is the very life of heaven—indeed of God—in human expression.

William Temple, *Readings in St. John's Gospel* (First and Second Series), Macmillan & Co. Ltd., 1947, p.47.

Heaven is the goal of man, and heaven gives the true perspective for our present life. Our belief in the goal of heaven goes with our belief in the infinite and eternal worth of every man, woman, and child created in God's own image, and reminds us that we are called to nothing less than the Christ-like perfection of the saints.
In the Communion of Saints, which is the family of Jesus, the Lord of the dead and the living, we are one with the saints in every age, and in that oneness with them we hold fast to the truth which belongs to no one age because it is timeless. In the Communion of Saints we are freed from the dominance of the contemporary, as well as of the past. We shall know "the glorious liberty of the children of God."

Michael Ramsey, *Through The Year With Michael Ramsey*, edited by Margaret Duggan, Hodder & Stoughton Ltd., 1975, p.253.

The final state of the Christian mystic, then, is not annihilation in the Absolute. It is a condition wherein we dwell wholly in God, one life and truth with Him; yet still "feel God *and* ourselves," as the lover feels his beloved, in a perfect union which depends for its joy on an invincible otherness. The soul, transfused and transfigured by the Divine Love as molten iron is by the fire, becomes, it is true, "one simple blessedness with God" yet ever retains its individuality: one with God beyond itself, yet other than God within itself. The "deified man" is fully human still, but spiritualised through and through; not by the destruction of his personality, but by the taking up of his manhood into God. There he finds, not a static beatitude, but a Height, a Depth, a Breadth of which he is made part, yet to which he can never attain: for the creature, even at its highest, remains finite, and is conscious that Infinity perpetually eludes its grasp and leads it on. So heaven itself is discovered to be no mere passive fulfillment, but rather a forward-moving life: an ever new loving and tasting, new exploring and enjoying of the Infinite Fulness of God that inexhaustible Object of our knowledge and delight. It is the eternal voyage of the adventurous soul on the vast and stormy sea of the Divine.

Evelyn Underhill, in *The Adornment of the Spiritual Marriage,* John of Ruysbroeck, translated by C.A. Wynschenk Dom. edited with an introduction and notes by Evelyn Underhill, John M. Watkins, 1951, p.xxxi.

I wish there be not, among some, such a light and poor esteem of heaven, as makes them more to seek after assurance of heaven only in the idea of it as a thing to come, than after heaven itself; which, indeed, we can never well be assured of, until we find it rising up within ourselves, and glorifying our own souls. When true assurance comes, heaven itself will appear upon the horizon of our souls, like a morning light, chasing away all our dark and gloom doubtings before it. We shall not need then to light up our candles to seek for it in corners; no: it will display its own lustre and brightness so before us, that we may see it in its own light, and ourselves the true possessors of it. We may be too nice and vain in seeking for signs and tokens of Christ's spiritual appearances in the souls of men, as well as the Scribes and Pharisees were in seeking for them at His first appearance in the world. When He comes into us, let us expect till the works that He shall do within us testify of Him; and be not over credulous, till we find that He doth those works there which none other could do. As for a true, well-grounded, assurance, say not so much, "Who shall ascend up into heaven," to fetch it down from thence? or, "who shall descend into the deep," to fetch it up from beneath? for in the growth of true, internal, goodness, and in the progress of true religion it will freely unfold itself within us. Stay till the grain of mustard-seed itself breaks forth from among the clods that buried it; till, through the descent of the heavenly dew, it sprouts up, and discovers itself openly. This holy assurance is, indeed, the budding and blossoming of felicity in our own souls; it is the inward sense and feeling of the true life, spirit, sweetness, and beauty of grace, powerfully expressing its own energy within us.

John Smith the Platonist, *Select Discourses,* Cambridge at the University Press, 1859, p.449.

HELL

Hell is not to love any more, Madame.

George Bernanos, *The Diary of a Country Priest,* translated by Pamela Morris, Boriswood Limited, 1937, p.177.

The heart of man is the place the devill dwels in; I feel sometimes a hell within my selfe.

Sir Thomas Browne, *The Works of Sir Thomas Browne,* edited by Geoffrey Keynes, Faber and Faber Limited, 1964, Volume One, *Religio Medici,* p.62.

The hell to be endured hereafter, of which theology tells, is no worse than the hell we make for ourselves in this world by habitually fashioning our characters in the wrong way.

William James, *The Principles of Psychology*, Macmillan & Co. Ltd., 1890, Volume II, p.127.

What is hell? Hell is oneself,
Hell is alone, the other figures in it
Merely projections. There is nothing to escape from
And nothing to escape to. One is always alone.

T.S. Eliot, *The Complete Poems and Plays of T.S. Eliot*, Faber and Faber Limited, 1975, *The Cocktail Party*, Act I. sc.iii. p.397.

On that hard Pagan world disgust
And secret loathing fell.
Deep weariness and sated lust
Made human life a hell.

Matthew Arnold, *The Poems of Matthew Arnold*, edited by Kenneth Allott, Longmans, Green & Co. Ltd., 1965, p.523, "Obermann Once More," l.93.

They (men) are not in hell because Father, Son and Holy Ghost are angry at them, and so cast them into punishment which their wrath had contrived for them; but they are in wrath and darkness because they have done to the light which infinitely flows forth from God as that man does to the light of the sun who puts out his own eyes.

William Law, *Selected Mystical Writings of William Law*, edited by Stephen Hobhouse, Rockliff, 1948, p.49.

It hath been said, that there is of nothing so much in hell as of self-will. The which is true, for there is nothing else there than self-will, and if there were no self-will, there would be no Devil and no hell. When it is said that Lucifer fell from Heaven, and turned away from God and the like, it meaneth nothing else than that he would have his own will, and would not be at one with the Eternal Will. So was it likewise with Adam in Paradise. And when we say Self-will, we mean, to will otherwise than as the One and Eternal Will of God willeth.

Theologia Germanica, translated by Susanna Winkworth, Stuart & Watkins Ltd., 1966, p.118.

See here the whole truth in short. All sin, death, damnation, and hell is nothing else but this kingdom of self, or the various operations of self-love, self-esteem, and self-seeking which separate the soul from God and end in eternal death and hell.

William Law, *Selected Mystical Writings* of William Law, edited by Stephen Hobhouse, Rockliff, 1948, p.92.

All misery arises out of *ourselves*. It is a most gross mistake, and men are of dull and stupid spirits who think that the state which we call Hell is an incommodious place only; and that God by His sovereignty throws men therein. Hell arises out of a man's self. And Hell's fuel is the guilt of a man's conscience. It is possible that any should be so miserable as Hell makes a man and as there a man is miserable by his own condemning of himself.

Rufus M. Jones, *Spiritual Reformers in the 16th and 17th Centuries*, Macmillan & Co. Ltd., 1914, p.302.

The one principle of hell is—"*I* am my own. *I* am my own king and my own subject. *I* am the centre from which go out my thoughts; *I* am the object and end of my thoughts; back upon *me* as the alpha and omega of life, my thoughts return. My own glory is, and ought to be, my chief care; my ambition, to gather the regards of men to the one centre, myself. My pleasure is *my* pleasure. My kingdom is—as many as I can bring to acknowledge my greatness over them. My judgement is the faultless rule of things. My right is—what I desire. The more I am all in all to myself, the greater I am. The less I acknowledge debt or obligation to another; the more I close my eyes to the fact that I did not make myself; the more self-sufficiency I feel or imagine myself—the greater I am. I will be free with the freedom that consists in doing whatever I am inclined to do, from whatever quarter may come the inclination. To do my own will so long as I feel anything to be my will, is to be free, is to live." To all these principles of hell, or of this world—they are the same thing, and it matters nothing whether they are asserted or defended so long as they are acted upon—the Lord, the king, gives the direct lie.

George Macdonald, *Unspoken Sermons,* Third Series, Longmans, Green, and Co. 1889, p.102.

HOLINESS

Worship the Lord in the beauty of holiness.
1 Chronicles 16.29 (A.V.).

There is no true Holiness, without Humility.
Thomas Fuller, M.D., *Gnomologia,* 1732, Dublin, p.214, No. 4924.

There is nothing holier, in this life of ours, than the first consciousness of love,—the first fluttering of its silken wings.
Henry Wadsworth Longfellow, *Hyperion,* George Routledge and Sons, 1887, p.215.

A true love to God must begin with a delight in his holiness, and not with a delight in any other attribute: for no other attribute is truly lovely without this.
Jonathan Edwards, *A Treatise Concerning Religious Affections,* Chalmers and Collins, 1825, p.323.

Think of a white cloud as being holy, you cannot love it; but think of a holy man within the cloud, love springs up in your thoughts, for to think of holiness distinct from man is impossible to the affections.
William Blake, *The Complete Writings of William Blake,* edited by Geoffrey Keynes, Oxford University Press, 1974, p.90, "Annotations to Swedenborg's Divine Love," p.12.

The measure of your holiness is proportionate to the goodness of your will. Consider then how good your will is, and the degree of your holiness will be clear to you. For every one is as holy, as he is good of heart.
John of Ruysbroeck, *The Seven Steps of the Ladder of Spiritual Love,* translated by F. Sherwood Taylor, Dacre Press, 1942, p.15.

He that sees the beauty of holiness, or true moral good, sees the greatest and most important thing in the world, which is the fulness of all things, without which all the world is empty.... Unless this is seen, nothing is seen that is worth the seeing; for there is no other true excellency or beauty.

Jonathan Edwards, *A Treatise concerning Religious Affections,* Chalmers and Collins, 1825, p.349.

Our progress in holiness depends on God and ourselves—on God's grace and on our will to be holy. We must have a real living determination to reach holiness. "I will be a saint" means I will despoil myself of all that is not God; I will strip my heart of all created things; I will live in poverty and detachment; I will renounce my will, my inclinations, my whims and fancies, and make myself a willing slave to the will of God.

Mother Teresa of Calcutta, in *Something Beautiful For God,* Malcolm Muggeridge, William Collins Sons & Co. Ltd., 1983, p.66.

The primary characteristic of the Church is neither its missionary enterprise which is the essence of Apostolicity, nor its universal scope which is its Catholicity, but the fact that it is constituted by the redeeming act of God in Christ and is sustained by the indwelling divine Spirit, or in short its Holiness. And the first way in which it is called to be itself is neither through missionary extension nor through influence upon national life but through inward sanctification.

William Temple, *Citizen and Churchman,* Eyre and Spottiswoode, Ltd., 1941, p.98.

All human love is a holy thing, the holiest thing in our experience. It is the chief mode of initiation into the mysteries of the divine life, the most direct point of contact with the nature of our Creator. "He prayeth best who loveth best." Pure affection "abides" in a sense in which nothing else abides. It is rooted in the eternal, and cannot be destroyed by any of the changes and chances of mortal life. It is a relation between immortal spirits, which in the eternal world are united together solely by likeness of nature; so that death not only makes no break in the ties of pure affection, but liberates it from adventitious obstacles which at present only impede its free action and dull its radiance. When we know even as we are known, we shall know our friends and be known by them, to a degree which we cannot even imagine now.

W.R. Inge, *Speculum Animae,* Longmans, Green & Co. Ltd., 1911, p.50.

HOLY SPIRIT

I will put my Spirit within you, and you shall live.

Ezekiel 37.14.

And the Spirit of the Lord shall rest upon him, the spirit of wisdom and understanding, the spirit of counsel and might, the spirit of knowledge and the fear of the Lord.

Isaiah 11.2.

And when he had said this, he breathed on them, and said to them, "Receive the Holy Spirit."

John 20.22.

There appeared to them tongues as of fire, distributed and resting on each one of them. And they were all filled with the Holy Spirit and began to speak in other tongues, as the Spirit gave them utterance.

Acts 2.3-4.

Now we have received not the spirit of the world, but the Spirit which is from God, that we might understand the gifts bestowed on us by God.

1 Corinthians 2.12.

Do you not know that you are God's temple and that God's Spirit dwells in you?

1 Corinthians 3.16.

The fruit of the Spirit is love, joy, peace, patience, kindness, goodness, faithfulness, gentleness, self-control; against such there is no law.

Galatians 5.22-23.

Spiritual experience is the supreme reality in man's life: in it the divine is not proven, it is simply shown.

Nicolas Berdyaev, *Christian Existentialism,* selected and translated by Donald A. Lowrie, George Allen & Unwin Ltd., 1965, p.39.

Holy Spirit ... was hardly recognised as distinct from the Word until the Word was uttered in a new fullness of expression, as Christians believe, in the historical Person, Jesus of Nazareth. That fuller objective self-manifestation of the divine called forth a new potency of responsive aspiration to which, as an experienced fact, was given the name Holy Spirit.

William Temple, *Nature, Man and God,* Macmillan & Co. Ltd., 1934, p.446.

From the beginning, the Spirit of God has been understood as God in the midst of men, God present and active in the world, God in his closeness to us as a dynamic reality shaping the lives and histories of men. The Spirit, in this sense, is not something other than God, but God in that manner of the divine Being in which he comes closest, dwells with us, acts upon us.

John Macquarrie, *Paths in Spirituality, S.C.M. Press Ltd.,* 1972, p.42.

He does not take the place of an absent Christ, or work in His stead; His mission is to bring Christ, to ensure His Presence. Before Christ had been *with* them; now, through the agency of the Holy Ghost, He is to be *in* them; His Presence and action is central, not on the circumference as before. The descent of the Holy Ghost at Pentecost was a change in the manner of His working, a change which may be described as both an extension and an intensification.

Frank H. Hallock, *The Gifts of the Holy Ghost,* S.P.C.K., 1936, p.7.

My own attempt to understand the Holy Spirit has convinced me He is active in precisely those experiences that are very common—experiences of recognition, sudden insight, an influx of awareness when you wake up and become alive to something. It may be another person, or a scientific problem, and suddenly the penny drops. Every time a human being cries "Ah! I see it now!", that's what I mean by the Holy Spirit.

John V. Taylor, in *Priestland's Progress*, Gerald Priestland, British Broadcasting Corporation, 1982, p.108.

I think the point of the Holy Spirit is this: a divine something in them, enabling their response to the divine above and about them. Now it is so today: if I believe in God and Jesus and want to respond to them—there is a divine something enabling me to do so.
To put it as simply as possible: where is God? God is above us and around us and everywhere, the world's creator. Where is God? God is particularly revealed in Jesus, the very image of God. Where is God? God is within me, enabling me to respond to God above me and around me. Why a person? Because God is always personal, not impersonal, so I find myself saying not that there's an *It* within me—but just as there is a *He* to whom I am responding, so there is a He within me enabling me to make that response.

Michael Ramsey, in *Priestland's Progress*, Gerald Priestland, British Broadcasting Corporation, 1982, p.111.

The mysteries of life, of love, of truth, run like a deep stream within our own natures, and beneath all the outward surface appearances which we see. It is a deep stream from which comes life and, as we open ourselves to its reality, we sense the mystery of our own being, and know ourselves to be part of a mysterious immensity, a tiny but great part of it.
In this awareness of mysterious reality, of ourselves, and of the world, we touch the fringes of the garment of Holy Being which we call God, the source and life of all that is. It is the Spirit of God to whom countless men and women have borne witness by their writings, but above all by their lives, and it is the origin and life force of our lives....
So the life of the Spirit is seen to be OUR LIFE LIVED IN ACCORD WITH THE SPIRIT OF GOD WHICH IS OUR TRUE END AND HAPPINESS.

Herbert Waddams, *The Life of the Spirit*, The Faith Press Ltd., 1969, p.18,21.

The outpouring of His Holy Spirit is really the outpouring of His love, surrounding and penetrating your little soul with a peaceful, joyful delight in His creature: tolerant, peaceful, a love full of long-suffering and gentleness, working quietly, able to wait for results, faithful, devoted, without variableness or shadow of turning. Such is the charity of God....
Love breaks down the barrier that shuts most of us from Heaven. That thought is too much for us really.... Yet it is the central truth of the spiritual life. And that loving, self-yielding to the Eternal Love—that willingness that God shall possess, indwell, fertilize, bring forth fruit of *His* Spirit in us instead of fruits of our spirit—is the secret of all Christian power and Christian peace.

Evelyn Underhill, *The Fruits of the Spirit*, Longmans, Green and Co. Ltd., 1949, p.3.

It was something more than a glorified Christ in the heavens in which they (the Apostles) believed. At the beginning John the Baptist had taught his disciples to expect from the Christ the baptism, not of water only as in his baptism, but of the Spirit. Before His death Jesus had sought to fill His disciples' minds with the expectation of this gift as the chief object of His coming. And that Spirit had come in sensible power upon them some ten days after Jesus had disappeared for the last time from their eyes, and after that first outpouring on the original group of brethren, He had come successively to all who had received baptism, normally through the laying-on of the hands of the apostles so that the reception could be looked back to as an event at a particular moment of their experience. And this Spirit was the Spirit of God, but also and therefore the Spirit of Jesus. Jesus was not to them merely a past example, or a remote Lord, but an inward presence and power. A mere example in past history becomes in experience a feebler and feebler power, all the more if the example is that of a genius, of a more than ordinary man. But the example of Jesus was something much more than a memory. For He who had taught them in the past how to live was alive in the heavenly places, and was working within them by His Spirit, moulding them inwardly in conformity with the pattern He had shown them outwardly.

Charles Gore, *The Philosophy of the Good Life,* John Murray Ltd., 1930, p.195.

When we pray "Come, Holy Ghost, our souls inspire," we had better know what we are about. He will not carry us to easy triumphs and gratifying successes; more probably He will set us to some task for God in the full intention that we shall fail, so that others, learning wisdom by our failure, may carry the good cause forward. He may take us through loneliness, desertion by friends, apparent desertion even by God; that was the way Christ went to the Father. He may drive us into the wilderness to be tempted of the devil. He may lead us from the mount of Transfiguration (if He ever lets us climb it) to the hill that is called the Place of a Skull. For if we invoke Him, it must be to help us in doing God's will, not ours. We cannot call upon the

"Creator Spirit, by whose aid
The world's Foundations first were laid"

in order to use omnipotence for the supply of our futile pleasures or the success of our futile plans. If we invoke Him, we must be ready for the glorious pain of being caught by His power out of our petty orbit into the eternal purposes of the Almighty, in whose onward sweep our lives are as a speck of dust. The soul that is filled with the Spirit must have become purged of all pride or love of ease, all self-complacence and self-reliance; but that soul has found the only real dignity, the only lasting joy. Come then, Great Spirit, come. Convict the world; and convict my timid soul.

William Temple, *Readings in St. John's Gospel* (First and Second Series), Macmillan & Co.Ltd., 1947, p.288.

The religion of the Spirit, that autonomous faith which rests upon experience and individual inspiration, has seldom had much of a chance in the world since the Christian revelation, in which it received its full and final credentials. We may call it the Platonic tradition, since the school of Plato ended by being completely dominant in the last age of classical antiquity. We may venture to call it the true heir of the original Gospel, while admitting that no direct Hellenic influence can be traced in our Lord's teaching. We may confidently call it Pauline and Johannine Christianity, though the theology of St. Paul is woven of many strands. We find it explicitly formulated by Clement and Origen, and we may appeal to one side of that strangely divided genius, Augustine. It lives on in the mystics, especially in the German mediaeval school, of which Eckhart is the greatest name. We find it again, with a new and exuberant life, in many of the Renaissance writers, so much so that our subject might as well be called the Renaissance tradition. Our own Renaissance poetry is steeped in Platonic thoughts. Later, during the civil troubles of the seventeenth century, it appears in a very pure and attractive form in the little group of Cambridge Platonists, Whichcote, Smith, Cudworth, and their friends. In the unmystical eighteenth century Jacob Böhme takes captive the manly and robust intellect of William Law, and inspires him to write some of the finest religious treatises in the English language. Meanwhile, the Quakers had the root of the matter in them, but they have only recently discovered their spiritual affinities with Plato. The tradition has never been extinct; or we may say more truly that the fire which, in the words of Eunapius, "still burns on the altars of Plotinus," has a perennial power of rekindling itself when the conditions are favourable. But the repressive forces of tyranny and bigotry have prevented the religion of the Spirit from bearing its proper fruits. The luck of history, we may say, has hitherto been unfavourable to what I, at least, hold to be the growth of the divine seed. It has either fallen on the rock or by the wayside, or the thorns have grown up with it and choked it. The religion of the Spirit has an intrinsic survival value, which is quite different from the extrinsic survival value of the religion of authority. Authority may for a time diminish the number of dissentients by burning their bodies or their books; but *"On ne tue pas des idées par coup de bâton."*

W.R. Inge, *The Platonic Tradition in English Religious Thought*, Longmans, Green & Co. Ltd., 1926, p.27.

HOPE

May the God of hope fill you with all joy and peace in believing, so that by the power of the Holy Spirit you may abound in hope.

Romans 15.13.

Hope in action is charity, and beauty in action is goodness.

Miguel de Unamuno, *The Tragic Sense of Life in Men and in Peoples*, Macmillan & Co. Ltd., 1921, p.203.

The virtue of hope is an orientation of the soul towards a transformation after which it will be wholly and exclusively love.

Simone Weil, *Gateway To God*, edited by David Raper, with the collaboration of Malcolm Muggeridge and Vernon Sproxton, William Collins Sons & Co. Ltd., 1974, p.131.

Hope is itself a species of happiness, and, perhaps, the chief happiness which this world affords.

Samuel Johnson, *Boswell's Life of Johnson,* edited by G.B. Hill, revised by L.F. Powell, Oxford at the Clarendon Press, 1934, Volume I, p.368.

To hope till Hope creates
From its own wreck the thing it contemplates.

Percy Bysshe Shelley, *The Poetical Works of Percy Bysshe Shelley,* edited with a memoir by H. Buxton Forman, George Bell & Sons, 1892, Volume III, p.257, *Prometheus Unbound,* Act IV, l.573.

I live on hope and that I think do all
Who come into this world.

Robert Bridges, *Poetical Works of Robert Bridges,* Humphrey Milford, Oxford University Press, 1913, p.218, Sonnet: "The Growth of Love," st. lxiii, l.1.

So, when dark thoughts my boding spirit shroud,
Sweet Hope, celestial influence round me shed.

John Keats, *The Poems of John Keats,* edited with an introduction and notes by E. de Selincourt, Methuen & Co. Ltd., 1907, p.19, "To Hope," concluding lines.

Hope springs eternal in the human breast:
Man never is, but always to be blest.

Alexander Pope, *An Essay on Man,* introduction by Henry Morley, Cassell and Company Limited, 1905, Epistle I, p.18.

Anything that is found to stimulate hope should be seized upon and made to serve. This applies to a book, a film, a broadcast, or a conversation with someone who can impart it.

Hubert van Zeller, *Considerations,* Sheed & Ward Ltd., 1974, p.100.

Christian Hope is the consecration of desire, and desire is the hardest thing of all to consecrate. That will only happen as you begin to think how lovely the life according to Christ is.

William Temple, *Christian Faith and Life,* S.C.M. Press Ltd., 1963, p.44.

For if you find hope in the ground of history, you are united with the great prophets who were able to look into the depth of their times, who tried to escape it, because they could not stand the horror of their visions, and who yet had the strength to look to an even deeper level and there to discover hope.

Paul Tillich, *The Shaking of the Foundations,* S.C.M. Press Ltd., 1949, p.59.

Hope like the gleaming taper's light
Adorns and cheers our way
And still as darker grows the night
Emits a brighter ray.

Oliver Goldsmith, *Collected Works of Oliver Goldsmith,* edited by Arthur Friedman, Oxford at the Clarendon Press, 1966, Volume IV, p.222, *The Captivity,* Act II. l.135.

Know then, whatever cheerful and serene
Supports the mind, supports the body too.
Hence the most vital movement mortals feel
Is Hope; the balm and life-blood of the soul.

John Armstrong, *The Art of Preserving Health*, 1756, Bk.IV. p.54.

Hope to the last.... Always hope;... Never leave off hoping; it don't answer.... Don't leave a stone unturned. It's always something to know you've done the most you could. But don't leave off hoping, or it's no use doing anything. Hope, hope, to the last!

Charles Dickens, *Nicholas Nickleby*, The Gresham Publishing Company, 1904, p.528.

HUMANISM

For at least half a century its predominant culture has been what is called Humanism, which consists, roughly speaking, in the acceptance of many Christian standards of life with a rejection or neglect of the only sources of power to attain them.

William Temple, *The Hope of a New World*, S.C.M. Press Ltd., 1940, p.64.

Humanism is a very old phenomenon which flowered wonderfully in the Greek world, and flowered again in the great scholars and writers of the Renaissance. And it has been flowering again in our own time. Humanism essentially means a great reverence for man, for man's dignity, and man's wonderful potentialities.
What is today called scientific humanism is a particular version of humanism, dominated by a faith in the sciences as able to make man competent to solve the problems of human existence, and capable of leading a happy and moral life in society.
Now we, as Christians, are bound to criticise the theses of scientific humanism, because, on the one hand, it does not diagnose properly the depth of man's trouble—that man as a creature is estranged from God his Creator—nor does it look high enough to the real heights of man's potentiality, not just to be a competent, moral, intelligent citizen of this world, but to be a saint reigning with Christ in glory in heaven, with the wonderful glow of humility, and the beauty of saintliness.
So we say that humanism does not see deep enough into the pit of man's predicament, nor high enough into the potentialities of man's glory.

Michael Ramsey, *Through the Year with Michael Ramsey*, edited by Margaret Duggan, Hodder & Stoughton Ltd., 1975, p.138.

I refer to the scientific humanist with great respect because as a Christian I share with him a great regard for man, for human dignity, for human worth, and human freedom. I believe that Christians and scientific humanists have much in common in their belief in the dignity of man and the service of mankind. But we part company on this. The scientific humanist believes that if the knowledge of the sciences develops as it should, and if all the sciences, duly developed, are applied to human affairs in the right way, then the human race can be made more progressive, better organised, more comfortable, more happy, and indeed more moral as well. The scientific humanist will reject religion and the religious dimension altogether, as being an unnecessary drag upon the rightful scientific progress which of itself can put the human race to rights.

My criticism is this: the evidence seems to show that the human race can become increasingly advanced in the knowledge of the sciences and the application of the sciences to human affairs, but can still go on being proud and selfish and cruel and insensitive. The tragic thing is that in the century in which the sciences have made the most stupendous strides, we have also seen the most terrible reactions in mass hysterical cruelty and selfishness.

The scientific humanist's diagnosis does not go deep enough. The trouble with man is not that he is not sufficiently progressive or scientifically enlightened, but that he is too deeply estranged from his Creator, and needs to be reconciled to his Creator in awe and humility—to be cured of his deep pride and selfishness.

Michael Ramsey, *Through the Year with Michael Ramsey*, edited by Margaret Duggan, Hodder & Stoughton Ltd., 1975, p.138.

The Renaissance began with the affirmation of man's creative individuality; it has ended with its denial. Man without God is no longer man: that is the religious meaning of the internal dialectic of modern history, the history of the grandeur and of the dissipation of humanist illusions. Interiorly divided and drained of his spiritual strength, man becomes the slave of base and unhuman influences; his soul is darkened and alien spirits take possession of him. The elaboration of the humanist religion and the divinization of man and of humanity properly forbodes the end of Humanism. The flowering of the idea of humanity was possible only so long as man has a deep belief in and consciousness of principles above himself, was not altogether cut off from his divine roots. During the Renaissance he still had this belief and consciousness and was therefore not yet completely separated; throughout modern history the European has not totally repudiated his religious basis. It is thanks to that alone that the idea of humanity remained consistent with the spread of individualism and of creative activity. The humanism of Goethe had a religious foundation, he kept his faith in God. The man who has lost God gives himself up to something formless and inhuman, prostrates himself before material necessity.

Nowadays there is none of that "renaissential" play and inter-play of human powers which gave us Italian painting and Shakespeare and Goethe; instead unhuman forces, spirits unchained from the deep, crush man and becloud his image, beating upon him like waves from every side. It is they, not man, who have been set free. Man found his form and his identity under the action of religious principles and energies; the confusion in which he is losing them cannot be re-ordered by purely human efforts.

Nicolas Berdyaev, *The End of our Time*, translated by Donald Attwater, Sheed & Ward Ltd., 1933, p.54.

HUMILITY

He has filled the hungry with good things, and the rich he has sent empty away.

Luke 1.53.

For every one who exalts himself will be humbled, and he who humbles himself will
be exalted.

Luke 14.11.

True humility,
The highest virtue, mother of them all.

Alfred, Lord Tennyson, *The Poems of Tennyson,* edited by Christopher Ricks, Longmans, Green & Co. Ltd., 1969,
p.1674, No 471, "The Holy Grail," l.445.

Show yourself humble in all things.

Thomas à Kempis, *The Imitation of Christ,* translated by Betty I. Knott, William Collins Sons & Co. Ltd., 1979,
p.150.

True humility is contentment.

Henri Frédéric Amiel, *Amiel's Journal,* translated by Mrs. Humphry Ward, Macmillan & Co. Ltd., 1918, p.46.

Humility like darkness reveals the heavenly lights.

Henry David Thoreau, *Walden,* The New American Library of World Literature, Inc., 1960, p.218.

He that is humble, ever shall
Have God to be his Guide.

John Bunyan, *The Pilgrim's Progress,* introduction & notes by G.B. Harrison, J.M. Dent & Sons, Ltd., 1964,
p.237.

The Holy Ghost flows into the soul as fast as she is poured forth in humility and so
far as she has gotten the capacity. He fills all the room he can find.

Meister Eckhart, *Meister Eckhart,* Franz Pfeiffer, translated by C. de B. Evans, John M. Watkins, 1956, Volume
I, p.158.

There must be feelings of humility, not from nature, but from penitence, not to rest
in them, but to go on to greatness.

Blaise Pascal, *Pensées,* translated by W.F. Trotter, Random House Inc., 1941, p.169.

You will find Angling to be like the virtue of humility, which has a calmness of spirit,
and a world of other blessings attending upon it.

Izaak Walton, *The Complete Angler,* Macmillan & Co. Ltd., 1906, p.37.

If thou wouldst become a pilgrim on the path
Of love
The first condition is
That thou become as humble as dust
And ashes.

Al-Ansari, *The Persian Mystics,* translated by Sardar Sir Jogendra Sing, John Murray Ltd., 1939, p.39.

O Saviour pour upon me thy Spirit of meekness & love!
Annihilate the Selfhood in me: be thou all my life!
Guide thou my hand, which trembles exceedingly upon the rock of ages.

William Blake, *The Complete Writings of William Blake,* edited by Geoffrey Keynes, Oxford University Press,
1974, p.623, *Jerusalem,* ch.I, plate 5, l.21.

Humility does not rest, in final count, upon bafflement and discouragement and self-disgust at our shabby lives, a brow-beaten, dog-slinking attitude. It rest upon the disclosure of the consummate wonder of God, upon finding that only God counts, that all our self-originated intentions are works of straw....

Humility rests upon a holy blindedness, like the blindedness of him who steadily looks into the sun. For wherever he turns his eyes on earth, there he sees only the sun. The God-blinded soul sees nought of self.

Thomas Kelly, *A Testament of Devotion*, Hodder & Stoughton Ltd., 1943, p.54.

I am sure it is no easier to pray than it is to create music or write a poem; it must be as hard to do as it is to build a bridge, or to discover a great scientific principle, or to heal the sick, or to understand another human being. It is surely as important as these to man in his search for his role in the universal scheme of things....

To pray.... It is so necessary and so hard. Hard not because it requires intellect or knowledge or a big vocabulary or special technics but because it requires of us humility. And that comes, I think, from a profound sense of one's brokenness, and one's need. Not the need that causes us to cry, "Get me out of this trouble, quick!" but the need that one feels every day of one's life—even though one does not acknowledge it—to be related to something bigger than one's self, something more alive than one's self, something older and something not yet born, that will endure through time.

Lillian Smith, *The Journey*, The Cresset Press, 1955, p.40.

Every person, when he first applies himself to the exercise of the virtue of humility, must ... consider himself as a learner, that is to learn something that is contrary to former tempers and habits of mind, and which can only be got by daily and constant practice.

He has not only as much to do as he that has some new art or science to learn, but he has also a great deal to unlearn: he is to forget and lay aside his own spirit, which has been a long while fixing and forming itself; he must forget and depart from abundance of passions and opinions, which the fashion, and vogue, and spirit of the world, has made natural to him.

He must lay aside his own spirit; because as we are born in sin, so in pride, which is as natural to us as self-love, and continually springs from it. And this is one reason why Christianity is so often represented as a new birth, and a new spirit.

He must lay aside the opinions and passions which he has received from the world; because the vogue and fashion of the world, by which we have been carried away as in a torrent, before we could pass right judgements of the value of things is, in many respects, contrary to humility; so that we must unlearn what the spirit of the world has taught us, before we can be governed by the spirit of humility....

To abound in wealth, to have fine houses, and rich clothes,... to be beautiful in our persons, to have title of dignity, to be above our fellow creatures,... to overcome our enemies with power, to subdue all that oppose us, to set out ourselves in as much splendour as we can, to live highly and magnificently, to eat, and drink, and delight ourselves in the most costly manner, these are the great, the honourable, the desirable things, to which the spirit of the world turns the eyes of all people. And many a man is afraid of standing still, and not engaging in the pursuit of these things, lest the same world should take him for a fool....

This is the mark of Christianity: you are to be dead, that is, dead to the spirit and temper of the world, and live a new life in the Spirit of Jesus Christ.

William Law, *A Serious Call to a Devout and Holy Life*, J.M. Dent & Co. Ltd., 1898, p.255.

The source of humility,... is the habit of realising the presence of God. Humility does not mean thinking less of yourself than of other people, nor does it mean having a low opinion of your own gifts. It means freedom from thinking about yourself one way or the other at all. It may be quite right that a man conscious of certain powers given him by God should desire the opportunities to exercise those powers for God. It may be quite right that under certain circumstances a man should insist that he is more capable than another man of doing something that must be done. No one would select as an example of humility the elder Pitt; but there was nothing contrary to humility in his alleged declaration to the Duke of Devonshire: "I know that I can save this country and I know that no one else can". He knew the political life of the time pretty well; he was conscious of power in himself, and in a few years he showed that he was right in what he said of himself; only if he set about his task in his own interest or for self-glorification did he fail in humility.

Humility means that you feel yourself, as a distinct person, out of count, and give your whole mind and thought to the object towards which they are directed, to God himself in worship and to the fulfilment of His will in Christian love; and humility, in that sense, is quite plainly a source of effectiveness. The humility which consists in being a great deal occupied about yourself, and saying you are of little worth, is not Christian humility. It is one form of self-occupation, and a very poor and futile one at that; but real humility makes for effectiveness because it delivers a man from anxiety, and we all know that in all undertakings, from the smallest to the greatest, the chief source of feebleness is anxiety. Even in a game we all know that nothing so much paralyses good play as anxiety. If you once begin to wonder whether you are going to catch the ball you will drop it, but if you just catch it without thinking about anything but catching it—not, above all, of what other people are going to think of you—probably you will hold it. That goes through everything, from such a simple act to the greatest. But there is nothing big enough to hold a man's soul in detachment from the centre of himself through all the occupations of life except the majesty of God and his love; and it is in worship, worship given to God because He is God, that man will most learn the secret of real humility.

William Temple, *Christ In His Church*, Macmillan & Co. Ltd., 1925, p.145.

I

IDEALS

The highest flights of charity, devotion, trust, patience, bravery to which the wings
of human nature have spread themselves have been flown for religious ideals.
William James, *The Varieties of Religious Experience,* William Collins Sons & Co. Ltd., 1974, p.258.

The Ideal is in thyself, the Impediment too is in thyself: thy condition is but the stuff
thou art to shape that same Ideal out of.
Thomas Carlyle, *Sartor Resartus,* Ward, Lock & Co. Ltd., p.131.

If one advances confidently in the direction of his dreams, and endeavours to live the
life which he has imagined, he will meet with a success unexpected in common hours.
Henry David Thoreau, *Walden,* The New American Library of World Literature, Inc., 1960, p.215.

For the idealist living wholly with people occupied with the concrete, existence is not
merely lonely, but fatiguing. It is as though he or she were for ever talking a foreign
language.
L. Falconer, in *The Note Books of a Woman Alone,* edited by M.G. Ostle, J.M. Dent & Sons Ltd., 1935, p.228.

In reverence for life my knowledge passes into experience.... My life carries its own
meaning in itself. This meaning lies in my living out the highest idea which shows
itself in my will-to-live, the idea of reverence for life. With that for a starting-point
I give value to my own life and to all the will-to-live which surrounds me, I persevere
in activity, and I produce values.
Albert Schweitzer, *The Philosophy of Civilization,* Part II, Civilization and Ethics, translated by C.T. Campion,
A.& C. Black Ltd., Third English Editon, revised by Mrs. E.B. Russell, 1946, p.xvii.

The ideals which have lighted my way, and time after time have given me new courage
to face life cheerfully, have been Kindness, Beauty, and Truth.
Without the sense of kinship with men of like mind, without the occupation with
the objective world, the eternally unattainable in the field of art and scientific endeavours, life would have seemed to me empty. The trite objects of human efforts—
possessions, outward success, luxury—have always seemed to me contemptible.
Albert Einstein, *Ideas and Opinions,* Souvenir Press (Educational & Academic) Ltd., 1973, p.9.

The essential nature of the will-to-live is determination to live itself to the full. It
carries within it the impulse to realize itself in the highest possible perfection. In the
flowering tree, in the strange forms of the medusa, in the blade of grass, in the crystal;
everywhere it strives to reach the perfection with which it is endowed. In everything
that exists there is at work an imaginative force, which is determined by ideals. In
us beings who can move about freely and are capable of pre-considered, purposive

working, the craving for perfection is given in such a way that we aim at raising to their highest material and spiritual value both ourselves and every existing thing which is open to our influence. How this striving originated within us, and how it has developed, we do not know, but it is given with our existence. We must act upon it, if we would not be unfaithful to the mysterious will-to-live which is within us.

Albert Schweitzer, *The Philosophy of Civilization,* Part II, "Civilization and Ethics," translated by C.T. Campion, A. & C. Black Ltd., Third English Edition, revised by Mrs. E. B. Russell, 1946, p.213.

Today there is an increased number of people who cherish communism as their ideal, but the type of communism thus coming into existence is woefully defective. Russia has established a Soviet-organised communism. But in order to carry out communism genuinely, there is no other way than for every man to return his possessions to God first of all. It is very important to give all our property back to God to whom everything belongs. Unless each of us has sufficient devotion to restore all things to God before we cry, "Workers, unite!" communism can never be a success. I do not believe that communism restricted to a single country can be called real and valid. To be real, communism must be changed into a God-centred undertaking. There is no other way to accomplish it. I often think that thieves maintain a kind of communism, too; that is, among themselves. So it can be said that there are two brands of communism: the God-centred type, and the thief type. It goes without saying that every genuine communist is seeking for God first of all. Paul dwelt on this condition. He expressed it in very marvellous words. According to him, Jesus Christ became poor, though he was rich, so that all men might be enriched through his poverty. If this ideal should be put into practice, heaven would descend upon earth. Dwelling upon this idea led Paul furthermore to declare that all men are made equal.

Toyohiko Kagawa, *Meditations,* translated by Jiro Takenaka, Harper & Brothers, 1950, No. 44.

It is innocence that is full and experience that is empty.
It is innocence that wins and experience that loses.
It is innocence that is young and experience that is old.
It is innocence that grows and experience that wanes.
It is innocence that is born and experience that dies.
It is innocence that knows and experience that does not know.
It is the child who is full and the man who is empty,
Empty as an empty gourd and as an empty barrel:
That is what I do with that experience of yours.
Now then, children, go to school.
And you men, go to the school of life.
Go and learn,
How to unlearn.

Charles Péguy, *Basic Verities,* translated by Ann and Julian Green, Kegan Paul, Trench, Trubner & Co. Ltd., 1943, p.223.

IMAGE OF GOD

Then the Lord God formed man of dust from the ground, and breathed into his nostrils the breath of life; and man became a living being.

Genesis 2.7.

Can we find such a man as this, in whom is the Spirit of God?

Genesis 41.38.

I have filled him with the Spirit of God, with ability and intelligence, with knowledge and all craftsmanship.

Exodus 31.3.

I have heard of you that the spirit of the holy gods is in you, and that light and understanding and excellent wisdom are found in you.

Daniel 5.14.

Just as we have borne the image of the man of dust, we shall also bear the image of the man of heaven.

1 Corinthians 15.49.

When God made man the innermost heart of the Godhead was put into man.

Meister Eckhart, *Meister Eckhart,* Franz Pfeiffer, translated by C. de B. Evans, John M. Watkins, 1956, Volume I, p.436.

The Difference then of a good and a bad Man does not lie in this, that the one wills that which is good, and the other does not, but solely in this, that the one concurs with the living inspiring Spirit of God within him, and the other resists it, and is and can be *only chargeable* with Evil, because he resists it.

William Law, *The Spirit of Love,* full text, edited with an introduction and notes by Sidney Spencer, James Clarke & Co. Ltd., 1969, p.207.

I have often said before that there is an agent in the soul, untouched by time and flesh, which proceeds out of the Spirit, and which remains forever in the Spirit and is completely spiritual. In this agent God is perpetually verdant and flowering with all the joy and glory that is in him. Here is joy so hearty, such inconceivably great joy that no one can ever fully tell it.... God glows and burns without ceasing, in all his fullness, sweetness, and rapture.

Meister Eckhart, *Meister Eckhart,* translated by Raymond B. Blakney, Harper & Row, Publishers, Inc., 1941, p.209.

You are a principal work, a fragment of God Himself, you have in yourself a part of Him. Why then are you ignorant of your high birth? Why do you not know whence you have come? Will you not remember, when you eat, who you are that eat, and whom you are feeding, and the same in your relations with women? When you take part in society, or training, or conversation, do you not know that it is God you are nourishing and training? You bear God about you,... and know it not. Do you think

---

I speak of some external god of silver or gold? No, you bear Him about within you and are unaware that you are defiling Him with unclean thoughts and foul actions. If an image of God were present, you would not dare to do any of the things you do; yet when God Himself is present within you and sees and hears all things, you are not ashamed of thinking and acting thus: O slow to understand your nature, and estranged from God!

Epictetus, *The Stoic and Epicurean Philosophers,* edited by Witney J. Oates, Random House, Inc., 1940, p.295.

There is something more in man than is apparent in his ordinary consciousness, something which frames ideals and thoughts, a finer spiritual presence, which makes him dissatisfied with mere earthly pursuits. The one doctrine that has the longest intellectual ancestry is the belief that the ordinary condition of man is not his ultimate being, that he has in him a deeper self, call it breath or ghost, soul or spirit. In each being dwells a light which no power can extinguish, an immortal spirit, benign and tolerant, the silent witness in his heart. The greatest thinkers of the world unite in asking us to know the self. Mencius declares: "Who knows his own nature knows heaven." St. Augustine writes: "I, Lord, went wandering like a strayed sheep, seeking thee with anxious reasoning without, whilst thou wast within me.... I went round the streets and squares of the city of this world seeking thee, and I found thee not, because in vain I sought without for him who was within myself." We make a detour round the universe to get back to the self. The oldest wisdom in the world tells us that we can consciously unite with the divine while in this body, for this is man really born. If he misses his destiny, Nature is not in a hurry; she will catch him some day and compel him to fulfil her secret purpose. Truth, beauty, peace, power, and wisdom are all attributes of a divine self which awaits our finding.

Sir Sarvepalli Radhakrishnan, *Eastern Religions and Western Thought,* Oxford University Press, 1940, p.25.

There is a divine element, an innermost essence in us, in the very structure of the soul, which is the starting-point of all spiritual progress, the mark of man's dignity, the real source of all religious experience, and the eternal basis of the soul's salvation and joy. He names this inward endowment by many names. It is the Word of God, the Power of God, Spirit, Mind of Christ, Divine Activity, Divine Origin, the inward Light, the true Light, the Lamp of the soul. "The Inward Light ... is nothing else than the Word of God, God Himself, by whom all things were made and by whom all men are enlightened." It is, in Franck's thought, not a capricious, subjective impulse or vision, and it is not to be discovered in sudden ecstatic experiences; nor, on the other hand, is the divine Word, for Franck, something purely objective and transcendent. It is rather a common ground and essence for God and man. It is God in His self-revealing activity; God in His self-giving grace; God as the immanent ground of all that is permanently real, and at the same time this divine endowment forms the fundamental nature of man's soul—and is the original substance of our being. Consciousness of God and consciousness of self have one fundamental source in this deep where God and man are unsundered. "No man can see or know himself unless he sees and knows, by the Light and Life that is in him, God the eternally true Light and Life; wherefore nobody can ever know God outside of himself, outside that region where he knows himself in the ground of himself.... Man must seek, find, and know God through an interrelation—he must find God in himself and himself in God." This deep ground of inner reality is in every person, so far as he is a person; it shines forth as a steady illumination in the soul, and, while everything else is transitory, this Word is eternal and has been the moral and spiritual guide of all peoples in all ages.

Rufus M. Jones, *Spiritual Reformers in the 16th and 17th Centuries*, Macmillan & Co. Ltd., 1914, p.53.

IMAGINATION

Imagination is the eye of the soul.

Joseph Joubert, *Pensées and Letters*, George Routledge & Sons, Ltd., 1928, p.48.

Imagination and fiction go to make up more than three-quarters of our real life.

Simone Weil, *Gravity and Grace*, Routledge & Kegan Paul Ltd., 1952, p.50.

Only in men's imagination does every truth find an effective and undeniable existence. Imagination, not invention, is the supreme master of art as of life.

Joseph Conrad, *A Personal Record*, J.M. Dent & Sons Ltd., 1923, p.25.

Imagination grows by exercise and contrary to common belief is more powerful in the mature than in the young.

W. Somerset Maugham, *The Summing Up*, Bernhard Tauchnitz, 1938, p.131.

The great instrument of moral good is the imagination.

Percy Bysshe Shelley, *The Prose Works of Percy Bysshe Shelley*, edited by H. Buxton Forman, Reeves and Turner, 1880, Volume III, p.111, "A Defence of Poetry."

It is the marriage of the soul with Nature that makes the intellect fruitful, that gives birth to imagination.

Henry David Thoreau, *The Journal of Henry D. Thoreau*, edited by Bradford Torrey and Francis H. Allen, Houghton Mifflin Company, Boston, The Riverside Press, 1949, Volume II, p.413.

There are no days in life so memorable as those which vibrated to some stroke of the imagination.

Ralph Waldo Emerson, *The Conduct of Life, Nature, and Other Essays*, J.M. Dent & Sons Ltd., 1911, p.298.

What is it that we ask of our ideal audience? It is imagination. And is not all our writing a profession of belief in the powers of the imagination?

Katherine Mansfield, in *Katherine Mansfield*, Anthony Alpers, Jonathan Cape Ltd., 1954, p.296.

I am certain of nothing but the holiness of the heart's affections, and the truth of Imagination. What the Imagination seizes as Beauty must be Truth, whether it existed before or not.

John Keats, *The Works of John Keats*, edited by H. Buxton Forman, Reeves & Turner, 1883, Volume III, p.90, Letter to Benjamin Bailey.

But how entirely I live in my imagination; how completely depend upon spurts of thought, coming as I walk, as I sit; things churning up in my mind and so making a perpetual pageant, which is to be my happiness.

Virginia Woolf, *A Writer's Diary*, edited by Leonard Woolf, The Hogarth Press, 1953, p.67.

The primary IMAGINATION I hold to be the living Power and prime Agent of all human Perception, and as a repetition in the finite mind of the eternal act of creation in the infinite I AM.

Samuel Taylor Coleridge, *Coleridge, Select Poetry & Prose*, edited by Stephen Potter, The Nonesuch Press, p.246, *Biographia Literaria*, Chapter XIII.

The virtue of the Imagination is its reaching, by intuition and intensity of gaze (not by reasoning, but by its authoritative opening and revealing power), a more essential truth than is seen at the surface of things.

John Ruskin, *Modern Painters*, George Allen & Sons, 1911, Volume II, p.201, Part III, sec. II, ch.III, sec. 29.

He realised in the entire sphere of human relations that imaginative sympathy which in the Sphere of Art is the sole secret of creation. He understood the leprosy of the leper, the darkness of the blind, the fierce misery of those who live for pleasure, the strange poverty of the rich.

Oscar Wilde, *The Works of Oscar Wilde*, edited by G.F. Maine, William Collins Sons & Co. Ltd., 1948, *De Profundis*, p.867.

The imagination—the divinest of mental faculties—is God's self in the soul. All our other faculties seem to me to have the brown touch of earth on them; but this one carries the very livery of heaven. It is God's most supernal faculty, interpreting to us the difference between the material and the immaterial, and the difference between the visible and the invisible; teaching us how to take material and visible things and carry them up into the realm of the invisible and the immaterial, and how to bring down immaterial and invisible things, and embody them in visible and material symbols;—and so being God's messenger and prophet, standing between our soul and God's.

Henry Ward Beecher, *Royal Truths*, Alexander Strahan & Co., 1862, p.47.

IMMORTALITY

God created man to be immortal, and made him to be an image of his own eternity.

Wisdom of Solomon 2.23 (A.V.).

The blazing evidence of immortality is our dissatisfaction with any other solution.

Ralph Waldo Emerson, *The Heart of Emerson's Journals*, edited by Bliss Perry, Constable & Co. Ltd., 1927, p.270.

I believe in the immortality of the soul, not in the sense in which I accept the demonstrable truths of science, but as a supreme act of faith in the reasonableness of God's work.

John Fiske, *The Destiny of Man*, Macmillan & Co. Ltd., 1884, p.116.

Our Creator would never have made such lovely days and have given us the deep hearts to enjoy them, above and beyond all thought, unless we were meant to be immortal.

Nathaniel Hawthorne, *Mosses From An Old Manse,* William Paterson, 1883, p.30.

The belief of immortality is impressed upon all men, and all men act under an impression of it, however they may talk, and though, perhaps, they may be scarcely sensible of it.

Samuel Johnson, *Boswell's Life of Johnson,* edited by G.B. Hill, revised by L.F. Powell, Oxford at the Clarendon Press, 1934, Volume II, p.358.

If you were to destroy the belief in immortality in mankind, not only love but every living force on which the continuation of all life in the world depended, would dry up at once.

Fyodor Dostoyevsky, *The Brothers Karamazov,* translated by David Magarshack, 1963, Volume I, p.77.

Cold in the dust this perished heart may lie,
But that which warmed it once shall never die!
That spark unburied in its mortal frame,
With living light, eternal, and the same.

Thomas Campbell, *The Pleasures of Hope,* edited with an introduction by Henry Morley, George Routledge & Sons, Ltd., 1892, p.50.

It is only true goodness and virtue in the souls of men, that can make them both to know and love, believe and delight themselves in their own immortality.... His soul being purged and enlightened by true sanctity, is more capable of those divine irradiations, whereby it feels itself in conjunction with God ... it knows that Almighty love which it lives by, to be stronger than death.... It knows that God will never forsake His own life which He hath quickened in it ... those breathings and gaspings after an eternal participation of Him are but the energy of His own breath within us.

John Smith the Platonist, *Select Discourses,* Cambridge at the University Press, 1859, p.102.

If the soul is really immortal, what care should be taken of her, not only in respect of the portion of time which is called life, but of eternity! And the danger of neglecting her from this point of view does indeed appear to be awful. If death had only been the end of all, the wicked would have had a good bargain in dying, for they would have been happily quit not only of their body, but of their own evil together with their souls. But now, inasmuch as the soul is manifestly immortal, there is no release or salvation from evil except the attainment of the highest virtue and wisdom.

Socrates, in *The Dialogues of Plato,* translated with analyses and introductions by B. Jowett, Oxford at the Clarendon Press, 1875, Volume I, p.488, "Phaedo," 107.

It must be so—Plato, thou reason'st well!—
Else whence this pleasing hope, this fond desire,
This longing after immortality?
Or whence this secret dread, and inward horror,
Of falling into nought? Why shrinks the soul
Back on herself, and startles at destruction?

'Tis the divinity that stirs within us;
'Tis heaven itself, that points out an hereafter,
And intimates eternity to man.
Eternity! thou pleasing, dreadful thought!

Joseph Addison, *The Works of Joseph Addison,* notes by Richard Hurd, edited and published by Henry G. Bohn, 1856, Volume I, *Cato,* Act V, p.220.

As to the supreme form of soul that is within us, we must believe that God has given it to each of us as a guiding genius—even that which we say, and say truly, dwells in the summit of our body and raises us from earth towards our celestial affinity, seeing we are of no earthly, but of heavenly growth: since to heaven, whence in the beginning was the birth of our soul, the diviner part attaches the head or root of us and makes our whole body upright. Now whoso is busied with appetites or ambitions and labours hard after these, all the thoughts of his heart must be altogether mortal; and so far as it is possible for him to become utterly mortal, he falls no whit short of this; for this is what he has been fostering. But he whose heart has been set on the love of learning and on true wisdom, and has chiefly exercised this part of himself, this man must without fail have thoughts that are immortal and divine, if he lay hold upon the truth; and so far as it lies in human nature to possess immortality, he lacks nothing thereof; and seeing that he ever cherishes the divinest part and keeps in good estate the guardian spirit that dwells in him, he must be happy above all.

Plato, *The Timaeus of Plato,* edited with an introduction and notes by F.D. Archer-Hind, Macmillan & Co. Ltd., 1888, p.337, 90A.

"I cannot see what harm would come of letting us know a little— as much at least as might serve to assure us that there was more of *something* on the other side."
"Just this ... that, their fears allayed, their hopes encouraged from any lower quarter, men would, as usual, turn away from the fountain to the cistern of life.... That there are thousands who would forget God if they could but be assured of such a tolerable state of things beyond the grave as even this wherein we now live, is plainly to be anticipated from the fact that the doubts of so many in respect of religion concentrate themselves nowadays upon the question whether there is any life beyond the grave; a question which ... does not immediately belong to religion at all. Satisfy such people, if you can, that they shall live, and what have they gained? A little comfort perhaps— but a comfort not from the highest source, and possibly gained too soon for their well-being. Does it bring them any nearer to God than they were before? Is he filling one cranny more of their hearts in consequence?"

George Macdonald, *Thomas Wingfold, Curate,* Chatto & Windus, 1883, p.486.

INCARNATION

In the beginning was the Word, and the Word was with God, and the Word was God.... And the Word became flesh and dwelt among us, full of grace and truth.

John 1.1,14.

No one has ever seen God; the only Son, who is in the bosom of the Father, he has made him known.

John 1.18.

All things have been delivered to me by my Father.

Matthew 11.27.

He who has seen me has seen the Father.

John 14.9.

If a man loves me, he will keep my word, and my Father will love him, and we will come to him and make our home with him.

John 14.23.

The Word of God, Jesus Christ our Lord: Who for His immense love's sake was made that which we are, in order that He might perfect us to be what He is.

S. Irenaeus, *Five Books of S. Irenaeus Against Heresies,* translated by the Rev. John Keble, James Parker & Co., 1872, p.449.

> Christ could be born
> a thousand times in Galilee—
> but all vain
> until He is born in me.

Angelus Silesius, *The Book of Angelus Silesius,* translated, drawn, and handwritten by Frederick Franck, Wildwood House Ltd., 1976, p.107.

At this time ... the renewal of Christianity depends solely on accepting the Incarnation in all its fulness. For without the realization of God's love for the world, we can love neither the world nor God.

Alan W. Watts, *Behold the Spirit,* John Murray Ltd., 1947, p.244.

As it is, there is one road, and one only, well secured against all possibility of going astray; and this road is provided by one who is himself both God and man. As God, he is the goal; as man, he is the way.

St. Augustine, *City of God,* translated by Henry Bettenson, edited, with an introduction by David Knowles, Penguin Books Ltd., 1972, p.431.

Christianity does mean getting down to actual ordinary life as the medium of the Incarnation, doesn't it, and our lessons in that get sterner, not more elegant as time goes on?

Evelyn Underhill, *The Letters of Evelyn Underhill,* edited with an introduction by Charles Williams, Longmans, Green & Co. Ltd., 1947, p.259.

"Man is the true Shekinah"—the visible presence, that is to say, of the divine. We are far too apt to limit and mechanize the great doctrine of the Incarnation which forms the centre of the Christian faith. Whatever it may mean, it means at least this—

that in the conditions of the highest human life we have access, as nowhere else, to the inmost nature of the divine.

A.S. Pringle-Pattison, *The Idea of God,* Oxford University Press, 1920, p.157.

Once the Creator Spirit became involved in matter and in developing life, once the spirit of man was created in the likeness of the divine Spirit, it would seem natural that he should become fully incarnate in a person, not only to manifest the divine life but also to be the prototype of human life. The union of the divine and human in Jesus speaks of the hope of man sharing in the divine life.

George Appleton, *Journey for a Soul,* William Collins Sons & Co. Ltd., 1976, p.135.

The Incarnation was not an isolated event, wonderful though it would have been if it was that and nothing more. It was the beginning of something new, perhaps rather the manifestation of something which had never been recognized, but which could now happen in a fully conscious and effective way. The Spirit of God, incarnate fully and supremely in Jesus, wishes to indwell every man, not only as an immanent force, but as an invited, personal guest.

George Appleton, *Journey for a Soul,* William Collins Sons & Co. Ltd., 1976, p.138.

For a Person came, and lived and loved, and did and taught, and died and rose again, and lives on by His Power and His Spirit for ever within us and amongst us, so unspeakably rich and yet so simple, so sublime and yet so homely, so divinely above us precisely in being so divinely near,—that His character and teaching require, for an ever fuller yet never complete understanding, the varying study, and different experiments and applications, embodiments and unrollings of all the races and civilizations, of all the individual and corporate, the simultaneous and successive experiences of the human race to the end of time.

Friedrich von Hügel, *The Mystical Element of Religion,* J.M. Dent & Co., 1909, Volume I, p.26.

There is one secret, the greatest of all—a secret which no previous religion dared, even in enigma, to allege fully—which is stated with the utmost distinctness by Our Lord and the Church; though this very distinctness seems to act as a thick veil, hiding the disc of the revelation as that of the Sun is hidden by its rays, and causing the eyes of men to avert themselves habitually from that one centre of all seeing. I mean the doctrine of the Incarnation, regarded not as an historical event which occurred two thousand years ago, but as an event which is renewed in the body of every one who is in the way to the fulfilment of his original destiny.

Coventry Patmore, *The Rod, The Root and the Flower,* The Grey Walls Press Ltd., 1950, p.124, "Homo," xix, 1.1.

The Incarnation is a proclamation that "the All-great is the All-loving too"—a doctrine which few, I think, accept who do not believe in the Incarnation of the Son of God in Christ. And if, with the Church of the Creeds and Fathers, we accept something like the Logos-doctrine already held by St. Paul and briefly summarised by St. John, we have the most inspiring thought that the laws of the universe, in their deepest meaning, are the expression of the character of the creating and sustaining Word who became flesh and tabernacled among us in the person of Jesus of Nazareth. I need not dwell on the consecration of the whole of nature which follows from this belief; on the final repudiation of that unfortunate dualism between the natural and supernatural which has introduced chaos into both spheres, natural and spiritual alike; on the sanction which it gives to the pursuits of poetry, art, and science, as being each, in their different ways, a priestly and prophetic office, revealing to us the God whom we know in our hearts as the Good, under His other attributes of the True and the Beautiful. The world is good, for God the Word made it; but it can be made better, for He came to redeem it. And His redeeming, transforming work did not come to an end when He left the earth; we are living under the dispensation which then began, a dispensation of progressive enlightenment and steady realisation of a great purpose—the achievement of a theophany in redeemed humanity itself.

W.R. Inge, *Speculum Animae,* Longmans, Green & Co. Ltd., 1911, p.19.

The Incarnation was to him the centre of all history, the blossoming of Humanity. The Life which followed the Incarnation was the explanation of the life of God, and the only solution of the problem of the life of man. He did not speak much of loving Christ; his love was fitly mingled with that veneration which makes love perfect; his voice was solemn, and he paused before he spoke His name in common talk; for what that Name meant had become the central thought of his intellect, and the deep realisation of his spirit. He had spent a world of study, of reverent meditation, of adoring contemplation on the gospel history. Nothing comes forward more vividly in his letters than the way in which he had entered into the human life of Christ. To that everything is referred—by that everything is explained. The gossip of a drawing-room, the tendencies of the time, the religious questions of the day, especially the Sabbath question, the loneliness and the difficulties of his work, were not so much argued upon or combated, as at once and instinctively brought to the test of a Life which was lived out eighteen centuries ago, but which went everywhere with him. Out of this intuitive reception of Christ, and from this ceaseless silence of meditation which makes the blessedness of great love, there grew up in him a deep comprehension of the whole, as well as a minute sympathy with all the delicate details of the character of Christ. Day by day, with passionate imitation, he followed his Master, musing on every action, revolving in thought the interdependence of all that Christ had said or done, weaving into the fibres of his heart the principles of the Life he worshipped, till he had received into his being the very impression and image of that unique Personality. His very doctrines were the Life of Christ expressed in words. The Incarnation, Atonement, and Resurrection of Christ were not dogmas to him. In himself he was daily realising them. They were in him a life, a power, a light. This was his Christian consciousness.

Stopford A. Brooke, said of Frederick W. Robertson in *Life and Letters of Frederick W. Robertson,* edited by Stopford A. Brooke, Smith, Elder & Co, 1865, Volume II, p.168.

INFLUENCE

Blessed influence of one true loving human soul on another!

George Eliot, *Scenes of Clerical Life*, "Janet's Repentance," Oxford University Press, 1909, p.369.

A teacher affects eternity; he can never tell where his influence stops.

Henry Adams, *The Education of Henry Adams*, Constable & Co. Ltd., 1919, p.300.

You can exert no influence if you are not susceptible to influence.

C.G. Jung, *Modern Man in Search of a Soul*, translated by W.S. Dell & Cary F. Baynes, Kegan Paul, Trench, Trubner & Co. Ltd., 1933, p.57.

God must act and pour in as soon as he finds that you are ready.

Meister Eckhart, *Meister Eckhart*, translated by Raymond B. Blakney, Harper & Row, Publishers, Inc., 1941, p.121.

No life
Can be pure in its purpose or strong in its strife
And all life not be purer and stronger thereby.

Owen Meredith, *Lucile*, Longmans, Green & Co. Ltd., 1893, Part II, canto vi, sec.40, p.333.

Thou art the framer of my nobler being;
Nor does there live one virtue in my soul,
One honourable hope, but calls thee father.

Samuel Taylor Coleridge, *The Poetical Works of Samuel Taylor Coleridge*, edited with a biographical introduction by James Dykes Campbell, Macmillan & Co. Ltd., 1893, p.401, "Zapolya," sc.i, l.73.

It is certainly often sad and depressing when one tries to effect something in life by one's words and sees in the end that one has effected nothing; but that the person in question obstinately perseveres in his opinion; but on the other hand there is something great in the fact that the other person, and in the same way everyone, is a world unto himself, has his holy of holies into which no strange hand can penetrate.

Søren Kierkegaard, *The Journals of Søren Kierkegaard*, a selection edited and translated by Alexander Dru, Oxford University Press, 1938, p.25.

Whose powers shed round him in the common strife,
Or mild concerns of ordinary life,
A constant influence, a peculiar grace;
But who, if he be called upon to face
Some awful moment to which Heaven has joined
Great issues, good or bad for human kind,
Is happy as a Lover; and attired
With sudden brightness, like a Man inspired;
And, through the heat of conflict, keeps the law
In calmness made, and sees what he foresaw.

William Wordsworth, *The Poetical Works of William Wordsworth*, edited by E. de Selincourt and Helen Darbishire, Oxford at the Clarendon Press, 1958, Volume IV, p.87, "Character of a Happy Warrior," l.45.

We can influence and direct others as we desire their good, but only when they are convinced, with the shrewd sense that all creatures have, that our motives are clean, our statements true, that we do seek their good, and not our advancement and elevation as their essential benefactors. All of us are individual spirits created to evolve into a common union. If we have made ourselves to grow, so that we are advanced some stages beyond the average intensity of individualism, we can directly influence those who wish to grow, and who are feeling the natural need to grow, in that direction. The spirit and character which is already advanced in constant creativeness, in wide compassion and unceasing illumination, knowing what life means and how to attain that meaning—such a spirit not only influences those among whom it is—but its influence spreads radioactively, telepathetically, and the limits of its force cannot be set, because the source on which it is drawing is itself illimitable. Being, therefore, is all, and doing merely the symptom and sign of being, as body is the appearance of spirit.

Anon.

Ask yourselves, Who are the people who have really helped me? You will find, I think, that they have been laymen more often than clergymen, women perhaps more often than men; that the occasions have been most trivial, that the words spoken and things done have been slight and unpremeditated. They have been sidelights upon the person's character, peeps into the inner life of one whom God hides privily by His own presence from the provoking of all men; whose mind is kept in perfect peace because it is stayed on God; of one who sees God because his heart is pure.
It is the sudden sting of self-reproach, the shame of the contrast, the longing to be like such an one, to see things as he sees them, that sticks in a man's mind, and sends him to his knees as soon as he is alone. Sometimes when such a man or woman dies, we learn for the first time, not without surprise, what he or she has been to many. Such persons have laid up a rich store of gratitude by being what God has helped them to be. A character can never be refuted or ignored; disinterestedness is always interesting.

W.R. Inge, *Personal Religion and the Life of Devotion*, Longmans, Green & Co. Ltd., 1924, p.72.

INNER LIFE

I within did flow
With Seas of Life, like Wine.

Thomas Traherne, *The Poetical Works of Thomas Traherne*, edited with preface and notes by Gladys I. Wade, P.J. & A.E. Dobell, 1932, p.5, "Wonder," st.iii, l.5.

The important matter was the increase of this inward life, the silent growth of this kingdom of God in the hearts of men, the spread of this invisible Church.

Rufus M. Jones, *Spiritual Reformers in the 16th and 17th Centuries*, Macmillan & Co. Ltd., 1914, p.85.

We must revolutionise this system of life, that is based on *outside* things, money, property, and establish a system of life which is based on *inside* things.

D.H. Lawrence, *The Letters of D.H. Lawrence,* edited by George T. Zytaruk & James T. Boulton, Cambridge University Press, 1981, Volume II, p.280.

Justice is like the kingdom of God—it is not without us as a fact, it is within us as a great yearning.

George Eliot, *Romola,* T. Nelson & Sons, Ltd., 1965, p.543.

God does not die on the day when we cease to believe in a personal deity, but we die on the day when our lives cease to be illumined by the steady radiance, renewed daily, of a wonder, the source of which is beyond all reason.

Dag Hammarskjold, *Markings,* translated by Leif Sjoberg and W.H. Auden, with a foreword by W.H. Auden, Faber and Faber Limited, 1964, p.64.

The life of Jesus was a calm. It was a life of marvellous composure. The storms were all about it, tumult and tempest, tempest and tumult, waves breaking over Him all the time.... But the inner life was as a sea of glass. It was a life of perfect composure ... the great calm is there.

Henry Drummond, *The Greatest Thing in the World,* William Collins Sons & Co. Ltd., 1978, p.169.

The indwelling of God is this—to have God ever in mind, established within us. We thus become temples of God whenever our recollection of Him is not interrupted by earthly thoughts, nor the mind disturbed by unexpected passions, but escaping all these, the lover of God withdraws to Him.

St. Basil the Great, in *Studies in Early Mysticism in the Near and Middle East,* Margaret Smith, Sheldon Press, 1931, p.59.

Such practice of inward orientation, of inward worship and listening, is no mere counsel for special religious groups, for small religious orders, for special "interior souls," for monks retired in cloisters. This practice is the heart of religion. It is the secret, I am persuaded, of the inner life of the Master of Galilee. He expected this secret to be freshly discovered in everyone who would be his follower.

Thomas Kelly, *A Testament of Devotion,* Hodder & Stoughton Ltd, 1943, p.31.

He that thus seeks shall find; he shall live in truth, and that shall live in him; it shall be like a stream of living waters issuing out of his own soul; he shall drink of the waters of his own cistern, and be satisfied; he shall every morning find this heavenly manna lying upon the top of his own soul, and be fed with it to eternal life; he will find satisfaction within, feeling himself in conjunction with truth, though all the world should dispute against him.

John Smith the Platonist, *Select Discourses,* Cambridge at the University Press, 1859, p.13.

For when the soul reaches the perfection of the Spirit, being completely purified from passion, and is joined and commingled with the Holy Spirit by that secret communion, and being united with the Spirit is deemed worthy to become spirit itself, then it becomes all light, all eye, all spirit, all joy, all rest, all exultation, all heart-felt love, all goodness and loving kindness. Such souls as these are strengthened within themselves by the virtues of the Spirit's power, for ever, being blameless within, and spotless and pure.

St. Macarius of Egypt, in *Studies in Early Mysticism in the Near and Middle East*, Margaret Smith, Sheldon Press, 1931, p.65.

The man who lives from the deep centre discovers a new dynamic. He is worked through, in a manner wholly different from "his previous experience."...
The energy coming from "the deep centre" is not subject to the law of opposites. It is quiet. This is not to say that the man through whom the energy flows lives a life of placid ease. He has to strive and agonize at the conscious level, more so than before, perhaps; but he does not agonize for nothing. New and creative springs of action arise in the depths; and in the midst of his striving the man finds himself serving as a channel by which they find their way into life.

P.W. Martin, *Experiment in Depth*, Routledge & Kegan Paul Ltd., 1967, p.225.

The divine mystery of this infinite God is revealed and discovered in the hearts of the sons of men, whom He hath chosen: and He hath given us, to enjoy and possess in us a measure of that fulness that is in Himself, even a measure of the same Love and Life, of the same Mercy and Power, and of the same divine Nature.... These things ye know, if ye be born from above, and if the immortal birth live in you, and you be constant in the faith, then are you heirs through it, of the everlasting inheritance of eternal life ... and all are yours, because you are Christ's, and he is God's, and you have the Father and the Son.

Edward Burroughs, *The Memorable Works of a Son of Thunder and Consolation*, 1672, p.698.

God dwells secretly in all souls and is hidden in their substance; for, were this not so, they would be unable to exist. But there is a difference between these two manners of dwelling, and a great one. For in some He dwells alone, and in others He dwells not alone; in some He dwells contented and in others He dwells displeased; in some He dwells as in His house, ordering it and ruling everything, while in others He dwells as a stranger in the house of another where He is not allowed to do anything or to give any commands. Where He dwells with the greatest content and most completely alone is in the soul wherein dwell fewest desires and pleasures of its own; here He is in His own house and rules and governs it. And the more completely alone does He dwell in the soul, the more secretly He dwells; and thus in this soul wherein dwells no desire, neither any other image or form or affection of aught that is created, the Beloved dwells most secretly, with more intimate, more interior and closer embrace, according as the soul, as we say, is the more purely and completely withdrawn from all save God.

St. John of the Cross, *Living Flame of Love*, translated, edited, with an introduction by E. Allison Peers, Image Books, Doubleday & Company, Inc., 1972, p.269.

INSPIRATION

When God intends doing some act of great charity in us, by us, or with us, first, He proposes it by inspiration; secondly, we are pleased with it; and thirdly, we give our full consent to it.

St. Francis de Sales, *Introduction to the Devout Life,* translated and edited by John K. Ryan, Longmans, Green & Co. Ltd., 1962, p.92.

Perpetual Inspiration, therefore, is in the Nature of the Thing as necessary to a Life of Goodness, Holiness, and Happiness, as perpetual Respiration of the Air is necessary to animal life.

William Law, *The Spirit of Love,* full text, edited with an introduction and notes by Sidney Spencer, James Clarke & Co. Ltd., 1969, p.206.

Now, this continual knocking of Christ at the door of the heart sets forth the case or nature of a continual, immediate divine inspiration within us; it is always with us, but there must be an opening of the heart to it; and though it is always there, yet it is only felt and found by those who are attentive to it, depend upon, and humbly wait for it.

William Law, *Selected Mystical Writings of William Law,* edited by Stephen Hobhouse, Rockliff, 1948, p.219.

What but God?
Inspiring God! who, boundless spirit all,
And unremitting energy, pervades,
Adjusts, sustains, and agitates the whole.

James Thomson, *The Seasons* and *The Castle of Indolence,* edited by J. Logie Robertson, Oxford at the Clarendon Press, 1891, "Spring," l.852, p.54.

Those divinely possessed and inspired have at least the knowledge that they hold some greater thing within them though they cannot tell what it is; from the movements that stir them and the utterances that come from them they perceive the power, not themselves, that moves them.

Plotinus, *The Enneads,* translated by Stephen Mackenna, Faber and Faber Limited, 1956, p.396.

Sometimes, when I have come to my work empty, I have suddenly become full, ideas being in an invisible manner showered upon me, and implanted in me from on high; so that through the influence of divine inspiration I have become filled with enthusiasm, and have known neither the place in which I was nor those who were present, nor myself, nor what I was saying, nor what I was writing, for then I have been conscious of a richness of interpretation, an enjoyment of light, a most keen-sighted vision, a most distinct view of the objects treated, such as would be given through the eyes from the clearest exhibition.

Philo, in *The Philosophy of Plotinus,* W.R. Inge, Longmans, Green & Co. Ltd., 1918, Volume II, p.154.

Thou, my all!
My theme! my inspiration! and my crown!
My strength in age! my rise in low estate!

My soul's ambition, pleasure, wealth! my world!
My light in darkness! and my life in death!
My boast thro' time! bliss thro' eternity!
Eternity, too short to speak thy praise,
Or fathom thy profound of love to man!

Edward Young, *Night Thoughts*, Thomas Nelson, 1841, p.59.

Already I am wavering in my absolute determination to shut myself up daily, wherever I am and in whatever external circumstances, for so-and-so many hours for my work's sake: I do not know whether it will really come now or whether I am just making the appropriate gestures, but remain unfilled.... Have I not known ever since I was in Russia, and with such great conviction, that prayer and its time and its reverent and unstinted gestures were the condition of God and of his return to all those who barely expect it, who only kneel down and stand up and are suddenly filled to the brim? So will I kneel down and stand up, daily, alone in my room, and will keep holy all that befalls me: even what has *not* come, even disappointment, even desertion. There is no poverty that is not fullness could we but accept it gravely and worthily, and not surrender or yield it up to bitterness....

Rainer Maria Rilke, *Selected Letters of Rainer Maria Rilke*, translated by R.F.C. Hull, Macmillan & Co. Ltd., 1946, p.98.

It is by long obedience and hard work that the artist comes to unforced spontaneity and consummate mastery. Knowing that he can never create anything on his own account, out of the top layers, so to speak, of his personal consciousness, he submits obediently to the workings of "inspiration"; and knowing that the medium in which he works has its own self-nature, which must not be ignored or violently overridden, he makes himself its patient servant and, in this way, achieves perfect freedom of expression. But life is also an art, and the man who would become a consummate artist in living must follow, on all the levels of his being, the same procedure as that by which the painter or the sculptor or any other craftsman comes to his own more limited perfection.

Aldous Huxley, *The Perennial Philosophy*, Chatto & Windus Ltd., 1974, p.135.

The Greek sculptor who wrought his statue, and, when it was finished, fell on his knees before it, felt that its beauty was no mere creation of his own, but something heavenly. Milton's passionate prayer to the celestial muse was not a poetic convention. And to Wordsworth what in literary phrase is named the consciousness of genius was in truth the consciousness of dependence upon, union with, and devotion to, the spirit of thought and love which manifests itself in nature and is more fully revealed in the thought and love of humanity. The man who is conscious of genius is generally a little man of talent. Men of genius are more often intensely conscious of their own littleness, and of the immeasurable heights above them. Here again we find the paradox of inspiration—that the greater the spiritual activity within a man, the less is he able to ascribe this activity to himself. And this fact, however paradoxical, is the root of religion....

In truth the man of genius (or rather the spirit which expresses itself in him under the limitations which belong to his individuality and diminish his greatness) is the main factor in human progress. Be his sphere that of religion, or science, or art, or of practice in morals or politics or even industry, he comes, and something as yet unrevealed breaks into the light. That which he brings, the new insight, begins its work upon the world, often, alas, in pain and conflict, struggling through clouds, and losing, as it conquers them and brightens on the general mind, much of the ineffable purity and radiance of its dawn. But even so it does its work. Like a stream from a mountain spring his idea divides and spreads. Slowly it distributes itself along the hundred channels of minds less original, and then along the thousand channels of minds less original still, till it has irrigated and fertilized a country or a continent, meeting again and again with like streams of influence from other springs, mixing with them and acquiring from its union a new virtue and a continued life. We *are* in our spiritual substance the spirits of the great dead.

A.C. Bradley, *A Miscellany*, Macmillan & Co. Ltd., 1931, p.235.

INTELLECT

Opinion is ultimately determined by the feelings, and not by the intellect.

Herbert Spencer, *Social Statics*, Williams & Norgate, 1892, p.244.

The greater intellect one has, the more originality one finds in men. Ordinary persons find no difference between men.

Blaise Pascal, *Pensées*, translated by W.F. Trotter, Random House Inc., 1941, p.6.

When Man has arrived at a certain ripeness of intellect any one grand and spiritual passage serves him as a starting-post towards all "the two-and-thirty Palaces."

John Keats, *The Works of John Keats*, edited by H. Buxton Forman, Reeves & Turner, 1883, Volume III, p.117, Letter to J. H. Reynolds, l.10.

For no creature, howsoever rational and intellectual, is lighted of itself, but is lighted by participation of eternal Truth.

St. Augustine, *An Augustine Synthesis*, arranged by Erich Przywara, S.J., Sheed & Ward Ltd., 1945, p.21.

We must shut the eye of sense, and open that brighter eye of our understandings, that other eye of the soul (as the philosopher calls our intellectual faculty) ... "which indeed all have, but few make use of."

John Smith the Platonist, *Select Discourses*, Cambridge at the University Press, 1859, p.16.

The uncertainty, however, lies always in the intellectual region, never in the practical. What Paul cares about is plain enough to the true heart, however far from plain to the man whose desire to understand goes ahead of his obedience.

George Macdonald, *Unspoken Sermons*, Third Series, Longmans, Green, & Co., 1889, p.43.

The mind will never unveil God to man. God is only found at a certain point on the road of experience. He speaks to man through his heart and when that happens man knows, and he never again questions the love of God.

Grace Cooke, *Spiritual Unfoldment*, The White Eagle Publishing Trust, 1961, p.113.

How often does the weak will obscure the clear call of conscience by resort to intellectual "difficulties!" Some of these are real enough; but some are sheer self-protection against the exacting claim of the holy love of God.

William Temple, *Readings in St. John's Gospel* (First and Second Series), Macmillan & Co. Ltd., 1947, p.68.

We should not pretend to understand the world only by the intellect; we apprehend it just as much by feeling. Therefore the judgement of the intellect is, at best, only the half of truth, and must, if it be honest, also come to an understanding of its inadequacy.

C.G. Jung, *Psychological Types*, translated by H. Godwin Baynes, Kegan Paul, Trench, Trubner & Co. Ltd., 1946, p.628.

The longest way to God
the indirect
lies through the intellect
Here is my journey's end
and here its start.

Angelus Silesius, *The Book of Angelus Silesius*, translated, drawn, and handwritten by Frederick Franck, Wildwood House, Ltd., 1976, p.104.

All these intellectual attitudes would have short shrift if Christianity had remained what it was, a communion, if Christianity had remained what it was, a religion of the heart. This is one of the reasons why modern people understand nothing of true, real Christianity, of the true, real history of Christianity and what Christendom really was.

Charles Péguy, *Basic Verities*, translated by Ann & Julian Green, Kegan Paul, Trench, Trubner & Co. Ltd., 1943, p.115.

It often seems to me when listening to the talk of clever people that they are in effect saying, "Unless I understand, unless I am let into all the secrets of the Creator, I shall refuse to believe in him at all." I am sure that such an attitude, even if it be unconscious, creates a strong barrier between man and his understanding of his true position. Anyone with the most elementary knowledge of physics knows that there are sounds which are too high in pitch for us to hear, and forms of light which are quite invisible to the human eye.... Yet for some curious reason we find it very difficult to believe that there may be sense higher than our sense, reason above our reason, and a total purpose quite beyond our comprehension. It seems to me perfectly possible that there may be supra-human wisdom, and we might well assume an attitude of wholesome humility when we reflect upon our relative insignificance. Can we not accept the suggestion that there are facts, even "scientific" facts, which we can never know because we are incapable of understanding them? Can we not be persuaded to believe that

specks of consciousness on this little planet cannot, in all reasonableness, be thought
of as accurate critics of the total purpose behind creation?

J.B. Phillips, *God Our Contemporary*, Hodder & Stoughton Ltd., 1961, p.54.

Perhaps the most dangerous by-product of the Age of Intellect is the unconscious growth of the idea that the human brain can solve the problems of the world. Even on the low level of practical affairs this is patently untrue. Any small human activity, the local bowls club or the ladies' luncheon club, requires for its survival a measure of self-sacrifice and service on the part of the members. In a wider national sphere, the survival of the nation depends basically on the loyalty and self-sacrifice of the citizens. The impression that the situation can be saved by mental cleverness, without
unselfishness or human self-dedication, can only lead to collapse.
Thus we see that the cultivation of the human intellect seems to be a magnificent ideal, but only on condition that it does not weaken unselfishness and human dedication to service. Yet this, judging by historical precedent, seems to be exactly what it does do. Perhaps it is not the intellectualism which destroys the spirit of self-sacrifice— the least we can say is that the two, intellectualism and the loss of a sense of duty,
appear simultaneously in the life-story of the nation.
Indeed it often appears in individuals, that the head and the heart are natural rivals. The brilliant but cynical intellectual appears at the opposite end of the spectrum from the emotional self-sacrifice of the hero or the martyr. Yet there are times when the perhaps unsophisticated self-dedication of the hero is more essential than the sarcasm
of the clever.

Sir John Glubb, *The Fate of Empires* and *Search For Survival*, William Blackwood & Sons Ltd., 1978, p.13.

INTERCESSION

Why has our sincere prayer for each other such great power over others? Because of the fact that by cleaving to God during prayer I become one spirit with Him, and unite with myself, by faith and love, those for whom I pray; for the Holy Ghost acting in me also acts at the same time in them, for He accomplishes all things. "We, being
many, are one bread, one body." "There is one body and one Spirit."

John of Cronstadt, in *A Treasury of Russian Spirituality*, edited by G.P. Fedotov, Sheed & Ward Ltd., 1977,
p.362.

In intercession as a whole we have the simplest example provided by the general religious life, of a vast principle which is yet largely unexplored by us. It is the principle, that man's emergent will and energy can join itself to, and work with, the supernatural forces for the accomplishment of the work of God: sometimes for this purpose even entering into successful conflict with the energies of the "natural world."

Evelyn Underhill, *Man and the Supernatural*, Methuen & Co Ltd., 1927, p.257.

If thou shouldst never see my face again,
Pray for my soul. More things are wrought by prayer
Than this world dreams of. Wherefore, let thy voice

Rise like a fountain for me night and day.
For what are men better than sheep or goats
That nourish a blind life within the brain,
If, knowing God, they lift not hands of prayer
Both for themselves and those who call them friend?
For so the whole round earth is every way
Bound by gold chains about the feet of God.

Alfred, Lord Tennyson, *The Poems of Tennyson,* edited by Christopher Ricks, Longmans, Green & Co. Ltd., 1969, p.1753, *The Idylls of the Kings,* No.475, "The Passing of Arthur," 1.414.

The first step in intercession is to make a definite "act" of union with this stream of God's love and power, which is flowing ceaselessly out of His heart, and back to Him again....

Making a conscious effort to unite our wills and hearts with the ever-flowing river of the love of God will give us a restful energy. As we realize that the love of God is flowing through us and using us as it passes, all merely natural strain will disappear. If suffering comes to us in our time of intercession, we must accept it, and still remain tranquilly surrendered to God for His purpose. If we experience difficulty in "getting going," it would be well to search our hearts to see whether after all we are praying that God will bless *our* efforts for His glory, rather than seeking to be united with *His* will. "The greatest works wrought by prayer have been accomplished, not by human effort but by human trust in God's effort." In prayer of this kind we are united with the very life of God, sharing in His work.

"It is the unseen, unknown part of intercession which makes our part both possible and important. It is the wind of the Holy Ghost blowing through us, it is the tide of God's providence, it is the current of the divine desire which really accomplish the work of intercession; and yet the human agent is essential for the accomplishment of the activity. Intercession is the expression of God's love and desire which He has deigned to share with man, and in which He uses man."...

The essence and heart of intercession is self-offering. The deeper our surrender to God, the more true and powerful will be our intercession. Intercession is indeed a basic principle of human living: it expresses that corporate sense of community which is the real nature of human life; and it expresses that instinct to give to the point of sacrifice which is one of the deepest elements in our nature, fulfilled once for all by Christ on the Cross.... Thus intercession covers the whole world: all the sins and cruelties and miseries of men; all the horrors of war; the sighing of prisoners and captives; the sufferings of the oppressed and the outcast; the despair of those who are far from God: "Christian intercession is the completion and expression of self-giving." We offer our poor imperfect love to God to be a channel of His perfect and redeeming love. We offer ourselves to be a way through which God will reach, and save and bless the whole world.

Olive Wyon, *The School of Prayer,* S.C.M. Press Ltd., 1943, p.115.

J

JESUS CHRIST

For in him the whole fulness of deity dwells bodily, and you have come to fulness of
life in him.
Colossians 2.9.

As Man alone, Jesus could not have saved us; as God alone, he would not; Incarnate,
he could and did.
Malcolm Muggeridge, *Jesus, The Man Who Lives,* William Collins Sons & Co. Ltd., 1981, p.31.

He does not say "No man knoweth God save the Son." That would be to deny the
truth of the Old Testament revelation. What He does say is that He alone has a deeper
secret, the essential Fatherhood of the Sovereign Power.
D.S. Cairns, *The Riddle of the World,* S.C.M. Press Ltd., 1937, p.321.

Jesus astonishes and overpowers sensual people. They cannot unite him to history, or
reconcile him with themselves. As they come to revere their intuitions and aspire to
live holily, their own piety explains every fact, every word.
Ralph Waldo Emerson, *Essays,* "History," Bernhard Tauchnitz, 1915, p.24.

If you accept that Jesus is the revelation and manifestation of the Father, then you
are a follower of Christ and so a Christian. If you move from that to asking in what
sense is Christ God, then I would think you have to come in the end to making that
act of faith which is recorded of St. Thomas the Doubtful: "My Lord and my God."
Basil Hume, in *Priestland's Progress,* Gerald Priestland, British Broadcasting Corporation, 1982, p.41.

When criticism has done its worst, the words and acts of Our Lord which remain are
not those of "a good and heroic man," but of one deliberately claiming unique authority
and insight, and conscious of a unique destiny.
Evelyn Underhill, *The Letters of Evelyn Underhill,* edited with an introduction by Charles Williams, Longmans,
Green & Co. Ltd., 1947, p.217.

If we refuse the invitation of Christ, some day our greatest pain will lie, not in the
things we suffer, but in the realization of the precious things which we have missed,
and of which we have cheated ourselves.
William Barclay, *The Gospel of Matthew,* The Saint Andrew Press, 1975, Volume 2, p.296.

That is the secret after all—to get to know and love Christ through love for *all* His
brothers and sisters, and not to expect to know Christ first and then begin to think
of them. St. Francis learnt first how to love everybody and everything for Christ's
sake, before he came really to know Christ Himself... I can see more, in the people

in church with me, to put me in a right frame for Communion than I can see in all the little "aids to devotion" given me at my confirmation.... In every person we meet, in whom we see something to love, we are seeing something of Christ. For what we recognize as Christ-like in them is due to the Holy Spirit in them, and the power to recognize it is the Holy Spirit in ourselves. God is Love, and His Spirit is the power to love and attract love. This changes one's whole outlook on life, and then we have a glimpse of heaven....

Edward Wilson, in *The Faith of Edward Wilson*, George Seaver, John Murray Ltd., 1949, p.35.

Christ was the Son of God. But remember in what sense He ever used this name— Son of God because Son of Man. He claims Sonship in virtue of His Humanity. Now, in the whole previous revelation through the Prophets, &c. one thing was implied— only through man can God be known; only through a perfect man, perfectly revealed. Hence He came, "the brightness of His Father's Glory, the *express image* of His person." Christ then must be loved as Son of Man before He can be adored as Son of God. In personal love and adoration of Christ the Christian religion consists, not in correct morality, or in correct doctrines, but in a homage to the King.

Frederick W. Robertson, in *Life and Letters of Frederick W. Robertson*, edited by Stopford A. Brooke, Smith, Elder, & Co., 1865, Volume II, p.169.

In the days of His earthly ministry, only those could speak to Him who came where He was. If He was in Galilee, men could not find Him in Jerusalem; if He was in Jerusalem, men could not find Him in Galilee. But His Ascension means that He is perfectly united with God; we are with Him wherever we are present to God; and that is everywhere and always. Because He is "in Heaven" He is everywhere on earth; because He is ascended, He is here now. Our devotion is not to hold us by the empty tomb; it must lift up our hearts to heaven so that we too "in heart and mind thither ascend and with Him continually dwell"; it must also send us forth into the world to do His will; and these are not two things, but one.

William Temple, *Readings in St. John's Gospel* (First and Second Series), Macmillan & Co. Ltd., 1947, p.382.

He is always seeking, *through* the historical Christ, to find the Eternal Christ—the ever-living, ever-present, personal Self-Revelation of God.... "I esteem Christ the Word of God above all else, for without Him there is no salvation, and without Him no one can enjoy God." "Christ ... has been called the Image, the Character, the Expression of God, yes, the Glory and Effulgence of His Splendour, the very Impression of His Substance, so that in Him God Himself is seen and heard and known. For it is God Himself whom we see and hear and perceive in Christ. In Him God becomes visible and His nature is revealed. Everything that God is, or knows, or wills or possesses, or can do, is incarnated in Christ and put before our eyes. Everything that can be said of God can as truly be said of Christ."

But this Christ, who is the very Nature and Character of God made visible and vocal, is, as we have seen, not limited to the historical Person who lived in Galilee and Judea. He is an eternal Logos, a living Word, coming to expression, in some degree, in all times and lands, revealing His Light through the dim lantern of many human lives—a Christ reborn in many souls, raised again in many victorious lives, and endlessly spreading His Kingdom through the ever-widening membership of the invisible Church.

Rufus M. Jones, *Spiritual Reformers in the 16th and 17th Centuries*, Macmillan & Co. Ltd., 1914, p.61.

Unless we know Christ experimentally so that "He lives within us spiritually, and so that all which is known of Him in the Letter and Historically is truly done and acted in our souls—until we experimentally verify all we read of Him—the Gospel is a mere tale to us." It is not saving knowledge to know that Christ was born in Bethlehem but to know that He is born in us. It is vastly more important to know experimentally that we are crucified with Christ than to know historically that He died in Jerusalem many years ago, and to feel Jesus Christ risen again within you is far more operative than to have "a notional knowledge" that He rose on the third day. "When thou begins to find and know not merely that He was conceived in the womb of a virgin, but that *thou* art that virgin and that He is more truly and spiritually, and yet as really, conceived in thy heart so that thou feelest the Babe beginning to be conceived in thee by the power of the Holy Ghost and the Most High overshadowing thee; when thou feelest Jesus Christ stirring to be born and brought forth in thee; when thou beginnest to see and feel all those mighty, powerful actions done in thee which thou readest that He did in the flesh—here is a Christ indeed, a real Christ who will do thee some good."

Rufus M. Jones, *Spiritual Reformers in the 16th and 17th Centuries*, Macmillan & Co. Ltd., 1914, p.244.

Anyone who ventures to look the historical Jesus straight in the face and to listen for what He may have to teach him in His powerful sayings, soon ceases to ask what this strange-seeming Jesus can still be to him. He learns to know Him as One who claims authority over him.
The true understanding of Jesus is the understanding of will acting on will. The true relation to Him is to be taken possession of by Him. Christian piety of any and every sort is valuable only so far as it means the surrender of our will to His.
Jesus does not require of men to-day that they be able to grasp either in speech or in thought Who He is. He did not think it necessary to give those who actually heard His sayings any insight into the secret of His personality, or to disclose to them the fact that He was that descendant of David who was one day to be revealed as the Messiah. The one thing He did require of them was that they should actively and passively prove themselves men who had been compelled by Him to rise from being as the world to being other than the world, and thereby partakers of His peace.

Albert Schweitzer, in *Albert Schweitzer: Christian Revolutionary*, George Seaver, James Clarke and Co. Ltd., 1944, p.18.

First of all, Jesus Christ was a Man, in the full psychological sense, sharing truly and fully in the conditions of our empirical humanity. The fact which confronts us in the New Testament in all the wonder of its perfection is an actual human life, which was at the same time true human life. He was no phantom, archangel or demi-god.... It is vitally important that we do not in any way jeopardize the truth that Jesus was a Man.... He not only ate and drank; he knew hunger, thirst and weariness. Consider his bravery, his sense of humour, his severity, his tenderness. To use Pilate's words, "Behold the Man"—poor, born in an outhouse, working, journeying, praying; tempted as we are tempted.... Behold him, healing and teaching the pathetic multitudes, touched with the feeling of men's infirmities, himself a Man of sorrows and acquainted with grief. He was human enough to weep over the woes of those whom he was not ashamed to call his brethren. Bearing on his heart the burden and shame of their sin, he nevertheless stood in with them and loved them to the end. Utterly clear-sighted, he was the vigorous debater, ruthlessly exposing and fiercely denouncing the shams of much conventional religion. Without a trace of self-pity he went deliberately to Jerusalem to die. His was the highest, holiest Manhood which this world has seen or can see, and at the last—we men and women being what we are—he was nailed to a gallows to die with criminals, the innocent victim of fear, bigotry, jealous hatred, political opportunism and legalized murder. He was crucified, dead and buried....

Here in this human life we meet the living God. It is God himself, personally present and redeemingly active, who comes to meet men in this Man of Nazareth. Jesus is more than a religious genius, such as George Fox, and more than a holy man, such as the lovable Lama in Kipling's *Kim*. He himself knows that he is more.... The Gospel story is a tree rooted in the familiar soil of time and sense; but its roots go down into the Abyss and its branches fill the Heavens; given to us in terms of a country in the Eastern Mediterranean no bigger than Wales, during the Roman Principate of Tiberius Caesar in the first century of our era, its range is universal; it is on the scale of eternity. God's presence and his very Self were made manifest in the words and works of this Man....

In short,... the Man Christ Jesus has the decisive place in man's ageless relationship with God. He is what God means by "Man." He is what man means by "God."

J.S. Whale, *Christian Doctrine,* Cambridge at the University Press, 1942, p.99.

We want to realize very definitely what Christ is to us, how we are to look upon Christ and what it was that induced Him to put on all the weakness and the pain that life brings to every one of us.

God is a law to Himself. All good men are a law to themselves; all the best men and women and children are those who live with principles. Principles are the laws of life which each person makes for himself, and the best people are those whose principles are so strong that they resist every temptation to anything lower, yet so pliant that they readily give way to anything higher. Like a cog-wheel with a catch, they can always be screwed a turn higher and never drop to where they were before.

Such should be the law of our lives, one tooth higher in the wheel every day. Such is God's Law of Nature, and such was Christ's Law of Life. So that when Christ as a Jew allowed that He was under the law bound to keep the Sabbath without working, when it came to a question of keeping it and turning a deaf ear to suffering, or breaking it and relieving suffering, He chose to break it—because the Law of Mercy is a tooth higher in the cog-wheel than the Law of keeping the Sabbath. But to neglect your work on Saturday night in order to amuse yourself, and to do your work in consequence on Sunday, this is holding the catch back and letting your cog-wheel slip the wrong way.

"We want to realize very definitely what Christ is to us."—What was He to Wilson? The divinity of Christ was fundamental to his faith. Yet Christ was for him no ready-made perfection, no *deus ex machina,* but a man like others who, though He were a Son, was made perfect through the discipline of suffering; not the Great Exception, but the Great Example; no half-brother or step-brother to mankind, but Elder Brother, with the blood of the human race in His veins, the first-fruits of every human creature, first-born among many brethren; perfect as we are not, healthy as a sick man is not, yet the Norm of perfectibility and wholeness for all men, who became like us that we might become like Him.
And equally fundamental to his faith in the divinity of Christ, because indissolubly bound up with it, was his faith in the potential divinity of man; Christ's nature being no different in kind from ours, from the least of His brethren, though immeasurably different in degree.... "Everyone that is perfected shall be as his Master." Not that he counted himself to have apprehended—very far indeed from that; but he pressed toward the mark, in confidence of the final consummation when all should come in the unity of the same faith, by the power of the same indwelling Spirit, "unto a perfect man, unto the measure of the stature of the man Christ Jesus."
This is the central theme which inspired all his thinking, and which he strove so faithfully to weave into the texture of his life; it was his reading of the true meaning of human existence—Christ-likeness, and nothing less than that.

Edward Wilson, in *The Faith of Edward Wilson,* George Seaver, John Murray Ltd., 1949, p.27.

JOY

The gladness of the heart is the life of man, and the joyfulness of a man prolongeth his days.
Ecclesiasticus 30.22 (A.V.).

Thou dost show me the path of life; in thy presence there is fulness of joy, in thy right hand are pleasures for evermore.
Psalm 16.11.

I will greatly rejoice in the Lord, my soul shall exult in my God.
Isaiah 61.10.

These things I have spoken to you, that my joy may be in you, and that your joy may be full.
John 15.11.

But now I am coming to thee; and these things I speak in the world, that they may have my joy fulfilled in themselves.
John 17.13.

Rejoice in the Lord always; again I will say, Rejoice. Let all men know your forbearance. The Lord is at hand. Have no anxiety about anything, but in everything by prayer and supplication with thanksgiving let your requests be made known to God. And the peace of God, which passes all understanding, will keep your hearts and your minds in Christ Jesus.

Philippians 4.4-7.

Joy rises in me, like a summer's morn.

Samuel Taylor Coleridge, *Coleridge's Poetical Works*, edited by Ernest Hartley Coleridge, Oxford University Press, 1978, p.340, "A Christmas Carol," st.viii, l.47.

Joy is prayer—Joy is strength—Joy is love ... A joyful heart is the normal result of a heart burning with love.

Mother Teresa of Calcutta, in *Something Beautiful For God*, Malcolm Muggeridge, William Collins Sons & Co. Ltd., 1983, p.68.

How good is man's life, the mere living! how fit to employ
All the heart and the soul and the senses for ever in joy!

Robert Browning, *The Poetical Works of Robert Browning*, Smith, Elder, & Co., 1899, Volume I, p.275, "Saul," st.ix. l.21.

This glory and honour wherewith man is crowned ought to affect every person that is grateful, with celestial joy: and so much the rather because it is every man's proper and sole inheritance.

Thomas Traherne, *Centuries*, The Faith Press Ltd., 1969, p.150.

Joy is everywhere; it is in the earth's green covering of grass; in the blue serenity of the sky; in the reckless exuberance of spring; in the severe abstinence of grey winter; in the living flesh that animates our bodily frame; in the perfect poise of the human figure, noble and upright; in living; in the exercise of all our powers; in the acquisition of knowledge; in fighting evils; in dying for gains we can never share. Joy is there everywhere.

Rabindranath Tagore, *Sadhana*, Macmillan & Co. Ltd., Indian Edition, 1930, p.116.

There are some people who have the quality of richness and joy in them and they communicate it to everything they touch. It is first of all a physical quality; then it is a quality of the spirit. With such people it makes no difference if they are rich or poor: they are really always rich because they have such wealth and vital power within them that they give everything interest, dignity, and a warm colour.

Thomas Wolfe, *The Web and the Rock*, The Sun Dial Press, 1940, p.377.

Given reasonable health and freedom from anxiety, the world is for most people a good place to live in, with much of interest, beauty and wonder. Contact with other people can bring friendship, co-operation, humour and enjoyment. Given the faith that the world is God's creation and that each man is made in the image of God in a unique and personal way, our enjoyment becomes increasingly right and satisfying. Add to this the availability of divine grace for every difficulty and opportunity, and our enjoyment becomes almost mandatory.

George Appleton, *Journey for a Soul*, William Collins Sons & Co. Ltd., 1976, p.39.

Joy is the triumph of *life;* it is the sign that we are living our true life as spiritual beings. We are sent into the world to become something and to make something. The two are in practice so closely connected as to be almost inseparable. Our personality expands by creativeness, and creates spontaneously as it expands. Joy is the signal that we are spiritually alive and active. Wherever joy is, creation has been; and the richer the creation, the deeper the joy....

A great work of art, or a great scientific discovery, gives greater joy to its maker than a work of merely technical or mechanical skill....

Joy was a characteristic of the Christian community so long as it was growing, expanding, and creating healthfully. The time came when the Church ceased to grow, except externally in wealth, power and prestige; and these are mere outward adornments, or hampering burdens, very likely. They do not imply growth, or creativeness....

God sent us into the world to create something, and to enrich our own personality in the process. In our wrestling with intractable material, we have to draw on what is *above* ourselves. We have to rely on God's help to make anything worth making. And in drawing upon this power above ourselves, we take this higher power *into* ourselves; we raise ourselves above ourselves. This is how creativeness and inner growth mutually condition each other.

I want you to think earnestly of the witness which Joy on the one hand, and its antithesis, Boredom, on the other, bear to the duty and happiness of creative work, that is to say, real work, on however small a scale. The happy people are those who are producing something; the bored people are those who are consuming much and producing nothing.... God punishes the useless by giving them pleasure without joy; and very wearisome they find it....

Joy will be ours, in so far as we are genuinely interested in great ideas outside ourselves. When we have once crossed the charmed circle and got outside ourselves, we shall soon realise that all true joy has an eternal and Divine soul and goal. We are immortal spirits, set to do certain things in time; were it not so, our lives would lack any rational justification. The joy of achievement is the recognition of a task understood and done. It is done, and fit to take its place—however lowly a place—in the eternal order.... To do our duty in our own sphere, to try to create something worth creating, as our life's work, is the way to understand what joy is in this life, and, by God's grace to earn the verdict: "Well done, good and faithful servant; enter thou into the joy of thy Lord."

W.R. Inge, *Personal Religion and the Life of Devotion,* Longmans, Green & Co. Ltd., 1924, p.64.

JUDGEMENT

Those who plow iniquity and sow trouble reap the same.
Job 4.8.

God is not mocked, for whatever a man sows, that he will also reap.
Galatians 6.7.

Those consequences which follow from our actions or characters by the operation of God's laws are His judgements upon us.

William Temple, *The Church Looks Forward,* Macmillan & Co. Ltd., 1944, p.176.

God casts no soul away, unless it cast itself away. Every soul is its own judgement.

Jacob Boehme, in *Selected Mystical Writings of William Law,* edited by Stephen Hobhouse, Rockliff, 1948, p.371.

At the judgement I shall be asked if I have loved. This will be the touchstone question. If I am not failed on this once and for all, I shall be asked further if I have believed and obeyed, accepted and trusted, prayed and followed as best I could the light that was given me.

Hubert van Zeller, *Considerations,* Sheed & Ward Ltd., 1974, p.116.

We tend to think of the Divine Judgement as being the infliction upon us by an irresistible Despot of penalties, not growing out of our characters and deeds, but imposed from without ... The Divine Judgement is the verdict upon us which consists in our reaction to *the light* (3.19) when it is offered to us.

William Temple, *Readings in St. John's Gospel* (First and Second Series), Macmillan & Co. Ltd., 1947, p.287.

A life devoted to the interests and enjoyments of this world, spent and wasted in the slavery of earthly desires, may be truly called a dream, as having all the shortness, vanity, and delusion of a dream; only with this great difference, that when a dream is over nothing is lost but fictions and fancies; but when the dream of life is ended only by death, all that eternity is lost, for which we were brought into being.

William Law, *Selected Mystical Writings of William Law,* edited by Stephen Hobhouse, Rockliff, 1948, p.67.

People often wonder about the end of the world and the consummation of human life. Conscience reminds us of past wrongs, foolish actions and childish ignorances. Scripture and preachers remind us of a judgement to come and some people are unscriptural enough to claim to predict the day and hour. The secret is to see ourselves in the light of God's holiness and love, to acknowledge our need of forgiveness, to accept God's forgiveness and his grace, so that when death or judgement comes we may be ready, trusting and unafraid.

George Appleton, *Journey for a Soul,* William Collins Sons & Co. Ltd., 1976, p.227.

Damnation is no foreign, separate, or imposed state that is brought in upon us, or adjudged to us by the will of God, but is the inborn, natural, essential state of our own disordered nature, which is absolutely impossible in the nature of the thing to be anything else but our own hell both here and hereafter, unless all sin be separated from us and righteousness be again made our natural state by a birth of itself in us. And all this, not because God will have it so by an arbitrary act of His sovereign will but because He cannot change His own nature or make anything to be happy and blessed, but only that which has its proper righteousness and is of one will and spirit with Himself.

William Law, *Selected Mystical Writings of William Law,* edited by Stephen Hobhouse, Rockliff, 1948, p.171.

K

KINDNESS

There is also a grace of kind listening, as well as a grace of kind speaking.
F.W. Faber, *Spiritual Conferences,* Thomas Richardson & Son, 1859, p.40.

What wisdom can you find that is greater than kindness?
Jean Jacques Rousseau, *Emile* or *Education,* translated by Barbara Foxley, J.M. Dent & Sons, Ltd., 1911, p.43.

Kindness is the principle of tact, and respect for others the first condition of *savoir-vivre.*
Henri Frédéric Amiel, *Amiel's Journal,* translated by Mrs. Humphry Ward, Macmillan & Co. Ltd., 1918, p.16.

'Twas a thief said the last kind word to Christ:
Christ took the kindness and forgave the theft.
Robert Browning, *The Poetical Works of Robert Browning,* Smith, Elder, & Co., 1910, Volume II, p.128, *The Ring and the Book,* Pt.VI, l.869.

Life is short, and we have never too much time for gladdening the hearts of those who are travelling the dark journey with us. Oh, be swift to love, make haste to be kind!
Henri Frédéric Amiel, *Amiel's Journal,* translated by Mrs. Humphry Ward, Macmillan & Co. Ltd., 1918, p.146.

I expect to pass through this world but once; any good thing therefore that I can do, or any kindness that I can show to any fellow-creature, let me do it now; let me not defer or neglect it, for I shall not pass this way again.
Attributed to Stephen Grellet.

On that best portion of a good man's life,
His little, nameless, unremembered, acts
Of kindess and of love.
William Wordsworth, *The Poetical Works of William Wordsworth,* edited by E. de Selincourt, Oxford at the Clarendon Press, 1944, Volume II, p.260, "Lines composed a few miles above Tintern Abbey," l.33.

My feeling is that there is nothing in life but refraining from hurting others, and comforting those that are sad.
Olive Schreiner, *The Letters of Olive Schreiner,* edited by S.C. Cronwright-Schreiner, T. Fisher Unwin Ltd., 1924, p.48.

Be kind and merciful. Let no one ever come to you without coming away better and happier. Be the living expression of God's kindness: kindness in your face, kindness in your eyes, kindness in your smile, kindness in your warm greeting.
Mother Teresa of Calcutta, in *Something Beautiful For God,* Malcolm Muggeridge, William Collins Sons & Co. Ltd., 1983, p.69.

More skilful in self-knowledge, even more pure,
As tempted more; more able to endure,
As more exposed to suffering and distress;
Thence, also, more alive to tenderness.

William Wordsworth, *The Poetical Works of William Wordsworth*, edited by E. de Selincourt & Helen Darbishire, Oxford at the Clarendon Press, 1958, Volume IV, p.87, "Character of a Happy Warrior," 1.23.

Kind thoughts are rarer than either kind words or kind deeds. They imply a great deal of thinking about others. This in itself is rare. But they imply also a great deal of thinking about others without the thoughts being criticisms. This is rarer still.

F.W. Faber, *Spiritual Conferences*, Thomas Richardson & Son, 1859, p.22.

When we have been absorbed in great music, I do not think we generally feel particularly charitable to the people we meet outside. They seem to be of a coarser fibre than that into which we have been entering. That could never be true of our worship if it has really been worship of God, not some indulgence of our own spiritual emotion, but the concentration of mind, heart and will on Him. You will be full of kindness for everybody as you go out from such worship.

William Temple, *Christian Faith and Life*, S.C.M. Press Ltd., 1963, p.28.

THE KINGDOM OF GOD

The time is fulfilled, and the kingdom of God is at hand; repent, and believe in the gospel.

Mark 1.15.

I must preach the good news of the kingdom of God to the other cities also; for I was sent for this purpose.

Luke 4.43.

Nor will they say, "Lo here it is!" or "There!" for behold, the kingdom of God is within you.

Luke 17.21.

Unless one is born of water and the Spirit, he cannot enter the kingdom of God.

John 3.5.

But seek first his kingdom and his righteousness, and all these things shall be yours as well.

Matthew 6.33.

This life, this kingdom of God, this simplicity of absolute existence, is hard to enter. How hard? As hard as the Master of salvation could find words to express the hardness.

George Macdonald, *Unspoken Sermons*, Second Series, Longmans, Green & Co. Ltd., 1885, p.38.

To keep alive the sense of wonder, to live in unquestioning trust, instinctively to obey, to forgive and to forget—that is the childlike spirit, and that is the passport to the Kingdom of God.

William Barclay, *The Gospel of Luke*, The Saint Andrew Press, 1964, p.236.

The outer world, with all its phenomena, is filled with divine splendour, but we must have experienced the divine within ourselves, before we can hope to discover it in our environment.

Rudolf Steiner, *Knowledge of the Higher Worlds*, Rudolf Steiner Press, 1963, p.22.

This Kingdom of God is now within us. The Grace of the Holy Spirit likewise shines forth and warms us, distils a multitude of fragrances in the air around us, and pervades our senses with heavenly delight, flooding our hearts with inexpressible joy.

Seraphim of Sarov, in *A Treasury of Russian Spirituality*, edited by G.P. Fedotov, Sheed & Ward Ltd., 1977, p.277.

The Kingdom of God was the main subject of the early preaching of Jesus. He claimed that in himself the Kingdom had drawn near, was in operation, and he called to men to accept this fact in faith and to change their attitudes, behaviour and world view. Many of his parables dealt with the meaning of the Kingdom, as if he were wanting to ensure that those who could not at first understand would remember one vivid human story, and that one day the penny would drop. He wanted everyone to share the treasure that he had brought.

George Appleton, *Journey for a Soul*, William Collins Sons & Co. Ltd., 1976, p.159.

The Kingdom is something within you which has the power of growth like a seed; something that you discover almost accidentally; something that you are searching for, and of whose value you become more confident and excited as the search proceeds, and you discover truer, lovelier things which are constantly being surpassed; something for which you have to give everything you have, no less yet no more, including the earlier finds with which you were once so completely delighted.

George Appleton, *Journey for a Soul*, William Collins Sons & Co. Ltd., 1976, p.160.

Poor Sinner! consider the Treasure thou hast within Thee, the Saviour of the World, the eternal Word of God lies hid in Thee, as a Spark of the Divine Nature, which is to overcome Sin and Death, and Hell within Thee, and generate the Life of Heaven again in thy Soul. Turn to thy Heart, and thy Heart will find its Saviour, its God within itself. Thou seest, hearest, and feelest nothing of God, because thou seekest for Him *abroad* with thy outward Eyes, thou seekest for Him in Books, in Controversies, in the Church, and outward Exercises, but *there* thou wilt not find Him, till thou hast *first* found Him in thy Heart. Seek for Him in thy Heart, and thou wilt never seek in vain, for there He dwells, there is the Seat of his Light and Holy Spirit.

William Law, *The Spirit of Prayer*, full text, edited with an introduction and notes by Sidney Spencer, James Clarke & Co. Ltd., 1969, p.43.

The Kingdom of God is within us. When Christ appears in the clouds He will simply be manifesting a metamorphosis that has been slowly accomplished under His influence in the heart of the mass of mankind. In order to hasten His coming, let us therefore concentrate upon a better understanding of the process by which the Holy Presence is born and grows within us. In order to foster its progress more intelligently, let us observe the birth and growth of the divine *milieu*, first in ourselves and then in the world that begins with us.

Pierre Teilhard de Chardin, *Le Milieu Divin*, William Collins Sons & Co. Ltd., 1960, p.118.

Gentlemen, when a man grows older and sees more deeply into life, he does not find, if he possesses any inner world at all, that he is advanced by the external march of things, by "the progress of civilisation." Nay, he feels himself, rather, where he was before, and forced to seek the sources of strength which his forefathers also sought. He is forced to make himself a native of the kingdom of God, the kingdom of the Eternal, the kingdom of Love; and he comes to understand that it was only this kingdom that Jesus Christ desired to speak and to testify, and he is grateful to him for it.

Adolf Harnack, *What is Christianity?* translated by Thomas Bailey Saunders, with an introduction by the Very Rev. W.R. Matthews, Ernest Benn Limited, 1958, p.93.

To discover the Kingdom of God exclusively within oneself is easier than to discover it, not only there, but also in the outer world of minds and things and living creatures. It is easier because the heights within reveal themselves to those who are ready to exclude from their purview all that lies without. And though this exclusion may be a painful and mortificatory process, the fact remains that it is less arduous than the process of inclusion, by which we come to know the fullness as well as the heights of spiritual life. Where there is exclusive concentration on the heights within, temptations and distractions are avoided and there is a general denial and suppression. But when the hope is to know God inclusively—to realize the divine Ground in the world as well as in the soul, temptations and distractions must not be avoided, but submitted to and used as opportunities for advance; there must be no suppression of outward-turning activities, but a transformation of them so that they become sacramental. Mortification becomes more searching and more subtle; there is need of unsleeping awareness and, on the levels of thought, feeling and conduct, the constant exercise of something like an artist's tact and taste.

Aldous Huxley, *The Perennial Philosophy*, Chatto & Windus Ltd., 1974, p.74.

No age has ever seen a more pressing need for world adjustment than the one we live in today. I am not referring, now, only to Europe or America, but my own country, which needs it above all others.

Suppose that we set about making this adjustment; with what sort of standard or intention should we make it? The answer to this initial question is very simple. I say, make a standard of the Kingdom of God that Jesus taught. To start with the intention of the Kingdom of God is the sole way of adjusting today's mismanaged world.

In the Kingdom of God the ideal of Jesus has already taken a concrete shape. Jesus Christ regarded himself as the King of the Kingdom of God. Among the heathen, men who have many employees, or wield authority, or exert the power of mammon are held in esteem; but in the Kingdom of God it is just the opposite. In this realm those are respected who labour, who are oppressed or despised, or who humble themselves to serve others. Here the proud and haughty are weeded out. Many schemes today are presented as infallible programmes for remedying the world's ills. But no promise of social reconstruction is so reliable and thoroughgoing as this.

Toyohiko Kagawa, *Meditations*, translated by Jiro Takenaka, Harper & Brothers, 1950, No. 18.

Modern faith finds the beginning of the Kingdom of God in Jesus and in the Spirit which came into the world with him. We no longer leave the fate of mankind to be decided at the end of the world. The time in which we live summons us to new faith in the Kingdom of God.

We are no longer content, like the generations before us, to believe in the Kingdom that comes of itself at the end of time. Mankind to-day must either realise the Kingdom of God or perish. The very tragedy of our present situation compels us to devote ourselves in faith to its realisation.

We are at the beginning of the end of the human race. The question before it is whether it will use for beneficial purposes or for purposes of destruction the power which modern science has placed in its hands. So long as its capacity for destruction was limited, it was possible to hope that reason would set a limit to disaster. Such an illusion is impossible to-day, when its power is illimitable. Our only hope is that the Spirit of God will strive with the spirit of the world and will prevail.

The last petition of the Lord's Prayer has again its original meaning for us as a prayer for deliverance from the dominion of the evil powers of the world. These are no less real to us as working in men's minds, instead of being embodied in angelic beings opposed to God. The first believers set their hope solely upon the Kingdom of God in expectation of the end of the world; we do it in expectation of the end of the human race.

The Spirit shows us the signs of the time and their meaning.

Belief in the Kingdom of God makes the biggest demands of all the articles of the Christian faith. It means believing the seemingly impossible,—the conquest of the spirit of the world by the Spirit of God. We look with confidence for the miracle to be wrought through the Spirit.

The miracle must happen in us before it can happen in the world. We dare not set our hope on our own efforts to create the conditions of God's Kingdom in the world. We must indeed labour for its realisation. But there can be no Kingdom of God in the world without the Kingdom of God in our hearts. The starting-point is our determined effort to bring every thought and action under the sway of the Kingdom of God. Nothing can be achieved without inwardness. The Spirit of God will only strive against the spirit of the world when it has won its victory over that spirit in our hearts.

Albert Schweitzer, in *The Theology of Albert Schweitzer*, E.N. Mozley, "Epilogue: The Conception of the Kingdom of God in the Transformation of Eschatology," translated by J.R. Coates, A. & C. Black, 1950, p. 106.

KNOWLEDGE

But if one loves God, one is known by him.
1 Corinthians 8.3.

By faith we know His existence; in glory we shall know His nature.
Blaise Pascal, *Pensées*, translated by W.F. Trotter, Random House Inc., 1941, p.80.

Knowledge comes, but wisdom lingers.
Alfred, Lord Tennyson, *The Poems of Tennyson*, edited by Christopher Ricks, Longmans, Green & Co. Ltd., 1969, p.697, No.271, "Locksley Hall," l.143.

To know is not to prove, nor to explain. It is to accede to vision.
Antoine de Saint-Exupéry, *Flight to Arras*, translated by Lewis Galantière, William Heinemann Ltd., 1942, p.33.

Knowledge is the action of the Soul.
Ben Jonson, *Ben Jonson*, edited by C.H. Herford, Percy and Evelyn Simpson, Oxford at the Clarendon Press, 1947, Volume VIII, *The Poems, The Prose Works*, p.588, "Explorata: or, Discoveries."

To *know;* to get into the truth of anything, is ever a mystic act,—of which the best Logics can but babble on the surface.
Thomas Carlyle, *Sartor Resartus*, "Lectures on Heroes," Chapman and Hall, 1840, p.227.

I arrived at Truth, not by systematic reasoning and accumulation of proofs but by a flash of light which God sent into my soul.
Al-Ghazali, cited by Vaswani, "The Sufi Spirit," in *The New Orient*, May-June, 1924, p.11.

Knowledge is proud that he has learn'd so much;
Wisdom is humble that he knows no more.
William Cowper, *The Poetical Works of Cowper*, edited by H.S. Milford, Oxford University Press, 1950, p.221, "The Task," Bk.VI. l.97.

An extensive knowledge is needful to thinking people; it takes away the heat and fever, and helps, by widening speculation, to ease the "burden of the Mystery."
John Keats, *The Works of John Keats*, edited by H. Buxton Forman, Reeves & Turner, 1883, Volume III, p.150, Letter to J.H. Reynolds.

There is therefore knowledge and knowledge. Knowledge that resteth in the bare speculation of things, and knowledge that is accompanied with the Grace of faith and love, which puts a man upon doing even the will of God from the heart.
John Bunyan, *The Pilgrim's Progress*, introduction and notes by G. B. Harrison, J. M. Dent & Sons Ltd., 1964, p.83.

To know God is to know Goodness. It is to see the beauty of infinite Love: To see it attended with Almighty Power and Eternal Wisdom; and using both those in the magnifying of its object. It is to see the Kingdom of Heaven and Earth take infinite delight in *Giving....* He is not an Object of Terror, but Delight. To know Him

---

therefore as He is, is to frame the most beautiful idea in all Worlds. He delighteth in our happiness more than we: and is of all other the most Lovely Object. An infinite Lord, who having all Riches, Honours, and Pleasures in His own hand, is infinitely willing to give them unto me. Which is the fairest idea that can be devised.

Thomas Traherne, *Centuries*, The Faith Press Ltd., 1969, p.8.

But the greatest error ... is the mistaking or misplacing of the last or furthest end of knowledge. For men have entered into a desire of learning and knowledge, sometimes upon a natural curiosity and inquisitive appetite; sometimes to entertain their minds with variety and delight; sometimes for ornament and reputation; and sometimes to enable them to victory of wit and contradiction; and most times for lucre and profession; and seldom sincerely to give a true account of their gift of reason to the benefit and use of men: as if there were sought in knowledge a couch whereupon to rest a searching and restless spirit; or a terrace for a wandering and variable mind to walk up and down with a fair prospect; or a tower of state, for a proud mind to raise itself upon; or a fort or commanding ground, for strife and contention; or a shop, for profit or sale; and not a rich storehouse for the glory of the Creator and the relief of man's estate.

Francis Bacon, *The Advancement of Learning*, introduction by Henry Morley, Cassell and Company Limited, 1905, p.38.

What then can give rise to a true spirit of peace on earth? Not commandments and not practical experience. Like all human progress, the love of peace must come from knowledge. All living knowledge as opposed to academic knowledge can have but one object. This knowledge may be seen and formulated by thousands in a thousand different ways, but it must always embody one truth. It is the knowledge of the living substance in us, in each of us, in you and me, of the secret magic, the secret godliness that each of us bears within him. It is the knowledge that, starting from this innermost point, we can at all times transcend all pairs of opposites, transforming white into black, evil into good, night into day. The Indians call it "Atman," the Chinese "Tao"; Christians call it "grace." Where that supreme knowledge is present (as in Jesus, Buddha, Plato, or Lao-tzu), a threshold is crossed beyond which miracles begin. There war and emnity cease. We can read of it in the New Testament and in the discourses of Gautama. Anyone who is so inclined can laugh at it and call it "introverted rubbish," but to one who has experienced it his enemy becomes his brother, death becomes birth, disgrace honour, calamity good fortune. Each thing on earth discloses itself twofold, as "of this world" and "not of this world." But "this world" means what is "outside us." Everything that is outside us can become enemy, danger, fear and death. The light dawns with the experience that this entire "outward" world is not only an object of our perception but at the same time the creation of our soul, with the tranformation of all outward into inward things, of the world into the self.

Herman Hesse, *If The War Goes On*, translated by Ralph Manheim, Pan Books Ltd., 1974, p.54.

It takes a long time for the average over-intellectualized person to realize that in this particular sphere of reality he must be prepared to receive illumination from the most unexpected quarters, to learn his lessons in completely unfamiliar terms, to strain his ear to catch overtones to which he previously paid little attention, to abandon some of his most cherished preconceptions, to bare himself to truths which he has not hitherto been prepared to face. Yet only at this price can spiritual be substituted for merely intellectual knowledge....

The point is that the particular kind of awareness which the educated derive from dealing with experience in its more intellectual aspects hardly comes into play at all when it is a question of the deeper laws of life. The attention then becomes concentrated upon a certain type of datum which the unsophisticated person can identify and handle just as effectively as can any other—often more effectively, indeed, than the person who is highly educated. We find ourselves in a region in which the vital issues are brought into focus by such factors as acts of devotion, simplicity of behaviour, humbleness of spirit....

We may draw from this an important conclusion. If anything in the nature of a religious revival ever takes place in this country... we shall be prudent not to expect the educated classes to play any more important a part in it than that which is played by people of quite humble origin and pretensions. Spiritual power, insight, and authority— these things are apt at such an epoch to manifest themselves in the most unexpected places, to the confusion of the orthodox. A tram-driver who has been spiritually quickened in the way in which certain slaves were once quickened at the beginning of the Christian era, or as certain Quakers were quickened in the seventeenth century, is a figure to be reckoned with—particularly in a society which, like our own, is beginning to regard the capacities of its intelligentsia with distrust.

Lawrence Hyde, *The Prospects of Humanism*, Gerald Howe Limited, 1931, p. 139.

L

LEADERSHIP

In the simplest terms, a leader is one who knows where he wants to go, and gets up
and goes.

John Erskine, *The Complete Life,* Andrew Melrose Ltd., 1945, p.134.

There are men, who, by their sympathetic attractions, carry nations with them, and
lead the activity of the human race.

Ralph Waldo Emerson, *The Conduct of Life, Nature and Other Essays,* J.M. Dent & Sons Ltd., 1911, p.175.

The real leader has no need to lead—he is content to point the way.

Henry Miller, *The Wisdom of the Heart,* New Directions Books, 1941, p.46.

He that would govern others, first should be

The master of himself.

Philip Massinger, *The Plays of Massinger,* Alfred Thomas Crocker, 1868, *The Bondman,* p.102, Act I. sc.iii.

The fire of God

Fills him: I never saw his like: there lives

No greater leader.

Alfred, Lord Tennyson, *The Poems of Tennyson,* edited by Christopher Ricks, Longmans, Green & Co. Ltd., 1969,

p.1629, *Idylls of the King,* No.470, "Lancelot and Elaine," 1.314.

No man is great enough or wise enough for any of us to surrender our destiny to.
The only way in which any one can lead us is to restore to us the belief in our own
guidance.

Henry Miller, *The Wisdom of the Heart,* New Directions Books, 1941, p.122.

We that had loved him so, followed him, honoured him,

Lived in his mild and magnificent eye,

Learned his great language, caught his clear accents,

Made him our pattern to live and to die!

Robert Browning, *The Poetical Books of Robert Browning,* Smith, Elder, & Co., 1899, Volume I, p.249, "The

Lost Leader," st.i. 1.12.

A leader of his people, unsupported by any outward authority: a politician whose
success rests neither upon craft nor the mastery of technical devices, but simply on
the convincing power of his personality; a victorious fighter who has always scorned
the use of force; a man of wisdom and humility, armed with resolve and inflexible
consistency, who has devoted all his strength to the uplifting of his people and the

betterment of their lot; a man who has confronted the brutality of Europe with the dignity of the simple human being, and thus at all times risen superior.
Generations to come, it may be, will scarce believe that such a one as this ever in flesh and blood walked upon this earth.
Albert Einstein, written of Mahatma Gandhi in *Ideas and Opinions*, Souvenir Press (Educational & Academic) Ltd., 1973, p.77.

However dedicated men may be, the success of their work inevitably depends on the quality of their leaders. I am convinced that the key to leadership lies in the principle: "He that is greatest among you, let him be as the younger; and he that is chief, as he that doth serve." Leadership should not bring privileges, but duties.
No man should ask his subordinates to do more than he does himself. If work begins at eight in the morning, the top man should be there on time. If the workers snatch a quick lunch in a cafeteria, the directors should do the same, and not absent themselves for two hours to eat at a restaurant.
Everyone should enjoy his or her daily work. Enjoyment depends on personal relations. It is the duty of the senior men to make their subordinates happy by knowing them personally and by producing a spirit of comradeship and of mutual pride in the work. Warm personal relationships can be used by senior men to discuss with their subordinates the progress of the work, their mutual achievements and the difficulties which lie ahead. Such intercourse and exchange of confidences foster a sense of comradeship and team-work.
Sir John Glubb, *The Fate of Empires* and *Search for Survival*, William Blackwood & Sons Ltd., 1978, p.39.

LIFE

If anyone thirst, let him come to me and drink. He who believes in me, as the scripture has said, "Out of his heart shall flow rivers of living water."
John 7.38.

I came that they may have life, and have it abundantly.
John 10.10.

Creative life is always on the yonder side of convention.
C.G. Jung, *Psychological Reflections*, selected and edited by Jolande Jacobi, Routledge & Kegan Paul Ltd., 1953, p.185.

The mystery of life is not a problem to be solved; it is a reality to be experienced.
J.J. van der Leeuw, *The Conquest of Illusion*, Alfred A. Knopf, 1928, p.9.

Life is its own journey; pre-supposes its own change and movement, and one tries to arrest them at one's eternal peril.
Laurens van der Post, *Venture to the Interior*, Penguin Books Ltd., 1968, p.124.

Is life so wretched? Isn't it rather your hands which are too small, your vision which is muddied? You are the one who must grow up.

Dag Hammarskjold, *Markings*, translated by Leif Sjoberg and W.H. Auden, with a foreword by W.H. Auden, Faber and Faber Limited, 1964, p.63.

To live as fully, as completely as possible, to be happy and again to be happy is the true aim and end of life. "Ripeness is all."

Llewelyn Powys, *Impassioned Clay*, Longmans, Green & Co. Ltd., 1931, p.94.

Reflect that life, like ev'ry other blessing,
Derives its value from its use alone.

Samuel Johnson, *The Yale Edition of the Works of Samuel Johnson*, edited by E.L. McAdam Jr., with George Milne, Yale University Press, 1964, Volume VI, *Poems*, p.162, "Irene," Act III. sc.viii. l.28.

The web of our life is of a mingled yarn, good and ill together; our virtues would be proud if our faults whipp'd them not, and our crimes would despair if they were not cherish'd by our virtues.

William Shakespeare, *All's Well That Ends Well*, Act IV. sc.iii. l.68.

We live in deeds, not years; in thoughts, not breaths;
In feelings, not in figures on a dial.
We should count time by heart-throbs. He most lives
Who thinks most; feels the noblest; acts the best.

P.J. Bailey, *Festus*, William Pickering, 1839, p.62.

What makes our lives worth while is stretching towards God who is love and truth. That we reach out beyond our capacity is at once our pain, our adventure, our hope.

Hubert van Zeller, *Considerations*, Sheed & Ward Ltd., 1974, p.69.

The true spiritual goal of life is the formation of a rightly fashioned will, the creation of a controlling personal love, the experience of a guiding inward Spirit, which keep the awakened soul steadily approximating the perfect Life which Christ has revealed.

Rufus M. Jones, *Spiritual Reformers in the 16th and 17th Centuries*, Macmillan & Co. Ltd., 1914, p.38.

Not a May-Game is this man's life; but a battle and a march, a warfare with principalities and powers. No idle promenade through fragrant orange-groves and green flowery spaces, waited on by coral Muses and rosy Hours: it is a stern pilgrimage through burning sandy solitudes, through regions of thick-ribbed ice.

Thomas Carlyle, *Past and Present*, Ward, Lock & Co. Ltd., p.198.

People are always blaming their circumstances for what they are. I don't believe in circumstances. The people who get on in this world are the people who get up and look for the circumstances they want, and, if they can't find them, make them.

George Bernard Shaw, *The Complete Plays of Bernard Shaw*, Paul Hamlyn Ltd., 1965, p.75, *Mrs. Warren's Profession*, Act II.

After all it is those who have a deep and real inner life who are best able to deal with the "irritating details of outer life."

Evelyn Underhill, *The Letters of Evelyn Underhill,* edited with an introduction by Charles Williams, Longmans, Green and Co. Ltd., 1947, p.219.

Man is a journey out of animal individuality to the human significance which is personality, and on to the life of God.... Man is able, "even here and now, vividly to conceive ... the timeless character ... of his own spirit," and of God, and of his experience of God who penetrates his own spirit.

Friedrich von Hügel, in *The Spirituality of Friedrich von Hügel,* Joseph P. Whelan, S.J., William Collins Sons & Co. Ltd., 1971, p.48.

You have striven so hard, and so long, to *compel* life. Can't you now slowly change, and let life slowly drift into you. Surely it is even a greater mystery and preoccupation even than willing, to let the invisible life steal into you and slowly possess you.

D.H.Lawrence, *The Selected Letters of D.H. Lawrence,* edited with an introduction by Diana Trilling, Farrar, Straus & Cudahy, Inc., 1958, p.210.

A man contains all that is needful to his government within himself. He is made a law unto himself. All real good or evil that can befall him must be from himself.... The purpose of life seems to be to acquaint a man with himself. He is not to live to the future as described to him, but to live to the real future by living the real present.
The highest revelation is that God is in every man.

Ralph Waldo Emerson, *The Heart of Emerson's Journals,* edited by Bliss Perry, Constable & Co. Ltd., 1927, p.79.

People "died" all the time in their lives. Parts of them died when they made the wrong kind of decisions—decisions against life. Sometimes they died bit by bit until finally they were just living corpses walking around. If you were perceptive you could see it in their eyes; the fire had gone out.... But you always knew when you made a decision against life. When you denied life you were warned. The cock crowed, always, somewhere inside you. The door clicked and you were safe inside—safe and dead.

Anne Morrow Lindbergh, *The Steep Ascent,* Chatto & Windus Ltd., 1945, p.57.

I do know that trying to be open to things that are good, and beautiful, and true, wherever they are to be found, brings to me a strength that is greater than my own. This is fortified by seeking out and finding reassurance from "good deeds in a naughty world," which encourages the belief that goodness, courage, generosity and heroism are possible. This remains true even when such virtues are partially disclosed. There have been many lives like those of St. Francis, Gandhi and Schweitzer, which have shown how great is the human potential for heroic living.

George H. Gorman, *Introducing Quakers,* Friends Home Service Committee, 1969, p.22.

If you don't know what man was made for, neither do you know what man can do. You don't know the heights to which he can rise, the fullness of living of which he is capable or the happiness which can come his way. The whole thing means a tremendous difference here and now, the difference of knowing what life really can be.

R.L. Smith, in *Man's Dilemma and God's Answer,* Broadcast Talks, S.C.M. Press Ltd., 1944, p.73.

There are real ends in life, and they are all in that realm which belongs to us in virtue of our spiritual and intellectual capacities, and not of our animal capacities. They all belong to the realm, for example, either of knowledge, or appreciation of beauty, or friendship, or family affection or loyalties, and courage, and love and joy and peace. They are all, in fact, in the wider sense of the term part of the fruit of the spirit; and those, and those only, are real ends. The whole economic sphere is concerned with means to those ends; and it must be judged, not primarily by its efficiency within itself, by its effectiveness in promoting the maximum output and the like; but primarily in the light of the question whether it is fostering the attainment of the real ends by the greatest number of people. We may take as our slogan, if you like; "Fullness of Personality in the widest possible Fellowship."

William Temple, *The Church Looks Forward*, Macmillan & Co. Ltd., 1944, p.117.

We too must have life in ourselves. We too must, like the Life himself, live. We can live in no way but that in which Jesus lived, in which life was made in him. That way is, to give up our life. This is the one supreme action of life possible to us for the making of life in ourselves. Christ did it of himself, and so became light to us, that we might be able to do it in ourselves, after him, and through his originating act. We must do it ourselves, I say. The help that he has given and gives, the light and the spirit—working of the Lord, the spirit, in our hearts, is all in order that we may, as we must, do it ourselves. Till then we are not alive; life is not made in us. The whole strife and labour and agony of the Son with every man, is to get him to die as he died. All preaching that aims not at this, is a building of wood and hay and stubble.

George Macdonald, *Unspoken Sermons*, Third Series, Longmans, Green, and Co., 1889,p.20.

LIGHT

In him was life, and the life was the light of men. The light shines in the darkness, and the darkness has not overcome it.

John 1.4-5.

The true light that enlightens every man was coming into the world.

John 1.9.

I am the light of the world; he who follows me will not walk in darkness, but will have the light of life.

John 8.12.

While you have the light, believe in the light, that you may become sons of light.

John 12.36.

You are the light of the world.

Matthew 5.14.

Let your light so shine before men, that they may see your good works and give glory to your Father who is in heaven.

Matthew 5.16.

For it is the God who said, "Let light shine out of darkness," who has shone in our hearts to give the light of the knowledge of the glory of God in the face of Christ.

2 Corinthians 4.6.

Those who have once been enlightened, who have tasted the heavenly gift, and have become partakers of the Holy Spirit, and have tasted the goodness of the word of God and the powers of the age to come.

Hebrews 6.4-5.

I am aware of something in myself *whose shine is my reason.* I see clearly that something is there, but what it is I cannot understand. But it seems to me, that, if I could grasp it, I should know all truth.

Meister Eckhart, *Meister Eckhart,* translated by Raymond B. Blakney, Harper & Row, Publishers, Inc., 1941, p.101.

Christ the Light of the World shines first upon the soul, and then from within the soul upon the path of life. He does not illumine our way while leaving us unconverted; but by converting us He illumines our way.

William Temple, *Readings in St. John's Gospel* (First and Second Series), Macmillan & Co. Ltd., 1947, p.179.

And I said to the man who stood at the gate of the year:
"Give me a light that I may tread safely into the unknown."
And he replied: "Go out into the darkness and put your hand into the hand of God.
That shall be to you better than light and safer than a known way."

Louise M. Haskins, "God Knows," quoted by King George VI in a Christmas Broadcast, 25 Dec. 1939.

Hast never come to thee an hour,
A sudden gleam divine, precipitating, bursting all these bubbles, fashions, wealth?
These eager business aims—books, politics, art, amours,
To utter nothingness?

Walt Whitman, *The Complete Poems,* edited by Francis Murphy, Penguin Books Ltd., 1982, p.303, "Hast Never Come to Thee an Hour," l.1.

This opening of the spiritual eyes is that glowing darkness and rich nothingness of which I spoke earlier. It may be called: Purity of soul and spiritual rest, inward stillness and peace of conscience, refinement of thought and integrity of soul, a lively consciousness of grace... the tasting of heavenly joys, the ardour of love and brightness of light, the entry into contemplation and reformation of feeling.

Walter Hilton, *The Ladder of Perfection,* translated with an introduction by Leo Sherley-Price, Penguin Books Ltd., 1957, p.223.

The world may be in darkness but this should not upset us. Christ is the light of the world. If we bring this truth into the context of our own experience we must know that light inaccessible has invited us to enter into this light. He has asked us not merely to reflect it but to *be* it. Otherwise his words "you are the light of the world, the city seated on a hill, the salt of the earth" are no more than an oratorical flourish. Jesus did not go in for oratorical flourishes.

Hubert van Zeller, *Considerations,* Sheed & Ward Ltd., 1974, p.51.

There is a Light in man which shines into his darkness, reveals his condition to him, makes him aware of evil and checks him when he is in the pursuit of it; gives him a vision of righteousness, attracts him towards goodness, and points him infallibly toward Christ from whom the Light shines. This Light is pure, immediate, and spiritual. It is of God, in fact is God immanently revealed.

Rufus M. Jones, *Spiritual Reformers in the 16th and 17th Centuries,* Macmillan & Co. Ltd., 1914, p.345.

But I will now show a little more distinctly, what this *Pearl of Eternity* is. First, It is the *Light* and *Spirit* of God within Thee, which has hitherto done Thee but little Good, because all the Desire of thy Heart has been after the Light and Spirit of this World. Thy Reason, and Senses, thy Heart and Passions, have turned all their Attention to the poor Concerns of this Life, and therefore thou art a Stranger to this Principle of Heaven, this Riches of Eternity within Thee. For as God is not, cannot be truly found by any Worshippers, but those who worship Him in *Spirit* and in *Truth,* so this Light and Spirit, though always within us, is not, cannot be found, felt, or enjoyed, but by those whose whole Spirit is turned to it.

William Law, *The Spirit of Prayer,* full text, edited with an introduction and notes by Sidney Spencer, James Clarke & Co. Ltd., 1969, p.45.

I do not believe that we can put into anyone ideas which are not in him already. As a rule there are in everyone all sorts of good ideas, ready like tinder. But much of this tinder catches fire, or catches it successfully, only when it meets some flame or spark from outside, i.e., from some other person. Often, too, our own light goes out, and is rekindled by some experience we go through with a fellow-man. Thus we have each of us cause to think with deep gratitude of those who have lighted the flames within us. If we had before us those who have thus been a blessing to us, and could tell them how it came about, they would be amazed to learn what passed over from their life into ours.

Albert Schweitzer, *Memoirs of Childhood and Youth,* translated by C.T. Campion, George Allen & Unwin Ltd., 1924, p.90.

Now the Lord God hath opened to me by his invisible power how that every man was enlightened by the divine light of Christ; and I saw it shine through all, and that they that believed in it came out of condemnation and came to the light of life and became children of it, but they that hated it, and did not believe in it, were condemned by it, though they made a profession of Christ. This I saw in the pure openings of the Light without the help of any man, neither did I then know where to find it in the Scriptures; though afterwards, searching the Scriptures, I found it. For I saw in that Light and Spirit which was before Scripture was given forth, and which led the holy men of God to give them forth, that all must come to that Spirit, if they would

know God, or Christ, or the Scriptures aright, which they that gave them forth were
led and taught.

George Fox, *The Journal of George Fox,* a revised edition by John L. Nickalls, Cambridge at the University Press, 1952, p.33.

Christ walked in the full light of God, we only have flashes of it. Hence, whereas Christ knew when His day was coming, we cannot know. Christ's life was marred by no error of judgement, because He had full light. Our lives are full of errors of judgement because our sight is dim, so that we often cannot see what is our right path.
If we have put our earthly life in God's hands—that is to say, if we are ready to die today, as we should be—we can have absolutely no fear, no matter what happens. For I know that once having given myself to God, to be in His hand a mere tool on earth, a tool with which some good work may be done while I live,—having once and for all done away with my own free-will and having put God's will in its place,—I know that no power of earth can do me any harm till God's day comes....
So I live, knowing that I am in God's hands, to be used to bring others to Him, if He so wills by a long life full of work, or to die tomorrow if He wills, having done nothing worth mentioning.... We must do what we can and leave the rest to Him....
My trust is in God, so that it matters not what I do nor where I go.

Edward Wilson, in *The Faith of Edward Wilson,* George Seaver, John Murray Ltd., 1949, p.43.

LISTENING

Give us grace to listen well.

John Keble, *The Christian Year,* edited by Ernest Rhys, J M Dent & Sons, Ltd., 1914, p.72.

By listening it is possible to bring a man's soul into being.

Anon., heard on the radio.

Basically the answer is simple, very simple. We need only listen to what Jesus has told us. It's enough to listen to the Gospel and put into practice what it tells us.

Carlo Carretto, *Letters from the Desert,* translated by Rose Mary Hancock, with a foreword by Ivan Illich, Darton, Longman and Todd, Orbis Books, 1972, p.40.

Difficult as it is really to listen to someone in affliction, it is just as difficult for him to know that compassion is listening to him.

Simone Weil, *Waiting on God,* translated by Emma Craufurd, William Collins Sons & Co. Ltd., 1974, p.106.

If we knew how to listen to God, we should hear him speaking to us. For God does speak. He speaks in his Gospel; he speaks also through life—that new Gospel to which we ourselves add a page each day.

Michel Quoist, *Prayers of Life,* translated by Anne Marie de Commaile & Agnes Mitchell Forsyth, Gill and Macmillan Ltd., 1963, p.2.

The boy Samuel was told by Heli to pray: "Speak, Lord, for your servant listens." He was not instructed to say: "Listen, Lord, for your servant speaks." If we listened more we would learn more about spirit and truth ... and in turn would be better able to worship in spirit and in truth.

Hubert van Zeller, *Considerations,* Sheed & Ward Ltd., 1974, p.88.

Listening to oneself is so difficult because this art requires another ability, rare in modern man: that of being alone with oneself....
Listening to the feeble and indistinct voice of our conscience is difficult also because it does not speak to us directly but indirectly and because we are often not aware that it is our conscience which disturbs us. We may feel only anxious (or even sick) for a number of reasons which have no apparent connection with our conscience.

Erich Fromm, *Man For Himself,* Routledge & Kegan Paul Ltd., 1975, p.161.

The most useful service we can do for anybody, says Laubach, is to link him with God. Our prayers to do this need not be long prayers. Laubach is a great advocate of the "flash prayer," made whenever the thoughts of somebody else comes to mind: linking him immediately with the thought of God!...
Most of us, in our praying, devote far less time and attention to "waiting upon God"— to the listening side of prayer—than we devote to the incessantly active and vocal form of praying that most of us indulge in. We ought ... to give more time to listening to God than we do to speaking to Him.

Dr. Cyril H. Powell, *Secrets of Answered Prayer,* Arthur James Ltd., 1958, p.114, 123.

There is a great need today for hearts that listen.
Martin Israel assures us that we do not have to rely upon ourselves alone when trying to solve the problems with which we are confronted. He says, "When we are able to listen in silence to the life story of another person and not respond with our own wisdom, a greater wisdom, that of the Holy Spirit who is the Advocate, will flow from our lips and will lead both that other person and ourselves into truth. From the lips of silence proceeds wisdom the Word of God, from the hushed heart flows love."

Elizabeth Bassett, *The Bridge is Love,* Darton, Longman and Todd Ltd., 1981, p.93.

LITERATURE

Literature is the Thought of thinking Souls.

Thomas Carlyle, *The Works of Thomas Carlyle,* Chapman and Hall Limited, 1899, *Critical and Miscellaneous Essays,* Volume IV, p.83.

He (Shakespeare) was the man who of all Modern, and perhaps Ancient Poets, had the largest and most comprehensive soul.

John Dryden, *The Works of John Dryden,* general editor, H.T. Swedenberg, Jr., University of California Press, 1971, Volume XVII, *Prose 1668-1691,* p.55, "Essay of Dramatic Poesy," l.20.

Of all literary pleasures, the reading of a poem is the highest and purest. Only pure lyric poetry can sometimes achieve the perfection, the ideal form wholly permeated by life and feeling, that is otherwise the secret of music.

Herman Hesse, *Reflections*, selected from his books and letters by Volker Michels, translated by Ralph Manheim, Jonathan Cape Ltd., 1977, p.109.

Books are the treasured wealth of the world and the fit inheritance of generations and nations.... Their authors are a natural and irresistible aristocracy in every society, and, more than kings or emperors, exert an influence on mankind!

Henry David Thoreau, *Walden*, The New American Library of World Literature, Inc., 1960, p.74.

It is chiefly through books that we enjoy intercourse with superior minds, and these invaluable means of communication are in the reach of all. In the best books, great men talk to us, give us their most precious thoughts, and pour their souls into ours. God be thanked for books. They are the voices of the distant and the dead, and make us heirs of the spiritual life of past ages. Books are the true levellers. They give to all, who will faithfully use them, the society, the spiritual presence of the best and greatest of our race.

William E. Channing, *Self-Culture*, Dutton and Wentworth, Printers, 1838, p.40.

To me it seems that the novels of Dostoievski derive almost the whole of their power and value from the fact that they are interpretations of life in its heights and its depths.... I do indeed regard them as among the greatest masterpieces with which I am acquainted, and I think that they show an interpretation of the real meaning both of human life and of the Christian religion in its dealing with human life, of which I know no equal in fiction or other literature.

William Temple, *The Resources and Influences of English Literature*, National Book Council, 1943, p.17.

Woe betide that nation whose literature is interrupted by the interference of force. This is not simply a violation of the "freedom of the press": it is the locking-up of the national heart, the carving-up of the national memory. Such a nation does not remember itself, it is deprived of its spiritual unity, and although its population supposedly have a common language, fellow-countrymen suddenly stop understanding each other. Mute generations live out their lives and die without telling their story either to their own or a future generation. If such geniuses as Akhmatova or Zamyatin are walled up alive for the duration of their lives, if they are condemned to create in silence until the grave, without hearing any response to what they have written, then this is not just their own personal misfortune but the deep tragedy of the whole nation— and, too, a threat to the whole nation. And in certain cases it is a danger for the whole of mankind, too: when the whole of history ceases to be understood because of that silence.

Alexander Solzhenitsyn, *"One Word of Truth ..."*, The Nobel Speech on Literature 1970, The Bodley Head, 1972, p.16.

It has been said by some that there is no religion in Shakespeare, or, what is the same thing, no element of the divine in his view of the world. To this it may be said, there is the same element of the divine which is to be seen in the world itself. Shakespeare's purpose is to give a section of the real world that we may read the whole world by it. He does not moralise himself, but lets the picture speak. But a poet may do much without moralising. He may indicate the presence of two elements, destiny, or what Christians call providence, and free-will, not always harmonising—for this would not be true—but always present, and therefore urging a wish for solution, which can only be found finally in a right view of God and of man. Next, he may indicate how moral faults and weaknesses bring catastrophes in good characters—irresolution in Hamlet, jealousy in Othello, parental partiality in Lear, etc. Further, he may make us prefer, like Cato, to share the lot of the good man in adversity rather than that of the bad man in success, to love the right and hate the wrong, whatever circumstances surround them. And lastly, he may give such views of man's nature as exalt our conceptions of it, admiring without deifying it in some of its aspects, condemning without despising it in others. Besides, there may be the introduction of touches of Christian truth, which make us feel that the heart of the author was with the speaker:

> "Those holy fields
> Over whose acres walk'd those blessed feet
> Which, fourteen hundred years ago, were nail'd
> For our advantage on the bitter cross."
> *King Henry IV, Part I,* Act I. sc.i.

John Ker, *Thoughts for Heart and Life,* David Douglas, 1888, p.62.

Just as words have two functions—information and creation—so each human mind has two personalities, one on the surface, one deeper down. The upper personality has a name. It is called S.T. Coleridge, or William Shakespeare, or Mrs. Humphry Ward. It is conscious and alert, it does things like dining out, answering letters, etc., and it differs vividly and amusingly from other personalities. The lower personality is a very queer affair. In many ways it is a perfect fool, but without it there is no literature, because, unless a man dips a bucket down into it occasionally he cannot produce first-class work. There is something general about it. Although it is inside S.T. Coleridge, it cannot be labelled with his name. It has something in common with all other deeper personalities, and the mystic will assert that the common quality is God, and that here, in the obscure recesses of our being, we near the gates of the Divine. It is in any case the force that makes for anonymity. As it came from the depths, so it soars to the heights, out of local questionings; as it is general to all men, so the works it inspires have something general about them, namely beauty. The poet wrote the poem no doubt, but he forgot himself while he wrote it, and we forget him while we read. What is so wonderful about great literature is that it transforms the man who reads it towards the condition of the man who wrote, and brings to birth in us also the creative impulse. Lost in the beauty where he was lost, we find more than we ever threw away, we reach what seems to be our spiritual home, and remember that it was not the speaker who was in the beginning but the Word.

E.M. Forster, *Anonymity. An Enquiry,* Leonard and Virginia Woolf at the Hogarth Press, 1925, p.16.

LONELINESS

We are born helpless. As soon as we are fully conscious we discover loneliness. We need others physically, emotionally, intellectually; we need them if we are to know anything, even ourselves.

C.S. Lewis, *The Four Loves*, William Collins Sons & Co. Ltd., 1960, p.7.

And lifting up mine eyes, I found myself
Alone, and in a land of sand and thorns.

Alfred, Lord Tennyson, *The Poems of Tennyson*, edited by Christopher Ricks, Longmans, Green & Co. Ltd., 1969, p.1673, *The Idylls of the King*, No.471, "The Holy Grail," l.375.

Loneliness is bred of a mind that has grown earthbound. For the spirit has its homeland, which is the realm of the meaning of all things.

Antoine de Saint-Exupéry, *The Wisdom of the Sands*, translated by Stuart Gilbert, Hollis & Carter Ltd., 1952, p.224.

When you close your doors and make darkness within, remember never to say that you are alone: you are not alone, God is within.

Epictetus, *The Stoic and Epicurean Philosophers*, edited by Witney J. Oates, Random House, Inc., 1940, p.251.

Our language has wisely sensed those two sides of man's being alone. It has created the word "loneliness" to express the pain of being alone. And it has created the word "solitude" to express the glory of being alone.

Paul Tillich, *The Eternal Now*, S.C.M. Press Ltd., 1963, p.11.

The knowledge of the ever-present Christ can reach down into the hidden depths and assure lonely modern man that he is not alone. More than that; it can draw him out of his loneliness to the rediscovery of the human race.

Stephen Neill, *The Church and Christian Union*, Oxford University Press, 1968, p.279.

In fact, we have developed a phobia of being alone; we prefer the most trivial and even obnoxious company, the most meaningless activities, to being alone with ourselves; we seem to be frightened at the prospect of facing ourselves. Is it because we feel we would be such bad company? I think the fear of being alone with ourselves is rather a feeling of embarrassment, bordering sometimes on terror at seeing a person at once so well known and so strange; we are afraid and run away.

Erich Fromm, *Man For Himself*, Routledge & Kegan Paul Ltd., 1975, p.161.

Yes: I am alone on earth: I have always been alone.... Do not think you can frighten me by telling me that I am alone. France is alone; and God is alone; and what is my loneliness before the loneliness of my country and my God? I see now that the loneliness of God is His strength: what would He be if He listened to your jealous little counsels? Well, my loneliness shall be my strength too: it is better to be alone with God: His friendship will not fail me, nor His counsel, nor His love. In His strength I will dare, and dare, and dare, until I die.

George Bernard Shaw, *The Complete Plays of Bernard Shaw*, Paul Hamlyn Ltd., 1965, p.989, *Saint Joan*, sc.v.

Essentially loneliness is the knowledge that one's fellow human beings are incapable of understanding one's condition and therefore are incapable of bringing the help most needed. It is not a question of companionship—many are ready to offer this and companionship is certainly not to be despised—but rather one of strictly sharing, of identifying. No two human beings can manage this, so to a varying extent loneliness at times is the lot of all.

Hubert van Zeller, *Considerations,* Sheed and Ward Ltd., 1974, p.18.

That Jesus was lonely is indisputable. Not only during his agony in the garden when his friends failed him, not only at every stage of his passion when again he had to endure his sufferings alone, not only when on the cross and he felt himself to be deserted by his Father, but also throughout his life when he looked for understanding and hardly ever met with it. If he allowed loneliness to be his lot, was it not to invite the lonely to unite their lot with his?

Hubert van Zeller, *Considerations,* Sheed and Ward Ltd., 1974, p.18.

LONGING

As a hart longs for flowing streams, so longs my soul for thee, O God.
Psalm 42.1.

The thing we long for, that we are
For one transcendent moment.

J.R. Lowell, *The Poetical Works of James Russell Lowell,* introduction by William Michael Rossetti, Ward, Lock & Co. Ltd., 1911, p.94, "Longing."

If there was one that I could trust and love and be so bound up with that he or she could share with me and understand my joys and my love, and my passion for beauty, for colour, for form, for pure joy in nature,—if he or she could enter into my thoughts and feel with me,—if my sorrow, my pain, my doubts, my unspoken thoughts and hopes and fancies and longings—my life and my love—if only—
If I could find such a one, shouldn't I bring every joy, every delight, every pain, every sorrow, every passion, every love to be shared and to open the whole before that one: I know that I should: but there exists not the person on earth with whom lies the power of even to a small extent feeling with me in one of the smallest of my joys. Now and again one can truly say that one has felt with another, in joy or pain, in love or sorrow. But it is only now and again, and for years the heart hungers in between.

Edward Wilson, in *Edward Wilson of the Antarctic,* George Seaver, John Murray Ltd., 1935, p.46.

Life is a search for this "something," a search for something or someone to give meaning to our lives, to answer the question, who am I, why am I here, what is the purpose of my life?
I believe that this great need we all feel is caused by a longing which cannot be satisfied by the usual goals we set ourselves in this journey of life. Even when they have been

achieved they so often fall short of our hopes and expectations. The longed-for objective is not something which can be possessed, it cannot be held or kept, can only be fleetingly glimpsed as it comes and goes.

It can only be hinted at, referred to obliquely; indescribable in words, it can only be felt, and all we know of it is that it is what we are looking for. The promise of it is there in our love for another person. In the glory of a sunrise or sunset, the silver path of the moon on the sea, the sad haunting cry of sea-birds, the touching protective courage of a wild thing for its young or its mate. In the mountains and the streams, in the flowers and the forests, in the sufferings and sorrows of mankind as well as in the joys and the laughter.

This longing is all bound up with memories too, it carries its light like a will-o'-the-wisp through the scents and sounds and sights which suddenly bring back to us the magical moments when we were very young and in love with life. But it is also there, playing its part in the despair and the sorrowing and the regrets and the remorse.

Sadly it seems that this yearning can become misdirected into channels which lead to drugs or drink or other excesses for excitement to assuage the longing when it has not been recognised for what it is.

There are countless ways in which the longing can be expressed, by poets and painters, musicians and dancers, and by so many of those whose talent is for living and loving in awe and worship.

Perhaps the whole of life is concerned with this yearning. Nothing can be left out, but it carries us on into death and beyond when we dare to hope that we shall come face to face with the source of all our longing.

Elizabeth Bassett, *The Bridge is Love*, Darton, Longman and Todd Ltd., 1981, p.31.

Men turn to prayer in the extremity of their fears, or anxieties, or helplessness before the perils of their day, and of all human existence. But they also turn to prayer because of the almost universal and unquenchable yearning they have for God, and for that fullness of life to be found in knowing, loving and serving Him.

This hunger for God will be described by every generation in its own language. In the seventeenth century, Henry Scougal, that bright and gentle young Scot, expressed it in saying, "The glorious things spoken of heaven may make even the carnal heart in love with it." For some modern minds, the statement of the psychologist, C.G. Jung, may be more intelligible: "Everyone's ultimate aim and strongest desire lie in developing the fullness of human existence that is called personality"—a goal, as he points out, to be realized through the establishment of a personal relation between the human personality and a Power outside itself. Dorothy Day, a distinguished Catholic laywoman, speaks experientially of this hunger, as she knew it even in her childhood, by quoting the words of Kiriloff, in Dostoevsky's novel *The Possessed:* "All my life I have been haunted by God." In every generation, this interior restlessness, this mingling of impassioned longing with the intimation of bright hope, rekindles the inward being in men and women, until they move out to seek Him by whom that being, and that hunger, first were given us.

Nor is this longing after God confined to high moments of ecstasy and vision. A young man sitting down to plan and dream for his future—his career, his marriage, his achievement of professional success and social status—may appear to be thinking in quite material terms. Income, prospects, and connections may seem to be the centre of his anticipation and his calculation as to how they are to be achieved and employed. Yet even as he speaks of these practical considerations, the light in his eyes and the nuance of his voice betrays a larger, unguessed hope, whose aura flames about his dreams.

John L. Casteel, *Rediscovering Prayer*, Hodder & Stoughton Ltd., 1955, p.13.

LOVE

You shall love the Lord your God with all your heart, and with all your soul, and with all your mind, and with all your strength.... You shall love your neighbour as yourself.

Mark 12.30-31.

A new commandment I give to you, that you love one another; even as I have loved you.

John 13.34.

As the Father has loved me, so have I loved you; abide in my love. If you keep my commandments, you will abide in my love, just as I have kept my Father's commandments and abide in his love.

John 15.9-10.

Let love be genuine; hate what is evil, hold fast to what is good; love one another with brotherly affection; outdo one another in showing honour. Never flag in zeal, be aglow with the Spirit, serve the Lord. Rejoice in your hope, be patient in tribulation, be constant in prayer. Contribute to the needs of the saints, practice hospitality.

Romans 12.9-13.

God is love, and he who abides in love abides in God, and God abides in him.

1 John 4.16.

We are all born for love,... It is the principle of existence and its only end.

Benjamin Disraeli, *Sybil* or *The Two Nations*, Peter Davies, 1927, p.354.

Whoever lives true life, will love true love.

E.B. Browning, *Elizabeth Barrett Browning's Poetical Works*, Smith, Elder, & Co., 1873, Volume V, p.39, *Aurora Leigh*, First Book.

For love is but the heart's immortal thirst
To be completely known and all forgiven.

Henry Van Dyke, *Music and Other Poems*, Hodder & Stoughton, 1904, Sonnet: "Love," p.51.

You give but little when you give of your possessions.
It is when you give of yourself that you truly give.

Kahlil Gibran, *The Prophet*, William Heinemann Ltd., 1970, p.24.

Love is rarer than genius itself. And friendship is rarer than love.
Charles Péguy, *Basic Verities*, translated by Ann & Julian Green, Kegan Paul, Trench, Trubner & Co. Ltd., 1943, p.51.

By love may He be gotten and holden; but by thought never.
The Cloud of Unknowing, introduction by Evelyn Underhill, John M. Watkins Ltd., 1956, p.77.

The greatest thing that can happen to any human soul is to become utterly filled with love; and self-sacrifice is love's natural expression.
William Temple, *Christian Faith and Life*, S.C.M. Press Ltd., 1963, p.106.

Love ... is the supreme badge of any true Christianity, and the traits of the beatitudes in a person's life are a surer evidence that he belongs in Christ's family, than is the fact that he holds current opinions on obscure questions of belief.
Rufus M. Jones, *Spiritual Reformers in the 16th and 17th Centuries*, Macmillan & Co. Ltd., 1914, p 96

That love shall in the end, as it is now in the eternal verities, be all in all, must remain for him (the Christian) a postulate not of knowledge but of faith. And that too is well, since faith is possible for all men, and knowledge is not.
L.W. Grensted, *The Philosophical Implications of Christianity*, Oxford at the Clarendon Press, 1930, p.17.

I always think that the best way to know God is to love many things. Love a friend, a wife, something, whatever you like, but one must love with a lofty and serious intimate sympathy, with strength, with intelligence, and one must always try to know deeper, better, and more.
Vincent van Gogh, *Dear Theo: An Autobiography of Vincent van Gogh*, edited by Irving Stone, Constable & Company Ltd., 1937, p.44.

Love is eager, sincere and kind; it is glad and lovely; it is strong, patient and faithful; wise, long-suffering and resolute; and it never seeks its own ends, for where a man seeks his own ends, he at once falls out of love.
Thomas à Kempis, *The Imitation of Christ*, translated by Betty I. Knott, William Collins Sons & Co. Ltd., 1979, p.118.

Love all God's creation, the whole of it and every grain of sand. Love every leaf, every ray of God's light! Love the animals, love the plants, love everything. If you love everything, you will perceive the divine mystery in things. And once you have perceived it, you will begin to comprehend it ceaselessly more and more every day.
Fyodor Dostoyevsky, *The Brothers Karamazov*, translated with an introduction by David Magarshack, Penguin Books Ltd., 1963, Volume I, p.375.

Would'st thou learn thy Lord's meaning in this thing? Learn it well: Love was His meaning. Who shewed it thee? Love. What shewed He thee? Love. Wherefore shewed it He? For Love. Hold thee therein and thou shalt learn and know more in the same.
Lady Julian of Norwich, *Revelations of Divine Love*, edited by Grace Warrack, Methuen & Co. Ltd., 1949, p.202.

Love is the cosmic energy that flames from the constellations and is concealed in the abyss of the atom; is whispered by the Holy Spirit in the heart, and placarded before men's eyes upon the Cross. It offers to us all that it has, and demands from us all that we can give.

Bishop Lumsden Barkway, in the introduction of *An Anthology of the Love of God,* Evelyn Underhill, edited by Bishop Barkway and Lucy Menzies, A.R. Mowbray & Co. Ltd., 1953, p.23.

Love, once kindled in the soul, is the mother of all heroic actions; love knows how to abound and overflow—the man who has lighted his life from Christ's love is constant in trials, patient in sufferings, courageous in assaults, prudent in difficulties, victorious and triumphant in action.

Rufus M. Jones, *Spiritual Reformers in the 16th and 17th Centuries,* Macmillan & Co. Ltd., 1914, p.334.

To make Love the ruling power of my life, the only power. To be kind, gentle, considerate and unselfish, to let nothing stand in the way of doing everyone a good turn, never to consider myself and my own feelings, but only other people's. To put myself out to any extent for the sake of others, especially for the sake of those who are not attractive.

Edward Wilson, in *The Faith of Edward Wilson,* George Seaver, John Murray Ltd., 1949, p.15.

Love is the best motivation and finally the only valid one. It is dynamic and strong; the secret of moral force. At its highest it also seems to be indivisible. If we truly loved anything—whether it be music, plants, mountains or primitive peoples—we would love all. And the precondition of all love is the escape from egoism. Preoccupation with the false self has to give way to love of the true self. Without that, our new and unprecedented destructive powers will sooner or later eliminate our species.

Ronald Higgins, *The Seventh Enemy,* Hodder & Stoughton Ltd., 1978, p.274.

True love's the gift which God has given
To man alone beneath the heaven:...
It is the secret sympathy,
The silver link, the silken tie,
Which heart to heart, and mind to mind,
In body and in soul can bind.

Sir Walter Scott, *The Poems and Plays of Sir Walter Scott,* introduction by Andrew Lang, J.M. Dent & Sons, Ltd., 1911, Volume I, "The Lay of the Last Minstrel," p.393.

In the world everything is problematic except one thing: charity, love. Love alone is not a problem for him who lives it.
I can only say, "Live love, let love invade you. It will never fail to teach you what you must do...."
I repeat again St. Augustine's words: "Love and do as you will." Don't worry about what you ought to do. Worry about loving.... Loving, you will listen to the Voice. Loving, you will find peace.
Love is the fulfillment of the law and should be everyone's rule of life; in the end it's the solution to every problem, the motive for all good.

Carlo Carretto, *Letters from the Desert,* translated by Rose Mary Hancock, with a foreword by Ivan Illich, Darton, Longman & Todd Ltd., 1972, p.24.

Be very sure that all are placed in the exact position in earth life where they are most needed and where they will have opportunities for doing the most good. The unknown man or woman may contribute more to the advancement of the human race than one whose name is in everyone's mouth. The whole purpose of spiritual unfoldment is for the individual man so to train himself that he becomes a more powerful centre from which the love of God can radiate. Then he no longer hankers after the wonderful things that the "I" can do. Instead he desires only that through him a greater love may be breathed forth into life.

Grace Cooke, Spiritual Unfoldment, The White Eagle Publishing Trust, 1961, p.16.

M

MAN

The spirit of God has made me, and the breath of the Almighty gives me life.
Job 33.4.

Yet thou hast made him little less than God, and dost crown him with glory and honour. Thou hast given him dominion over the works of thy hands; thou hast put all things under his feet.
Psalm 8.5-6.

I am fearfully and wonderfully made.
Psalm 139.14 (A.V.).

A man is a god in ruins.
Ralph Waldo Emerson, *The Works of Ralph Waldo Emerson,* edited by George Sampson, George Bell & Sons, Ltd., 1906, Volume II, *English Traits: The Conduct of Life: Nature,* p.412.

Man found his form and his identity under the action of religious principles and energies; the confusion in which he is losing them cannot be re-ordered by purely human efforts.
Nicolas Berdyaev, *The End of Our Time,* translated by Donald Attwater, Sheed and Ward Ltd., 1933, p.56.

Man is a Wonder to himself; he can neither *govern,* nor *know* himself.
Benjamin Whichcote, *Moral and Religious Aphorisms,* 1930, p.23, Century II, No.186.

We may pause in sorrow and silence over the depths of darkness that are in man; if we rejoice in the heights of purer vision he has attained to. Such things were and are in man; in all men; in us too.
Thomas Carlyle, *Sartor Resartus,* "Lectures on Heroes," Chapman and Hall, 1840, p.187.

How poor, how rich, how abject, how august,
How complicate, how wonderful, is man!
Edward Young, *Night Thoughts,* Thomas Nelson, 1841, p.3.

We know, and it is our pride to know, that man is by his constitution a religious animal.
Edmund Burke, *Reflections on the Revolution in France,* edited by Conor Cruise O'Brien, Penguin Books Ltd., 1969, p.187.

To please God ... to be a real ingredient in the divine happiness ... to be loved by God, not merely pitied, but delighted in as an artist delights in his work or a father in a son—it seems impossible, a weight or burden of glory which our thoughts can hardly sustain. But so it is.

C.S. Lewis, *Screwtape Proposes a Toast*, William Collins Sons & Co. Ltd., 1982, p. 104.

I say no man has ever yet been half devout enough,
None has ever yet adored or worship'd half enough,
None has begun to think how divine he himself is, and how certain the future is.

Walt Whitman, *The Complete Poems*, edited by Francis Murphy, Penguin Books Ltd., 1982, p. 54, *Leaves of Grass*, "Starting from Paumanok," l. 107.

When we talk of "spirit" in man, we are pointing to that extra dimension of being that belongs to him and that makes him more than a mere physical organism or a highly complicated animal.

John Macquarrie, *Paths in Spirituality*, S.C.M. Press Ltd., 1972, p. 43.

What piece of work is a man, how noble in reason, how infinite in faculties, in form and moving how express and admirable, in action how like an angel, in apprehension how like a god: the beauty of the world, the paragon of animals.

William Shakespeare, *Hamlet*, Act II. sc. ii. l. 303.

Since modern man experiences himself both as the seller and as the commodity to be sold on the market, his self-esteem depends on conditions beyond his control. If he is "successful," he is valuable; if he is not, he is worthless.

Erich Fromm, *Man For Himself*, Routledge & Kegan Paul Ltd., 1975, p. 72.

Nature tels me I am the Image of God as well as Scripture; he that understands not thus much, hath not his introduction or first lesson, and is yet to begin the Alphabet of man.

Sir Thomas Browne, *The Works of Sir Thomas Browne*, edited by Geoffrey Keynes, Faber and Faber Limited, 1964, Volume One, *Religio Medici*, p. 87.

For a man is not as God,
But then most Godlike being most a man.

Alfred, Lord Tennyson, *The Poems of Tennyson*, edited by Christopher Ricks, Longmans, Green & Co. Ltd., 1969, p. 729, No. 279, "Love and Duty," l. 30.

I Am a little world made cunningly
Of Elements, and an Angelike spright.

John Donne, *Poetical Works*, edited by Sir Herbert Grierson, Oxford University Press, 1971, *Divine Poems*, V, p. 295.

No human being is meant to be a carbon copy, a double, an understudy,... a shadow. Each must be his own man, much as this may mean resembling someone else's. This is not egocentricity or independence of the herd. It is the incommunicable response to the particular summons of God.

Hubert van Zeller, *Considerations*, Sheed & Ward Ltd., 1974, p. 15.

Man is a microcosmos and contains all things within himself; but of these only what is distinctly individual and characteristic acquires tangible form. He is, moreover, a being who lives in many dimensions, and I have always been conscious of this within myself.

Nicolas Berdyaev, *Dream and Reality*, translated by Katharine Lampert, Geoffrey Bles, Ltd., 1950, p.1.

Man with all his noble qualities, with sympathy which feels for the most debased, with benevolence which extends not only to other men but to the humblest living creature, with his god-like intellect which has penetrated into the movements and constitution of the solar system—with all these exalted powers—Man still bears in his bodily frame the indelible stamp of his lowly origin.

Charles Darwin, *The Descent of Man*, Part I, C.A. Watts & Co. Limited, 1930, p. 244.

I see the marks of God in the heavens and the earth, but how much more in a liberal intellect, in magnanimity, in unconquerable rectitude, in a philanthropy which forgives every wrong, and which never despairs of the cause of Christ and human virtue. I do and I must reverence human nature. Neither the sneers of a worldly scepticism, nor the groans of a gloomy theology, disturb my faith in its godlike powers and tendencies. I know how it is despised, how it has been oppressed, how civil and religious establishments have for ages conspired to crush it. I know its history. I shut my eyes on none of its weaknesses and crimes.... But injured, trampled on, and scorned as our nature is, I still turn to it with intense sympathy and strong hope. The signatures of its origin and its end are impressed too deeply to be ever wholly effaced. I bless it for its kind affections, for its strong and tender love. I honour it for its struggles against oppression, for its growth and progress under the weight of so many chains and prejudices, for its achievements in science and art, and still more for its examples of heroic and saintly virtue. These are marks of a divine origin and pledges of a celestial inheritance; and I thank God that my own lot is bound up with that of the human race.

William E. Channing, *Complete Works*, Routledge & Sons, 1884, "Likeness to God," p.235.

Man is both animal and spiritual. On one side he is the most fully developed of the animals; but if that were all, he would present, and know, no problems. Upon him is stamped the Image of God; he is capable of that communion with God which is eternal life. But here again we find two-sidedness; for the Image of God in man is blurred and distorted. How or why this should be so is a question too large for discussion here. The fact is certain. Man, capable by his nature as God made it of communion with God as the author, centre, and goal of his being, does always in greater or less degree conduct himself as though he were himself his own beginning and end, the centre of his own universe. His "sin" is not a mere survival or disproportionate development of animal tendencies, or an inadequate development of rational control. It is a perversion of reason itself. His capacity for divine communion is become a usurpation of divine authority. The worst, the most typical sin, from which all other sin flows, is not sensuality but pride.

William Temple, *Citizen and Churchman*, Eyre & Spottiswoode, Ltd., 1941, p.44.

MARRIAGE

It is not good that the man should be alone; I will make him a helper fit for him.
Genesis 2.18.

None can be eternally united who have not died for each other.
Coventry Patmore, *The Rod, the Root and the Flower*, The Grey Walls Press Ltd., 1950, p.215, "Aphorisms and Extracts."

Love is a glass which shatters if you hold it too tightly or too loosely.
Russian Proverb.

Being married is something that takes everything you've got.
Henrik Ibsen, *The League of Youth*, edited & translated by James Walter McFarlane & Graham Orton, Oxford University Press, 1963, Volume IV, p.99, Act IV.

It takes patience to appreciate domestic bliss; volatile spirits prefer unhappiness.
George Santayana, *The Life of Reason*, Archibald Constable & Co. Ltd., 1905, Volume II, "Reason in Society," p.45.

I ... chose my wife as she did her wedding gown, not for a fine glossy surface, but such qualities as would wear well.
Oliver Goldsmith, *Collected Works of Oliver Goldsmith*, edited by Arthur Friedman, Oxford at the Clarendon Press, 1966, Volume IV, p.18, *The Vicar of Wakefield*, Ch.I, 1.8.

Life has taught us that love does not consist in gazing at each other but in looking outward together in the same direction.
Antoine de Saint-Exupéry, *Wind, Sand and Stars*, translated by Lewis Galantière, William Heinemann Ltd., 1939, p.268.

When marrying, one should ask oneself this question: Do you believe that you will be able to converse well with this woman into your old age?
Friedrich Nietzsche, *The Portable Nietzsche*, translated by Walter Kaufmann, Penguin Books Ltd., 1976, p.59.

Unless marriage is thought of in terms of supernatural vocation even the natural side of it will be incomplete. The material and physical will outweigh the natural and spiritual.
Hubert van Zeller, *Considerations*, Sheed & Ward Ltd., 1974, p.93.

Affection, companionship, common interests, mutual respect and enduring devotion: these are the temporal elements in a good marriage. Temporal elements have their eternal dimension.
Hubert van Zeller, *Considerations*, Sheed and Ward Ltd., 1974, p.94.

Love does not cause suffering: what causes it is the sense of ownership, which is love's opposite.
Antoine de Saint-Exupéry, *The Wisdom of the Sands*, translated by Stuart Gilbert, Hollis & Carter Ltd., 1952, p.152.

Love is a recent discovery, and requires a new law. Easy divorce is the vulgar solution.
The true solution is some undiscovered security for true marriage.

Coventry Patmore, *The Rod, the Root and the Flower,* The Grey Walls Press Ltd., 1950, p.51, "Aurea Dicta,"
CXXXV.

Suitability helps the security of a marriage, but spirituality, by calling for mutual
self-sacrifice, ensures it.

Hubert van Zeller, *Considerations,* Sheed & Ward Ltd., 1974, p.94.

Seldom, or perhaps never, does a marriage develop into an individual relationship
smoothly and without crises; there is no coming to consciousness without pain.

C.G. Jung, *Contributions to Analytical Psychology,* translated by H.G. and Cary F. Baynes, Kegan Paul, Trench,
Trubner & Co. Ltd., 1928, p.193.

Love is not getting, but giving; not a wild dream of pleasure, and a madness of desire—
oh, no, love is not that—it is goodness, and honour, and peace, and pure living—
yes, love is that; and it is the best thing in the world, and the thing that lives longest.

Henry Van Dyke, *Little Rivers,* David Nutt, 1903, p.132.

Marriage is a terrifying responsibility. Marriage is a unique wholeness and completeness
and having a best friend to confide in, to hurt, a friend who will understand, argue,
fight, but still make love and be friends.

A young housewife.

Affinity of nature founded on worship of the same ideal, and perfect in proportion to
perfectness of soul, is the only affinity which is worth anything. True love is that
which ennobles the personality, fortifies the heart, and sanctifies the existence. And
the being we love must not be mysterious and sphinx-like, but clear and limpid as a
diamond; so that admiration and attachment may grow with knowledge.

Henri Frédéric Amiel, *Amiel's Journal,* translated by Mrs. Humphry Ward, Macmillan & Co. Ltd., 1918, p.284.

Love, indeed, is an affair of maturity. I don't believe that a man, in this country, can
love before forty or a woman before thirty-five. They may marry before that and have
children; and they will love their children, but very rarely each other. I am thinking
now of love at its highest rating, as that passion which is able to lift a man to the
highest flight of which the soul is capable here on earth—a flight, mind you, which
it may take without love, as the poet's takes it, or the musician's, but which the
ordinary man's can only take by means of love.

Maurice Hewlett, in *The Note Books of a Woman Alone,* edited by M.G. Ostle, J.M. Dent & Sons Ltd., 1935,
p.228.

Only in marriage can human beings fully know one another—the miracle of feeling,
touching, seeing another's personality—and this is as wonderful and as unique as the
mystic's knowledge of God. It is for this reason that before marriage man hovers about
life, observes it from without; only in marriage does he plunge into it, entering it

through the personality of another. This joy of knowledge and real life gives us that feeling of achieved plenitude and satisfaction for which we are richer and wiser.

Father Yelchaninov, in *A Treasury of Russian Spirituality*, edited by G.P. Fedotov, Sheed and Ward Ltd., 1977, p.446.

Marriage is the beginning and the pinnacle of all culture. It makes the savage gentle, and it gives the most cultivated the best occasion for demonstrating his gentleness. It has to be indissoluble: it brings so much happiness that individual instances of unhappiness do not come into account. And why speak of unhappiness at all? Impatience is what it really is, ever and again people are overcome by impatience, and then they like to think themselves unhappy. Let the moment pass, and you will count yourself happy that what has so long stood firm still stands. As for separation, there can be no adequate grounds for it. The human condition is compounded of so much joy and so much sorrow that it is impossible to reckon how much a husband owes a wife or a wife a husband. It is an infinite debt, it can be paid only in eternity. Marriage may sometimes be an uncomfortable state. I can well believe that, and that is as it should be. Are we not also married to our conscience, and would we not often like to be rid of it because it is more uncomfortable than a husband or a wife could ever be?

Johann Wolfgang von Goethe, *Elective Affinities*, translated with an introduction by R.J. Hollindale, 1971, Penguin Books Ltd., 1982, p.89.

What are the facts and principles upon which monogamy rests?
Male and female—the differences of gender belongs to many parts of nature as well as humanity. It links humanity with nature, and also serves humanity's divine goal, which reaches far beyond nature. The delicate division of gifts and qualities leaves man eager for woman, and woman eager for man. Eros, or love, is the desire of the one for the other, as the one feels incomplete without the other; it is a desire to possess and be possessed. Venus is the pleasurable act in which union is expressed; it serves Eros, and Eros craves for it.
But Eros and Venus together do not exhaust the meaning of man and woman in their togetherness. Man and woman are selves, they are persons; they bring to one another a wealth of thoughts, actions, interests, concerns, and these are to become the stuff of the unity between them, without individuality disappearing. What monogamy does is not only unite Eros and Venus to one another, but unite them both within the whole realm of unities in which man and woman can be joined.
Thus it is that these are linked with *Philia* (friendship), the whole range of comradeship in life, together with all that this involves, and as God is the giver and God is the goal, there comes also within the relationship of man and woman the *Agape* (the word which is usually translated as "love" in the New Testament, especially in 1 Cor: 13) which is the divine self-giving kind of love without which the rest may go astray. Such is monogamy. Its emergence in history, its interior depth, and its stable continuance require the sacrifice of a great restraint.

Michael Ramsey, *Through the Year with Michael Ramsey*, edited by Margaret Duggan, Hodder & Stoughton Ltd., 1975, p.93.

People get from books the idea that if you have married the right person you may expect to go on "being in love" for ever. As a result, when they find they are not, they think this proves they have made a mistake and are entitled to a change—not realising that, when they have changed, the glamour will presently go out of the new love just as it went out of the old one. In this department of life, as in every other, thrills come at the beginning and do not last....

Let the thrill go—let it die away—go on through that period of death into the quieter interest and happiness that follow—and you will find you are living in a world of new thrills all the time. But if you decide to make thrills your regular diet and try to prolong them artificially, they will all get weaker and weaker, and fewer and fewer, and you will be a bored, disillusioned old man for the rest of your life. It is because so few people understand this that you find many middle-aged men and women maundering about their lost youth, at the very age when new horizons ought to be appearing and new doors opening all round them. It is much better fun to learn to swim than to go on endlessly (and hopelessly) trying to get back the feeling you had when you first went paddling as a small boy.

C.S. Lewis, *Mere Christianity*, William Collins Sons & Co. Ltd., 1961, p.97.

And what of Marriage?...
And he answered saying:
You were born together, and together you shall be for evermore.
You shall be together when the white wings of death scatter your days.
Aye, you shall be together even in the silent memory of God.
But let there be spaces in your togetherness.
And let the winds of the heavens dance between you.

Love one another, but make not a bond of love:
Let it rather be a moving sea between the shores of your souls.
Fill each other's cup but drink not from one cup.
Give one another of your bread but eat not from the same loaf.
Sing and dance together and be joyous, but let each one of you be alone,
Even as the strings of a lute are alone though they quiver with the same music.

Give your hearts, but not into each other's keeping.
For only the hand of Life can contain your hearts.
And stand together yet not too near together:
For the pillars of the temple stand apart,
And the oak tree and the cypress grow not in each other's shadow.

Kahlil Gibran, *The Prophet*, William Heinemann Ltd., 1970, p.16.

MATERIALISM

As having nothing, and yet possessing everything.
2 Corinthians 6.10.

Happily for our blessedness, the joy of possession soon palls.
George Macdonald, *Wilfred Cumbermede,* Hurst and Blackett, Publishers, 1872, Volume I, p.170.

It is preoccupation with possessions, more than anything else, that prevents men from living freely and nobly.
Bertrand Russell, *Principles of Social Reconstruction,* George Allen & Unwin Ltd., 1971,p.162.

High thinking is inconsistent with complicated material life based on high speed imposed on us by Mammon worship. All the graces of life are possible only when we learn the art of living nobly.
Mohandas K.Gandhi, *Non-Violence in Peace & War,* Navajivan Publishing House, 1949, Volume II, p.121.

We consume, as we produce, without any concrete relatedness to the objects with which we deal; we live in a world of things, and our only connection with them is that we know how to manipulate or to consume them.
Erich Fromm, *The Sane Society,* Routledge & Kegan Paul Ltd., 1956, p.134.

No country has had a more splendid succession of inspiring teachers, whether poets, philosophers, or men of letters. The idealistic tradition in England is much older and more deeply rooted in the national character than our temporary and partly accidental addiction to material success. In proportion as our people can be taught to interest themselves in those treasures of the soul, in which one man's gain is not another man's loss, and which are increased by being shared with others, we may hope that the bitterness and narrowness of economic strife may be assuaged, and that something like a really harmonious civilization may come in sight.
W.R.Inge, *England,* Ernest Benn Ltd.,1926, p.289.

The art of living is not best understood by highly industrialised communities, where men are too busy to think, and where the cult of efficiency makes them reluctant to waste time, as they put it, by considering whether their standards of value correspond with the nature of things and with their own best selves. But we ought not to evade these questions. For it is an unpleasant reflection that the same motives which make big business hostile to sensual gratifications must make it antagonistic to all the higher interests of life—to art, science, philosophy, and religion. For all these are in one way like drink—they "make men desire fewer things." A philosopher was once asked by a vulgar fellow whether his philosophy had ever brought him in any money. The answer, intended to be intelligible to the questioner, was: "It has saved me a great many expenses." Consumptionism plainly has no use for philosophy!
W.R.Inge, *Lay Thoughts of a Dean,* G.P. Putnam's Sons, 1926, p.194.

We must begin to organise our industry with the supply of need as the primary aim and the making of profits as entirely incidental. This is a return to the "natural order"

---

as it exists in the mind of the Creator; but of course it is a reversal of the order natural to the selfishness of men! The Church cannot say how it is to be done; but it is called to say that it must be done, and to demand of those upon whom the change will impose sacrifices that they accept those with goodwill in the name of fellowship and service.

There the Church stops, and the State, moved by its citizens and by the Christian impulse communicated through them from the Church, takes up the task. There is room for abundance of divergent opinions.

William Temple, *Citizen and Churchman,* Eyre & Spottiswoode, Ltd., 1941, p.84.

For in our age all men are separated into self-contained units, everyone crawls into his own hole, everyone separates himself from his neighbour, hides himself away and hides away everything he possesses, and ends up by keeping himself at a distance from people and keeping other people at a distance from him. He accumulates riches by himself and thinks how strong he is now and how secure, and does not realize, madman that he is, that the more he accumulates the more deeply does he sink into self-destroying impotence. For he is used to relying on himself alone and has separated himself as a self-contained unit from the whole. He has trained his mind not to believe in the help of other people, in men and mankind, and is in constant fear of losing his money and the rights he has won for himself. Everywhere today the mind of man has ceased, ironically, to understand that true security of the individual does not lie in isolated personal efforts but in general human solidarity. But an end will most certainly come to this dreadful isolation of man, and everyone will realize all at once how unnaturally they have separated themselves from one another. Such will be the spirit of the time, and everyone will be surprised at having remained so long in darkness and not having seen the light. And then the sign of the Son of Man will appear in the heavens.... But till then we must still keep the banner flying and, even if he has to do it alone, a man has to set an example at least once and draw his soul out of its isolation and work for some great act of human intercourse based on brotherly love, even if he is to be regarded as a saintly fool for his pains. He has to do so that the great idea may not die....

Fyodor Dostoyevsky, *The Brothers Karamazov,* translated with an introduction by David Magarshack, Penguin Books Ltd., 1963, Volume I, p.357.

MEDITATION

Meditation is a contented but perfectly conscious dwelling of the mind on something likely to elevate our life.

Ernest Dimnet, *What We Live By,* Jonathan Cape Ltd., 1932, p.185.

Our duty is not primarily to strive and to brace up our wills, but primarily to fasten our attention upon the divine love, that it may do its own work upon us and within us.

William Temple, *The Preacher's Theme To-day,* S.P.C.K., 1936, p.60.

The art of meditation may be exercised at all hours, and in all places; and men of genius, in their walks, at table, and amidst assemblies, turning the eye of the mind inwards, can form an artificial solitude; retired amidst a crowd, calm amidst distraction, and wise amidst folly.

Isaac Disraeli, *Literary Character of Men of Genius,* edited by The Earl of Beaconsfield, Frederick Warne and Co., 1881, p.131.

Scarcely is there anything which the understanding can know of God,—only the will can greatly love Him. Let a man imprison himself within his own self, in the centre of his soul, wherein is the image of God, and there let him wait upon Him, as one listens to another speaking from some high tower, or as though he had Him within his heart, and as if in all creation there were no other thing save God and his soul.

St. Peter of Alcantara, in *Studies of the Spanish Mystics,* E. Allison Peers, Sheldon Press, 1930, Volume II, p.114.

People need to discover their own self-identity. Many go to drugs, not to forget the miseries of life, but to discover its secrets, to explore an inner life of identity, liberation and happiness. The mystics tell us that this experience can be gained from the discipline of meditation, entering into silence, stilling the activity of the mind, allowing feelings and intuitions to rise from the depths of our being.

George Appleton, *Journey for a Soul,* William Collins Sons & Co. Ltd., 1976, p.38.

Meditation is a channel for continuous reconstitution of the self, to prepare it that it may move into the new.... The entire nervous system and the vital processes rest as in deep sleep, while there is a condition of alert attention in the mind, a listening to the world of being. We are then open to the qualities of the Higher Self, which essentially are peace, love, gentleness, courage and joy.
While these fill the soul, there is simply no room for the negative qualities of the lower self, which include remorse, regret, disappointment, anger, resentment for things past, and fear, anxiety and doubt about the future. These negative emotions cannot enter, any more than darkness can remain in a room when we switch on the light.

George Trevelyan, *A Vision of the Aquarian Age,* Coventure Ltd., 1977, p.87.

Since I learned how to enter the forest of meditation, I have received sweet dewlike drops from that forest. I have found that the door to meditation is open everywhere and any time, at midnight or at noonday, at dawn or at dusk. Everywhere, on the street, on the trolley, on the train, in the waiting room, or in the prison cell, I am given a resting place of meditation, wherein I can meditate to my heart's content on the Almighty God who abides in my heart.
It is said that Francis of Assisi meditated and prayed, looking up at the sun in broad daylight. Plato has told how Socrates suddenly would pause and stand erect to meditate for a few minutes while walking with his disciples.... Jesus withdrew into the wilderness and meditated forty days and forty nights. Sometimes he was lost in meditation and prayer all night long in the mountains of Galilee. Those who draw water from the wellspring of meditation know that God dwells close to their hearts. For those who wish to discover the quietude of old amid the hustle and bustle of today's machine civilization, there is no way save to rediscover this ancient realm of meditation. Since

the loss of my eyesight I have been as delighted as if I had found a new wellspring
by having arrived at this sacred precinct.

Toyohiko Kagawa, *Meditations,* translated by Jiro Takenaka, Harper & Brothers, 1950, p.1, No.1.

There is an act of the mind, natural to the earnest and the wise, impossible only to
the sensual and the fool, healthful to all who are sincere, which has small place in
modern usage, and which few can now distinguish from vacuity. Those who knew
what it was, called it *meditation.* It is not *reading,* in which we apprehend the thoughts
of others, and bring them to our critical tribunal. It is not *study,* in which we strive
to master the known and prevail over it, till it lies in order beneath our feet. It is
not *reasoning,* in which we seek to push forward the empire of our positive conceptions.... It is not *deliberation,* which computes the particular problems of action, reckons
up the forces that surround our individual lot, and projects accordingly the expedient
or the right. It is not *self-scrutiny,* which by itself is only shrewdness or at most science
turned within instead of without, and analyzing mental feelings instead of physical
facts. Its view is not personal and particular, but universal and immense.... It brings,
not an intense self-consciousness and spiritual egotism, but almost a renunciation of
individuality.... It gives us no matter for criticism and doubt, but everything for
wonder and for love. It does not suggest indirect demonstration, but furnishes immediate perception of things divine, eye to eye with the saints, spirit to spirit with God,
peace to peace with Heaven. In thus being alone with the truth of things, and passing
from shows and shadows into communion with the everlasting One, there is nothing
at all impossible and out of reach.... Let any true man go into silence; strip himself
of all pretence, and selfishness, and sensuality and sluggishness of soul; lift off thought
after thought, passion after passion till he reaches the inmost depth of all... and it
will be strange if he does not feel the Eternal Presence as close upon his soul, as the
breeze upon his brow; if he does not say, "O Lord, art Thou ever near as this, and
have I not known Thee?"

James Martineau, *Endeavours after the Christian Life,* Longmans, Green, Reader, and Dyer, 1876, p.186.

MERCY

May mercy, peace, and love be multiplied to you.

Jude 2.

Who will not mercie unto others shew
How can he mercy ever hope to have?

Edmund Spenser, *Spenser's Faerie Queene,* edited by J.C. Smith, Oxford at the Clarendon Press, 1964, p.322,
Bk.VI, Canto I, st.xlii. l.1.

Wilt thou draw near the nature of the gods?
Draw near them then in being merciful;
Sweet mercy is nobility's true badge.

William Shakespeare, *Titus Andronicus,* Act I. sc.i. l.118.

Does it never come into your mind to fear, lest He should demand of you why you had not exercised towards your brother a little of that mercy, which He, Who is your Master, so abundantly bestows upon you?

F. de la M. Fénelon, *Letters and Reflections of Fénélon,* edited by B.W. Randolph, A. R. Mowbray & Co. Ltd., 1906, p.128.

I saw soothfastly that our Lord was never wroth, nor ever shall be. For He is God: Good, Life, Truth, Love, Peace; His Charity and His Unity suffereth Him not to be wroth. For I saw truly that it is against the property of His Might to be wroth, and against the property of His Wisdom, and against the property of His Goodness.

Lady Julian of Norwich, *Revelations of Divine Love,* edited by Grace Warrack, Methuen & Co. Ltd., 1949, p.97.

> Teach me to feel another's Woe;
> To hide the Fault I see;
> That Mercy I to others show,
> That Mercy show to me.

Alexander Pope, *The Poems of Alexander Pope,* Volume VI, *Minor Poems,* edited by Norman Ault and compiled by John Butt, Methuen & Co. Ltd., 1954, p.148, "The Universal Prayer," st.10, l.37.

> Then I see the Saviour over me
> Spreading his beams of love & dictating the words of this mild song....
> I am not a God afar off, I am a brother and friend;
> Within your bosoms I reside, and you reside in me:
> Lo! we are One, forgiving all Evil, Not seeking recompense.

William Blake, *The Complete Writings of William Blake,* edited by Geoffrey Keynes, Oxford University Press, 1974, p.622, *Jerusalem,* Ch.I, Plate 4, l.4,18.

> For Mercy has a human heart,
> Pity a human face,
> And Love, the human form divine,
> And Peace, the human dress.

William Blake, *The Complete Writings of William Blake,* edited by Geoffrey Keynes, Oxford University Press, 1974, p.117, *Songs of Innocence,* "The Divine Image," st.iii, l.9.

The words "Be ye perfect, even as your Father which is in heaven is perfect," coming immediately after the words "Your Father which is in heaven, who maketh his sun to rise on the evil and on the good, and sendeth rain on the just and on the unjust" imply a whole doctrine which, as far as I know, is not developed anywhere. For Christ cites as the supreme characteristic of God's justice precisely what is always brought forward (example of Job) with the object of accusing him of injustice, namely, that he favours the good and the wicked indifferently.

There must have been in Christ's teaching the notion of a certain virtue attaching to indifference, similar to that which may be found in Greek stoicism and Hindu thought. These words of Christ remind one of the supreme cry uttered by Prometheus: "Heaven by whom for all the common light revolves...."

(Moreover, this light and this rain also possess probably a spiritual significance, that is to say, that all—both in Israel and outside it, both in the Church and outside it— have grace showered upon them *equally,* although the majority reject it.)

That is absolutely contrary to the current conception whereby God arbitrarily sends down more grace on one man, less on another man, like some capricious sovereign; and that on the pretext that he does not owe it to any man! He owes it to his own infinite goodness to give to every creature good in all its fulness. We ought rather to believe that he showers continually on each one the fulness of his grace, but that we consent to receive it to a greater or lesser extent. In purely spiritual matters, God grants all desires. Those that have less have asked for less.

Simone Weil, *Gateway to God,* edited by David Raper, with the collaboration of Malcolm Muggeridge and Vernon Sproxton, William Collins Sons & Co. Ltd., 1974, p.137.

MIND

You shall love the Lord your God ... with all your mind.

Mark 12.30.

I appeal to you therefore, brethren, by the mercies of God, to present your bodies as a living sacrifice, holy and acceptable to God, which is your spiritual worship. Do not be conformed to this world but be transformed by the renewal of your mind, that you may prove what is the will of God, what is good and acceptable and perfect.

Romans 12.1-2.

"For who has known the mind of the Lord so as to instruct him?" But we have the mind of Christ.

1 Corinthians 2.16.

Finally, brethren, whatever is true, whatever is honourable, whatever is just, whatever is pure, whatever is lovely, whatever is gracious, if there is any excellence, if there is anything worthy of praise, think about these things.

Philippians 4.8.

The mind grows always by intercourse with a mind more mature than itself. That is the secret of all teaching.

William Temple, *Christian Faith and Life,* S.C.M. Press Ltd., 1963, p.36.

Engage and then the mind becomes heated. Only begin, and then the task will be completed.

Anon.

The mind of man is capable of anything—because everything is in it, all the past as well as all the future.

Joseph Conrad, *Heart of Darkness,* included in *Youth, a Narrative & Two Other Stories,* J.M. Dent & Sons Ltd., 1923, p.96.

Our minds are finite, and yet even in these circumstances of finitude we are surrounded by possibilities that are infinite, and the purpose of human life is to grasp as much as we can out of that infinitude.

Alfred North Whitehead, *Dialogues of Alfred North Whitehead*, as recorded by Lucien Price, Max Reinhardt, 1954, p.160.

The life of Christ is not simply a thing written. It is a thing lived. My sanctification lies in re-living this life in the context of my own life. It lies in identifying myself with the mind of Christ which is primarily the mind of love.

Hubert van Zeller, *Considerations*, Sheed & Ward Ltd., 1974, p.67.

Man is distinguished from the animals by possessing, among other things, a conscious mind, with the ability to think, reason, remember, imagine, understand and express himself. He is not just mind, nor is mind just a machine that he uses. It is a vital part of man's personality but not the whole of it. It needs to be brought under the inspiration and guidance of God.

George Appleton, *Journey for a Soul*, William Collins Sons & Co. Ltd., 1976, p.18.

The mind of man is meant to be a microcosm of the mind of God. This was shown supremely, in terms of a human life, in Jesus Christ. We therefore need to study the records of that divine and human life, recognizing the faith of the writers but reaching back as far as possible to the life itself. Also, by communion with the ever-living, ever-present Christ, we can experience direct, intuitive contact and illumination.

George Appleton, *Journey for a Soul*, William Collins Sons & Co. Ltd., 1976, p.19.

I call that mind free which jealously guards its intellectual rights and powers, which calls no man master, which does not content itself with a passive or hereditary faith, which opens itself to light whencesoever it may come, which receives new truth as an angel from heaven, which, whilst consulting others, inquires still more of the oracle within itself, and uses instructions from abroad not to supersede but to quicken and exalt its own energies.

William E. Channing, *The Complete Works of William Ellery Channing*, "Spiritual Freedom," Routledge & Sons, 1884, p.166.

MIRACLES

Love ... is always in the mood of believing in miracles.

John Cowper Powys, *The Meaning of Culture*, Jonathan Cape Ltd., 1932, p.170.

Miracles happen only to those who believe in them.

French Proverb.

A portent (miracle), therefore, does not occur contrary to nature, but contrary to what is known of nature.

St. Augustine, *City of God*, translated by Henry Bettenson, edited, with an introduction by David Knowles, Penguin Books Ltd., 1972, p.980.

The miracles of Jesus were the ordinary works of his Father, wrought small and swift that we might take them in.

George Macdonald, *Unspoken Sermons,* Second Series, Longmans, Green, & Co. Ltd., 1885, p.52.

The divine art of miracle is not an art of suspending the pattern to which events conform but of feeding new events into that pattern.

C.S. Lewis, *Miracles,* William Collins Sons & Co. Ltd., 1974, p.64.

It is Christ Himself, rather than any of the things which He did, who is the supreme miracle and the chief attestation of the truth of the biblical revelation.

Alan Richardson, *Christian Apologetics,* S.C.M. Press Ltd., 1947, p.156.

Disbelief in the miracles is usually the result of disbelief in the biblical conception of God as the source of all power or in Christ as the veritable incarnation of the *dunamis* of God.

Alan Richardson, in *A Theological Word Book of the Bible,* edited by Alan Richardson, S.C.M. Press Ltd., 1969, p.152, "Miracle."

Men talk about Bible miracles because there is no miracle in their lives. Cease to gnaw that crust. There is ripe fruit over your head.

Henry David Thoreau, *The Journal of Henry D. Thoreau,* edited by Bradford Torrey and Francis H. Allen, 1949, Houghton Mifflin Company, Boston, The Riverside Press, Volume II, p.33.

The essence of Jesus' religion is not its miraculous character. Miracles themselves did not constitute the religion of Jesus. It is a gross mistake to take his miracles for the essence of Christianity.
Jesus never made his miracle the central point of his teaching. He simply used this power as a means of manifesting his personality.
The salient feature of Jesus' religion is neither his virgin birth nor his resurrection. The gist of his religion is the uplift of conscience wrought through God and Christ. This implies that, recovering our benumbed divine sense, we enter into that sacred precinct where God and man are united, and there revel in the love of our Heavenly Father. This is the religion of Jesus.
The Miracles were only an addendum, an afterthought.
Christianity would continue unimpaired even if all the miracles were to be completely eliminated from it. Nevertheless, it is a certainty that Jesus Christ could perform miracles, and did perform them. The only question for criticism to decide is how far we are to depend upon their acceptance.

Toyohiko Kagawa, *Meditations,* translated by Jiro Takenaka, Harper & Brothers, 1950, No.36.

It is not necessary to go far afield in search for miracles. I am myself a miracle. My physical birth and my soul's existence are miracles. First and foremost the fact that I was ever born is a miracle. The fact that I am still alive despite my shadow-like, weakened body battling a host of devils of disease is a miracle.
Yet the greatest miracle of all is the reality of my soul. That I should be made victorious in temptations, be the object of God's care in a ruined world, be given assurance to go forward into the world of the devout, this is to me a master miracle. At times the

storms of passion shake my soul to its depths, but a purer power, stronger a thousand times, has possession of my being and holds sway over me. When I think of this state of my soul it appears, even to me, a miracle.

To my heart value immediately takes on reality, and prayer ere long is reproduced in realization. In the depths of my soul I am daily conscious of the miracle of creation. The miracle of the resurrection becomes not a matter of yesterday, but takes place to-day in this soul of mine. A virgin conceiving and bearing God in her bosom becomes not an ancient tale in far-off Bethlehem but a present-day fact within me.

Toyohiko Kagawa, in *Kagawa*, William Axling, S.C.M. Press Ltd., 1946, p.10.

But now if all things whatsoever that we look upon are emblems to us of the Highest God, I add that more so than any of them is man such an emblem. You have heard of St. Chrysostom's celebrated saying, in reference to the Shekinah, or Ark of Testimony, visible Revelation of God, among the Hebrews: "The true Shekinah is Man!" Yes, it is even so: this is no vain phrase; it is veritably so. The essence of our being, the mystery in us that calls itself "I,"—ah, what words have we for such things?— is a breath of Heaven; the Highest Being reveals himself in man. This body, these faculties, this life of ours, is it not all as a vesture for that Unnamed? "There is but one temple in the Universe," says the devout Novalis, "and that is the Body of Man. Nothing is holier than that high form. Bending before men is a reverence done to this Revelation in the Flesh. We touch Heaven when we lay our hand on a human body!" This sounds much like a mere flourish of rhetoric; but it is not so. If well meditated, it will turn-out to be a scientific fact; the expression, in such words as can be had, of the actual truth of the thing. *We* are the miracle of miracles.

Thomas Carlyle, *Sartor Resartus*, "Lectures on Heroes," Chapman & Hall, 1840, p.192.

Why, who makes much of a miracle?
As to me I know of nothing else but miracles,
Whether I walk the streets of Manhattan,
Or dart my sight over the roofs of houses toward the sky,
Or wade with naked feet along the beach just in the edge of the water,
Or stand under trees in the woods,
Or talk by day with any one I love, or sleep in the bed at night with any one I love,
Or sit at table at dinner with the rest,
Or look at strangers opposite me riding in the car,
Or watch honey-bees busy around the hive of a summer forenoon,
Or animals feeding in the fields,
Or birds, or the wonderfulness of insects in the air,
Or the wonderfulness of the sundown, or of stars shining so quiet and bright,
Or the exquisite delicate thin curve of the new moon in spring;
These with the rest, one and all, are to me miracles,
The whole referring, yet each distinct and in its place.

To me every hour of the light and dark is a miracle,
Every cubic inch of space is a miracle,

Every square yard of the surface of the earth is spread with the same,
Every foot of the interior swarms with the same.

To me the sea is a continual miracle,
The fishes that swim—the rocks—the motion of the waves—the ships with men in them,
What stranger miracles are there?

Walt Whitman, *The Complete Poems,* edited by Francis Murphy, Penguin Books Ltd., 1982, p.409, "Miracles,"
l.1.

MISSION

Jesus said to them again, "Peace be with you. As the Father has sent me, even so I send you."

John 20.21.

Kindness has converted more sinners than either zeal, eloquence, or learning.

F.W. Faber, *Spiritual Conferences,* Thomas Richardson & Son, 1859, p.6.

Every life is a profession of faith, and exercises an inevitable and silent propaganda.

Henri Frédéric Amiel, *Amiel's Journal,* translated by Mrs. Humphry Ward, Macmillan & Co. Ltd., 1918, p.24.

The appeal of Christ to us is not so much to consider how we will be punished as it is to see what we miss, if we will not take his way of things.

William Barclay, *The Gospel of Matthew,* The Saint Andrew Press, 1975, Volume 2, p.296.

The members of the Church are impelled to engage in this activity because of the charity with which they love God and by which they desire to share with all men in the spiritual goods of this life and the life to come.

Vatican Council II, *The Conciliar and Post Conciliar Documents,* 1981 Edition, general editor, Austin Flannery, O.P., Fowler Wright Books Ltd., p.821.

When a man genuinely and humbly feels he has discovered the buried treasure of the gospel he naturally wants to spread the good news to others and so to bring them closer to God. He must be on guard, however, not to let them stop short of himself.

Hubert van Zeller, *Considerations,* Sheed and Ward Ltd., 1974, p.15.

There is no expeditious road,
To pack and label men for God,
And save them by the barrel-load.

Francis Thompson, *The Works of Francis Thompson,* Burns & Oates·Ltd., 1913, Volume I, p.190, Epilogue to A Judgement in Heaven, l.22.

I would spend my best efforts to make them follow him whose first servants were the fishermen of Galilee, for with all my heart I believe that that Man holds the secret of life, and that only the man who obeys him can ever come to know the God who is the root and crown of our being, and whom to know is freedom and bliss.

George Macdonald, *The Marquis of Lossie,* Everett & Co. Ltd., 1912, p.269.

I often ask myself why a "Christian instinct" often draws me more to the religionless people than to the religious, by which I do not in the least mean with any evangelizing intention, but, I might almost say, "in brotherhood." While I am often reluctant to mention God by name to religious people—because that name somehow seems to me here not to ring true, and I feel myself to be slightly dishonest (it is particularly bad when others start to talk in religious jargon; I then dry up almost completely and feel awkward and uncomfortable)—to people with no religion I can on occasion mention him by name quite calmly and as a matter of course.

Dietrich Bonhoeffer, *Letters and Papers from Prison*, edited by Eberhard Bethge, S.C.M. Press Ltd., Second Revised Edition, 1967, p.154.

Some say that it is pure presumption to urge repentance upon people and proclaim a gospel of salvation. They insist that only he who is out of step with the times indulges in such arrogant conduct. Among those who argue in this fashion, the wayward, the egoist, the wilful, and those who press for their own selfish way abound.

Others, again, contend that it is wrong to urge repentance upon one's fellows and attempts to save them, because such action issues from a sense of superiority.

Were it possible for men to live an isolated, sundered life, repentance and salvation might not be necessary. In that case the individual might be left to settle his own affairs. But where the syphilitic disease of a debauchee poisons his descendants even to the fourth generation, and where the alcohol which men drink smites with a curse even to the tenth generation, one cannot but implore people to repent.

Even more imperative is the necessity of urging repentance upon moneyed men who, because of their unawakened state, tyrannize over tens of thousands of toilers and treat them as wage-slaves.

From this individualistic standpoint there may be no need to press for repentance and preach salvation, but where life takes on a social aspect, these two moral activities become imperative.

For the individualist in whose consciousness society is still unborn, a world where self-gratification is the norm may seem right, but society will never come to its own on that basis.

Because the building of a moral social order known as the Kingdom of God was explicit and inherent in the teachings of Jesus, His religion and the way of the present-day proponents of individualism naturally clash. He who calls evangelism antiquated is a novice as regards life. When the destiny of mankind as a whole is considered, we must acknowledge that Christ made no mistake in His passionate effort to save.

Toyohiko Kagawa, in *Kagawa*, William Axling, S.C.M. Press Ltd., 1946, p.128.

The dismissal (at the end of a service) means this: You have been on the Mount of Transfiguration, you have seen the glory of God, you have been on the road to Damascus, you have faced the living God, you have been in the upper chamber, you have been here and there in Galilee and Judaea, all the mysterious places where one meets God, and now having spent several days with him, he says now that so much has been given—go, your joy will never abandon you. What you have acquired, you will never lose as long as you remain faithful. Go now, and if truly you have discovered joy, how can you not give joy to others? If truly you have come nearer to truth, how can you keep it for yourself? If truly something has been kindled in you which is life, are you going to allow anyone not to have a spark of this life? It does not mean go round and tell everyone specifically religious things or use clerical phrases. It means that you should go into the world which is yours with a radiance, with a joy, with an intensity that will make everyone look at you and say "He has something he hadn't before. Is it that truly God has come near? He has something he never had before and which I do not possess—joy, life, certainty, a new courage, a new daring, a vision, where can I get it?"

People will also say to you, "Mad you are." I answer in those cases, and there are many, I say "I am mad, but one thing I find strange. You who are wise call to the mad man, and the mad man is happy, alive and you feel dead; let us share my folly, it is God's folly."

You are now going to start. With God you go now, with him on all the ways, on all the roads; you can dance on the Mount of Transfiguration, you can bring concreteness of life for others. May God bless you in it with joy. I don't know any other words than "with joy"—go with joy, bring joy, and then you will have brought everything else, because God is joy, he is life, he is intensity.

Anthony Bloom, *God and Man*, Darton, Longman & Todd Ltd., 1971, p.124.

MONEY

Do not lay up for yourselves treasures on earth, where moth and rust consume and where thieves break in and steal, but lay up for yourselves treasures in heaven, where neither moth nor rust consumes and where thieves do not break in and steal. For where your treasure is, there will your heart be also.

Matthew 6.19-21.

No man can serve two masters; for either he will hate the one and love the other, or he will be devoted to the one and despise the other. You cannot serve God and mammon.

Matthew 6.24.

It will be hard for a rich man to enter the kingdom of heaven ... it is easier for a camel to go through the eye of a needle than for a rich man to enter the kingdom of God.

Matthew 19.23-24.

He has filled the hungry with good things, and the rich he has sent empty away.

Luke 1.53.

But those who desire to be rich fall into temptation, into a snare, into many senseless and hurtful desires that plunge men into ruin and destruction. For the love of money is the root of all evils; it is through this craving that some have wandered away from the faith and pierced their hearts with many pangs.

1 Timothy 6.9-10.

Great Wealth and Content seldom live together.
Thomas Fuller, M.D., *Gnomologia*, 1732, Dublin, p.68.

Money—money, like everything else—is a deception and a disappointment.
H.G. Wells, *Kipps*, Thomas Nelson and Sons, 1909, p.260.

Money is human happiness in the abstract: he, then, who is no longer capable of enjoying human happiness in the concrete devotes himself utterly to money.
Arthur Schopenhauer, in *A Certain World*, W.H. Auden, Faber and Faber Limited, 1971, p.266.

Ill fares the land, to hastening ills a prey,
Where wealth accumulates, and men decay.
Oliver Goldsmith, *Collected Works of Oliver Goldsmith*, edited by Arthur Friedman, Oxford at the Clarendon Press, 1966, Volume IV, p.289, "The Deserted Village," l.51.

The two things which, of all others, most want to be under a strict rule, and which are the greatest blessings both to ourselves and others, when they are rightly used, are our time and our money. These talents are continual means and opportunities of doing good.
William Law, *A Serious Call to a Devout and Holy Life*, J.M. Dent & Co. Ltd., 1898, p.88.

We have not driven home upon men His clear intuition that though, if wealth comes, it ought to be accepted and used as an opportunity, yet it must be recognised as rather a snare to the spiritual life than an aim which the Christian may legitimately set before himself to pursue.
William Temple, *Christian Faith and Life*, S.C.M. Press Ltd., 1963, p.131.

Selecting jobs for the pseudo independence that higher pay seems to offer, instead of for autonomous reasons —i.e., the job offering deepest satisfaction because it has intrinsic meaning for the person and adds to his self-respect—is likewise due to neurotic tendencies, namely the unrecognized equation of money with true status. Here, too, the outer security (what money can buy) is accepted in lieu of inner security; the impersonal coin of exchange is given more relevance than the particular product of one's labour. Matters are, of course, much worse when not even a semblance of freedom exists in choosing occupations.
Bruno Bettelheim, *The Informed Heart*, Thames and Hudson, 1960, p.82.

Can a rich man be saved? Can a rich society be saved? We must first notice that the Christian gospel has never said that material abundance was in itself evil. The Old Testament constantly reiterated that abundance was the fruit that came of following the ways of the Lord; the Son of Man ate and drank with sinners and publicans, though he had nowhere to lay his head; and the Church has constantly prayed for abundance and prosperity for its members and their societies.
The evils of riches, to the Christian, are the evils of distraction (the distraction that keeps men from thinking about God), the evils of a false dependence on the created order, and a would-be security that fails to take account of the inevitable fragility of human destiny on this earth. They are spiritual evils, not material evils, and it may

be that they lead men to inadequate, not excessive, appreciation and enjoyment of the glories of the material universe; we tend to use, and abuse, material things, rather than to enjoy them.

D.L. Munby, *God and the Rich Society,* Oxford University Press, 1961, p.55.

If we look at the Gospels with a firm intention to discover the *emphasis* of Christ's morality, we shall find that it did not lie at all along the lines laid down by the opinion of highly placed and influential people. Disreputable people who knew they were disreputable were gently told to "go and sin no more"; the really unparliamentary language was reserved for those thrifty, respectable, and sabbatarian citizens who enjoyed Caesar's approval and their own. And the one and only thing that ever seems to have roused the "meek and mild" Son of God to a display of outright physical violence was precisely the assumption that "business was business." The money-changers in Jerusalem drove a very thriving trade, and made as shrewd a profit as any other set of brokers who traffic in foreign exchange; but the only use Christ had for these financiers was to throw their property down the front steps of the Temple.

Dorothy L. Sayers, *Unpopular Opinions,* Victor Gollancz Ltd., 1946, p.10.

There does not appear to be any doubt that money is the agent which causes the decline of the strong, brave and self-confident people. The decline in courage, enterprise and a sense of duty is, however, gradual.

The first direction in which wealth injures the nation is a moral one. Money replaces honour and adventure as the objective of the best young men. Moreover, men do not normally seek to make money for their country or their community, but for themselves. Gradually, and almost imperceptibly, the Age of Affluence silences the voice of duty. The object of the young and the ambitious is no longer fame, honour or service, but cash.

Education undergoes the same gradual transformation. No longer do schools aim at producing brave patriots ready to serve their country. Parents and students alike seek the educational qualifications which will command the highest salaries. The Arab moralist, Ghazali (1058-1111), complains in these very same words of the lowering of objectives in the declining Arab world of his time. Students, he says, no longer attend college to acquire learning and virtue, but to obtain qualifications which will enable them to grow rich. The same situation is everywhere evident among us in the West today.

Sir John Glubb, *The Fate of Empires* and *Search for Survival,* William Blackwood & Sons Ltd., 1978, p.10.

MORALS

Men are great in proportion as they are moral.

Henry David Thoreau, *The Journal of Henry D. Thoreau,* edited by Bradford Torrey and Francis H. Allen, 1949, Houghton Mifflin Company, Boston, The Riverside Press, Volume IV, p.128.

Morality, when vigorously alive, sees farther than intellect.

J.A. Froude, *Short Studies on Great Subjects,* Longmans, Green, & Co. Ltd., 1907, Volume IV, p.265.

If your morals make you dreary, depend upon it they are wrong.

Robert Louis Stevenson, *Across the Plains*, T. Nelson & Sons, Ltd., 1892, p.276.

Conduct is three-fourths of our life and its largest concern.

Matthew Arnold, *The Complete Prose Works of Matthew Arnold*, Volume VI, *Dissent and Dogma*, edited by R.H. Super, Ann Arbor, The University of Michigan Press, 1968, "Literature and Dogma," Ch.I, p.180.

To make our idea of morality centre on forbidden acts is to defile the imagination and to introduce into our judgements of our fellow-men a secret element of gusto.

Robert Louis Stevenson, *Across the Plains*, T. Nelson & Sons, Ltd., 1892, p.272.

His (Jesus') system of morality was the most benevolent and sublime probably that has been ever taught.

Thomas Jefferson, *The Writings of Thomas Jefferson*, Taylor & Maury, 1854, Volume IV, p.476.

Morality, said Jesus, is kindness to the weak; morality, said Nietzsche, is the bravery of the strong; morality, said Plato, is the effective harmony of the whole. Probably all three doctrines must be combined to find a perfect ethic; but can we doubt which of the elements is fundamental?

Will Durant, *The Story of Philosophy*, Ernest Benn Ltd., 1946, p.55.

It is not strange if we are tempted to despair of good. We ask too much. Our religions and moralities have been trimmed to flatter us, till they are all emasculate and sentimentalized, and only please and weaken. Truth is of a rougher strain. In the harsh face of life, faith can read a bracing gospel.

Robert Louis Stevenson, *Across the Plains*, T. Nelson & Sons, Ltd., 1892, p.259.

No society has yet solved the problem of how to teach morality without religion. So the law must base itself on Christian morals and to the limit of its ability enforce them, not simply because they are the morals of most of us, nor simply because they are the morals which are taught by the established Church—on these points the law recognizes the right to dissent—but for the compelling reason that without the help of Christian teaching the law will fail.

Lord Devlin, *The Enforcement of Morals*, Oxford University Press, 1970, p.25.

The great secret of morals is love; or a going out of our own nature, and an identification of ourselves with the beautiful which exists in thought, action, or person, not our own. A man, to be greatly good, must imagine intensely and comprehensively; he must put himself in the place of another and of many others; the pains and pleasures of his species must become his own.

Percy Bysshe Shelley, *The Prose Works of Percy Bysshe Shelley*, edited by H. Buxton Forman, Reeves and Turner, 1880, Volume III, "A Defence of Poetry," p.111.

The standard of morals is the mind of Christ; that is our great principle if we are Christian. It will not help you at once to solve each particular problem; it will give you a touch-stone. As you seek to live in the constant companionship of Christ, you will find yourself knowing ever more fully what your duty is in accordance with His mind. Your moral authority is not a principle, but a Person. It is the mind of Christ.

William Temple, *Christian Faith and Life*, S.C.M. Press Ltd., 1963, p.60.

> The things that will destroy us are:
> Politics without principle;
> Pleasure without conscience;
> Wealth without work;
> Knowledge without character;
> Business without morality;
> Science without humanity, and
> Worship without sacrifice.
>
> Anon.

Morality is character and conduct, such as is required by the circle or community in which the man's life happens to be placed. It shews how much good *men* require of us. Religion is the endeavour of a man with all his mind, and heart, and soul, to form his life and his character upon the true elements of love and submission to God, and love and good will to man. A spiritual Christian is like a man who learns the principles of music, and then goes on to the practice. A moralist is like a man who learns nothing of the principles, but only a few airs by rote, and is satisfied to know as many tunes as common people do. Morality is good, and is accepted of God, as far as it goes; but the difficulty is, it does not go far enough. "Is not my fifty fathom cable as good as your hundred fathom one?" says the sailor. Yes, as far as it goes; but in water a hundred fathoms deep, if it does not go within fifty fathoms of anchorage, of what use will it be in a storm?

Henry Ward Beecher, *Life Thoughts*, Alexander Strahan & Co., 1859, p.145.

If the evil-doing of men should arouse your indignation and uncontrollable grief, even to make you wish to revenge yourself upon the evil-doers, fear most of all that feeling; go at once and seek suffering for yourself just as if you were yourself guilty of that villainy. Accept that suffering and bear it, and your heart will be appeased, and you will understand that you, too, are guilty, for you might have given light to the evil-doers, even as the one man without sin and you have not given them light. If you had, you would have lighted a path for them too, and he who had committed the felony would not have committed it if you had shown him a light. And even if you showed a light but saw that men are not saved even by your light, you must remain steadfast and doubt not the power of the heavenly light; believe that if they were not saved now, they will be saved afterwards. And if they are not saved afterwards, their sons will be saved, for your light will not die, though you were to die yourself. The righteous man departs, but his light remains. People are always saved after the death of him who came to save them. Men do not accept their prophets and slay them, but they love their martyrs and worship those whom they have tortured to death. You are working for the whole, you are acting for the future. Never seek reward, for your reward on earth is great as it is: your spiritual joy which only the righteous find....

Love all men, love everything, seek that rapture and ecstasy. Water the earth with the tears of your joy and love those tears. Be not ashamed of that ecstasy, prize it, for it is a gift of God, a great gift, and it is not given to many, but only to the chosen ones.

Fyodor Dostoyevsky, *The Brothers Karamazov*, translated with an introduction by David Magarshack, Penguin Books Ltd., 1963, Volume I, p.379.

MUSIC

Organ playing ... is the manifestation of a will filled with a vision of eternity.

Widor, in *Music in the Life of Albert Schweitzer*, selections from his writings translated and edited by Charles R. Joy, A. & C. Black Limited, 1953, p.157.

Music is a higher revelation than all wisdom and philosophy.

J.W.N. Sullivan, *Beethoven*, Jonathan Cape Ltd., 1931, p.13.

Who hears music, feels his solitude
Peopled at once.

Robert Browning, *The Poetical Works of Robert Browning*, Smith, Elder & Co., 1899, Volume I, p.631, "Balaustion's Adventure."

The soul continues as an instrument of God's harmony, a tuned instrument of divine joy for the Spirit to strike on.

William Law, *Selected Mystical Writings of William Law*, edited by Stephen Hobhouse, Rockliff, 1948, p.246.

The language of tones belongs equally to all men, and that melody is the absolute language in which a musician addresses every heart.

Richard Wagner, *Beethoven*, translated by Edward Dannreuther, William Reeves, 1880, p.1.

Music, the greatest good that mortals know,
And all of heaven we have below.

Joseph Addison, *The Works of Joseph Addison*, notes by Richard Hurd, edited and published by Henry G. Bohn, 1856, Volume I, "A Song for St. Cecilia's Day," p.21.

But God has a few of us whom he whispers in the ear;
The rest may reason and welcome: 'tis we musicians know.

Robert Browning, *The Poetical Works of Robert Browning*, Smith, Elder & Co., 1899, Volume I, p.580, *Dramatis Personae*, "Abt Vogler," st.xi, l.12.

It is in Music, perhaps, that the soul most nearly attains the great end for which, when inspired by the Poetic Sentiment, it struggles—the creation of supernal Beauty.

Edgar Allan Poe, *The Portable Poe*, selected and edited with an introduction and notes by Philip Van Doren Stern, Penguin Books Ltd., 1973, p.574, "The Poetic Principle."

For even that vulgar and Taverne Musicke, which makes one man merry, another mad, strikes me into a deepe fit of devotion, and a profound contemplation of the first Composer; there is something in it of Divinity more than the eare discovers.

Sir Thomas Browne, *The Works of Sir Thomas Browne*, edited by Geoffrey Keynes, Faber and Faber Limited, 1964, Volume One, *Religio Medici*, p.84.

Who is there that, in logical words, can express the effect music has on us? A kind of inarticulate unfathomable speech, which leads us to the edge of the Infinite, and lets us for moments gaze into that!

Thomas Carlyle, *Sartor Resartus*, "Lectures on Heroes," Chapman and Hall, 1840, p.247.

There is no truer truth obtainable
By Man than comes of music.

Robert Browning, *The Poetical Works of Robert Browning*, Smith, Elder & Co., 1910, Volume II, p.726, "Parleyings with Certain People," with Charles Avison, st.vi, l.2.

See deep enough, and you see musically; the heart of Nature *being* everywhere music, if you can only reach it.

Thomas Carlyle, *Sartor Resartus*, "Lectures on Heroes," Chapman and Hall, 1840, p.247.

Yea, music is the Prophets' art;
Among the gifts that God hath sent,
One of the most magnificent!

Henry Wadsworth Longfellow, *The Writings of Henry Wadsworth Longfellow*, Riverside Edition, George Routledge and Sons, 1886, Volume VII, p.295, *Christus: A Mystery*, Pt.iii, Interlude 2.

Musical training is a more potent instrument than any other, because rhythm and harmony find their way into the secret places of the soul, on which they mightily fasten, imparting grace, and making the soul graceful of him who is rightly educated, or ungraceful of him who is ill-educated.

Plato, *The Republic of Plato*, translation, analysis and introduction by B. Jowett, Oxford at the Clarendon Press, 1881, p.85, Bk.III, 401D.

Preposterous ass, that never read so far
To know the cause why music was ordain'd!
Was it not to refresh the mind of man
After his studies or his usual pain?

William Shakespeare, *The Taming of the Shrew*, Act III. sc.i. l.9.

I lost myself in a Schubert Quartet at the end of a Crowndale Road concert, partly by ceasing all striving to understand the music, partly by driving off intruding thoughts, partly feeling the music coming up inside me, myself a hollow vessel filled with sound.

Joanna Field, *A Life of One's Own*, Chatto and Windus Ltd., 1934, p.29.

(Music) is a principal means of glorifying our merciful Creator, it heightens our devotion, it gives delight and ease to our travails, it expelleth sadness and heaviness of spirit, preserveth people in concord and amity, allayeth fierceness and anger; and lastly, is the best physic for many melancholy diseases.

Henry Peacham, *The Compleat Gentleman*, Da Capo Press, Theatrum Orbis Terrarum Ltd., 1968, p.104.

Now, what is music? This question occupied me for hours before I fell asleep last night. Music is a strange thing. I would almost say it is a miracle. For it stands halfway between thought and phenomenon, between spirit and matter, a sort of nebulous mediator, like and unlike each of the things it mediates—spirit that requires manifestation in time, and matter that can do without space.

We do not know what music is.

Heinrich Heine, in *Pleasures of Music,* edited by Jacques Barzun, Michael Joseph Ltd., 1952, p.268.

Musical order, as recognized and evaluated by our mind, is not an end in itself. It is an image of a higher order which we are permitted to perceive if we proceed one step further to the sixth degree on our scale of musical assimilation: if we put our enjoyment of such knowledge ("enjoyment, the weight of the soul!") into the side of the balance that tends towards the order of the heavens and towards the unification of our soul with the divine principle.

Paul Hindemith, *A Composer's World,* Harvard University Press, distributed in Great Britain by Geoffrey Cumberlege, Oxford University Press, 1952, p.4.

Music seems to say something but we can never put into words just what it is saying. It seems to take us beyond words. The composer Mahler once wrote, "As long as my experience can be summed up in words, I write no music about it; my need to express myself musically ... begins at the door which leads into the 'other world'—the world in which things are no longer separated by space and time." And a contemporary Christian, Ulrich Simon, has stated the same thought in these words, "For me the D minor quartet and the G minor quintet of Mozart evoke in every bar the truth about God, but I do not know how to express the truth. Perhaps it is a *musical* truth, for what do words like *tragic* and *searing* mean even if I related them to my chosen bars, themes and developments? Rather these empty words are fulfilled by the music. We owe everything to Mozart because he has revealed the priority of music in theology." Music, then, seems to lead us into another world, to make us aware of the spiritual dimension, in a way words so often fail to do.

Richard Harris, *Prayers of Grief and Glory,* Lutterworth Press, 1979, p.86.

You say, you should like to know my way of composing, and what method I follow in writing works of some extent. I can really say no more on this subject than the following; for I myself know no more about it, and cannot account for it. When I am, as it were, completely myself, entirely alone, and of good cheer—say, travelling in a carriage, or walking after a good meal, or during the night when I cannot sleep; it is on such occasions that my ideas flow best and most abundantly. *Whence* and *how* they come, I know not; nor can I force them. Those ideas that please me I retain in memory, and am accustomed, as I have been told, to hum them to myself....

All this fires my soul, and, provided I am not disturbed, my subject enlarges itself, becomes methodised and defined, and the whole, though it be long, stands almost complete and finished in my mind, so that I can survey it, like a fine picture or a beautiful statue, at a glance. Nor do I hear in my imagination the parts *successively*, but I hear them, as it were, all at once. What a delight this is I cannot tell! All this inventing, this producing, takes place in a pleasing lively dream. Still the actual hearing of the *tout ensemble* is after all the best. What has been thus produced I do not easily forget, and this is perhaps the best gift I have my Divine Maker to thank for.

Edward Holmes, *The Life of Mozart,* Chapman & Hall, 1845, p.317, Letter written by Mozart.

MYSTICS AND MYSTICISM

Mystic. One who seeks by contemplation and self-surrender to obtain union with or absorption into the Deity, or who believes in spiritual apprehensions of truths beyond the understanding.

The Concise Oxford Dictionary.

The mystics are not only themselves an incarnation of beauty, but they reflect beauty on all who with understanding approach them.

Havelock Ellis, *Selected Essays,* J.M. Dent & Sons Ltd., 1936, p.186.

If you can enjoy the sun and flowers and music where there is nothing except darkness and silence you have proved the mystic sense.

Helen Keller, *My Religion,* Hodder & Stoughton Ltd., 1927, fronticepiece.

Mysticism is that type of religion which puts the emphasis on immediate awareness of relation with God, on direct and immediate consciousness of the Divine Presence. It is religion in its most acute, intense, and living stage.

Rufus Jones, in *The Awakening of the Soul,* W.R. Inge, edited by Prebendary A.F. Judd, A.R. Mowbray & Co. Ltd., 1959, p.10.

... by love, by the willing loss of self, we realize our true nature and become partakers in the being of God. The ego may be said to represent a stage in a spiritual process. By breaking out of its shell we can be born again, into a boundless freedom. That is the doctrine implied in all mystical philosophy.

Gerald Bullett, *The English Mystics,* Michael Joseph Ltd., 1950, p.17.

The highest thought ... is ineffable; it must be felt from one person to another but cannot be articulated. All the most essential and thinking part of thought is done without words. It is not till doubt and consciousness enter that words become possible. Our profoundest and most important convictions are unspeakable.

Samuel Butler, in *The English Mystics,* Gerald Bullett, Michael Joseph Ltd., 1950, p.227.

We are always in presence of mysticism when we find a human being looking upon the division between earthly and super-earthly, temporal and eternal, as transcended, and feeling himself, while still externally amid the earthly and temporal, to belong to the super-earthly and eternal.

Albert Schweitzer, *The Mysticism of Paul the Apostle,* translated by William Montgomery, prefatory note by F.C. Burkitt, A. & C. Black, 1931, p.1.

"In the time of the philosophers," he (Al-Ghazzali) writes, "as at every other period, there existed some of these fervent mystics. God does not deprive this world of them, for they are its sustainers." It is they who, dying to themselves, become capable of perpetual inspiration and so are made the instruments through which divine grace is mediated to those whose unregenerate nature is impervious to the delicate touches of the Spirit.

Aldous Huxley, *The Perennial Philosophy,* Chatto & Windus Ltd., 1974, p.345.

The most beautiful and most profound emotion we can experience is the sensation of the mystical. It is the sower of all true science. He to whom this emotion is a stranger, who can no longer wonder and stand wrapt in awe, is as good as dead. To know that what is impenetrable to us really exists, manifesting itself as the highest wisdom and the most radiant beauty which our dull faculties can comprehend only in their most primitive forms—this knowledge, this feeling is at the centre of true religiousness.

Albert Einstein, in *The Universe and Dr. Einstein,* Lincoln Barnett, Victor Gollancz Ltd., 1949, p.95.

The mystics—to give them their short, familiar name—are men and women who insist that they know for certain the presence and activity of that which they call the Love of God. They are conscious of that Fact which is there for all, and which is the true subject-matter of religion; but of which the average man remains either unconscious or faintly and occasionally aware. They know a spiritual order, penetrating, and everywhere conditioning though transcending the world of sense. They declare to us a Reality most rich and living, which is not a reality of time and space; which is something other than everything we mean by "nature," and for which no merely pantheistic explanation will suffice.

Evelyn Underhill, *Man and the Supernatural,* Methuen & Co. Ltd., 1927, p.21.

It is a central idea of mysticism that there is a way to God through the human soul. The gate to Heaven is thus kept, not by St. Peter or by any other saint of the calendar; it is kept by each individual person himself as he opens or closes within himself the spiritual circuit of connection with God. The door into the Eternal swings within the circle of our own inner life, and all things are ours if we learn how to use the key that opens, for "to open" and "to find God" are one and the same thing.

Rufus M. Jones, *Spiritual Reformers in the 16th and 17th Centuries,* Macmillan & Co. Ltd., 1914, p.133.

Mysticism is a spiritual philosophy which demands the concurrent activity of thought, will, and feeling. It assumes from the outset that these three elements of our personality, which in real life are never sundered from each other, point towards the same goal, and if rightly used will conduct us thither. Further, it holds that only by the consecration of these three faculties in the service of the same quest can a man become effectively what he is potentially, a partaker of the Divine nature and a denizen of the spiritual world. There is no special organ for the reception of Divine or spiritual truth, which is simply the knowledge of the world as it really is. Some are better endowed with spiritual gifts than others, and are called to ascend greater heights; but the power which leads us up the pathway to reality and blessedness is, as Plotinus says, one which all possess, though few use it.

W.R. Inge, *The Philosophy of Plotinus,* Longmans, Green & Co. Ltd., 1918, Volume I, p.5.

At the core of our personality is a spark lighted at the altar of God in heaven—a something too holy ever to consent to evil, an inner light which can illuminate our whole being. To purify the eyes of the understanding by constant discipline, to detach ourselves from hampering worldly or fleshly desires, to accustom ourselves to ascend in heart and mind to the kingdom of the eternal values which are the thoughts and purposes of God—this is the quest of the mystic and the scheme of his progress through its earthly life. It carries with it its own proof and justification, in the increasing clearness and certainty with which the truths of the invisible world are revealed to him who diligently seeks for them. The experience is too intimate, and in a sense too formless, to be imparted to others. Language was not made to express it, and the imagination which recalls the hours of vision after they have passed paints the vision in colours not its own. Remembered revelation always tends to clothe itself in mythical or symbolic form. But the revelation was real; and it is here and here only—in the mystical act *par-excellence,* the act of prayer—that faith passes for a time into sight. Formless and vague and fleeting as it is, the mystical experience is the bedrock of religious faith.

W.R. Inge, *Outspoken Essays,* Second Series, Longmans, Green & Co. Ltd., 1922, p.14.

The real fact of the matter is, that the great mystics are religious geniuses. They make their contribution to religion in ways similar to those in which the geniuses in other fields raise the level of human attainments and achievements. They swiftly seize upon and appreciate the specific achievements of the race behind them; they are profoundly sensitive to the aspirations of their time and to the deep-lying currents of their age; they are suggestible in an acute degree, through heightened interest, to certain ideas or truths or principles which they synthesise by such leaps of insight that slow-footed logic seems to be transcended. Then these unifying and intensifying experiences to which they are subject give them irresistible conviction, "a surge of certainty," a faith of the mountain-moving order, and an increasing dynamic of life which, in the best cases, is manifest in thoughts and words and deeds. Their mystical experience seldom supplies them with a new intellectual content which they communicate, but their experience enables them rather to *see* what they know, to get possession of themselves, and to fuse their truth with the heat of conviction. The mystical experience is thus a way of heightening life and of increasing its dynamic quality rather than a way to new knowledge.

Rufus M. Jones, *Spiritual Reformers in the 16th and 17th Centuries,* Macmillan & Co. Ltd., 1914, p.xxiv.

N

NATURE

All things are artificiall, for Nature is the Art of God.

Sir Thomas Browne, *The Works of Sir Thomas Browne,* edited by Geoffrey Keynes, Faber and Faber Limited, 1964, Volume One, *Religio Medici,* p.26.

The course of nature is the art of God.

Edward Young, *Night Thoughts,* Thomas Nelson, 1841, p.229.

Joy in looking and comprehending is nature's most beautiful gift.

Albert Einstein, *Ideas and Opinions,* Souvenir Press (Educational & Academic) Ltd., 1973, p.28.

Laws of nature are God's thoughts thinking themselves out in the orbits and the tides.

Charles H. Parkhurst, *The Pattern in the Mount and Other Sermons,* R.D. Dickinson, 1890, p.14.

Those honour Nature well, who teach that she can speak on everything, even on theology.

Blaise Pascal, *Pensées,* translated by W.F. Trotter, Random House Inc., 1941, p.12.

Nature has some perfections to show that she is the image of God, and some defects to show that she is only his image.

Blaise Pascal, *Pensées,* translated by W.F. Trotter, Random House Inc., 1941, p.190.

Come forth into the light of things,
Let Nature be your Teacher.

William Wordsworth, *The Poetical Works of William Wordsworth,* edited by E. de Selincourt and Helen Darbishire, Oxford at the Clarendon Press, 1958, Volume IV, p.57, "The Tables Turned," st.iv, l.15.

Nature is full of genius, full of divinity; so that not a snowflake escapes its fashioning hand.

Henry David Thoreau, *The Journal of Henry D. Thoreau,* edited by Bradford Torrey and Francis H. Allen, 1949, Houghton Mifflin Company, Boston, The Riverside Press, Volume VIII, p.88.

Nature is but a name for an effect,
Whose cause is God.

William Cowper, *The Poetical Works of Cowper,* edited by H.S. Milford, Oxford University Press, 1950, p.224, "The Task," Bk.VI, l.224.

Nature stamped us in a heavenly mould.

Thomas Campbell, *The Pleasures of Hope,* edited, with an introduction by Henry Morley, George Routledge & Sons, Ltd., 1892, p.30.

To me the meanest flower that blows can give
Thoughts that do often lie too deep for tears.

William Wordsworth, *The Poetical Works of William Wordsworth*, edited by E. de Selincourt and Helen Darbishire, Oxford at the Clarendon Press, 1958, Volume IV, p.285, Ode: "Intimations of Immortality," xi, l.203.

There is undoubtedly a deep affinity, probably both psychic and chemical, between every individual human being and some particlar type of landscape. It is well to find out as soon as possible what kind this is; and then to get as much of it as you can.

John Cowper Powys, *The Meaning of Culture*, Jonathan Cape Ltd., 1932, p.177.

O Nature all-sufficient! over all!
Enrich me with the knowledge of thy works.
Snatch me to heaven.

James Thomson, *The Seasons* and *The Castle of Indolence*, edited by J. Logie Robertson, Oxford at the Clarendon Press, 1891, "Autumn," p.152, l.1352.

The losing of Paradise is enacted over and over again by the children of Adam and Eve. We clothe our souls with messages and doctrines and lose the touch of the great life in the naked breast of Nature.

Rabindranath Tagore, *Letters to a Friend*, George Allen & Unwin Ltd., 1928, p.138.

I do not count the hours I spend
In wandering by the sea;
The forest is my loyal friend,
Like God it useth me.

Ralph Waldo Emerson, *The Works of Ralph Waldo Emerson*, edited by George Sampson, George Bell & Sons Ltd., 1906, Volume V, *Poems*, "Waldeinsamkeit," p.180.

His are the mountains, and the vallies his,
And the resplendent rivers. His t'enjoy
With a propriety that none can feel,
But who, with filial confidence inspir'd,
Can lift to heaven an unpresumptuous eye,
And smiling say—My Father made them all!

William Cowper, *The Poetical Works of Cowper*, edited by H.S. Milford, Oxford University Press, 1950, p.216, "The Task," Bk.V, l.742.

The year's at the spring
And day's at the morn;
Morning's at seven;
The hill-side's dew-pearled;
The lark's on the wing;
The snail's on the thorn:
God's in his heaven—
All's right with the world!

Robert Browning, *The Poetical Works of Robert Browning*, Smith, Elder, & Co., 1899, Volume I, p.202, "Pippa Passes," Pt.I.

In looking at objects of Nature while I am thinking, as at yonder moon dim-glimmering through the dewy window-pane, I seem rather to be seeking, as it were *asking* for, a symbolical language for something within me that already and for ever exists, than observing anything new. Even when that latter is the case, yet still I have always an obscure feeling as if that new phenomena were the dim awaking of a forgotten or hidden truth of my inner nature.

Samuel Taylor Coleridge, *Coleridge, Select Poetry & Prose,* edited by Stephen Potter, The Nonesuch Press, p.175, Notebooks: 14th April, 1805.

The same stream of life that runs through my veins night and day runs through the world and dances in rhythmic measures.
It is the same life that shoots in joy through the dust of the earth in numberless blades of grass and breaks into tumultuous waves of leaves and flowers.
It is the same life that is rocked in the ocean-cradle of birth and of death, in ebb and in flow.
I feel my limbs are made glorious by the touch of this world of life. And my pride is from the life-throb of ages dancing in my blood at this moment.

Rabindranath Tagore, *Gitanjali,* Macmillan & Co. Ltd., 1971, p.64.

There is a pleasure in the pathless woods,
There is a rapture on the lonely shore,
There is society, where none intrudes,
By the deep Sea, and music in its roar:
I love not Man the less, but Nature more,
From these our interviews, in which I steal
From all I may be, or have been before,
To mingle with the Universe, and feel
What I can ne'er express, yet can not all conceal.

Lord Byron, *The Complete Poetical Works,* edited by Jerome J McCann, Oxford at the Clarendon Press, 1980, Volume II, p.184, "Childe Harold's Pilgrimage," Canto IV, st.clxxviii, l.1594.

All are but parts of one stupendous whole,
Whose body Nature is, and God the soul;
That, changed through all, and yet in all the same;
Great in the earth, as in the ethereal frame;
Warms in the sun, refreshes in the breeze,
Glows in the stars, and blossoms in the trees,...
As full, as perfect, in vile man that mourns,
As the rapt seraph that adores and burns:
To him no high, no low, no great, no small:
He fills, he bounds, connects, and equals all.

Alexander Pope, *An Essay on Man,* introduction by Henry Morley, Cassell and Company, Limited, 1905, Epistle I, p.23.

The beauty of nature is a distinct revelation made to the human mind, from that of its use.... When the materialist has exhausted himself in efforts to explain utility in nature, it would appear to be the peculiar office of beauty to rise up suddenly as a confounding and baffling *extra,* which was not even formally provided for in his scheme.... The glory of nature in reality resides in the mind of man; there is an inward intervening light through which the material objects pass, a transforming medium which converts the physical assemblage into a picture. It must be remarked that the whole of what any scene of earth or sky is materially, is stamped upon the retina of the brute, just as it is upon the man's; and that the brute sees all the same objects which are beautiful to man, only without their beauty: which aspect is inherent in man, and part of his reason. He possesses the key to the sight; and that which makes the appearance what it is, resides in him; and is an inner light or splendour reflected from his reason upon the surface of the universal frame of things.

J.B. Mozley, *University and Other Sermons,* Rivingtons, 1876, p.124.

NEIGHBOUR

This love of our neighbour is the only door out of the dungeon of self.

George Macdonald, *Unspoken Sermons,* First Series, Alexander Strahan, Publisher, 1867, p.214.

You cannot love a fellow-creature fully till you love God.

C.S. Lewis, *The Great Divorce,* William Collins Sons & Co. Ltd., 1982, p.84.

We are made *one for another;* and each is to be a Supply to his Neighbour.

Benjamin Whichcote, *Moral and Religious Aphorisms,* 1930, p.16, Century II, No.122.

All is well with him, who is beloved of his neighbours.

George Herbert, *The Works of George Herbert,* edited by F.E. Hutchinson, Oxford at the Clarendon Press, 1972, p.321, "Outlandish Proverbs," No.10.

We cannot be sure if we are loving God, although we may have good reasons for believing that we are, but we can know quite well if we are loving our neighbour.

St. Teresa of Avila, *Complete Works of St. Teresa of Jesus,* translated by E. Allison Peers, Sheed & Ward Ltd., 1978, p.261, "Interior Castle."

The good neighbour looks beyond the external accidents and discerns those inner qualities that make all men human and, therefore, brothers.

Martin Luther King, *Strength to Love,* William Collins Sons & Co. Ltd., 1980, p.29.

A man must not choose his neighbour; he must take the neighbour that God sends him.... The neighbour is just the man who is next to you at the moment, the man with whom any business has brought you into contact.

George Macdonald, *Unspoken Sermons,* First Series, Alexander Strahan, Publisher, 1867, p.210.

The desert is not remote in southern tropics,
The desert is not only around the corner,

The desert is squeezed in the tube-train next to you,
The desert is in the heart of your brother.

T.S. Eliot, *The Complete Poems and Plays of T.S. Eliot,* Faber and Faber Limited, 1975, Choruses From "The Rock," 1934, I, p.149.

Today there is an inescapable duty to make ourselves the neighbour of every man, no matter who he is, and if we meet him, to come to his aid in a positive way, whether he is an aged person abandoned by all, a foreign worker despised without reason, a refugee, an illegitimate child wrongly suffering for a sin he did not commit, or a starving human being who awakens our conscience by calling to mind the words of Christ: "As you did it to one of the least of these my brethren, you did it to me."
(Mt.25.40)

Vatican Council II, *The Conciliar and Post Conciliar Documents,* 1981 Edition, general editor, Austin Flannery, O.P., Fowler Wright Books Ltd., p.928.

The second great commandment of the Law of the Lord was a miracle of inspiration, combining divine inspiration and human perception. To love my neighbour as myself, to give him equal value and equal rights, to do nothing to him which I would not want done to myself, and more positively to do to him only those deeds that I would like done to me, is a principle that makes for a human and satisfying society, and it makes for a heart at peace and moving out in love.

George Appleton, *Journey for a Soul,* William Collins Sons & Co. Ltd., 1976, p.59.

True neighbourliness must begin within our own psychological attitudes. I must accept my neighbour for what he is, I must let him be himself, respect his "isness" and self-understanding. I must not impose my pattern on him or exploit him for my own purposes. I must be interested in him as a person, so that our relationship will encourage mutual development in maturity. I must be ready to take initiatives, to engage in adventures of understanding and friendship.

George Appleton, *Journey for a Soul,* William Collins Sons & Co. Ltd., 1976, p.60.

By love, I do not mean natural tenderness, which is more or less in people, according to their constitutions; but I mean a larger principle of the soul, founded in reason and piety, which makes us tender, kind, and benevolent to all our fellow creatures as creatures of God, and for His sake.
It is this love, that loves all things in God, as His creatures as the images of His power, as the creatures of His goodness, as parts of His family, as members of His society, that becomes a holy principle of all great and good actions.
The love, therefore, of our neighbour, is only a branch of our love to God. For when we love God with all our hearts, and with all our souls, and with all our strength, we shall necessarily love those beings that are so nearly related to God, that have everything from Him, and are created by Him to be objects of His own eternal love.

William Law, *A Serious Call to a Devout and Holy Life,* J.M. Dent & Co., 1898, p.334.

People can sense when we are concerned and interested. Sometimes it may be that we are preoccupied with some problems or too much under pressure of time, or it may be that we cannot take the trouble. We need to give our whole attention to our neighbour, to identify ourselves with him, to have an open ear, an open mind and an open heart. This applies not only to individual relationships, but also to the relationship of our social, national and religious groupings as we meet similar neighbourhood groups.

George Appleton, *Journey for a Soul,* William Collins Sons & Co. Ltd., 1976, p.73.

NEW CREATION

Therefore, if any one is in Christ, he is a new creation; the old has passed away, behold, the new has come.

2 Corinthians 5.17.

For neither circumcision counts for anything, nor uncircumcision, but a new creation.

Galatians 6.15.

Put off your old nature which belongs to your former manner of life and is corrupt through deceitful lusts, and be renewed in the spirit of your minds, and put on the new nature, created after the likeness of God in true righteousness and holiness.

Ephesians 4.22-24.

Do not lie to one another, seeing that you have put off the old nature with its practices and have put on the new nature, which is being renewed in knowledge after the image of its creator.

Colossians 3.9-10.

And ah for a man to arise in me,
That the man I am may cease to be!

Alfred, Lord Tennyson, *The Poems of Tennyson,* edited by Christopher Ricks, Longmans, Green & Co. Ltd., 1969, p.1060, No.316, "Maud," X. vi. 1.396.

So long as a man is capable of self-renewal he is a living being.... If we are to remain among the living there must be a perpetual revival of youth within us, brought about by inward change and by love.

Henri Frédéric Amiel, *Amiel's Journal,* translated by Mrs. Humphry Ward, Macmillan & Co. Ltd., 1918, p.186.

We will never change men from the outside. New houses, new conditions, better material things only change the surface. It is the task of Christianity to make, not new things, but new men. And once the new men are created the new world will surely follow. That is why the Church is the most important institution in the world, for it is the factory where *men* are produced.

William Barclay, *The Gospel of Luke,* The Saint Andrew Press, 1964, p.187.

St. Paul sees in Jesus the coming of a new man, man as God meant him to be. Jesus is not just one lonely individual but the beginning of a new creation, the spearhead of a new humanity. By our participation in the old humanity we share its mortality.

Incorporated with Christ, we share his deathless life. More than this, Paul sees an eternal purpose, unperceived in past ages, to bring all things and all men into a unity in Christ.

George Appleton, *Journey for a Soul*, William Collins Sons & Co. Ltd., 1976, p.68.

While we were yet sinners, Christ died for us. So it is written in the epistles to the Romans. This is love. Some people are proud of having given little bits of charity to others, but such meagre doles cannot represent true love.
This love of Christ cannot be understood by those who think only in the moral terms of give and take, who dwell only on the struggle for existence and its amelioration through mutual aid. The love of Christ has little to do with physiological and psychological considerations. It is his intention to restore the moral ruin at the bottom of a soul. Such love must utilize the power with which God originally created light out of darkness. That creative power is required to create a new soul out of the darkness of sin. Why then must sinners be forgiven? Redemption means that the ego is resmelted in the crucible that is Christ and poured forth anew. When this new creation appears, sins are dissolved and banished by this very process.

Toyohiko Kagawa, *Meditations*, translated by Jiro Takenaka, Harper & Brothers, 1950, No.37.

To be inspired in our thoughts by divine knowledge, to be moved in our will by the divine purpose, to mould our emotions into harmony with divine bliss, to get at the great self of truth, goodness, and beauty to which we give the name of God as a spiritual presence, to raise our whole being and life to the divine status, is the ultimate purpose and meaning of human living. Some exceptional individuals have achieved this status and harmony. They are the highest type of humanity yet reached and indicate the final shape which humanity has to assume. They are the forerunners of the new race.
These men with wisdom and vitality, constant awareness and unremitting social effort, are not members of limited groups based on blood and soil but citizens of a world yet unborn, still in the womb of time.
Whatever the individual has done, the race, too, may and should eventually succeed in doing. When the incarnation of God is realized, not only in a few individuals but in the whole of humanity, we will have the new creation, the new race of men and women, mankind transformed, redeemed, and reborn, and a world created anew. This is the destiny of the world, the supreme spiritual ideal. It alone can rouse the deepest creative energies, rescue us from cold reason, inspire us with constructive passion, and unite us mentally, morally, and spiritually in a world fellowship.

Sir Sarvepalli Radhakrishnan, *Eastern Religions and Western Thought*, Oxford University Press, 1940, p.57.

O

OBEDIENCE

Teach me thy way, O Lord.
Psalm 27.11.

We must obey God rather than men.
Acts 5.29.

What you have learned and received and heard and seen in me, do.
Philippians 4.9.

Obedience is the key to every door.
George Macdonald, *The Marquis of Lossie,* Everett & Co. Ltd., 1912, p.207.

Henceforth I learn, that to obey is best,
And love with fear the only God, to walk
As in his presence, ever to observe
His providence, and on him sole depend.
John Milton, *The Poetical Works of John Milton,* edited by the Rev. H.C. Beeching, Oxford at the Clarendon Press, 1900, p.446, *Paradise Lost,* Bk. XII, l.561.

God does not desire that we should abound in spiritual lights, but that in all things we should submit to His will.
Henry Suso, in *On Conformity with the Will of God,* St. Alphonsus de Liguori, translated by the Rev. James Jones, Catholic Truth Society, 1892, p.7.

Had he done as the Master told him, he would soon have come to understand. Obedience is the opener of eyes.
George Macdonald, *Unspoken Sermons,* Second Series, Longmans, Green, & Co. Ltd., 1885, p.22.

If a man does not keep pace with his companions, perhaps it is because he hears a different drummer. Let him step to the music which he hears, however measured or far away.
Henry David Thoreau, *Walden,* The New American Library of World Literature, Inc., 1960, p.216.

Obedience is a complicated act of virtue, and many graces are exercised in one act of obedience. It is an act of humility, of mortification and self-denial, of charity to God, of care of the public, of order and charity to ourselves and all our society, and a great instance of a victory over the most refractory and unruly passions.
Jeremy Taylor, *Holy Living,* abridged by Anne Lamb, The Langford Press, 1970, p.85.

We have no code of rules that can only be obeyed in the circumstances of their origin, no scheme of thought which can only be understood in the terms in which it was first conceived, but a Person to whom we can be loyal in all circumstances whatever, with that infinite flexibility and delicacy of adjustment which are compatible with a loyalty that remains absolute and unalterable.

William Temple, *Thoughts On Some Problems Of The Day*, Macmillan & Co. Ltd., 1931, p.28.

True and perfect obedience is a virtue above all virtues. No great work can be accomplished without it; nor can there be any task, however small or insignificant, which will not be done to better purpose in obedience…. Obedience brings out the best of everything; it never fails or errs in any matter; and no matter what you do, if you do it in true obedience, it will not miss being good.
Obedience has no cares; it lacks no blessing. Being obedient, if a man purifies himself, God will come into him in course; for when he has no will of his own, then God will command for him what God would command for himself.

Meister Eckhart, *Meister Eckhart*, translated by Raymond B. Blakney, Harper & Row, Publishers, Inc., 1941, p.3.

I dislike talk about obeying God, as if he were some Stalin or Hitler: I cannot think that he wants me to obey him: what he wants, I think, is that I should learn to co-operate, quietly and in complete freedom, with his blessed and blessing will, that will of his which I discover deep in my own heart as my own will also—as the best, essential me—and which, discovering it also deep in the heart of everything else, I find to be not only vaster, but also saner and more fruitful of life and peace and joy, than the self-regarding wilfulness that would deceive me with its appearance of leading me to my goal, but would in fact cut me off, if it had its way, from my birthright of unity with all things.

Victor Gollancz, *From Darkness to Light*, Victor Gollancz Ltd., 1965, p.245.

So many people need to learn that Obedience must often come before Faith; that it is by going on patiently obeying the commandments of God and the teaching of Christ that faith will come to them; that faith is neither something to which they are entitled nor something which is either given or withheld, but something which has to be earned by a life of discipline and obedience. It is really no good saying: "I find it so difficult to believe" when we are doing little or nothing to build up faith by using the means of grace which God has provided for us and by bringing our lives under the control of his will. And if we are to practise obedience we can scarcely do better than begin with the three commands which Jesus gave to Peter in the boat. "Thrust out a little from the land"; do not allow yourself to become earthbound, your life dominated by things of this world; withdraw a little from the pleasures and interests and anxieties of what happens in this life and devote a little more of your time to the things of eternity. And then "launch out into the deep" and explore the depths of God's love; consider his nature, his goodness, his strength; let the thought of his majesty and of his tender mercy and compassion flow into your heart; learn to be alone with him in the deep. And then "Let down your nets for a draught"; learn to accept what God gives of his grace, his peace, his strength; spread the nets wide for that miraculous draught of all that your soul can need.

J.R.H. Moorman, *The Path to Glory*, S.P.C.K., and Seabury Press, 1960, p.54.

But there are hours, and they come to us all at some period of life or other, when the hand of Mystery seems to lie heavy on the soul— when some life-shock scatters existence, leaves it a blank and dreary waste henceforth for ever, and there appears nothing of hope in all the expanse which stretches out, except that merciful gate of death which opens at the end—hours when the sense of misplaced or ill-requited affection, the feeling of personal worthlessness, the uncertainty and meanness of all human aims, and a doubt of all human goodness, unfix the soul from all its old moorings—and leave it drifting—drifting over the vast Infinitude, with an awful sense of solitariness. Then the man whose faith rested on outward Authority and not on inward life, will find it give away: the authority of the Priest: the authority of the Church: or merely the authority of a document proved by miracles and backed by prophecy: the soul— conscious life hereafter—God—will be an awful desolate Perhaps. Well! in such moments you doubt all—whether Christianity be true: whether Christ was man, or God, or a beautiful fable. You ask bitterly, like Pontius Pilate, What is Truth? In such an hour what remains? I reply, Obedience. Leave those thoughts for the present. Act—be merciful and gentle—honest: force yourself to abound in little services: try to do good to others: be true to the Duty that you know. *That* must be right whatever else is uncertain. And by all the laws of the human heart, by the word of God, you shall not be left to doubt. Do that much of the will of God which is plain to you, and "You shall know of the doctrine, whether it be of God."

F.W. Robertson, *Sermons*, Kegan Paul, Trench, Trubner & Co. Ltd., 1897, Second Series, p.104.

OPPORTUNITY

Observe the opportunity.

Ecclesiasticus 4.20 (A.V.).

A man must make his opportunity, as oft as find it.

Francis Bacon, *The Advancement of Learning* and *New Atlantis*, edited by Arthur Johnston, Oxford at the Clarendon Press, 1974, p.172.

No great man ever complains of want of opportunity.

Ralph Waldo Emerson, *The Heart of Emerson's Journals*, edited by Bliss Perry, Constable & Co. Ltd., 1927, Volume V, p.534.

God often gives in one brief moment what he has long been keeping from you.

Thomas à Kempis, *The Imitation of Christ*, translated by Betty I. Knott, William Collins Sons & Co. Ltd., 1979, p.244.

A wise man will make more opportunities than he finds.

Francis Bacon, *The Moral and Historical Works of Francis Bacon*, introductory dissertation and notes (critical, explanatory, and historical) by Joseph Devey, Henry G. Bohn, 1852, p.140.

To improve the golden moment of opportunity, and catch the good that is within
our reach, is the great art of life.

Samuel Johnson, *The Works of Samuel Johnson,* Talboys and Wheeler, 1825, Volume VI, p.214, "The Patriot."

Who seeks and will not take, when once 'tis offer'd,
Shall never find it more.

William Shakespeare, *Anthony and Cleopatra,* Act II. sc.vii. l.83.

Yet he who grasps the moment's gift,
He is the proper man.

Johann Wolfgang von Goethe, *Faust,* introduction by Dennis Wheatley, translated by Bayard Taylor, Sphere
Books Ltd., 1974, p.78, Part I, Act I. sc.iv. l.2017.

For age is opportunity no less
Than youth itself, though in another dress,
And as the evening twilight fades away
The sky is filled with stars, invisible by day.

Henry Wadsworth Longfellow, *The Poetical Works of Longfellow,* Humphrey Milford, Oxford University Press,
1913, p.708, "Morituri Salutamus," final stanza.

There is a tide in the affairs of men,
Which, taken at the flood, leads on to fortune;
Omitted, all the voyage of their life
Is bound in shallows and in miseries.
On such a full sea are we now afloat,
And we must take the current when it serves,
Or lose our ventures.

William Shakespeare, *Julius Caesar,* Act IV. sc.iii. l.217.

To every man there openeth
A Way, and Ways, and a Way,
And the High Soul climbs the High Way,
And the Low Soul gropes the Low,
And in between, on the misty flats,
The rest drift to and fro.
But to every man there openeth
A High Way, and a Low.
And every man decideth
The Way his soul shall go.

John Oxenham, *The King's High Way, Some More Helpful Verse,* Methuen & Co. Ltd., 1916, "The Ways," p.10.

OTHER FAITHS

If we believe in God as Creator we must surely think of him as wanting to make an
impact on all, through their history, their experience, their prophets. We believe that

he is the source of all truth, goodness and love, so where we see signs of these we must surely believe that he has been active.

George Appleton, *Journey for a Soul*, William Collins Sons & Co. Ltd., 1976, p.71.

People of other faiths are our spiritual neighbours in the journey of life and in the search for spiritual dimensions and values. The outgoing Christian mission has made them neighbours and has stimulated them to examine their own religious traditions. The ease of travel and the development of trade brings them to our countries, so they are now physical as well as spiritual neighbours. Their presence makes them our neighbours, as well as their interest in religious questions. We have to interpret the second great commandment in our attitude towards them.

George Appleton, *Journey for a Soul*, William Collins Sons & Co. Ltd., 1976, p.70.

After long study and experience I have come to these conclusions that: 1) all religions are true; 2) all religions have some error in them; 3) all religions are almost as dear to me as my own Hinduism. My veneration for other faiths is the same as for my own faith. Consequently, the thought of conversion is impossible.... Our prayer for others ought never to be: "God! give them the light thou has given to me!" But: "Give them all the light and truth they need for their highest development!"

Mohandas K. Gandhi, in *Discovery of India*, Jawaharlal Nehru, Meridian Books Limited, 1951, p.340.

These people (Indians) will never hear of Christ in my lifetime. What has God been doing in them all these centuries? Is God absent from them? I must recognise God at work in their laughter, in their love, in their coming to terms with their sufferings, in their prayers. Travel suddenly opens the windows of the soul to the reality of God in other people. If the humble Hindu on the Ganges can't be saved unless he becomes C. of E. or Baptist or R.C., then God is not the God *I* want to believe in. Your faith depends literally on where you stand. If you stand in France you are a Catholic. If you stand in Burma you are a Buddhist. If most of the people in Ulster who are vehemently Protestant had been born in the south, they would have been Roman Catholics.

Colin James, in *Priestland's Progress*, Gerald Priestland, British Broadcasting Corporation, 1982, p.95.

Once some blind men chanced to come near an animal that someone had told them was an elephant. They were asked what the elephant was like. The blind men began to feel its body. One of them said the elephant was like a pillar; he had touched only its leg. Another said it was like a winnowing-fan; he had touched only its ear. In this way the others, having touched its tail or belly, gave their different versions of the elephant. Just so, a man who has seen only one aspect of God limits God to that alone. It is his conviction that God cannot be anything else.

Sri Ramakrishna, *Ramakrishna: Prophet of New India*, translated by Swami Nikhilananda, Rider & Company, 1951, p.163.

I see God as a vast mountain with its top vanishing into the clouds and its circumference disappearing over the horizon. We do not know what its limits are. Each of us stands in a slightly different position in relation to that mountain; each of us gets a somewhat different view of it. The nearest we—as a human race—can hope to get to a conspectus of the mountain is by adding together our different views, not by pretending (what is impossible) that we can all stand on the same spot: for we were not put on the same spot.

Increasingly we have learned, and we are able, to visit one another's points of view. By doing that we can appreciate why some people say the mountain is green and gentle, others that it is fierce and rocky, others again that it is clad with pine forests. It is all the same mountain, seen from different angles; and to deny any of those points of view is to diminish the true nature of the mountain.

Equally, to endeavour to approach or climb the mountain as if we could tackle all those features simultaneously is to doom ourselves to an ineffectual and possibly disastrous expedition. It is not impossible to move over to a different base-camp, a different route. But fundamentally I believe that each of us has been set an appropriate route to climb and would do best to follow it. (Incidentally, that does not rule out the possibility that some views of the mountain are deceptive and even dangerous). But we can all witness together to the existence, majesty and glory of the mountain.

Most of us, if we are wise, will follow a guide who speaks our language—though there will always be some who insist they can follow their own lonely way. Some of the routes toward that unseen and here-unknowable summit lie adjacent to one another; some may cross or eventually run together. One party may call across to another, help another out of difficulty, donate some provisions, offer advice on the way ahead. One party may find a harder, steeper and loftier route than another; or again, may settle down to picnic idly on a plateau and cease climbing altogther. Most of our expeditions have been climbing for centuries; the climbers are the great-great-great-grandchildren of men and women who set out long ago. How futile it is to criticise each other for not having arrived on precisely the same path together! We cannot turn back (though some are tempted to). We can only do our best from where we are. But we are still on the same mountain.

Gerald Priestland, *Priestland's Progress*, British Broadcasting Corporation, 1982, p. 101.

P

PACIFISM

We ought not to retaliate or render evil for evil to any one, whatever evil we may
have suffered from him.

Socrates, *The Dialogues of Plato,* translated with analyses and introductions by B. Jowett, Oxford at the Clarendon
Press, 1875, Volume I, p.390, "Crito," 49.

(Non-violence) is not a garment to be put on and off at will. Its seat is in the heart,
and it must be an inseparable part of our very being.

Mohandas K. Gandhi, *Non-Violence in Peace & War,* Navajivan Publishing House, 1948, Volume I, p.61.

A nation, following the way of Christ, might feel called upon to adopt a policy of
total disarmament. But it would do so, in the first instance, not with the deliberate
purpose of courting martyrdom, but with the conviction that the best safety from the
perils against which nations arm is to be found in a new national way of life, which
would remove causes of provocation and lead progressively to reconciliation and peace.
It, too, would risk everything on the conviction that God's way would work. But
such a nation must also be willing, if necessary, to incur the risk of national martyrdom
by refusing to equip itself against the possibility of aggression. And it may be that
the world must wait for its redemption from warfare until one nation is ready to risk
crucifixion at the hands of its possible enemies. It might lose its own national life;
but it would set free such a flood of spiritual life as would save the world.

G.H.C. Macgregor, *The New Testament Basis of Pacificism,* James Clarke & Co. Ltd., 1936, p.103.

Through the centuries probably only a minority of considering Christians have held
that Christ's teaching demands the totally pacifist position. I would hold myself that
the injunction to turn the other cheek and to offer no resistance to evil, like many
other of Christ's injunctions, concerns motive. Faced with a violent attack the follower
of Christ must have total selflessness in motive; so far as his own pride or comfort or
security is concerned he must be ready to accept death and have no self-concern. But
given that selflessness in motive which Christ demands, he may strike, or risk killing,
or even kill if his concern is to protect others, whether family, friends, neighbours,
enemies, or the community itself. It has been found possible, however hazardous, to
strike in defence of others without hatred, anger, or self-concern; and conversely it is
possible to be physically passive while bearing anger and hatred. It is such considerations which cause many conscientious Christians not to endorse total pacifism.

Michael Ramsey, *Canterbury Pilgrim,* S.P.C.K., 1974, p.129.

PAIN

He has seen but half the universe who never has been shown the House of Pain.
Ralph Waldo Emerson, *The Works of Ralph Waldo Emerson*, edited by George Sampson, George Bell & Sons,
Ltd., 1906, Volume IV, "Miscellaneous Pieces," p.189.

Those who do not feel pain, seldom think that it is felt.
Samuel Johnson, *The Yale Edition of the Works of Samuel Johnson*, edited by W.J. Bate and Albrecht B. Strauss,
Yale University Press, 1969, Volume III, p.259, "The Rambler," No.48.

Pain is no evil
Unless it conquers us.
Charles Kingsley, *The Life and Works of Charles Kingsley*, Macmillan & Co. Ltd., 1902, Volume XVI, *Poems*,
"St. Maura," p.271.

"If God were good, He would wish to make His creatures perfectly happy, and if God were almighty He would be able to do what He wished. But the creatures are not happy. Therefore God lacks either goodness, or power, or both." This is the problem of pain, in its simplest form. The possibility of answering it depends on showing that the terms "good" and "almighty," and perhaps also the term "happy" are equivocal: for it must be admitted from the outset that if the popular meanings attached to these words are the best, or the only possible, meanings, then the argument is unanswerable.
C.S. Lewis, *The Problem of Pain*, The Centenary Press, 1941, p.14.

What is the meaning of pain? How does it find a place in a world created by a loving God? If we are to face that tormenting question as Christians we must take care that we are not prejudiced by our natural attitude to pain. For we naturally tend to think of it as the first, if not the worst, of evils. In recent discussions of the problem of evil, suffering has bulked larger than sin. But here, at the foot of the Cross, we learn once for all that pain—agonising pain—may find a place in the perfect life. It did have place there. But no sin has any place there—no form of selfishness, whether hatred, lust or greed. The perfect life and death were sinless; they were not painless. On the contrary, the pain directly contributed to the perfection of the life and death. It was in the endurance of the pain that the supreme courage was perfected; it was in the selfless endurance of pain that the supreme love was perfected. Take away pain from life, and you take heroism with it: the result is to make life poorer, not richer. Of course this truth must never be made an excuse for lack of sympathy towards sufferers; we must relieve them if we can; so we shew love—the very best thing in life. But here, paradoxically, is another justification of pain. It is the chief occasion of sympathy. Our hearts are not easily drawn to others by their joy or their laughter, their virtues or their talents; but pain claims sympathy wherever it occurs. It is the great binder of hearts. And sympathy, being a form of love, is so precious that the cost of pain is not worthy to be compared with it.
We see how false our standards are when we reflect how much of our perplexity about pain is due to the suffering of the innocent. The assumption is that pain is at all costs to be avoided and averted unless it comes as a just penalty for wrong-doing. But this

ignores the refining power of pain for those who accept it in gentleness and love. Observation shews that pain either purifies or coarsens the character, according to the degree of its development towards selflessness. From a Christian standpoint it is harder to justify the pain that further coarsens a brutal character which has earned it as a punishment, than the pain which comes to an innocent sufferer and is used as the material of spiritual growth. For there is no unselfishness so great as the unselfish endurance of pain; and when it is so used it becomes something for which the sufferer gives thanks.

The world is full of pain to-day; each of us has a share; for some it is but a slight burden, for others it is crushing. But every Christian can turn it into a blessing if he will seek the companionship of Christ in his suffering; then pain becomes a new point of fellowship with Christ; and even our suffering becomes part of the price of the world's redemption as we fill up what is left over of the sufferings of the Christ. Pain does not then cease to be pain; but it ceases to be barren pain; and in fellowship with Christ upon the Cross we find new strength for bearing it and even for making it the means by which our hearts are more fully cleansed of selfishness and grow towards perfect love.

William Temple, *Palm Sunday to Easter*, Pamphlet, S.C.M. Press Ltd., 1948, p.32.

Revelation, the "object" of Christian conviction, is not a foolproof system of divine answers to human questions. It is not a system at all, but a destiny—the destiny of men with God and of God among men. So we have to take into account that God has revealed to us only as much as we need in order to dare the next step towards him through the darkness, trusting that for us his light will not be extinguished for ever. God has revealed to us everything that will help us to get to heaven—all of it, but no more.

There are many questions to which Revelation gives no answer at all. God quite simply proves his love for us right to the end, to the Cross. This self-sacrificing love is God's uttermost, ultimate openness of being, the revelation, too, of what God has not yet given us as revelation and perhaps never will. Unfortunately the questions not answered by revelation are exactly the ones that most bitterly torment us. Such, for example, is the question of suffering, which is never given theoretical "treatment" in the Bible. The book of Job is the supreme song of humanity silent in the face of suffering. People often try to provide a rational justification for suffering. For instance, that suffering is as important for life as shadow and darkness, in order to bring out the light. If we had only this lamentable, threadbare and superficial answer to human suffering, we should have good reason to resist it. Anyone who has even once seen a child suffer, a child in mortal pain, a child screaming for help we cannot give, will have understood once and for all that all the beauty in the world, all the joy and all the radiance of creation cannot justify the suffering of this one child. We Christians should not listen to those people who can explain everything, who can give a quick answer precisely when they don't really have one. We should do better to admit honestly that we do not understand God, that we cannot conceive why God has created pain, so much howling, senseless pain. We do not understand why, at the end, the eyes of Christ were so filled with sorrow and weeping that he could not recognize even God. God does not give an answer to human suffering—he takes it upon himself. He lets the ocean of pain that surrounds him burn through to the very centre of his incarnate being. St. Matthew writes: "He began to be sorrowful and troubled" (Matthew 26.37). St. Mark puts it even more strongly: "He began to be greatly distressed and troubled" (Mark 14.33). Luke said that Christ was "in an agony" (Luke 22.44). In Christ's agony in the Garden of Olives his entire physical and mental self shrank from life to such an extent that "his sweat became like great drops of blood falling down upon the ground" (Luke 22.44).

In the face of this act of God all questioning stops, even though there is no answer. This falling silent is one of the creative experiences of Christian prayer. The most beautiful words, those that give the most genuine help, are often born in a silence filled with suffering. Silence is the glowing furnace of the word, the forge of true speech and sensitivity. The people who have won the right to speak to us at the worst moments in our lives are those who have suffered in silence, before God, with God, and for his sake. God speaks to us through men whom—like his own Son—he has led into the desert, into the loneliness of suffering, of inner hunger and unquenchable yearning, and who have become quite silent there. For them their suffering has become an election and a mission; they feel inwardly linked to all sufferers; God lets them suffer human need in order that they may be able to sit down alongside a stranger, on the dreary bed of his inner prison and say, "You are not alone." Such people have the right to bear another's pain and to seek out God in their hesitant prayer. Their words are more than "true." They are words of solidarity.

Ladislaus Boros, *In Time of Temptation,* translated by Simon and Erika Young, Burns & Oates Ltd., 1968, p.104.

PARADISE

And he said, "Jesus, remember me when you come into your kingdom." And he said to him, "Truly, I say to you, today you will be with me in Paradise."

Luke 23.42-43.

The world is a mirror of infinite beauty, yet no man sees it. It is a Temple of Majesty, yet no man regards it. It is a region of Light and Peace, did not men disquiet it. It is the Paradise of God.

Thomas Traherne, *Centuries,* The Faith Press Ltd., 1969, p.15.

Too much of words or yet too few! What to thy Godhead easier than One little glimpse of Paradise to ope the eyes and ears of man?

Sir Richard Burton, *The Kasidah of Haji Abdu Al-Vazdi,* H.J. Cook, 1900, p.3.

The meanest flowret of the vale,
The simplest note that swells the gale,
The common Sun, the air, and skies,
To him are opening Paradise.

Thomas Gray, *Poetry and Prose,* introduction and notes by J. Crofts, Oxford at the Clarendon Press, 1971, "Ode on the Pleasure Arising from Vicissitude," l.49.

What is Paradise? All things that are; for all are goodly and pleasant, and therefore may fitly be called a Paradise. It is said also, that Paradise is an outer court of Heaven. Even so this world is verily an outer court of the Eternal, or of Eternity, and specially whatever in Time, or any temporal things or creatures, manifesteth or remindeth us of God or Eternity; for the creatures are a guide and a path unto God and Eternity. Thus this world is an outer court of Eternity, and therefore it may well be called a Paradise, for it is such in truth.

Theologia Germanica, translated by Susanna Winkworth, Stuart & Watkins Ltd., 1966, p.119.

Now was I come up in spirit through the flaming sword into the paradise of God. All things were new, and all the creation gave another smell unto me than before, beyond what words can utter. I knew nothing but pureness, and innocency, and righteousness, being renewed up into the image of God by Jesus Christ, so that I say I was come up to the state of Adam which he was in before he fell. The creation was opened to me, and it was showed me how all things had their names given them according to their nature and virtue.

George Fox, *The Journal of George Fox*, a revised edition by John L. Nickalls, Cambridge at the University Press, 1952, p.27.

"Since I am coming to that Holy roome
Where, with thy Quire of Saints, for evermore
I shall be made thy music; as I come
I tune the instrument here at the door,
And what I must doe then, thinke here before."

These words by John Donne direct our attention to the very heart of the purpose of our life on this earth. They stir our imagination and provoke what Wordsworth calls "obstinate questionings." How are we to set about this tuning of our instrument, here in the ante-room of earth-life, before joining the great orchestra in the next dimension? Donne's powerful poetic imagery sets fire to our imagination. He is suggestive, not dogmatic, and we are left free to speculate and to undertake our own "adventures in ideas." Whatever our beliefs or prejudices about survival after physical death may be, we shall probably be familiar with the concept of many different levels of consciousness; and it is in this direction that we may find an interpretation of Donne's poem.

A wise teacher has said that even a little knowledge and understanding of the next sphere (for which we are all bound, whether we like it or not) will be of great value to us. If the next world is indeed largely a thought-world, Donne's words are fraught with a sense of urgency that underlines the spiritual law of cause and effect: as we think now, so shall we *be* when we discard the body. The metaphor of music, implying a vast orchestra in which we all participate, draws our attention to the possibility of unity in diversity, and to the underlying quality of harmony. Any orchestra would be the poorer if all the instruments were playing the same line of music: the secret lies in perfect blending. Implicit in Donne's image is the suggestion that each one of us will contribute a degree of harmony, or lack of it, according to the quality of thought and character built up through a possible succession of lives. "As a man thinketh in his heart, so is he."

Belle Valerie Gaunt and George Trevelyan, *A Tent in which to Pass a Summer Night*, Coventure Ltd., 1977, p.61.

PATIENCE

But they who wait for the Lord shall renew their strength, they shall mount up with wings like eagles, they shall run and not be weary, they shall walk and not faint.

Isaiah 40.31.

We have peace with God through our Lord Jesus Christ. Through him we have obtained access to this grace in which we stand, and we rejoice in our hope of sharing the glory of God. More than that, we rejoice in our sufferings, knowing that suffering produces endurance, and endurance produces character, and character produces hope, and hope does not disappoint us, because God's love has been poured into our hearts through the Holy Spirit which has been given to us.

Romans 5. 1-5.

Possess your soul with patience.

John Dryden, *The Poems of John Dryden*, edited by James Kinsley, Oxford at the Clarendon Press, 1958, Volume II, p.525, "The Hind and the Panther," The Third Part, 1.839.

Calumnies are answer'd best with silence.

Ben Jonson, *Ben Jonson*, edited by C.H. Herford and Percy Simpson, Oxford at the Clarendon Press, 1965, Volume V, p.50, *Volpone*, Act II. sc.ii.

Endurance is nobler than strength, and patience than beauty.

John Ruskin, *The Two Paths*, George Allen, 1905, p.179.

I worked with patience, which means almost power.

E.B. Browning, *Elizabeth Barrett Browning's Poetical Works*, Smith, Elder, & Co., 1873, Volume V, p.96, *Aurora Leigh*, Third Book.

One of the principal parts of faith is patience.

George Macdonald, *Weighed and Wanting*, Sampson Low, Marston, Searle & Rivington, 1882, Volume III, p.191.

Endurance is the crowning quality,
And patience all the passion of great hearts.

J.R. Lowell, *The Poetical Works of James Russell Lowell*, introduction by William Michael Rossetti, Ward, Lock & Co. Ltd., 1911, p.58, "Columbus."

Patience is not passive; on the contrary, it is active; it is concentrated strength.

Anon.

One moment of patience may ward off great disaster, one moment of impatience may ruin a whole life.

Chinese wisdom.

Sorrow and silence are strong, and patient endurance is godlike.

Henry Wadsworth Longfellow, *The Poetical Works of Longfellow*, Humphrey Milford, Oxford University Press, 1913, p.158, *Evangeline*, Part the Second, I, l.60.

Let patience have her perfect work. Statue under the chisel of the sculptor, stand steady to the blows of his mallet. Clay on the wheel, let the fingers of the divine potter model you at their will. Obey the Father's lightest word; hear the Brother who knows you, and died for you.

George Macdonald, *Unspoken Sermons*, Third Series, Longmans, Green, and Co., 1889, p.227.

God is unwearied patience, a meekness that cannot be provoked; He is an ever-enduring mercifulness; He is unmixed goodness, impartial, universal love; His delight is in the communication of Himself, His own happiness to everything according to its capacity. He does everything that is good, righteous, and lovely for its own sake, because it is good, righteous and lovely. He is the good from which nothing but good comes, and resisteth all evil only with goodness. This ... is the nature and Spirit of God.

William Law, *Selected Mystical Writings of William Law*, edited by Stephen Hobhouse, Rockliff, 1948, p.113.

The patient man is already experiencing a deep and healthful purging. When he receives an injury, he is more distressed for the other's unkind thought than for the hurt he has received; he gladly prays for those who put obstacles in his path, forgives others their faults from his heart, and is not slow in seeking their forgiveness. He is more ready to feel pity for others than anger, but his own feelings he often treats roughly, and he tries to keep his natural impulses obedient to his spirit.

Thomas à Kempis, *The Imitation of Christ*, translated by Betty I. Knott, William Collins Sons & Co. Ltd., 1979, p.75.

PEACE

If possible, so far as it depends upon you, live peaceably with all.

Romans 12.18.

And the peace of God, which passes all understanding, will keep your hearts and your minds in Christ Jesus.

Philippians 4.7.

What you have learned and received and heard and seen in me, do; and the God of peace will be with you.

Philippians 4.9.

And let the peace of Christ rule in your hearts, to which indeed you were called in the one body.

Colossians 3.15.

May the God of peace himself sanctify you wholly; and may your spirit and soul and body be kept sound and blameless at the coming of our Lord Jesus Christ.

1 Thessalonians 5.23.

Live in peace yourself and then you can bring peace to others.

Thomas à Kempis, *The Imitation of Christ,* translated by Betty I. Knott, William Collins Sons & Co. Ltd., 1979, p.87.

Peace is always beautiful.

Walt Whitman, *The Complete Poems,* edited by Francis Murphy, Penguin Books Ltd., 1982, p.447, "The Sleepers," l.147.

Where there is peace, God is.

George Herbert, *The Works of George Herbert,* edited by F.E. Hutchinson, Oxford at the Clarendon Press, 1972, p.345, "Outlandish Proverbs," No.733.

You touched me, and I am inflamed with love of your peace.

St. Augustine, *Confessions,* translated with an introduction by R.S. Pine-Coffin, Penguin Books Ltd., 1964, p.232.

The more a man gives up his heart to God, to his vocation and to men, forgetful of himself and of that which belongs to him—the greater poise he will acquire, until he reaches peace, quiet, joy—the apanage of simple and humble souls.

Father Yelchaninov, in *A Treasury of Russian Spirituality,* edited by G.P. Fedotov, Sheed and Ward Ltd., 1977, p.445.

To thee, O God, we turn for peace ... but grant us too the blessed assurance that nothing shall deprive us of that peace, neither *ourselves,* nor our foolish, earthly desires, nor my wild longings, nor the anxious cravings of my heart.

Søren Kierkegaard, *The Journals of Søren Kierkegaard,* a selection edited and translated by Alexander Dru, Oxford University Press, 1938, p.85.

A soul divided against itself can never find peace. Peace cannot exist where there are contrary loyalties. For true peace there has to be psychological and moral harmony. Conscience must be at rest.

Hubert van Zeller, *Considerations,* Sheed and Ward Ltd., 1974, p.43.

People are always expecting to get peace in heaven; but you know whatever peace they get there will be ready made. Whatever making of peace *they* can be blest for, must be on earth here.

John Ruskin, *The Eagle's Nest,* George Allen & Sons, 1910, p.222.

My son, I will teach you the way of peace and true liberty ... try to do another's will rather than your own. Always choose to have less rather than more. Always choose the lowest place and to be less than everyone else. Always long and pray that the will of God may be fully realized in your life. You will find that the man who does all this walks in the land of peace and quietness.

Thomas à Kempis, *The Imitation of Christ,* translated by Betty I. Knott, William Collins Sons & Co. Ltd., 1979, p.147.

Children, that peace which is found in the spirit and the inner life is well worth our care, for in that peace lies the satisfaction of all our wants. In it the Kingdom of God is discovered and His righteousness is found. This peace a man should allow nothing to take from him, whatever betide, come weal or woe, honour or shame.

John Tauler, *The History and Life of the Reverend Doctor John Tauler,*
translated by Susanna Winkworth, Smith, Elder, and Company, 1857, p.381.

Every good man, in whom religion rules, is at peace and unity with himself, is as a city compacted together. Grace doth more and more reduce all the faculties of the soul into a perfect subjection and subordination to itself. The union and conjunction of the soul with God, that primitive Unity, is that which is the alone original and fountain of all peace, and the centre of rest.

John Smith the Platonist, *Select Discourses,* Cambridge at the University Press, 1859, p.421.

Reflect now, how Our Lord Himself spoke of Peace. He said to His disciples, "Peace I leave with you, my peace I give unto you." Did He mean peace as we think of it: the kingdom of England at peace with its neighbours, the barons at peace with the King, the householder counting over his peaceful gains, the swept hearth, his best wine for a friend at the table, his wife singing to the children? Those men His disciples knew no such things: they went forth to journey afar, to suffer by land and sea, to know torture, imprisonment, disappointment, to suffer death by martyrdom. What then did He mean? If you ask that, remember then that He said also,"Not as the world gives, give I unto you." So then, He gave to His disciples peace, but not peace as the world gives.

T.S. Eliot, *The Complete Poems and Plays of T.S. Eliot,* Faber and Faber Limited, 1975, *Murder in the Cathedral,*
p.260, Interlude.

PENITENCE

It can take less than a minute to commit a sin. It takes not as long to obtain God's forgiveness. Penitence and amendment should take a lifetime.

Hubert van Zeller, *Considerations,* Sheed & Ward Ltd., 1974, p.48.

He who is truly penitent and really sorry shall receive pardon without doubt or delay. The prayer that is made by a contrite and humble heart is quickly granted, a heart contrite by fear and humbled by sorrow.

Richard of Saint-Victor, *Selected Writings on Contemplation,* translated by Clare Kirchberger, Faber and Faber Limited, 1957, p.87.

We have heard that *the way is narrow that leads to life.* This is the way of penance and few find it."Narrow" is what it is called, and called rightly; through it the flesh sheds its unlawful things and the worldly comforts; through it the soul is held back from degenerate delights and decadent thoughts; through it the soul is totally given over to love of the divine. Yet it is not often found among men, because scarcely any have taste for the things of God, but look for earthly joys, and find their pleasure there. So they have recourse to sensual lusts, and neglect the mental: they detest any way that would lead to spiritual well-being, and reject it as narrow and rough, and to their lust intolerable.

Richard Rolle, *The Fire of Love*, introduced and translated by Clifton Wolters, Penguin Books Ltd., 1981, p.103.

It is penitence which creates intimacy with Our Lord. No one can know Him intimately who has not realised the sickness of his own soul and obtained healing from the physician of souls. Our virtues do not bring us near to Christ—the gulf between them and His holiness remains unbridgeable. Our science does not bring us near Him, nor our art. Our pain may give us a taste of fellowship with Him, but it is only a taste unless the great creator of intimacy—penitence—is also there. For in my virtue, my art, my knowledge, there is sure to be some pride—probably, indeed, a great deal of pride. But I cannot be proud of sin which is really admitted to be sin. I can be proud of my dare-devilry; oh, yes, and of anything I do to shock respectability. But then I am not admitting to myself that it is sin—only that other people think it so. When I find something in myself of which I really am ashamed, I cannot at the time be proud of that—though, alas! I may be proud of my shame at it, and so make this, too, worthless. In straightforward shame at my own meanness there is no pride and no expectation of forgiveness except through trust in the love of Him who forgives. So it is penitence which brings me in all simplicity to appeal to the sheer goodness and love of God. And we can turn our very sins into blessings if we will let them empty us of pride and cast ourselves upon the generosity of God. "We receive the due reward of our sins: Jesus, remember me."

"To-day shalt thou be with me in Paradise." To-day. We do not have to wait for "some far-off divine event." When true penitence opens our hearts to the love of God, forthwith He enters there to reign. Because His Kingdom is spiritual, the sovereignty of His love over hearts that are open to its claim and its appeal, we do not have to wait for Him to come in His kingdom. No doubt its perfection, when all hearts are open and respond, is in the future. But the power of His Kingdom is focussed in His Cross. He reigns from the Tree. Let us come with hearts ready to respond to that shining forth of the Love of God. Let us see how we look in that Presence. Then let us acknowledge our unfitness to be near Him, and hear Him say in answer: "To-day shalt thou be with Me."

William Temple, *Palm Sunday to Easter*, Pamphlet, S.C.M. Press Ltd., 1948, p.20.

PERFECTION

You, therefore, must be perfect, as your heavenly Father is perfect.
Matthew 5.48.

God's purpose is to lead man into perfection of growth, which is the attainment of a unity comprehending an immense manifoldness.

Rabindranath Tagore, *Letters to a Friend*, George Allen & Unwin Ltd., 1928, p.116.

We always find a restless appetite within ourselves which craves for some supreme
and chief good, and will not be satisfied with any thing less than infinity itself.
John Smith the Platonist, *Select Discourses*, Cambridge at the University Press, 1859, p.138.

So slow
The growth of what is excellent; so hard
T'attain perfection in this nether world.
William Cowper, *The Poetical Works of Cowper*, edited by H.S. Milford, Oxford University Press, 1950, p.131,
"The Task," Bk.I, 1.83.

The very best and utmost of attainment in this life is to remain still and let God act
and speak in thee.
Meister Eckhart, *Meister Eckhart*, Franz Pfeiffer, translated by C. de B. Evans, John M. Watkins, 1956, Volume
I, p.6.

Perfection is finally attained not when there is no longer anything to add but when
there is no longer anything to take away.
Antoine de Saint-Exupéry, *Wind, Sand and Stars*, translated by Lewis Galantière, William Heinemann Ltd.,
1939, p.54.

The great aim of culture (is) the aim of setting ourselves to ascertain what perfection
is and to make it prevail.
Matthew Arnold, *The Complete Prose Works of Matthew Arnold*, Volume V, *Culture and Anarchy*, edited by R.H.
Super, Ann Arbor, The University of Michigan Press, 1965, "Sweetness and Light," p.93.

He has made the soul according to his own most perfect nature, pouring into her the
whole of his own light in all its pristine purity, while he himself remains all undefiled.
Meister Eckhart, *Meister Eckhart*, Franz Pfeiffer, translated by C. de B. Evans, John M. Watkins, 1956, Volume
I, p.222.

In this broad earth of ours,
Amid the measureless grossness and the slag,
Enclosed and safe within its central heart,
Nestles the seed perfection.
Walt Whitman, *The Complete Poems*, edited by Francis Murphy, Penguin Books Ltd., 1982, p.255, "Song of
the Universe," st.i, l.4.

The Church recalls to mind that culture must be subordinated to the integral development of the human person, to the good of the community and of the whole of
mankind. Therefore one must aim at encouraging the human spirit to develop its
faculties of wonder, of understanding, of contemplation, of forming personal judgements and cultivating a religious, moral and social sense.
Vatican Council II, *The Conciliar and Post Conciliar Documents*, 1981 Edition, general editor, Austin Flannery,
O.P., Fowler Wright Books Ltd., p.963.

All that can be expected from the most perfect institutions is that they should make
it possible for individual excellence to develop itself, not that they should produce
the excellent individual. Virtue and genius, grace and beauty, will always constitute

a *noblesse* such as no form of government can manufacture. It is of no use, therefore, to excite oneself for or against revolutions which have only an importance of the second order—an importance which I do not wish either to diminish or to ignore, but an importance which, after all, is mostly negative.

Henri Frédéric Amiel, *Amiel's Journal,* translated by Mrs. Humphry Ward, Macmillan & Co. Ltd., 1918, p.177.

I suppose others feel the same intense delight, which one cannot describe any more than one can explain how it comes, when some verse in the Gospels which one has read for years and years without a second thought suddenly expands in some new direction of thought and goes on from point to point of one's whole idea of the beginning and method and ultimate object of the great fact of Life, from birth and beginning to death and completion. Everything in life which comes anywhere near this delight has the same foundation; it is just simply the realization of beauty, just a glimpse of something nearing perfection, just a momentary sense of the presence of something which will last, which cannot be done away with or lost, something, however little, of the perfect Love of God.

Edward Wilson, in *The Faith of Edward Wilson,* George Seaver, John Murray Ltd., 1949, p.16.

We acknowledge that there are broken lives, pieces of lives which have begun in this world to be completed, as we believe, in another state of being. And some of them have been like fragments of ancient art, which we prize not for their completeness but for their quality, and because they seem to give us a type of something which we can hardly see anywhere upon earth. Of such lives we must judge, not by what the person said or wrote or did in the short span of human existence, but by what they were: if they exercised some peculiar influence on society and on friends, if they had some rare grace of humility, or simplicity, or resignation, or love of truth, or self-devotion, which was not to be met with in others. God does not measure men's lives only by the amount of work which is accomplished in them. He who gave the power to work may also withhold the power. And some of these broken lives may have a value in His sight which no bustle or activity of ordinary goodness could have attained. There have been persons confined to a bed of sickness, blind, palsied, tormented with pain and want, who yet may be said to have led an almost perfect life. Such persons afford examples to us, not indeed of a work carried out to the end (for their circumstances did not admit of this), but of a work, whether finished or unfinished, which at any moment is acceptable to God. And we desire to learn of them, and to have an end like theirs when the work of active life is over and we sit patiently waiting for the will of God.

Benjamin Jowett, *Select Passages from the Theological Writings of Benjamin Jowett,* edited by Lewis Campbell, John Murray, 1902, p.231.

PERSONALITY

Nothing endures but personal qualities.

Walt Whitman, *The Complete Poems,* edited by Francis Murphy, Penguin Books Ltd., 1982, p.218, "Song of the Broad-Axe," section 4, l.99.

The secret of the universe, as by slow degrees it reveals itself to us, turns out to be personality.

John Cowper Powys, *The Complex Vision*, Dodd, Mead and Company, Inc., 1920, p.194.

Man's main task in life is to give birth to himself, to become what he potentially is. The most important product of his effort is his own personality.

Erich Fromm, *Man For Himself*, Routledge & Kegan Paul Ltd., 1975, p.237.

One whose greatest power lay in unfolding the love of God by speech and action, and in helping individual men and women to find the meaning and the glory, the purpose and the joy of life, in that surrender to the all-pervading presence of God which for him gave earth the character of heaven.

G.A. Studdert Kennedy, *By his Friends*, Hodder and Stoughton Ltd., 1929, p.63.

Here is the genuine beginning in modern times of what has come to be the deepest note of present-day Christianity, *the appreciation of personality as the highest thing in earth or heaven,* and the initiation of a movement to find the vital sources and resources for the inner kindling of the spirit, and for raising the whole personal life to higher functions and to higher powers.

Rufus M. Jones, *Spiritual Reformers in the 16th and 17th Centuries*, Macmillan & Co. Ltd., 1914, p.xlix.

The present state of the world calls for a moral and spiritual revolution, revolution in the name of personality, of man, of every single person. This revolution should restore the hierarchy of values, now quite shattered, and place the value of human personality above the idols of production, technics, the state, the race or nationality, the collective.

Nicolas Berdyaev, *The Fate of Man in the Modern World*, translated by Donald A. Lowrie, S.C.M. Press Ltd., 1935, p.83.

To live is the rarest thing in the world. Most people exist.... Have we ever seen the full expression of a personality?... A perfect man is one who develops under perfect conditions; one who is not wounded, or worried, or maimed, or in danger. Most personalities have been obliged to be rebels. Half their strength has been wasted in friction ... and these battles do not always intensify strength, they often exaggerate weakness.... The note of the perfect personality is not rebellion but peace.

Oscar Wilde, in *The Note Books of a Woman Alone*, edited by M.G. Ostle, J.M. Dent & Sons Ltd., 1935, p.160.

It is by the body that we come into contact with Nature, with our fellow-men, with all their revelations of God to us. It is through the body that we receive all the lessons of passion, of suffering, of love, of beauty, of science. It is through the body that we are both trained outwards from ourselves, and driven inwards into our deepest selves to find God. There is glory and might in this vital evanescence, this slow glacier-like flow of clothing and revealing matter, this ever uptossed rainbow of tangible humanity. It is no less of God's making than the spirit that is clothed therein.

George Macdonald, *Unspoken Sermons*, First Series, Alexander Strahan, Publisher, 1867, p.238.

It is as a body that I am most aware of myself, and my strongest and most elemental instincts are directed to satisfy the needs and desires of the body. The body is a wonderful organism—breathing, circulation of the blood, digestion and sewerage, sexual feeling and the capacity for union and the procreation of children. The body has a marked effect on the feeling tone of its owner. It is an integral part of our being; it is basically good because given us by God. It must be the servant of the total personality, through which the person expresses himself in demeanour and behaviour.

George Appleton, *Journey for a Soul*, William Collins Sons & Co. Ltd., 1976, p.15.

The achievement of personality means nothing less than the optimum development of the whole individual human being. It is impossible to foresee the endless variety of conditions that have to be fulfilled. A whole lifetime, in all its biological, social, and spiritual aspects, is needed. Personality is the supreme realization of the innate idiosyncrasy of a living being. It is an act of high courage flung in the face of life, the absolute affirmation of all that constitutes the individual, the most successful adaptation to the universal conditions of existence coupled with the greatest possible freedom for self-determination. To educate a man to *this* seems to me no light matter. It is surely the hardest task the modern mind has set itself. And it is dangerous too.... It is as dangerous as the bold and hazardous undertaking of nature to let women bear children....

Just as the child must develop in order to be educated, so the personality must begin to sprout before it can be trained. And this is where the danger begins. For we are handling something unpredictable, we do not know how and in what direction the budding personality will develop, and we have learned enough of nature and the world to be somewhat chary of both. On top of that, we were brought up in the Christian belief that human nature is intrinsically evil. But even those who no longer adhere to the Christian teaching are by nature mistrustful and not a little frightened of the possibilities lurking in the subterranean chambers of their being. Even enlightened psychologists like Freud give us an extremely unpleasant picture of what lies slumbering in the depths of the human psyche. So it is rather a bold venture to put in a good word for the development of personality.... "Anything might happen then," people say. Or they dish up the old, feebleminded objection to "individualism." But individualism is not and never has been a natural development; it is nothing but an unnatural usurpation, a freakish, impertinent pose that proves its hollowness by crumpling up·before the least obstacle. What we have in mind is something very different.... The development of personality means ... fidelity to the law of one's own being.... Fidelity to the law of one's own being is a trust in this law, a loyal perseverence and confident hope; in short, an attitude such as a religious man should have towards God. It can now be seen how portentous is the dilemma that emerges from behind our problem: personality can never develop unless the individual chooses his own way, consciously and with moral deliberation. Not only the causal motive—necessity—but conscious moral decision must lend its strength to the process of building the personality. If the first is lacking, then the alleged development is a mere acrobatics of the will; if the second, it will get stuck in unconscious automatism. But a man can make a moral decision to go his own way only if he holds that way to be the best. If any other way were held to be better, then he would live and develop that other personality instead of his own. The other ways are conventionalities of a moral, social, political, philosophical, or religious nature. The fact that the conventions always flourish in one form or another only proves that the vast majority of mankind do not choose their own way, but convention, and consequently develop not themselves but a method and a collective mode of life at the cost of their own wholeness....

To develop one's own personality is indeed an unpopular undertaking, a deviation that is highly uncongenial to the herd.... Small wonder, then, that from earliest times only the chosen few have embarked upon this strange adventure. Had they all been fools, we could safely dismiss them as, *idiotai,* mentally "private" persons who have no claim on our interest. But, unfortunately, these personalities are as a rule the legendary heroes of mankind, the very ones who are looked up to, loved, and worshipped, the true sons of God whose names perish not. They are the flower and the fruit, the ever fertile seeds of the tree of humanity.... They towered up like mountain peaks above the mass that still clung to its collective fears, its beliefs, laws, and systems, and boldly chose their own way. To the man in the street it has always seemed miraculous that anyone should turn aside from the beaten track with its known destinations, and strike out on the steep and narrow path leading into the unknown. Hence it was always believed that such a man, if not actually crazy, was possessed by a daemon or a god....

What is it, in the end, that induces a man to go his own way and to rise out of unconscious identity with the mass as out of a swathing mist? Not necessity, for necessity comes to many, and they all take refuge in convention. Not moral decision, for nine times out of ten we decide for convention likewise. What is it, then, that inexorably tips the scales in favour of the *extra-ordinary?*

It is what is commonly called *vocation:* an irrational factor that destines a man to emancipate himself from the herd and from its well-worn paths. True personality is always a vocation and puts its trust in it as in God, despite its being, as the ordinary man would say, only a personal feeling. But vocation acts like a law of God from which there is no escape. The fact that many a man who goes his own way ends in ruin means nothing to one who has a vocation. He *must* obey his own law as if it were a daemon whispering to him of new and wonderful paths. Anyone with a vocation hears the voice of the inner man: he is *called.* That is why the legends say that he possesses a private daemon who counsels him and whose mandates he must obey. The best known example of this is Faust, and an historical instance is provided by the daemon of Socrates....

The original meaning of "to have a vocation" is "to be addressed by a voice." The clearest examples of this are to be found in the avowals of the Old Testament prophets.... Vocation, or the feeling of it, is not, however, the prerogative of great personalities; it is also appropriate to the small ones all the way down to the "midget" personalities, but as the size decreases the voice becomes more and more muffled and unconscious ... until finally it merges indistinguishably with the surrounding society, thus surrendering its own wholeness and dissolving into the wholeness of the group. In the place of the inner voice is the voice of the group with its conventions, and vocation is replaced by collective necessities....

(Likewise) to become a personality is not the absolute prerogative of the genius, for a man may be a genius without being a personality. In so far as every individual has the law of his life inborn in him, it is theoretically possible for any man to follow this law and so become a personality, that is, to achieve wholeness....

Only the man who can consciously assent to the power of the inner voice becomes a personality; but if he succumbs to it he will be swept away by the blind flux of psychic events and destroyed. That is the great and liberating thing about any genuine personality: he voluntarily sacrifices himself to his vocation, and consciously translates into his own individual reality what would only lead to ruin if it were lived unconsciously by the group.

One of the most shining examples of the meaning of personality that history has preserved for us is the life of Christ.... Obeying the inner call of his vocation, Jesus voluntarily exposed himself (in the Temptations) to the assaults of the imperialistic madness that filled everyone, conqueror and conquered alike. In this way he recognized the nature of the objective psyche which had plunged the whole world into misery and had begotten a yearning for salvation that found expression even in the pagan poets. Far from suppressing or allowing himself to be suppressed by this psychic onslaught, he let it act on him consciously, and assimilated it. Thus was world-conquering Caesarism transformed into spiritual kingship, and the Roman Empire into the universal kingdom of God that was not of this world. While the whole Jewish nation was expecting an imperialistically minded and politically active hero as a Messiah, Jesus fulfilled the Messianic mission not so much for his own nation as for the whole Roman world, and pointed out to humanity the old truth that where force rules there is no love, and where love reigns force does not count. The religion of love was the exact psychological counterpart to the Roman devil-worship of power.

The example of Christianity is perhaps the best illustration of my previous abstract argument. This apparently unique life became a sacred symbol because it is the psychological prototype of the only meaningful life, that is, of a life that strives for the individual realization— absolute and unconditional—of its own particular law. Well may we exclaim with Tertullian: *anima naturaliter christiana!*

Just as the great personality acts upon society to liberate, to redeem, to tranform, and to heal, so the birth of personality in oneself has a therapeutic effect. It is as if a river that had run to waste in sluggish side-streams and marshes suddenly found its way back to its proper bed, or as if a stone lying on a germinating seed were lifted away so that the shoot could begin its natural growth.

C.G. Jung, *The Collected Works of C.G. Jung*, Volume 17, *The Development of Personality*, translated by R.F.C. Hull, Routledge & Kegan Paul Ltd., 1954, p.171.

PHILOSOPHY

That untaught innate philosophy.

Lord Byron, *The Complete Poetical Works*, edited by Jerome J. McCann, Oxford at the Clarendon Press, 1980, Volume II, p.90, "Childe Harold's Pilgrimage," canto III, st.xxxix, l.344.

The example of good men is visible philosophy.

English Proverb.

The object of studying philosophy is to know one's mind, not other people's. Philosophy means thinking things out for oneself.

W.R. Inge, *Outspoken Essays*, Second Series, Longmans, Green & Co. Ltd., 1922, p.1.

Philosophy makes us wiser, but Christianity makes us better men.

Henry Fielding, *The History of Tom Jones*, introduction by George Sainsbury, J.M. Dent & Sons Ltd., 1957, Volume I, p.377.

Every philosophy is tinged with the colouring of some secret imaginative background, which never emerges explicitly into its trains of reasoning.

Alfred North Whitehead, *Science and the Modern World*, Cambridge at the University Press, 1932, p.9.

Any genuine philosophy leads to action and from action back again to wonder, to the enduring fact of mystery.

Henry Miller, *The Wisdom of the Heart*, New Directions Books, 1941, p.93.

Philosophical knowledge is a spiritual act, where not only the intellect is active, but the whole of man's spiritual power, his emotions and his will.

Nicolas Berdyaev, *Christian Existentialism*, selected and translated by Donald A. Lowrie, George Allen & Unwin Ltd., 1965, p.119.

To be a philosopher is not merely to have subtle thoughts, nor even to found a school, but so to love wisdom as to live according to its dictates, a life of simplicity, independence, magnanimity, and trust.

Henry David Thoreau, *Walden*, The New American Library of World Literature, Inc., 1960, p.15.

"Come unto me ... and I will give you rest"; it is not Philosophy that can estimate the right of the Speaker to issue that invitation or to make that promise; that right can be proved or disproved only by the experiment of life.

William Temple, *Nature, Man and God*, Macmillan & Co. Ltd., 1934, p.520.

A Christian cannot live by philosophy. Only the light of Christian revelation gives the end as well as the means of life. It is the same for you as for me and the man in the street. If one has more learning, another has more grace, it is all one.

John Chapman, *The Spiritual Letters of Dom John Chapman*, Sheed and Ward Ltd., 1946, p.205.

Pretend what we may, the whole man within us is at work when we form our philosophical opinions. Intellect, will, taste, and passion co-operate just as they do in

---

practical affairs; and lucky it is if the passion be not something as petty as a love of personal conquest over the philosopher across the way.

William James, *The Will To Believe*, Longmans, Green & Co. Ltd., 1904, p.92.

The philosophy which is so important in each of us is not a technical matter; it is our more or less dumb sense of what life honestly and deeply means. It is only partly got from books; it is our individual way of just seeing and feeling the total push and pressure of the cosmos.

William James, *Pragmatism*, Longmans, Green & Co. Ltd., 1943, p.4.

The highest triumphs of philosophy are possible only to those who have achieved in themselves a purity of soul. This purity is based upon a profound acceptance of experience, realised only when some point of hidden strength within man, from which he can not only inspect but comprehend life, is found. From this inner source the philosopher reveals to us the truth of life, a truth which mere intellect is unable to discover. The vision is produced almost as naturally as a fruit from a flower out of the mysterious centre, where all experience is reconciled.

Sir Sarvepalli Radhakrishnan, *Indian Philosophy*, George Allen & Unwin Ltd., 1923, Volume I, p.44.

The Challenge of Death is the summary challenge addressed by the universe to man. It is the spear-point of the Challenge of Life, not to be evaded on any terms, as the fashion now is with many to evade it. To find a good in life which is worth achieving in spite of the fact, consciously realized, that this visible scene on which we operate, and we, the visible agents who operate, will presently be gathered to the dark death-kingdoms and enfolded in the everlasting Silence—that is the spear-point of the Challenge, the acid test of philosophy, the point where philosophy must either pass into religion or retire, beaten, from the field. The philosopher may be unaware of this, often is, or will even go out of his way to repudiate all interest in the matter; but in the audience that gathers round his feet there is always a vague hope, and sometimes a poignant one, that he will come at last to the critical point where Life and Death stand confronting one another in a "fell incensèd opposition," that he will let fall the word of wisdom which is to end that conflict and release the mind from the tension it involves—perhaps by teaching contentment with annihilation, perhaps by an argument for *carpe diem,* perhaps by proving personal immortality. Without that motive, subtly operating in all our curiosities about "mind and matter," "good and evil," "reality and appearance," there would be no market for the philosopher's goods; his performance would be offered to an empty house.

L.P. Jacks, *The Faith of a Worker*, Hodder and Stoughton Ltd., 1925, p.24.

He thought that to be a Philosopher, a Christian, and a Divine, was to be one of the most illustrious creatures in the world; and that no man was a man in act, but only in capacity, that was not one of these, or rather all. For either of these three include the other two. A Divine includes a Philosopher and a Christian; a Christian includes a Divine and a Philosopher; a Philosopher includes a Christian and a Divine. Since no man therefore can be a man unless he be a Philosopher, nor a true Philosopher unless he be a Christian, nor a perfect Christian unless he be a Divine, every man ought to spend his time in studying diligently Divine Philosophy.

This last principle needs a little explication. Not only because Philosophy is condemned for vain, but because it is superfluous among inferior Christians, and impossible, as some think, unto them. We must distinguish therefore of philosophy and of Christians also. Some philosophy, as Saint Paul says, is vain. But then it is vain philosophy. But there is also a Divine Philosophy, of which no books in the world are more full than his own. That we are naturally the Sons of God (I speak of primitive and upright nature), that the Son of God is the first beginning of every creature, that we are to be changed from glory to glory into the same Image, that we are spiritual Kings, that Christ is the express Image of His Father's person, that by Him all things are made whether they are visible or invisible, is the highest Philosophy in the world; and so it is also to treat, as he does, of the nature of virtues and Divine Laws. Yet no man, I suppose, will account these superfluous, or vain, for in the right knowledge of these Eternal Life consisteth. And till we see into the beauty and blessedness of God's Laws, the glory of His works, the excellency of our soul, &c. we are but children of darkness, at least but ignorant and imperfect: neither able to rejoice in God as we ought, nor to live in communion with Him.

Rather we should remember that Jesus Christ is the Wisdom of the Father, and that since our life is hid with Christ in God, we should spend our days in studying Wisdom, that we might be like unto Him; that the treasures of Heaven are the treasures of Wisdom, and that they are hid in Christ. As it is written, *In Him are hid all the treasures of Wisdom and Knowledge.*

Thomas Traherne, *Centuries*, The Faith Press Ltd., 1969, p.167.

POETRY

A poem is the very image of life expressed in its eternal truth.

Percy Bysshe Shelley, *The Prose Works of Percy Bysshe Shelley*, edited by H. Buxton Forman, Reeves and Turner, 1880, Volume III, p.108, "A Defence of Poetry."

God is the perfect poet,
Who in his person acts his own creations.

Robert Browning, *The Poetical Works of Robert Browning*, Smith, Elder, & Co., 1899, Volume I, *Paracelsus*, II, p.36.

Most people do not believe in anything very much and our greatest poetry is given us by those who do.

Cyril Connolly, in *The Making of a Poem*, Stephen Spender, Hamish Hamilton Ltd., 1955, p.26, in a review of Keat's Collected Letters.

Poetry is the record of the best and happiest moments of the happiest and best minds.

Percy Bysshe Shelley, *The Prose Works of Percy Bysshe Shelley*, edited by H. Buxton Forman, Reeves and Turner, 1880, Volume III, p.138, "A Defence of Poetry."

It (poetry) was ever thought to have some participation of divineness, because it doth raise and erect the mind.

Francis Bacon, *The Advancement of Learning,* introduction by Henry Morley, Cassell and Company Ltd., 1905, p.79.

Poetry, therefore, we will call *musical Thought.* The Poet is he who *thinks* in that manner.

Thomas Carlyle, *Sartor Resartus,* "Lectures on Heroes," Chapman and Hall, 1840, p.247.

Poetry should be vital—either stirring our blood by its divine movement, or snatching our breath by its divine perfection. To do both is supreme glory; to do either is enduring fame.

Augustine Birrell, *Obiter Dicta,* Elliot Stock, 1884, "Mr. Browning's Poetry," p.92.

The essence of all poetry is to be found, not in high-wrought subtlety of thought, nor in pointed cleverness of phrase, but in the depths of the heart and the most sacred feelings of the men who write.

John Keble, *Keble's Lectures on Poetry,* translated by E.K. Francis, Oxford at the Clarendon Press, 1912, Volume II, p.201.

Poetry should be great and unobtrusive, a thing which enters into one's soul, and does not startle it or amaze it with itself, but with its subject.

John Keats, *The Works of John Keats,* edited by H. Buxton Forman, Reeves and Turner, 1883, Volume III, p.113, Letter to J.H. Reynolds.

When a poet takes words as his instruments ... the very sound of the words is now part of the meaning; that meaning can never be apprehended or recovered except by re-hearing physically or in imagination the actual sound of the words.... Here we are near to a sacrament.

William Temple, *Nature, Man and God,* Macmillan & Co. Ltd., 1934, p.484.

Poetry turns all thing to loveliness; it exalts the beauty of that which is most beautiful, and it adds beauty to that which is most deformed; it marries exultation and horror, grief and pleasure, eternity and change; it subdues to union, under its light yoke, all irreconcilable things. It transmutes all that it touches, and every form moving within the radiance of its presence is changed by wondrous sympathy to an incarnation of the spirit which it breathes: its secret alchemy turns to potable gold the poisonous waters which flow from death through life; it strips the veil of familiarity from the world, and lays bare the naked and sleeping beauty, which is the spirit of its forms.... It purges from our inward sight the film of familiarity which obscures from us the wonder of our being. It compels us to feel that which we perceive, and to imagine that which we know.

Percy Bysshe Shelley, *The Prose Works of Percy Bysshe Shelley,* edited by H. Buxton Forman, Reeves and Turner, 1880, Volume III, p.139, "A Defence of Poetry."

What is a Poet? To whom does he address himself? And what language is to be expected from him?—He is a man speaking to men: a man, it is true, endowed with more lively sensibility, more enthusiasm and tenderness, who has a greater knowledge of human nature, and a more comprehensive soul, than are supposed to be common among mankind; a man pleased with his own passions and volitions, and who rejoices more than other men in the spirit of life that is in him....

The Poet writes under one restriction only, namely, the necessity of giving immediate pleasure to a human Being possessed of that information which may be expected from him, not as a lawyer, a physician, a mariner, an astronomer, or a natural philosopher, but as a Man....

He is the rock of defence for human nature; an upholder and preserver, carrying everywhere with him relationship and love. In spite of difference of soil and climate, of language and manners, of laws and customs: in spite of things silently gone out of mind, and things violently destroyed; the Poet binds together by passion and knowledge the vast empire of human society, as it is spread over the whole earth, and over all time. The objects of the Poet's thoughts are everywhere; though the eyes and senses of man are, it is true, his favourite guides, yet he will follow wheresoever he can find an atmosphere of sensation in which to move his wings. Poetry is the first and last of all knowledge—it is as immortal as the heart of man.

William Wordsworth, *The Poems of William Wordsworth*, edited with an introduction and notes by Nowell Charles Smith, Methuen & Co., 1908, Volume III, Preface to the Second Edition of Lyrical Ballads, p.490.

The most beautiful poem there is, is life—life which discerns its own story in the making, in which inspiration and self-consciousness go together and help each other, life which knows itself to be the world in little, a repetition in miniature of the divine universal poem. Yes, be man; that is to say, be nature, be spirit, be the image of God, be what is greatest, most beautiful, most lofty in all the spheres of being, be infinite will and idea, a reproduction of the great whole. And be everything while being nothing, effacing thyself, letting God enter into thee as the air enters an empty space, reducing the *ego* to the mere vessel which contains the divine essence. Be humble, devout, silent, that so thou mayest hear in the depths of thyself the subtle and profound voice; be spiritual and pure, that so thou mayest have communion with the pure spirit. Withdraw thyself often into the sanctuary of thy inmost consciousness; become once more point and atom, that so thou mayest free thyself from space, time, matter, temptation, dispersion,—that thou mayest escape thy very organs themselves and thine own life. That is to say, die often, and examine thyself in the presence of this death, as a preparation for the last death.

Henri Frédéric Amiel, *Amiel's Journal*, translated by Mrs. Humphry Ward, Macmillan & Co. Ltd., 1918, p.28.

Browning's poetry ... deals with what is essentially the business of prayer, the responsive Yes that a man must endeavour to make in those moments when the engagement is offered to him, when to be truly himself he must speak the truth in love, when he is presented with the opportunity and the responsibility of framing his reply "in spirit and in truth." Browning knew that the eternal Word waited to be embodied in human speech. In such moments all the divine events from the Nativity to the Passion are in our human key re-enacted. The Word may be given no room, may be misunderstood, treated with contempt, entirely rejected, but it is certain that, because of His love, it will not cease to be uttered. It is in this sense that the language of poetry is the serious speech to which all prayer aspires. The poet knows only too well that he himself is failing again and again to speak as he should, now wrestling with unmanageable perceptions, now giving way to the deceptions of easy speech, now intruding a false self-consciousness into the area where openness should prevail. The poet can just as easily get in the way of the movement of the Word as anyone else. He may be all that Shelley said so magnificently about the poet and still betray his calling. None the less, he shares in the forgiveness extended to us all. It is his job to enable words to become bearers of the Word, to permit the Word to take our flesh and dwell among us, to speak the words that hallow all that God has given and man has received, to translate them all into a Yes to God.

Alan Ecclestone, *Yes To God*, Darton, Longman & Todd Ltd., 1975, p.69.

POLITICS

Those who say that religion has nothing to do with politics do not know what religion means.

Mohandas K. Gandhi, *The Story of My Experiments with Truth, An Autobiography*, translated by Mahadur Desai, Phoenix Press, 1949, p.420.

Everything begins in mysticism and ends in politics.

Charles Péguy, *Basic Verities*, translated by Ann & Julian Green, Kegan Paul, Trench, Trubner & Co. Ltd., 1943, p.107.

No society can be run on the basis that its members are saints. Any state has to take into account that it has to govern sinners, which means there are going to be tensions between one group and another—but it's better to work that out than have bloody revolution.

Harry Williams, in *Priestland's Progress*, Gerald Priestland, British Broadcasting Corporation, 1982, p.55.

The issue of Church involvement in politics hinges on the fact that *we* are concerned with people as politics are concerned with people; and you can't divide people up into secular and religious. Whenever the poor are afflicted, or whenever human dignity and freedom is not respected, then the Church has a duty to sound a prophetic note; and it must be prepared to be unpopular on matters which concern politicians as well.

Basil Hume, in *Priestland's Progress*, Gerald Priestland, British Broadcasting Corporation, 1982, p.55.

I can't see any future for a church that in God's world doesn't accept that it must be involved in that part of it which is political and economic. A church which claims that the world is for Christ must be up to its neck in politics. I don't say party politics—that is more complex. But very often, when people say, "Let's keep the Church out of politics," they mean, "Let's keep it out of left-wing politics."

Lord Soper, in *Priestland's Progress*, Gerald Priestland, British Broadcasting Corporation, 1982, p.54.

Examining our own position—whatever it may be—from the Christian point of view we must come to the conclusion ... that, quite apart from our own personal interests,

we hold our accomplishments in trust from God to offer them in His service, and
that service on earth is, as Christ taught us so thoroughly, to bring happiness and
well-being to our fellow-men—to make our best contribution.

Sir Stafford Cripps, *God in our Work*, Thomas Nelson and Sons Ltd., 1949, p.4.

But the Church and the official representatives must keep themselves free from the
entanglements of party politics. There will come times when they should support or
resist a specific measure; but they should not take any share in the strife of parties.
Their business is something far more fundamental and important; it is the formation
of that mind and temper in the whole community which will lead to wholesome
legislation by any party and all parties.

William Temple, *The Kingdom of God*, Macmillan & Co. Ltd., 1912, p.89.

Christianity insists that man is an end because he is a child of God, made in God's
image. Man is more than a producing animal guided by economic forces; he is a being
of spirit, crowned with glory and honour, endowed with the gift of freedom. The
ultimate weakness of Communism is that it robs man of that quality which makes
him man. Man, says Paul Tillich, is man because he is free. This freedom is expressed
through man's capacity to deliberate, decide, and respond. Under Communism, the
individual soul is shackled by the chains of conformity; his spirit is bound by the
manacles of party allegiance. He is stripped of both conscience and reason.

Martin Luther King, *Strength to Love*, William Collins Sons & Co. Ltd., 1980, p.98.

I feel we are here to complement the political parties and knock their heads together
occasionally. I think the ministry of Christ is basically reconciliation, and there are
times when we can't afford party politics. Our movement is political, but it's non-
party-political. We want to get rid of this Red Clydeside image and present the image
of a reasonable community trying to work together. If man is made in God's image,
he's got to share in God's creative power—not just for his own benefit, but for the
benefit of all mankind and for the glory of God. He's got to develop his talents or
he's not fully human. Now if he's unemployed, what are we going to do about this?
He's going to become not an image but a caricature of God.

James McShane, in *Priestland's Progress*, Gerald Priestland, British Broadcasting Corporation, 1982, p.56.

Prayer and politics, far from being alternative modes of discipleship or even opposites,
are necessary to each other. If they are divided, the result is either a superficial "Christian radicalism" which stresses action and service at the expense of awe and vision, or
a pietism which reduces spirituality to the private sector.
At the turn of the century Nicolas Berdyaev observes that Christian piety had all too
often become a withdrawal from the world and from men, an unwillingness to share
human suffering. The world has risen in protest against this form of piety, this indifference to the world's sorrow. Yet against this protest Berdyaev insisted, only a reborn
piety can stand. The choice is not between spirituality and action, but between true
spirituality and false.
Christian prayer is rooted in a revolutionary vision, it is Kingdom-directed prayer. It
is therefore marked by a sense of unfulfilment, of yearning, of stretching out into the

future and tasting the powers of the age to come. It is never the prayer of security, ease, and the smug certainty. It is a crying out for the Kingdom that is coming. Prayer and politics meet at the point at which this vision of the new age comes into collision, as it must, with political structures based upon a different view of man and of human life. At the heart of our Gospel and our prayer there lies an inescapable core of conflict. This core of conflict is central to the Kingdom which must be the motive force and the visionary cumulus for Christian action.

Christian prayer is rooted also in the materiality of creation, incarnation, resurrection, and eucharist. It has a materialistic basis. Gnostic spirituality, so popular at present in the West, offers a way of living and praying which bypasses or despises the created order, and sees matter as an obstacle to the spiritual life. Christian prayer takes place within the framework of an incarnational theology which sees all matter as the potential vehicle of grace. This materialistic basis for prayer is of the greatest importance if we are to rescue Christian spirituality from the harmful influences of Neo-Platonism and other forms of dualism. The principle that grace comes through the flesh is central to orthodox Christianity. The centrality of the Eucharist in Christian worship involves the rejection of the false dichotomy between spirit and matter. Christian spirituality is a spirituality of broken bread and outpoured wine, an earthly, common spirituality. Christian prayer is concerned with insight. A central element in prayer is listening, waiting on God in silence, gazing on God, striving to see more clearly. This dimension of clarity and insight contrasts sharply with the blurring of vision and the obscuring of reality which comes through what the fourteenth-century mystic Ruysbroeck called "false vacancy." This sense of seeing more clearly is one of the essential criteria in discernment of true prayer from false.

Finally, Christian prayer is concerned with transformation. Many Christians accept that, at a personal level, grace changes and transforms us, that in Christ there is a new creation. But people do not exist in a vacuum, nor is the relationship between personal change and socio-political change a simple one of cause and effect. The Christian virtues of love, forgiveness, gentleness and so on are public virtues. The fruits of the Spirit cannot be insulated in a private realm cut off from the world of political reality.

There is then an inescapable link between prayer and politics, between the mystical and the prophetic dimensions of faith. The renewal to which we are being called today is basically concerned with the restoration of that lost unity. It is very probable that the decay of a genuine mystical life in the Western church has not been unconnected with the decay of prophetic witness. While many see these two traditions as poles apart, they are in fact very close. For without clear vision there can be no authentic struggle. The hands raised in prayer and the hands raised in revolt are often the same hands. Out of prayer comes the spirit of resistance. Karl Barth puts it well. "To clasp the hands in prayer is the beginning of an uprising against the disorder of the world."

Kenneth Leech, "The Meeting of Prayer and Politics," article in *The Times*, Saturday February 13, 1982.

POVERTY

Blessed are you poor, for yours is the kingdom of God.
Luke 6.20.

The greatest man in history was the poorest.
Ralph Waldo Emerson, *The Works of Ralph Waldo Emerson*, edited by George Sampson, George Bell & Sons, Ltd, 1906, Volume III, *Society and Solitude: Letters and Social Aims: Addresses*, p.62.

There is nothing perfectly secure but poverty.
Henry Wadsworth Longfellow, *Final Memorials*, edited by Samuel Longfellow, Ticknor and Company, 1887, p.197.

The town's poor seem to me often to live the most independent lives of any.
Henry David Thoreau, *Walden*, The New American Library of World Literature, Inc., 1960, p.218.

I want nothing whatever. I am quite happy.
William Blake, cited in Crabb Robinson's Diary for 10th December, 1825.

Oh Poverty, high wisdom! to be subject to nothing, and by despising all to possess all created things....
God will not lodge in a narrow heart; and it is as great as thy love. Poverty has so ample a bosom that Deity Itself may lodge therein....
Poverty is naught to have, and nothing to desire: but all things to possess in the spirit of liberty.
Jacopone da Todi, in *Mysticism*, Evelyn Underhill, Methuen & Co. Ltd, 1912, p.250, footnote, "Lauda," l.ix.

"Blessed are the poor in spirit" means: Blessed is the man who has realised his own utter helplessness, and has put his whole trust in God.
If a man has realised his own utter helplessness, and has put his whole trust in God, there will enter into his life two things which are opposite sides of the same thing. He will become completely *detached from things,* for he will know that things have not got it in them to bring happiness or security; and he will become completely *attached to God,* for he will know that God alone can bring him help, and hope, and strength. The man who is poor in spirit is the man who has realised that things mean nothing, and that God means everything.
William Barclay, *The Gospel of Matthew*, The Saint Andrew Press, 1974, Volume One, p.86.

Theologians and philosophers have no special expertise at all, except in the asking of awkward questions, and a certain acquaintance with the answers that men in past generations have offered themselves. But this is precisely why they are needed now, to ask us what our objects are, what we are aiming at, what sort of society we really want to create, what sort of people we really want to be....
The point I am trying to make is excellently illustrated by the moon landings. Nothing could demonstrate better the capacity of human hearts to accomplish what they set their hearts on, and their equal capacity to set their hearts on the wrong things. The moon landings are, of course, magnificent. But to the underprivileged, undernourished

two-thirds of the world they are a magnificent irrelevance. We are clever enough to reach the moon, but not sensible enough to share out the world's resources with anything approaching equity.

Henry McKeating, *Living with Guilt*, S.C.M. Press Ltd; 1970, p.65.

POWER

But as for me, I am filled with power, with the Spirit of the Lord, and with justice and might.

Micah 3.8.

All power is given unto me in heaven and earth.

Matthew 28.18 (A.V.).

But you shall receive power when the Holy Spirit has come upon you.

Acts 1.8.

Who will change our lowly body to be like his glorious body, by the power which enables him even to subject all things to himself.

Philippians 3.21.

May you be strengthened with all power, according to his glorious might, for all endurance and patience with joy, giving thanks to the Father, who has qualified us to share in the inheritance of the saints in light.

Colossians 1.11-12.

For God did not give us a spirit of timidity but a spirit of power and love and self-control.

2 Timothy 1.7.

Energy is Eternal Delight.

William Blake, *The Complete Writings of William Blake*, edited by Geoffrey Keynes, Oxford University Press, 1974, p.149, *The Marriage of Heaven and Hell*, Plate 4, "The voice of the Devil."

The strongest man in the world is the man who stands alone.

Henrik Ibsen, *An Enemy of the People*, translated and edited by James Walter McFarlane, Oxford University Press, 1960, Volume VI, p.126, Act V.

Patience and Gentleness is Power.

Leigh Hunt, *The Poetical Works of Leigh Hunt*, edited by H.S. Milford, Oxford University Press, 1923, p.247, Sonnet: "On a lock of Milton's hair."

Right and Truth are greater than any *Power;* and all Power is limited by Right.

Benjamin Whichcote, *Moral and Religious Aphrisms*, 1930, p.5, Century I, No.34.

From the summit of power men no longer turn their eyes upward, but begin to look about them.

J.R. Lowell, *Among My Books*, J.M. Dent & Sons Ltd., 1914, p.182, "New England Two Centuries Ago."

Concentration is the secret of strength in politics, in war, in trade, in short, in all management of human affairs.

Ralph Waldo Emerson, *The Conduct of Life, Nature and Other Essays,* J.M. Dent & Sons Ltd., 1911, p.186.

Self-reverence, self-knowledge, self-control,
These three alone lead life to sovereign power.

Alfred, Lord Tennyson, *The Poems of Tennyson,* edited by Christopher Ricks, Longmans, Green & Co. Ltd., 1969, p.392, No. 164, "Oenone," l.142.

To know the pains of power, we must go to those who have it; to know its pleasures, we must go to those who are seeking it: the pains of power are real, its pleasures imaginary.

C.C. Colton, *Lacon,* William Tegg, 1866, p.243.

Life engenders life. Energy creates energy. It is by spending oneself that one becomes rich.

Sarah Bernhardt, in *Madam Sarah,* Cornelia Otis Skinner, Michael Joseph Ltd., 1967, p.xvi.

We are the wire, God is the current. Our only power is to let the current pass through us. Of course, we have the power to interrupt it and say "no." But nothing more.

Carlo Carretto, *Letters from the Desert,* translated by Rose Mary Hancock, with a foreword by Ivan Illich, Darton, Longman & Todd Ltd., 1972, p.19.

A non-violent revolution is not a programme of "seizure of power." It is a programme of transformation of relationships ending in a peaceful transfer of power.

Mohandas K. Gandhi, *Non-Violence in Peace & War,* Navajivan Publishing House, 1949, Volume II, p.8.

He (Christ) stimulates us, as other great men stimulate us, but we find a power coming from Him into our lives that enables us to respond. That is the experience that proves Him to be the universal Spirit. It does not happen with others.

William Temple, *Christian Faith and Life,* S.C.M. Press Ltd., 1963, p.45.

Justice without might is helpless; might without justice is tyrannical... We must then combine justice and might, and for this end make what is just strong, or what is strong just.

Blaise Pascal, *Pensées,* translated by W.F. Trotter, Random House Inc., 1941, p.103.

Give me the strength lightly to bear my joys and sorrows.
Give me the strength to make my love fruitful in service.
Give me the strength never to disown the poor or bend my knees before insolent might.
Give me the strength to raise my mind high above daily trifles.
And give me the strength to surrender my strength to thy will with love.

Rabindranath Tagore, *Gitanjali,* Macmillan & Co. Ltd., 1971, p.28.

You have lost the knack of drawing strength from God: and vain strivings after communion of the *solitude à deux* sort will do nothing for you at this point. Seek contact with Him now in the goodness and splendour which is in other people, in *all* people, for those who have the art to find it.

Evelyn Underhill, *The Letters of Evelyn Underhill,* edited with an introduction by Charles Williams, Longmans, Green & Co. Ltd., 1947, p.98.

Be still and cool in thy own mind and spirit from thy own thoughts, and then thou wilt feel the principle of God to turn thy mind to the Lord God, whereby thou wilt receive his strength and power from whence life comes, to allay all tempests, against blusterings and storms. That is it which moulds up into patience, into innocency, into soberness, into stillness, into stayedness, into quietness, up to God, with his power.

George Fox, *The Journal of George Fox,* a revised edition by John L. Nickalls, Cambridge at the University Press, 1952, p.346.

At the highest point of his inner self, his soul, man is more God than creature: however much he is the same as creature in his nature, in mind he is like God more than any creature. To the soul at rest in God in her potential, her essential, intellectual nature, everything comes natural as though she were created not at the will of something else but solely at her own. In this point creatures are her subjects, all submitting to her as though they were her handiwork. It was in this power the birds obeyed St. Francis and listened to his preaching. And Daniel took refuge in this power, trusting himself to God alone, when he sat among the lions. Moreover, in this power it has been the custom of the saints to offer up their sufferings which, in the greatness of their love, are to them no suffering.

Meister Eckhart, *Meister Eckhart,* Franz Pfeiffer, translated by C. de B. Evans, John M. Watkins, 1956, Volume I, p.290.

What then does Pentecost represent? What change is effected by the outpouring of the Spirit?

The change lies in the relation of the Holy Spirit to the human spirit. This relation was made quite new. Previously the Holy Spirit had acted on men from without, like an external force; as the prophet Ezekiel describes it, "the hand of the Lord was upon me." But now the Holy Spirit acts from within. He is in man (Jn xiv. 17). Before Pentecost his manifestations had been transient and exceptional: now his presence in man's heart is an "abiding" one and regular. This change had become possible because the Holy Spirit is "the Spirit of Jesus" (Jn xvi. 7). It was the union of the divine and human natures in the person of Jesus Christ which first made it possible for the divine Spirit to dwell in a human personality. When the Word was made flesh, the Holy Ghost became the Spirit of the man Jesus; and now that Jesus was glorified the Spirit of Jesus was become the Spirit of consummated humanity, and through the channel of that humanity he could be poured out upon the brethren of Jesus. This new presence of the Spirit has also a corresponding effect on human society. Being the Spirit of the Son of Man, the church which his indwelling creates is a universal church: no longer the church of a small select race but the church of humanity.

On earth then the day of Pentecost marks the beginning of this new relation. It is the beginning of the new spiritual life of the church—its second birth. And the characteristic of this life is Power. A transformation takes place, the apostles are new men, all fear of the Jews is gone. Peter, but now afraid of a servant girl, stands up boldly before all the people. The apostles' tongues are loosed and three thousand are converted. The work of the church begins.

R.B. Rackham, *The Acts of the Apostles,* Methuen & Co. Ltd., 1901, p.14.

PRAISE

Thou awakest us to delight in Thy praise.

St. Augustine, *The Confessions of St. Augustine,* revised from a former translation by the Rev. E.B. Pusey, Library of the Fathers, Volume I, J.G. and F. Rivington, 1838, p.1.

The whole wood-world is one full peal of praise.

Alfred, Lord Tennyson, *The Poems of Tennyson,* edited by Christopher Ricks, Longmans, Green & Co. Ltd., 1969, p.1588, No.468, Balin and Balan, l.444.

Praised be God who has given us a mind that cannot be satisfied with the temporal.

Nicolas Cusanus, *Of Learned Ignorance,* translated by Fr. Germain Heron, Routledge & Kegan Paul Ltd., 1954, p.168.

Our meditation in this present life should be in the praise of God; for the eternal exultation of our life hereafter will be the praise of God; and none can become fit for the future life, who hath not practiced himself for it now.

St. Augustine, *An Augustine Synthesis,* arranged by Erich Przywara, S.J., Sheed and Ward Ltd., 1945, p.397.

What else can a lame old man as I am do but chant the praise of God? If, indeed, I were a nightingale I should sing as a nightingale, if a swan, as a swan: but as I am a rational creature I must praise God. This is my task, and I do it: and I will not abandon this duty, so long as it is given me; and I invite you all to join in this same song.

Epictetus, *The Stoic and Epicurean Philosophers,* edited, with an introduction by Witney J. Oates, Random House Inc., 1940, p.253.

Man's chief work is but to praise God. To Him it belongs to satisfy thee by His beauty, to thee to praise Him in acts of thanksgiving. If thy works be not the praise of God, thou art beginning to love thyself.... Be dissatisfied with thyself; find satisfaction in Him Who made thee, in that thou art dissatisfied with that in thee which thou thyself hast made. Let therefore thy work be the praise of God. For it is not He that increaseth by our praise, but we. God is neither the better if thou praise Him, nor worse if thou disparage Him; but thou, by praising Him that is good, art the better; by disparaging thou art the worse, for He remaineth good, as He is.

St. Augustine, *An Augustine Synthesis,* arranged by Erich Przywara, S.J., Sheed and Ward Ltd., 1945, p.398.

We should praise God by means of everything that we can offer to Him. To praise God, means that all his life long a man glorifies, reverences and venerates the Divine Omnipotence. The praise of God is the meet and proper work of the angels and the saints in heaven, and of loving men on earth. God should be praised by desire, by the lifting up of all our powers, by words, by works, with body and with soul, and with whatsoever one possesses; in humble service, from without and from within. He who does not praise God while here on earth shall in eternity be dumb. To praise God is the dearest and most joyous work of every loving heart; and the heart which is full of praise desires that every creature should praise God. The praise of God has no end, for it is our bliss; and most justly shall we praise Him in eternity.

John of Ruysbroeck, *The Adornment of the Spiritual Marriage,* translated by C.A. Wynshenk Dom, edited with an introduction and notes by Evelyn Underhill, John M. Watkins, 1951, p.65.

We are on retreat. Very cold morning.... I left for the woods before dawn, after a conference on sin. Pure dark sky, with only the crescent moon and planets shining: the moon and Venus over the barns, and Mars over in the west over the hills and the fire tower.
Sunrise is an event that calls forth solemn music in the very depths of man's nature, as if one's whole being had to attune itself to the cosmos and praise God for the new day, praise Him in the name of all the creatures that ever were or ever will be. I look at the rising sun and feel that now upon me falls the responsibility of seeing what all my ancestors have seen, in the Stone Age and even before it, praising God before me. Whether or not they praised Him then, for themselves, they must praise Him now in me. When the sun rises each one of us is summoned by the living and the dead to praise God.

Thomas Merton, *Conjectures of a Guilty Bystander,* Burns & Oates Ltd., 1968, p.256.

As it becometh you to retain a glorious sense of the world, because the Earth and the Heavens and the Heaven of Heavens are the magnificent and glorious territories of God's Kingdom, so are you to remember always the unsearchable extent and illimited greatness of your own soul; the length and breadth and depth, and height of your own understanding. Because it is the House of God, a Living Temple, and a Glorious Throne of the Blessed Trinity: far more magnificent and great than the Heavens; yea, a person that in Union and Communion with God, is to see Eternity, to fill His Omnipresence, to possess His greatness, to admire His love; to receive His gifts, to enjoy the world, and to live in His Image. Let all your actions proceed from a sense of this greatness, let all your affections extend to this wideness, let all your prayers be animated by this spirit and let all your praises arise and ascend from this fountain. For you are never your true self, till you live by your soul more than by your body, and you never live by your soul till you feel its incomparable excellency, and rest satisfied and delighted in the unsearchable greatness of its comprehension.

Thomas Traherne, *Centuries,* The Faith Press Ltd., 1969, p.100.

PRAYER

And in the morning, a great while before day, he rose and went out to a lonely place, and there he prayed.

Mark 1.35.

But when you pray, go into your room and shut the door and pray to your Father who is in secret.

Matthew 6.6.

You pray in your distress and in your need; would that you might pray also in the fullness of your joy and in your days of abundance.

Kahlil Gibran, *The Prophet*, William Heinemann Ltd., 1970, p.78.

Prayer is the nearest approach to God, and the highest enjoyment of Him, that we are capable of in this life.

William Law, *A Serious Call to a Devout and Holy Life*, J.M. Dent & Co., 1898, p.191.

Prayer, crystallised in words, assigns a permanent wavelength on which the dialogue has to be continued, even when our mind is occupied with other matters.

Dag Hammarskjold, *Markings*, translated by Leif Sjoberg and W.H. Auden, with a foreword by W.H. Auden, Faber and Faber Limited, 1964, p.97.

Lift up your heart to Him, sometimes even at your meals and when you are in company; the least little remembrance will always be acceptable to Him. You need not cry very loud; He is nearer to us than we are aware of.

Brother Lawrence, *The Practice of the Presence of God*, A.R. Mowbray & Co. Ltd., 1977, p.47.

Prayer is not an old woman's idle amusement. Properly understood and applied, it is the most potent instrument of action.

Mohandas K. Gandhi, *Non-Violence in Peace & War*, Navajivan Publishing House, 1949, Volume II, p.77.

In our Lord's teaching about petitionary prayer there are three main principles. The first is confidence, the second is perseverence and the third, for lack of a better word, I will call correspondence with Christ.

William Temple, *Christian Faith and Life*, S.C.M. Press Ltd., 1963, p.115.

He prayeth best, who loveth best
All things both great and small;
For the dear God who loveth us,
He made and loveth all.

Samuel Taylor Coleridge, *Coleridge, Poetry & Prose*, edited by Stephen Potter, The Nonesuch Press, p.57, *The Ancient Mariner*, Pt.VII. st.xlvii.

The Lord's prayer is the prayer above all prayers, a prayer which the most high Master taught us, wherein are comprehended all spiritual and temporal blessings, and the strongest comforts in all trials, temptations, and troubles, even in the hour of death.

Martin Luther, *Table-Talk*, translated and edited by William Hazlitt, George Bell & Sons Ltd., 1895, p.125.

Believe and trust that as it is easy for you to breathe the air and live by it, or to eat and drink, so it is easy and even still easier for your faith to receive all spiritual gifts from the Lord. Prayer is the breathing of the soul; prayer is our spiritual food and drink.

John of Cronstadt, in *A Treasury of Russian Spirituality*, edited by G.P. Fedotov, Sheed & Ward Ltd., 1977, p.354.

Prayer is a fundamental style of thinking, passionate and compassionate, responsible and thankful, that is deeply rooted in our humanity and that manifests itself not only among believers but also among serious-minded people who do not profess any religious faith.

John Macquarrie, *Paths in Spirituality*, S.C.M. Press Ltd., 1972, p.30.

The word "prayer" is applied to at least four distinct procedures—petition, intercession, adoration, contemplation. Petition is the asking of something for ourselves. Intercession is the asking of something for other people. Adoration is the use of intellect, feeling, will and imagination in making acts of devotion directed towards God in his personal aspect or as incarnated in human form. Contemplation is that condition of alert passivity in which the soul lays itself open to the divine Ground within and without, the immanent and transcendent Godhead.

Aldous Huxley, *The Perennial Philosophy*, Chatto & Windus Ltd., 1974, p.251.

He knows what we want before we ask it. Then why ask? Why, because there may be blessings which only are effectively blessings to those who are in the right condition of mind; just as there is wholesome food which is actually wholesome only to those who are healthy in body. If you give the best beef to somebody in typhoid fever, you do him great harm. The worst of all diseases of the soul is forgetfulness of God; and if everything that we need came to us while we forgot God, we should only be confirmed in our forgetfulness of Him, in our sense of independence of Him.... Over and over again, it will happen that, whether or not God can give the blessing which, in His love, He desires to give, will depend on whether or not we recognise the source from which it comes. The way to recognise that He is the source of the blessings, and that we need them, is to ask.

William Temple, *Christian Faith and Life*, S.C.M. Press Ltd., 1963, p.111.

If we ask of the saints how they achieved spiritual effectiveness, they are only able to reply that, in so far as they did it themselves, they did it by love and prayer. A love that is very humble and homely; a prayer that is full of adoration and of confidence. Love and prayer, on their lips, are not mere nice words; they are the names of tremendous powers, able to transform in a literal sense human personality and make it more and more that which it is meant to be—the agent of the Holy Spirit in the world. Plainly then, it is essential to give time or to get time somehow for self-training in this love and this prayer. It is true that in their essence they are "given," but the gift is only fully made our own by a patient and generous effort of the soul. Spiritual achievement costs much, though never as much as it is worth. It means at the very least the painful development and persevering, steady exercise of a faculty that most of us have allowed to get slack. It means an inward if not an outward asceticism: a virtual if not an actual mysticism.

People talk about mysticism as if it were something quite separate from practical religion; whereas, as a matter of fact, it is the intense heart of all practical religion, and no-one without some touch of it is contagious and able to win souls.

What *is* mysticism? It is in its widest sense the reaching out of the soul to contact with those eternal realities which are the subject matter of religion. And the mystical life is the complete life of love and prayer which transmutes those objects of belief into living realities.

Evelyn Underhill, *Concerning the Inner Life,* Methuen & Co. Ltd., 1926, p.31.

I had spent some weeks or months without saying any prayers because I had come to consider them a useless waste of time. But everything else seemed to be becoming also a useless waste of time, excepting always the seeing of beauty in nature and the attempt to fix something of it on paper. But it seemed a funny thing that this should be the object for which life was given to us, and I began to wonder how one could find out what one was really put here for; and then it struck me that in the New Testament, and especially in the teaching of Christ, one might be able to write down in one's own words once and for all whatever definite directions one could make out from His teaching. Then, whatever the disciples gave us. So I started a book, and wrote down Christ's directions for life, and then the apostles' and disciples', word for word when the meaning was clear, and my own reading of whatever wasn't clear. Well, I have done this off and on now for a year, and my insight into the meaning of the Gospels has increased enormously, and though there are many directions which are definite and many which are contradictory, it seems to me that across every page may be written as a summary of its teaching— *Love one another* in Truth and Purity, as children, impulsively and uncalculatingly, not with reasoning and quibbling over what is the best way under the circumstances, but as though I were alone with God in everyone I met, not influenced therefore by any human law or convention, but faithfully offering them a true love in act and example, and at all costs to myself. Offer them the best, let them take it or leave it, never the second best or half best or best under the circumstances, but the best always.

Edward Wilson, in *The Faith of Edward Wilson,* George Seaver, John Murray Ltd., 1949, p.16.

PREACHING

For I will not venture to speak of anything except what Christ has wrought through me.

Romans 15.18.

Preach the word, be urgent in season and out of season, convince, rebuke, and exhort, be unfailing in patience and in teaching.

2 Timothy 4.2.

I like the silent church before the service begins, better than any preaching.

Ralph Waldo Emerson, *Essays,* Bernhard Tauchnitz Edition, 1915, p.52, "Self-Reliance."

A good honest and painful sermon.

Samuel Pepys, *The Diary of Samuel Pepys,* edited by Robert Latham and William Matthews, G. Bell and Sons Ltd., 1970, Volume II, 1661, p.55.

Every man is a priest, even involuntarily; his conduct is an unspoken sermon, which is for ever preaching to others.

Henry Frédéric Amiel, *Amiel's Journal,* translated by Mrs. Humphry Ward, Macmillan & Co. Ltd., 1918, p.25.

The design of preaching is to lead men into the experience of eternal life, to bring them into contact with the promised life of God.

William Barclay, *The Plain Man Looks at the Apostles' Creed,* William Collins Sons & Co. Ltd., 1967, p.376.

The best preaching is a fruit of constant pastoral visiting; it springs out of the relationship between pastor and people.

William Temple, *Readings in St. John's Gospel* (First and Second Series), Macmillan & Co. Ltd., 1947, p.167.

The pencil of the Holy Ghost hath laboured more in describing the afflictions of Job than the felicities of Solomon.

Francis Bacon, *The Moral and Historical Works of Francis Bacon,* introductory dissertation and notes (critical, explanatory, and historical), by Joseph Devey, Henry G. Bohn, 1852, p.14.

One may sometimes attend Church for a year, and hear excellent discourses on international peace, on industrial justice, on civil liberties, sex relations, social ethics in every phase; but rarely or never a word to help one's poor little old soul in its effort to enter into commerce with the Eternal.

Vida D. Scudder, *The Privilege of Age,* J.M. Dent & Sons Ltd., 1939, p.216.

The preacher possesses no magical efficacy. His only power lies in his spiritual experience, his clarified vision, and his organic connection with Christ the Head of the Church and the source of its energy. If his life is spiritually poor and weak and thin, if it lacks moral passion and insight, his ministry will be correspondingly ineffective and futile, for the dynamic spiritual impact of a life is in proportion to its personal experience and its moral capacity to transmit divine power.

Rufus M. Jones, *Spiritual Reformers in the 16th and 17th Centuries,* Macmillan & Co. Ltd., 1914, p.79.

His (John Everard) new way of preaching—vivid, concrete, touched with subtle humour, grounded in experience and filling old texts with new meaning—appealed powerfully to the common people and to an elect few of the more highly privileged who had won a large enough freedom of spirit to go with him into new paths.... he poured out the best he had in his treasury to any, even the simplest and most ordinary, who cared to hear of this "spiritual, practical experiment of life."

Rufus M. Jones, *Spiritual Reformers in the 16th and 17th Centuries,* Macmillan & Co. Ltd., 1914, p.240.

He only is able to declare with spirit and power any truths or bear a faithful testimony of the reality of them who preaches nothing but what he has first seen and felt and found to be true by a living sensibility and true experience of their reality and power

in his own soul. All other preaching, whether from art, hearsay, books, or education,
is, at best, but playing with words and mere trifling with sacred things.

William Law, *Selected Mystical Writings of William Law,* edited by Stephen Hobhouse, Rockliff, 1948, p.118.

There is an old story of a boy who joined the Franciscan Order longing to become a friar preacher. He was put to work in the kitchen for the first months and got more and more restive and impatient to get on with learning to preach. Finally Francis himself drew him by the arm one day and asked him if he would like to go into the village with him to preach. The boy's heart was full as they set out. They stopped on the way to see a man whose son needed work in the town, then to call on an old woman who was sick and lonely, and to visit with a peasant at work in the fields. In the town, they saw a merchant about a post for the son, they begged some food for the brothers at home, they talked with some people in the market place, and then Francis turned to the boy and gaily proposed that they return to the friary. "But when are we going to preach?" asked the boy in an anguish of concern. Francis slipped his arm about him and said, "Why, my brother, we've been preaching all the time."

Douglas Steere, *Where Words Come From,* Swarthmore Lecture, 1955, George Allen & Unwin Ltd., p.47.

PRESENCE

Fear not, for I am with you, be not dismayed, for I am your God; I will strengthen
you, I will help you, I will uphold you with my victorious right hand.

Isaiah 41.10.

I am with you always, to the close of the age.

Matthew 28.20.

If you abide in me, and my words abide in you, ask whatever you will, and it shall
be done for you.

John 15.7.

All who keep his commandments abide in him, and he in them. And by this we know
that he abides in us, by the Spirit which he has given us.

1 John 3.24.

Though God be everywhere present, yet He is only present to Thee in the deepest,
and most central Part of thy Soul.

William Law, *The Spirit of Prayer,* full text, edited with an introduction and notes by Sidney Spencer, James Clarke & Co. Ltd., 1969, p.44.

Speak to Him thou for He hears, and Spirit with Spirit can meet—
Closer is He than breathing, and nearer than hands and feet.

Alfred, Lord Tennyson, *The Poems of Tennyson,* edited by Christopher Ricks, Longmans, Green & Co. Ltd., 1969, p.1205, No.353, "The Higher Pantheism," l.11.

The doctrine of the presence of God, to be realized here and now, should give to the habitually unhappy both the light to see what Christian hope is all about and the grace to act upon this light.

Hubert van Zeller, *Considerations,* Sheed & Ward Ltd., 1974, p.100.

The time of business does not with me differ from the time of prayer; and in the noise and clutter of my kitchen, while several persons are at the same time calling for different things, I possess God in as great tranquillity as if I were upon my knees at the Blessed Sacrament.

Brother Lawrence, *The Practice of the Presence of God,* A.R. Mowbray & Co. Ltd., 1977, p.23.

The practice of the presence of God may involve very many hours of hard work; but the reward is great; for this is the joy that no man can take from us; this is the faith which is the human of side divine grace, an experiment which is becoming an experience, a foretaste and assurance of the rest that remaineth for the people of God.

W.R. Inge, *Personal Religion and the Life of Devotion,* Longmans, Green and Co. Ltd., 1924, p.32.

What if it be true that the key to the correct understanding of the Second Coming is indeed to be found in John's Gospel in the words which tell how Father and Son will come and make their dwelling in the loving and the obedient heart? (John 14.23). The cosmic upheaval may well stand for the destruction of the old life and the creation of the new when Christ enters into life. The judgement may well stand for the confrontation of the soul with Christ. The blessedness may well stand for the new life which is the life lived in Christ. For us it may well be that the Second Coming is not meant to be a dream of the future but a challenge to each individual Christian to make that sort of submission which will bring the coming again of the Spirit and the presence of Jesus Christ into his own soul.

William Barclay, *The Plain Man Looks at the Apostles' Creed,* William Collins Sons & Co. Ltd., 1967, p.197.

You ought to know yourself as you really are ... so that you may understand of what nature you are and whence you have come into this world, and for what purpose you were created, and in what your happiness and your misery consist, for within you are combined the qualities of the animals and the wild beasts and the angels, but the spirit is your real essence and all beside it is, in fact, foreign to you.... So strive for the knowledge of your origin, so that you may know how to attain to the Divine Presence and the contemplation of the Divine Majesty and Beauty, and deliver yourself from the fetters of lust and passion ... for God did not create you to be their captive, but that they should be your thralls, under your control, for the journey which is before you, to be your steed and your weapon, so that you may therewith pursue your happiness and then cast them under your feet.

Al-Ghazali, in *Al-Ghazali, The Mystic,* Margaret Smith, Luzac & Co., 1944, p.151.

In those rare glimpses of Christ's own life and prayer which the Gospels vouchsafe to us, we always notice the perpetual reference to the unseen Father; so much more vividly present to Him than anything that is seen. Behind that daily life into which He entered so generously, filled as it was with constant appeals to His practical pity and help, there is ever the sense of that strong and tranquil Presence, ordering all things and bringing them to their appointed end; not with a rigid and mechanical precision, but with the freedom of a living, creative, cherishing thought and love. Throughout His life, the secret, utterly obedient conversation of Jesus with His Father goes on. He always snatches opportunities for it, and at every crisis He returns to it as the unique source of confidence and strength; the right and reasonable relation between the soul and its source.

Evelyn Underhill, *Abba*, Longmans, Green & Co. Ltd., 1940, p.12.

It is easier to attain knowledge of this presence by personal experience than by reading books, for it is life and love, strength and light, joy and peace to a chosen soul. A soul that has once experienced it cannot therefore lose it without pain; it cannot cease to desire it, because it is so good in itself, and brings such comfort....
The awareness of special grace that accompanies the invisible presence of God and makes the soul perfect in love, does not always continue at its highest intensity, but comes and goes unpredictably.... Sometimes He comes secretly when you are least aware of Him, but you will recognize Him unmistakably before He goes, for He stirs your heart in a wonderful way, and moves it strongly to contemplate His goodness. Then your heart melts with delight at the tenderness of His love like wax before the fire, and this is the sound of His voice.

Walter Hilton, *The Ladder of Perfection*, translated with an introduction by Leo Sherley-Price, Penguin Books Ltd., 1957, p.233.

I went out one afternoon for a walk alone. I was in the empty unthinking state in which one saunters along country lanes, simply yielding oneself to the casual sights around which give a town-bred lad with country yearnings such intense delight. Suddenly I became conscious of the presence of some one else. I cannot describe it, but I felt that I had as direct a perception of the being of God all about me as I have of you when we are together. It was no longer a matter of inference, it was an immediate act of spiritual (or whatever adjective you like to employ) apprehension. It came unsought, absolutely. I remember the wonderful transfiguration of the far-off woods and hills as they seemed to blend in the infinite being with which I was thus brought into relation. This experience did not last long. But it sufficed to change all my feeling. I had not found God because I had never looked for him. But He had found me; he had, I could not but believe, made himself personally known to me. I had not gone in search of a satisfying emotion, I did not work myself up into this state by any artificial means. But I felt that God had come to me, I could now not only believe in him with my mind, but love him with my heart. I cannot tell you how often this has come back to me both with thankfulness and with humiliation.... I am often perplexed to know why such revealings do not come to other souls. But I cannot regard this as a mere piece of romanticism, though I shall not be surprised or offended if you do. This event has never happened to me again.... It was not necessary. The sense of a direct relation to God then generated in my soul has become a part of my habitual thought and feeling.

Joseph Carpenter, *Joseph Estlin Carpenter*, edited by C.H. Herford, Oxford at the Clarendon Press, 1929, p.9.

PRIDE

The beginning of human pride is to desert the Lord, and to turn one's heart away
from one's maker.
Since the beginning of pride is sin, whoever clings to it will pour forth filth.
Ecclesiasticus 10.12-13 (Jerusalem Bible).

A *Proud* man hath no *God*.
Benjamin Whichcote, *Morals and Religious Aphorisms*, 1930, p.90, Century IX, No.801.

Pride is over-estimation of oneself by reason of self-love.
Spinoza, *Spinoza's Ethics and De Intellectus Emendatione*, introduction by T.S. Gregory, J.M. Dent & Sons Ltd.,
1955, p.134.

Evil can have no beginning, but from pride; nor any end, but from humility.
William Law, *Selected Mystical Writings of William Law*, edited by Stephen Hobhouse, Rockliff, 1948, p.107.

Pride is therefore pleasure arising from a man's thinking too highly of himself.
Spinoza, *Spinoza's Ethics and De Intellectus Emendatione*, introduction by T.S. Gregory, J.M. Dent & Sons Ltd.,
1955, p.102.

The whole trouble is that we won't let God help us.
George Macdonald, *The Marquis of Lossie*, Everett & Co. Ltd., 1912, p.91.

There are two states or conditions of pride. The first is one of self-approval, the second
one of self-contempt. Pride is seen probably at its purest in the last.
Henri Frédéric Amiel, *Amiel's Journal*, translated by Mrs. Humphry Ward, Macmillan & Co. Ltd., 1918, p.45.

Every good thought that we have, every good action that we do, lays us open to pride,
and exposes us to the assaults of vanity and self-satisfaction.
William Law, *A Serious Call to a Devout and Holy Life*, J.M. Dent & Co. Ltd., 1898, p.246.

He that is proud eats up himself: pride is his own glass, his own trumpet, his own
chronicle; and whatever praises itself, but in the deed, devours the deed in the praise.
William Shakespeare, *Troilus and Cressida*, Act II. sc.iii. 1.156.

Of all the Causes which conspire to blind
Man's erring Judgement, and misguide the Mind,
What the weak Head with strongest Byass rules,
Is *Pride*, the *never failing Vice of Fools*.
Alexander Pope, *The Poems of Alexander Pope*, Volume I, *Pastoral Poetry and An Essay on Criticism*, edited by E.
Audra and Aubrey Williams, Methuen & Co. Ltd., 1961, p.263, "An Essay on Criticism," 1.201.

Nothing hath separated us from God but our own will, or rather our own will is our
separation from God.... The fall of man brought forth the kingdom of this world; sin
in all shapes is nothing else but the will of man driving on in a state of self-motion
and self-government, following the workings of a nature broken off from its dependency

upon, and union with, the divine will. All the evil and misery in the creation arises
only and solely from this one cause.

William Law, *Selected Mystical Writings of William Law,* edited by Stephen Hobhouse, Rockliff, 1948, p.25,29.

There is one vice of which no man in the world is free; which every one in the world
loathes when he sees it in someone else; and of which hardly any people, except
Christians, ever imagine that they are guilty themselves....
The essential vice, the utmost evil, is Pride. Unchastity, anger, greed, drunkenness,
and all that, are mere fleabites in comparison: it was through Pride that the devil
became the devil: Pride leads to every other vice: it is the complete anti-God state of
mind....
If I am a proud man, then, as long as there is one man in the whole world more
powerful, or richer, or cleverer than I, he is my rival and my enemy....
As long as you are proud you cannot know God. A proud man is always looking down
on things and people: and, of course, as long as you are looking down, you cannot
see something that is above you....
The real test of being in the presence of God is that you either forget about yourself
altogether or see yourself as a small, dirty object. It is better to forget about yourself
altogether.

C.S. Lewis, *Mere Christianity,* William Collins Sons & Co. Ltd., 1961, p.106.

Does the world as a whole possess the value and meaning that we constantly attribute
to certain parts of it (such as human beings and their works); and, if so, what is the
nature of that value and meaning? This is a question which, a few years ago, I should
not even have posed. For, like so many of my contemporaries, I took it for granted
that there was no meaning. This was partly due to the fact that I shared the common
belief that the scientific picture of an abstraction from reality was a true picture of
reality as a whole; partly also to other, non-intellectual reasons. I had motives for not
wanting the world to have a meaning; consequently assumed that it had none, and
was able without any difficulty to find satisfying reasons for this assumption.
Most ignorance is vincible ignorance. We don't know because we don't want to know.
It is our will that decides how and upon what subjects we shall use our intelligence.
Those who detect no meaning in the world generally do so because, for one reason or
another, it suits their books that the world should be meaningless....
For myself, as, no doubt, for most of my contemporaries, the philosophy of meaninglessness was essentially an instrument of liberation. The liberation we desired was
simultaneously liberation from a certain political and economic system and liberation
from a certain system of morality. We objected to the morality because it interfered
with our sexual freedom.

Aldous Huxley, *Ends and Means,* Chatto and Windus Ltd., 1965, p.269.

PROGRESS

I consider that the way of life in urbanised, rich countries, as it exists today, and as it is likely to go on developing, is probably the most degraded and unillumined ever to come to pass on earth.

Malcolm Muggeridge, *Jesus Rediscovered,* William Collins Sons & Co. Ltd., 1982, p.52.

So long as all the increased wealth which modern progress brings goes but to build up great fortunes, to increase luxury and make sharper the contrast between the House of Have and the House of Want, progress is not real and cannot be permanent.

Henry George, *Progress and Poverty,* Kegan Paul & Co., 1881, p.9.

It is therefore the opinion of the present writer that even in this age there are no supersonic flights to the Celestial City or even to the Palace Beautiful. Increased awareness can be obtained only by a journey on foot by way of the Slough of Despond, the Hill of Difficulty, Doubting Castle, and the rest.

H.A. Williams, in *Soundings,* edited by A.R. Vidler, Cambridge at the University Press, 1962, p.72.

A man's ability to be a pioneer of progress, that is, to understand what civilization is and to work for it, depends, therefore, on his being a thinker and on his being free. He must be the former if he is to be capable of comprehending his ideals and putting them into shape. He must be free in order to be in a position to launch his ideals out into the general life. The more completely his activities are taken up in any way by the struggle for existence, the more strongly will the impulse to improve his own condition find expression in the ideals of his thought. Ideals of self-interest then get mixed up with and spoil his ideals of civilization. Material and spiritual freedom are closely bound up with one another. Civilization presupposes free men, for only by free men can it be thought out and brought to realization.

Albert Schweitzer, *The Philosophy of Civilization,* Part I, "The Decay and Restoration of Civilization," translated by C.T. Campion, A. & C. Black Ltd., 1932, p.16.

When a Christian hath begun to think of spiritual progress, he beginneth to suffer from the tongues of adversaries. Whoever hath not yet suffered from these, hath not yet made progress; and whoever suffereth them not, doth not even endeavour to progress. Doth he wish to know what we mean? Let him experience at the same time what we have to listen to. Let him begin to progress, let him begin to wish to ascend, to wish to despise earthly, perishable, temporal things, to hold the happiness of this world as nothing, to think of God alone, not to rejoice in gain, not to pine at losses, to wish to sell all his goods and give them to the poor, and to follow Christ; let us see how he suffereth the tongues of detractors and many things from opponents, and— a still graver thing—the efforts of pretended counsellors who lead him away from salvation.

St. Augustine, *An Augustine Synthesis,* arranged by Erich Przywara, S.J., Sheed & Ward Ltd., 1945, p.430.

The world is a-building. This is the basic truth which must first be understood so thoroughly that it becomes an habitual and as it were natural springboard for our thinking. At first sight, beings and their destinies might seem to us to be scattered haphazard or at least in an arbitrary fashion over the face of the earth; we could very easily suppose that each of us might *equally well* have been born earlier or later, at this place or that, happier or more ill-starred, as though the universe from the beginning to end of it's history formed in space-time a sort of vast flower-bed in which the flowers could be changed about at the whim of the gardener. But this idea is surely untenable. The more one reflects, with the help of all that science, philosophy and religion can teach us, each in its own field, the more one comes to realize that the world should be likened not to a bundle of elements artificially held together but rather to some organic system animated by a broad movement of development which is proper to itself. As the centuries go by it seems that a comprehensive plan is indeed being slowly carried out around us. A process is at work in the universe, an issue is at stake, which can best be compared to the processes of gestation and birth; the birth of that spiritual reality which is formed by souls and by such material reality as their existence involves. Laboriously, through and thanks to the activities of mankind, the new earth is being formed and purified and is taking on definition and clarity. No, we are not like the cut flowers that make us a bouquet: we are like the leaves and buds of a great tree on which everything appears at its proper time and place as required and determined by the good of the whole.

Pierre Teilhard de Chardin, *Hymn of the Universe,* William Collins Sons & Co. Ltd., 1961, p.92.

In the great mystics we see the highest and widest development of that consciousness to which the human race has yet attained. We see its growth exhibited to us on a grand scale, perceptible to all men.... The germ of that same transcendent life, the spring of the amazing energy which enables the great mystic to rise to freedom and dominate his world, is latent in all of us; an integral part of our humanity. Where the mystic has a genius for the Absolute, we have each a little buried talent, some greater, some less; and the growth of this talent, this spark of the soul, once we permit its emergence, will conform in little, and according to its measure, to those laws of organic growth, those inexorable conditions of transcendence which we found to govern the Mystic Way.

Every person, then, who awakens to consciousness of a Reality which transcends the normal world of sense ... is put of necessity upon a road which follows at low levels the path which the mystic treads at high levels....

I do not care whether the consciousness be that of artist or musician, striving to catch and fix some aspect of the heavenly light or music, and denying all other aspects of the world in order to devote themselves to this: or of the humble servant of Science, purging his intellect that he may look upon her secrets with innocence of eye: whether the higher reality be perceived in the terms of religion, beauty, suffering; of human love, of goodness, or of truth. However widely these forms of transcendence may seem to differ, the mystic experience is the key to them all....

Each brings the self who receives its revelation in good faith, does not check it by self-regarding limitations, to a humble acceptance of the universal law of knowledge: the law that "we behold that which we are"; and hence that "only the Real can know

Reality." Awakening, Discipline, Enlightenment, Self-surrender, and Union, are the essential processes of life's response to this fundamental fact: the conditions of our attainment of Being....

Evelyn Underhill, *Mysticism*, Methuen & Co. Ltd., 1912, p.532.

PROPHETS

If there is a prophet among you, I the Lord make myself known to him in a vision, I will speak with him in a dream.

Numbers 12.6.

Prophecy consists in catching the best of God's thoughts and telling them.

Charles H. Parkhurst, *The Pattern in the Mount and Other Sermons*, R.D. Dickinson, 1890, p.14.

Every honest man is a Prophet; he utters his opinion both of private & public matters. Thus: If you go on So, the result is So. He nevers says, such a thing shall happen let you do what you will. A Prophet is a seer, not an Arbitrary Dictator.

William Blake, *The Complete Writings of William Blake*, edited by Geoffrey Keynes, Oxford University Press, 1974, p.392, Annotations to Watson.

The prophet is primarily the man, not to whom God has communicated certain divine thoughts, but whose mind is illuminated by the divine spirit to interpret aright the divine acts; and the act is primary.

William Temple, *The Preacher's Theme To-day*, S.P.C.K., 1936, p.21.

The prophets were not Gifford Lecturers with the advantage of some special "guidance." They were men faced with practical problems of political, moral and spiritual life.... As the prophet faces some actual human need, that truth of God which bears upon it irradiates his mind and he proclaims it in words that thrill our hearts today.

William Temple, *Nature, Man and God*, Macmillan & Co. Ltd., 1934, p.340.

It is just because the prophets and apostles are so indwelt by the Spirit of God that they are so robustly, freely, independently, and concretely human. The incoming of God's Spirit does not eliminate their human qualities so that they become mere puppets of God, but in the fullest sense it makes them *men* of God.

James D. Smart, *The Interpretation of Scripture*, The Westminster Press, 1961, p.196

No pronouncement of a prophet is ever his own; he is an interpreter prompted by Another in all his utterances, when knowing not what he does, he is filled with inspiration, as the reason withdraws and surrenders the citadel of the soul to a new visitor and tenant, the Divine Spirit which plays upon the vocal organism and raises sounds from it, which clearly express its prophetic message.

Philo, in *Three Jewish Philosophers*, selections, edited by Hans Lewy, Harper & Row, Publishers, Inc., 1945, p.75.

Unlike the priest, pagan or Christian, the prophet is always alone; he always experiences a phase of sharp separation from the religious collective, from the milieu of the people among whom he lives. By his spiritual type, the prophet is always the bearer of the subjective element in religious life, as compared with the objective element whose bearer is the religious collective. And only later those spiritual elements, first expressed by the prophetic individual, take on objective significance, and religious life enters the objective stage. Religious life is born in propheticism and is precipitated in the priesthood.... Always oriented to the future, the prophet is always dissatisfied with the present, denounces the evil in the life about him, and awaits the future triumph of higher spiritual elements which are revealed to him in prophetic visions....

The prophet breathes the air of freedom, he smothers in the hardened world about him, but in his own spiritual world he breathes freely. He always visions a free spiritual world and awaits its penetration into this stifling world. The prophet foresees the fate of man and of the world, and through contemplation of the spiritual he unriddles the events of the empirical world. The prophetic gnosis is always a philosophy of history, and a philosophy of history is possible only as free prophecy. Unlike the saint, the prophet is submerged in the life of the world and of his own people; he shares the fate of both. But he renounces and denounces the life of the world and of his people; he foretells its ruin....

The prophet belongs to the human hierarchy, he is a man inspired by God. The prophet does not strive for personal perfection, saintliness or salvation, although he may rise to the highest degree of spiritual perfection, he may or may not be a saint.... The prophetic is always a spiritually explosive psychology. The prophet does not calm men's spirits, or bring peace to their souls. Hence the prophetic cannot be the sole or even the predominant element in religious life. The world could not bear the ardent and consuming spirit of prophecy and it must guard itself against such domination.

But without the spirit of prophecy, spiritual life would die out in this world....

A Christian renaissance will require not only a consecrated, priestly spirit of the sanctification of life, but a prophetic spirit as well, a spirit of transfiguration, the real alteration of life. The Christian movement proceeds not only from the popular collective, but also from the prophetic individuals of various hierarchical ranks. The priestly hierarchy is the necessary foundation of Christianity, but it must not dominate completely and throttle prophecy. Orientation to the Coming Christ is the prophetic side of Christianity, and cannot be eliminated from it. Through centuries of objectivization, Christianity has become so congealed into a racial, national, collective religion that the spirit of prophecy has dried up and has come to be considered almost as heresy....

At the summit of the spiritual life of humanity are two figures: the image of the prophet and that of the saint. Man has never risen higher than these two images. And both are needed for God's work in the world, for the coming of the Kingdom of God. Both these spiritual ways, the way of sanctity and that of prophecy, are part of the final appearance of Divine-humanity, both are part of the integral life of the Church, of the Church's fulfilment and completion. For the time being, in the mysterious plan of God, prophecy is active outside the visible body of the Church. But the time will come when the prophetic spirit will be recognized as the spirit of the Church, as proceeding out of the Church's depths. So man's religious fate is accomplished in tragedy, in apparent separation, in tormenting conflict. But mankind moves toward fulfilment, toward deification, toward the Kingdom of God....

Christian prophecies are not optimistic; they do not justify the theory of progress; they denounce severely the evil coming into this world. But they are not pessimistic; they are above human pessimism and optimism. They await the coming of Christ in power and glory.

Nicolas Berdyaev, *Christian Existentialism*, selected and translated by Donald A. Lowrie, George Allen & Unwin Ltd., 1965, p.228.

PROVIDENCE

Accept the place the divine providence has found for you, the society of your contemporaries, the connection of events.

Ralph Waldo Emerson, *Essays*, Bernhard Tauchnitz Edition, 1915, p.36, "Self-Reliance."

We ought to live with the gods. This is done by him who always exhibits a soul contented with the appointments of Providence, and obeys the orders of that divinity which is his deputy and ruler, and the offspring of God. Now this divine authority is neither more nor less than that soul and reason which every man possesses.

Marcus Aurelius, *The Meditations of Marcus Aurelius*, translated by Jeremy Collier, with an introduction by Alice Zimmern, Walter Scott, p.78.

What in me is dark
Illumine, what is low raise and support;
That to the height of this great Argument
I may assert Eternal Providence,
And justify the ways of God to men.

John Milton, *The Poetical Works of John Milton*, edited by the Rev. H.C. Beeching, Oxford at the Clarendon Press, 1900, p.182, *Paradise Lost*, Bk.I, l.22.

Providence has a thousand means to raise the fallen and support the prostrate. Sometimes our fate resembles a fruit tree in winter. Who would think at beholding so sad a sight that these rigid branches, these jagged twigs, would turn green again in the spring and blossom and bear fruit? But we hope it, we know it!

Johann Wolfgang von Goethe, *Wisdom and Experience*, selections by Ludwig Curtius, translated and edited, with an introduction by Hermann J. Weigand, Routledge & Kegan Paul Ltd., 1949, p.166.

It is a perfectly correct view of things—and strictly consonant with the Gospel—to regard Providence across the ages as brooding over the world in ceaseless effort to spare that world its bitter wounds and to bind up its hurts. Most certainly it is God Himself who, in the course of the centuries, awakens the great benefactors of humankind, and the great physicians, in ways that agree with the general rhythm of progress. He it is who inspires, even among those furthest from acknowledging His existence, the quest for every means of comfort and every means of healing.

Pierre Teilhard de Chardin, *Le Milieu Divin*, William Collins Sons & Co. Ltd., 1960, p.63.

What, then, is the nature of that spiritual law of life under the direction of which, as he saw it, man should order his life if he would truly live?—It was his steadfast and unalterable conviction that for a man who has wrapped his will in God's will, put his life consciously in the stream of the divine life, freed his soul from all personal ambitions, taken his life on trust as a divine gift—that for such a man there is an overruling Providence which guards and guides him in every incident of his life, from the greatest to the least. He held that all annoyances, frustrations, disappointments, mishaps, discomforts, hardships, sorrows, pains, and even finally disaster itself, are simply God's ways of teaching us lessons that we could never else learn. That circumstances do not matter, are nothing; but that the response of the spirit that meets them is everything; that there is no situation in human life, however apparently adverse, nor any human relationship, however apparently uncongenial, that cannot be made, if God be in the heart, into a thing of perfect joy; that in order to attain this ultimate perfection, one must accept every experience and learn to love all persons; that the love particular should lead up to the love universal; that the worth of life is not to be measured by its results in achievement or success, but solely by the motive of one's heart and the effort of one's will; that the value of experience depends not so much upon its variety or duration as upon its intensity; and that by one single concentrated effort a brief life might attain a level that ages of ordinary development would fall short of, so that a man who lives his life thus "having become perfect in a little while fulfils long years."

George Seaver, said of Edward Wilson in *The Faith of Edward Wilson*, John Murray Ltd., 1949, p.10.

PSYCHOLOGY

The human psyche is the meeting ground between God and man. It is possible, I think, that some of the meaning of the mystery of Divine Grace may be revealed when we understand better the working of the subconscious mind, where buried memories and buried guilts and buried impulses germinate for years and then break out into a strange flowering.... I must encourage competent men inside the Church to pursue this study, and to co-operate with those outside it, to make the best use possible of their discoveries....
The sick mind is a defective instrument in the great instrument which is God's dialogue with man. Here perhaps we may see a fuller revelation of the meaning of human responsibility and God's compassion for His creatures. Here we may be able to illuminate the difference between formal guilt and the true status of the soul in the sight of God.

Morris West, *The Shoes of the Fisherman*, William Heinemann Ltd., 1963, p.79.

It is in this aiding of people to find meaning for their lives that religion and depth-psychology are in partnership. The field of meaning in life is essentially the religious area, but the technique of discovering why persons fail to find meaning—why they suffer hindrances, complexes, irrational fears—is the modern contribution of depth-psychology.
But many modern persons have been unable to quench their thirst for meaning in the stream of organized religion. Numerous reasons could be given for this—the stagnation

that results from any large organization, the preaching of dry forms in which the vitality has run dry, and the great upheavals in our Western culture of the last century, and so forth. Whatever the reason, multitudes of modern intelligent people have been unable to find the guidance they wished in conventional religion. They have been told so oppressively often to believe in life and love their neighbours, that the words ring with the cant of mere verbal repetition.

And so at the threshold of the present century, a new endeavour to understand the human personality sprang up as an answer to a great need. Beginning with the sage of Vienna, Sigmund Freud, this "psychoanalysis" was an attempt to be scientific about the human soul. We cannot achieve health or happiness, Freud pointed out, by the dishonest means of repressing all tendencies that our Victorian moralism finds unpalatable, and we are deceiving ourselves if we think that our arrogant "egos" standing at the thresholds of our minds can arbitrarily decide the great issues of life as the whim strikes them.... The new understanding of human motives worked out in Vienna constitutes probably the outstanding discovery of the twentieth century....

(The practical application of the knowledge which depth-psychology has discovered was developed through various contributions) by Dr.C.G. Jung, who terms his subject "analytical psychology," Alfred Adler, who calls his work, "individual psychology," Fritz Kunkel, Otto Rank, and others. The fact that so many of Freud's disciples have dissented from the master, rather than a mutiny of the ranks, was like the independent searching for gold of a number of prospectors—since there was so much gold to be found....

In the past twenty years it has become recognized that most psychological problems are intertwined with religious, and that religious problems have in most cases a very clear psychological aspect.... Dr. Jung expresses in vivid and perhaps extreme fashion what psychologists of all sorts were beginning to observe: "Among all my patients in the second half of life— that is to say over thirty-five—there has not been one whose problem in the last resort was not that of finding a religious outlook on life. It is safe to say that every one of them fell ill because he had lost that which the living religions of every age have given to their followers, and none of them has been really healed who did not regain his religious outlook." Dr. Jung goes on to caution us that this has nothing to do with the dogmas of a particular church; it is rather ... the reaching out of the human soul for basic meaning by which it can live....

The psychoanalyst, or consulting psychologist, or whatever he may call himself, is concerned with helping the individual overcome fears and rationalizations and inhibitions so that he can move ahead with success.... This neurotic man who refuses to meet people and who holds that all women are demons must first understand the detours in his background that have led him to the impasse—here the sheer technique of analysis comes into its own. But then, having been helped back on the road, he must believe in the worth of love and friendship in order that he may move down the road with courage.... So psychotherapy, the technique, points inevitably toward religion, the goal and meaning....

Dr. Adler holds in his last book that we should view life *sub specie aeternitatis* and at the time of his death he was engaged in collaborating with clergymen in work on

pastoral psychology. "The best conception hitherto gained," he writes, "for the elevation of humanity is the idea of God."
"It is doubtless true," writes Dr. Menninger, "that religion has been the world's
psychiatrist throughout the centuries...." One can be coldly scientific in segments of
the technique of analysis; but the closer the treatment comes to completion, the more
the therapist must take into consideration aspects of life which are by no means coldly
scientific, such as faith, hope, and love. "The patient needs a world view," Dr. Otto
Rank aptly puts it, "and will always need it, because man always needs belief, and
this so much more, the more increasing self-consciousness brings him to doubt.

Rollo May, *The Springs of Creative Living*, Abingdon Press, 1940.

PURITY

The body is not meant for immorality, but for the Lord, and the Lord for the body.

1 Corinthians 6.13.

To the pure all things are pure.

Titus 1.15.

Chastity is a wealth that comes from abundance of love.

Rabindranath Tagore, *Stray Birds*, Macmillan & Co. Ltd., Indian Edition, 1941, p.19.

Chastity—spiritually it is the devotion of all powers of body and soul to the service
of God.

E.R. Hardy, in *A Dictionary of Christian Ethics*, edited by John Macquarrie, S.C.M. Press Ltd., 1967, p.53,
"Chastity."

Even from the body's purity the mind
Receives a secret sympathetic aid.

James Thomson, *The Seasons* and *The Castle of Indolence*, edited by J. Logie Robertson, Oxford at the Clarendon
Press, 1891, p.99, "Summer," l.1267.

My strength is as the strength of ten,
Because my heart is pure.

Alfred, Lord Tennyson, *The Poems of Tennyson*, edited by Christopher Ricks, Longmans, Green & Co. Ltd., 1969,
p.610, No.234, "Sir Galahad," l.3.

Man flows at once to God as soon as the channel of purity, physical, intellectual, and
moral, is open.

Henry David Thoreau, *The Journal of Henry D.Thoreau*, edited by Bradford Torrey and Francis H. Allen, 1949,
Houghton Mifflin Company, Boston, The Riverside Press, Volume II, p.4.

The essence of chastity is not the suppression of lust, but the total orientation of one's
life towards a goal. Without such a goal, chastity is bound to become ridiculous.
Chastity is the *sine qua non* of lucidity and concentration.

Dietrich Bonhoeffer, *Letters and Papers from Prison*, William Collins Sons & Co. Ltd., 1963, p.163.

Bless'd are the pure in heart,
For they shall see our God,
The secret of the Lord is theirs,
Their soul is Christ's abode.

Still to the lowly soul
He doth Himself impart,
And for His cradle and His throne
Chooseth the pure in heart.

John Keble, *The Christian Year,* edited by Ernest Rhys, J.M. Dent & Sons, Ltd., 1914, p.185.

It is not necessary to search for God in heaven and earth and to send out our mind to seek Him in different places. Purify thy soul, o man, and strip thyself from the thought of recollections which are unnatural and hang before thy impulses the curtain of chastity and humility. Thereby thou wilt find Him that is within thee. For to the humble the mysteries are revealed.

Isaac of Nineveh, *Mystical Treatises of Isaac of Nineveh,* translated by E.J. Wensinck, 1923, p.36.

The supreme reality is incomprehensible in the sense that it cannot be expressed in logical propositions but it is increasingly apprehensible by the purified mind. This apprehension is reached not so much by the exercise of reason as by the purification of the heart, by the process of turning the attention of the soul to its own central necessities. The conception of the ground of all existence in God and of the kinship of the human spirit to the divine is at the basis of the idea that the human spirit is an exile always longing for home. It is the source of the urge in the heart towards union with the beloved.

Sir Sarvepalli Radhakrishnan, *Eastern Religions and Western Thought,* Oxford University Press, 1940, p.128.

Unchangeableness and complete detachment from creatures, that sets me nearest to God and to the summit of perfection. Purity makes me all unmindful of things, and by purity God is always kept in me. Purity makes me uniform with God, purity forces me into the inner being of creatures, purity means farewell to all creatures. None but the pure in heart can see God. In purity only is God to be found. Intellect teaches me about things, purity makes me see God. By purity God is made captive in me, purity makes me God-conscious and conscious of naught beside God, purity begets detachment. The pure soul has a light-birth as it were, purity is satisfied with God alone.

Meister Eckhart, *Meister Eckhart,* Franz Pfeiffer, translated by C. de B. Evans, John M. Watkins, 1952, Volume II, p.143.

He will shake heaven and earth, that only the unshakeable may remain: he is a consuming fire, that only that which cannot be consumed may stand forth eternal. It is the nature of God, so terribly pure that it destroys all that is not pure as fire, which demands like purity in our worship. He will have purity. It is not that the fire will burn us if we do not worship thus; but that the fire will burn us until we worship thus; yea, will go on burning within us after all that is foreign to it has yielded to its force, no longer with pain and consuming, but as the highest consciousness of life, the presence of God.

George Macdonald, *Unspoken Sermons,* First Series, Alexander Strahan, Publisher, 1867, p.31.

Love is the forgetfulness of self in the thought of the interests of another.... What do "my" wishes, "my" feelings, "my" wants matter? Why on earth should I bother about *them?*... Why "me"—when there are so many others?
Pierce beneath the outer coverings of human sinfulness and see the real, though ruined, beauty of human souls.
Pure strong love let me have for what is still natural in my fellow creatures. Corrupt and artificial we have made ourselves, but the sweeter and more lovely is the glimpse of what we were as children in God's hands.
Pure and lovely were we when we left God's hands; let me hunt in everyone for traces of this beauty and purity; and for myself let me try and get back to it, back to my childhood with God....

Edward Wilson, in *The Faith of Edward Wilson,* George Seaver, John Murray Ltd., 1949, p.23.

PURPOSE

Purpose is what gives life a meaning.... A drifting boat always drifts down-stream.

Charles H. Parkhurst, *The Pattern in the Mount and Other Sermons,* R.D. Dickinson, 1890, p.8.

What makes life dreary is the want of motive.

George Eliot, *Daniel Deronda,* introduction by Emrys Jones, J.M. Dent & Sons Ltd., 1964, Volume 2, p.580, Bk.VIII, ch.65.

Continuity of purpose is one of the most essential ingredients of happiness in the long run, and for most men this comes chiefly through their work.

Bertrand Russell, *The Conquest of Happiness,* George Allen & Unwin Ltd., 1984, p.48.

The man who consecrates his hours
By vig'rous effort and honest aim,
At once he draws the sting of life and death.

Edward Young, *Night Thoughts,* Thomas Nelson, 1841, p.17.

How could there be any question of acquiring or possessing, when the one thing needful for a man is to *become*—to *be* at last, and to die in the fullness of his being.

Antoine de Saint-Exupéry, *The Wisdom of the Sands,* translated by Stuart Gilbert, Hollis & Carter Ltd., 1952, p.127.

Many persons have a wrong idea of what constitutes true happiness. It is not attained through self-gratification but through fidelity to a worthy purpose.

Helen Keller, *Helen Keller's Journal,* Michael Joseph Ltd., 1938, p.64.

To those who worship Thee; to see Thee is our end,
Who art our source and maker, lord and path and goal.
Boethius, *De Consolatione Philosophiae,* translated with an introduction by V.E. Watts, Penguin Books Ltd., 1969, p.98.

The need for devotion to something outside ourselves is even more profound than the need for companionship. If we are not to go to pieces or wither away, we all must have some purpose in life; for no man can live for himself alone.
Ross Parmenter, *The Plant in My Window,* Geoffrey Bles Ltd., 1951, p.39.

What is the meaning of human life, or, for that matter, of the life of any creature? To know an answer to this question means to be religious. You ask: Does it make any sense, then, to pose this question? I answer: The man who regards his own life and that of his fellow creatures as meaningless is not merely unhappy but hardly fit for life.
Albert Einstein, *Ideas and Opinions,* Souvenir Press (Educational & Academic) Ltd., 1973, p.11.

Obstacles cannot bend me.
Every obstacle yields to effort.
Not to leave the furrow.
He who fixes his course by a star changes not.
Leonardo da Vinci, *The Notebooks of Leonardo da Vinci,* arranged, rendered into English, with an introduction by Edward MacCurdy, Jonathan Cape Ltd., 1977, Volume I, p.89.

The object of life ... is the discovery ... by a deepening of the self, of the centre of the self that constitutes our unique and personal essence, and which we always run the risk of missing so long as we remain on the surface of things, and think only of self-aggrandisement.
Louis Lavelle, in *Existentialism,* Paul Foulquié, translated by Kathleen Raine, Dennis Dobson Ltd., 1947, p.118.

Life does not need comfort, when it can be offered meaning, nor pleasure, when it can be shown purpose. Reveal what is the purpose of existence and how he may attain it—the steps he must take—and man will go forward again hardily, happily, knowing that he has found what he must have—intentional living—and knowing that an effort, which takes all his energy because it is worth his full and constant concentration, is the only life deserving the devotion, satisfying the nature and developing the potentialities of a self-conscious being.
Anon.

What is the course of the life
Of mortal men on the earth?
Most men eddy about
Here and there—eat and drink,
Chatter and love and hate,
Gather and squander, are raised
Aloft, are hurled in the dust,
Striving blindly, achieving

Nothing; and then they die—
Perish; and no one asks
Who or what they have been.

Matthew Arnold, *The Poems of Matthew Arnold,* edited by Kenneth Allott, Longmans, Green & Co. Ltd., 1965, p.447, "Rugby Chapel," l.58.

Scientists tell us that matter has been in existence for over a thousand million years. Throughout that near eternal age of time God has been at work with unfailing wisdom and patience, taming the recalcitrance of matter, enabling each species of life to find its own goal of beauty and usefulness, training men in mind and spirit, drawing them together in unity, and in Jesus Christ showing them the prototype of human maturity as well as the image of divine love. We know from his revelation of himself that his purpose is good, loving, wise, the most effective thing to be done in every situation, and that his creative and redemptive work will continue until his eternal purpose is achieved.

George Appleton, *Journey for a Soul,* William Collins Sons & Co. Ltd., 1976, p.233.

Our analysis of (William) Temple's thoughts concerning the Kingdom of God makes manifest that the doctrine in question is not only the central message of Christianity, i.e., the original Gospel according to Temple's interpretation, but that in everything essential it really represents the fundamental principles of Temple's view of the world and thus may be characterised as the most adequate expression of the basic principle of reality, from the point of view of men's life. As we saw, it is the principle of purpose which plays the central role in Temple's understanding of the universe: in the creative will of God, guiding the process of the world toward His goal, he sees the only self-explanatory principle. This principle or power, by virtue of its essence, also expresses the true nature of everything. It is at work in the world of men who are created to be free, responsible beings, choosing what seems good to them, i.e., what is of value to them, according to their understanding. In accordance with this principle God realises His goal—and thus also expresses His nature—by means of His sacramental universe. This necessitates divine revelation in the general sense of the word. But owing to the nature of men it also necessitates the incarnation as an indispensable means of redemption for the realisation of the purpose of God. Because the incarnation thus essentially serves the purpose of God for men, the life and work of Christ—His inauguration of the Kingdom—are to be seen in the light of the said purpose, which reflects the true meaning and character of the universe. Thus the Kingdom of God shows what man's life should be, i.e., the true principles of life. Therefore, it is the Kingdom of freedom and the sovereignty of love. And since the purpose of God is the explanation of the whole creation, His purpose expressed in the Kingdom is the explanation of the life and history of mankind. The will of God, revealed in the principles of the Kingdom, is the primary goal for His entire world and thus also for men: when men live in accordance with the true spirit of the Kingdom, they live in accordance with the true nature of everything. God aims at the consecration of the world—the whole creation is to express His nature—and thereby the Kingdom is both the means and the goal. It is a value which is and yet needs to be realised or actualised.

This process, the actualisation of the value in question, implies that the will of God as a living energy permeates all life and that the Highest in His sacramental universe makes Himself manifest through what is lower. The Kingdom cannot, however, be separated from its King, who thus above all expresses the nature of the Creator and whose spirit should guide the lives of men as citizens of the Kingdom. The more the Kingdom is actualised, the more is the true nature of the world made manifest. The principles of the Kingdom, are, therefore to be made to bear upon the life of mankind.

W.R. Rinne, The Kingdom of God in the thought of William Temple, The Purpose of God for Mankind, 1966, p.81.

After experience had taught me that all things which frequently take place in ordinary life are vain and futile; when I saw that all the things I feared and which feared me had nothing good or bad in them in so far as the mind was affected by them, I determined at last to inquire whether there might be anything which might be truly good and able to communicate its goodness, and by which the mind might be affected to the exclusion of all other things: I determined, I say, to inquire whether I might discover and acquire the faculty of enjoying throughout eternity continual supreme happiness.

I say "I determined at last," for at the first sight it seemed ill advised to lose what was certain in the hope of attaining what was uncertain. I could see the many advantages acquired from honour and riches, and that I should be debarred from acquiring these things if I wished seriously to investigate a new matter, and if perchance supreme happiness was in one of these I should lose it; if, on the other hand, it were not placed in them and I gave them the whole of my attention, then also I should be wanting in it.

I therefore turned over in my mind whether it might be possible to arrive at this new principle, or at least at the certainty of its existence, without changing the order and common plan of my life: a thing which I had often attempted in vain. For the things which most often happen in life and are esteemed as the greatest good of all, as may be gathered from their works, can be reduced to these three headings: to wit, Riches, Fame, and Pleasure. With these three the mind is so engrossed that it cannot scarcely think of any other good. As for pleasure, the mind is so engrossed in it that it remains in a state of quiescence as if it had attained supreme good, and this prevents it from thinking of anything else. But after that enjoyment follows pain, which, if it does not hold the mind suspended, disturbs and dullens it. The pursuit of fame and riches also distracts the mind not a little, more especially when they are sought for their own sake, inasmuch as they are thought to be the greatest good. By fame the mind is far more distracted, for it is supposed to be always good in itself, and as an ultimate aim to which all things must be directed....

But the love towards a thing eternal and infinite alone feeds the mind with pleasure, and it is free from all pain; so it is much to be desired and to be sought out with all our might.... although I could perceive all this quite clearly in my mind, I could not lay aside at once all greed, pleasure, and honour....

One thing I could see, and that was that as long as the mind was employed with these thoughts, it turned away from its former subjects of thought and meditated seriously on this new plan: which was a great comfort to me. For I saw that those evils were not of such a state that they could not be cured by remedies. And although at the commencement these intervals were rare and lasted for a very short space of time, yet afterwards the true good became more apparent to me, and these intervals more frequent and of longer duration.

Spinoza, *Spinoza's Ethics and De Intellectus Emendatione,* introduction by T.S. Gregory, J.M. Dent & Sons Ltd., 1955, p.227.

Q

QUIETNESS

In returning and rest you shall be saved; in quietness and in trust shall be your strength.

Isaiah 30.15.

Study to be quiet.

1 Thessalonians 4.11 (A.V.).

In silence alone does a man's truth bind itself together and strike root.

Antoine de Saint-Exupéry, *The Wisdom of the Sands,* translated by Stuart Gilbert, Hollis & Carter Ltd., 1952, p.45.

I have discovered that all the unhappiness of men arises from one single fact, that they cannot stay quietly in their own chamber.

Blaise Pascal, *Pensées,* translated by W.F. Trotter, Random House Inc., 1941, p.48.

Tranquillity! thou better name
Than all the family of Fame!

Samuel Taylor Coleridge, *Coleridge's Poetical Works,* edited by Ernest Hartley Coleridge, Oxford University Press, 1978, p.360, "Ode to Tranquillity," l.1.

To go up alone into the mountain and come back as an ambassador to the world, has ever been the method of humanity's best friends.

Evelyn Underhill, *Mysticism,* Methuen & Co. Ltd., 1912, p.210.

Silence is the element in which great things fashion themselves together, that at length they may emerge, full-formed and majestic, into the daylight of Life, which they are henceforth to rule.

Maurice Maeterlinck, *The Treasure of the Humble,* translated by Alfred Sutro, George Allen, 1897, p.3.

All I can prescribe out of my own experience is to abide patiently till the soul relaxes—it is sprung up. It needs to be let free from all thought and strain, and simply to bathe itself in the ocean of God's love. Do nothing itself—but let God do it all. Utter surrender. Then it becomes still, tranquil, and goes out to God and rests.

William of Glasshampton, *William of Glasshampton, Friar: Monk: Solitary,* Geoffrey Curtis, C.R., S.P.C.K., 1947, p.148.

Christ's existence was ruled by a great silence. His soul was "listening." It was given over to the needs of others. In his innermost being he was silent, not asserting himself, detached. He did not grasp at anything in the world. Thus he overcame in his life the power of habit and daily routine, of dullness and fatigue, and created within himself a carefree tranquillity, a place for every encounter.

Ladislaus Boros, *In Time of Temptation,* translated by Simon & Erika Young, Burns & Oates Ltd., 1968, p.18.

The more we receive in silent prayer, the more we can give in our active life. We need silence in order to be able to touch souls. The essential thing is not what we say, but what God says to us and through us. All our words will be useless unless they come from within—words which do not give the light of Christ increase the darkness.

Mother Teresa of Calcutta, in *Something Beautiful for God,* Malcolm Muggeridge, William Collins Sons & Co. Ltd., 1983, p.66.

> Come now, little man,
> turn aside for a while from your daily employment,
> escape for a moment from the tumult of your thoughts.
> Put aside your weighty cares,
> let your burdensome distractions wait,
> free yourself awhile for God
> and rest awhile in him.
> Enter the inner chamber of your soul,
> shut out everything except God
> and that which can help you in seeking him,
> and when you have shut the door, seek him.

St. Anselm, *The Prayers and Meditations of Saint Anselm,* Penguin Books Ltd., 1973, p.239.

Let your mind be quiet, realising the beauty of the world, and the immense the boundless treasures that it holds in store.
All that you have within you, all that your heart desires, all that your Nature so specially fits you for—that or the counterpart of it waits embedded in the great Whole, for you. It will surely come to you.
Yet equally surely not one moment before its appointed time will it come. All your crying and fever and reaching out of hands will make no difference.
Therefore do not begin that game at all.
Do not recklessly spill the waters of your mind in this direction and in that, lest you become like a spring lost and dissipated in the desert.
But draw them together into a little compass, and hold them still, so still;
And let them become clear, so clear,—so limpid, so mirror-like;
At last the mountains and sky shall glass themselves in peaceful beauty,
And the antelope shall descend to drink,and to gaze at his reflected image, and the lion to quench his thirst,
And Love himself shall come and bend over, and catch his own likeness in you.

Edward Carpenter, *Towards Democracy,* George Allen & Unwin Ltd., 1931, p.372.

R

RECONCILIATION

He can never therefore be reconciled to your sin, because sin itself is incapable of being altered: but He may be reconciled to your person, because that may be restored: and, which is an infinite wonder, to greater beauty and splendour than before.

Thomas Traherne, *Centuries,* The Faith Press Ltd., 1969, p.72.

It is certain that, at the moment of His death, He (Christ) was likewise forsaken and, as it were, annihilated in His soul, and was deprived of any relief and consolation, since His Father left Him in the most intense aridity, according to the lower part of His nature. Wherefore He had perforce to cry out, saying: "My God! My God! Why hast Thou forsaken Me?" This was the greatest desolation, with respect to sense, that He had suffered in His life. And thus He wrought herein the greatest work that He had ever wrought, whether in miracles or in mighty works, during the whole of His life, either upon earth or in Heaven, which was the reconciliation and union of mankind, through grace, with God.

St. John of the Cross, *Ascent of Mount Carmel,* translated and edited, with an introduction by E. Allison Peers, Image Books, Doubleday & Company, Inc., 1958, p.193, Book II, Ch.VII, sec.II.

The Church is called to a ministry of reconciliation which involves breaking down such impersonal problems as "race" or "delinquency" into people. There is, first, a preventative task. By the quality of its life-together the Church has the power to reconcile men across racial and other barriers. Joost de Blank at his enthronement service in Cape Town said: "I suffer from an incurable disease: I am colour blind." And Alec Fraser of Achimota said: "I have yet to meet the man for whom Christ did not die."

Secondly, it is a task of healing the wounds which hatred and prejudice have inflicted on people in mind and heart. We have spoken above of this work in the church-community and in groups of Christians. Reconciliation ... is a work which has power to heal, not only relationships, but also broken hearts, minds and bodies.

In the Church of today we are faced with denominational divisions which greatly weaken our power to reconcile different races. So the Church is broken. But her ministry of reconciliation is even now going on in East Harlem and Notting Hill, just as when Paul wrote to admonish the Corinthians for their party factions, the work of reconciling Jew and Gentile, master and slave, was continuing. The world is in the Church dividing Christians from one another; but the Church is also in the world, suffering, healing and reconciling men to each other.

Michael Wilson, *The Church is Healing,* S.C.M. Press Ltd., 1966, p.47.

REDEMPTION

Christ lifted up in our heart will redeem our feelings, emotions and passions by the love, grace, and understanding of the Son of God. Inharmony has no hold on us, passion no place in us, hatred nor misunderstanding no expression through us when Christ is lifted up in our heart.

Anon.

Man cannot meet his own deepest need, nor find for himself release from his profoundest trouble. What he needs is not progress, but redemption. If the Kingdom of God is to come on earth, it must be because God first comes on earth Himself.

William Temple, *Nature, Man and God,* Macmillan and Co. Ltd., 1934, p.513.

Remember that Christianity is not just another religion of individual salvation, differing only in having a different plan of salvation to offer. It is the one and only religion of world-redemption. We are members of the family of God; when we come to Him in Christ, it must always be in the company of our brothers and sisters.

William Temple, *Christian Faith and Life,* S.C.M. Press Ltd., 1963, p.45.

By His suffering, our Lord did make it possible for us to avoid suffering continual alienation from God and the consequences of this; and therefore, in a sense, His suffering is substituted for ours; but it is not a transferred penalty: it is something in the nature of a price paid; it is something which He gave, by means of which we are set free. It is a real redemption; but what He is concerned with all the time is delivering us, not from the consequences of sin, but from sin; and the centre of sin is self. So He is delivering us out of self-centredness into a life that finds its centre in God.

William Temple, *Christian Faith and Life,* S.C.M. Press Ltd., 1963, p.86.

The entire work of redemption is, thus, to restore man to himself, to bring him once more to the Tree of Life, to enable him to discover the glory all about him, to reveal to him the real values of things, and to bring to birth within him an immortal love. The true healing of the soul is always through the birth of love. Before a soul loves, it lives only to itself; as soon as love is born it lives beyond itself and finds its life in the object of its love. It is Christ who first reveals the full measure of love, who makes us see the one adequate Object of love and who forges within our human spirits the invisible bonds of a love that binds us forever to Him who *so* loved us. Here in him— "a Man loving to all the world, a God dying for mankind" we see that we are infinitely prone to love, and that true love spares nothing for the sake of what it loves—"O miraculous and eternal Godhead suffering on a Cross for me!" "That Cross is a tree set on fire with invisible flame which illuminateth all the world. The flame is love: the love in His Bosom that died upon it."

But there is no salvation for us in the Cross until it kindles the same flame of love in us, until that immeasurable love of His becomes an irresistible power in us, so that we henceforth live unto Him that loved us. It must, if it is to be efficacious, shift all our values and set us to loving as he loved—"He who would not in the same cases do the same things Jesus Christ hath done can never be saved," for love is never timorous. The love of Christ is to dwell within us and every man is to be the object of it. God and we are to become one spirit, that is, one in will and one in desire. Christ must live within us. We must be filled with the Holy Ghost, which is the God of Love; we must be of the same mind with Christ Jesus and led by His Spirit, and we must henceforth treat every man in respect to the greatness of Christ's love— this is salvation in Traherne's conception of it, and holiness and happiness are the same thing. The Cross has not done its complete work for us until we can say: "O Christ, I see thy crown of thorns in every eye; thy bleeding, naked wounded body in every soul; thy death liveth in every memory; thy crucified person is embalmed in every affection; thy pierced feet are bathed in every one's tears and it is my privilege to enter with thee into every soul."

Rufus M. Jones, *Spiritual Reformers in the 16th and 17th Centuries,* Macmillan & Co. Ltd., 1914, p.332.

RELATIONSHIPS

Talk not of wasted affection, affection never was wasted;
If it enrich not the heart of another, its waters, returning
Back to their springs, like the rain, shall fill them full of refreshment.

Henry Wadsworth Longfellow, *The Poetical Works of Longfellow,* Humphrey Milford, Oxford University Press, 1913, p.158, *Evangeline,* Part the Second, I, l.55.

I have often wondered why it is that men should be so fearful of new ventures in social relationships.... Most of us fear, actually fear, people who differ from ourselves, either up or down the scale.

David Grayson, *The Friendly Road,* Andrew Melrose Ltd., 1946, p.117.

Forgiving love is a possibility only for those who know that they are not good, who feel themselves in need of divine mercy, who live in a dimension deeper and higher than that of moral idealism.

Reinhold Niebuhr, *An Interpretation of Christian Ethics,* S.C.M. Press Ltd., 1936, p.236.

There is hardly anything that can make one happier than to feel that one counts for something with other people. What matters here is not numbers, but intensity. In the long run, human relationships are the most important things in life.

Dietrich Bonhoeffer, *Letters and Papers from Prison,* edited by Eberhard Bethge, S.C.M. Press Ltd., 1967, second revised edition, p.212.

The life and destiny of the least of human beings has an absolute meaning in respect of eternity: his life and his destiny are everlasting. For that reason one may not do away with a single human creature and escape punishment; we must consider the divine image and likeness in every one, from the most noble to the most despicable.

Nicolas Berdyaev, *Dostoievsky,* translated by Donald Attwater, Sheed & Ward Ltd., 1934, p.106.

The first (danger) is that a man lives for himself alone, deciding everything in the light of his own advantage, disregarding the rights and needs of his fellow-men. The second (danger) is that we should think of people impersonally, in the mass, with numbers rather than names, thinking of them as cast in the same mould, with no individuality of their own. Each man wants value in himself, wants to be himself, thinking of others in the same way. Neither individualism or collectivism is the right way of human relationship.

George Appleton, *Journey for a Soul*, William Collins Sons & Co. Ltd., 1976, p.27.

The woman is increasingly aware that love alone can give her her full stature, just as the man begins to discern that spirit alone can endow his life with its highest meaning. Fundamentally, therefore, both seek a psychic relation one to the other; because love needs the spirit, and the spirit, love, for their fulfilment.

C.G. Jung, *Contributions to Analytical Psychology*, translated by H.G. and Cary F. Baynes, Kegan Paul, Trench, Trubner & Co. Ltd., 1928, p.185.

No matter how genuine a relationship may be, there will always be stresses and storms, to bring unexpected words, to make one impotent and afraid, to make one feel the terribleness of not being able to count on the other person, to create the despairing feeling that breaks in love can never be repaired. But one lives and loves, and suffers and forgets, and begins again—perhaps even thinking that this time, this new time, is to be permanent. But man is not permanent and man is not predictable.

Clark Moustakas, *Creativity and Conformity*, D. Van Nostrand Company Inc., 1967, p.21.

In order to attain the being-with in love, our own existence must, so to speak, be given up; it must give up making use of the other person and treating him as a possession. Quite simply, man is meant to come to a personal fulfilment. His existence has not yet really come "to be"; it has first to be created in a community of persons, in the last analysis that means—in love; but love means powerlessness.
To love means, of course, to renounce any exercise of power and desire to interfere with, to "manage," to gain for oneself or to "possess" any other person. Love leaves the other person free; indeed love creates freedom in the other person; and in this case, creating freedom means self-effacement and renunciation. Love is realized in a great movement of self-emptying and, when once realized, is no more "our own" love, but comes to us from the other person; it is pure gift. In this gift and as gift we become what we "are"; that is, it is as gift that we begin "to be." The soul's trusting readiness to surrender itself and be at another's disposal ... creates the possibility of love and, therefore, of being. In order to be, one must surrender oneself.

Ladislaus Boros, *The Moment of Truth*, Burns & Oates Ltd., 1962, p.43.

The deepest need of man ... is the need to overcome his separateness, to leave the prison of his aloneness....
The full answer lies in the achievement of interpersonal union, of fusion with another person, in *love*.
This desire for interpersonal fusion is the most powerful striving in man. It is the most fundamental passion, it is the force which keeps the human race together, the clan, the family, society....
Mature *love* is *union under the condition of preserving one's integrity,* one's individuality.

Love is an active power in man; a power which breaks through the walls which separate man from his fellow men, which unites him with others; love makes him overcome the sense of isolation and separateness, yet it permits him to be himself, to retain his integrity. In love the paradox occurs that two beings become one yet remain two.... Envy, jealousy, ambition, any kind of greed are passions; love is an action, the practice of a human power, which can be practised only in freedom and never as the result of a compulsion.

Love is an activity, not a passive affect.... The active character of love can be described by stating that love is primarily *giving,* not receiving....

Giving is more joyous than receiving, not because it is a deprivation, but because in the act of giving lies the expression of my aliveness....

Whoever is capable of giving himself is rich...

Beyond the element of giving, the active character of love becomes evident in the fact that it always implies certain basic elements, common to all forms of love. These are *care, responsibility, respect* and *knowledge.*

Erich Fromm, *The Art of Loving,* George Allen & Unwin Ltd., 1974, pp.14-25.

RELIGION

Religion, that voice of the deepest human experience.

Matthew Arnold, *The Complete Prose Works of Matthew Arnold,* Volume V, *Culture and Anarchy,* edited by R.H. Super, Ann Arbor, The University of Michigan Press, 1965, "Sweetness and Light," p.93.

True religion is the establishment by man of such a relation to the Infinite Life around him, as, while connecting his life with this Infinitude and directing his conduct, is also in agreement with his reason and with human knowledge.

Leo Tolstoy, *What is Religion?* The Free Age Press, 1902, p.16.

For Wilson ... religion was a divine life, not a divine science; and embodied person-alities and examples, not philosophical systems and doctrinal formulas.

Dr. H.S. Pennington, said of Edward Wilson in *The Faith of Edward Wilson,* George Seaver, John Murray Ltd., 1949, p.5.

Religion is something infinitely simple, simple-souled. It is not knowledge, not the content feeling ... it is not duty and not renunciation, it is not a limitation: but, within the perfect amplitudes of the universe it is—a direction of the heart.

Rainer Maria Rilke, *Selected Letters of Rainer Maria Rilke,* translated by R.F.C. Hull, Macmillan & Co. Ltd., 1946, p.336.

Religion is not a test to judge by, but an immense aid for those who use it to live by. The main thing is whether a person has the Spirit of God in him, which to my mind means simply the power to love and be kind and unselfish; and many people have this in a very perfect form without professing any religious belief at all, or using any religious practices to keep it.

Edward Wilson, in *The Faith of Edward Wilson,* George Seaver, John Murray Ltd., 1949, p.19.

It is not religious experiences, but religious experience as a whole, that is of chief concern.... For the religious man is not only religious when he prays; his work is religiously done, his recreation religiously enjoyed, his food and drink religiously received; the last he often emphasises by the custom of "grace before meat."

William Temple, *Nature, Man and God*, Macmillan & Co. Ltd., 1934, p.334.

Religion, wherever it exists as a concrete and spiritually effective force, requires the exercise of the faculty of intuitive perception, the leap of the mind across and beyond all the data and methods of rational and logical analysis to grasp directly and in concrete experience some element in the nature of things which reason cannot describe or identify. Faith is the substance of things hoped for, the evidence of things not seen.

Anon.

It is well to have specifically holy places, and things, and days, for, without these focal points or reminders, the belief that all is holy and "big with God" will soon dwindle into a mere sentiment. But if these holy places, things, and days cease to remind us, if they obliterate our awareness that all ground is holy and every bush (could we but perceive it) a Burning Bush, then the hallows begin to do harm. Hence both the necessity, and the perennial danger, of "religion."

C.S. Lewis, *Letters to Malcolm*, Geoffrey Bles Ltd., 1964, p.100.

It is well said, in every sense, that a man's religion is the chief fact with regard to him.... By religion I do not mean here the church-creed which he professes.... This is not what I call religion.... But the thing a man does practically believe;... the thing a man does practically lay to heart, and know for certain, concerning his vital relations to this mysterious Universe, and his duty and destiny there,... That is his *religion.*

Thomas Carlyle, *Sartor Resartus, "Lectures on Heroes,"* Chapman & Hall, 1840, p.186.

True religion is always inward and spiritual, is directly initiated within the soul, is independent of form and letter, is concerned solely with the eternal and invisible, and verifies itself by producing within man a nature like that of God as He is seen in Christ. The "law" of true religion is a new and divinely formed disposition towards goodness—a law written in the heart; its temple is not of stone or wood, but is a living and spiritual temple, its worship consists entirely of spiritual activities, i.e., the offering of genuine praise from appreciative hearts, the sacrifice of the self to God, and the partaking of divine food and drink through living communion with Christ the Life. Religion, of this true and saving sort, never comes through hearsay knowledge, or along the channels of tradition, or by a head knowlege of texts of the written word. It comes only with inward experience of the Word of God, and it grows and deepens as the will of man lives by the Will of God, and as the kingdom of God comes, not in some faraway Jerusalem, or in some remote realm above the sky, but *in a man's own heart.*

Rufus M. Jones, *Spiritual Reformers in the 16th and 17th Centuries*, Macmillan & Co. Ltd., 1914, p.109.

Some people say that social and religious movements are two different things. This, however, is said by those who fail to think of religion as an art concerned with the whole of life. If the material and the spiritual are separate entities, and if there is no relation between God and the world, this contention may be true. To him, however, who makes life the realization of the supremest good it is impossible to separate social and religious effort.

If religion is the whole of life in action, how can social movements alone exist apart from religion? It is only the timid who interpret God and the world as a dualism. Until even the Stock Exchange is filled to saturation with God there is little hope for genuine religion.

Toyohiko Kagawa, in *Kagawa, William Axling*, S.C.M. Press Ltd., 1946, p.56.

It is no good asking for a simple religion. After all, real things are not simple. They look simple, but they are not. The table I am sitting at looks simple: but ask a scientist to tell you what it is really made of—all about the atoms and how the light waves rebound from them and hit my eye and what they do to the optic nerve and what it does to my brain— and, of course, you find that what we call "seeing a table" lands you in mysteries and complications which you can hardly get to the end of. A child saying a child's prayer looks simple. And if you are content to stop there, well and good. But if you are not—and the modern world usually is not—if you want to go on and ask what is really happening—then you must be prepared for something difficult. If we ask for something more than simplicity, it is silly then to complain that the something more is not simple.

C.S. Lewis, *Mere Christianity*, William Collins Sons and Co. Ltd., 1961, p.42.

I am convinced that moral standards can only be raised by a revival of religion. The proliferation of "isms" in our own times proves that no intellectual panacea can command general support. A group of clever people produce a theory of society which they are convinced will result in an earthly paradise, but it is impossible to build a dream society with violent, selfish people. Their theories are bitterly attacked by other groups, and conflict and hatred result.

Religion alone can persuade men to abandon their immediate, short-term selfishness and to dedicate themselves to the common good in complete self-oblivion. By religion, I mean the conviction that this life is not the end; that there is a spiritual world which, though invisible, penetrates all creation, and which can strike a sympathetic note in every human heart.

To accept the existence of this vast spiritual world immensely enlarges our horizon and enables us to see the pettiness of our quarrels and our attempts to grab for ourselves. It can result in a gradual transformation of our characters. But, more often than not, pride in our own cleverness closes our minds to the spiritual world which everywhere surrounds and envelopes us.

Sir John Glubb, *The Fate of Empires and Search for Survival*, William Blackwood & Sons Ltd., 1978, p.44.

Religion, this feeling of contact with a Greater Power beyond the self, seems to be some fundamental feature in the natural history of man. As one travels through the English countryside, taking the lesser by-ways rather than the great, one cannot, if one goes slowly and is prepared to stop, but be struck by the beauty of the old parish churches and be made to marvel that such glories could be built by such small groups of people, just as one marvels at the great medieval cathedrals in towns which, at the time of their building, must have had only moderate populations. If one goes inside such an old country church one cannot help feeling that here is something fashioned with real love and reverence; elements of superstition there may well be, but in spite of this, surely here is something created not just by an ignorant craving for magic, but by something of profound depth. A naturalist coming from another planet, if his space-ship had the ability to drift across the countryside like a balloon, could not but be struck by the prominence of these buildings in each small community. Amidst the little groups of houses their spires and towers stand up like the sporangia of some organism and he might well be excused for first thinking them to have the importance of some such reproductive process. Indeed they had an equal importance in the past when devotion to God was as real to the population as was that of sexuality. They hardly have the same significance today and some, alas, stand forsaken like fossil skeletons of the past; this, however, may only be a temporary phase due to the accelerated growth of a physical science, whose findings are difficult to reconcile with many of the old doctrinal dogmas. I say temporary because I believe the dogmas on both sides may be revised as theology becomes more natural and science's mechanistic interpretation of life is shown not to be the whole truth.

Religion indeed seems to be some fundamental feature in Man's make-up: something which can be as powerful as any other urge. Few can doubt that the wars of religion or of rival ideologies are more bitter than those fought for just economic ends; and we must not forget that those on the two sides of a conflict may well, through the lack of a generally accepted scientific theology, be propelled by different ideas of God that they both, in their prejudice, passionately feel to be right. It would not surprise me if the roots of religion went much deeper down into biological history than is generally conceded, and that it *is* part of the very nature of the living stream.

Sir Alistair Hardy, *The Living Stream*, William Collins Sons & Co. Ltd., 1965, p.274.

RENEWAL

So we do not lose heart. Though our outer nature is wasting away, our inner nature is being renewed every day.

2 Corinthians 4.16.

By the reading of Scripture I am so renewed that all nature seems renewed around me and with me. The sky seems to be a pure, a cooler blue, the trees a deeper green, light is sharper on the outlines of the forest and the hills and the whole world is charged with the glory of God and I feel fire and music in the earth under my feet.

Thomas Merton, *The Sign of Jonas*, Sheldon Press, 1976, p.215.

It behoves the doctor, if he will be called a doctor, to study the whole process, how God has restored the *universal* in man; which is fully clear and manifest in the person of Christ, from his entrance into the humanity, even to his ascension, and sending of the Holy Ghost.

Let him follow this entire process, and then he may find the universal, provided he be born again of God.

Jacob Boehme, *The Signature of All things and Other Discourses,* Everyman's Library 1912-1934, (from Wm Law's English Edition—4 volumes), p.110.

If men can be found who revolt against the spirit of thoughtlessness, and who are personalities sound enough and profound enough to let the ideals of ethical progress radiate from them as a force, there will start an activity of the spirit which will be strong enough to evoke a new mental and spiritual disposition in mankind.

Albert Schweitzer, *My Life and Thought,* translated by C.T. Campion, George Allen & Unwin Ltd., 1924, p.281.

Regeneration or the renewal of our first birth and state is something entirely distinct from this first sudden conversion or call to repentance ... it is not a thing that is done in an instant, but is a certain process, a gradual release from our captivity and disorder, consisting of several stages and degrees, both of death and life, which the soul must go through before it can have thoroughly put off the old man.

William Law, *Selected Mystical Writings of William Law,* edited by Stephen Hobhouse, Rockliff, 1948, p.25.

Remember, the supreme wonder of the history of the Christian Church is that always in the moments when it has seemed most dead, out of its own body there has sprung up new life; so that in age after age it has renewed itself, and age after age by its renewal has carried the world forward into new stages of progress, as it will do for us in our day, if only we give ourselves in devotion to its Lord and take our place in its service.

William Temple, *Christian Faith and Life,* S.C.M. Press Ltd., 1963, p.133.

To have learned through enthusiasms and sorrows what things there are within and without the self that make for more life or less, for fruitfulness or sterility; to hold to the one and eschew the other; to seek to persuade and reveal and convince; to be ready to readjust one's values at the summons of a new truth that is known and felt; to be unweary in learning how to discriminate more sharply between the false and the true, the trivial and the significant, in life and in men and in works; to be prepared to take a risk for what seems the finer and better thing—that is, perhaps all we can do. Yet somehow, as I write the words, that "perhaps all we can do" seems a very meagre phrase. The endeavour to be true to experience strikes me at this moment as the most precious privilege of all. To have found a loyalty from which one cannot escape, which one must for ever acknowledge—no, one cannot ask for more.

John Middleton Murry, *To An Unknown God,* Jonathan Cape Ltd., 1924, p.22.

RENUNCIATION

I shrink to give up my life, and thus do not plunge into the great waters of life.

Rabindranath Tagore, *Gitanjali,* Macmillan & Co. Ltd., 1971, p.72.

Wherefore forsake all things for God, and then God will be truly given unto you in all things.

John Tauler, *The History and Life of the Reverend Doctor John Tauler,* translated by Susanna Winkworth, Smith, Elder, and Company, 1857, p.311.

My son, you cannot have complete freedom unless you deny your own claims entirely....
Hold on to the brief saying that sums this up—Leave everything and you will find everything.

Thomas à Kempis, *The Imitation of Christ*, translated by Betty I. Knott, William Collins Sons & Co. Ltd., 1979, p.161.

The only value which Christianity sees in voluntary renunciation is that which relates it to love. True renunciation renounces that which is opposed to love, and embraces that which leads to it.

Hubert van Zeller, *Considerations*, Sheed & Ward Ltd., 1974, p.69.

I know that for the right practice of it the heart must be empty of all other things, because GOD will possess the heart *alone;* and as He cannot possess it *alone,* without emptying it of all besides, so neither can He act *there,* and do in it what He pleases, unless it be left vacant to Him.

Brother Lawrence, *The Practice of the Presence of God*, A.R. Mowbray & Co. Ltd., 1977, p.42.

This pearl of eternity is the peace and joy of God within thee, but can only be found by the manifestation of the life and power of Jesus Christ in thy soul. But Christ cannot be thy power and thy life till, in obedience to His call, thou deniest thyself, takest up thy daily cross and followest Him in the regeneration. This is peremptory, it admits of no reserve or evasion, it is the one way to Christ and eternal life. But be where thou wilt, either here or at Rome or Geneva, if self is undenied, if thou livest to thine own will, to the pleasures of thy natural lust and appetites, senses, and passions, and in conformity to the vain customs and spirit of this world, thou art dead whilst thou livest ... a stranger to all that is holy and heavenly within thee and utterly incapable of finding the peace and joy of God in thy soul.

William Law, *Selected Mystical Writings of William Law*, edited by Stephen Hobhouse, Rockliff, 1948, p.90.

Therefore if a heart is to be ready for him, it must be emptied out to nothingness, the condition of its maximum capacity. So, too, a disinterested heart, reduced to nothingness, is the optimum, the condition of maximum sensitivity.
Take an illustration from nature. If I wish to write on a white tablet, then no matter how fine the matter already written on it, it will confuse me and prevent me from writing down (my thoughts); so that, if I still wish to use the tablet, I must first erase all that is written on it, but it will never serve me as well as for writing as when it is clean. Similarly, if God is to write his message about the highest matters on my heart, everything to be referred to as "this or that" must first come out and I must be disinterested. God is free to do his will on his own level when my heart, being disinterested, is bent on neither this nor that.

Meister Eckhart, *Meister Eckhart*, translated by Raymond B. Blakney, Harper & Row, Publishers, Inc., 1941, p.88.

It is by losing the egocentric life that we save the hitherto latent and undiscovered life which, in the spiritual part of our being, we share with the Divine Ground. This new-found life is "more abundant" than the other, and of a different and higher kind. Its possession is liberation into the eternal, and liberation is beatitude. Necessarily so; for the Brahman, who is one with the Atman, is not only Being and Knowledge, but also Bliss, and, after Love and Peace, the final fruit of the Spirit is Joy. Mortification is painful, but that pain is one of the pre-conditions of blessedness. This fact of spiritual experience is sometimes obscured by the language in which it is described. Thus, when Christ says that the Kingdom of Heaven cannot be entered except by those who are as little children, we are apt to forget (so touching are the images evoked by the simple phrase) that a man cannot become childlike unless he chooses to undertake the most strenuous and searching course of self-denial. In practice the command to become as little children is identical with the command to lose one's life.

Aldous Huxley, *The Perennial Philosophy*, Chatto & Windus Ltd., 1974, p.124.

To die—for this into the world you came.
Yes, to abandon more than you ever conceived as possible:
All ideals, plans—even the very best and most unselfish—all hopes and desires,
All formulas of morality, all reputation for virtue or consistency or good sense; all cherished theories, doctrines, systems of knowledge,
Modes of life, habits, predilections, preferences, superiorities, weaknesses,indulgences,
Good health, wholeness of limb and brain, youth, manhood, age—nay life itself—in one word: To die—
For this into the world you came.
All to be abandoned, and when they have been finally abandoned,
Then to return to be used—and then only to be rightly used, to be free and open for ever.

Edward Carpenter, *Towards Democracy*, George Allen & Unwin Ltd., 1931, p.353.

To every man comes, sooner or later, the great renunciation. For the young, there is nothing unattainable; a good thing desired with the whole force of a passionate will, and yet impossible, is to them not credible. Yet, by death, by illness, by poverty, or by the voice of duty, we must learn, each one of us, that the world was not made for us, and that, however beautiful may be the things we crave, Fate may nevertheless forbid them. It is the part of courage, when misfortune comes, to bear without repining the ruin of our hopes, to turn away our thoughts from vain regrets. This degree of submission to Power is not only just and right: it is the very gate of wisdom.
But passive renunciation is not the whole of wisdom; for not by renunciation alone can we build a temple for the worship of our own ideals. Haunting foreshadowings of the temple appear in the realm of imagination, in music, in architecture, in the untroubled kingdom of reason, and in the golden sunset magic of lyrics, where beauty shines and glows, remote from the touch of sorrow, remote from the fear of change, remote from the failures and disenchantments of the world of fact. In the contemplation of these things the vision of heaven will shape itself in our hearts, giving at once a touchstone to judge the world about us, and an inspiration by which to fashion to our needs whatever is not incapable of serving as a stone in the sacred temple.

Except for those rare spirits that are born without sin, there is a cavern of darkness to be traversed before that temple can be entered. The gate of the cavern is despair, and its floor is paved with the gravestones of abandoned hopes. There Self must die; there the eagerness, the greed of untamed desire must be slain, for only so can the soul be freed from the empire of Fate. But out of the cavern the Gate of Renunciation leads again to the daylight of wisdom, by whose radiance a new insight, a new joy, a new tenderness, shine forth to gladden the pilgrim's heart.

Bertrand Russell, *Mysticism and Logic, and Other Essays,* Longmans, Green & Co. Ltd., 1919, p.52.

REPENTANCE

Then the spirit of the Lord will come mightily upon you, and you shall prophesy with them and be turned into another man.

1 Samuel 10.6.

Repent therefore, and turn again, that your sins may be blotted out, that times of refreshing may come from the presence of the Lord.

Acts 3.19.

"But how can God bring this about in me?"—Let him do it, and perhaps you will know.

George Macdonald, *Unspoken Sermons,* Third Series, Longmans, Green, and Co., 1889, p.226.

Often we shall have to change the direction of our thinking and our wishing and our striving. That is what repentance really means—taking our bearings afresh and trying a new road.

Harry Williams, *The True Wilderness,* Constable and Company, 1965, p.27.

If you have behaved badly, repent, make what amends you can and address yourself to the task of behaving better next time. On no account brood over your wrongdoing. Rolling in the muck is not the best way of getting clean.

Aldous Huxley, *Brave New World,* Chatto & Windus Ltd., 1970, p.vii.

The soul in its nature loves God and longs to be at one with Him in the noble love of a daughter for a noble father; but coming to human birth and lured by the courtships of this sphere, she takes up with another love, a mortal, leaves her father and falls. But one day coming to hate her shame, she puts away the evil of earth, once more seeks her father, and finds her peace....
The soul takes another life as it approaches God; thus restored it feels that the dispenser of true life is There to see, that now we have nothing to look for but, far otherwise, that we must put aside all else and rest in This alone, This become....
Thus we have all the vision that may be of Him and of ourselves; but it is of a self wrought to splendour, brimmed with the Intellectual light, become that very light, pure, buoyant, unburdened, raised to Godhood or, better, knowing its Godhood, all aflame.

Plotinus, *The Enneads,* translated by Stephen MacKenna, Faber and Faber Limited, 1956, p.623.

Repentance is but a kind of table-talk, till we see so much of the deformity of our inward nature as to be in some degree frightened and terrified at the sight of it. There must be some kind of an earthquake within us, something that must rend and shake us to the bottom, before we can be enough sensible either of the state of death we are in or enough desirous of that Saviour, who alone can raise us from it.... Sooner or later repentance must have a broken and a contrite heart; we must with our blessed Lord go over the brook Cedron, and with Him sweat great drops of sorrow before He can say for us, as He said for Himself: "It is finished."

William Law, *Selected Mystical Writings of William Law,* edited by Stephen Hobhouse, Rockliff, 1948, p.13.

To repent is to adopt God's viewpoint in place of your own. There need not be any sorrow about it. In itself, far from being sorrowful, it is the most joyful thing in the world, because when you have done it you have adopted the viewpoint of truth itself, and you are in fellowship with God. It means a complete revaluation of all things we are inclined to think good. The world, as we live in it, is like a shop window in which some mischievous person has got in overnight and shifted all the price-labels round so that the cheap things have the high price labels on them, and the really precious things are priced low. We let ourselves be taken in. Repentance means getting those price-labels back in the right place.

William Temple, *Christian Faith and Life,* S.C.M. Press Ltd., 1963, p.74.

Above all things beware of taking this desire of repentance to be the effect of thy own natural sense and reason, for in so doing thou losest the key of all the heavenly treasure that is in thee, thou shuttest the door against God, turnest away from Him, and thy repentance (if thou hast any) will be only a vain, unprofitable work of thy own hands, that will do thee no more good than a well that is without water.... When, therefore, the first spark of a desire after God arises in thy soul, cherish it with all thy care, give all thy heart into it, it is nothing less than a touch of the divine loadstone that is to draw thee out of the vanity of time into the riches of eternity. Get up, therefore, and follow it as gladly as the Wise Men of the East followed the star from Heaven that appeared to them. It will do for thee as the star did for them: it will lead thee to the birth of Jesus, not in a stable at Bethlehem in Judea, but to the birth of Jesus in the dark centre of thy own fallen soul.

William Law, *Selected Mystical Writings of William Law,* edited by Stephen Hobhouse, Rockliff, 1948, p.91, 103.

We have shown that every soul, though it may be burdened with sins, caught in the net of evil habits, taken captive by the allurements of sinful pleasures; though it be as a captive in exile, confined in the body as in a prison, submerged and fixed fast in mud and clay, closely bound to its members, weighed down by cares, absorbed in business, saddened by fears, afflicted by sorrows, led astray by errors, anxious because of forebodings, uneasy through suspicions, and, lastly, an alien on the earth, in which it finds so many enemies, and, according to the saying of a prophet, defiled with the dead and counted with them that go down into hell (Baruch 3.11); although a soul, I say, be thus under condemnation and thus despairing, yet, as I have shown, it is able to find in itself, not only reason for breathing freely in the hope of mercy and forgiveness, but also for daring to aspire to the heavenly nuptials of the Word; nor does it fear to enter into alliance with God, and to bear the sweet yoke of love with Him who is the King of Angels. For why should it not venture to come confidently into the presence of Him by whose image and likeness it sees and knows that it is still honoured and ennobled? Why should even a Majesty so great be a cause of distrust to a being to whom its own origin gives a ground for confidence? All that it has to do is to preserve with care the original purity of its nature by a pure and honourable life; or, rather, to study to adorn and embellish by good and virtuous thoughts and actions, as by rich colours, that illustrious image which has been impressed upon the depths of its nature at its creation.

St. Bernard, *Life and Works of Saint Bernard,* edited by Dom John Mabillon, translated and edited with additional notes by Samuel J. Eales, John Hodges, 1896, Volume IV, p.507, Sermon lxxxiii.

RESURRECTION

That I may know him and the power of his resurrection, and may share his sufferings, becoming like him in his death, that if possible I may attain the resurrection from the dead.

Philippians 3.10-11.

If then you have been raised with Christ, seek the things that are above, where Christ is, seated at the right hand of God. Set your minds on things that are above, not on things that are on earth.

Colossians 3.1-2.

It has never at any time been possible to fit the resurrection of Jesus into any world view except a world view of which it is the basis.

Lesslie Newbigin, *Honest Religion for Secular Man,* S.C.M. Press Ltd., 1966, p.53.

Christian theology has never suggested that the "fact" of Christ's resurrection could be known apart from faith.

Alan Richardson, *History Sacred and Profane,* S.C.M. Press Ltd., 1964, p.206.

You believe in the resurrection, not because it is reported by the apostles but because the resurrected One himself encounters you in a living way as he who unites you with God, as the living Mediator. Now you yourself know it: he lives, he, the Reconciler and Redeemer.

Emil Brunner, *I Believe in the Living God,* translated and edited by John Holden, Lutterworth Press, 1961, p.93.

The New Testament promises us that our physical body shall be transmuted into a spiritualized body, like the body of the risen Christ, released from the domination of the material, the spatial and the temporal. Yet in some mysterious way it will be recognizable perhaps with its most significant features, as the nail-marks and the spear-wound on our Lord's resurrection body. We may think of the body as a life-long comrade, who will survive death and in some spiritualized form be our comrade still.

George Appleton, *Journey for a Soul*, William Collins Sons & Co. Ltd., 1976, p.16.

Jesus revealed God to them and became so utterly the central form that they were clinging to Him. But that could not go on for ever. They had to make a painful transition to a new relationship in which they clung to Him as something within their own lives, and not just as a nostalgic kind of thing. The great story that marks this transition is that of Jesus saying to Mary Magdalen on the Resurrection Day: "Do not cling to Me, as in the past. It really is Me, but you and my other followers are passing on to a new relationship of a very tremendous kind."

Michael Ramsey, in *Priestland's Progress*, Gerald Priestland, British Broadcasting Corporation, 1982, p.111.

Christ has conquered death, not only by suppressing its evil effects, but by reversing its sting. By virtue of Christ's rising again, nothing any longer kills inevitably but everything is capable of becoming the blessed touch of the divine hands, the blessed influence of the will of God upon our lives. However marred by our faults, or however desperate in its circumstances, our position may be, we can, by a total re-ordering, completely correct the world that surrounds us, and resume our lives in a favourable sense. "To those who love God all things are turned to God." That is the fact which dominates all explanation and all discussion.

Pierre Teilhard de Chardin, *Le Milieu Divin*, William Collins Sons & Co. Ltd., 1960, p.61.

The word "resurrection" has for many people the connotation of dead bodies leaving their graves or other fanciful images. But resurrection means the victory of the New state of things, the New Being born out of the death of the Old. Resurrection is not an event that might happen in some remote future, but it is the power of the New Being to create life out of death, here and now, today and tomorrow. Where there is a New Being, *there* is resurrection, namely, the creation into eternity out of every moment of time. The Old Being has the mark of disintegration and death. The New Being puts a new mark over the old one. Out of disintegration and death something is born of eternal significance. That which is immersed in dissolution emerges in a New Creation. Resurrection happens *now,* or it does not happen at all. It happens in us and around us, in soul and history, in nature and universe. ◯

Paul Tillich, *The New Being*, S.C.M. Press Ltd., 1956, p.24.

The resurrection of Jesus had a far deeper significance than what happened to the flesh. It meant the resurrection of spirit beyond the needs of any carnal body. Therefore, it was not necessary for the disciples to see the resurrected Jesus, nor for the tomb-keepers to observe him. The Roman soldiers guarded the sepulcher least his body should be stolen away, but they were not able to testify to his resurrection either. Much less were casual passers-by.

The first person to discover the resurrection of Jesus that morning was Mary Magdalene whose soul had once been possessed with seven devils. The resurrection of Jesus was a resurrection for such miserable persons as she, for ruined souls. To those who cannot grasp this meaning, resurrection remains an insoluble enigma, an empty falsehood, a prick of doubt. It is an ever-lasting secret. Not a few of us seem inclined to deny this miracle. If we are reluctant to accept sinners as friends, it means that we belong to the sceptics who deny the fact of resurrection. Let us, therefore, remember that the first witness who saw the figure of Jesus the morning of his resurrection had been a prostitute.

Toyohiko Kagawa, *Meditations*, translated by Jiro Takenaka, Harper & Brothers, 1950, No.35.

If my mind can't quite take certain things—such as the physical Resurrection—does it matter, so long as it doesn't get in the way of belief in Christ as master and saviour and helper, to be sought and served? I know it mattered to the early church, and was perhaps the only way in which they could be convinced—but should one try to force or persuade one's mind to it, if one feels one doesn't need it? You say "we cannot be expected to do more than yield to God the minds which we actually possess," so I suppose God takes them and does what he can with them. And of course in time they might develop new powers of faith; as you say, it depends on what happens to make connections. He keeps showing us new things, new lights on the past, new roads for the future, and one hopes for new powers. But what moors, fens, crags and torrents lie all about....

It seems almost better ... that God should have sent his Incarnation on earth in form fully human, with human birth and death. I would almost *rather* think He was born like us and died like us, and that it was His spirit only that lived after death, taking the form His friends would recognise. But of course this is no argument at all, and I don't try to make up my mind about it. I don't feel either way that it could make any difference to what I value more and more—the relationship that one tries to keep. But I will keep my mind open about it, and try to think it out. I felt, at the Easter mass, that here was Christ risen and with us, and I didn't care how.

Rose Macaulay, *Letters to a Friend*, edited by Constance Babington Smith, William Collins Sons & Co. Ltd., 1961, p.74, 107.

In the earliest days of Christianity an "apostle" was first and foremost a man who claimed to be an eye-witness of the Resurrection. Only a few days after the Crucifixion when two candidates were nominated for the vacancy created by the treachery of Judas, their qualification was that they had known Jesus personally both before and after His death and could offer first-hand evidence of the Resurrection in addressing the outer world (Acts 1.22)....

The Resurrection is the central theme in every Christian sermon reported in the Acts. The Resurrection, and its consequences, were the "gospel" or good news which the Christians brought: what we call the "gospels," the narratives of Our Lord's life and death, were composed later for the benefit of those who had already accepted the *gospel*. They were in no sense the basis of Christianity: they were written for those already converted. The miracle of the Resurrection, and the theology of that miracle, comes first: the biography comes later as a comment on it....

When modern writers talk of the Resurrection they usually mean one particular moment—the discovery of the Empty Tomb and the appearance of Jesus a few yards away from it. The story of that moment is what Christian apologists now chiefly try to support and sceptics chiefly try to impugn. But this almost exclusive concentration on the first five minutes or so of the Resurrection would have astonished the earliest Christian teachers. In claiming to have seen the Resurrection they were not necessarily claiming to have seen *that*. Some of them had, some of them had not. It had no more importance than any of the other appearances of the risen Jesus— apart from the poetic and dramatic importance which the beginning of things must always have. What they were claiming was that they had all, at one time or another, met Jesus during the six or seven weeks that followed His death. Sometimes they seem to have been alone when they did so, but on one occasion twelve of them saw Him together, and on another occasion about five hundred of them. St. Paul says that the majority of the five hundred were still alive when he wrote the *First Letter to the Corinthians*, i.e., in about 55 AD.

C.S. Lewis, *Miracles*, William Collins Sons & Co. Ltd., 1974, p.147.

In writing in this way about Jesus we must not distort the fact that he was a man, born of human parents. He undoubtedly made a tremendous impact on many people, some of whom found relief from physical illness as a result of their trust in him. In their desire to emphasise his supreme value to them, some of his followers in later years described his life and activities in miraculous terms. Whether we accept this explanation is not important; what matters is the greatness of his personality and his spiritual insight. Because his teaching and way of life ran counter to the convictions and practices of the religious leaders of his time, they, with the consent of the populace, engineered his trial and execution. Men do not like goodness if it challenges their moral failure, or loyalty to truth that calls for a revolutionary change of mind. They killed Jesus because they were afraid of him.

As in his life, so in his approach to death Jesus never faltered in his trust in love, and forgave those who rejected him. By this creative attitude Jesus radically changed a most heinous act of human wickedness into an event that has released love and forgiveness into a dark world. For ever after men know that such love can overcome evil, and in this knowledge have found freedom to live.

Many Friends are sceptical about the New Testament accounts of the physical resurrection of Jesus, although for some this is a crucial element in their faith. Most would agree that the essential meaning behind the story of the first Easter is that death could not destroy all that was of real value in the earthly life of Jesus. The love experienced by his disciples could not be taken from them by his death, because they recognised that it was of an infinite and eternal quality. In fact, it was only after his death that they came to understand and to appreciate fully the deep meaning of his life and to be set free by it.

George H. Gorman, *Introducing Quakers*, Friends Home Service Committee, 1969, p.19.

REVELATION

It was not that this man sinned, or his parents, but that the works of God might be made manifest in him.

John 9.3.

I have raised you up for the very purpose of showing my power in you.
Romans 9.17.

But when he who had set me apart before I was born, and had called me through his grace, was pleased to reveal his Son in me.
Galatians 1.15-16.

The one obvious, unmistakable manifestation of the Deity is the law of good and evil disclosed to men by revelation.
Leo Tolstoy, *Anna Karenin*, translated with an introduction by Rosemary Edmonds, Penguin Books Ltd., 1983, p.851, Part VIII, ch.19.

For each truth revealed by grace, and received with inward delight and joy, is a secret murmur of God in the ear of a pure soul.
Walter Hilton, *The Ladder of Perfection*, translated with an introduction by Leo Sherley-Price, Penguin Books Ltd., 1957, p.252.

If you only say, you have a Revelation from God; I must have a Revelation from God too, before I can believe you.
Benjamin Whichcote, *Moral and Religious Aphorisms*, 1930, p.51, Century V, No.443.

The first and most important fact that we can know about God is ever this: *we* know nothing of Him, except what He Himself has revealed to us.
Emil Brunner, *Our Faith*, translated by John W. Rilling, Charles Scribner's Sons Ltd., 1936, p.11.

That which we really know about God, is not what we have been clever enough to find out, but what the Divine Charity has secretly revealed.
Evelyn Underhill, *The School of Charity*, Longmans, Green & Co. Ltd., 1956, p.12.

My own mind is the direct revelation which I have from God and far least liable to mistake in telling his will of any revelation.
Ralph Waldo Emerson, *The Heart of Emerson's Journals*, edited by Bliss Perry, Constable & Co. Ltd., 1927, p.53.

Instead of complaining that God had hidden Himself, you will give Him thanks for having revealed so much of Himself.
Blaise Pascal, *Pensées*, translated by W.F. Trotter, Random House Inc., 1941, p.98.

The knowledge of man is as the waters, some descending from above, and some springing from beneath: the one informed by the light of nature, the other inspired by divine revelation.
Francis Bacon, *The Advancement of Learning*, introduction by Henry Morley, Cassell and Company, Ltd., 1905, p.81.

God is revealed as the God of love, and henceforth every morally good act, that is, every act formed by charity, is a revelation of God. Every word of truth and love, every hand extended in kindness, echoes the inner life of the Trinity.
Gabriel Moran, F.S.C., *Theology of Revelation*, Burns & Oates Ltd., 1967, p.127.

To see a World in a Grain of Sand
And a Heaven in a Wild Flower,
Hold Infinity in the palm of your hand
And Eternity in an hour.

William Blake, *The Complete Writings of William Blake*, edited by Geoffrey Keynes, Oxford University Press, 1974, p.431, "Auguries of Innocence," l. 1.

In nature we find God; we do not only infer from Nature what God must be like, but when we see Nature truly, we see God self-manifested in and through it. Yet the self-revelation so given is incomplete and inadequate. Personality can only reveal itself in persons. Consequently it is specially in Human Nature—in men and women—that we see God.

William Temple, *Nature, Man and God*, Macmillan & Co. Ltd., 1934, p.266.

For two reasons the event in which the fullness of revelation is given must be the life of a Person: the first is that the revelation is to persons who can fully understand only what is personal; the second is that the revelation is of a personal Being, who accordingly cannot be adequately revealed in anything other than personality. Moreover, if the Person who is Himself the revelation is to be truly adequate to that function, He must be one in essence with the Being whom He reveals.

William Temple, *Nature, Man and God*, Macmillan & Co. Ltd., 1934, p.319.

Love, whether in its most exalted form as the love between husband and wife, or in the less ardent experience of affection and sympathy, unlocks the doors of our prison-house and reveals to us something of the breadth and length and depth and height of the spiritual world which surrounds us. In various degrees, all cordial human intercourse is a liberation and an enhancement of our personality; it is a channel of revelation.

W.R. Inge, *Personal Religion and the Life of Devotion*, Longmans, Green & Co. Ltd., 1924, p.16.

In order that the revelation may effectively reveal or disclose the Divine Purpose there must be men attuned to it so as to discern and in part to understand it. The Apostles were necessary to the effectual disclosure of the Divine Nature which the Incarnation was designed to offer. If none had "beheld His glory" it would still have been there; the Life and the Death and the Resurrection are in themselves the manifestation of God in the flesh. But though the manifestation would have occurred, it would have been sterile unless some could apprehend it. So it had been with the prophets. If none had been able to interpret the mighty acts of God as what they were, they would have been wrought partly in vain. The essential condition of effectual revelation is the coincidence of a divinely controlled event and minds divinely illumined to read it aright.

William Temple, in *Revelation*, edited by John Baillie and Hugh Martin, Faber and Faber Limited, 1937, p.107.

By divine revelation is meant the entrance of truth into the depth of living. As long as the truth does not hold sway over the whole of life, cognition and life are two separate entities, God and man are living apart from each other. When the truth penetrates into the whole warp and woof of life, then for the first time God becomes man's motive power and the guiding spirit of all his ways.

Therefore, he who seeks for the divine revelation will not find God through the theory of cognition. First of all let him endeavour to create values. Let him liberate those who are oppressed, feed those who are in want, give sight to the blind, find a way to enrich the poor. Then will he be able to see divine revelations every day.

This is the truth. The emancipators see God daily. God whispers to them. They stand in His presence. While the religionists of the study are seeking for divine revelation through cognition the God of life reveals Himself in the midst of life itself. The divine revelation is not closed. False scholars and false religious teachers are setting it at naught.

Toyohiko Kagawa, in *Kagawa*, William Axling, S.C.M. Press Ltd., 1946, p.144.

In the infant period of the race, both among the Hebrews and the Gentile peoples, God has used, like a wise Teacher, the symbol and picture-book method. He has disciplined them with external laws and with ceremonies which would move their child-minded imaginations; but all this method was used only because they were not ripe and ready for the true and higher form of goodness. "They used the face of Moses until they could come to the full Light of the truth and righteousness of God, for which all the time their spirits really hungered and thirsted." The supreme instance of the divine pictorial method was the sending of Christ to reveal God visibly. Before seeing God in Christ men falsely thought of Him as hostile, stern, and wrathful; now they may see Him in this unveiling of Himself as He actually is, eternally loving, patiently forgiving, and seeking only to draw the world into His love and peace: "When the Abba-crying spirit of Christ awakens in our hearts we commune with God in peace and love." But no one must content himself with Christ after the flesh, Christ historically known. That is to make an idol of Him. We can be saved through Him only when by His help we discover the essential nature of God and when He moves us to go on living in the spirit and power as Christ Himself lived. His death as an outward, historical fact does not save us; it is the supreme expression of His limitless love and the complete dedication of His spirit in self-giving, and it is effective for our salvation only when it draws us into a similar way of living, unites us in spirit with Him and makes us in reality partakers of His blood spiritually apprehended. Christ is our Mediator in that He reveals the love of God towards us and moves our will to appreciate it."

Every step of human progress and of spiritual advance is marked by a passage from the dominion of the external to the sway and power of inward experience. God is training us for a time when images, figures, and picture-book methods will be no longer needed, but all men will live by the inward Word and have the witness—"the Abba-crying voice"—in their own hearts.

Rufus M. Jones, *Spiritual Reformers in the 16th and 17th Centuries*, Macmillan & Co. Ltd., 1914, p.37.

S

SACRAMENTS

An outward and visible sign of an inward and spiritual grace.
Book of Common Prayer, Catechism.

Embodied acts, such as the Sacramental act, are beneath acts purely *mental* and spiritual;
such as Prayer is.
Benjamin Whichcote, *Moral and Religious Aphorisms,* 1930, p.124, Century XI, No.1082.

Whatever we see, wherever we look, whether we recognize it as true or not, we cannot
touch or handle the things of earth and not, in that very moment, be confronted with
the sacraments of heaven.
C.A. Coulson, *Science and Christian Belief,* Oxford University Press, 1955, p.102.

A sacrament is something more than a divine poem, because it conveys (as is believed
by those who make use of it) not only God's meaning to the mind, but God Himself
to the whole person of the worshipper.
William Temple, *Nature, Man and God,* Macmillan & Co. Ltd., 1934, p.484.

When faith exists as a struggle to believe in spite of empirical and temperamental
pressure to unbelief, when the whole life of feeling is dead, when nothing is left but
stark loyalty to God as He is dimly and waveringly apprehended to be—then the sheer
objectivity, even the express materialism, of a sacrament gives it a value that nothing
else can have.
William Temple, *Nature, Man and God,* Macmillan & Co. Ltd., 1934, p.491.

The particular sacraments are meant to teach us that all life is sacramental. Every
deliberate act should be, in a sense, the outward sign of inward grace. A sacrament
is more than a symbol. A symbol leads us from the lower to the higher; a sacrament
brings us back again to earth, but infuses a heavenly meaning and divine potency into
common things and actions.
W.R. Inge, *Personal Religion and the Life of Devotion,* Longmans, Green & Co. Ltd., 1924, p.47.

Let me ask you a question: are we still able to understand what a sacrament means?
The more we are estranged from nature, the less we can answer affirmatively. That
is why, in our time, the sacraments have lost so much of their significance for individuals and Churches. For in the sacraments nature participates in the process of
salvation. Bread and wine, water and light, and all the great elements of nature become
the bearers of spiritual meaning and saving power. Natural and spiritual powers are
united—reunited—in the sacrament. The word appeals to our intellect and may move

our will. The sacrament, if its meaning is still alive, grasps our unconscious as well as our conscious being. It grasps the creative ground of our being. It is the symbol of nature and spirit, united in salvation.

Paul Tillich, *The Shaking of the Foundations*, S.C.M. Press Ltd., 1949, p.86.

When psalmist or prophet calls Israel to lift their eyes to the hills, or to behold how the heavens declare the glory of God, or to listen to that unbroken tradition, which day passes to day and night to night, of the knowledge of the Creator, it is not proofs to doubting minds which he offers: it is spiritual nourishment to hungry souls. These are not arguments—they are sacraments.
When we Christians go to the Lord's Supper, we go not to have the Lord proved to us, but to feed upon a life and a love of whose existence we are past all doubt. Our sacrament fills all the mouths by which needy faith is fed—such as outward sight, and imagination, and memory, and wonder, and love. Now very much what the Lord's Supper is to us for fellowship with God and feeding upon Him, that were the glory of the heavens, and the everlasting hills, and the depths of the sea, and the vision of the stars to the Hebrews. They were the sacraments of God. By them faith was fed, and the spirit of man entered into the enjoyment of God, whose existence indeed he had never doubted, but whom he had lost, forgotten, or misunderstood.

George Adam Smith, *The Book of Isaiah*, Hodder and Stoughton Ltd., 1927, Volume II, p.91.

The sacraments are a perpetual witness that man thus needs something done to him, here and now. They declare that an access of Supernature is needed, which he cannot get alone: and that this access of Supernature will reach him most easily along natural paths. Their whole emphasis is on this given-ness. They remind us that our innate thirst for the Infinite is not the governing fact of our religious life, and cannot be satisfied by any effort we are able to make. That Infinite must come to us before we can go to it; and it is within the sensory and historical frame of human experience that such supernatural gifts are best and most surely received by our successive and sense-conditioned souls. Thus the sacramental principle continues to press upon us that profound truth which the Incarnation so vividly exhibits: that the whole of man's spiritual history, both corporate and solitary, involves and entirely rests in the free self-giving of God—is conditioned from first to last by the action of His all-penetrating, prevenient and eternal love.... Through the Christian sacraments that self-giving, of which the Incarnation is the supreme example, finds another and a continuous expression: sense here becoming the vehicle through which the very Spirit of Life enters into the little lives of men.

Evelyn Underhill, *Man and the Supernatural*, Methuen & Co. Ltd., 1927, p.180.

SACRIFICE

There is no man who has left house or wife or brothers or parents or children, for the sake of the kingdom of God, who will not receive manifold more in this time, and in the age to come eternal life.

Luke 18.29.

Greater love has no man than this, that a man lay down his life for his friends.

John 15.13.

Present your bodies as a living sacrifice, holy and acceptable to God, which is your spiritual worship.

Romans 12.1.

Sacrifice is the first element of religion, and resolves itself in theological language into the love of God.

J.A. Froude, *Short Studies on Great Subjects,* Longmans, Green & Co. Ltd., 1907, Volume IV, p.176.

In common things the law of sacrifice takes the form of positive duty.

J.A. Froude, *Short Studies on Great Subjects,* Longmans, Green & Co. Ltd., 1907, Volume IV, p.175.

Was anything real ever gained without sacrifice of some kind?

Arthur Helps, *Friends in Council,* George Routledge & Sons, Ltd., 1907, p.165.

Inwardness, mildness, and self-renouncement do make for man's happiness.

Matthew Arnold, *The Complete Prose Works of Matthew Arnold,* Volume VI, *Dissent and Dogma,* edited by R.H. Super, Ann Arbor, The University of Michigan Press, 1968, "Literature and Dogma," ch.3, p.229.

Too long a sacrifice,
Can make a stone of the heart.

W.B. Yeats, *The Collected Poems of W.B. Yeats,* Macmillan & Co. Ltd., 1973, p.204, "Easter 1916."

Standing before God the only thing we have to offer him is ourselves. And the extraordinary part is that this is exactly what he wants.

Hubert van Zeller, *Considerations,* Sheed and Ward Ltd., 1974, p.123.

The church's glory is not its power and numerical superiority, nor its system or its discipline or its theology. Its glory lies in its willingness to sacrifice.

Hubert van Zeller, *Considerations,* Sheed and Ward Ltd., 1974, p.79.

Without sacrifice there is no resurrection. Nothing grows and blooms save by giving. All you try to save in yourself wastes and perishes.

André Gide, *Fruits of the Earth,* Penguin Books Ltd., in association with Secker & Warburg, 1976, p.156.

Measure thy life by loss instead of gain;
Not by the wine drunk, but the wine poured forth;
For love's strength standeth in love's sacrifice;
And whoso suffers most hath most to give.

Harriet Eleanor Hamilton King, *The Disciples,* Kegan Paul & Co., 1880, p.100.

The vine lives to give its life-blood. Its flower is small, its fruit abundant; and when that fruit is mature and the vine has for a moment become glorious, the treasure of the grapes is torn down and the vine is cut back to the stem and next year blooms again,
Not bitter for the torment undergone.

Not barren for the fulness yielded up.

William Temple, *Readings in St. John's Gospel* (First and Second Series), Macmillan & Co. Ltd., 1947, p.252.

If sacrifice, total self-giving to God's mysterious purpose, is what is asked of us, His answer to that sacrifice is the gift of power. Easter and Whitsuntide complete the Christian Mystery by showing us first Our Lord Himself and then His chosen apostles possessed of a new power— the power of the Spirit—which changed every situation in which they were placed. That supernatural power is still the inheritance of every Christian, and our idea of Christianity is distorted and incomplete unless we rely on it. It is this power and only this which can bring in the new Christian society of which we hear so much. We ought to pray for it; expect it and trust it; and as we do this, we shall gradually become more and more sure of it.

Evelyn Underhill, *The Fruits of the Spirit*, Longmans, Green & Co. Ltd., 1949, p.71.

SAINTS

God creates out of *nothing*, wonderful, you say: yes, to be sure, but he does what is still more wonderful: he makes saints out of sinners.

Søren Kierkegaard, *The Journals of Søren Kierkegaard*, a selection edited and translated by Alexander Dru, Oxford University Press, 1938, p.59.

Grace is indeed needed to turn a man into a saint; and he who doubts it does not know what a saint or a man is.

Blaise Pascal, *Pensées*, translated by W.F. Trotter, Random House Inc., 1941, p.165.

They may have had their trials too—failing health, declining years, the ingratitude of men—but they have endured as seeing Him who is invisible.

Benjamin Jowett, *College Sermons*, edited by W.H. Fremantle, John Murray Ltd., 1895, p.317.

The power of the Soul for good is in proportion to the strength of its passions. Sanctity is not the negation of passion but its order.... Hence great Saints have often been great sinners.

Coventry Patmore, *The Rod, the Root and the Flower*, Grey Walls Press Ltd., 1950, p.51, "Aurea Dicta," cxxxii.

They were men of intense religious faith, of marked mystical type, characterized by interior depth of experience, but at the same time they were men of scholarship, breadth and balance.

Rufus M. Jones, *Spiritual Reformers in the 16th and 17th Centuries*, Macmillan & Co. Ltd., 1914, p.336.

This man is known by five signs. First, he never complains. Next, he never makes excuses: when accused, he leaves the facts to vindicate him. Thirdly, there is nothing he wants in earth or heaven but what God wills himself. Fourthly, he is not moved in time. Fifthly, he is never rejoiced: he is joy itself.

Meister Eckhart, *Meister Eckhart*, Franz Pfeiffer, translated by C. de B. Evans, John M. Watkins, 1956, Volume I, p.327.

I have met in my life two persons, one a man, the other a woman, who convinced me that they were persons of sanctity. Utterly different in character, upbringing and interests as they were, their effect on me was the same. In their presence I felt myself to be ten times as nice, ten times as intelligent, ten times as good-looking as I really am.

W.H. Auden, *A Certain World*, Faber and Faber Limited, 1971, p.331.

A saint is not so much a man who realizes that he possesses virtues and sanctity as one who is overwhelmed by the sanctity of God. God is holiness. And therefore things are holy in proportion as they share what He is. All creatures are holy insofar as they share in His being, but men are called to be holy, in a far superior way—by somehow sharing His transcendence and rising above the level of everything that is not God.

Thomas Merton, *The Sign of Jonas*, Sheldon Press, 1976, p.262.

What is a Saint? A particular individual completely redeemed from self-occupation; who, because of this, is able to embody and radiate a measure of Eternal Life. His whole life, personal, social, intellectual, mystical, is lived in supernatural regard. What is he for? To help, save, and enlighten by his loving actions and contemplations; to oppose in one way or another, by suffering, prayer and work upon heroic levels of love and self-oblation, the mysterious downward drag within the world, which we call sin.

Evelyn Underhill, *Man and the Supernatural*, Methuen & Co. Ltd., 1927, p.237.

The saints are men and women of prayer to whom we owe our deepest revelations of the Supernatural—those who give us real news about God— are never untrained amateurs or prodigies. Such men and women as Paul, Augustine, Catherine, Julian, Ruysbroeck, are genuine artists of eternal life. They have accepted and not scorned the teachings of tradition: and humbly trained and disciplined their God-given genius for ultimates.

Evelyn Underhill, *Man and the Supernatural*, Methuen & Co. Ltd., 1927, p.211.

There is after all something in Christian saintliness which eludes analysis. For saintliness is the partial expression, the reflection in the external life, of the hidden man of the heart, who is not fully known even by the saint himself; and it is always imperfect, because it is always going on to perfection. I will not have my portrait painted, said a holy man; for which man do you want to paint? One of them is not worth painting, and the other is not finished yet.

W.R. Inge, *Types of Christian Saintliness*, Longmans, Green & Co., 1915, p.92.

Saints are people who have had an encounter with God, however they name him, and have had their lives changed as a consequence. This can be seen significantly in the call of the first disciples, their training by Jesus and their sending out to serve the world in witness and love. None of them were men of wisdom by human standards, none of them from the noblest families or in positions of power. But because of their devotion and faithfulness to our Lord they made their contribution to God's purpose of love. This is repeated in every generation by faithful followers who live for Jesus, if necessary die for him and whatever be the manner of their death die in him.

George Appleton, *Journey for a Soul,* William Collins Sons & Co. Ltd., 1976, p.190.

Praise be unto God, Who hath consumed the hearts of His saints in the fire of His love and hath taken captive their desires and their spirits by the longing to meet with Him and to look upon Him and hath fixed their sight and their insight upon the vision of the Beauty of His Presence, until by the inbreathing of the spirit of Union, they have become rapt beyond themselves and their hearts have become distraught by the contemplation of the splendours of the Divine Glory, so that they see naught but Him in this world or the world to come, and they remember none in heaven or earth save Him alone.... Their grief is only in Him and their longing is only for that which is to be found in his Presence, they are aroused only for Him, and their going to and fro is round about Him alone. For from Him is all that they hear and it is to Him that they give heed, since He hath closed their eyes to all but Himself and hath made them deaf to all words save His. These are they whom God hath called to be His saints, having claimed them for Himself from among His chosen and His elect.

Al-Ghazali, *Al-Ghazali, The Mystic,* Margaret Smith, Luzac & Co., 1944, p.196.

Ours is an age of violence and disbelief. But in spite of that, or perhaps because of it, the earth's interest in virtuous accomplishment is stronger now than it has been at any time since the Age of Reason began ousting religion from its seat of authority. God may be dead insofar as theological concepts no longer direct political and economic affairs. But His heroes still interest the race. They are quoted by columnists, cited by historians, their names taken not always in vain by novelists, biographers, and agnostic tractarians. Thomas More was not long ago the protagonist of a noble play, a notable film; as was Becket twice in a decade. Joan of Arc never fails the playwright. Not long ago in the sober *New York Times* an editorial recommended that in our dealings with nature we try, for the sake of conservation, to become more like Francis of Assisi who considered all living creatures his brothers.
In times of crisis we need saints; and we often breed them, too. They appeared by hundreds in the first centuries of Christianity when Europe was struggling out of nearly universal darkness into what then passed for the light of civilization. They flourished during the Reformation on both sides of the conflict. Wherever and whenever an evil has existed, from slave-trading to the miseries of famine and war, saints have sprung up to mitigate those evils. They may well be rising among us now, preparing to lead us out of the onrushing night which so threateningly descends. As a matter of fact, I think I number two or three among my acquaintance.
One of them spends himself among impoverished Negroes of the South, one wears himself out in Northern slums, the third (completely without personal possessions) by some sleight of hand and heart feeds and lodges hundreds of Bowery derelicts each week.

Phyllis McGinley, *Saint-Watching,* William Collins Sons & Co. Ltd., 1970, p.15,28.

SALVATION

For the gate is narrow and the way is hard, that leads to life, and those who find it are few.

Matthew 7.14.

Work out your own salvation with fear and trembling; for God is at work in you, both to will and to work for his good pleasure.

Philippians 2.12-13.

For you were straying like sheep, but have now returned to the Shepherd and Guardian of your souls.

1 Peter 2.25.

Christ died to save us, not from suffering, but from ourselves; not from injustice, far less from justice, but from being unjust. He died that we might live—but live as he lives, by dying as he died who died to himself that he might live unto God.

George Macdonald, *Unspoken Sermons*, Third Series, Longmans, Green and Co., 1889, p.96.

The notion that the salvation of Jesus is a salvation from the consequences of our sins is a false mean, low notion.... Jesus did not die to save us from punishment; He was called Jesus because he should save his people from their sins.

George Macdonald, *Unspoken Sermons*, Third Series, Longmans, Green and Co., 1889, p.132.

What is most contrary to salvation is not sin but habit.

Charles Péguy, *Basic Verities*, translated by Ann & Julian Green, Kegan Paul, Trench, Trubner & Co. Ltd., 1943, p.181.

There is but one salvation for all mankind, and that is the life of God in the soul. God has but one design or intent towards all mankind and that is to introduce or generate His own life, light, and Spirit in them, that all may be as so many images, temples and habitations of the Holy Trinity.... There is not one for the Jew, another for a Christian, and a third for the heathen. No; God is one, human nature is one, salvation is one, and the way to it is one; and that is, the desire of the soul turned to God.

William Law, *Selected Mystical Writings of William Law*, edited by Stephen Hobhouse, Rockliff, 1948, p.102.

The true aim of the soul is not its own salvation; to make that the chief aim is to ensure its perdition ("Whosoever would save his soul shall lose it."—St. Matthew 16.25); for it is to fix the soul on itself as centre. The true aim of the soul is to glorify God; in pursuing that aim it will attain to salvation unawares. No one who is convinced of his own salvation is as yet even safe, let alone "saved." Salvation is the state of him who has ceased to be interested whether he is saved or not, provided that what takes the place of that supreme self-interest is not a lower form of self-interest but the glory of God.

William Temple, *Nature, Man and God*, Macmillan & Co. Ltd., 1934, p.390.

Consider yourself a refractory pupil for whom you are responsible as mentor and tutor. To sanctify sinful nature, by bringing it gradually under control of the angel within us, by the help of a holy God, is really the whole of Christian pedagogy and of religious morals. Our work—my work—consists in taming, subduing, evangelising and *angelising* the evil self; and in restoring harmony with the good self.

Salvation lies in abandoning the evil self in principle, and in taking refuge with the other, the divine self,—in accepting with courage and prayer the task of living with one's own demon, and making it into a less and less rebellious instrument of good. The Abel in us must labour for the salvation of the Cain. To undertake it is to be converted, and this conversion must be repeated day by day. Abel only redeems and touches Cain by exercising him constantly in good works. To do right is in one sense an act of violence: it is suffering, expiation, a cross, for it means the conquest and enslavement of self. In another sense it is the apprenticeship to heavenly things, sweet and secret joy, contentment and peace.

Henri Frédéric Amiel, *Amiel's Journal,* translated by Mrs. Humphry Ward, Macmillan & Co. Ltd., 1918, p.70.

Who are you who go about to save them that are lost?
Are you saved yourself?
Do you not know that who would save his own life must lose it?
Are you then one of the "lost"?
Be sure, very sure, that each one of these can teach you as much as, probably more than, you can teach them.
Have you then sat humbly at their feet, and waited on their lips that they should be the first to speak—and been reverent before these children— whom you so little understand?
Have you dropped into the bottomless pit from between yourself and them all hallucination of superiority, all flatulence of knowledge, every shred of abhorrence and loathing?
Is it equal, is it free as the wind between you?
Could you be happy receiving favours from one of the most despised of these?
Could you be yourself one of the lost?
Arise, then, and become a saviour.

Edward Carpenter, *Towards Democracy,* George Allen & Unwin Ltd., 1931, p.180.

The future (of mankind) will be dependant on a saving group, embodied in one nation or crossing through all nations. There is saving power in mankind, but there is also the hidden will to self-destruction. It depends on every one of us which side will prevail. There is no divine promise that humanity will survive this or next year. But it may depend on the saving power effective in you or me, whether it will survive. (It may depend on the amount of healing and liberating grace which works through any of us with respect to social justice, racial equality, and political wisdom.) Unless many of us say to ourselves: Through the saving power working in me, mankind may be saved or lost—it will be lost.

But in order to be the bearers of saving power, we must be saved ourselves; the wall separating us from eternal life must be broken through. And here is one thing which strengthens the wall and keeps us sick and enslaved. It is our estrangement and guilt which are the impediments which keep us from reaching eternal life here and now. The judgement against us which we confirm in our conscience is the sickness unto death, the despair of life, from which we must be halted in order to say *yes* to life. Healed life is new life, delivered from the bondage of the evil one. Here the last two petitions of our Lord's Prayer become one petition: forgive our trespasses, and deliver us from the evil one—this is one and the same thing. And if we call Jesus, the Christ, our saviour, then we mean that in him we see the power which heals us by accepting us and which liberates us by showing us in his being a new being—a being in which there is reconciliation with ourselves, with our world, and with the divine ground of our world and ourselves.

And now the last question: Who shall be saved, liberated, healed? The fourth gospel says: The world! The reunion with the eternal from which we come, from which we are separated, to which we shall return, is promised to everything that is. We are saved not as individuals but in unity with all others and with the universe. Our own liberation does not leave the enslaved ones alone, our own healing is a part of the great healing of the world. Therefore, two other petitions of our Lord's Prayer also ask the same: Save us from the evil one, and thy Kingdom come! This Kingdom is his creation, liberated and healed. This is what we hope for when we look from time to eternity. Deliver us—heal us—that is the cry of everything that is; of each of us in unity with all mankind and in unity with the whole universe. The divine answer is: I shall return to me what is separated from me because it belongs to me. I am liberating you today as I did before and will do in the future. Today, when you hear these words, "I am liberating you, I am healing you," do not resist!

Paul Tillich, *The Eternal Now*, S.C.M. Press Ltd., 1963, p. 101.

SANCTIFICATION

For this is the will of God, your sanctification.

1 Thessalonians 4.3.

All that should be sought for in the exercise of prayer is conformity of our will with the Divine Will; assuredly in this consists the highest perfection.

St. Teresa of Avila, in *On Conformity with the Will of God*, translated by the Rev. James Jones, Catholic Truth Society, 1892, p.8.

Sanctity is not getting noticeably nicer as you go along. It is a revolution. It is continuous conversion.

Hubert van Zeller, *Considerations*, Sheed & Ward Ltd., 1974, p.32.

Even when the marks of it are patently obvious to other people, holiness is not something which the saint sees in himself. It is something he sees by. His prayer and charity give him the right perspectives.

Hubert van Zeller, *Considerations*, Sheed and Ward Ltd., 1974, p.31.

Every heroic devotion to beauty, truth, goodness, every ungrudging sacrifice, is a crucifixion of self-interest, and thus lies in the direction of sanctity; and wherever we find sanctity we find the transforming act of God, of supernature, upon the creature, irrespective of that creature's dogmatic belief. All Saints, that "glorious touching Company," will doubtless include many whom the world classed among its irreligious men.

Evelyn Underhill, *Man and the Supernatural*, Methuen & Co. Ltd., 1927, p.237.

There is nothing that so sanctifies the heart of man, that keeps us in such habitual love, prayer, and delight in God; nothing that so kills all the roots of evil in our nature, that so renews and perfects all our virtues, that fills us with so much love, goodness, and good wishes to every creature as this faith that God is always present in us with His light and Holy Spirit.

William Law, *Selected Mystical Writings of William Law*, edited by Stephen Hobhouse, Rockliff, 1948, p.32.

All gardeners know the importance of good root development before we force the leaves and flowers. So our life in God should be deeply rooted and grounded before we presume to expect to produce flowers or fruits; otherwise we risk shooting up into one of those lanky plants which never do without a stick. We are constantly beset by the notion that we ought to perceive ourselves springing up quickly, like the seed on stony ground; showing striking signs of spiritual growth. But perhaps we are only required to go on quietly, making root, growing nice and bushy; docile to the great slow rhythm of life. When we see no startling marks of our own religious progress or our usefulness to God, it is well to remember the baby in the stable and the little boy in the streets of Nazareth. The very life was there present, which was to change the whole history of the human race; the rescuing action of God. At that stage there was not much to show for it; yet there is perfect continuity between the stable and the Easter garden, and the thread that unites them is the hidden Will of God. The childish prayer of Nazareth was the right preparation for the awful prayer of the Cross. So it is that the life of the Spirit is to unfold gently and steadily within us; till at the last the full stature for which God designed us is attained.

Evelyn Underhill, *The School of Charity*, Longmans, Green & Co. Ltd., 1956, p.48.

Lastly: although there was no definite religious sentiment mingled with it, there was a continual perception of Sanctity in the whole of nature, from the slightest thing to the vastest;—an instinctive awe, mixed with delight; an indefinable thrill, such as we sometimes imagine to indicate the presence of a disembodied spirit. I could only feel this perfectly when I was alone; and then it would often make me shiver from head to foot with the joy and fear of it, when after being some time away from hills, I first got to the shore of a mountain river, where the brown water circled among the pebbles, or when I first saw the swell of distant land against the sunset, or the first low broken wall, covered with mountain moss. I cannot in the least *describe* the feeling; but I do not think this is my fault, nor that of the English language, for I am afraid, no feeling *is* describable. If we had to explain even the sense of bodily hunger to a person who had never felt it, we should be hard put to it for words; and the joy in nature seemed to me to come of a sort of heart-hunger, satisfied with the presence of a Great and Holy Spirit. These feelings remained in their full intensity till I was eighteen or twenty, and then, as the reflective and practical power increased, and the "cares of this world" gained upon me, faded gradually away, in the manner described by Wordsworth in his Intimations of Immortality.

John Ruskin, *Modern Painters,* George Allen & Sons, 1910, Volume III, p.309, Part IV, ch.xvii, sec.19.

SCIENCE AND RELIGION

Science may have found a cure for most evils; but it has found no remedy for the worst of them all—the apathy of human beings.

Helen Keller, *My Religion,* Hodder & Stoughton Ltd., 1927, p.162.

The means by which we live have outdistanced the ends for which we live. Our scientific power has outrun our spiritual power. We have guided missiles and misguided man.

Martin Luther King, *Strength to Love,* William Collins Sons & Co. Ltd., 1980, p.74.

Science investigates; religion interprets. Science gives man knowledge which is power; religion gives man wisdom which is control.

Martin Luther King, *Strength to Love,* William Collins Sons & Co., Ltd., 1980, p.11.

Anybody who has been seriously engaged in scientific work of any kind realizes that over the entrance to the gates of the temple of science are written the words: *Ye must have faith.* It is a quality which the scientist cannot dispense with.

Max Planck, *Where is Science Going?* translated and edited by James Murphy, George Allen & Unwin Ltd., 1933, p.214.

The simple and plain fact is that the scientific method wins its success by ignoring parts of reality as given in experience; it is perfectly right to do this for its own purposes; but it must not be permitted by a kind of bluff to create the impression that what it ignores is non-existent.

William Temple, *Nature, Man and God,* Macmillan & Co. Ltd., 1934, p.216.

The theologian who quarrels with science on its own ground is but a presumptuous fool. But the scientist who quarrels with theology on its own ground is no better. If there is mutual respect and common reverence for truth in all its forms there may still be divergence and even what we have called tension; but there will be no quarrel.

William Temple, *Nature, Man and God,* Macmillan & Co., Ltd., 1934, p.288.

Science cannot solve the ultimate mystery of nature. And that is because, in the last analysis, we ourselves are part of nature and therefore part of the mystery that we are trying to solve. Music and art are, to an extent, also attempts to solve or at least to express the mystery. But to my mind the more we progress with either the more we are brought into harmony with all nature itself. And that is one of the great services of science to the individual.

Max Planck, *Where Is Science Going?* translated and edited by James Murphy, George Allen & Unwin Ltd., 1933, p.217.

You will hardly find one among the profounder sort of scientific minds without a religious feeling of his own.... His religious feeling takes the form of a rapturous amazement at the harmony of natural law, which reveals an intelligence of such superiority that, compared with it, all systematic thinking and acting of human beings is an utterly insignificant reflection. This feeling is the guiding principle of his life and work, in so far as he succeeds in keeping himself from the shackles of selfish desire. It is beyond question closely akin to that which has possessed the religious geniuses of all ages.

Albert Einstein, *Ideas and Opinions*, Souvenir Press (Educational & Academic) Ltd., 1973, p.40.

The scientist has a faith ... which is reflected in the fact that he would never consider that an experiment begun on a Wednesday would yield entirely different results from one undertaken on a Friday. He believes in the orderliness of the universe. He stakes his shirt on his faith that everything happens in such a reasonable and well-ordered fashion that the same experiment will give the same result.... If the contents of our universe did not behave in so regular and predictable a fashion no real scientific research would be possible.

Roger Pilkington, *World Without End*, Macmillan & Co. Ltd., 1960, p.13.

It is, I think, of the very essence of the unseen world that the conception of personality should dominate it. Force, energy, dimensions belong to the world of symbols; it is out of such conceptions that we have built up the external world of physics. What other conceptions have we? After exhausting physical methods we returned to the inmost recesses of consciousness, to the voice that proclaims our personality; and from there we entered on a new outlook. We have to build the spiritual world out of symbols taken from our own personality, as we build the scientific world out of the symbols of the mathematician. I think therefore we are not wrong in embodying the significance of the spiritual world to ourselves in the feeling of a personal relationship, for our whole approach to it is bound up with those aspects of consciousness in which personality is centred.

Arthur S. Eddington, *Science and the Unseen World*, George Allen & Unwin Ltd., 1929, p.50.

We all know that there are regions of the human spirit untrammelled by the world of physics. In the mystic sense of the creation around us, in the expression of art, in a yearning towards God, the soul grows upward and finds the fulfilment of something implanted in its nature. The sanction for this development is within us, a striving born with our consciousness or an Inner Light proceeding from a greater power than ours. Science can scarcely question this sanction, for the pursuit of science springs from a striving which the mind is impelled to follow, a questioning that will not be suppressed. Whether in the intellectual pursuits of science or in the mystical pursuits of the spirit, the light beckons ahead and the purpose surging in our nature responds.

Arthur S. Eddington, *The Nature of the Physical World*, Cambridge at the University Press, 1928, p.327.

Every scientific statement in the long run, however complicated it looks, really means something like, "I pointed the telescope to such and such a part of the sky at 2.20 a.m. on January 15th and saw so-and-so," or, "I put some of this stuff in a pot and heated it to such-and-such a temperature and it did so-and-so." Do not think I am saying anything against science: I am only saying what its job is. And the more scientific a man is, the more (I believe) he would agree with me that this is the job of science—and a very useful and necessary job it is too. But why anything comes to be there at all, and whether there is anything behind the things science observes—something of a different kind—this is not a scientific question. If there is "Something Behind," then either it will have to remain altogether unknown to men or else make itself known in some different way. The statement that there is any such thing, and the statement that there is no such thing, are neither of them statements that science can make.... Supposing science ever became complete so that it knew every single thing in the whole universe. Is it not plain that the question, "Why is there a universe?" "Why does it go on as it does?" "Has it any meaning?" would remain just as they were?

C.S. Lewis, *Mere Christianity*, William Collins Sons & Co. Ltd., 1961, p.30.

All science has God as its author and giver. Much is heard of the conflict between science and religion, and of the contrast between sacred and secular. There may be aspects of truth to which religion is the gate, as indeed there are aspects of truth to which particular sciences are the gate. But if there be a Creator, and if truth be one of his attributes, then everything that is true can claim his authorship, and every search for truth can claim his authority.

When science has appeared to be anti-religious it generally has meant that one or two particular sciences were exaggerating their claim to a sort of omnicompetence for reading the whole meaning of the universe, even though one particular science is, of course, not competent to do more than read one particular aspect of the universe. But the more we Christians are ready to see and acknowledge God in the sciences—God in the truly scientific spirit—the more we shall be witnessing to what is true to the presence of God in the world, and the more entitled we shall be to go on to point out that there can indeed be a certain sort of scientifically trained mentality which is narrow and unperceptive, and robbing itself of a real chance of interpreting the universe aright.

Michael Ramsey, *Through the Year with Michael Ramsey*, edited by Margaret Duggan, Hodder & Stoughton Ltd., 1975, p.147.

What is sometimes called the conflict between religion and science often proves to be not between religion and science as such, but between bad religion making wrong claims and a bad scientific outlook also making false claims.

A narrow kind of religion that can see God only in biblical literalism, and is blind to the presence of God in the sciences (which, if we could learn from them, would help us to understand the Bible itself better)—that sort of narrowness is a positive invitation to the scientific man to take an anti-religious standpoint, because we are taking a less than truly religious standpoint ourselves in our claim.

We may complain that the scientific mind—by which I think we really mean the technological kind of mind—is very often blind to spiritual values because it practises a sort of omnicompetence which so blinds it.

But we are not now talking about certain sorts of scientific mind, but about the sciences themselves. Take a genuine human science practised with skill and knowledge and integrity. Its author is said to be Mr. So-and-so, or Sir Somebody-Somebody, or Lord Somebody the great biologist, the great geologist, the great astronomer—or whatnot. But the real author of any science is God—the divine Spirit, the Spirit of Truth at work.

It is for us Christians to be far more sensitive to the presence of God in the very middle of all human sciences, and to be more ready to acknowledge God there.

If scientists sometimes are not Christians or believers, we do not help by being blind to God in their work. No, we must all the more acknowledge that God is the author and sustainer of the sciences.

Michael Ramsey, *Through the Year with Michael Ramsey*, edited by Margaret Duggan, Hodder & Stoughton Ltd., 1975, p.148.

SECULAR

Secularism is a form of opinion which concerns itself only with questions the issues of which can be tested by the experience of this life.

G.J. Holyoake, *The Origin and Nature of Secularism*, Watts & Co., 1896, p.63.

If only we knew how to look at life as God sees it, we should realize that nothing is secular in the world, but that everything contributes to the building of the kingdom of God.

Michel Quoist, *Prayers of Life*, translated by Anne Marie de Commaile & Agnes Mitchell Forsyth, Gill & Macmillan Ltd., 1963, p.10.

St. John saw no temple in his vision of the new Jerusalem. The temple as the symbol of the sacred is no longer needed, because its mission has been accomplished. God is in everything. In one way the eternal city is a secular city; in another way the secular city has been permeated and become sacred.

George Appleton, *Journey for a Soul*, William Collins Sons & Co. Ltd., 1976, p.146.

Secular conformism, presentation of a false image, ambition at the expense of others, emphasis on money and position: these are the marks of "living in the flesh." Leaving the disposal of life to God, referring decisions to gospel principles, trying to reflect Christ's life: these are marks of "living in the spirit."

Hubert van Zeller, *Considerations*, Sheed and Ward Ltd., 1974, p.85.

In the Holy Communion service we take the bread and wine—man's industrial and commercial life in symbol—and offer it to God; because we have offered it to Him, He gives it back to us as the means of nurturing us, not in our animal nature alone, but as agents of His purpose, limbs of a body responsive to His will; and as we receive it back from Him, we share it with one another in true fellowship. If we think of the service in this way, it is a perfect picture of what secular society ought to be.

William Temple, *The Hope of a New World*, S.C.M. Press Ltd., 1940, p.70.

Many religious people are troubled about the secularization of modern life. In one way this is good and right, for values which were once thought of as religious have now passed into the texture of society. Also there are areas of human life which have their own distinctive laws which ought not to be governed by religious views or ecclesiastical direction. On the other hand, Christians must question the assumption that man's relation to the objective world is the whole of life. There is a spiritual dimension of life which people ignore at their peril. The aim for the Christian is to humanize the sacred and to regard the whole of life as good and God-given.

George Appleton, *Journey for a Soul*, William Collins Sons & Co. Ltd., 1976, p.144.

SEEKING

Those who seek me diligently find me.
Proverbs 8.17.

You will seek me and find me; when you seek me with all your heart, I will be found by you.
Jeremiah 29.13-14.

Seek, and you will find.
Matthew 7.7.

A man travels the world over in search of what he needs and returns home to find it.
George Moore, *The Brook Kerith*, William Heinemann Ltd., 1927, p.121.

Even in the midst of the lowest pleasures, the most abandoned voluptuary is still seeking God; nay more, as far as regards what is positive in his acts, that is to say in all that makes them an analogue of the true Love, it is God Himself Who, in him and for him, seeks Himself.
Etienne Gilson, *The Spirit of Mediaeval Philosophy*, translated by A.H.C. Downes, Sheed and Ward, Ltd., 1950, p.274.

Know that, by nature, every creature seeks to become like God.... Nature's intent is neither food nor drink, nor clothing, nor comfort, nor anything else in which God is left out. Covertly, nature seeks, hunts, tries to ferret out the track on which God may be found.
Meister Eckhart, *Meister Eckhart*, translated by Raymond B. Blakney, Harper & Row, Publishers, Inc., 1941, p.167.

Hold fast to God and he will add every good thing. Seek God and you shall find him and all good with him.... To the man who cleaves to God, God cleaves and adds virtue. Thus, what you have sought before, now seeks you; what once you pursued, now pursues you; what once you fled, now flees you. Everything comes to him who truly comes to God, bringing all divinity with it, while all that is strange and alien flies away.
Meister Eckhart, *Meister Eckhart*, translated by Raymond B. Blakney, Harper & Row, Publishers, Inc., 1941, p.7.

Seek and ye shall find. But what is one to seek? A conscious and living communion with the Lord. This is given by the grace of God, but it is also essential that we ourselves should work, that we ourselves should come to meet Him. How? By always remembering God, who is near the heart and even present within it. To succeed in this remembrance it is advisable to accustom oneself to the continual repetition of the Jesus Prayer, "Lord Jesus Christ, Son of God, have mercy upon me," holding in mind the thought of God's nearness, His presence in the heart. But it must also be understood that in itself the Jesus Prayer is only an outer oral prayer; inner prayer is to stand before the Lord, continually crying out to Him without words.

By this means remembrance of God will be established in the mind, and the countenance of God will be in your soul like the sun. If you put something cold in the sun it begins to grow warm, and in the same way your soul will be warmed by the remembrance of God, who is the spiritual sun. What follows on from this will presently appear.

Your first task is to acquire the habit of repeating the Jesus Prayer unceasingly. So begin: and continually repeat and repeat, but all the time keep before you the thought of our Lord. And herein lies everything.

Theophan the Recluse, in *The Art of Prayer, An Orthodox Anthology,* compiled by Igumen Chariton of Valamo, translated by E. Kadloubovsky & E.M. Palmer, edited and introduced by Timothy Ware, Faber and Faber Limited, 1973, p.121.

I remember one day in the early spring-time I was listening to the sounds of a wood, and thinking only of one thing, the same of which I had constantly thought for two years—I was again seeking for a God.

I said to myself, "It is well, there is no God, there is none that has a reality apart from my own imaginings, none as real as my own life—there is none such. Nothing, no miracles can prove there is, for miracles only exist in my own unreasonable imagination."

And then I asked myself, "But my conception of the God whom I seek, whence comes it?" And again life flashed joyously through my veins. All around me seemed to revive, to have a new meaning. My joy, though, did not last long, for reason continued its work: "The conception of God is not God. Conception is what goes on within myself; the conception of God is an idea which I am able to rouse in my mind or not, as I choose; it is not what I seek, something without which life could not be." Then again all seemed to die around and within me, and again I wished to kill myself.

After this I began to retrace the process which had gone on within myself, the hundred-times-repeated discouragement and revival. I remembered that I had lived only when I believed in a God. As it was before so it was now; I had only to know God, and I lived; I had only to forget Him, not to believe in Him, and I died. What was this discouragement and revival? I do not live when I lose faith in the existence of a God; I should long ago have killed myself if I had not had a dim hope of finding Him. I only really live when I feel and seek Him. "What more, then, do I seek?" A voice seemed to cry within me, "This is He, He without whom there is no life! To know God and to live are one. God is life! Live to seek God, and life will not be without

Him." And stronger than ever rose up life within and around me, and the light that
then shone never left me again.

Leo Tolstoy, *How I Came to Believe*, C.W. Daniel, Limited, 1922, p.50.

THE SELF

We are potentially all things; our personality is what we are able to realise of the
infinite wealth which our divine-human nature contains hidden in its depths.

W.R. Inge, *The Philosophy of Plotinus*, Longmans, Green & Co. Ltd., 1918, Volume I, p.248.

The true value of a human being is determined primarily by the measure and the sense
in which he has attained liberation from the self.

Albert Einstein, *Ideas and Opinions*, Souvenir Press (Educational & Academic) Ltd., 1973, p.12.

Begin to search and dig in thine own Field for this *Pearl of Eternity*, that lies hidden
in it; it cannot cost Thee too much, nor canst thou buy it too dear, for it is *All*, and
when thou hast found it, thou wilt know, that all which thou hast sold or given away
for it, is as mere a Nothing, as a Bubble upon the Water.

William Law, *The Spirit of Prayer*, full text, edited with an introduction and notes by Sidney Spencer, James
Clarke & Co. Ltd., 1969, p.44.

> Not in the clamour of the crowded street,
> Not in the shouts and plaudits of the throng,
> But in ourselves, are triumph and defeat.

Henry Wadsworth Longfellow, *The Poetical Works of Longfellow*, Humphrey Milford, Oxford University Press,
1913, p.717, "The Poets," l.12.

But can one actually find oneself in someone else? In someone else's love? Or even in
the mirror someone else holds up for one? I believe that true identity is found, as
Eckhart once said, by "going into one's own ground and knowing oneself." It is found
in creative activity springing from within. It is found, paradoxically, when one loses
oneself. One must lose one's life to find it.

Anne Morrow Lindbergh, *Gift from the Sea*, Chatto & Windus Ltd., 1974, p.68.

Sincerity is the act whereby each of us at once knows and makes himself....
It is the quality of sincerity to oblige me to be myself, that is to become, by my own
agency, what I am. It is a search for my own essence, which begins to be adulterated
as soon as I borrow from outside the motives of my actions. For this essence is never
an object that I contemplate, but a work that I carry out, the bringing into play of
certain powers that are within me, and which atrophy if I cease to exercise them.
Sincerity consists in a certain tranquil courage by which we dare to enter existence,
as we are.

Louis Lavelle, in *Existentialism*, Paul Foulquié, translated by Kathleen Raine, Dennis Dobson, Ltd., 1947, p.119.

The all-one idea can definitely be realized or embodied only in the fulness of completed
individualities, this means that the final aim of the whole matter is the higher devel-

opment of each individuality in the perfected unity of all, but this latter necessarily comprises in itself also our own life-aim, which for us therefore no consideration or possibility separates or isolates from the aim common to all. We are just as necessary to the world, as the world is to us. The universe from time immemorial is interested in the preservation, development and perpetuation of all that is really necessary and desirable for us, all that is absolute and of worth in our individuality. And it remains to us only to accept, if possible more consciously and actively, our share in the general historical process—for our own selves and for all others *inseparably*.

Vladimir Solovyev, *The Meaning of Love*, translated by Jane Marshall, Geoffrey Bles, The Centenary Press, 1945, p.72.

The question is always: *Who am I?* and until that is discovered I don't see how one can really direct anything in one's self. *Is there a me?* One must be certain of that before one has a real unshakeable leg to stand on. And I don't believe for one moment these questions can be settled by the head alone. It is this life of the head, this intellectual life at the expense of all the rest which has got us into this state. How can it get us out of it? I see no hope of escape except by learning to live in our emotional and instinctive being as well, and to balance all three.
You see, if I were allowed one single cry to God, that cry would be: *I want to be REAL*. Until I am that I don't see why I shouldn't be at the mercy of old Eve in her various manifestations for ever... At this present moment all I know really, really, is that though one thing after another has been taken from me, I am not annihilated, and that I hope—more than hope—believe. It is hard to explain.

Katherine Mansfield, *The Letters of Katherine Mansfield*, edited by J. Middleton Murry, Constable & Co. Ltd., 1928, Volume II, p.266.

SELFISHNESS

A covetous man's eye is not satisfied with his portion; and the iniquity of the wicked drieth up his soul.

Ecclesiasticus 14.9 (A.V.).

The more selfish you are, the more involved life becomes.

Thomas Merton, *The Sign of Jonas*, Sheldon Press, 1976, p.102.

Man seeks his own good at the whole world's cost.

Robert Browning, *The Poetical Works of Robert Browning*, Volume I, Smith, Elder, & Co., 1899, p.441, *Luria*, Act I.

No man is more cheated than the selfish man.

Henry Ward Beecher, *Proverbs From Plymouth Pulpit*, Charles Burnett & Co., 1887, p.191.

The selfish heart deserves the pains it feels.

Edward Young, *Night Thoughts*, Thomas Nelson, 1841, p.8.

Selfish persons are incapable of loving others, but they are not capable of loving themselves either.

Erich Fromm, *Man For Himself*, Routledge and Kegan Paul Ltd., 1975, p.131.

Selfish men may possess the earth; but it is the meek who inherit it, and enjoy it as an inheritance from their heavenly Father, free from all the defilements and perplexities of unrighteousness.

John Woolman, *The Journal of John Woolman*, Edward Marsh, 1857, p.311.

If a man is centred upon himself, the smallest risk is too great for him, because both success and failure can destroy him. If he is centred upon God, then no risk is too great because success is already guaranteed—the successful union of Creator and creature beside which everything else is meaningless.

Morris West, *The Shoes of the Fisherman*, William Heinemann Ltd., 1963, p.296.

Anyone who from time to time will sit quiet with himself and survey his life and present state will be conscious of failure. He will remember things of which he is now ashamed. He will see his secret selfishness, his carefully controlled ambitions, his secret lusts. He will know the power of temptations—from without and within. He will recognize times of wilful choice of wrong attitudes and deeds. When he compares himself with the perfection of Jesus, he will realize his need of forgiveness, a fresh start and continuing grace.

George Appleton, *Journey for a Soul*, William Collins Sons & Co. Ltd., 1976, p.121.

For the self-centred spirit there can be no eternal life. Even if it should exist for ever, its existence could only be an ever deepening chill of death. Because it seeks its satisfaction in itself, where none is to be found, it must suffer an always intenser pang of spiritual hunger, which cannot be allayed until that spirit turns to another source of satisfaction. In the self which it contemplates there can only be successive states. The self is not sufficient to inspire a dedication such as brings purposive unity into life.

William Temple, *Nature, Man and God*, Macmillan & Co. Ltd., 1934, p.424.

The great evils of society do not result from the startling and appalling wickedness of some few individuals; they are the result of a few million people like ourselves living together; and if anyone wants to see the picture of his sin, let him look at slums, and wars, and the like. These things have their origin in characters like ours, ready, no doubt, to be generous with superfluities, but in the last resort self-centred with alike the defensiveness and aggressiveness that go with that self-centredness.

William Temple, *The Preacher's Theme To-day*, S.P.C.K., 1936, p.52.

High though his titles, proud his name,
Boundless his wealth as wish can claim;
Despite those titles, power, and pelf,
The wretch, concentrated all in self,
Living, shall forfeit fair renown,

And, doubly dying, shall go down
To the vile dust, from whence he sprung,
Unwept, unhonour'd, and unsung.

Sir Walter Scott, *The Poems and Plays of Sir Walter Scott,* introduced by Andrew Lang, J.M. Dent & Sons, Ltd., 1911, Volume I, "The Lay of the Last Minstrel," p.401.

To be a Christian is to be very closely united to Christ as living Lord, not alone but in the fellowship of the Church. It means an existence in which our self-centredness is constantly challenged and defeated. The more Christ becomes your true centre, the less can your own selfish pride be the centre. The more you are drawn into the fellowship of those who belong to Christ, the less are you entangled in your selfish pride. That is why again and again the Christian life has been called a "death to self"; it is the growth in us of Christ's own self-giving unto death. The Sacraments depict this: *Baptism* was from the beginning the means whereby the convert *died* to the old life whose centre was the self; and, having been buried symbolically beneath the water, he stepped out into a new life whose centre was Christ in the midst of the Church's fellowship. *Holy Communion* deepens our unity with Christ who, through the media of bread and wine, feeds us with himself. But it is always his self as given to death. It is his broken body, his blood poured and offered. These are the great realities upon which Christian people have laid hold. Some have grasped them, once, and forgotten them. Some have grasped them only in a conventional and unreal way. Some have grasped them, and courageously try to be true to them amid much conflict with the reassertions of self and of pride. Some have grasped them and have shewn it in lives in which, notwithstanding humiliating failures, Christ really has been apparent. It all happens through Calvary judging us, Calvary bringing forgiveness to us, and Calvary defeating the pride which rules us.

Michael Ramsey, *Introducing the Christian Faith,* S.C.M. Press Ltd., 1970, p.53.

SERENITY

You made us for yourself and our hearts find no peace until they rest in you.

St. Augustine, *Confessions,* translated with an introduction by R.S. Pine-Coffin, Penguin Books Ltd., 1964, p.21.

All men who live with any degree of serenity live by some assurance of grace.

Reinhold Niebuhr, *Reflections on the End of an Era,* Charles Scribner's Sons, 1936, p.284.

He who would be serene and pure needs but one thing, detachment.

Meister Eckhart, *Meister Eckhart,* Franz Pfeiffer, translated by C. de B. Evans, John M. Watkins, 1956, Volume I, p.341.

Serenity of Mind, and Calmness of Thought are a better Enjoyment; than any thing *without* us.

Benjamin Whichcote, *Moral and Religious Aphorisms,* 1930, Century III, No.280.

Serene yet strong, majestic yet sedate,
Swift without violence, without terror great.

Matthew Prior, *The Poetical Works of Matthew Prior,* edited by Charles Cowden Clarke, William P. Nimmo, 1868, p.116, "Carmen Seculare for the Year MDCC," l.282.

He who is of a calm and happy nature will hardly feel the pressure of age, but he who is of an opposite disposition will find youth and age equally a burden.

Plato, *The Republic of Plato,* translation, analysis and introduction by B. Jowett, Oxford at the Clarendon Press, 1881, p.3, Bk.I, 329.

Calm's not life's crown, though calm is well.
'Tis all perhaps which man acquires,
But 'tis not what our youth desires.

Matthew Arnold, *The Poems of Matthew Arnold,* edited by Kenneth Allott, Longmans, Green & Co. Ltd., 1965, p.225, "Youth and Calm," l.23.

Serene will be our days and bright,
And happy will our nature be,
When love is an unerring light,
And joy its own security.

William Wordsworth, *The Poetical Works of William Wordsworth,* edited by E. de Selincourt and Helen Darbishire, Oxford at the Clarendon Press, 1958, Volume IV, p.84, "Ode to Duty," l.17.

A sense of rest, of deep quiet even. Silence within and without. A quietly-burning fire. A sense of comfort ... I am not dazed or stupid, but only happy in this peaceful morning. Whatever may be the charm of emotion, I do not know whether it equals the sweetness of those hours of silent meditation, in which we have a glimpse and foretaste of the contemplative joys of Paradise. Desire and fear, sadness and care, are done away. Existence is reduced to the simplest form, the most ethereal mode of being, that is, to pure self-consciousness. It is a state of harmony, without tension and without disturbance, the dominical state of the soul, perhaps the state which awaits it beyond the grave. It is happiness as the Orientals understand it, the happiness of the anchorite, who neither struggles nor wishes any more, but simply adores and enjoys. It is difficult to find words in which to express this moral situation, for our languages can only render the particular and localised vibrations of life; they are incapable of expressing this motionless concentration, this divine quietude, this state of the resting ocean, which reflects the sky, and is master of its own profundities. Things are then re-absorbed into their principles; memories are swallowed up in memory; the soul is only soul, and is no longer conscious of itself in its individuality and separateness. It is something which feels the universal life, a sensible atom of the Divine, of God. It no longer appropriates anything to itself, it is conscious of no void. Only the Yoghis and Soufis perhaps have known in its profundity this humble and yet voluptuous state, which combines the joys of being and of non-being, which is neither reflection nor will, which is above both the moral existence and the intellectual existence, which is the return to unity, to the pleroma, the vision of Plotinus and of Proclus,—Nirvana in its most attractive form.

It is clear that the western nations ... know very little of this state of feeling. For them life is devouring and incessant activity. They are eager for gold, for power, for dominion; their aim is to crush men and to enslave nature. They show an obstinate interest in means, and have not a thought for the end. They confound being with individual being, and the expansion of the self with happiness,—that is to say, they do not live by the soul; they ignore the unchangeable and the eternal; they live at the periphery of their being, because they are unable to penetrate to its axis. They are excited, ardent, positive, because they are superficial. Why so much effort, noise, struggle, and greed?—it is all a mere stunning and deafening of the self. When death comes they recognise that it is so,—why not then admit it sooner? Activity is only beautiful when it is holy—that is to say, when it is spent in the service of that which passeth not away.

Henri Frédéric Amiel, *Amiel's Journal,* translated by Mrs. Humphry Ward, Macmillan & Co. Ltd., 1918, p.263.

SERVICE

When you have done all that is commanded of you, say, "We are unworthy servants; we have only done what was our duty."

Luke 17.10.

I am among you as one who serves.

Luke 22.27.

In Jesus the service of God and the service of the least of the brethren were one.

Dietrich Bonhoeffer, *The Cost of Discipleship,* revised and abridged edition, S.C.M. Press Ltd., 1959, p.118.

Be useful where thou livest.

George Herbert, *The Works of George Herbert,* edited by F.E. Hutchinson, Oxford at the Clarendon Press, 1972, p.19, *The Temple,* "The Church Porch," st.55, l.1.

They also serve who only stand and wait.

John Milton, Sonnet on his Blindness.

You have not done enough, you have never done enough, so long as it is still possible that you have something of value to contribute.

Dag Hammarskjold, *Markings,* translated by Leif Sjoberg and W.H. Auden, with a foreword by W.H. Auden, Faber and Faber Limited, 1964, p.135.

When a man turns to Him, desiring to serve Him, God directs his attention to the world and its need. It is His will that our service of Him should be expressed as our service to the world, through Him, and for His sake.

Emil Brunner, *The Divine Imperative,* translated by Olive Wyon, Lutterworth Press, 1942, p.189.

The giving of self to the service of God is not like making a single offer, handing over a single gift, receiving a single acknowledgement. It is a continued action, renewed all the time.

Hubert van Zeller, *Considerations,* Sheed and Ward Ltd., 1974, p.124.

An act of prayer at the heart of every act of service—a self-offering to His purpose so that the action may be His and not our own. That, in its perfection, is the secret of the saints. *I live—yet not I!* Christ is the boundless source of energy and love.

Evelyn Underhill, *The Light of Christ*, Longmans, Green and Co. Ltd., 1944, p.94.

> A servant with this clause
> Makes drudgery divine:
> Who sweeps a room, as for thy laws,
> Makes that and th' action fine.

George Herbert, *The Works of George Herbert*, edited by F.E. Hutchinson, Oxford at the Clarendon Press, 1972, p.185, "The Church—The Elixir," st.5, l.1.

> Love seeketh not Itself to please,
> Nor for itself hath any care,
> But for another gives its ease,
> And builds a Heaven in Hell's despair.

William Blake, *The Complete Writings of William Blake*, edited by Geoffrey Keynes, Oxford University Press, 1974, p.211, *Songs of Innocence and of Experience*, "The Clod and the Pebble," st.i, l.1.

> Small service is true service while it lasts:
> Of humblest Friends, bright Creature! scorn not one:
> The Daisy, by the shadow that it casts,
> Protects the lingering dew-drop from the Sun.

William Wordsworth, *The Poetical Works of William Wordsworth*, edited by E. de Selincourt and Helen Darbishire, Oxford at the Clarendon Press, 1958, Volume IV, p.178, "To a Child, written in her Album, 1835," l.1.

There came to me, as I awoke, the thought that I must not accept this happiness as a matter of course, but must give something in return for it.... I settled with myself before I got up, that I would consider myself justified in living till I was thirty for science and art, in order to devote myself from that time forward to the direct service of humanity.

Albert Schweitzer, *My Life and Thought*, translated by C.T. Campion, George Allen & Unwin Ltd., 1933, p.103.

Think not that God will be always caressing His children, or shine upon their head, or kindle their hearts, as He does at the first. He does so only to lure us to Himself, as the falconer lures the falcon with its gay hood. Our Lord works with His children so as to teach them afterwards to work themselves; as He bade Moses to make the tables of stone after the pattern of the first which He had made Himself. Thus, after a time, God allows a man to depend upon himself, and no longer enlightens, and stimulates, and rouses him. We must stir up and rouse ourselves, and be content to leave off learning, and no more enjoy feeling and fire, and must now serve the Lord with strenuous industry and at our own cost.

John Tauler, *The History and Life of the Reverend Doctor John Tauler*, translated by Susanna Winkworth, Smith, Elder, & Company, 1857, p.280.

SEX

The first necessity for a truly Christian philosophy of sex is to pass from the phase where sex is a matter of shame to that where it becomes an object of reverence. Through it God allows to men the incomparable privilege of co-operating with Him in the creation of His own sons and daughters, called to eternal fellowship with Him. How sacred a thing is this!

William Temple, *Thoughts On Some Problems Of The Day*, Macmillan & Co. Ltd., 1931, p.42.

Sex, being a strong natural appetite in animals, and being enormously strengthened in man by the use of imagination, is very liable in human nature to grow in a degree entirely disproportionate. So there is a peculiar difficulty in maintaining, in this respect, that true economy of nature in which to every impulse there is given its own proper, but no more than its own proper, exercise. If our ancestors were wrong in their suggestions that there was about sex something wrong, they were quite right in thinking there was about it something which gave the greatest ground for the most anxious caution.

William Temple, *Christian Faith and Life*, S.C.M. Press Ltd., 1963, p.55.

Chastity is the most unpopular of the Christian virtues. There is no getting away from it: the Christian rule is, "Either marriage, with complete faithfulness to your partner, or else total abstinence." Now this is so difficult and so contrary to our instincts, that obviously either Christianity is wrong or our sexual instinct, as it now is, has gone wrong. One or the other. Of course, being a Christian, I think it is the instinct which has gone wrong.

C.S. Lewis, *Mere Christianity*, William Collins Sons & Co. Ltd., 1961, p.85.

One thing, however, marriage has done for me. I can never again believe that religion is manufactured out of our unconscious, starved desires and is a substitute for sex. For those few years H. and I feasted on love; every mode of it—solemn and merry, romantic and realistic, sometimes as dramatic as a thunderstorm, sometimes as comfortable and unemphatic as putting on your soft slippers. No cranny of heart or body remained unsatisfied. If God were a substitute for love we ought to have lost all interest in Him. Who'd bother about substitutes when he has the thing itself? But that isn't what happens. We both knew we wanted something besides one another—quite a different kind of something, a quite different kind of want.

C.S. Lewis, *A Grief Observed*, Faber and Faber Limited, 1961, p.10.

The monstrosity of sexual intercourse outside marriage is that those who indulge in it are trying to isolate one kind of union (the sexual) from all the other kinds of union which were intended to go along with it and make up the total union. The Christian attitude does not mean that there is anything wrong about sexual pleasure, any more than about the pleasure of eating. It means that you must not isolate that pleasure and try to get it by itself, any more than you ought to try to get the pleasures of taste without swallowing and digesting, by chewing things and spitting them out again.

C.S. Lewis, *Mere Christianity*, William Collins Sons & Co. Ltd., 1961, p.92.

Sex-love, if it is love at all, is a personal communion in which a man and a woman meet in the full integrity of their personal reality. And the law of reality in the relationship of persons is this. "The integrity of persons in inviolable. You shall not use a person for your own ends, or indeed for any ends, individual or social. To use another person is to violate his personality by making an object of him; and in violating the integrity of another you violate your own." In all enjoyment there is a choice between enjoying the other and enjoying yourself through the instrumentality of the other. The first is the enjoyment of love, the second is the enjoyment of lust. When people enjoy themselves through each other, that is merely mutual lust. They do not meet as persons at all; their reality is lost. They meet as ghosts of themselves and their pleasure is a ghostly pleasure that cannot begin to satisfy a human soul, and which only vitiates its capacity for reality.

John Macmurray, *Reason and Emotion*, Faber and Faber Limited, 1972, p.141.

The practice of Christian sex ethics is not to be recovered by preaching the ethics.... A renewed, creative and fully personal fulfilment of sexuality will only come from people who are aware of the pressure of a debilitated civilisation, and without contracting out of it, can put down their roots in an alternative culture. Christianity is such a culture. Its moral demands are not its main contribution. Underneath those demands is a whole way of life, of deep emotional power bringing its believers in touch with the ultimate mystery of existence, more permanent than the ups and downs of histories and culture. Religion and sex have been closely linked in the history of the human race. That is the ground upon which I assert that religion provides the kind of security and resources which men and women are now vainly seeking by an exaltation of sex in order to counterbalance the impoverishing influence of an over-sophisticated culture. You can only really live in the world fruitfully, happily and co-operatively if you have resources not given by the world. You can only appreciate fruitfully the good things of the world—and sexual love is one of the greatest—if you don't trust them overmuch or seek salvation in them.

V.A. Demant, *Christian Sex Ethics*, Hodder & Stoughton Ltd., 1963, p.121.

SIN

Be sure your sin will find you out.
Numbers 32.33.

The way of the faithless is their ruin.
Proverbs 13.15.

For from within, out of the heart of man, come evil thoughts, fornication, theft, murder, adultery, coveting, wickedness, deceit, licentiousness, envy, slander, pride, foolishness. All these evil things come from within, and they defile a man.
Mark 7.21-23.

Poor soul, the centre of my sinful earth.
William Shakespeare, Sonnet 146, l.1.

A sinful heart makes feeble hand.
Sir Walter Scott, *The Poems and Plays of Sir Walter Scott*, introduction by Andrew Lang, J.M. Dent & Sons, Ltd., 1911, Volume I, *Marmion*, p.543.

Men may securely sin, but safely never.
Ben Jonson, *Ben Jonson*, edited by C.H. Herford, Percy and Evelyn Simpson, Oxford at the Clarendon Press, 1947, Volume VIII, *The Poems, The Prose Works*, p.113, "The Forest," xi, Epode, l.116.

Sin is a fearful thing, and unrighteousness is the sorest ailment of the soul, secretly sapping its sinews ... a self-chosen evil, the offspring of a man's set purpose of mind.
Cyril of Jerusalem, *The Catechetical Lectures of St. Cyril*, J.G. and F. Rivington, 1838, p.14.

You have ordained and so it is with us, that every soul that sins brings its own punishment upon itself.
St. Augustine, *Confessions*, translated with an introduction by R.S. Pine-Coffin, Penguin Books Ltd., 1964, p.33.

Sin is something inside our fallen selves trying to come out and be free to hurt. The evil outside ourselves in the fallen world is something which is trying to come in— also to hurt.
Hubert van Zeller, *Considerations*, Sheed and Ward Ltd., 1974, p.49.

The safest road to Hell is the gradual one—the gentle slope, soft underfoot, without sudden turnings, without milestones, without signposts.
C.S. Lewis, *The Screwtape Letters*, William Collins Sons & Co. Ltd., 1960, p.65.

The worst sin towards our fellow creatures is not to hate them, but to be indifferent to them; that's the essence of inhumanity.
George Bernard Shaw, *The Complete Plays of Bernard Shaw*, Paul Hamlyn, 1965, p.230, *The Devil's Disciple*, Act II.

One shall not kill "the evil impulse," the passion, in oneself, but one shall serve God *with it;* it is the power which is destined to receive its direction from man.
Martin Buber, *Hasidism*, The Philosophical Library, Inc., 1948, p.71.

St. Paul says that the wages of sin is death, not that God condemns us to death for our sins, but that sin kills the life of the spirit. Sin is a sickness that leads to spiritual death unless it is cured by forgiveness and the soul kept healthy by grace.
George Appleton, *Journey for a Soul*, William Collins Sons & Co. Ltd., 1976, p.122.

Whenever you fight against the root of sin in general or any sin in particular, hold fast to this desire, and fix your mind upon Jesus Christ for whom you long rather than upon the sin which you are fighting.
Walter Hilton, *The Ladder of Perfection*, translated with an introduction by Leo Sherley-Price, Penguin Books Ltd., 1957, p.109.

Such harmony is in immortal souls,
But whilst this muddy vesture of decay
Doth grossly close it in, we cannot hear it.

William Shakespeare, *The Merchant of Venice*, Act V. sc.i. l.64.

Over and over again, as we break some rule which seems rather arbitrary and mean-ingless, we discover the principle which had dictated it. We set in motion the causes and effects from which we understand, for the first time, why there had ever been that prohibition; then it is too late. The discovery is called the Fall of Man.

William Temple, *Christian Faith and Life*, S.C.M. Press Ltd., 1963, p.65.

The smallest atom of good realized and applied to life, a single vivid experience of love, will advance us much further, will far more surely protect our souls from evil, than the most arduous *struggle* against sin, than the resistance to sin by the severest ascetic methods of chaining the dark passions within us.

Father Yelchaninov, in *A Treasury of Russian Spirituality*, edited by G.P. Fedotov, Sheed and Ward Ltd., 1977, p.461.

Sin is the putting of self in the centre where God alone should be. Sin is acting from the self instead of from God. It is falling short of the will and glory of God. Often it is more than that—it is setting one's will against God's will, consciously (where guilt is involved) or unconsciously (when the sinful consequences are equally disastrous).

George Appleton, *Journey for a Soul*, William Collins Sons & Co. Ltd., 1976, p.122.

In the Creation story God says: "Let us make man in our image, after our likeness" (Genesis 1.26). And sin may well be said to be man's failure to reach the object and the purpose for which he was created. As G.K. Chesterton put it: "Whatever else is true of man, man is not what he was meant to be." So, then,... sin is failure.... Sin is the failure to be what we should have been and what we ought to have been, what we could have been and what we might have been.

William Barclay, *The Plain Man Looks at the Apostles' Creed*, William Collins Sons & Co. Ltd., 1967, p.304.

All sins are contained in this one category, that one turns away from things divine and truly enduring, and turns towards those which are mutable and uncertain. And although the latter are rightly placed each in its order, and work out that beauty proper to them it is nevertheless the mark of a perverted and ungoverned mind to be in subjection to them as things to be pursued, when by the divine order and law it is set above them as things to be directed.

St. Augustine, *An Augustine Synthesis*, arranged by Erich Przywara, S.J., Sheed and Ward Ltd., 1945, p.124.

Eden is on no map, and Adam's fall fits no historical calendar. Moses is not nearer the Fall than we are, because he lived three thousand years before our time. The Fall refers not to some datable aboriginal calamity in the historic past of humanity, but to a dimension of human experience which is always present—namely, that we who have been created for fellowship with God repudiate it continually; and that the whole of mankind does this along with us. Everyman is his own "Adam," and all men are solidarily "Adam." Thus, Paradise before the Fall, the *status perfectionis,* is not a period of history, but our "memory" of a divinely intended quality of life, given to us along with our consciousness of guilt.

J.S. Whale, *Christian Doctrine,* Cambridge at the University Press, 1942, p.52.

I think sin is anything which leads to a greater deadening of one's mind, one's personality, one's feelings. God is ultimately interested in my being totally alive: everything that comes from Him is life-giving. I think that my belief in the Devil—call him what you like— sees him as the personification of the inbuilt false promise that goes with a great many experiences—they hold out false hopes of greater vitality. We think: if I do that, I'll get a kick out of it. Well, each time you get less and less of a kick, and it ends up making you deader instead of more alive. Whatever we do that creates deadness is a sin. And in terms of society, if I organise some institution the end result of which is the greater deadening of the human community, then that is a gigantic sin.

John V. Taylor, in *Priestland's Progress,* Gerald Priestland, British Broadcasting Corporation, 1982, p.70.

I'm very much of a Jungian, and I feel Jung's concept of the dark side in all of us is very near the truth. If we equate that dark side with the Devil, we are not far wrong in our understanding of what the Devil is up to.
The interesting thing about the dark side, or the Devil, is that he was a fallen angel— he belongs to God really—and our problem is to reconcile the dark side and make use of its energy. It's always recognised that the Devil is walking up and down the earth, full of energy. In education I used to find the apparently wicked boy was full of it. You've got to understand it, come to terms with it and make use of it. In other words, bring the Devil back into God's Kingdom.

Kenneth Barnes, in *Priestland's Progress,* Gerald Priestland, British Broadcasting Corporation, 1982, p.72.

The first Light which shined in my Infancy in its primitive and innocent clarity was totally eclipsed: insomuch that I was fain to learn all again. If you ask me how it was eclipsed? Truly by the customs and manners of men, which like contrary winds blew it out: by an innumerable company of other objects, rude, vulgar, and worthless things, that like so many loads of earth and dung did overwhelm and bury it: by the impetuous torrent of wrong desires in all others whom I saw or knew that carried me away and alienated me from it: by a whole sea of other matters and concernments that covered and drowned it: finally by the evil influence of a bad education that did not foster and cherish it. All men's thoughts and words were about other matters. They all prized new things which I did not dream of. I was a stranger and unacquainted with them; I was little and reverenced their authority; I was weak, and easily guided by their example: ambitious also, and desirous to approve myself unto them. And finding no one syllable in any man's mouth of those things, by degrees they vanished, my thoughts (as indeed what is more fleeting than a thought?) were blotted out; and at last all the celestial great and stable treasures to which I was born, as wholly forgotten, as if they had never been.

Thomas Traherne, *Centuries,* The Faith Press, 1969, p.114.

SOCIETY

The spirit of truth and the spirit of freedom—*these* are the pillars of society.

Henrik Ibsen, *Pillars of Society,* translated and edited by James Walter McFarlane, Oxford University Press, 1961, Volume V, Act IV, Last lines.

We know, and what is better we feel inwardly that religion is the basis of civil society, and the source of all good and of all comfort.

Edmund Burke, *Reflections on the Revolution in France,* edited by Conor Cruise O'Brien, Penguin Books Ltd., 1969, p.186.

The first duty of society is to give each of its members the possibility of fulfilling his destiny. When it becomes incapable of performing this duty it must be transformed.

Alexis Carrel, *Reflections on Life,* translated by Antonia White, Hamish Hamilton Ltd., 1952, p.132.

The test of every religious, political, or educational system, is the man which it forms. If a system injures the intelligence it is bad. If it injures the character it is vicious. If it injures the conscience it is criminal.

Henri Frédéric Amiel, *Amiel's Journal,* translated by Mrs. Humphry Ward, Macmillan & Co. Ltd., 1918, p.27.

All our rational investigation and rational planning of the economic and political and social spheres is without meaning unless it is the means to one end—the living of the personal life of community in joy and freedom. To sacrifice life to its own conditions is the ultimate insincerity and the real denial of God.

John Macmurray, *Reason and Emotion,* Faber and Faber Limited, 1972, p.254.

More potent than school, or even than home, as a moral influence, is the whole structure of society, and especially its economic structure. This fixes for all their place in the general scheme; and the way in which they gain and keep that place of necessity determines a great deal of their conduct and profoundly influences their outlook upon life.

William Temple, *The Hope of a New World,* S.C.M. Press Ltd., 1940, p.49.

If we let the economic aim become predominant, we shall find that it disintegrates our society, that it treats every individual primarily as so much labour power to be used where he most conduces to efficiency of output, irrespective of all his social ties and traditional roots. The economic approach to life atomises society.

William Temple, *The Church Looks Forward,* Macmillan & Co. Ltd., 1944, p.128.

There are large proportions of our fellow citizens for whom the bottom is liable to fall out of life through no action of their own, but simply through the way in which our economic system is worked or works, and it is a shocking evil and we must fight against it.

William Temple, *The Church Looks Forward,* Macmillan & Co., Ltd., 1944, p.121.

We concentrate on social reform and economic justice and better standards of life, of housing, of health, of education.... Will they even work if we ignore our own complete make-up? A recent writer has put it better than I can. "What do all these promises of material Utopias amount to?" he asks, "that people can get good results without bothering to be good—that you can build a good society out of bad men."

R.L. Smith, in *Man's Dilemma and God's Answer*, Broadcast Talks, S.C.M. Press Ltd., 1944, p.76.

You cannot bring about prosperity by discouraging thrift; you cannot strengthen the weak by weakening the strong; you cannot help the wage-earner by pulling down the wage-payer; you cannot further the brotherhood of man by encouraging class hatred; you cannot help the poor by destroying the rich; you cannot establish sound security on borrowed money; you cannot keep out of trouble by spending more than you earn; you cannot build character and courage by taking away man's initiative and independence; you cannot help men permanently by doing for them what they could and should do for themselves.

Attributed to Abraham Lincoln.

Happiness lies in the fulfilment of the spirit through the body. Thus humanity has already evolved from an animal life to one more civilized. There can be no complete return to nature, to nudism, desert-islandry: city life is the subtlest ingredient in the human climate. But we have gone wrong over the size of our cities and over the kind of life we lead in them; in the past the clods were the peasants, now the brute mass of ignorance is urban. The village idiot walks in Leicester Square. To live according to nature we should pass a considerable time in cities, for they are the glory of human nature, but they should never contain more than two hundred thousand inhabitants; it is our artificial enslavement to the large city, too sprawling to leave, too enormous for human dignity, which is responsible for half our sickness and misery. Slums may well be breeding-grounds of crime, but middle-class suburbs are incubators of apathy and delirium. No city should be too large for a man to walk out of in a morning.

Cyril Connolly, *The Unquiet Grave*, Hamish Hamilton Ltd., 1945, Part I, Ecce Gubernator, p.26.

Our present economic, social and international arrangements are based, in large measure, upon organized lovelessness. We begin by lacking charity towards Nature, so that instead of trying to co-operate with Tao or the Logos on the inanimate and sub-human levels, we try to dominate and exploit, we waste the earth's mineral resources, ruin its soil, ravage its forests, pour filth into its rivers and poisonous fumes into its air. From lovelessness in relation to Nature we advance to lovelessness in relation to art—a lovelessness so extreme that we have effectively killed all the fundamental or useful arts and set up various kinds of mass-production by machines in their place. And of course this lovelessness in regard to art is at the same time a lovelessness in regard to the human beings who have to perform the fool-proof and grace-proof tasks imposed by our mechanical art-surrogates and by the interminable paperwork connected with mass-production and mass-distribution. With mass-production and mass-distribution go mass-financing, and the three have conspired to expropriate ever-increasing numbers of small owners of land and productive equipment, thus reducing the sum of freedom among the majority and increasing the power of a minority to exercise a coercive control over the lives of their fellows. This coercively controlling minority is composed of private capitalists or governmental bureaucrats or of both classes of bosses acting in collaboration—and, of course, the coercive and therefore essentially loveless nature of the control remains the same, whether the bosses call themselves "company directors" or "civil servants." The only difference between these two kinds of oligarchical rulers is that the first derive more of their power from wealth than from position within a conventionally respected hierarchy, while the second derive more power from position than from wealth.

Aldous Huxley, *The Perennial Philosophy*, Chatto & Windus Ltd., 1974, p.109.

SONS OF GOD

You are gods, sons of the Most High.

Psalm 82.6.

But to all who received him, who believed in his name, he gave power to become children of God; who were born, not of blood nor of the will of the flesh nor of the will of man, but of God.

John 1.12-13.

For all who are led by the Spirit of God are sons of God. For you did not receive the spirit of slavery to fall back into fear, but you have received the spirit of sonship. When we cry, "Abba! Father!" it is the Spirit himself bearing witness with our spirit that we are children of God, and if children, then heirs, heirs of God and fellow heirs with Christ, provided we suffer with him in order that we may also be glorified with him.

Romans 8.14-17.

And because you are sons, God has sent the Spirit of his Son into our hearts, crying, "Abba! Father!" So through God you are no longer a slave but a son, and if a son then an heir.

Galatians 4.6-7.

See what love the Father has given us, that we should be called children of God; and so we are.

1 John 3.1.

To the thirsty I will give from the fountain of the water of life without payment. He who conquers shall have this heritage, and I will be his God and he shall be my son.

Revelation 21.6-7.

Our Lord recalls us to our original being, our intimate being. We are children of God all through our lives, however young, however old, however experienced or disillusioned. We have to return to this original being, assured now of what we first felt in unquestioning intuition or received trustingly from others.

George Appleton, *Journey for a Soul*, William Collins Sons & Co. Ltd., 1976, p.82.

He is the Son of God in that sense (among others) in which we say of a man that he is the son of his father, meaning that in him the father's character is reproduced. So supremely is our Lord the Son because in Him we truly see the Father.

William Temple, *Christian Faith and Life*, S.C.M. Press Ltd., 1963, p.35.

The writers of the New Testament all observe a certain use of language which has deep significance. They often imply that God is the Father of all men; but they do not speak of all men as His children; that expression is reserved for those who, by the grace of God, are enabled in some measure to reproduce His character.

William Temple, *Readings in St. John's Gospel* (First and Second Series), Macmillan & Co. Ltd., 1947, p.12.

I cannot explain the mystery of how someone who is a human being just like I am can also be worshipped. And yet the more real the mystery has become for me, it isn't that Jesus has become more like God, but that all my brothers and sisters have. It is through Him that I recognise God in my neighbour—through Jesus I've discovered the uniqueness of everyone. And there was in Him a quality of willingness to be defeated and destroyed by His enemies, and to go on loving them, that alone made possible a new quality of life afterwards....
But so special that in Him those who loved Him were able to recognise something they had to call God; it was divine. If others have somehow come through this Jesus to share aspects of His holiness, that mysteriously makes us one with God. There is a sense in which every man becomes divine. I would not want to draw hard, dogmatic lines between the rest of humanity and this Jesus.

Paul Oestreicher, in *Priestland's Progress*, Gerald Priestland, British Broadcasting Corporation, 1982, p.43.

(Was Jesus the Son of God?) To think it is a clear-cut concept which can be dealt with in that sort of way seems to me to be a total misunderstanding. Anybody who had read scriptural history and so on would know that the phrase "Son of God" has so many different concepts, indicating one who is in a very special relationship to God, focal for other men's faith towards God. What our book (The Myth of God Incarnate) was feeling after was something which would keep the positive implications of a great deal of the traditional religious language, but free people from thinking it had to be understood in ways which I honestly believe diminish the effective reality of Jesus for our continuing faith.

Maurice Wiles, in *Priestland's Progress*, Gerald Priestland, British Broadcasting Corporation, 1982, p.40.

SORROW

A deep distress hath humanised my Soul.

William Wordsworth, *The Poetical Works of William Wordsworth*, edited by E. de Selincourt and Helen Darbishire, Oxford at the Clarendon Press, 1958, Volume IV, p.259, "Elegaic Stanzas," l.36.

The busy bee has no time for sorrow.

William Blake, *The Complete Writings of William Blake*, edited by Geoffrey Keynes, Oxford University Press, 1974, p.151, *The Marriage of Heaven and Hell*, Plate 7, "Proverbs of Hell," l.11.

362

Where there is sorrow there is holy ground.

Oscar Wilde, *The Works of Oscar Wilde*, edited by G.F. Maine, William Collins Sons & Co. Ltd., 1948, *De Profundis*, p.854.

Sorrow makes us all children again,—destroys all differences of intellect. The wisest knows nothing.

Ralph Waldo Emerson, *The Heart of Emerson's Journals*, edited by Bliss Perry, Constable & Co. Ltd., 1927, p.173.

The groundwork of life is sorrow. But that once established, one can start to build. And until that is established one can build nothing: no life of any sort.

D.H. Lawrence, *The Selected Letters of D.H. Lawrence*, edited with an introduction by Diana Trilling, Farrar, Straus and Cudahy, Inc., 1958, p.188.

True sorrow makes a silence in the heart.

Robert Natham, *A Cedar Box*, The Bobbs-Merrill Company, Publishers, 1929, p.35.

Take this sorrow to thy heart, and make it a part of thee, and it shall nourish thee till thou art strong again.

Henry Wadsworth Longfellow, *Hyperion*, George Routledge and Sons, 1887, p.245.

Sorrow is the most tremendous of all realities in the sensible world, but the transfiguration of sorrow after the manner of Christ is a more beautiful solution of the problem than the extirpation of sorrow.

Henry Frédéric Amiel, *Amiel's Journal*, translated by Mrs. Humphry Ward, Macmillan & Co., Ltd., 1918, p.285.

We wasters of sorrows!
How we stare away into sad endurance beyond them,
trying to foresee their end! Whereas they are nothing else
than our winter foliage, our sombre evergreen, *one*
of the seasons of our interior year,—not only
season—they're also place, settlement, camp, soil, dwelling.

Rainer Maria Rilke, *Duino Elegies*, translated with an introduction and commentary by J.B. Leishman and Stephen Spender, Chatto & Windus Ltd., 1975, p.91.

If it were possible for us to see further than our knowledge extends and out a little over the outworks of our surmising, perhaps we should then bear our sorrows with greater confidence than our joys. For they are the moments when something new, something unknown, has entered into us; our feelings grow dumb with shy confusion, everything in us retires, a stillness supervenes, and the new thing that no one knows stands silent there in the midst.

Rainer Maria Rilke, *Letters to a Young Poet*, translation, introduction and commentary by Reginald Snell, Sidgwick & Jackson, 1945, p.35.

Sorrow is one of the things that are lent, not given. A thing that is lent may be taken away; a thing that is given is not taken away. Joy is given; sorrow is lent. We are not our own, we are bought with a price, "and our sorrow is not our own" (Samuel Rutherford said this a long time ago), it is lent to us for just a little while that we may use it for eternal purposes. Then it will be taken away and everlasting joy will be our Father's gift to us, and the Lord God will wipe away all tears from off all faces. So let us use this "lent" thing to draw us nearer to the heart of Him Who was once a Man of Sorrows (He is not that now, but He does not forget the feeling of sorrow). Let us use it to make us more tender with others, as He was when on earth and is still, for He is touched with the feeling of our infirmities.

Amy Carmichael, *Edges Of His Ways*, S.P.C.K., 1955, p.193.

SOUL

... the One who shaped him, who breathed an active soul into him, and inspired a living spirit.

Wisdom of Solomon 15.11 (Jerusalem Bible).

My soul magnifies the Lord.

Luke 1.46.

I count life just a stuff
To try the soul's strength on.

Robert Browning, *The Poetical Works of Robert Browning*, Smith, Elder & Co., 1899, Volume I, p.559, "In A Balcony."

By the word soul, or psyche, I mean that inner consciousness which aspires. By prayer I do not mean a request for anything preferred to a deity; I mean intense soul-emotion, intense aspiration.

Richard Jefferies, *The Story of My Heart*, Duckworth & Co., 1923, p.143.

"I tell you these things, not because you know them not, but because ye know them."
All living instruction is nothing but corroboration of intuitive knowledge.

Coventry Patmore, *The Rod, the Root and the Flower*, The Grey Walls Press Ltd., 1950, p.47, "Aurea Dicta," cxiv.

And see all sights from pole to pole,
And glance, and nod, and bustle by,
And never once possess our soul
Before we die.

Matthew Arnold, *The Poems of Matthew Arnold*, edited by Kenneth Allott, Longmans, Green & Co. Ltd., 1965, p.460, "A Southern Night," st.18, l.69.

It seems to me that what one aims at is to work with one's mind and one's soul *together*. By soul I mean that "thing" that makes the mind really important. I always picture it like this. My mind is a very complicated, capable instrument. But the interior is dark. It *can* work in the dark and throw off all kinds of things. But behind that instrument like a very steady gentle light is the soul. And it's only when the soul *irradiates* the mind that what one does matters.... What I *aim* at is that state of mind when I feel my soul and my mind are one. It's awfully, terribly difficult to get at. Only solitude will do it for me.

Katherine Mansfield, *The Letters of Katherine Mansfield,* edited by J. Middleton Murry, Constable & Co. Ltd., 1928, Volume II, p.203.

Highly ought we to rejoice that God dwelleth in our soul, and much more highly ought we to rejoice that our soul dwelleth in God. Our soul is *made* to be God's dwelling-place; and the dwelling-place of the soul is God, which is *unmade.* And high understanding it is, inwardly to see and know that God, which is our Maker, dwelleth in our soul; and an higher understanding it is, inwardly to see and to know that our soul, that is made, dwelleth in God's Substance: of which Substance, God, we are that we are.

Lady Julian of Norwich, *Revelations of Divine Love,* edited by Grace Warrack, Methuen & Co. Ltd., 1949, p.130.

Either we have an immortal soul, or we have not. If we have not, we are beasts; the first and wisest of beasts, it may be; but still true beasts. We shall only differ in degree, and not in kind; just as the elephant differs from the slug. But by the concession of all the materialists of all the schools, or almost all, we are not of the same kind as beasts—and this also we say from our own consciousness. Therefore, methinks, it must be the possession of a soul within us that makes the difference.

Samuel Taylor Coleridge, *Table Talk of Samuel Taylor Coleridge,* introduction by Henry Morley, George Routledge and Sons, 1884, p.33.

Thus the Lord, the spirit, becomes the soul of our souls, becomes spiritually what he always was creatively; and as our spirit informs, gives shape to our bodies, in like manner his soul informs, gives shape to our souls. In this there is nothing unnatural, nothing at conflict with our being. It is but that the deeper soul that willed and wills our souls, rises up, the infinite Life, into the Self we call *I* and *me,* but which lives immediately from him, and is his very own property and nature—unspeakably more his than ours ... until at length the glory of our existence flashes upon us, we face full to the sun that enlightens what it sent forth, and know ourselves alive with an infinite life, even the life of the Father; know that our existence is not the moonlight of a mere consciousness of being, but the sun-glory of a life justified by having become one with its origin, thinking and feeling with the primal Sun of life, from whom it was dropped away that it might know and bethink itself, and return to circle for ever in exultant harmony around him. Then indeed we *are;* then indeed we have life; the life of Jesus has, through light, become life in us; the glory of God in the face of Jesus, mirrored in our hearts, has made us alive; we are one with God for ever and ever.

George Macdonald, *Unspoken Sermons,* Third Series, Longmans, Green, & Co., 1889, p.53.

SUFFERING

When you pass through the waters I will be with you; and through the rivers, they shall not overwhelm you; when you walk through fire you shall not be burned, and the flame shall not consume you.

Isaiah 43.2.

Although he was a Son, he learned obedience through what he suffered; and being made perfect he became the source of eternal salvation to all who obey him.

Hebrews 5.8-9.

He who suffers much will know much.

Greek Proverb.

In time of sickness the soul collects itself anew.

Latin Proverb.

Although the world is full of suffering, it is full also of the overcoming of it.

Helen Keller, *Optimism*, George G. Harrop, 1903, p.17.

Know how sublime a thing it is
To suffer and be strong.

Henry Wadsworth Longfellow, *The Poetical Works of Longfellow*, Humphrey Milford, Oxford University Press, 1913, p.4, "The Light of Stars," st.xi, l.3.

Understood in its deepest sense, being Christ's follower means suffering that is unendurable to the great majority of mankind.

C.G. Jung, *The Collected Works of C.G. Jung*, translated by R.F.C. Hull, Routledge & Kegan Paul, Ltd., 1953, Volume 12, *Psychology and Alchemy*, p.22.

I wonder why we suffer so strangely—to bring out something in us, I try to believe, which can't be brought out in any other way.

A.C. Benson, *Extracts from the Letters of Dr. A.C. Benson to M.E.A.*, Jarrolds Publishers London Limited, 1927, p.13.

It *did* come—the day when the grief became small. For what had befallen me and seemed so hard to bear became insignificant in the light of the demands which God was now making. But how difficult it is to feel that this was also, and for that very reason, the day when the joy became great.

Dag Hammarskjold, *Markings*, translated by Leif Sjoberg and W.H. Auden, with a foreword by W.H. Auden, Faber and Faber Limited, 1964, p.87.

The mark of the spiritually mature man is that he can endure sorrow without bitterness, bewilderment without fuss, loss without envy or recrimination or self-pity. Above all, whatever the set-backs and misunderstandings, public and private, that he maintains a belief in the essential goodness of mankind.

Hubert van Zeller, *Considerations*, Sheed and Ward Ltd., 1974, p.122.

Shut out suffering, and you see only one side of this strange and fearful thing, the life of man. Brightness, and happiness, and rest—that is not life. It is only one side of life: Christ saw both sides.

F.W. Robertson, *Sermons,* Kegan Paul, Trench, Trubner, and Co. Ltd., 1890, Fifth Series, p.17.

Sooner or later suffering, misfortune, trouble come to every life. Some of it comes from our own ignorance, some from our own mistakes, some is a consequence of our own sin. But in almost every life there is a residue which seems inexplicable. Our Christian faith does not completely explain the mystery of suffering. It teaches us how to deal with suffering. It assures us that God does not will suffering, but he is in it, to redeem it and to turn it into good and blessing. Let us also remember that the perfect life was not exempt from suffering.

George Appleton, *Journey for a Soul,* William Collins Sons & Co. Ltd., 1976, p.50.

When trouble hits us we can react to it in a variety of ways. We can let it knock us out, so that we lose all hope and stamina. We can rebel and refuse to accept the rightness or merit of it. We can fill our lives with feverish activity so that we have no time to think about it. Or we can accept it—without defeat, rebellion or evasion—trusting that God will make clear tomorrow what is so difficult to understand today.

George Appleton, *Journey for a Soul,* William Collins Sons & Co. Ltd., 1976, p.51.

Creative suffering—and this alone is real suffering—is positively non-resistant. It is a spiritual act, not a physical or mental reaction. And we cannot truly perform it until we wholly consent to the situation in which we find ourselves, however painful or disconcerting it may be, regarding it as the price we must pay for spiritual growth. By thus consenting to suffer we learn how to live by dying, how to surrender our existence to our being, until it is informed, more and more, by the eternal light of our essence.
To suffer thus is to pass through the defensive warfare of pain and pleasure to the pure joy in which we wholly accept and are accepted by life. And this is, also, to live from moment to moment in peaceful communion with death. For only by thus dying to what is resistant in ourselves can we enjoy the inexhaustible originality of life when it is left free to act in us from its true centre.

Hugh L'Anson Fausset, *Fruits of Silence,* Abelard-Schuman Ltd., 1963, p.197.

In page after page of the New Testament we are told that in so far as we share in Christ's sufferings we are made partakers here and now of His resurrection. This is the great and glorious paradox of Christian experience: that it is by dying that we live, that it is by sharing with Jesus the horror of His agony that we live with Him reigning indestructibly in peace. Once we are willing to see and feel the desert in which we live, the desert becomes fertile, bringing forth every tree whose fruit shall be for meat, and the leaf thereof for healing. Once we know that we are poor, the Kingdom of Heaven is ours. So when our lot is cast with somebody who is finding his cross, his desert, his poverty overwhelming, we are on holy ground. For it is precisely here that God is present to save, to save us as well as them. So our iden-

tification with the other person brings to our lives and to their's the power, the joy, the victory which is already ours and all mankind's in Christ Jesus our Lord.
That, I believe, is the message which our age is waiting to hear—a realistic recognition of suffering and evil in the universe, not trying apologetically to pretend that things are better than they are, together with the first-hand affirmation of this suffering and evil as the place where the Son of Man is glorified and with Him we and all mankind.

Harry Williams, *The True Wilderness,* Constable and Company Ltd., 1965, p.102.

The logical mind can never cease from questioning the necessity of suffering. It is perhaps the greatest metaphysical mystery of all. But no answer can be given by logic itself. The answer can perhaps be felt in a new state, but the knowing comes with the doing, not before, and then remains incommunicable.
"Who then devised the torment? Love." What can a man make of that in his ordinary self-willed state? But let him silence the self, the silence will be invaded by love, and for a fraction of a second he might know. A drop of that portion will strengthen him for long years.

Anon: On the Four Quartets of T.S. Eliot.

One night a man had a dream. He dreamt he was walking along the beach with his Lord. Across the sky flashed scenes from his life. For each scene he noticed two sets of footprints in the sand, one belonging to him, the other to the Lord. When the last scene in his life flashed before him he looked back at the footprints on the sand. He noticed that many times along the path of his life there was only one set of footprints. He also noticed that it happened at the very lowest and saddest times of his life. This really bothered him, and he questioned the Lord about it. "Lord, you said that, once I decided to follow you, you would walk with me all the way. But I've noticed that during the most difficult times in my life there is only one set of footprints. I don't understand why, in times when I needed you most, you would leave me." The Lord replied, "My precious child, I love you and would never leave you during your trials and sufferings; when you see only one set of footprints, it was then that I carried you.

Said to have been written by a young cancer patient.

I should like this to be accepted as my confession.
There is no limit to human suffering. When one thinks: "Now I have touched the bottom of the sea—now I can go no deeper," one goes deeper. And so it is for ever. I thought last year in Italy, any shadow more would be death. But this year has been so much more terrible that I think with affection of the Casetta! Suffering is boundless, it is eternity. One pang is eternal torment. Physical suffering is—child's play. To have one's breast crushed by a great stone—one could laugh!
I do not want to die without leaving a record of my belief that suffering can be overcome. For I do believe it. What must one do? There is no question of what is called "passing beyond it." This is false.
One must *submit.* Do not resist. Take it. Be overwhelmed. Accept it fully. Make it *part of life.*

Everything in life that we really accept undergoes a change. So suffering must become Love. This is the mystery. This is what I must do. I must pass from personal love to greater love. I must give to the whole of life what I gave to one. The present agony will pass—if it doesn't kill. It won't last. Now I am like a man who has had his heart torn out—bear it—bear it! As in the physical world, so in the spiritual world, pain does not last for ever. It is only so terribly acute now. It is as though a ghastly accident had happened. If I can cease reliving all the shock and horror of it, cease going over it, I will get stronger.

Here, for a strange reason, rises the figure of Doctor Sorapure. He was a good man. He helped me not only to bear pain, but he suggested that perhaps bodily ill-health is necessary, is a repairing process, and he was always telling me to consider how man plays but a part in the history of the world. My simple kindly doctor was pure of heart as Tchehov was pure of heart. But for these ills one is one's own doctor. If "suffering" is not a repairing process, I will make it so. I will learn the lesson it teaches. These are not idle words. These are not the consolations of the sick.

Life is a mystery. The fearful pain will fade. I must turn to work. I must put my agony into something, change it. "Sorrow shall be changed into joy."

It is to lose oneself more utterly, to love more deeply, to feel oneself part of life,— not separate.

Oh Life! accept me—make me worthy—teach me.

Katherine Mansfield, *Journal of Katherine Mansfield,* edited by J. Middleton Murry, Constable & Co. Ltd., 1927, p. 163.

T

TEMPTATION

My son, if you aspire to serve the Lord, prepare yourself for an ordeal. Be sincere of heart, be steadfast, and do not be alarmed when disaster comes. Cling to him and do not leave him, so that you may be honoured at the end of your days. Whatever happens to you, accept it, and in the uncertainties of your humble state, be patient, since gold is tested in the fire, and chosen men in the furnace of humiliation. Trust him and he will uphold you, follow a straight path and hope in him.

Ecclesiasticus 2.1-6 (Jerusalem Bible).

No temptation has overtaken you that is not common to man. God is faithful, and he will not let you be tempted beyond your strength, but with the temptation will also provide the way of escape, that you may be able to endure it.

1 Corinthians 10.13.

Blessed is the man who endures trial, for when he has stood the test he will receive the crown of life which God has promised to those who love him.

James 1.12.

Every evil to which we do not succumb is a benefactor.

Ralph Waldo Emerson, *Essays*, Bernhard Tauchnitz Edition, 1915, p.84, "Compensation."

Subdue your appetites,... and you've conquered human nature.

Charles Dickens, *Nicholas Nickleby*, The Gresham Publishing Company, 1904, p.36.

No man is tempted so, but may o'recome,
If that he has a will to Masterdome.

Robert Herrick, *The Poetical Works of Robert Herrick*, edited by F.W. Moorman, Oxford at the Clarendon Press, 1915, p.389, "Temptations."

Ay me, how many perils doe enfold
The righteous man, to make him daily fall?
Were not, that heavenly grace doth him uphold,
And stedfast truth acquit him out of all.

Edmund Spenser, *Spenser's Faerie Queene*, edited by J.C. Smith, Oxford at the Clarendon Press, 1964, p.95, Bk.I, Canto VIII, st.i. l.1.

The story of the Temptations is, of course, a parable of His spiritual wrestlings, told by Himself to His disciples. It represents the rejection, under three typical forms, of all existing conceptions of the Messianic task, which was to inaugurate the Kingdom of God.

William Temple, *Readings in St. John's Gospel* (First and Second Series), Macmillan & Co. Ltd., 1947, p.xxvi.

In the very overcoming of temptation ... we may draw out a hidden spiritual sweetness, as the bees suck honey from the thorn-bushes as well as from all other flowers. He who has not been tempted, knows nothing, nor lives as yet, say the wise man Solomon, and the holy teacher St. Bernard. We find more than a thousand testimonies in Scripture to the great profit of temptation; for it is the special sign of the love of God towards a man for him to be tempted and yet kept from falling; for thus he must and shall of a certainty receive the crown.

John Tauler, *The History and Life of the Reverend Doctor John Tauler*, translated by Susanna Winkworth, Smith, Elder, and Company, 1857, p.404.

There are but two things that we can do against temptations. The first is to be faithful to the light within us, in avoiding all exposure to temptation, which we are at liberty to avoid. I say, all that we are at liberty to avoid, because it does not always depend upon ourselves, whether we shall escape occasions of sin. Those that belong to the situation in life in which Providence has placed us, are not under our control. The other is to turn our eyes to God in moments of temptation, to throw ourselves immediately upon the protection of heaven, as a child, when in danger, flies to the arms of its parent.

The habitual conviction of the Presence of God is the sovereign remedy; it supports, it consoles, it calms us. We must not be surprised that we are tempted. We are placed here to be proved by temptations. Everything is temptation to us.

F. de la M. Fénelon, *Letters and Reflections of Fénelon*, edited by B.W. Randolph, A.R. Mowbray & Co. Limited, 1906, p.93.

The starting-point of all evil temptings lies in inconstancy of mind and small confidence in God. The slack man who abandons his fixed resolve is battered by all kinds of temptation like a ship with no steersman, driven to and fro by the waves.

Iron is proved in the fire, and the upright man in temptation. We often do not know what we are capable of till temptation reveals what kind of persons we are.

All the same, when temptation first appears, we must be especially alert, because it is easier to defeat the enemy if we do not allow him to set foot inside the door of the mind but meet him on the step as he knocks. As an ancient writer once said: Resist the beginnings—cure is provided too late. (Ovid, *Remedium Amoris*, 1.91). For first of all, a thought simply crosses the mind, then it grows stronger and takes shape; then comes pleasure, an evil impulse, and consent. So our malignant enemy gradually obtains complete entry if we do not resist him at the start. If a man is slow in stirring himself up to resist, he will grow weaker every day, while the enemy forces grow stronger.

Thomas à Kempis, *The Imitation of Christ*, translated by Betty I. Knott, William Collins Sons & Co. Ltd., 1979, p.54.

THANKSGIVING

Rejoice always, pray constantly, give thanks in all circumstances; for this is the will of God in Christ Jesus for you. Do not quench the Spirit.
1 Thessalonians 5.16-19.

Let us, therefore, be thankful for health and a competence; and above all, for a quiet conscience.
Izaak Walton, The Complete Angler, Macmillan & Co. Ltd., 1906, p.172.

To wake at dawn with a winged heart and give thanks for another day of loving.
Kahlil Gibran, The Prophet, William Heinemann Ltd., 1970, p.15.

Gratitude is a fruit of great cultivation; you do not find it among gross people.
Samuel Johnson, Boswell's Life of Johnson, edited by G.B. Hill, revised by L.F. Powell, Oxford at the Clarendon Press, 1950, Volume V, p.232.

Let never day nor night unhallow'd pass,
But still remember what the Lord hath done.
William Shakespeare, King Henry VI, Part II, Act II. sc.i. 1.85.

Thank God every morning, when you get up, that you have something to do that day which must be done, whether you like it or not. Being forced to work, and forced to do your best, will breed in you temperance and self-control, diligence and strength of will, cheerfulness and content and a hundred virtues which the idle man never knows.
Charles Kingsley, Town and Country Sermons, Macmillan & Co. Ltd., 1868, p.99.

Cultivate the thankful spirit—it will be to thee a perpetual feast. There is, or ought to be, with us no such things as small mercies. A really thankful heart will extract motive for gratitude from everything, making the most even of scanty blessings.
Anon.

It is probable that in most of us the spiritual life is impoverished and stunted because we give so little place to gratitude. It is more important to thank God for blessings received than to pray for them beforehand. For that forward-looking prayer, though right as an expression of dependence upon God, is still self-centred in part, at least, of its interest; there is something which we hope to gain by our prayer. But the backward-looking act of thanksgiving is quite free from this. In itself it is quite selfless. Thus it is akin to love. All our love to God is in response to His love for us; it never starts on our side. "We love, because He first loved us" (1 John 4.19).
William Temple, Readings in St. John's Gospel (First and Second Series), Macmillan & Co. Ltd., 1947, p.189.

Almighty God, Father of all mercies, We thine unworthy servants do give thee most humble and hearty thanks For all thy goodness and loving-kindness To us, and to all men. We bless thee for our creation, preservation, and all the blessings of this life; But above all, for thine inestimable love In the redemption of the world by our Lord

---

Jesus Christ; For the means of grace, And for the hope of glory. And, we beseech thee, give us that due sense of all thy mercies, That our hearts may be unfeignedly thankful, And that we shew forth thy praise, Not only with our lips, but in our lives; By giving up ourselves to thy service, And by walking before thee in holiness and righteousness all our days; through Jesus Christ our Lord, to whom with thee and the Holy Ghost be all honour and glory, world within end. Amen.

The Book of Common Prayer: General Thanksgiving.

If any one would tell you the shortest, surest way to all happiness, and all perfection, he must tell you to make a rule to yourself, to thank and praise God for everything that happens to you. For it is certain that whatever seeming calamity happens to you, if you thank and praise God for it, you turn it into a blessing. Could you therefore work miracles, you could not do more for yourself than by this thankful spirit; for it heals with a word speaking, and turns all that it touches into happiness....

And although this be the highest temper that you can aim at, though it be the noblest sacrifice that the greatest saint can offer unto God, yet is it not tied to any time, or place, or great occasion, but is always in your power, and may be the exercise of every day. For the common events of every day are sufficient to discover and exercise this temper, and may plainly show you how far you are governed in all your actions by this thankful spirit.

William Law, *A Serious Call to a Devout and Holy Life*, J.M. Dent & Co. Ltd., 1898, p.232.

Inward devotion often brings forth gratitude; for none can thank and praise God so well as the inward and devout man. And it is just that we should thank and praise God, because He has created us as reasonable creatures, and has ordained and destined heaven and earth and the angels to our service; and because He became man for our sins, and taught us, and lived for our sake, and showed us the way; and because He has ministered to us in humble raiment, and suffered an ignominious death for the love of us, and promised us His eternal kingdom and Himself also for our reward and for our wage. And He has spared us in our sins, and has forgiven us or will forgive us; and has poured His grace and His love into our souls, and will dwell and remain with us, and in us, throughout eternity. And He has visited us and will visit us all the days of our lives with His noble sacraments, according to the need of each, and has left us His Flesh and His Blood for food and drink, according to the desire and the hunger of each; and has set before us nature and the Scriptures and all creatures, as examples, and as a mirror, that therein we may look and learn how we may turn all our deeds to works of virtue; and has given us health and strength and power, and sometimes for our own good has sent us sickness; and in outward need has established inward peace and happiness in us; and has caused us to be called by Christian names and to have been born of Christian parents. For all these things we should thank God here on earth, that hereafter we may thank Him in eternity.

John of Ruysbroeck, *The Adornment of the Spiritual Marriage*, translated by C.A. Wynschenk Dom, edited with an introduction and notes by Evelyn Underhill, John M. Watkins, 1951, p.64.

THINKING

What is the hardest task in the world? To think.

Ralph Waldo Emerson, *Essays*, Bernhard Tauchnitz Edition, 1915, p.191, "Intellect."

Reading is sometimes an ingenious device for avoiding thought.

Arthur Helps, *Friends in Council*, George Routledge & Sons, Ltd., 1907, p.169.

My own thoughts
Are my companions.

Henry Wadsworth Longfellow, *The Poetical Works of Longfellow*, Humphrey Milford, Oxford University Press, 1913, p.688, *The Masque of Pandora*, Part III.

It is thy very energy of thought
Which keeps thee from thy God.

John Henry Newman, *The Dream of Gerontius*, Burns and Oates, 1886, p.25.

One thought fills immensity.

William Blake, *The Complete Writings of William Blake*, edited by Geoffrey Keynes, Oxford University Press, 1974, p.151, *The Marriage of Heaven and Hell*, Plate 8, "Proverbs of Hell," l.15.

It is thoughts of God's thinking which we need to set us right, and, remember, they are not as our thoughts.

W.M. Macgregor, *Jesus Christ the Son of God*, T. & T. Clark, 1907, p.99.

Thought that can emerge wholly into feeling, feeling that can merge wholly into thought—these are the artist's highest joy.

Thomas Mann, *Death in Venice*, translated by H.T. Lowe-Porter, Penguin Books Ltd., 1978, p.52.

Christianity has need of thought that it may come to the consciousness of its real self.

Albert Schweitzer, *Out of My Life and Thought*, Henry Holt and Company, Inc., 1949, p.236.

When we ask the ultimate questions, whether about the direction of our own lives or about the meaning of existence, the outcome of thinking is not an answer but a transformed way of thinking, not propositions to assent to but heightened power of apprehension.

Helen Merrell Lynd, *On Shame and the Search for Identity*, Routledge & Kegan Paul Ltd., 1958, p.251.

Elemental thinking is that which starts from the fundamental questions about the relations of man in the universe, about the meaning of life, and about the nature of goodness. It stands in the most immediate connexion with the thinking which impulse stirs in everyone. It enters into that thinking, widening and deepening it.

Albert Schweitzer, *My Life and Thought*, translated by C.T. Campion, George Allen & Unwin Ltd., 1933, p.260.

Today we overrate the rational values and behave as if thinking were a substitute for living. We have forgotten that thought and the intuition that feeds it only become whole if the deed grows out of it as fruit grows from the pollen on a tree.

So everywhere in our civilized world there tends to be a terrible cleavage between thinking and doing.

Laurens van der Post, *The Lost World of the Kalahari,* Penguin Books Ltd., 1983, p.61.

Full well aware that all has failed, yet, side by side with the sadness of that knowledge, there lives on in me an unquenchable belief, thought burning like the sun, that there is yet something to be found, something real, something to give each separate personality sunshine and flowers in its own existence now. Something to shape this million-handed labour to an end and outcome, leaving accumulated sunshine and flowers to those who shall succeed. It must be dragged forth by might of thought from the immense forces of the universe.

Richard Jefferies, *The Story of My Heart,* Duckworth & Co., 1923, p.73.

None the less strong than the will to truth must be the will to sincerity. Only an age which can show the courage of sincerity can possess truth which works as a spiritual force within it.

Sincerity is the foundation of the spiritual life.

With its depreciation of thinking our generation has lost its feeling for sincerity and with it that for truth as well. It can therefore be helped only by its being brought once more on to the road of thinking.

Because I have this certainty I oppose the spirit of the age, and take upon myself with confidence the responsibility of taking my part in the rekindling of the fire of thought.

Albert Schweitzer, *My Life and Thought,* translated by C.T. Campion, George Allen & Unwin Ltd., 1933, p.259.

It seems, indeed, little better than mockery that we should urge men to anything so remote as a return to reflection about the meaning of life at a time when the passions and the follies of the nations have become so intense and so extended, when unemployment and poverty and starvation are rife, when power is being used on the powerless in the most shameless and senseless way, and when organized human life is dislocated in every direction. But only when the general population begins to reflect in this way will forces come into being which will be able to effect something to counterbalance all this chaos and misery. Whatever other measures it is attempted to carry out will have doubtful and altogether inadequate results.

When in the spring the withered grey of the pastures gives place to green, this is due to the millions of young shoots which sprout up freshly from the old roots. In like manner the revival of thought which is essential for our time can only come through a transformation of the opinions and ideals of the many brought about by individual and universal reflection about the meaning of life and of the world.

Albert Schweitzer, *The Philosophy of Civilization,* Part I, "The Decay and the Restoration of Civilization," translated by C.T. Campion, A. & C. Black Ltd., 1932, p.100.

TIME

Time is the great physician.

Benjamin Disraeli, *Henrietta Temple,* John Lane, The Bodley Head, 1906, p.430.

The more a person is able to direct his life consciously, the more he can use time for constructive benefits.

Rollo May, *Man's Search For Himself*, George Allen & Unwin Ltd., 1953, p.259.

Both in thought and in feeling, even though time be real, to realise the unimportance of time is the gate of wisdom.

Bertrand Russell, *Mysticism and Logic and Other Essays*, Longmans, Green & Co. Ltd., 1919, p.21.

Dost thou love Life? then do not squander Time;
for that's the Stuff Life is made of.

Benjamin Franklin, *Poor Richard's Almanacks*, Richard Saunders, Paddington Press Ltd., 1976, p.132.

If time is not to be either hoarded or pressed out of existence it must be spent as possessions are spent; not solely for personal use but for others.

Hubert van Zeller, *Considerations*, Sheed and Ward Ltd., 1974, p.60.

Time lost is time when we have not lived a full human life, time unenriched by experience, creative endeavour, enjoyment and suffering.

Dietrich Bonhoeffer, *Letters and Papers from Prison*, William Collins Sons & Co. Ltd., 1963, p.134.

Man's greatest disease is the consciousness of transcience. Nothing is so likely to produce despair as the awareness of the contingency and vanity of life. A powerful and time-honoured cure is to seek a perception of eternity.

Peter Munz, *Problems of Religious Knowledge*, S.C.M. Press Ltd., 1959, p.129.

If the doors of perception were cleansed, every thing would appear to man as it is, infinite.
For man has closed himself up, till he sees all things thro' narrow chinks of his cavern.

William Blake, *The Complete Writings of William Blake*, edited by Geoffrey Keynes, Oxford University Press, 1974, p.154, *The Marriage of Heaven and Hell*, Plate 14, "A Memorable Fancy."

Time ... is what keeps the light from reaching us. There is no greater obstacle to God than time. He means not time alone but temporalities: not only temporal things but temporal affections; not only temporal affections but the very taint and aroma of time.

Meister Eckhart, *Meister Eckhart*, Franz Pfeiffer, translated by C. de B. Evans, John M. Watkins, 1956, Volume I, p.237.

What is Time? The shadow on the dial, the striking of the clock, the running of the sand, day and night, summer and winter, months, years, centuries—these are but arbitrary and outward signs, the measure of Time, not Time itself. Time is the Life of the soul. If not this, then tell me, what is Time?

Henry Wadsworth Longfellow, *Hyperion*, George Routledge and Sons, 1887, p.123.

Everything is in the mind; time and beyond time, hell and heaven, death and life. The key to understanding is awareness in the now. But awareness of the moment is not a state that comes naturally to man. Usually, if at all, it comes and goes, elusively, with happiness or suffering; it comes with the creative urge, in abstract thought, through the love of God, or the love of creatures.

Anon: On the Four Quartets of T.S. Eliot.

The happy moments of life have continually escaped my grasp. I could never be reconciled to the fact that time is in a perpetual flux and that each moment is devoured by, and vanishes into, the succeeding one. This terrible aspect of time has caused me intense and unspeakable pain. To part with people, with things, with places, has been a source of agony to me as dreadful as death....
The problem of time may well be the fundamental problem of philosophy, especially of the philosophy of existence.

Nicolas Berdyaev, *Dream and Reality*, translated by Katharine Lampert, Geoffrey Bles Ltd., 1950, p.29.

Once I said: "They are not always happy who set their hearts on time."
St. Paul says: "Rejoice in the Lord always." St. Augustine says: "To rejoice always is to find your joy above or beyond time." One Scripture says that three things there are, that prevent a person from knowing anything about God at all. The first is time, the second, materiality, the third, multiplicity. As long as these three are in me, God is not mine nor is his work being done.... All these things must be got rid of before God comes in and then you may have them in a higher and better way, namely, that the many are made one in you.

Meister Eckhart, *Meister Eckhart*, translated by Raymond B. Blakney, Harper & Row, Publishers, Inc., 1941, p.151.

The word "time" is used in two ways in the New Testament. The first is in the sense of duration, time by the clock or the calendar, a purely impersonal, chronological idea. The second is judged by rightness, ripeness, achievement of purpose, which is determined by reference to God, in his goodwill, in his love and patience. Those who believe in God try to live their lives in chronological time with ever-deepening understanding of God's purpose, God's timelessness and their own keen eye for opportunity.

George Appleton, *Journey for a Soul*, William Collins Sons & Co. Ltd., 1976, p.221.

Take Time to THINK ...
It is the source of power.
Take Time to PLAY ...
It is the secret of perpetual youth.
Take Time to READ ...
It is the fountain of wisdom.
Take Time to PRAY ...
It is the greatest power on earth.
Take Time to LOVE and BE LOVED ...
It is a God-given privilege.
Take Time to BE FRIENDLY ...
It is the road to happiness.
Take Time to LAUGH ...
It is the music of the soul.

Take Time to GIVE ...
It is too short to be selfish.
Take Time to WORK ...
It is the price of success.
Take Time to DO CHARITY ...
It is the key to heaven.

Anon., found on a bookmark.

TRANSFORMATION

The central idea in Christianity is not justification, but transfiguration.

Nicolas Berdyaev, *Christian Existentialism*, selected and translated by Donald A. Lowrie, George Allen & Unwin Ltd., 1965, p.248.

It is far more important that one's life should be perceived than that it should be transformed; for no sooner has it been perceived, than it transforms itself of its own accord.

Maurice Maeterlinck, *The Treasure of the Humble*, translated by Alfred Sutro, George Allen, 1897, p.185.

Life should be a giving birth to the soul, the development of a higher mode of reality. The animal must be humanised: flesh must be made spirit; physiological activity must be transmuted into intellect and conscience, into reason, justice, and generosity, as the torch is transmuted into life and warmth. The blind, greedy selfish nature of man must put on beauty and nobleness. This heavenly alchemy is what justifies our presence on the earth; it is our mission and our glory.

Henri Frédéric Amiel, *Amiel's Journal*, translated by Mrs. Humphry Ward, Macmillan & Co. Ltd., 1918, p.285.

The mainspring of life is in the heart. Joy is the vital air of the soul... To make anyone happy, then, is strictly to augment his store of being, to double the intensity of his life, to reveal him to himself, to ennoble him and transfigure him. Happiness does away with ugliness, and even makes the beauty of beauty. The man who doubts it, can never have watched the first gleams of tenderness dawning in the clear eyes of one who loves;—sunrise itself is a lesser marvel.... Heroism, ecstasy, prayer, love, enthusiasm, weave a halo round the brow, for they are a setting free of the soul, which through them gains force to make its envelope transparent and shine through upon all around it;... intense life and supreme joy can make the most simple mortal dazzlingly beautiful. Man, therefore, is never more truly man, than in these divine states.

Henri Frédéric Amiel, *Amiel's Journal*, translated by Mrs. Humphry Ward, Macmillan & Co. Ltd., 1918, p.104.

"Justification is not only forgiveness of sins, but it is more, it is the actual healing and renewing of the inward man." It must involve a real and radical transformation of man's nature—man must cease from sin and the love of it, he must receive from beyond himself a passion for goodness and a power to enable him to achieve it. The *passion* for goodness ... is created through the vision of the God-Man who has suffered and died on the Cross for us, and has been glorified in absolute newness of life; and the *power* for moral holiness is supplied to the soul by the direct inflowing of divine Life-streams from this new Adam, who is henceforth the Head of the spiritual order of humanity, the Life-giving Spirit who renews all who receive Him in faith. "Faith … is a penetrating stream of light flowing out from the central divine Light and Fire, which is God Himself, into our hearts, by which we are inflamed with love for God and for our neighbour, and by which we see both what we lack in ourselves and what can abundantly supply our lack, so that we may be made ready for the Kingdom of God and be prepared to become children of God." "Real faith … that is to say, justifying faith, can come from nothing external. It is a gracious and gratuitous gift of God through the Holy Spirit. It is an emanation from the eternal Life of God, and is of the same essence and substance as God Himself." It is, in fact, the Eternal Word of God become vocal and vital within the inner region of our own lives.

Rufus M. Jones, *Spiritual Reformers in the 16th and 17th Centuries,* Macmillan & Co. Ltd., 1914, p.77.

TRINITY

The three persons in the Godhead are Three in one sense, and One in another. We cannot tell how; and that is the mystery!

Samuel Johnson, *Boswell's Life of Johnson,* edited by G.B. Hill, revised by L.F. Powell, Oxford at the Clarendon Press, 1950, Volume V, p.88.

The Holy Spirit is the Person in the Trinity with whom we are most constantly in conscious contact.

William Temple, *Christian Faith and Life,* S.C.M. Press Ltd., 1963, p.94.

Our doctrine, teaching, experience of the Church, must be, so to speak, in a comatose state, unless there be an active, experimental, loving knowledge of the Name of the Holy Trinity, which is the living power wherewith the Church is bound together by the Holy Ghost.

R.M. Benson, *Further Letters of Richard Meux Benson,* edited by W.H. Longridge, A.R. Mowbray & Co. Ltd., 1920, p.220.

We are enclosed in the Father, and we are enclosed in the Son, and we are enclosed in the Holy Ghost. And the Father is enclosed in us, and the Son is enclosed in us, and the Holy Ghost is enclosed in us: Almightiness, All-Wisdom, All-Goodness: one God, one Lord.

Lady Julian of Norwich, *Revelations of Divine Love,* edited by Grace Warrack, Methuen & Co., Ltd., 1949, p.131.

I believe in the Father, the Son, and the Holy Ghost, as three distinct Persons: but I believe that above our knowledge there is a point of coincidence and unity between them. What it is I do not know. That is the unrevealed part. The revealed part is that the Divine nature stands forth to us as separate, individual Father—separate, individual Son—and separate, individual Spirit; and that in the vast recess of the being of God, which transcends our knowledge, there is a coming together of the three.

Henry Ward Beecher, *Royal Truths,* Alexander Strahan & Co., 1862, p.45.

My thoughtless youth was wing'd with vain desires,
My manhood, long misled by wandring fires,
Follow'd false lights; and when their glimps was gone,
My pride struck out new sparkles of her own.
Such was I, such by nature still I am,
Be thine the glory, and be mine the shame.
Good life be now my task: my doubts are done,
(What more could fright my faith, than Three in One?)

John Dryden, *The Poems of John Dryden,* edited by James Kinsley, Oxford at the Clarendon Press, 1958, Volume II, p.452, "The Hind and the Panther," The First Part, l.72.

God is especially present in the hearts of His people, by His Holy Spirit: and indeed the hearts of holy men are temples in the truth of things, and in type and shadow they are heaven itself. For God reigns in the hearts of His servants: there is His Kingdom. The power of grace hath subdued all His enemies: there is His power. They serve Him night and day, and give Him thanks and praise: that is His glory. The temple itself is the heart of man; God dwells in our heart by faith, and Christ by His Spirit, and the Spirit by His purities: so that we are also cabinets of the mysterious Trinity and what is this short of heaven itself, but as infancy is short of manhood and letters of words.

Jeremy Taylor, *Holy Living,* abridged by Anne Lamb, The Langford Press, 1970, p.22.

An ordinary simple Christian kneels down to say his prayers. He is trying to get into touch with God. But if he is a Christian he knows that what is prompting him to pray is also God: God, so to speak, inside him. But he also knows that all his real knowledge of God comes through Christ, the Man who was God—that Christ is standing beside him, helping him to pray, praying for him. You see what is happening. God is the thing to which he is—the goal he is trying to reach. God is also the thing inside him which is pushing him on—the motive power. God is also the road or bridge along which he is being pushed to that goal. So that the whole three-fold life of the three-personal Being is actually going on in that ordinary little bedroom where an ordinary man is saying his prayers. The man is being caught up into the higher kinds of life—what I called *Zoe* or spiritual life: he is being pulled into God, by God, while still remaining himself.

C.S. Lewis, *Mere Christianity,* William Collins Sons & Co. Ltd., 1961, p.138.

How wonderful is it that God by being Love should prepare a Redeemer to die for us? But how much more wonderful, that by this means Himself should be, and be God by being Love! By this means also he refineth our nature, and enableth us to purge out the poison and the filthy plague of Sin. For love is so amiable and desirable to the Soul that it cannot be resisted. Love is the Spirit of God. In Himself it is the Father, or else the Son, for the Father is in the Son, and the Son is in the Father: In us it is the Holy Ghost. The Love of God being seen, being God in us: Purifying, illuminating, strengthening, and comforting the soul of the seer. For God by shewing communicateth Himself to men and angels. And when He dwelleth in the soul, dwelleth in the sight. And when He dwelleth in the sight achieving all that love can do for such a soul. And thus the world serveth you as it is a mirror wherein you contemplate the Blessed Trinity. For it plainly sheweth that God is Love, and in His being Love you see the unity of the Blessed Trinity, and a glorious Trinity in the Blessed Unity.

Thomas Traherne, *Centuries*, The Faith Press Ltd., 1969, p.78.

TRUST

In God I trust without a fear,
What can man do to me?

Psalm 56.11.

Thou dost keep him in perfect peace, whose mind is stayed on thee, because he trusts in thee.

Isaiah 26.3.

I send you out as sheep in the midst of wolves; so be wise as serpents and innocent as doves.

Matthew 10.16.

I will never fail you nor forsake you.

Hebrews 13.5.

God provides for him that trusteth.

George Herbert, *The Works of George Herbert*, edited by F.E. Hutchinson, Oxford at the Clarendon Press, 1972, p.345, "Outlandish Proverbs," No. 728.

Trust men, and they will be true to you; treat them greatly, and they will show themselves great, though they make an exception in your favour to all their rules of trade.

Ralph Waldo Emerson, *The Works of Ralph Waldo Emerson*, edited by George Sampson, George Bell & Sons Ltd., 1906, Volume I, *Essays and Representative Men*, p.128.

We can trust Him wholly with His world. We can trust Him with ourselves. We are sure He cares far more to make the best of us, and to do the most through us, than we have ever cared ourselves. He is ever trying to make us understand that He yearns to be to us more than aught in the universe besides. That He really wants us, and needs us, is the wonder and strength of our life.

A.W. Robinson, *The Personal Life of the Clergy*, Longmans, Green & Co. Ltd., 1902, p.157.

Trust, which is always on the way to being love, must be spontaneous or non-existent. It grows of itself within our hearts as we come to appreciate the character and wisdom of someone whose record we know; and it grows most surely when we come to know personally in actual companionship someone who, the more we know him, inspires in us more trust and confidence in his character and wisdom.

William Temple, *The Hope of a New World*, S.C.M. Press Ltd., 1940, p.28.

What is very startling to the philosopher whose mental habit is controlled by scientific interests is the abundance of testimony given by those who have had intimate experience of men's spiritual life to the conviction that in the early stages prayer receives literal fulfilment with great frequency; that later on this becomes less frequent, until it seems almost to cease, as though God at first gives encouragement of the most obvious kind and later withdraws this in order to evoke a deeper trust.

William Temple, *Nature, Man and God,* Macmillan & Co. Ltd., 1934, p.297.

In all your affairs rely wholly on God's Providence.... Imitate little children, who, as they with one hand hold fast to their father, with the other gather strawberries or blackberries along the hedges. So too, as you gather and handle the goods of this world with one hand, you must with the other always hold fast the hand of your heavenly Father, turning yourself towards Him from time to time to see if your actions or occupations be pleasing to Him. Above all things, take heed that you never leave His hand and His protection or think to gather more or to gain some advantage. For should He forsake you, you will not be able to go a step further without falling to the ground.

St. Francis de Sales, *Introduction to the Devout Life,* translated and edited by John K. Ryan, Longmans, Green & Co. Ltd., 1962, p.147.

If the universe was created by God and human life planned by God, then we should see principles of goodness and wisdom embedded in both. The writer of the book of Genesis pictures God looking at his creation and finding it good. He is emphatic that man is akin to God, made in the divine image. He is conscious of man's ignorance, foolishness and wilfulness, but never does he think of man as being so depraved as not to be able to hear God speaking within himself. There may be a lot of original sin but there is also original goodness to which God and men can appeal. In spite of occasional natural catastrophes, for most of the time we think life is good. So we can trust life, both empirically from experience, and also because we trust the Creator.

George Appleton, *Journey for a Soul,* William Collins Sons & Co. Ltd., 1976, p.84.

"Abraham trusted in God" (Gen.xv.6). To trust in God alone and join no other with Him is no easy matter, by reason of our kinship with our yokefellow, mortality, which works upon us to keep our trust placed in riches and repute and office and friends and health and strength and many other things. To purge away each of these, to distrust created being, which in itself is wholly unworthy of trust, to trust in God, and in Him alone, even as He alone is truly worthy of trust—this is a task for a great and celestial understanding which has ceased to be ensnared by aught of the things that surround us.

Philo, in *Three Jewish Philosophers,* selections edited by Hans Lewy, Harper & Row, Publishers, Inc., 1945, p.89.

The whole world is yours ... the whole life, present and future, not parts of it. These important words speak of scientific knowledge and its passion, artistic beauty and its excitement, politics and their use of power, eating and drinking and their joy, sexual love and its ecstasy, family life and its warmth and friendship with its intimacy, justice with its clarity, nature with its might and restfulness, the man-made world above nature, the technical world and its fascination, philosophy with its humility—daring only to call itself love of wisdom—and its profundity—daring to ask ultimate questions. In all of these things is wisdom of this world and power of this world and all these things are ours. They belong to us and we belong to them; we create them and they fulfill us.

Paul Tillich, *The New Being*, S.C.M. Press Ltd., 1956, p.111.

TRUTH

Behold, thou desirest truth in the inward being; therefore teach me wisdom in my secret heart.

Psalm 51.6.

Grace and truth came through Jesus Christ. No one has ever seen God; the only Son, who is in the bosom of the Father, he has made him known.

John 1.17-18.

You will know the truth, and the truth will make you free.

John 8.32.

As thou didst send me into the world, so I have sent them into the world. And for their sake I consecrate myself, that they also may be consecrated in truth.

John 17.18-19.

Truth is given, not to be contemplated, but to be done. Life is an action—not a thought.

F.W. Robertson, *Sermons*, Kegan Paul, Trench, Trubner & Co. Ltd., 1893, First Series, p.289.

Truth lies in character. Christ did not simply *speak* truth: He *was* truth: true through and through; for truth is a thing, not of words, but of Life and Being.

F.W. Robertson, *Sermons*, Kegan Paul, Trench, Trubner & Co. Ltd., 1893, First Series, p.286.

"I cannot hear what you say for listening to what you are." Teaching and preaching are both "truth through personality."

William Barclay, *The Gospel of Luke*, The Saint Andrew Press, 1964, p.79.

The friend of Truth obeys not the multitude *but the Truth*.

Rufus M. Jones, *Spiritual Reformers in the 16th and 17th Centuries*, Macmillan & Co. Ltd., 1914, p.90.

Rather than love, than money, than fame, give me truth.

Henry David Thoreau, *Walden*, The New American Library of World Literature, Inc., 1960, p.219.

Say not, "I have found the truth," but rather, "I have found a truth."

Kahlil Gibran, *The Prophet*, William Heinemann Ltd., 1970, p.66.

But it is not enough to possess a truth; it is essential that the truth should possess us.

Maurice Maeterlinck, *The Treasure of the Humble*, translated by Alfred Sutro, George Allen, 1897, p.187.

The highest thing a man is capable of is to make an eternal truth true.... Did Christ ever undertake to prove some truth or another, or to prove the truth? No, but He made the truth true....

Søren Kierkegaard, *Christian Discourses,* translated with an introduction by Walter Lowrie, Princeton University Press, 1974, p.104.

God offers to every mind its choice between truth and repose. Take which you please— you can never have both.

Ralph Waldo Emerson, *Essays,* Bernhard Tauchnitz Edition, 1915, p.198, "Intellect."

When man is, with his whole nature, loving and willing the truth, he is then a live truth. But this he has not originated in himself. He has seen it and striven for it, but not originated it. The one originating, living, visible truth, embracing all truths in all relations, is Jesus Christ. He is true; he is the live Truth.

George Macdonald, *Unspoken Sermons,* Third Series, Longmans, Green & Co., 1889, p.79.

The inquiry of truth, which is the love-making, or wooing of it, the knowledge of truth, which is the presence of it, and the belief of truth, which is the enjoying of it, is the sovereign good of human nature.

Francis Bacon, *The Moral and Historical Works of Francis Bacon,* introductory dissertation, and notes, critical, explanatory, and historical, by Joseph Devey, Henry G. Bohn, 1852, p.2.

The gospel story, whether historically true or not, could still be regarded as a parable: that is, as a working model, cast in fictitious form, of the way things really are.

Sydney Carter, *Dance in the Dark,* William Collins Sons & Co. Ltd., 1980, p.26.

When a man is true, if he were in hell he could not be miserable. He is right with himself because right with him whence he came. To be right with God is to be right with the universe; one with the power, the love, the will of the mighty Father, the cherisher of joy, the lord of laughter, whose are all glories, all hopes, who loves everything, and hates nothing but selfishness.

George Macdonald, *Unspoken Sermons,* Third Series, Longmans, Green, & Co., 1889, p.81.

Truth is the perfect correlation of mind and reality; and this is actualised in the Lord's Person. If the Gospel is true and God is, as the Bible declares, a Living God, the ultimate truth is not a system of propositions grasped by a perfect intelligence, but is a Personal Being apprehended in the only way in which persons are ever fully apprehended, that is, by love.

William Temple, *Readings in St. John's Gospel* (First and Second Series), Macmillan & Co. Ltd., 1947, p.230.

To the question, "what is a primrose?" several valid answers may be given. One person says:

A primrose by the river's brim
A yellow primrose was to him,
And it was nothing more.

Just that, and no more. Another person, the scientist, says "a primrose is a delicately balanced biochemical mechanism, requiring potash, phosphates, nitrogen and water in definite proportions." A third person says "a primrose is God's promise of spring." All three descriptions are correct.

C.A. Coulson, *Science and Christian Belief*, Oxford University Press, 1955, p.70.

Not only in Jesus Christ does *the Spirit of Truth* touch the hearts of men. He spoke to and through Plato, as the early Christian Fathers fully recognised; and has spoken through many a seer, poet and prophet both within and outside the Canon of Holy Scripture. Wherever there is response in the hearts of men to the manifested glory of God, whether that manifestation be in nature or in history, there the Spirit of Truth is at work. He inspires all Science and all Art, and speaks in the conscience of the heathen child. Yet it is also true that the Son sends Him. For only in the Word made flesh is the glory of God truly displayed. *We beheld his glory* (1.14); that is the condition of receiving the Holy Spirit in His power. He "proceedeth from the Father and (or through) the Son."

William Temple, *Readings in St. John's Gospel* (First and Second Series), Macmillan & Co. Ltd., 1947, p.275.

From my youth I have held the conviction that all religious truth must in the end be capable of being grasped as something that stands to reason. I, therefore, believe that Christianity, in the contest with philosophy and with other religions, should not ask for exceptional treatment, but should be in the thick of the battle of ideas, relying solely on the power of its own inherent truth.

Albert Schweitzer, *Christianity and the Religions of the World*, translated by Joanna Powers, George Allen & Unwin Ltd., 1924, p.18.

There is an Indian saying: "The bee came to suck the honey, but his feet got stuck in it." We can only avoid the fate of the bee if we regard our lives as a perpetual search for meaning, an exercise in discrimination between the real and the unreal. In that spirit, we shall welcome all kinds of experience, both pleasant and painful, and it will never harm us. For the Truth lies hidden everywhere, within every experience and every object of the universe. Everything that happens to us, no matter how seemingly trivial, throughout the day, offers some tiny clue which could lead us toward wider spiritual knowledge and eventual liberation.

How to Know God, The Yoga Aphorisms of Patangali, translated with a New Commentary by Swami Prabhavananda and Christopher Isherwood, The New American Library, Inc., 1969, p.91.

The more we try the clearer becomes our insight, and the more we use our thinking faculties the quicker they become in their power of grasping points of Truth. Truths are not things we can pick up without taking trouble to hunt for them. And when we find a truth we really possess it, because it is bound to our heart by the process by which we reached it ... through trouble, difficulty, or sorrow ... a man binds it into his life. But what is easily come by is easily lost.
Every bit of truth that comes into a man's heart burns in him and forces its way out, either in his actions or in his words. Truth is like a lighted lamp in that it cannot be hidden away in the darkness because it carries its own light.

Edward Wilson, in *The Faith of Edward Wilson*, George Seaver, John Murray Ltd., 1949, p.17.

Truth is within ourselves; it takes no rise
From outward things, whate'er you may believe.
There is an inmost centre in us all,
Where truth abides in fulness; and around,
Wall upon wall, the gross flesh hems it in,
This perfect, clear perception—which is truth.
A baffling and perverting carnal mesh
Binds it, and makes all error: and to KNOW
Rather consists in opening out a way
Whence the imprisoned splendour may escape,
Than in effecting entry for a light
Supposed to be without.

Robert Browning, *The Poetical Works of Robert Browning*, Smith, Elder, & Co. 1899, Volume I, *Paracelsus*, I, p.26.

At every stage of religious development man may rebel, if not without violence to his own nature, yet without absurdity. He can close his spiritual eyes against the Numinous, if he is prepared to part company with half the great poets and prophets of his race, with his own childhood, with the richness and depth of uninhibited experience. He can regard the moral law as an illusion, and so cut himself off from the common ground of humanity. He can refuse to identify the Numinous with the righteous, and remain a barbarian, worshipping sexuality, or the dead, or the life-force, or the future. But the cost is heavy. And when we come to the last step of all, the historical Incarnation, the assurance is strongest of all. The story is strangely like many myths which have haunted religion from the first, and yet it is not like them. It is not transparent to the reason: we could not have invented it ourselves. It has not the suspicious *a priori* lucidity of Pantheism or of Newtonian physics.... If any message from the core of reality ever were to reach us, we should expect to find in it just that unexpectedness, that wilful, dramatic anfractuosity which we find in the Christian faith. It has the master touch—the rough, male taste of reality, not made by us, or, indeed, for us, but hitting us in the face.

C.S. Lewis, *The Problem of Pain*, The Centenary Press, 1941, p.12.

U

UNDERSTANDING

I shall light a candle of understanding in thine heart, which shall not be put out.
2 Esdras 14.25.

Wisdom is the principal thing; therefore get wisdom: and with all thy getting get understanding.
Proverbs 4.7 (A.V.).

All the glory of greatness has no lustre for people who are in search of understanding.
Blaise Pascal, *Pensées,* translated by W.F. Trotter, Random House Inc., 1941, p.277.

That which enables us to know and understand aright in the things of God, must be a living principle of holiness within us.
John Smith the Platonist, *Select Discourses,* Cambridge at the University Press, 1859, p.3.

If one is master of one thing and understands one thing well, one has at the same time insight into and understanding of many things.
Vincent van Gogh, *Dear Theo: An Autobiography of Vincent van Gogh,* edited by Irving Stone, Constable & Company Ltd., 1937, p.28.

Of course *understanding* of our fellow-beings is important. But this understanding becomes fruitful only when it is sustained by sympathetic feeling in joy and in sorrow.
Albert Einstein, *Ideas and Opinions,* Souvenir Press (Educational & Academic) Ltd, 1973, p.53.

I want, by understanding myself, to understand others. I want to be all that I am capable of becoming.... This all sounds very strenuous and serious. But now that I have wrestled with it, it's no longer so. I feel happy—deep down. *All is well.*
Katherine Mansfield, *Journal of Katherine Mansfield,* edited by John Middleton Murry, Constable & Co. Ltd., 1927, p.251.

UNION

Every rational soul should desire with all its strength to draw close to God, and to be united to Him by its awareness of His unseen presence.
Walter Hilton, *The Ladder of Perfection,* translated with an introduction by Leo Sherley-Price, Penguin Books Ltd., 1957, p.233.

As long as the soul has not thrown off all her veils, however thin, she is unable to see God. Any medium, but a hair's-breadth, in betwixt the body and the soul stops actual union.
Meister Eckhart, *Meister Eckhart,* Franz Pfeiffer, translated by C. de B. Evans, John M. Watkins, 1956, Volume I, p.114.

We come closest to Him (God) not when, with our mind, we obtain a wide conspectus of truth, but when in our purposes we are united with His righteous purpose.
William Temple, *The Preacher's Theme To-day*, S.P.C.K., 1936, p.8.

In the terms employed by Christian theology we may define realization as the soul's union with God as a Trinity, a three in one. It is simultaneously union with the Father, the Son, and the Holy Ghost— union with the source and Ground of all being, union with the manifestation of that Ground in a human consciousness and union with the spirit which links the Unknowable to the known.
Aldous Huxley, *The Devils of Loudun*, Penguin Books Ltd., 1973, p.74.

No unity with God is possible except by an exceedingly great love. This we can see from the story of the woman in the Gospel, who was a sinner: God in His great mercy granted her the forgiveness of her sins and a firm union with Him, "for she loved much" (Luke 7.47). He loves those who love Him, He cleaves to those who cleave to Him, gives Himself to those who seek Him, and abundantly grants fullness of joy to those who desire to enjoy His love.
To kindle in his heart such a divine love, to unite with God in an inseparable union of love, it is necessary for a man to pray often, raising the mind to Him. For as a flame increases when it is constantly fed, so prayer, made often, with the mind dwelling ever more deeply in God, arouses divine love in the heart. And the heart, set on fire, will warm all the inner man, will enlighten and teach him, revealing to him all its unknown and hidden wisdom, and making him like a flaming seraph, always standing before God within his spirit, always looking at Him within his mind, and drawing from this vision the sweetness of spiritual joy....
The principal thing is to stand with the mind in the heart before God, and to go on standing before Him unceasingly day and night, until the end of life.
St. Dimitri of Rostov and Theophan the Recluse, in *The Art of Prayer, An Orthodox Anthology*, compiled by Igumen Chariton of Valamo, translated by E. Kadloubovsky and E.M. Palmer, edited with an introduction by Timothy Ware, Faber and Faber Limited, 1973, pp.47, 63.

Who can tell of the intimacy of this union with God, for it is beyond compare!... God, when He is united with the soul, penetrates it wholly and enters all its secret chambers, till He is made one with its inmost being; and herein, when He has become soul of its soul and is straitly entwined with it, He enfolds it in the most intimate union....
And not merely in great part is God united with the soul, but He is united wholly; and not gradually, one part succeeding another, but all together and at once, with no waiting of one part for the other; which is the reverse of that which takes place with the body, the good things of which (or that which it holds to be good things) come to it slowly and gradually, one after the other, now this, now that, so that before it can enjoy the second it has already lost the first...
From all this it may be concluded that not only is there delight in this betrothal and union of the soul with God, but that it is a delight which, from whatsoever aspect it be regarded, is greater than any other. For neither is it mingled with necessity, nor

diluted with sorrow, nor is it given partially, nor corrupted in any degree soever. Neither is it born of lesser favours, nor of indifferent or weak embraces; neither is it a base delight nor lightly apprehended, as are the delights of our base and superficial senses. But it is wealth divine, and intimate fruition, abundance of delight, unsullied happiness, which bathes the whole soul, and inebriates it, and overwhelms it in such wise that its state can be described by none.

Luis de Leon, in *Studies of the Spanish Mystics,* E. Allison Peers, Sheldon Press, 1927, Volume I, p.336.

That life is difficult, I have often bitterly realised. I now had further cause for serious reflection. Right up to the present I have never lost the feeling of contradiction that lies behind all knowledge. My life has been miserable and difficult, and yet to others and sometimes to myself, it has seemed rich and wonderful. Man's life seems to me like a long, weary night that would be intolerable if there were not occasionally flashes of light, the sudden brightness of which is so comforting and wonderful, that the moments of their appearance cancel out and justify the years of darkness.
The gloom, the comfortless darkness, lies in the inevitable course of our daily lives. Why does one repeatedly rise in the morning, eat, drink, and go to bed again? The child, the savage, the healthy young person does not suffer as a result of this cycle of repeated activities. If a man does not think too much, he rejoices at rising in the morning, and at eating and drinking. He finds satisfaction in them and does not want them to be otherwise. But if he ceases to take things for granted, he seeks eagerly and hopefully during the course of the day for moments of real life, the radiance of which makes him rejoice and obliterates the awareness of time and all thoughts on the meaning and purpose of everything. One can call these moments creative, because they seem to give a feeling of union with the creator, and while they last, one is sensible of everything being necessary, even what is seemingly fortuitous. It is what the mystics call union with God. Perhaps it is the excessive radiance of these moments that makes everything else appear so dark, perhaps it is the feeling of liberation, the enchanting lightness and the suspended bliss that make the rest of life seem so difficult, demanding and oppressive. I do not know. I have not travelled very far in thought and philosophy.

However I do know that if there is a state of bliss and a paradise, it must be an uninterrupted sequence of such moments, and if this state can be attained by suffering and dwelling in pain, then no sorrow or pain can be so great that one should attempt to escape from it.

Herman Hesse, *Gertrude,* Peter Owen Ltd., & Vision Press Ltd., 1955, p.134.

UNITY

The unity of Christendom which alone we can desire and rationally seek to promote is not the unity of a world-wide centralised government, but unity of spirit based on a common faith and a common desire to see the Kingdom of God, which is "right-eousness and peace and joy in the Holy Ghost," established on earth. There will be diversities of gifts, but the same Spirit; differences of ecclesiastical organisation, but the same Lord. We must not expect that India, China, and Japan, if they ever adopt Christianity, will be European Christians. They have their ancient traditions, unlike the Graeco-Roman traditions which formed Catholicism; they must build their national churches upon these, in complete independence.

The sole bond of a spiritually united Christendom is the Person and the Gospel of the Divine Founder.

W.R. Inge, *Lay Thoughts of a Dean*, G.P. Putnam's Sons, 1926, p.300.

The time may come—and I hope will come—when the immense majority of English Christians may be content to worship under the same roof; but assuredly we shall not live to see it, and overtures to the Protestant bodies seem to me, I regret to say, quite premature.

Reunion then, in the same sense of fusion with any other Church or Churches, is not a question of practical politics. But let us remember that all good Christians in England are our brethren and have a claim to individual recognition as good Christians. I entirely agree with the words—I forget who uttered them—that the idea of a common Christianity, behind all denominational loyalties, is one which we should steadily hold before ourselves, and encourage by every means in our power.

Let us further remember, with a view to hastening the happy healing of our unhappy divisions—which we pray and hope for, but shall not live to see— how very partial, how very external, almost superficial, those divisions are. Has the Church of Christ ever been divided in the chambers where men shut their door and pray to their Father who is in secret? Do we not all pray the same prayers—at least the same prayer of prayers? Has it ever been divided in the service of praise and thanksgiving? How many of us know or care which hymns in "Ancient and Modern" were written by Roman Catholics, which by Anglicans, and which by Dissenters? Has it ever been divided in the shelves where we keep our books of devotion? The *Imitation of Christ*, Taylor's *Holy Living and Dying, The Counsels of Father John Sergieff of Cronstadt,* Penn's *No Cross no Crown* jostle each other near our bedhead, and do not quarrel. The mystics all tell the same tale. They have climbed the same mountain, and their witness agrees together. All ages, denominations, and languages are blended harmoniously on that Jacob's ladder which scales the heavens in far other fashion than is ever dreamed of by the builders of Babel. Has Christendom ever been divided in the world of letters? Do not Biblical scholars, historians, philosophers forget their denominational differences, and work side by side in the cause of truth? Lastly, are we divided in philanthropy and social service? Do we not unite, naturally and spontaneously, in the warfare against vice, crime, and injustice? These are no slight bonds of union. They embrace by far the greater part of our life as children of God and brethren to each other. Is it not much that we already have in common? Let us not magnify the institutional barriers which part us at public worship, but at no other times. If the Church of the future will, we hope, be co-extensive with all who love the Lord Jesus Christ in incorruptness; if this is the goal towards which we are moving, however slowly; if this is the idea of the Church which already exists in the mind of God as a fact; let us press forward thither in heart and mind; let us anticipate that which will surely come to pass, and which, when it has come to pass, will make what is now the present appear in quite a new light; let us keep that "ideal of a Christian Church" ever before us, gazing upon it with that eye of faith which gives substance to things hoped for, and conviction to things not seen.

W.R. Inge, *The Church and the Age,* Longmans, Green and Co. Ltd., 1912, p.63.

V

VISION

Golden hours of vision come to us in this present life, when we are at our best, and our faculties work together in harmony.

Charles Fletcher Dole, *The Hope of Immortality,* Houghton Mifflin Company, The Riverside Press, 1906, p.59.

The simple vision of pure love, which is marvellously penetrating, does not stop at the outer husk of creation; it penetrates to the divinity which is hidden within.

Malaval, in *Mysticism,* Evelyn Underhill, Methuen & Co. Ltd., 1912, p.305.

Hundreds of people can talk for one who can think, but thousands can think for one who can see. To see clearly is poetry, prophecy, and religion,—all in one.

John Ruskin, *Modern Painters,* George Allen & Sons, 1910, Volume III, p.278, Part IV, ch.16, sec.28.

An eternal trait of men is the need for vision and the readiness to follow it; and if men are not given the right vision, they will follow wandering fires.

Sir Richard Livingstone, *On Education,* Cambridge at the University Press, 1954, p.151.

And thus you have a Gate, in the prospect even of this world, whereby you may see into God's Kingdom.

Thomas Traherne, *Centuries,* The Faith Press Ltd., 1969, p.71.

Now, this state of "spiritual unrest" can never bring you to a state of vision, of which the essential is peace. And struggling to see does not help one to see. The light comes, when it does come, rather suddenly and strangely I think. It is just like falling in love; a thing that never happens to those who are always trying to do it.

Evelyn Underhill, *The Letters of Evelyn Underhill,* edited with an introduction by Charles Williams, Longmans, Green & Co. Ltd., 1947, p.51.

I but open my eyes,—and perfection, no more and no less,
In the kind I imagined, full-fronts me, and God is seen God
In the star, in the stone, in the flesh, in the soul and the clod.

Robert Browning, *The Poetical Works of Robert Browning,* Volume I, Smith, Elder, & Co., 1899, p.278, "Soul," st.xvii, l.21.

All that is sweet, delightful, and amiable in this world, in the serenity of the air, the fineness of seasons, the joy of light, the melody of sounds, the beauty of colours, the fragrancy of smells, the splendour of precious stones, is nothing else but Heaven breaking through the veil of this world, manifesting itself in such a degree and darting forth in such variety so much of its own nature.

William Law, *Selected Mystical Writings of William Law,* edited by Stephen Hobhouse, Rockliff, 1948, p.44.

This made it the more likely that he had seen a true vision; for instead of making common things look commonplace, as a false vision would have done, it had made common things disclose the wonderful that was in them.

George Macdonald, *Cross Purposes* and *The Shadows*, Blackie & Son, Ltd., 1891, p.62.

It is only in exceptional moods that we realise how wonderful are the commonest experiences of life. It seems to me sometimes that these experiences have an "inner" side, as well as the outer side we normally perceive. At such moments one suddenly sees everything with new eyes; one feels on the brink of some great revelation. It is as if we caught a glimpse of some incredibly beautiful world that lies silently about us all the time. I remember vividly my first experience of the kind when, as a boy, I came suddenly upon the quiet miracle of an ivy-clad wall glistening under a London street-lamp. I wanted to weep and I wanted to pray; to weep for the Paradise from which I had been exiled, and to pray that I might yet be made worthy of it. Such moments are rare, in my experience. But their influence is permanent. They import a tinge of unreality into our normal acceptances; we suspect them for the dull and purblind things that they are. There are analagous moments when one suddenly sees the glory of people. On some unforgettable evening one's friend is suddenly seen as the unique, irreplaceable, and utterly delightful being that he is. It is as if he had been freshly created. One is no longer concerned with his relations to oneself, with his *pragmatic* value. He exists wholly in his own right; his significance is eternal, and the essential mystery of his being is as fathomless as that of God Himself.

J.W.N. Sullivan, *But For the Grace of God*, Jonathan Cape Ltd., 1932, p.133.

Religion is the vision of something which stands beyond, behind, and within, the passing flux of immediate things; something which is real, and yet waiting to be realised; something which is a remote possibility, and yet the greatest of present facts; something that gives meaning to all that passes, and yet eludes apprehension; something whose possession is the final good, and yet is beyond all reach; something which is the ultimate ideal, and the hopeless quest.

The immediate reaction of human nature to the religious vision is worship. Religion has emerged into human experience mixed with the crudest fancies of barbaric imagination. Gradually, slowly, steadily the vision recurs in history under nobler form and with clearer expression. It is the one element in human experience which persistently shows an upward trend. It fades and then recurs. But when it renews its force, it recurs with an added richness and purity of content. The fact of the religious vision, and its history of persistent expansion, is our one ground for optimism. Apart from it, human life is a flash of occasional enjoyments lighting up a mass of pain and misery, a bagatelle of transient experience.

The vision claims nothing but worship; and worship is a surrender to the claim for assimilation, urged with the motive force of mutual love. The vision never overrules. It is always there, and it has the power of love presenting the one purpose whose fulfilment is eternal harmony. Such order as we find in nature is never force—it presents itself as the one harmonious adjustment of complex detail. Evil is the brute motive force of fragmentary purpose, disregarding the eternal vision. Evil is overruling, retarding, hurting. The power of God is the worship He inspires. That religion is strong which in its ritual and its modes of thought evokes an apprehension of the commanding vision. The worship of God is not a rule of safety, it is an adventure of the spirit, a flight after the unattainable. The death of religion comes with the repression of the high hope of adventure.

Alfred North Whitehead, *Science and the Modern World*, Cambridge at the University Press, 1932, p.238.

VOCATION

You did not choose me, but I chose you and appointed you that you should go and bear fruit and that your fruit should abide.

John 15.16.

Forgetting what lies behind and straining forward to what lies ahead, I press on toward the goal for the prize of the upward call of God in Christ Jesus.

Philippians 3.13-14.

Do not despise your situation; in it you must act, suffer, and conquer. From every point on earth we are equally near to heaven and to the infinite.

Henri Frédéric Amiel, *Amiel's Journal*, translated by Mrs. Humphry Ward, Macmillan & Co. Ltd., 1918, p.45.

Vocation is not the exceptional prerogative of a few specially good or gifted people.... All men and women are called to serve God.

F.R. Barry, *Vocation and Ministry*, James Nisbet & Co. Ltd., 1958, p.8.

All things are produced more plentifully and easily and of a better quality when one man does one thing which is natural to him and at the right time, and leaves other things.

Plato, *The Republic of Plato*, translation, analysis and introduction by B. Jowett, Oxford at the Clarendon Press, 1881, p.49, Bk.II, 370B.

Each man has his own vocation. The talent is the call. There is one direction in which all space is open to him. He has faculties silently inviting him thither to endless exertion. He is like a ship in a river: he runs against obstructions on every side but one; on that side all obstruction is taken away, and he sweeps serenely over a deepening channel into an infinite sea.

Ralph Waldo Emerson, *Essays*, Bernhard Tauchnitz Edition, 1915, p.120, "Spiritual Laws."

What are you going to do with your lives? To choose your career for selfish reasons is a worse sin than, let us say, committing adultery, for it is the withdrawal of the greater part of your time and energy from the service of God. Of course you are not going to be turned out of a club for doing it, but you will turn yourself out of the fellowship of Christ by doing it.

William Temple, *Christian Faith and Life*, S.C.M. Press Ltd., 1963, p.44.

Whatever the work you do for a living, it must be a form of service of some kind, for no one will pay you for your work if he does not want it done. What makes all the difference is what you are thinking of first and foremost, as you consider the spirit and temper in which you carry out your work. Is it your livelihood or is it God's service? The work in itself is both. But which do you think of first? Nothing would bring nearer the promised day of God than that all Christian people should enter on their profession in the spirit of those who regard it as their chief sphere of serving God.

William Temple, *Christian Faith and Life*, S.C.M. Press Ltd., 1963, p.107.

When Christ calls a man, he bids him come and die. It may be a death like that of the first disciples who had to leave home and work to follow him, or it may be a death like Luther's, who had to leave the monastery and go out into the world. But it is the same death every time— death in Jesus Christ, the death of the old man at his call. Jesus' summons to the rich young man was calling him to die, because only the man who is dead to his own will can follow Christ. In fact every command of Jesus is a call to die, with all our affections and lusts. But we do not want to die, and therefore Jesus Christ and his call are necessarily our death as well as our life.

Dietrich Bonhoeffer, *The Cost of Discipleship*, revised and abridged edition, S.C.M. Press Ltd., 1959, p.79.

There is a will for career as well as for character. There is a will for *where*—in what place, viz., in this town or another town—I am to become like God, as well as *that* I am to become like God. There is a will for where I am to be, and what I am to be, and what I am to do to-morrow. There is a will for what scheme I am to take up, and what work I am to do for Christ, and what business arrangements to make, and what money to give away. This is God's private will for me, for every step I take, for the path of life along which He points my way: God's will for my *career*.

Henry Drummond, *The Greatest Thing in the World*, William Collins Sons & Co. Ltd., 1978, p.291.

He that is choice of his time will also be choice of his company, and choice of his actions....

God hath given to man a short time here upon earth, and yet upon this eternity depends....

We must remember that the life of every man may be so ordered, and indeed must, that it may be a perpetual serving of God. For God provides the good things of the world to serve the needs of nature by the labours of the ploughman, the skill and pains of the artisan, and the dangers and traffic of the merchant: these men are, in their calling, the ministers of the Divine Providence, and the stewards of the creation, and servants of a great family of God, the world, in the employment of procuring necessaries for food and clothing, ornament and physic. In their proportions also a king and a priest and a prophet, a judge and an advocate,... are doing the work of God. So that no man can complain that his calling takes him off from religion; his calling itself, and his employment in honest trades and offices is a serving of God.

Jeremy Taylor, *Holy Living*, abridged by Anne Lamb, The Langford Press, 1970, p.9.

But if you are in doubt how you may best lay out your life, and if you are quite clear in your acceptance of Jesus Christ as your Saviour and your God, then the mere circumstances of the time constitute a call to the Church's direct service in its ministry which you must face; for there is no sphere of life in which a man can more certainly lay out all his talents in the service of God. It will call for every capacity; it will bring you into touch with human beings in every conceivable relation. There is no life so rich or so full of all those joys which come from serving people at the point of their greatest need.

William Temple, *Christian Faith and Life*, S.C.M. Press Ltd., 1963, p.139.

People ought not to consider so much what they are to do as what they *are;* let them but *be* good and their ways and deeds will shine brightly. If you are just, your actions will be just too. Do not think that saintliness comes from occupation; it depends rather on what one is. The kind of work we do does not make us holy but we may make it holy. However "sacred" a calling may be, as it is a calling, it has no power to sanctify; but rather as we *are* and have the divine being within, we bless each task we do, be it eating, or sleeping, or watching, or any other. Whatever they do, who have not much of (God's) nature, they work in vain.

Meister Eckhart, *Meister Eckhart,* translated by Raymond B. Blakney, Harper & Row, Publishers, Inc., 1941, p.6.

WAR

There is nothing that war has ever achieved we could not achieve without it.
Havelock Ellis, *Selected Essays,* J.M. Dent & Sons, Ltd., 1936, p.221, (footnote).

We used to wonder where war lived, what it was that made it so vile. And now we realize that we know where it lives, that it is inside ourselves.
Albert Camus, *Carnets 1935-42,* translated with an introduction and notes by Philip Thody, Hamish Hamilton Ltd., 1962, p.79.

We (Christians in war) are called to the hardest of all tasks: to fight without hatred, to resist without bitterness, and in the end, if God grant it so, to triumph without vindictiveness.
William Temple, *The Hope of a New World,* S.C.M. Press Ltd., 1940, p.81.

What we now need to discover in the social realm is the moral equivalent of war: something heroic that will speak to men as universally as war does, and yet will be as compatible with their spiritual selves as war has proved itself to be incompatible.
William James, *The Varieties of Religious Experience,* William Collins Sons & Co. Ltd., 1974, p.356.

The Church knows nothing of a sacredness of war. The struggle for existence is carried on here with inhuman means. The church which prays the "Our Father" asks God only for peace.
Dietrich Bonhoeffer, *No Rusty Swords, Lectures, Lectures and Notes 1928-1936,* from *The Collected Works,* Volume I, edited with an introduction by Edwin H. Robertson, translated by Edwin H. Robertson and John Bowden, William Collins Sons & Co. Ltd., 1965, p.145.

It is not merely cruelty that leads men to love war, it is excitement. It is not merely excitement, it is the excitement that discloses to them depths of power and averages of manhood far more in certain cases than belong to ordinary avocations in peace.
Henry Ward Beecher, *Proverbs From Plymouth Pulpit,* Charles Burnet & Co., 1887, p.51.

I believe that Christianity does not necessarily demand pacifism. I believe that Christians can encourage and participate in a just war— that is, a war conducted by a state or states against oppression, for the protection of the weak, and for the restoration of justice.
But in order to have a just war it is necessary that there should be some prospect of the outcome being just. That's why, on a world scale, it is very hard to see how today there *could* be a just war, because the result would be indiscriminate destruction.
As for a rebellion or revolution, there can, I believe, be a just revolution or rebellion which Christian people should support. But the condition of its justice must include

the prospect that from it there is going to emerge not only the destruction of a bad order, but also the substitution for it of an order that is good and just.

Such conditions are very difficult indeed to foresee, but this is an area in which Christian thought must work out more precisely what *are* the conditions of a just rebellion, bearing in mind that all the conclusions of a just war are not necessarily admirable.

Michael Ramsey, *Through the Year with Michael Ramsey,* edited by Margaret Duggan, Hodder and Stoughton Ltd., 1975, p.133.

The more I have reflected on the experience of history the more I have come to see the instability of solutions achieved by force and to suspect even those instances where force has had the appearance of resolving difficulties. But the question remains whether we can afford to eliminate force in the world as it is without risking the loss of such ground as reason has gained....

There is at least one solution that has yet to be tried—that the masters of force should be those who have mastered all desire to employ it....

If armed forces were controlled by men who have become convinced of the wrongness of using force there would be the nearest approach to a safe assurance against its abuse. Such men might also come closest to efficiency in its use, should the enemies of civilization compel this. For the more complex that war becomes the more its efficient direction depends on understanding its properties and effects; and the deeper the study of modern war is carried the stronger grows the conviction of its futility.

Sir Basil Liddell Hart, *Why Don't We Learn from History?* George Allen & Unwin Ltd., 1971, p.72.

Undoubtedly, armaments are not amassed merely for use in wartime. Since the defensive strength of any nation is thought to depend on its capacity for immediate retaliation, the stockpiling of arms which grows from year to year serves, in a way hitherto unthought of, as a deterrent to potential attackers. Many people look upon this as the most effective way known at the present time for maintaining some sort of peace among nations.

Whatever one may think of this form of deterrent, people are convinced that the arms race, which quite a few countries have entered, is no infallible way of maintaining real peace and that the resulting so-called balance of power is no sure and genuine path to achieving it. Rather than eliminate the causes of war, the arms race serves only to aggravate the position. As long as extravagant sums of money are poured into the development of new weapons, it is impossible to devote adequate aid in tackling the misery which prevails at the present day in the world. Instead of eradicating international conflict once and for all, the contagion is spreading to other parts of the world. New approaches, based on reformed attitudes, will have to be chosen in order to remove this stumbling block, to free the earth from its pressing anxieties, and give back to the world a genuine peace.

Vatican Council II, *The Conciliar and Post Conciliar Documents,* 1981 Edition, general editor, Austin Flannery, O.P., Fowler Wright Books Ltd., p.990.

It is our clear duty to spare no effort in order to work for the moment when all war will be completely outlawed by international agreement. This goal, of course, requires the establishment of a universally acknowledged public authority vested with the effective power to ensure security for all, regard for justice, and respect for law. But before this desirable authority can be constituted, it is necessary for existing international bodies to devote themselves resolutely to the exploration of better means for obtaining common security. But since peace must be born of mutual trust between peoples instead of being forced on nations through dread of arms, all must work to put an end to the arms race and make a real beginning of disarmament, not unilaterally indeed but at an equal rate on all sides, on the basis of agreements and backed up by genuine and effective guarantees.

Vatican Council II, *The Conciliar and Post Conciliar Documents,* 1981 Edition, general editor, Austin Flannery, O.P., Fowler Wright Books Ltd., p.991.

THE WAY

I am the way.

John 14.6.

That He would teach men the perfect way.
And there has never come, before Him nor after Him, any man who has taught anything divine approaching to this.

Blaise Pascal, *Pensées,* translated by W.F. Trotter, Random House, Inc., 1941, p.261.

"Thou must thyself be the way. The spiritual understanding must be born in thee." "A Christian is a new creature in the ground of the heart." "The Kingdom of God is not from without, but it is a new man, who lives in love, in patience, in hope, in faith and in the Cross of Jesus Christ."

Rufus M. Jones, *Spiritual Reformers in the 16th and 17th Centuries,* Macmillan & Co. Ltd., 1914, p.171.

Every man and woman has two journeys to make through life. There is the outer journey, with its various incidents, and the milestones of youth, marriage, middle age, and senility. There is also an inner journey, a spiritual Odyssey, with a secret history of its own.

W.R. Inge, *More Lay Thoughts of a Dean,* G.P. Putnam's Sons, 1931, p.69.

It is easy enough, assuming we have read the gospels, to know what the way stands for. It is less easy to stand for that way ourselves. It is extremely difficult to direct our thinking and living along that way and no other.

Hubert van Zeller, *Considerations,* Sheed and Ward Ltd., 1974, p.120.

To be committed to the way which is Christ means being committed to whatever aspects of it he may introduce me to. It will probably involve opposition and frustration and disappointment, it will possibly involve shame and guilt, it will most certainly mean the cross and obedience "even unto death."

Hubert van Zeller, *Considerations,* Sheed and Ward Ltd., 1974, p.120.

I do not feel that the Christian myth has anything left to tell Western man unless he understands it outside-in. He must discover that what seemed to be the far-off edges of time, where God is Alpha and Omega, are the present, and that the pilgrimage from earth to Heaven is not a journey into the future but into the Centre. He must realize that the "death" through which we must pass before God can be seen does not lie ahead of us in time. "Death" is the point at which "I" come to an end, and beyond which lies the unknown, and this point is not "on" but "in." "The Kingdom of God is within you." For if I explore myself a little way, I come to a point where I do not understand or recognize myself any more. The "I was" which I know becomes the "I am" which I never see. The roots of my consciousness disappear into an unknown region where I am as foreign to myself as to the pulse of my heart and the currents of my nerves. For what is most truly and inwardly myself is ever beyond that small area of knowledge and control which is called the ego. Paradoxically, the most central and fundamental region of my being seems to be most "other"—like the God of theistic imagery. Thus while I think of the ego as my actual *self,* I am off-centre. I am "beside myself," so that the coursing of my blood and all the deeper processes of body and mind seem to be the work of someone or something else, giving a sensation of strange-ness and "the creeps" when I feel them.

This basic "shift" in the position of God from the periphery of the world to the centre requires also a shift of faith. We have to recognize that the totally undefinable and incomprehensible "something" which is our most inward self is—in all important respects—beyond our control. For the self which knows and controls is never, at the same time, the known and controlled. This is the most important lesson in the world for a civilization which aspires to omnipotence, to the control of *everything.* For every attempt to establish total control on the part of the conscious ego starts a vicious circle. Thus our culture becomes a system of controls in which the solution of each new problem simply multiplies the number of problems to be solved, as in the myth of the Hydra monster who grows seven new heads for each one cut off. The complete control of life is impossible for the reason that we are part of it, and that, in the last analysis, the system is not a thing controlled but a thing controlling.

We are therefore compelled to have faith in something which is at once ourselves, in the most basic sense, and not ourselves, in the sense of the ego, the remembered "I." But this faith cannot have any tangible content, such as a system of beliefs, for the simple reason that the fundamental Self cannot be defined. Therefore it is not to be verbalized positively as a believing in or about. It is to be expressed negatively, as a *not* trying to control and to grasp, as a "letting-go" and not as a "holding-to." Further-more, such "letting-go" faith must come about not as a positive work to be done, but through the realization that there is really nothing else to do, since it is actually impossible to grasp the inmost Self.

The positive consequences of this faith in terms of love, joy, and illumination are strictly gratuitous. They emerge unpredictably and uncontrollably from the inner depths. The "letting-go" removes the obstacle to their coming, but the actual coming, the Second Advent, is "like a thief in the night," and we "know not the day nor the hour." Generally speaking, they follow immediately upon the act of release. The apparent delay is usually due to the fact that one is trying to force their arrival, so that the release is not actually complete. And the mind stops "forcing" only through the clear conviction of its uselessness.

As soon as one gets used to looking at the Christian images from this outside-in point of view, it becomes obvious that, in this way, they make sense as they never did before. God returns to his temple, the heart, the centre of all things—of man, of time, of space. Heaven is no longer in the place of Hell, the "outer darkness" of the most distant spaces and far-off times, but appears in the place of the most intense reality—the *now*. Christ actually rises from the dead, and is revealed in *this* moment, and is no more locked up in the tomb of the remote past, in the dead letter of the written Gospels. The Mass is for once effectively sacrificed, for the Body of Christ, the Church, is really willing to be broken, finding no further need to hold itself together with definitions and claims. The Faith becomes actual *faith*, which is self-surrender, as distinct from all anxious clinging to dogmatic rocks and doctrinal idols. The authority of the Church becomes self-evident, which is to say that the Church actually realizes authority, so that there is no more necessity to prove it, to convince itself, by exaggerated proselytism and preposterous claims of spiritual monopoly. The dispensation of the Law, in which virtue is forced, actually gives way to the dispensation of Grace, in which virtue happily "happens," and is not grotesquely imitated.

So understood, the marvellous symbols of Christianity might still—one is tempted to say, might begin to—have a message for Western man, that anxious and restless eccentric who has "no time" because he has reduced his present to an abstract dividing line between past and future, and who confuses his very self with a past which is no more and a future which is not yet. He, too, needs to be turned outside-in, to live in the real world which he thinks is abstract, instead of in the abstract world which he takes for reality. And for this he must know that the true place of Bethlehem, Calvary and Olivet is no more in history, and that Death, the Second Advent, and Heaven are not in a time to come. His "sin," his missing of the point, can only be forgiven if he repents—turns back—from his past, as from the future which it implies, and returns again to his Creator, the present reality from which he "ex-ists." Whereupon the life which had seemed momentary would be found momentous, and that present which had seemed to be no time at all would be found to be eternity.

Alan W. Watts, *Myth and Ritual in Christianity,* Thames & Hudson, 1953, p.232.

WHOLENESS

Until we all attain to the unity of the faith and of the knowledge of the Son of God, to mature manhood, to the measure of the stature of the fulness of Christ.

Ephesians 4.13.

When we rejoice in our fulness, then we can part with our fruits with joy.

Rabindranath Tagore, *Stray Birds,* Macmillan & Co. Ltd., 1941, Indian Edition, p.42.

I wished for all things that I might enjoy life, and was granted life that I might enjoy all things.

Anon.

Nothing can be sole or whole
That has not been rent.
W.B. Yeats, *Collected Poems of W.B. Yeats*, Macmillan & Co. Ltd., 1973, p.295, "Words for Music Perhaps."

Knowledge, love, power,—there is the complete life.
Henri Frédéric Amiel, *Amiel's Journal*, translated by Mrs. Humphry Ward, Macmillan & Co. Ltd., 1918, p.42.

The cure for all the illness of life is stored in the inner depth of life itself, the access to which becomes possible when we are alone. This solitude is a world in itself, full of wonders and resources unthought of. It is so absurdly near, yet so unapproachably distant.
Rabindranath Tagore, *Letters to a Friend*, George Allen & Unwin Ltd., 1928, p.55.

Many of us do not grow an inner health and maturity as we grow in bodily health, mental ability and control over outside things. Few of us devote to the study of God and his will the same time and application that we give to worldly studies and professional training. The writers of the New Testament frequently lament the lack of maturity in the Christians for whom they are writing. That spiritual maturity is essential for inner health, right attitudes and right decisions and is creative for a dimension of life beyond the physical and the material.
George Appleton, *Journey for a Soul*, William Collins Sons & Co. Ltd., 1976, p.110.

Yesterday I met a whole man. It is a rare experience but always an illuminating and ennobling one. It costs so much to be a full human being that there are very few who have the enlightenment, or the courage, to pay the price.... One has to abandon altogether the search for security, and reach out to the risk of living with both arms. One has to embrace the world like a lover, and yet demand no easy return of love. One has to accept pain as a condition of existence. One has to court doubt and darkness as the cost of knowing. One needs a will stubborn in conflict, but apt always to the total acceptance of every consequence of living and dying.
Morris West, *The Shoes of the Fisherman*, William Heinemann Ltd., 1963, p.204.

I keep on saying Our Lord was the first psychiatrist, with a penetrating awareness of human beings ten times better than psychological theory. And finally, what He did on the Cross was to take all the human ingredients and transform them into both a human wholeness and a divine wholeness. Only Christ could achieve that.
What Our Lord could do was to take the fulness of being divine and transform it in terms which we could understand. He could, on the Cross, express His fear of being abandoned with the certainty that He was not. None of us, as human beings, has that hundred-per-cent certainty of the divine presence. It was only God that could have this awareness of the Father.
Jack Dominion, in *Priestland's Progress*, Gerald Priestland, British Broadcasting Corporation, 1982, p.82.

Most men have a dual interpretation of themselves—two pictures of their two selves in separate rooms. In one room are hung all the portraits of their virtues, done in bright, splashing, glorious colours, but with no shadows and no balance. In the other room hangs the canvas of self-condemnation ... painted equally as unrealistically with dark and morbid greens, blacks, and no lights or relief.

Instead of keeping these two pictures isolated from one another, we must look at them together and gradually blend them into one. In our exalted moods we are afraid to admit guilt, hatred, and shame as elements of our personality; and in our depressed moods we are afraid to credit ourselves with the goodness and the achievement which really are ours.

We must begin now to draw a new portrait and accept and know ourselves for what we are. We are relative, and not *absolute,* creatures; everything we do is tinged with imperfection. So often people foolishly try to become rivals of God and make demands of themselves which only God could make of Himself—rigid demands of absolute perfection....

A splendid freedom awaits us when we realize that we need not feel like moral lepers or emotional pariahs because we have some aggressive, hostile thoughts and feelings toward ourselves and others. When we acknowledge these feelings we no longer have to pretend to be that which we are not. It is enough to know what we *are!* We discover that rigid pride is actually the supreme foe of inner victory, while flexible humility, the kind of humility that appears when we do not demand the impossible or the angelic of ourselves, is the great ally of psychic peace....

We should learn to accept this pluralism in ourselves, to rejoice in the truth that we human beings consist of a variety of moods, impulses, traits, and emotions....

If we become pluralistic in thinking about ourselves, we shall learn to take the depressed mood or the cruel mood or the unco-operative mood for what it is, one of many, fleeting, not permanent. As pluralists we take ourselves for worse as well as for better, cease demanding a brittle perfection which can lead only to inner despair.

There are facets of failure in every person's make-up and there are elements of success. Both must be accepted while we try to emphasize the latter through self-knowledge. The attainment of proper self-love must become the concern of every wise religion because as long as human beings are enslaved to wrong attitudes toward themselves they cannot help expressing wrong attitudes toward others. If the self is not loved, how can the neighbour be loved as oneself?

Joshua Loth Liebman, *Peace of Mind,* William Heinemann Ltd., 1946, p.53.

The Christian mystical tradition teaches men to find God's presence within.... The metaphor which is for me the most satisfying of all is that of the soul's centre as the focus of the divine action. The centre of a circle is equidistant from all the points on the circumference; and to say that God acts upon the soul from the centre suggests that the sweep of his action takes in the whole personality and not merely the narrow area of consciousness. The metaphor also suggests that the experience of God within is an experience of being integrated, centred, made one. But I believe the centre is best understood as a potentiality that needs to be actualised if we are to grow to full maturity. Men tend to be pulled first one way then another by opposite tendencies, there is the urge to dominate and the urge to submit, to turn outwards to other people and to withdraw into your shell, there is the aspiration for the spiritual and there is the equally strong counter-pull of the flesh. As the centre becomes actualized the opposed tendencies are held in a creative tension and harnessed in the service of the personality as a whole. I regard this centre, once actualized, as both a point of focus to help concentration on God's action within and also the centre through which God guides us. The symbol of the centre can help a man in practice to cooperate with God. God rules us through the whole of what we are, through our conscious thinking and deciding and through the unconscious that balances and corrects our conscious attitudes. As I learn to find God in the centre, this occillation, this pendulum swing, is slowed down. In perplexity I turn to the centre for guidance; in weakness I turn to the centre for strength. I don't mean that God does not guide and strengthen me from outside. He addresses me through my brother, through the community of faith to which I belong, through every soul I meet. He speaks to me through the Scriptures, through the wisdom of the past, through prophets and wise men today. But the wisdom and help that comes from outside are only truly assimilated and made my own when I have referred them to the centre within. It is through the centre, I believe, that the Holy Spirit enlightens the mind, fires the heart, makes firm the will. It is the focus of God's action, the sanctuary where he dwells.

C.R. Bryant, S.S.J.E., "The Psychology of Prayer" (an unpublished lecture), p.10.

WILL

Not my will, but thine, be done.
Luke 22.42.

In His will is our peace.
Dante Alighieri, *The Divine Comedy,* translated, with a commentary by Charles S. Singleton, Princeton University Press, Bollingen Series LXXX, 1977, Volume I, "Paradisio," Canto III, 1.85.

The unconquerable Will.
John Milton, *The Poetical Works of John Milton,* edited by the Rev. H.C. Beechjng, Oxford at the Clarendon Press, 1900, p.184, *Paradise Lost,* Bk.I, p.106.

Great things are not done by impulse, but by a series of small things brought together. And great things are not something accidental, but must certainly be *willed.*
Vincent van Gogh, *Dear Theo: An Autobiography of Vincent van Gogh,* edited by Irving Stone, Constable and Company Ltd., 1937, p.187.

The one complete cure for the sense of frustration and futility is to know and do the will of God. Everyone to whom this becomes a reality is at once supplied with a purpose in life and one which covers the whole of life.
William Temple, *The Hope of a New World,* S.C.M. Press Ltd., 1940, p.114.

He (Christ) hangs all true acquaintance with divinity upon the doing of God's will: "If any man will do His will, he shall know of the doctrine, whether it be of God" (John 7.17).
John Smith the Platonist, *Select Discourses,* Cambridge at the University Press, 1859, p.9.

He gave man the power to thwart his will, that, by means of that same power, he might come at last to do his will in a higher kind and way than would otherwise have been possible.

George Macdonald, *Unspoken Sermons*, Third Series, Longmans, Green, & Co., 1889, p.229.

The star of the unconquered will,
He rises in my breast,
Serene, and resolved, and still
And calm, and self-possessed.

Henry Wadsworth Longfellow, *The Poetical Works of Longfellow*, Humphrey Milford, Oxford University Press, 1913, p.4, "The Light of Stars," st.vii, l.1.

Remember our great principles: 1) That there is nothing so small or apparently trifling, even the fall of a leaf, that is not ordained or permitted by God; 2) That God is sufficiently wise, good, powerful and merciful to turn the most seemingly disastrous events to the good and profit of those who are capable of adoring and humbly accepting all these manifestations of his divine and adorable will.

Jean Pierre de Caussade, S.J., *Self-Abandonment to Divine Providence*, edited by Father John Joyce, S.J., with an introduction by David Knowles, Burns & Oates Ltd., 1962, p.123.

God's will is not just goodwill towards men in the sense of a benevolent disposition, though it is certainly that. It is a determined, dynamic force, working to achieve his purpose, ceaselessly opposed to evil, constantly countering the mistaken or sinful moves of men, always ready to guide those who take his will as the purpose of their lives, immediately generous to supply more than abundant grace to carry it out. "Thy will be done!" is a cry of glad acceptance of the rightness, goodness and love of God. "Thy will be done" is an equally joyful conviction.

George Appleton, *Journey for a Soul*, William Collins Sons & Co. Ltd., 1976, p.234.

"I will arise and go to my Father," and so develop in itself the highest *Divine* of which it is capable—the will for the good against the evil—the will to be one with the life whence it has come, and in which it still is—the will to close the round of its procession in its return, so working the perfection of reunion—to shape in its own life the ring of eternity—to live immediately, consciously, and active-willingly from its source, from its own very life—to restore to the beginning the end that comes of that beginning—to be the thing the maker thought of when he willed, ere he began to work its being.

George Macdonald, *Unspoken Sermons*, Second Series, Longmans, Green, & Co. Ltd., 1885, p.168.

Men have always wanted to handle their lives as they plan their careers. Money, power, pleasure, women, drink or other enjoyments attract them on earth. Many people would be willing to renounce worldly pleasures if they received convincing proofs that the ultimate rewards would make the deal worthwhile. But if such a deal could be made, it would not be due to love, but to business discernment. The object of the training can only be achieved by a loving donation of ourselves, uncertain of reward. Christ himself put the matter exactly. "My doctrine," he said, "is not mine but his that sent

me. If any man will do his will, he shall know of the doctrine whether it be of God."
The abandonment of our own interests and our surrender to his guidance must be the
first step. After that, our trust will grow.
Evelyn Underhill has a good illustration of the situation. She supposes someone looking
at a great cathedral, a mass of gray stone with the windows showing a dark dusty
colour. It does not look very cheerful. But if we push open the doors and go in, we
suddenly see that all the windows are really brightly coloured glass, which light up
all the walls and, through which the beams of the sun shine with dazzling light,
staining the stone floors with brilliant patterns of red, blue, green and gold. You
cannot see the glory if you stand outside, asking sneeringly what proof there is that
inside is beautiful. You have got to go in yourself.

Sir John Glubb, *The Way of Love,* Hodder and Stoughton Ltd., 1974, p.66.

WISDOM

Happy is the man who finds wisdom, and the man who gets understanding.

Proverbs 3.13.

Wisdom inspireth life into her children, and protecteth them that seek after her, and
will go before them in the way of justice.
And he that loveth her, loveth life....
If he trust her, he shall inherit her, and his generation shall be in assurance.
For she walketh with him in temptation, and at the first she chooseth him.
She will bring upon him fear and dread and trial: and she will scourge him with the
affliction of her discipline, till she try him by her laws, and trust his soul.
Then she will strengthen him, and make a straight way to him, and give him joy.
And will disclose her secrets to him, and will heap upon him treasures of knowledge
and understanding of justice.
But if he go astray, she will forsake him, and deliver him into the hands of his enemy.

Ecclesiasticus 4.11-19.

Wisdom is oftimes nearer when we stoop
Than when we soar.

William Wordsworth, *The Poetical Works of William Wordsworth,* edited by E. de Selincourt and Helen Darbishire,
Oxford at the Clarendon Press, 1959, Volume V, p.82, "The Excursion," Bk.III, 1.231.

Some people hold ... that there is a wisdom of the Head, and that there is a wisdom
of the Heart.

Charles Dickens, *Hard Times,* The Gresham Publishing Company, 1904, p.155.

More wisdom is latent in things-as-they-are than in all the words men use.

Antoine de Saint-Exupéry, *The Wisdom of the Sands,* translated by Stuart Gilbert, Hollis & Carter Ltd., 1952,
p.89.

The wisdom of the wise is an uncommon degree of common sense.

W.R. Inge, in *Wit and Wisdom of Dean Inge,* selected and arranged by Sir James Marchant, Longmans, Green and Co. Ltd., 1927, p.112.

Wisdom cometh by suffering.

Aeschylus, *Agamemnon,* translated by Herbert Weir Smyth, William Heinemann Ltd., 1952, p.19.

The only wisdom we can hope to acquire
Is the wisdom of humility: humility is endless.

T.S. Eliot, *The Complete Poems and Plays of T.S. Eliot,* Faber and Faber Limited, 1975, *Four Quartets,* "East Coker II," p.179.

We do well to believe less than we are told, and to keep a wary eye on our own impulses; whatever it is, we should think the matter over slowly and carefully, referring it to God.

Thomas à Kempis, *The Imitation of Christ,* translated by Betty I. Knott, William Collins Sons & Co. Ltd., 1979, p.43.

To know
That which before us lies in daily life,
Is the prime wisdom.

John Milton, *The Poetical Works of John Milton,* edited by the Rev. H.C. Beeching, Oxford at The Clarendon Press, 1900, p.339, *Paradise Lost,* Bk.VIII, l.192.

The spirit of Savouring Wisdom ... is a ghostly touch or stirring within the unity of our spirit; and it is an inpouring and a source of all grace, all gifts and all virtues.... And we feel this touch in the unity of our highest powers, above reason, but not without reason.

John of Ruysbroeck, *The Adornment of the Spiritual Marriage,* translated by C.A. Wynschenk Dom, edited with an introduction and notes by Evelyn Underhill, John M. Watkins, 1951, p.146.

By "a new nativity," initiated by obedient response to the inward Light ... of God the indwelling Spirit—he may put on the new man, created after the likeness of God, and become the recipient of heavenly Wisdom springing up within him from the Life of the Spirit.

Rufus M. Jones, *Spiritual Reformers in the 16th and 17th Centuries,* Macmillan & Co. Ltd., 1914, p.150.

Tracing out Wisdom, Power, and Love,
In earth or sky, in stream or grove.

John Keble, *The Christian Year,* edited by Ernest Rhys, J.M. Dent & Sons, Ltd., 1914, p.6.

The true sage is not he who sees, but he who, seeing the furthest, has the deepest love for mankind.

Maurice Maeterlinck, *Wisdom and Destiny,* translated by Alfred Sutro, George Allen, 1898, p.38.

And we shall be truly wise if we be made content; content, too, not only with what we can understand, but, content with what we do not understand—the habit of mind which theologians call—and rightly—faith in God.

Charles Kingsley, *Health and Education,* W. Isbister & Co., 1874, p.194.

Knowledge dwells
In heads replete with thoughts of other men;
Wisdom in minds attentive to their own.

William Cowper, *The Poetical Works of Cowper,* edited by H.S. Milford, Oxford University Press, 1950, p.221, "The Task," Bk.VI, l.89.

Wisdom alone is true Ambition's aim,
Wisdom the Source of Virtue, and of Fame,
Obtain'd with Labour, for Mankind employ'd,
And then, when most you share it, best enjoy'd.

William Whitehead, *Miscellaneous Poems,* 1744, "On Nobility," p.12.

Here is the test of wisdom,
Wisdom is not finally tested in schools,
Wisdom cannot be pass'd from one having it to another not having it,
Wisdom is of the soul, is not susceptible of proof, is its own proof.

Walt Whitman, *The Complete Poems,* edited by Francis Murphy, Penguin Books Ltd., 1982, p.182, "Song of the Open Road," section 6, l.77.

So, from this glittering world with all its fashion,
Its fire, and play of men, its stir, its march,
Let me have wisdom, Beauty, wisdom and passion,
Bread to the soul, rain where the summers parch.
Give me but these, and, though the darkness close
Even the night will blossom as the rose.

John Masefield, *Collected Poems,* William Heinemann Ltd., 1926, p.671, On Growing Old, l.23.

What is the price of Experience? do men buy it for a song?
Or wisdom for a dance in the street? No, it is bought with the price
Of all that a man hath, his house, his wife, his children.
Wisdom is sold in the desolate market where none come to buy,
And in the wither'd field where the farmer plows for bread in vain.

William Blake, *The Complete Writings of William Blake,* edited by Geoffrey Keynes, Oxford University Press, 1974, p.290, "Vala or the Four Zoas," l.397.

The whole secret of remaining young in spite of years, and even of gray hairs, is to cherish enthusiasm in oneself, by poetry, by contemplation, by charity,—that is, in fewer words, by the maintenance of harmony in the soul. When everything is in its right place within us, we ourselves are in equilibrium with the whole work of God. Deep and grave enthusiasm for the eternal beauty and the eternal order, reason touched with emotion and a serene tenderness of heart—these surely are the foundations of wisdom.

Henri Frédéric Amiel, *Amiel's Journal,* translated by Mrs. Humphry Ward, Macmillan & Co. Ltd., 1918, p.95.

This love of wisdom (or philosophy) is the illumination of the intelligent mind by that pure wisdom (defined as the self-sufficient living mind and sole primaeval reason of all things), and is a kind of return and recall to it, so that it seems at once the pursuit of wisdom, the pursuit of divinity and the friendship of that pure mind. So that this wisdom gives to the whole class of minds the reward of its own divinity and returns it to its proper constitution and purity of nature.

Migne, in *The Consolation of Philosophy*, Boethius, translated and with an introduction by V.E. Watts, Penguin Books Ltd., 1969, p.21.

Then said a teacher, Speak to us of Teaching. And he said:
No man can reveal to you aught but that which already lies half asleep in the dawning of your knowledge.
The teacher who walks in the shadow of the temple, among his followers, gives not of his wisdom but rather of his faith and lovingness.
If he is indeed wise he does not bid you enter the house of his wisdom, but rather leads you to the threshold of your own mind.
The astronomer may speak to you of his understanding of space, but he cannot give you his understanding.
The musician may sing to you of the rhythm which is in all space, but he cannot give you the ear which arrests the rhythm, nor the voice that echoes it.
And he who is versed in the science of numbers can tell of the regions of weight and measure, but he cannot conduct you thither.
For the vision of one man lends not its wings to another man.
And even as each one of you stands alone in God's knowledge, so must each one of you be alone in his knowledge of God and in his understanding of the earth.

Kahlil Gibran, *The Prophet*, William Heinemann Ltd., 1970, p.67.

WONDER

To be surprised, to wonder, is to begin to understand.

José Ortega Y Gasset, *The Revolt of the Masses*, George Allen & Unwin Ltd., 1932, p.12.

Wonder is involuntary praise.

Edward Young, *Cumberland's British Theatre*, Volume XV, John Cumberland, 1827, "The Revenge," p.35.

Wonder (which is the seed of knowledge).

Francis Bacon, *The Advancement of Learning*, introduction by Henry Morley, Cassell and Company Ltd., 1905, p.16

Wonder ... is essentially an "opening" attitude—an awareness that there is more to life than one has yet fathomed, an experience of new vistas in life to be explored as well as new profundities to be plumbed.

Rollo May, *Man's Search For Himself*, George Allen & Unwin Ltd., 1953, p.212.

The most beautiful experience we can have is the mysterious. It is the fundamental emotion which stands at the cradle of true art and science. Whoever does not know it and can no longer wonder, no longer marvel, is as good as dead, and his eyes are dimmed. It was the experience of mystery—even if mixed with fear—that engendered religion. A knowledge of the existence of something we cannot penetrate, our perceptions of the profoundest reason and the most radiant beauty, which only in their most primitive forms are accessible to our minds—it is this knowledge and this emotion that constitutes true religiosity.

Albert Einstein, *Ideas and Opinions*, Souvenir Press (Educational & Academic) Ltd., 1973, p. 11.

No man or woman begins to live a full life until they realise they live in the presence of something greater, outside and beyond themselves. Self-consciousness truly means that you are standing over against that other than yourself and you cannot be living in truth. Wonder is at the base of true living, and wonder leads to worship and after that the great other than self; it is yet kin to you, you are one with it. Then you begin to live more completely and realise the kinship between you and nature, that out of nature you came and are part and parcel with it, this brings nearer faith which is self-conscious life (opposed to birds, trees, etc.), reaching out to perfection.

G.A. Studdert Kennedy, *The New Man in Christ*, edited by the Dean of Worcester, Hodder and Stoughton Ltd., 1932, p. 132.

Now if it is these moments of recognition and awareness that change our minds and change our lives, if these can be the true turning points of human history, then something of enormous power must be at work in such commonplace experiences. One might say that a flash of recognition has a higher voltage than a flash of lightning, that the power that makes us suddenly aware is the secret of all evolution and the spark that sets off most revolutions.

But what is this force which causes me to see in a way in which I have not seen? What makes a landscape or a person or an idea come to life for me and become a presence towards which I surrender myself? I recognize, I respond, I fall in love, I worship—yet it was not I who took the first step. In every such encounter there has been an anonymous third party who makes the introduction, acts as a go-between, makes two beings aware of each other, sets up a current of communication between them. What is more, this invisible go-between does not simply stand between us but is activating each of us from inside. Moses approaching the burning bush is no scientific observer; the same fiery essence burns in his own heart also. He and the thorn-bush are caught and held, as it were, in the same magnetic field.

John V. Taylor, *The Go-Between God*, S.C.M. Press Ltd., 1972, p. 16.

The spirit has its own senses by which to see, feel and be guided; these grow out of our ordinary ones and are related to them, as inward eyes, ears and feelings, which as yet are only partly formed and rudimentary, but which develop as we dare to trust them. Mystical experience and knowledge of guidance are becoming commoner in these times and perhaps this is because the great Unseen is building up power to help us in these dark days. At last we are ready on a great scale to begin to understand what is happening in the polarization of old and new. I believe it will not be too many years ahead before we begin to educate children in a fuller use of their mind's and spirit's potential....

This way is open to every one; the seed of divine consciousness of which Christ's incarnation is the herald is not out in space but here, right under our hands to be experienced in fullness of life as we learn to look for it: as we dig in the garden, sit by the bedside of the dying, hold a young baby in our arms, study the patterns of nature through microscope and telescope, puzzle over philosophical problems and above all as we sit in the silence both alone and together in the meeting for worship.

Damaris Parker-Rhodes, *Truth: A Path and not a Possession*, Swarthmore Lecture, 1977, Friends Home Service Committee, p.51.

WORD OF GOD

But the word is very nigh you; it is in your mouth and in your heart, so that you can do it.

Deuteronomy 30.14.

And the Word became flesh and dwelt among us, full of grace and truth.

John 1.14.

Let the word of Christ dwell in you richly.

Colossians 3.16.

And you show that you are a letter from Christ delivered by us, written not with ink but with the Spirit of the living God, not on tablets of stone but on tablets of human hearts.

2 Corinthians 3.3.

In the midst of the silence there was spoken in me a secret Word.

Meister Eckhart, *Meister Eckhart*, Franz Pfeiffer, translated by C. de B. Evans, John M. Watkins, 1956, Volume I, p.4.

Our reading of the Gospel story can be and should be an act of personal communion with the living Lord.

William Temple, *Readings in St. John's Gospel* (First and Second Series), Macmillan & Co. Ltd., 1947, p.15.

And so the Word had breath, and wrought
With human hands the creed of creeds
In loveliness of perfect deeds,
More strong than all poetic thought.

Alfred, Lord Tennyson, *The Poems of Tennyson*, edited by Christopher Ricks, Longmans, Green & Co. Ltd., 1969, p.894, No. 296, "In Memoriam A.H.H.," st. xxxvi, l.9.

"A still small voice" comes through the wild,
(Like a Father consoling his fretful child),
Which banishes bitterness, wrath, and fear,—
Saying—MAN IS DISTANT, BUT GOD IS NEAR!

Thomas Pringle, *Afar in the Desert: and Other South African Poems*, edited by John Noble, Longmans, Green, and Co. Ltd., 1881, p.53.

Infallible direction for practical action is not to be had either from Bible or Church or Pope or individual communing with God; and this is not through any failure of a wise and loving God to supply it, but because in whatever degree reliance upon such infallible direction comes in, spirituality goes out. Intelligent and responsible judgement is the privilege and burden of spirit or personality.

William Temple, *Nature, Man and God,* Macmillan & Co. Ltd., 1934, p.353.

For it is impossible for language, miracles, or apparitions to teach us the infallibility of God's word, or to shew us the certainty of true religion, without a clear sight into truth itself, that is into the truth of things. Which will themselves when truly seen, by the very beauty and glory of them, best discover, and prove religion.

Thomas Traherne, *Centuries,* The Faith Press, 1969, p.134.

I prefer the Holy Scriptures before all Human Treasure; yet I do not so much esteem them as I do the Word of God which is living, potent, and eternal, and which is free from all elements of this world: For that is God Himself, Spirit, and no letter, written without pen or ink, so that it can never be obliterated. True Salvation is in the Word of God; it is not tied up to the Scriptures. They alone cannot make a bad heart good, though they may supply it with information. But a heart illumined with the Light of God is made better by everything.

Rufus M. Jones, *Spiritual Reformers in the 16th and 17th Centuries,* Macmillan & Co. Ltd., 1914, p.242.

We sometimes think that God spoke to men in the past in a more objective, external way than he speaks to us today. He speaks as he has always done, within the heart of man, in direct intuitive communication or through making relevant to us today, words that he spoke to prophets, saints, and thinkers, recorded in Scripture. Above all he speaks through his eternal word, who became man in Jesus our Christ, whose words and teaching as they were remembered and handed down are recorded in the gospels, and who is ever present with men.

George Appleton, *Journey for a Soul,* William Collins Sons & Co. Ltd., 1976, p.199.

There is no man in the world in whom this *logos,* this Word of God, this rational principle of all things, does not speak. The veriest atheist of them all thinks by the power of that which is perfectly revealed in Jesus Christ. It is the light that lighteth every man. You never get away from it, and there is nobody who is without it. That light which lighteth every man, and which shone by fits and starts elsewhere, that Word which was spoken in divers portions and divers manners in the prophets, shone out supremely and found perfect utterance in the Son.

William Temple, *Christian Faith and Life,* S.C.M. Press Ltd., 1963, p.35.

WORK

A man can be so busy making a living that he forgets to make a life.

William Barclay, *The Gospel of Matthew,* The Saint Andrew Press, 1976, Volume Two, p.296.

The real essence of work is concentrated energy.

Walter Bagehot, *Biographical Studies,* edited by Richard Holt Hutton, Longmans, Green, and Co., 1907, p.370.

I don't like work—no man does—but I like what is in the work,—the chance to find yourself. Your own reality—for yourself, not for others—what no other man can ever know.

Joseph Conrad, *Heart of Darkness*, included in *Youth, a Narrative and Two Other Stories*, J.M. Dent & Sons Ltd., 1923, p.85.

Every citizen should have a voice in the conduct of the business or industry which is carried on by means of his labour, and the satisfaction of knowing that his labour is directed to the well-being of the community.

William Temple, *Christianity and Social Order*, Penguin Books Ltd., 1942, p.73.

The work of the Church is done, not by ecclesiastical officials nor under the direction of ecclesiastical committees, but by members of the Church who do the ordinary work of the world in the inspiration of Christian faith and in a spirit sustained by Christian prayer and worship.

William Temple, *Citizen and Churchman*, Eyre and Spottiswoode, Ltd., 1941, p.48.

Capitalism is an evil thing, because it is based on what is called enlightened self-interest, and that is a baptismal name for selfishness. Poverty is a crime. The Church has been very specific on other matters. It hasn't hesitated to speak arbitrarily on most intimate affairs like sex. I don't see why it should restrict its particularity to those and not extend them to the world of the unemployed.

Lord Soper, in *Priestland's Progress*, Gerald Priestland, British Broadcasting Corporation, 1982, p.54.

Commitment does not stop with contemplation. It seeks issue in work. For the God discovered thus is a God at work, reconciling the world to Himself. And those who worship in spirit and truth find themselves called to a ministry of reconciliation. A world unfinished and broken is to be made whole. Ultimately, it is God, not we, who must heal it, but in our small measure, we may be co-labourers with God. That is our calling. Worship sends us out to work. But work in turn, through frustration or consummation, may continually tend again toward worship, wherein illumination and renewal are to be found. Such, in part, is man's way toward God.

Robert Lowry Calhoun, *God and the Common Life*, The Shoe String Press, 1954, p.240.

Perhaps if the Churches had had the courage to lay their emphasis where Christ laid it, we might not have come to this present frame of mind in which it is assumed that the value of all work, and the value of all people, is to be assessed in terms of economics. We might not so readily take for granted that the production of anything (no matter how useless or dangerous) is justified so long as it issues in increased profits and wages; that so long as a man is well paid, it does not matter whether his work is worth-while in itself or good for his soul; that so long as a business deal keeps on the windy side of the law, we need not bother about its ruinous consequences to society or the individual. Or at any rate, now that we have seen the chaos of bloodshed which follows upon economic chaos, we might at least be able to listen with more confidence to the voice of an untainted and undivided Christendom.

Dorothy L. Sayers, *Unpopular Opinions*, Victor Gollancz Ltd., 1946, p.11.

There is no prospect that machine work will ever make anything like the demand on character from the ordinary worker that the old crafts used to make and some skilled work in some callings makes today; the craftsman who knows something of what beauty is because his own hands bring it into being, the farmer whose work trains him in observation and sympathy, the small trader with his wide range of contacts with people, the sailor, the nurse, the teacher, all get more from their work as well as giving more to it than the modern factory worker ever can.... If the factory worker is ever in his life to meet the experiences that call upon his purposiveness, his creative capacity, his sense of perfection, and to be conscious of carrying significant responsibility in society, it must be in his leisure....

This involves a profound re-thinking of the balance of life. We have been accustomed to think that the challenge that develops character is met in work; that work is the adventure in which you find yourself, for the sake of which you have to grow, in which you find the chief interest of life and its paramount duties. This is the Puritan conception of work; it is not true of all periods of history.

Civilisation, in the sense of spiritual achievement, has largely been the creation of human leisure; music, art, philosophy, science, have owed much to men who had time to spare from bread winning. Working-class leisure has already made its not insignificant contributions: peasant communities have developed folk dance, embroi-
dery, wood-carving, and ballad; town-dwellers have their chapels, trade unions, and brass bands.... Today we think of leisure as the margin of life that may rightly be spared for relaxation or enjoyment after a good day's work. But for thousands of people there will never be a good day's work to be done, there will only be a lever to be pulled (or the like) for eight or nine or ten hours. If work in the sense of breadwinning means machine minding, work that is the making of a man must be done in leisure from breadwinning. Leisure must become the most truly strenuous part of life, a tonic rather than a sedative.

Constance Reaveley and John Winnington, *Democracy and Industry,* Chatto & Windus Ltd., 1947, p.135.

We have known an honour of work exactly similar to that which in the Middle Ages ruled hand and heart. The same honour had been preserved, intact underneath. We have known this care carried to perfection, a perfect whole, perfect to the last infin-
itesimal detail. We have known this devotion to *l'ouvrage bien faite,* to the good job, carried and maintained to its most exacting claims. During all my childhood I saw chairs being caned exactly in the same spirit, with the same hand and heart as those with which this same people fashioned its cathedrals....

Those bygone workmen did not serve, they worked. They had an absolute honour, which is honour proper. A chair rung had to be well made. That was an understood thing. That was the first thing. It wasn't that the chair had to be well made for the salary or on account of the salary. It wasn't that it was well made for the boss, nor for connaisseurs, nor for the boss' clients. It had to be well made itself, in itself, for itself, in its very self. A tradition coming, springing from deep within the race, a history, an absolute, an honour, demanded that this chair rung be well made. Every part of the chair which could not be seen was just as perfectly made as the parts which could be seen. This was the selfsame principle of cathedrals....

There was no question of being seen or of not being seen. It was the innate being of
work which needed to be well done....
All the honours converged towards that honour. A decency and a delicacy of speech.
A respect for home. A sense of respects, of all the respects, of respect itself. A constant
ceremony, as it were. Besides, home was still very often identified with the work-
room, and the honour of home and the honour of the work-room were the same honour.
It was the honour of the same place. It was the honour of the same hearth. What has
become of all this? Everything was a rhythm and a rite and a ceremony from the
moment of rising in the early morning. Everything was an event; a sacred event.
Everything was a tradition, a lesson, everything was bequeathed, everything was a
most saintly habit. Everything was an inner elevation and a prayer. All day long,
sleep and wake, work and short rest, bed and board, soup and beef, house and garden,
door and street, courtyard and threshold, and the plates on the table.
Laughing, they used to say, and that to annoy the priests, that *to work is to pray* and
little did they know how true that was.
So much of their work was a prayer, and the work-room an oratory.

Charles Péguy, *Basic Verities*, translated by Ann & Julian Green, Kegan Paul, Trench, Trubner & Co. Ltd.,
1943, p.79.

WORLDLINESS

What will it profit a man, if he gains the whole world and forfeits his life?
Matthew 16.26.

Do not love the world or the things in the world. If any one loves the world, love
for the Father is not in him. For all that is in the world, the lust of the flesh and the
lust of the eyes and the pride of life, is not of the Father but is of the world. And
the world passes away.
1 John 2.15-17.

Where wealth and freedom reign contentment fails,
And honour sinks where commerce long prevails.

Oliver Goldsmith, *Collected Works of Oliver Goldsmith*, edited by Arthur Friedman, Oxford at the Clarendon Press,
1966, Volume IV, p.252, "The Traveller," l.91.

One belongs to the world as long as one is more ashamed of a faux pas, a display of
ignorance, a wrong turn of phrase, a misquotation than of an unloving action.

Theodor Haecker, *Journal in the Night*, translated by Alexander Dru, The Harvill Press Ltd., 1950, p.39.

The things which most often happen in life and are esteemed as the greatest good of
all, as may be gathered from their works, can be reduced to these three headings: to
wit, Riches, Fame, and Pleasure. With these three the mind is so engrossed that it
cannot scarcely think of any other good.

Spinoza, *Spinoza's Ethics and De Intellectus Emendatione*, introduction by T.S. Gregory, J.M. Dent & Sons Ltd.,
1955, p.227.

More people are kept from a true sense and taste of religion, by a regular kind of sensuality and indulgence, than by gross drunkenness. More men live regardless of the great duties of piety, through too great a concern for worldly goods, than through direct injustice.

William Law, *A Serious Call to a Devout and Holy Life,* J.M. Dent & Co. Ltd., 1898, p.85.

> The world is too much with us; late and soon,
> Getting and spending, we lay waste our powers:
> Little we see in Nature that is ours;
> We have given our hearts away, a sordid boon!

William Wordsworth, *The Poetical Works of William Wordsworth,* edited by E. de Selincourt and Helen Darbishire, Oxford at the Clarendon Press, 1954, Volume III, *Miscellaneous Sonnets,* p.18, xxxiii: "The World is Too Much with us," l.1.

The world expresses itself in magnificence, the spirit in magnaminity. The one means making big, inflating. The other means greatness (or openness) of mind, heart, soul. It is the difference between false and true generosity.

Hubert van Zeller, *Considerations,* Sheed and Ward Ltd., 1974, p.10.

> My name is Ozymandias, king of kings:
> Look on my works, ye Mighty, and despair!
> Nothing beside remains. Round the decay
> Of that colossal wreck, boundless and bare
> The lone and level sands stretch far away.

Percy Bysshe Shelley, *The Poetical Works of Percy Bysshe Shelley,* edited with a memoir by H. Buxton Forman, George Bell & Sons, 1892, Volume II, p.294, "Ozymandias," l.13.

Fathers and teachers, what is a monk? Among the educated this word is nowadays uttered with derision by some people, and some even use it as a term of abuse. And it is getting worse as time goes on. It is true, alas, it is true that there are many parasites, gluttons, voluptuaries and insolent tramps among the monks. Educated men of the world point this out: "You are idlers and useless members of society," they say, "You live on the labour of others. You are shameless beggars." And yet think of the many meek and humble monks there are, monks who long for solitude and fervent prayer in peace and quiet. These attract their attention less and they even pass them over in silence, and how surprised they would be if I told them that the salvation of Russia would perhaps once more come from these meek monks who long for solitary prayer! For they are verily prepared in peace and quiet "for an hour, and a day, and a month, and a year." In their solitude they keep the image of Christ pure and undefiled for the time being, in the purity of God's truth, which they received from the Fathers of old, the apostles and martyrs, and when the time comes they will reveal it to the wavering righteousness of the world. That is a great thought. That star will shine forth from the East.

That is what I think of the monk, and is it false, is it arrogant? Look at the worldly and all those who set themselves above God's people on earth, has not God's image and God's truth been distorted in them? They have science, but in science there is nothing but what is subject to the senses. The spiritual world, however, the higher half of man's being, is utterly rejected, dismissed with a sort of triumph, even with hatred. The world has proclaimed freedom, especially in recent times, but what do we see in this freedom of theirs? Nothing but slavery and self-destruction! For the world says: "You have needs, and therefore satisfy them, for you have the same rights as the most rich and most noble. Do not be afraid of satisfying them, but multiply them even." That is the modern doctrine of the world. In that they see freedom. And what is the outcome of this right of multiplication of needs? Among the rich *isolation* and spiritual suicide and among the poor envy and murder, for they have been given the rights, but have not been shown the means of satisfying their needs. We are assured that the world is getting more and more united and growing into a brotherly community by the reduction of distances and the transmission of ideas through the air. Alas, put no faith in such a union of peoples. By interpreting freedom as the multiplication and the rapid satisfaction of needs, they do violence to their own nature, for such an interpretation merely gives rise to many senseless and foolish desires, habits and most absurd inventions. They live only for mutual envy, for the satisfaction of their carnal desires and for showing off. To have dinners, horses, carriages, rank, and slaves to wait on them is considered by them as a necessity, and to satisfy it they sacrifice life, honour, and love of mankind. Why, they even commit suicide, if they cannot satisfy it. We see the same thing among those who are not rich, while the poor drown their unsatisfied needs and envy in drink. But soon they will drown it in blood instead of in drink—that's where they are being led. I ask you: is such a man free? I knew one "fighter for an idea," who told me himself that when he was deprived of tobacco in prison he was so distressed by this privation that he nearly went and betrayed his "idea" just to get a little tobacco! And it is such a man who says, "I'm fighting for humanity!" How can such a man fight for anything and what is he fit for? For some rash action, perhaps, for he cannot hold out long. And it is no wonder that instead of gaining freedom, they have fallen into slavery, and instead of serving the cause of brotherly love and the union of humanity, they have, on the contrary, sunk into *separation* and isolation, as my mysterious visitor and teacher said to me in my youth. And that is why the idea of service to humanity, of brotherhood and of the solidarity of men is more and more dying out in the world. Indeed, this idea is even treated with derision, for how can a man give up his habits, where can such a slave go, if he is so used to satisfying his innumerable needs which he has himself created? He lives in isolation, and what does he care for the rest of mankind? And they have now reached the point of having more and more things and less and less joy in life.

The monastic way is different. People even laugh at obedience, fasting and prayer, and yet it is through them that the way lies to real, true freedom: I cut off all superfluous and unnecessary needs, I subdue my proud and ambitious will and chastise it with obedience, and, with God's help, attain freedom of spirit and with it spiritual joy! Which of them is more capable of conceiving a great idea and serving it—the rich man in his isolation or the man *freed* from the tyranny of material things and habits? The monk is reproached for his solitude: "You have sought solitude to find salvation within the walls of the monastery, but you have forgotten the brotherly service of humanity." But we shall see which will be more zealous in the cause of brotherly love. For it is they and not we who live in isolation, but they don't see that. In the olden times leaders of men came from our midst, so why cannot it happen again now? The same meek and humble monks, living a life of fasting and silence, will rise again and go forth to work for the great cause. The salvation of Russia comes from the people. And the Russian monastery has from time immemorial been on the side of the people. If the people are isolated, then we too are isolated. The people believe as we do. An unbelieving leader will never achieve anything in Russia, even if he were sincere at heart and a genius in intelligence. Remember that. The people will meet the atheist and overcome him, and Russia will be one and orthodox. Therefore, take care of the people and guard their heart. Educate them quietly. That is your great task as monks, for this people is a Godbearer.

Fyodor Dostoyevsky, *The Brothers Karamazov,* translated with an introduction by David Magarshack, Penguin Books Ltd., 1963, Volume I, p.368.

WORSHIP

We *Worship* God best; when we Resemble Him most.

Benjamin Whichcote, *Moral and Religious Aphorisms,* 1930, p.30, Century III, No. 248.

God in us worships God.

Ralph Waldo Emerson, *The Heart of Emerson's Journals,* edited by Bliss Perry, Constable & Co. Ltd., 1927, p.51.

Wonder ... is the basis of Worship.

Thomas Carlyle, *Sartor Resartus,* Ward, Lock & Co. Ltd., p.52.

So long as the letter is the servant of the spirit and not its master, the spirit gives life to the letter. Hence public worship. Hence vocal prayer.

Hubert van Zeller, *Considerations,* Sheed and Ward Ltd., 1974, p.86.

When our Lord told the Samaritan woman that worship of the Father should be in spirit and in truth he was not ruling out considerations of place, ceremonial, formulas. He was saying that these factors were useless unless animated by spirit and truth.

Hubert van Zeller, *Considerations,* Sheed and Ward Ltd., 1974, p.87.

Who worship God shall find him. Humble love,
And not proud reason, keeps the door of heav'n;
Love finds admission, where proud science fails.

Edward Young, *Night Thoughts,* Thomas Nelson, 1841, p.244.

For worship is the submission of all our nature to God. It is the quickening of conscience by His holiness; the nourishment of mind with His truth; the purifying of imagination by His beauty; the opening of the heart to His love; the surrender of will to His purpose—and all of this gathered up in adoration, the most selfless emotion of which our nature is capable.

William Temple, *Readings in St. John's Gospel* (First and Second Series), Macmillan & Co. Ltd., 1947, p.68.

One of the reasons why communal worship or private prayer seem to be so dead or so conventional is that the act of worship, which takes place in the heart communing with God, is too often missing. Every expression, either verbal or in action, may help, but they are only expressions of what is essential, namely, a deep silence of communion ... if we want to worship God, we must first of all learn to feel happy, being silent together with him.

Anthony Bloom, *Living Prayer*, Darton, Longman & Todd Ltd., 1966, p.vii.

All our external religious activities—services, communions, formal devotions, good works—these are either the expressions or the support of this inward life of loving adherence. We must have such outward expressions and supports, because we are not pure spirits but human beings, receiving through our senses the messages of Reality. But all their beauty is from within; and the degree in which we can either exhibit or apprehend that beauty depends on our own inward state.

Evelyn Underhill, *Concerning the Inner Life*, Methuen & Co. Ltd., 1926, p.32.

The word "worship" comes from an old English word meaning worthship—giving to God his true worth as Creator, Redeemer, and indwelling Spirit. Worship is man's response to these divine activities. As we realize the greatness, the goodness and the "allness" of God, we forget ourselves and our hearts break forth in praise. Yet worship is not just an expression in words or music of feeling, but the outgoing of our hearts and the acceptance of God as the governing reality of our lives. He becomes our chiefest good and our lives are henceforth offered to him in loving obedience.

George Appleton, *Journey for a Soul*, William Collins Sons & Co. Ltd., 1976, p.215.

Here, in the heart and love and life of Nature, and with Christ by my side, I cannot bring myself to go to church, when the whole of creation calls me to worship God in such infinitely more beautiful and inspiring light and colour and form and sound. Not a single thing out here but suggests love and peace and joy and gratitude.... If I didn't feel and know that He was there with me always, natural things—trees, skies, flowers, and animals—would have no fascination for me whatever. But I know that every joy I feel in a wood is understood and felt more perfectly by Christ at my side; I feel always as though He were leading me about and showing me things, and for everything I thank Him—in fact, it's a running conversation all the time. When I am with other people or in a bad temper, I don't feel this; but oh, the joy of getting away alone and getting Him to show you things.

Edward Wilson, in *The Faith of Edward Wilson*, George Seaver, John Murray Ltd., 1949, p.33.

The Christian hope of the future is that this, the true meaning and message of the Incarnation, will come to be more deeply understood: and the demand on man's worshipping love and total self-offering, will receive a more complete response—a response stretching upward in awestruck contemplation to share that adoring vision of the Principle which is "the inheritance of the saints in light," and downwards and outwards in loving action, to embrace and so transform the whole world. When this happens, Christian sacramental worship will at last disclose its full meaning, and enter into its full heritage. For it will be recognized as the ritual sign of our deepest relation with Reality, and so of the mysterious splendour of our situation and our call: the successive life of man freely offered in oblation, and the abiding life of God in Christ received, not for our own sakes, but in order to achieve that transfiguration of the whole created universe, that shining forth of the splendour of the Holy, in which the aim of worship shall be fulfilled.

Evelyn Underhill, Worship, Nisbet & Co. Ltd., 1943, p.343.

If the Church has emphasized the function of art in her public prayer, it has been because she knew that a true and valid aesthetic formation was necessary for the wholeness of Christian living and worship. The liturgy and the chant and Church art are all supposed to form and spiritualize man's consciousness, to give him a tone and a maturity without which his prayer cannot normally be either very deep or very wide or very pure.

There is only one reason why this is completely true: art is not an end in itself. It introduces the soul into a higher spiritual order, which it expresses and in some sense explains. Music and art and poetry attune the soul to God because they induce a kind of contact with the Creator and Ruler of the Universe. The genius of the artist finds its way by the affinity of creative sympathy, or connaturality, into the living law that rules the universe. This law is nothing but the secret gravitation that draws all things to God as to their centre. Since all true art lays bare the action of this same law in the depths of our own nature, it makes us alive to the tremendous mystery of being, in which we ourselves, together with all other living and existing things, come forth from the depths of God and return again to Him.

Thomas Merton, No Man Is An Island, Burns & Oates Ltd., 1974, p.30.

Y

YOUTH

Our most important are our earliest years.
William Cowper, *The Poetical Works of Cowper,* edited by H.S. Milford, Oxford University Press, 1950, p.25, "The Progress of Error," l.354.

The thoughts of youth are long, long thoughts.
Henry Wadsworth Longfellow, *The Poetical Works of Longfellow,* Humphrey Milford, Oxford University Press, 1913, p.308, "My Lost Youth," st.i, l.10.

Heaven lies about us in our infancy!
Shades of the prison-house begin to close
Upon the growing Boy.
William Wordsworth, *The Poetical Works of William Wordsworth,* edited by E. de Selincourt and Helen Darbishire, Oxford at the Clarendon Press, 1958, Volume IV, p.281, "Intimations of Immortality," V, l.66.

One other thing stirs me when I look back at my youthful days, viz. the fact that so many people gave me something or were something to me without knowing it.
Albert Schweitzer, *Memoirs of Childhood and Youth,* translated by C. T. Campion, George Allen & Unwin Ltd., 1924, p.89.

Bliss was it in that dawn to be alive,
But to be young was very Heaven.
William Wordsworth, *The Prelude,* edited by E. de Selincourt, Second Edition revised by Helen Darbishire, Oxford at the Clarendon Press, 1959, p.407, Bk.XI, l.108.

The imagination of a boy is healthy, and the mature imagination of a man is healthy; but there is a space of life between, in which the soul is in a ferment, the character undecided, the way of life uncertain, the ambition thick-sighted.
John Keats, *The Poems of John Keats,* edited with an introduction and notes by E. de Selincourt, Methuen & Co. Ltd., 1907, p.52, "Preface to Endymion."

Science, philosophy, theology, literature, art, education: all are in the quest for truth. In the last analysis it is not a matter of culture but of religion. It is a matter of rightly ordered spirituality. Why is this not more frankly put to the young?
Hubert van Zeller, *Considerations,* Sheed and Ward Ltd., 1974, p.64.

"Youth is full of sunshine and love. Youth is happy, because it has the ability to see beauty. When this ability is lost, wretched old age begins, decay, unhappiness."
"So age excludes the possibility of happiness?"

"No, happiness excludes age." Smiling, he bent his head forward, as if to hide it between his hunched shoulders. "Anyone who keeps the ability to see beauty never grows old."

Gustav Janouch, *Conversation with Kafka*, translated by Goronwy Rees, S. Fischer Verlag GmbH, 1968, p.30.

Youth is not a time of life... it is a state of mind.
Nobody grows old by merely living a number of years;
people grow old only by deserting their ideals.
Years wrinkle the skin, but to give up enthusiasm wrinkles
the soul. Worry, doubt, self-distrust, fear and despair ...
these turn the long, long years that bow the head and turn
the growing spirit back to dust.
Whether seventy or sixteen, there is in every being's
heart the love of wonder, the sweet amazement at the stars
and the starlike things and thoughts, the undaunted
challenge of events, and unfailing childlike appetite for what next,
and the joy of the game of life.
You are as young as your faith, as old as your doubt;
as young as your self-confidence, as old as your fear;
as young as your hope, as old as your despair.

Anon.

The future belongs to the young.
It is a young and new world which is now under process of development
and it is the young who must create it.
But it is also a world of truth, courage, justice, lofty aspirations and straight-forward
fulfillment which we seek to create.
Our ideal is a new birth of humanity into the spirit;
our life must be a spiritually inspired effort
to create a body of action for the great new birth and creation.
Our ideal is not the spirituality that withdraws from life but the conquest of life by
the power of the spirit.
It is to accept the world as an effort of manifestation of the Divine,
but also to transform humanity
by greater effort of manifestation than has yet been accomplished,
one in which the veil between man and God shall be removed,
the divine manhood of which we are capable shall come to birth
and our life shall be remolded in the truth and light and power of the spirit.
It is the young who are free in mind and heart
to accept a completer truth and labour for a greater ideal.
There must be men who will dedicate themselves not to the past or the present but
to the future.
They will need to consecrate their lives to an exceeding of their lower self,
to the realisation of God in themselves and in all human beings
and to a whole-hearted and indefatigable labour for the nation and for humanity.

422

This ideal can be as yet only a little seed and the life that embodies it a small nucleus,
but it is our fixed hope that the seed will grow into a tree
and the nucleus be the heart of an ever-extending formation.
It is with a confident trust in the spirit that inspires us that we take our place among
the standard-bearers of the new humanity that is struggling to be born.

Sri Aurobindo, published in the Auroville magazine, *One,* in *A Vision of the Aquarian Age,* George Trevelyan, Coventure Ltd., 1977, p.75.

ACKNOWLEDGEMENTS

GEORGE ALLEN & UNWIN LTD.
Thomas F. Green, *Preparation for Worship (Swarthmore Lecture)*. Reprinted by permission of the publisher.
Rollo May, *Man's Search for Himself*. Reprinted by permission of the publisher.
Bertrand Russell, *The Conquest of Happiness*. Reprinted by permission of the publisher.
Erich Fromm, *The Art of Loving*. Reprinted by permission of the publisher.
Copyright © 1971 by Lady Kathleen Sullivan Liddell Hart. B.H. Liddell Hart, *Why Don't We Learn from History*. Reprinted by permission of the publisher.

GEOFFREY BLES LTD.
Nicholas Berdyaev, *Dream and Reality*. Translated by Katherine Lampert. Reprinted by permission of the publisher.
Copyright © 1963, 1964 by C.S. Lewis. *Letters to Malcolm*. Reprinted by permission of the publisher.

GEOFFREY BLES, THE CENTENARY PRESS.
Nicholas Berdyaev, *The Destiny of Man*. Translated by Natalie Duddington. Reprinted by permission of the publisher.
Nicholas Berdyaev, *Freedom and the Spirit*. Translated by Oliver Fielding. Reprinted by permission of the publisher.
Vladamir Socovyeu, *The Meaning of Love*. Translated by Jane Marshall. Reprinted by permission of the publisher.

BURNS & OATES LTD.
Thomas Merton, *Conjectures of a Guilty Bystander*. Reprinted by permission of the publisher.
Copyright © 1955 by The Abbey of Our Lady of Gethsemane. Thomas Merton, *No Man is an Island*. Reprinted by permission of the publisher.
Copyright © 1967 by Walter-Verlag AG Olten and Freiburg, and english translation by Burns & Oates Ltd. Ladislaus Boros. *In Time of Temptation*. Translated by Simon and Erika Young. Reprinted by permission of the publisher.
Ladislaus Boros, *The Moment of Truth*. Reprinted by permission of the publisher.
Jean Pierre De Caussade, S.J., *Self Abandonment to Divine Providence*. Edited by Father John Joyce, S.J., Introduction by David Knowles. Reprinted by permission of the publisher.

G. BELL & SONS LTD.
Herbert Butterfield, *Christianity and History*. Reprinted by permission of the publisher.

ERNEST BENN LTD.
Adolf Harnack, *What is Christianity?* Translated by Thomas Bailey. Reprinted by permission of the publisher.

A & C BLACK LTD.
Albert Schweitzer, *The Quest of the Historical Jesus*. Reprinted by permission of the publisher.
E.N. Mozley, *The Theology of Albert Schweitzer*. Reprinted by permission of the publisher.

THE BODLEY HEAD
Copyright © 1972 by The Nobel Foundation. Alexander Solzhenitsyn, *One Word of Truth*. The Nobel Speech of Literature, 1970. Reprinted by permission of the publisher.

THE CENTENARY PRESS
C.S. Lewis, *The Problem of Pain*. Reprinted by permission of the Centenary Press. Reprinted by permission of William H. Collins.

CONSTABLE & COMPANY LTD.
Vincent Van Gogh, *Dear Theo: An Autobiography of Vincent Van Gogh*. Edited by Irving Stone. Reprinted by permission of the publisher.
Copyright © Harry Williams, *The True Wilderness*. Reprinted by permission of the publisher.
David Cecil, *Visionary and Dreamer*. Reprinted by permission of the publisher.

THE CRESSET PRESS LTD.
Lillian Smith, *The Journey*. Reprinted by permission of the publisher.

DENNIS DOBSON LTD.
Paul Foulquie, *Existentialism*. Translated by Kathleen Raine. Reprinted by permission of the publisher.

THE EPWORTH PRESS
J.B. Phillips, *Your God is Too Small*. Reprinted by permission of the publisher.

EYRE & SPOTTISWOODE LTD.
William Temple, *Citizen and Churchman*. Reprinted by permission of the publisher.

THE FAITH PRESS LTD.
Copyright © 1969 by Herbert Waddams. *The Life of the Spirit*. Reprinted by permission of the publisher.
